Contents

5. Foreword by Ian Ashbee
6. Note from the author
8. Cast (in order of appearance)
10. Formation to Second World War
13. 1945 to 1960
18. 1960s and 1970s
33. 1980s
65. 1990s
110. January to May 2000
115. 2000 to 2001 season
134. 2001 to 2002 season
152. 2002 to 2003 season
184. 2003 to 2004 season
213. 2004 to 2005 season
240. 2005 to 2006 season
255. 2006 to 2007 season
281. 2007 to 2008 season
313. The play-offs
359. 2008 to 2009 season
411. August to December 2009
424. 2010 onwards
437. Thank you

© 2019 Richard Gardham. All rights reserved.
All profits from this book will be donated to Dove House Hospice.

For Joshua and Theo.

I know you'll be growing up in north London, but there's no way you can support Arsenal or Spurs now I've gone to all this effort.

Love Dad. xx

Foreword by Ian Ashbee

When I signed for Hull City, I knew the club was a sleeping giant. I'd seen that they were getting crowds around the 50,000 mark in the 1950s. I arrived at a dilapidated Boothferry Park where all the business was done in Portakabins, but the new ground was imminent. I felt that there was something rumbling, ready to explode. I knew it was the club for me.

I saw the club grow for the better under Peter Taylor. It was a stroke of genius by Adam Pearson to bring him in. Peter could have gone to a club in a higher division but, like me, he could see what Hull was ready to do. His professionalism worked wonders on us. Everyone was trying to push the football club forward. Adam had all the right ingredients. We were a bottle of fizzy pop that had been shaken up. Once the top came off we exploded.

I was the captain at the club, and believed that we had a responsibility to our community. I believed that we needed to build the club up within the city and the rest of the region. We had a lot of people in that time who were brilliant at building relationships with the community. We'd always turn up at school visits or meeting fan groups, and we were glad to do so. We were a family club. Even as we evolved we managed to keep that family feel to the club.

That laid the foundation for what was to follow in 2008. Phil Brown had us amazingly well organised and motivated. I was living in Hull and so could identify with the fans. I could identify with the city. If we lost on a Saturday I was in among people who'd let me know that we hadn't been good enough. But round that time you could sense that everyone was getting behind City in a way that they hadn't done for years. That, of course, led to Wembley.

When I was stood at the balcony waiting to lift the play-off trophy, I just felt relief. I'd had promotions before at Hull City and elsewhere, but to get a club that I had taken on as my own – I'm a Hull City fan – into the top flight for the first time… I knew I'd achieved something special, for not just a football club but also for a city that I had such strong feelings for. We'd put ourselves on the map. When I was walking up those steps, all I was thinking about was the people in the background that had worked so hard over the club's history to save it, and then bring it to a stage like this. To get a club that I cared about so much in the Premier League, the over-riding feeling was one of relief. We'd done it. I could walk around the city for the rest of my life with my head held high and with a smile on my face.

Seeing the impact that win had on Hull, and what Hull has achieved since as a city, has been incredible. Hull has always had a bad ride in the press. I grew up on a council estate in Birmingham, and I know that Hull can be a tough place. But people in Hull are proud of being from Hull, and rightly so – I feel that way now. I'm proud to live in Hull, I'm proud that my children were raised here, and I'm proud with the way in which that win seemed to kick-start things for the city, which has been added to by people like Luke Campbell and Tommy Coyle. Is it a coincidence that in the years after that win, Hull saw investments such as the Siemens factory and the city was awarded the City of Culture title? I like to think not. The win at Wembley and what we did the following season seemed to put an end to a bad run for the city. It gave Hull a belief that it's taken and run with. People from Hull come together in bad times and good. We helped provide the good.

When I look back on my career at Hull City, I feel immensely proud to have contributed to such a big part of the club's history. It was such a brilliant, poignant time. I lived among the people – I still live among them – and I'll be forever grateful to the fans, to my fellow players, to my managers and to the owners and staff at the club from that time. Hopefully I did them proud, as every week I'd put blood and sweat on the shirt, along with a bit of thunder. It was a privilege to have been a part of it.

Note from the author

The idea to write this book has been with me for a long time. In 2012 I read Thomas Hauser's oral history of Muhammad Ali's life, and a few months later I came across Loose Balls by Terry Pluto, which uses a similar style to retell the tale of the American Basketball Association's short life in the 1970s. I loved the way both writers let the stories tell themselves through a series of interviews, with a bit of guidance where it was needed.

I knew that as a Hull City fan we'd been privileged to see the club do what it had done from around the Great Escape to the first experience of top-flight football in 2008. I knew that achieving so many monumental firsts in such a short space of time was special. I knew that the stories of Ian Ashbee, Dean Windass, Nick Barmby, Ryan France and co had a fairytale element to them. I knew there was a brilliant book in there. I'd initially intended to focus solely on the decade from 2000 to 2010, but when you've got the likes of Waggy, Chillo, Ken Houghton, Terry Neill, John Kaye, Garreth, Skip, Big Billy, Little Billy, Keithy, Les Mutrie, Jobbo and co discussing their careers with you… well, they had to go in the book. Happily, I think that chronicling the events leading up to the decade in question – all those near misses and periods of underachievement – help to show why the events of 2000 to 2010 were so special.

John Fieldhouse had written a book chronicling the club's rise in this time that was released when most of those interviewed were still connected with the club. When Paul McShane left City in 2015 no one from that decade was still attached to the club other than Dean Windass, who was the club's ambassador (though Fraizer Campbell was to rejoin after I interviewed him). There were a few more years separating these monumental events from the interviews, which meant that the players, managers, owners and fans could speak with a bit more clarity and freedom than when they were in the heat of the battle or didn't want to rock the boat too much.

Fittingly, I managed to contact Chris Chilton in the summer of 2015 and he became my first interviewee. I was terrified, kept running out of breath and didn't quite know what I was doing. Thankfully Chris was amazing; patient, reassuring and generous with his time. He's a great man in so many ways. Buoyed by this I ransacked Twitter for former players.

I somehow managed to get an interview with Adam Pearson. When I arrived for my interview with Adam, I was told that he'd be 10 minutes late as he was in a meeting with someone. Ten minutes later, Nick Barmby walked out of his office. I pounced. Nick seemed shocked. I left him, non-plussed, with my number and a plea for an interview. The next day he rang me. You need those strokes of luck. Both Adam and Nick are everything a Hull City fan could wish them to be. Nick has been hugely encouraging throughout the course of writing this book, for which I can't thank him enough.

The interviews kept coming. I'd set myself an initial target of 30. I'd smashed that within a few months of the first interview. Peter Taylor agreed to meet me in a gym in Basildon. Paul Duffen met me in the Ivy in London's West End. City fan and coach of the England women's cricket team Mark Robinson – who'd taken me to my first ever Hull City game in 1982 – spoke to me in a Chelmsford hotel while the players sat around us in their pyjamas watching Wales play Portugal in the Euro 2016 semi-final. My interview with Waggy was interrupted by two cars crashing into each other outside the Lambwath pub. Phil Brown was incredibly patient with me as our interview took place over four separate car journeys while he was on the way to various race meetings. If anyone ever doubts Phil's sheer, utter love of Hull City and the city of Hull, send them my way.

Still the interviews came. I had about 20 minutes-worth of questions for Terry Neill. An hour-and-a-half later he's still regaling me with anecdotes about George Best. Les Mutrie knew he had weeks to live and was insisting on contributing to the book. Getting to know Les and his family was and still is an honour that will never be lost on me. Sitting opposite Ian Ashbee for a couple of hours while he describes his career to you… Wow. The passion and pride with which Ash talks about his time at Hull City hits you like a double-decker bus. He's another legend whose help and support for the book was priceless.

I'll take such memories with me to the grave. What an incredible privilege. I retired on just over 120 interviews with players, fans, backroom staff, owners, media figures and fans. Thank you to all of them. Only Jan Molby evaded me out of those I badly wanted.

Just a few notes for the reader. The divisions kept changing their names from the mid-1990s onwards. I've tried to make it clear which division is being referred to through extensive use of 'second-tier', 'third-tier' and so on. From the year 2000 onwards, to make the reader's life easier (hopefully), the four divisions are simply referred to as League 2, League 1, the Championship and the Premier League. I've denoted which quotes are fan contributions on thir first mention as I'm hopeful that the players, managers, owners and so on will need no introduction. My narration is in italics, the rest is in non-italics. I have also been keen to not allow my opinions or version of events prejudice the book. Each interviewee has told their truth. You may not agree with them but this is how they recounted their time associated with Hull City to me. I haven't tried to alter anything or skew the narrative in a certain direction. I have ended the book in 2010 (other than tying up a few loose ends) as there started to be a level of acrimony surrounding the club not long after that and I wanted the book to be a celebration of a wonderful time; a reminder of what the club can achieve when everyone is pulling together.

I hope the book raises a great deal of money for a wonderful cause – Dove House Hospice. I hope it helps remind many fans who have fallen by the wayside in recent years of why they love Hull City and, deep down, always will. I hope it's the first thing that the legends within this book reach for when their grandkids ask them about their careers. Most of all I hope you enjoy reading the book as much as I have enjoyed putting it together.

Richard Gardham
March 2019

Cast (in order of appearance)

Players/managers
Chris Chilton
Ken Wagstaff
Ken Houghton
Tom Wilson
Terry Neill
John Kaye
Keith Edwards
Pete Skipper
Garreth Roberts
Billy Whitehurst
Les Mutrie
Colin Appleton
Neil Buckley
Billy Askew
Brian Horton
Richard Jobson
John Eyre
Nick Barmby
Dean Windass
Peter Swan
Steve Wilson
Alan Fettis
Adam Lowthorpe
Mark Greaves
Mark Hateley
Neil Mann
Mike Edwards
David Brown
Warren Joyce
Justin Whittle
Jon Whitney
Mark Bonner
Gary Brabin
Brian Little
Paul Musselwhite
Kevin Francis
Rodney Rowe
Andy Holt
Lawrie Dudfield
Gary Alexander
Stuart Green
Ian Ashbee
Greg Strong
Stuart Elliott
Dean Keates
Peter Taylor
Damien Delaney
Colin Murphy
Marc Joseph
Michael Ingham (opposition keeper)
Ben Burgess

Danny Allsopp
Jason Price
Andy Dawson
Ryan France
Boaz Myhill
Junior Lewis
Matt Duke
Leon Cort
Michael Keane
Craig Fagan
Jon Parkin
Phil Parkinson
Dean Marney
Michael Turner
Sam Ricketts
Phil Brown
Bryan Hughes
Henrik Pedersen
Richard Garcia
Wayne Brown
Caleb Folan
Fraizer Campbell
George Boateng
Geovanni
Paul McShane
Steven Hunt

Owners/chairmen/staff
Martin Fish
Jeff Radcliffe
Don Robinson
Rob Smith
John Cooper
Terry Dolan
Andy Daykin
Adam Pearson
Brendon Smurthwaite
Dave Richardson
Simon Maltby
Sean Rush
Paul Duffen

Fans/media figures
Roy Bly (son of keeper Billy Bly)
Bernard Noble (former chair of Official Supporters Club)
Shirley Dent
Raich Carter Junior (son of legend)
Roy North (actor)
Frank and Margaret Beill
Mark Herman (film director/writer)
Ian Thomson (HCSS)
Martin Batchelor (HCSS)
Paul Denman (musician)
Robert Crampton (journalist)
Gary Clark (author of various City books)
Ian Farrow (fanzine editor)
Mark Robinson (former cricketer and coach of England women's cricket team)
Matt Rudd (radio DJ and fanzine writer)
Ian Bunton (author of 46 and Counting…)
Rich Lusmore (fanzine editor)
Andy Medcalf (fanzine editor)
Dave Burns (Radio Humberside)
James Richardson (founder of Twitter feeds Tiger Tube/Crap 90s Football)
Les Motherby (fanzine editor, founder of Hull City Kits)
Tom McVie (councillor)
Mike Hall
Craig Sargent
Nick Turner (author of Now Tigers! and Boothferry Park The Early Years)
Mike White (Radio Humberside)
Rob Harmer (not606)
Alfie Potts Harmer (journalist)
Steve Lee (musician)
Phil Buckingham (Hull Daily Mail)
Gary Johnson (Bristol City manager)
Alan Wiley (referee)

Craig Sargent
A few months before this book was released, one of the contributors, my friend Craig Sargent, passed away aged only 42, leaving his wife Jo and sons Josh (8) and Sammy (5). Craig was a fellow member of the Hull City Southern Supporters, a hardcore City fan and one of the finest men and doting dads you could wish to meet. This book, and his contributions within it, stand as a testament to his love for Hull City.

We'll miss you, mate.

Formation to Second World War

Numerous association football clubs had existed in Hull before Hull City AFC came into existence on June 28th, 1904. Hull Town, Hull Comet and numerous others had tried (and failed) to bring high level football to Hull. The desire for the City to host professional football was still burning in the AGM of the East Riding of Yorkshire Football Association on June 23rd, 1904. It was here that association president Alfred E Spring made reference to a team with ambitions to play in the Football League starting up before the end of the 1904/05 season. He added that local businessmen were willing to cover start-up costs. Five days later an official announcement was made that Hull City Association Football Club Co Ltd had been formed. All that was needed was a ground, players and a league to play in...

The announcement had come too late for the club to be admitted to the Football League for the 1904/05 season, but a season of much-needed preparation work would now take place. Friendlies with the bigger teams across Yorkshire, Lancashire and the Midlands could be arranged. An agreement was reached to share the Boulevard with Hull FC. Local players were signed along with others who'd already played in the Football League. On September 4th, 1904, at 5pm, Hull City took on Notts County at the Boulevard in front of a crowd estimated to be in excess of 5,000. The game finished 2-2 and Hull City's odyssey was under way.

Further friendlies were arranged against illustrious opposition. Crowds rose to pass the 10,000 mark. The club, unable to use the Boulevard at certain points, started to play matches at the cricket ground known as 'the Circle'. Local MP Sir Seymour King was appointed as the club's president. Football League membership – and with it admission to Division Two – was applied for. The nickname 'the Tigers' was settled upon – suggested by Hull Daily Mail reporter Athleo in reference to the club's black and amber stripes. Sheffield Wednesday veteran Ambrose Langley was appointed player-manager in April 1905. Everything seemed to be in place.

In late May 1905, Hull City's application for league membership was considered alongside that of Burslem Port Vale, Burton United, Chelsea, Clapton Orient, Doncaster Rovers, Leeds City and Stockport County. Three places were available but when the votes were counted City came in fourth. However, a motion was then passed to extend the number of teams in the league. This meant that Hull City were now a Football League club.

The 1905/06 season kicked off on September 2nd. City were developing some land on Anlaby Road to play on, but had the option of the Circle and the Boulevard in the interim period. In early September, an estimated 8,000 people saw City beat Barnsley 4-1 at the Circle, with goals coming from 'Geordie' Spence, the club's first ever league scorer, 'Soldier' Wilson and a brace from Davy Gordon. City then won their first ever away game too, 1-0 at Clapton Orient. Next up was the first ever league game at Stamford Bridge, where City lost 5-1 to Chelsea. The Tigers soon recovered and were putting pressure on the Division 2 leaders by January. However, a dip in form – along with a move to the Anlaby Road ground – awaited, leaving City ending their inaugural season in a creditable fifth position. The new team had taken to league football like ducks to water, and it would surely only be a matter of time until promotion to Division One was earned. Ahem...

Finishes of ninth, eighth and fourth followed as City established themselves as a team to be reckoned with. The 'three Smiths', the Browell brothers, Davy Gordon, Arthur Temple and Alf Toward were thriving, with Eddie Roughley proving to be one of the division's finest goalkeepers. Best of all, however, was EDG 'Gordon' Wright. Wright was a Cambridge blue for football and played as an amateur on City's left wing while teaching at Hymers College. In 1906 he was picked to play for the full England team. Sadly, as he was keen to retain his amateur status, Wright was registered to Cambridge University and not City. So while a case can be made for Wright being City's first (and, to date, only) England player, the truth is that we can't really claim him.

Regardless, Wright was a key part of the first great City team, one that was to come agonisingly close to achieving top-flight football in the 1909/10 season. With one game left City stood in second position – one of two promotion spots – on 53 points, above Derby on 52 and Oldham on 51. City were to travel to Oldham, who had bought City's star striker, Alf Toward, for £350 earlier that season, while Derby went to mid-table West Brom. A win and City were up. A draw would leave promotion possible depending on what Derby did. A defeat, however, would mean that Oldham would overtake the Tigers by virtue of having a superior goal difference. Defeat came. Oldham won 3-0 with Toward inevitably opening the scoring and City finishing third. Still, surely it wouldn't be long before the Tigers reached the promised land. Surely...

A fifth-place finish followed the season after but City began to fall away as a Division Two force, in spite of the emergence of the free-scoring Sammy Stevens. This period also saw Ambrose Langley resign and EGD Wright retire. The Great War then brought about a suspension of the league programme until 1919/20.

Though players that were to become club greats were added to the squad in the immediate post-war years – the likes of Matt Bell, David Mercer, Tommy Bleakley, William Mercer, Jack Collier, Jock Gibson, Paddy Mills and George Maddison – City remained in the bottom half of Division Two for the most part. A low point came in the 1929/30 season when, under the management of Bill McCracken, City finished 21st out of 22 teams and endured a first ever relegation. However, in the same season City came agonisingly close to an FA Cup final appearance.

City beat Plymouth, Blackpool and Manchester City, who were near the top of the First Division, before coming up against another top-flight side – Newcastle – in the quarter-finals. More than 63,000 packed into St James' Park to see a 1-1 draw played out. In the replay at

Anlaby Road, a then-record 32,930 crowd saw City beat the Geordies 1-0 thanks to a Jimmy Howieson piledriver. This led to a semi-final against Arsenal. Within the Gunners' ranks were David Jack – the most expensive player in the world, costing somewhere between £10,000 and £11,500 – England defensive lynchpin Eddie Hapgood, and goalscorer extraordinaire Cliff Bastin. In the match at Elland Road, Howieson gave City the lead after 15 minutes with Dally Duncan adding a second on the half-hour mark. Matt Bell then went off injured, to return later, but Arsenal were to make their superior numbers count. David Jack scored with less than half-an-hour to go, and with several City players now carrying injuries, Cliff Bastin netted a late equaliser. In the replay at Villa Park, City had Arthur Childs sent off – a first in an FA Cup semi-final – and David Jack scored the only goal of the game to give the Gunners a 1-0 win. A visit to Wembley would have to wait. And wait. And wait.

Meanwhile City would have to adjust to life in Division Three (North). Paddy Mills, Dally Duncan and Stan Alexander were scoring freely but the defence was proving porous. City finished sixth in the 1930/31 season and eighth the season after. In the summer of 1932 City – now managed by Haydn Green – signed Bill McNaughton from Gateshead. His club record 41 goals in 41 games – added to by Russell Wainscoat's 24 – saw City romp to the Division Three (North) title, remaining unbeaten at home. The dip into third-tier football had been a brief one. However, there wasn't quite enough quality to challenge for honours back in Division Two, as City endured two stop-start seasons that ended in mid-table finishes before the Tigers again succumbed to relegation in the 1935/36 season. Despite handing out notable thrashings – 10-1 at home to Southport, to add to a record 11-1 at home to Carlisle in January 1935 – and adding legend-in-the-making Billy Bly to the club's ranks, City were to stay in the third tier until events on the European mainland, which were to culminate in the Second World War, saw league football again suspended.

1945 to 1960

Hull took a battering in the Second World War. Easy for bombers to identify given its location on such a vast river, and a convenient dumping ground for any Luftwaffe pilots carrying a surplus of bombs on the way home from raids on the big cities of Yorkshire, Lancashire and the Midlands, from 1939 to 1945 1,200 Hullensians were killed, 3,000 injured, 152,000 made homeless and 86,715 buildings (about 95% of the housing stock) were in some way bomb damaged. As the people of Hull celebrated the Allies' victory in Europe in May 1945, the city around them lay in ruins.

The people of our great city had stood tall against anything Hitler could throw at them in the war years with a defiance and pride that had been the hallmarks of Hull going back for generations. But thoughts now had to turn to the future. In many respects, given the bloodshed and loss experienced, sport shouldn't have really mattered in the mid to late 1940s. But an escape was needed. A return to relative normality was craved. The joy that sport can bring made the role of football – as well as rugby league and cricket – an important part of life in Hull in 1946.

However, whether the 'football' part of Hull's post-war world would involve Hull City was uncertain. A local businessman by the name of Harold Needler had been planning to create a new sports complex along with his brothers – complete with a new Hull-based professional football team – in the north of the city. This plan was to eventually be turned down by the Football League, leaving Needler with no choice other than to form a consortium to buy Hull City. In December 1945 the deal was finalised and Needler became the club's chairman. He wasted no time in launching a share offering in the club – which raised £60,000 within a month – and announcing that a new stadium would be built. The new ground, soon to be known as Boothferry Park, would be ready for the start of the new Football League season in August 1946.

When the day came, on August 31st, City drew 0-0 against Lincoln in front of 25,586 fans. In goal that day was a keeper who'd played in a handful of games pre-war, but who was to become a legendary figure over the next decade-and-a-half.

Roy Bly: Billy Bly came from Walker in Newcastle and came down to Hull on his own aged 17. He was always proud to go out to the schools to present cups and trophies. He loved being part of the local community. He was a very lightweight goalkeeper, but very agile, and in those days, because of the laws of the game, the goalkeepers got battered by the forwards. He was passionate about what he did and a loyal servant. Billy was a very brave goalkeeper. He proved that by becoming the most injured player in the Football League! He had back luck after bad luck after bad luck. But he kept coming back for more. Billy spent 20 years with Hull City, Chris Chilton did about half that period. Chris played 500-plus games, Billy just 400 or so.

Bernard Noble (Hull City fan since 1950s): Billy Bly – the elastic man – was always my hero. I wanted to be him when I was growing up. I always insisted on playing in goal.

Shirley Dent (Hull City fan since 1940s): Such a slender chap but he made such amazing saves.

City used a staggering 43 players that season as new manager Major Frank Buckley attempted to build a squad to meet Harold Needler's ambitions. The season also saw City playing in a new kit – orange shirts, white shorts and blue socks, to match the city's civic colours – as well as donning a new crest. This proved to be short lived, however, as Harold Needler noted the fans' opposition and reverted to the black and amber for the 1947/48 season.

City had finished 11th in Division Three (North) in the first season after the war, and went on to improve further the season after. Important names such as Jimmy Greenhalgh, Norman Moore and Ken Harrison were added to the squad, but the best of all arrived with only six games of the season to go. His name? Horatio Stratton Carter. You can call him Raich.

Raich Carter Junior: My dad started as a professional in 1930 with Sunderland. He'd previously been for a trial with Leicester, who said he was too small and would never make it. Within two years he was in Sunderland's first team and was captain by the age of 23. They then won the league in 1936 and the FA Cup in 1937. During the Second World War he was stationed at Loughborough with the RAF as a rehabilitation officer. In that time he made some guest appearances for Derby County, and then after the war, when Sunderland didn't want him back – which really shocked him – he was offered terms at Derby, and then they won the FA Cup, making him the only footballer to win winners medals before and after the war. As he was getting on a bit – in 1947 he was 34 – he was thinking about a coaching role. He came to Hull City as an understudy to Major Frank Buckley, but then within days Major Buckley had resigned and Raich was left as player-manager and told to get on with it.

Shirley Dent: Raich was brilliant. What used to amuse me was that he was so good, he would get the ball, stand there with his foot on it and either tell the referee that he'd missed something or tell his team-mates what they should be doing. He was a real character. He came at just the right time for the city. He gave us a lift after the Second World War. We hadn't had such a footballer at the club before. He'd been in the higher divisions, but even though he came at the end of his career he was still brilliant.

Roy North (actor and Hull City fan since 1950s): He was very bossy and a big personality, very confident. He'd wag his finger at the players if they weren't doing what he wanted. That amused the crowd. He was a wonderful personality. You'd see a lot of the players working on building sites in the summer, and a lot of them would get the bus to training.

Raich's impact wasn't to see the club achieve instant success, however. A poor end to the 1947/48 season – in which City had spent much of the time in the promotion places – saw the club finish fifth. However, a with a household name such as Raich in the manager's office and on the pitch, there was a buzz around the city ahead of the 1948/49 season. Winger Eddie Burbanks was added to the squad, to be joined a few months later by the great Viggo Jensen, fresh from the Denmark Olympics team. City won the league at a canter, with attendances regularly topping the 40,000 mark.

Raich Carter Junior: In the first season they did alright, and picked up a bit after he took over, but the next season, 1948/49, was the one that set the crowds records and so on.

My dad was a bit of a big-head! He was used to playing in front of big crowds, and in that first full season the average was 37,001. My mum's from Hull – she met my dad through Hull

City – and her parents were big Hull City fans, and they were the ones who'd tell me more about the buzz Raich brought to Hull. When my dad was seeing my mum, people were wanting tickets for games and the like, which meant the family lived quite well. The butcher would provide some lovely meat in exchange for tickets. In those days to get promoted you had to finish top of the league, and they only lost four games all season. It was a hard slog but Raich loved it.

He was the David Beckham of his day. He appeared in adverts for men's hairstyle product New Fix, and girls would have pictures of him on their bedroom wall.

Raich was lucky in that he was able to play and lead the team out on the pitch. But I've been told by numerous people that fans near the touchline would put their hands over their kids' ears whenever Raich passed someone the ball, as he'd really rip into them if they did anything wrong. He struggled to understand why people couldn't do certain things that he could. He was so good that he once dribbled round the pitch because he'd lost his chewing gum and couldn't find it, so he was taking players on looking for it. But he got good players in, the likes of Norman Moore, Viggo Jensen, Eddie Burbanks, and he had some good young lads at the time. So it came quite easy for him. And they had a good cup run that season.

Indeed, a sixth-round FA Cup tie against Manchester United in the February saw a record home crowd for Hull City that is unlikely to ever be beaten, as 55,019 people packed into Boothferry Park to see the Red Devils beat City 1-0.

Raich Carter Junior: The ground looked a bit different with a temporary stand in the North Stand and the crowd huddled right up to the pitch. But I think dad's lasting impression of the day was a regret that they didn't win.

With Division Three (North) won, the expectation levels for the coming season went into overdrive. Raich was the name on everyone's lips. City's total attendances had topped 1 million for the first time and a full-on assault at top-flight football was demanded. Raich added defender Gerrie Bowler to the squad for the 1949/50 season, and was to bring in midfielder Don Revie in November for a club record £20,000. At one point City stood second in the Second Division, but from February only won one match and fell away to seventh. Norman Moore's departure to Blackburn in the March hadn't helped matters.

Raich Carter Junior: Dad always said that if the board had left him alone they'd have been in the top flight in no time. But then he was quite a big head! He was very confident in his own abilities.

Martin Fish: I started supporting Hull City in 1950 when I was eight years old. I just saw Raich at the end of his career, but also saw players of the calibre of Roy Shiner, Jackie Sewell, Alf Ackerman, Tom Berry, Billy Bly, Eddie Burbanks, Dennis Durham, Paul Feasey, Bill Bradbury, Brian Bulless, Les Collinson and many more. Players like that really shone. I have vivid memories of Stanley Matthews taking a corner right next to where I was stood in Boothferry Park when he was playing for Blackpool.

At the start of the 1950/51 season, Raich had moved to replace Norman Moore with South Africa-born striker Alf Ackerman. Though another prolific forward – Syd Gerrie – came along as well as former England centre-back Neil Franklin, the season was a disappointing one, though City had to cope without Billy Bly for the most part, who was suffering from one of the many injuries that would afflict his career.

The season also saw the 'Boothferry Halt' railway platform being used for the first time. While such developments meant that City were widely regarded as one of the most innovative and ambitious clubs in the country, Raich Carter's time at Boothferry Park came to an abrupt halt five games into the 1951/52 season. He announced his resignation on September 5th, 1951, over what he called a "disagreement on matters of a general nature in the conduct of the club's affairs". Alf Ackerman had just left for Norwich, and Don Revie was to leave weeks later. The club, it seemed, was in turmoil.

Raich Carter Junior: There are lots of official reasons why Raich left… He did have a fall out with the board and not necessarily for football matters.

Carter was replaced as manager with a strange hybrid of the coaching team and the directors. It didn't work, somewhat predictably, and City went 12 games without victory in the run up to December 1951. With relegation looking a distinct possibility, the directors asked Raich to return as a player, which he duly agreed to. With Carter back in the team, City beat Doncaster 2-0 and went on to stave off relegation, with Carter only missing one game and weighing in with eight crucial goals. Indeed, City never lost when Raich scored. This was to be Raich's last act as a City player, however, as in the summer of 1952 he left for Cork Athletic.

Raich Carter Junior: He went away for a bit – they were sixth or seventh – then City lost a load of games on the trot, were in relegation trouble and they asked him to come back for the last few games. They stayed up, but then he decided he'd had enough. He was on about £8 a week when he left Hull City, and Cork Athletic offered him £100 a game.

Dad always followed Sunderland the most, but Hull is where he ended up. He liked it here. He liked going to Boothferry Park. Everybody would want to talk to him. It would take ages to get to our seats. He got on really well with the people of Hull. He'd go out to take the dog for a walk and be out for hours!

City moved to appoint Bob Jackson – who'd recently won league titles with Portsmouth – as manager in the summer of 1952. Jackson inherited what was still an impressive team. Starting from the back, Billy Bly was still a terrific goalkeeper who was acquiring an increasing number of admirers.

Roy Bly: Billy was selected to play for England B when he was in his mid-30s, along with the likes of Duncan Edwards and Harry Gregg. On the Wednesday night before the England B game, Hull City announced a last-minute friendly, and told Billy he had to play. He asked Bob Chapman if he could be excused but was told no. He played in it, went up for a ball and snapped his wrist against the crossbar. This ruled him out of playing for the England team. Then because he only played half a game, they only gave him £1.50, instead of the £3 he'd have got for a full game. He complained about that, and eventually got his £3 from Harold Needler.

Billy was joined in the team by the likes of Eddie Burbanks, Dennis Durham, Syd Gerrie and Viggo Jensen, each of whom would have walked into the starting XIs of most teams at that level. However, injuries hit the team hard and Jackson couldn't inspire his charges to much beyond the middle to lower reaches of Division Two. Two notable developments did occur in this time, however. First, the legendary Andy 'Jock' Davidson played his first game for City (as a centre-forward!) on September 8th, 1952. He was to go on to represent Hull City a record 579 times in league and cup matches, a club record. This came in spite of him breaking his leg three times. The other development was the installation of floodlights at Boothferry Park, first used in a friendly against Dundee in January 1953. City were among the first clubs in the country to use such artificial lighting, and the six free-standing towers were to be unique in English football.

In spite of Andy Davidson's introduction, the emergence of Paul Feasey and the signings of Wilf Mannion, Stan Mortensen and Doug Clarke, City were relegated in the 1955/56 season.

Jackson had been sacked in the March of 1955, but his replacement, Bob Brocklebank, had been unable to avoid relegation the following season. City had signed the prolific Bill Bradbury, however, and in this time had beaten crack Hungarian side Vasas in a friendly – much to the surprise of the national press, who'd asked for the game to be cancelled fearing a humiliation for both City and English football. None of this prevented Hull City from finishing rock bottom of the table come May 1956, having won just 10 games all season, conceding 97 goals.

Brocklebank was given the chance to make amends the following season back in Division Three (North). With Billy Bly fully fit, Andy Davidson and Paul Feasey marshalling the defence, Brian Bulless leading a midfield augmented by Les Collinson and Brian Crispey, and Bradbury and Clarke banging in the goals, City reversed what had been a gradual decline in the previous seasons to finish a creditable eighth in the 1956/57 season, and once again the Tigers resembled a progressive club. The regionalisation of the third tier was abandoned for the 1958/59 season, meaning City were now plying their trade in what was simply 'Division Three'.

It was to prove a memorable season, though not immediately. City won only one of their first seven games. A 6-1 defeat to Southampton in mid-September saw star players Bradbury, Bulless and Crispey all make transfer requests, which were granted. City won the next game 5-0 against Notts County and never looked back. Bradbury and Bulless elected to stay at the club and City stormed to a second-placed finish and promotion. Bradbury and Colin Smith shared 56 goals between them.

Much was expected for the 1958/59 season in Division 2, but City floundered badly. Bradbury and Smith were hit by injury and managed just eight goals between them all season, with Bradbury departing for Bury in the February. City were relegated, and at the end of the season Billy Bly was released. The 1950s had promised so much, but in spite of the efforts of Harold Needler, Raich Carter, Jock Davidson and company, the club was heading back to playing third-tier football.

1960s and 1970s

It took a while for the 1960s to start swinging for Hull City. The joy of the previous season's promotion to Division Two had been sapped by a disastrous start to affairs in 1959/60. The first game of the decade saw Liverpool win 1-0 at Boothferry Park, and it was to be mid-February before victory was to be tasted. City ended up finishing second-bottom of the table and immediately returned to Division Three. City's leading scorer of the season was Roy Shiner, who'd scored a paltry nine goals, so it was evident that improvement was needed in the goalscoring stakes. That improvement arrived in the summer of 1960 in the shape of Chris Chilton.

Chris Chilton: I left school at 16. I got a phone call from Hull City after playing for Bilton. I was there as ground staff initially on £3 a week. After I'd got my two buses there and two home I didn't have any money left! I was sweeping and digging the pitch, cleaning the toilets. Then in 1960 I was in the first team after playing a few games in pre-season.

Chris couldn't inspire City back to Division Two, however, with the club finishing 11th in the 1960/61 season, in spite of Chillo's 19 goals. This disappointing return led to Bob Brocklebank being sacked as manager and Cliff Britton, who'd previously managed Everton and Preston North End, replacing him.

Chris Chilton: The club didn't feel ambitious when I first joined. The type of people that were there – there was a hierarchy among the players that didn't create a good atmosphere. Everything improved after Cliff Britton took over. The younger players were breaking into the team and it felt much better.

Cliff couldn't inspire an immediate turnaround in the club's fortunes, with the next three seasons all bringing mid-table finishes. This was in spite of players of the calibre of Ray Henderson, John McSeveney, Chris Simpkin, Billy Wilkinson and Maurice Swan joining the ranks.

By late 1964, there was a social revolution in the offing throughout much of the Western world, and cultural icons were cropping up all over the place, from the beat clubs of Liverpool, from the beaches of California, from Carnaby Street, from the East End of London, from Cuba, and, in Hull at least, from Field Mill, Mansfield.

Ken Wagstaff: When Raich Carter came to watch me play initially, it was a cup final and I think he'd come to watch someone else. He then asked me to have trials at Mansfield. He was a fine man and treated me like a son. He got me to Hull City, as he was still a big friend of the chairman at the time, Harold Needler. I could have gone to a few clubs, Forest and Tottenham were in for me, but Raich told me to go to Hull City. He looked after me all my life, always called me 'boy'.

Raich Carter Junior: Dad got a phone call when he was at Mansfield to say there's a lad we want you to come and look at, we think he could make it. So he went down to the local pitch, saw him the once and signed him up. My dad played him whenever he could. Later he got in touch with someone at City to say you should sign this lad. But then my dad would also say that if Waggy had left Hull City he'd have played for England. He thought he was good enough, he just wasn't getting the exposure in Hull.

Ken Wagstaff: I went in for training at Mansfield and Raich said to me that he wanted me to come in with a suit on the next day. I did that – I only had one! – and I thought we were going to Nottingham Forest. When we were going along the Humber he told me that I was being sold to Hull City. I met Harold Needler – I had a meal in the Station Hotel with him – and that's how I became a Hull City player. Raich said that he knew they'd look after me and that this 'big lad' they had playing for them would be a good partner for me. He meant Chris Chilton.

Chris Chilton: I was living on North Road and I saw a bloke who I thought I recognised – he looked a scruffy get – and it was Waggy. We've been friends ever since. We struck up a partnership very quickly. In one of our early games he played a ball out to me on the right wing and it had too much pace on it and went for a throw in. He turned to the crowd as if to say: "What a pillock!" At half-time I said a few quiet words in his ear, and from that day on we were fine. He'd do nothing in some games and then he'd score twice and before you knew it you'd won 2-1. But you don't score the amount of goals he scored without being able to play. He was a magician.

Waggy scored on his league debut against Exeter, then scored in his next two games too. In his sixth league game for City he scored a hat-trick against Port Vale. City started a charge up the table that was to take them into the promotion places (after being near the relegation spots early in the season), and were to gain even more momentum when Ken Houghton and Ian Butler were brought in in January 1965 from Rotherham.

Ken Houghton: It came out of the blue. We were doing well at Rotherham with a young forward line that scored a lot of goals. The manager at the time said to us: "No one's going to leave here, because we're building for the future." Inside a month, four of us had gone. Money talks and Rotherham couldn't afford to turn the money down, and me and Ian Butler came to Hull.

I'd heard that Hull City were interested. I went through with the Rotherham manager of the time – Danny Williams – and we spoke to Cliff Britton. Cliff sold me the club and we signed there and then.

Frank and Margaret Beill (Hull City fans): Ken Houghton was a class midfield schemer who deserved to be playing at a much higher level.

Mark Herman (film director/writer and Hull City fan): In 1964/65, Cliff Britton's City were starting on a bit of a roll, and there was suddenly a winning team only 30 miles down the road which, if my brothers and I pestered our Dad relentlessly enough, we could actually go and see. We went a few times, but it was the arrival of Wagstaff, Ian Butler and Ken Houghton that finally got me hooked and led to this life sentence, now in its sixth decade. With freedom still not an option.

Bernard Noble: Ian Butler shouldn't be forgotten. He put so many crosses in for Waggy and Chillo to score. A lot of First Division clubs – the big ones from London – came in for him, but he told me you just never got told about it in those days.

City came close to promotion in the 1964/65 season, but two defeats, a draw and a solitary win in the final four games of the season resulted in an anti-climactic fourth-placed finish. Everything was in place now, however. The 'famous five' frontline of Waggy, Chillo, Ken Houghton, Ian Butler and Ray Henderson were all in the building (though wouldn't start a game together until September the following season in a game against Reading), but it was the Wagstaff-Chilton partnership that really caught the eye.

Bernard Noble: If Paul Pogba is worth £90m these days then Waggy and Chillo wouldn't have been far off that. They were amazing. They knew each other so well; it was like clockwork.

Ian Thomson (Hull City fan): Waggy was simply magical to watch. Every time he received the ball in an attacking position you always felt that surge of anticipation. Say what you like about the game being quicker now, but the deadliness of his finishing, his coolness and that never-overplayed but clearly perceptible swagger were and still are totally captivating. Obviously Chillo was a tremendous striker but Waggy just had that little extra bit of style.

Ken Wagstaff: It was a super partnership from the beginning. There wasn't a better partnership than me and Chillo. Chillo was so powerful.

Martin Batchelor (Hull City fan): I always expected us to win and for Waggy or Chillo to be among the scorers, and so often that was the case. Even if we didn't win, and that became more and more the case, you could rely on one or both of them scoring.

Martin Fish: Chris Chilton, Ken Wagstaff, Ken Houghton, Ian Butler… that was the forward line and they were so exciting. You'd see plenty of goals – I believe they broke the league record for goals scored when they were promoted. Those were very good times.

Ken Wagstaff: I could play football, I wasn't just a goalscorer. I'd make them as well. Chillo was the same. If I got through with the goalie to beat, nine out of 10 times I'd score.

Paul Denman (Hull City fan and musician): There was no one to touch Waggy. Not now. Not ever. Arrogant, talented, rotund! He put Gordon Banks on his arse twice. You always thought we could win when he played, he was so confident and so calm. And he stayed with us. He could have gone elsewhere, I'm sure. Waggy, Chillo and Ian Butler were amazing to watch. I was nine when I first saw them play together at home to Coventry, in the North Stand under the clock and everyone had a hat on and was smoking a pipe. Maurice Swan was in goal and he let one in through his legs! I was hooked.

Robert Crampton (Hull City fan and journalist): I was a slightly overweight child, and Waggy was a slightly overweight footballer – sorry Ken – much like Franny Lee at that time, so he was my first hero. When you get a player that skilful, with that low centre of gravity, they're almost unbeatable.

Gary Clark (Hull City fan and author): Waggy and Chilton are the best pair of strikers I have ever seen don the famous black and amber at the same time. They were magnificent and if we had bought a goalkeeper and a centre half I have no doubt that Cliff Britton's Hull City would have reached the promised land a lot sooner than we did.

Mark Herman: Neither could have been the player they were without the other. They were simply the best we've ever had, in my time anyway, and I suspect the best we ever will have.

Roy North: Waggy and Chillo were fabulous. Chillo was so brave – a big lad and he was like a movie star. You got hammered as a big centre-forward then. There was a famous picture that was in the children's football books of him and Stoke's Denis Smith wrestling on the ground. But he took some stick. Waggy was a natural, just amazing. He had the power and the talent and the skill, a low sense of gravity but really fast. Cloughie supposedly wanted him at Derby, but Terry Neill wouldn't let him go.

Everyone in Hull knew that both Waggy and Chillo were good enough for England honours, but the call never came.

Bernard Noble: Just before the 1966 World Cup, Martin Peters apparently said to Ian Butler that he couldn't believe that both he and Geoff Hurst were in the England squad but Butler wasn't. Had he been playing for a West Ham he'd have been in that World Cup squad, without a doubt.

Ken Wagstaff: We played England in a warm-up game and Chris Chilton scored a couple of goals. Jack Charlton said: "Who the hell's that?"

Chris Chilton: There were scouts watching in London, at Watford or QPR, but me and Ken Wagstaff only got to tour Australia with the England League side. It would have been wonderful, but I enjoyed my trip to Australia.

Ken Wagstaff: We were unlucky when it came to England. If we'd been at a better club in the First Division – not to talk Hull City down – we'd have played for England. We were told we were close. We went with the League 22 to Australia in 1971. But you just didn't have Second or Third Division players playing for England.

City started the 1965/66 season in barnstorming fashion. It was to be late October before they failed to score in a game, and by Christmas the Tigers were top of Division Three.

Gary Clark: One abiding memory is being part of a 40,000-plus crowd a day or two after Boxing Day in a game against Millwall at Boothferry Park in 1965. We were top and they were hot on our heels in second place and we beat them 1-0. You just had to try not to listen to the Doubting Thomases in the corner – "City will never get to the First Division, they can't afford it." They were everywhere, bringing us all down to earth, whether we wanted to be brought down or not.

Martin Batchelor: I'd been pestering my Dad all season to be taken to see a match and finally he relented. The last game of one of the greatest seasons, pushed to a Friday night late in May because of our cup run. It was a night game with over 30,000 there; I'll never forget how green the grass was under the floodlights and how loud the crowd was. I forget the details of the game but Ian Butler got the single winning goal, there was a sending off of a Southend player, a whistle in the crowd, a bottle on the pitch – all it missed was a dog chasing the ball! I was hooked and thought it would always be like that.

Away from their exploits in the league, City made it to the sixth round of the FA Cup, and landed a plum away tie at First Division Chelsea. City drew the game 2-2, with Waggy scoring both, but were to lose the replay at Boothferry Park 3-1.

Ken Wagstaff: We didn't fear them, despite being the underdogs. With me, Chris, Ken Houghton and Ian Butler they had to worry a bit about us. The first goal I tapped in from an Ian Butler cross. For the second the centre-half headed it on to the back of my head, it dropped down and I went round the centre-half, went round the keeper and it was in. That's what I could do. Goalkeepers were non-existent. It was all taught to me by Raich Carter.

City didn't just win promotion, they romped to it. Only being shut out three times all season, City scored 109 goals in the league (and 122 in all competitions) to win Division Three by four clear points. In the league, Waggy scored 27 goals, Chillo 23, Ken Houghton 22, and Ian Butler and Ray Henderson weighed in with 13 apiece. The rest of the team scored four goals between them.

Chris Chilton: Promotion just felt inevitable. There were very few team changes. We just got on with the job. We knew what the pattern was. The players knew what they had to do. This was all down to Cliff Britton. We'd play up into one striker, then the midfielders would be buzzing around. Then they'd knock it in the spaces for us to run into.

Ken Houghton: It was a great season. In the 1964/65 season when I arrived with Waggy and Ian Butler, we went 20-odd games undefeated and only just missed out on promotion. I think we'd been about fifth from bottom when Waggy came, so it was a good climb up the table. But after that run, a lot of people were tipping us to go up in the 1965/66 season. We had a good forward line. People said we weren't as strong defensively but we were a team that liked to go on the attack. Sometimes the defence got blamed for leaking goals but it's a team effort so I found that unfair.

Ken Wagstaff: Cliff was a good organiser, everything was well planned, and he had some good players that he'd brought in. He was strict though, didn't like you drinking after Tuesdays! When you played away from home, you stayed in the best hotels, had the best food and so on.

Ken Houghton: Cliff was one of the best. You listened to him – he was an old-school type of manager. His knowledge of the game was first class. We had a good side but he won us a lot of games because of his tactical knowledge and his knowledge of the opposition's weaknesses. He'd go in the gym with us on Tuesday afternoons and we'd have team talks about the game on the previous Saturday. Cliff would put his trainers on – he was 60-odd – and would demonstrate certain parts of the game that he wanted us to do. He was a very good manager.

Gary Clark: I've been a Hull City fan since 1964, with no breaks of service. I witnessed the glory days of the Cliff Britton era when Ken Wagstaff and Chris Chilton were almost household names, like Toilet Duck. Nineteen sixty-six was the coming of age; England won the World Cup, Yorkshire ruled the cricketing world and Hull City romped away with the Third Division title. All five forwards scored double figures and City were a colossal club.

Ian Farrow (Hull City fan and fanzine editor): There were always goals and excitement. The excitement and the crowds as a young boy were what got me most. It also seemed a much more innocent time for football and I don't think that was just because of my age. Being honest I couldn't see much of the games. I recall my feet were always freezing cold. The rest of me was kept warm with a Hull City balaclava, Hull City gloves and a Hull City scarf. Still, I just loved the atmosphere and what I could see, usually Ian Butler cheered as he sped down the wing before putting over a cross. I occasionally saw Chris Chilton power in headers from these and I remember the Bunkers end surging forward as Waggy swerved and jigged inside the opposition box before getting in a shot. Did City score six and win every home game in those days? It seemed that way. I don't remember going home disappointed and recall goals raining in.

Ian Thomson: It's probably fair to say that it's unlikely that City will ever field such a lethal striking partnership again, and certainly not for as long as the six or seven years that Waggy and Chillo were together. But there were other fine players at that time who, overshadowed by Waggy and Chillo, never quite got the recognition that they deserved. That is especially true of Ken Houghton, whom I have always regarded as the most underrated player to have worn the amber and black in the 50 years I have been going to City. Other players of that era who would have graced any City side were Chris Simpkin and Ian Butler. Conversely, that fine attacking side was often woeful defensively. And I'm sorry if this sounds like heresy, but despite meriting almost-legendary status because he was such a massive character, Ian McKechnie was dreadfully erratic between the posts.

Frank and Margaret Beill: We had a feeling that everything was possible – especially as England had just won the World Cup. Next stop Division One.

When the promotion became mathematically certain, the celebrations were a little more understated than they would be 40 years later.

Chris Chilton: It wasn't that exciting. The crowd got excited but in the dressing room Cliff insisted on no drinking, no smoking. It was a little bit dour! Among the players there were a few hugs and that was about it.

Ken Wagstaff: Cliff took us to Scarborough to see the Black and White Minstrels. That was our gift from the club.

The last time City had been in the second tier was for a single season in 1959/60. This time, however, City were a different proposition altogether. The previous season's FA Cup run had shown that City could mix it with anyone on their day. The Tigers started the 1966/67 season with a 1-0 defeat at Coventry but then returned to their freescoring ways, being shut out only five more times in the season. City scored 77 times in finishing 12th – three more than champions Coventry. However, they also conceded 72 goals. Only the three relegated teams conceded more.

Ken Houghton: It was still a team in development. We weren't out of our depth but people kept saying if we'd bought defenders we'd have been promoted. But Cliff thought we were good enough and strong enough with what we had.

Halfway through the following season, Cliff Britton made a move to shore up his defence. Scotsman Tom Wilson was a legend at Millwall, and was mentoring future Lions great, Barry Kitchener. City had struggled in the first few months of the 1967/68 season, twice conceding six goals in a single game. This meant that Tom, upon signing for City, had his work cut out.

Tom Wilson: I joined the club in November 1967. Ken Wagstaff insisted that it was him that got me to Hull City, as he'd told Cliff Britton that he'd found me so hard to play against at Millwall. At the time Cliff was playing a very strict 'W' formation. He was a very old-fashioned English manager. He was strict on man-marking – you'd mark your opponent wherever they went. In my first game against Norwich the full-backs were running all over the place to stay with their men, so I told Cliff at half-time that I couldn't play like this. He said to me: "Tom you're a number 5, you go to the halfway line and you stay there. If the ball comes your way, send it back in the other direction. Stay with your man wherever he goes." I just couldn't play man for man; I could lose my wife in a supermarket. A couple of weeks later Cliff took us to Lilleshall for a week and he told me to organise 4-4-2. For five days, six or seven hours a day, that's all we did. We came back and played Rotherham and Derby, won games. That side at the time would score goals but also let in goals. We went on a great run playing this system, but then Cliff decided to change it back. I had discussions with him saying I couldn't play that way, and I talked my way out of the team in the end.

Frank and Margaret Beill: Tom Wilson was the best buy City ever made. He pulled a very leaky defence together saving City from almost certain relegation.

With Tom at the back, City finished 17th, two points above the relegation places. Waggy and Chillo had continued to knock the goals in, as they did in the 1968/69 season to see City finish 11th. A mid-table finish came the season after too. But with City failing to kick on in spite of having an embarrassment of goalscoring riches, Cliff Britton took on the role of general manager in the summer of 1970, and played a prominent role in selecting his successor. The man for the job would be 28-year-old Northern Ireland international Terry Neill, who joined from Arsenal as player-manager.

Terry Neill: I'd had hepatitis so it was evident that my time at the Arsenal was as good as over. I'd been out of football for about four months. Bertie Mee knew that I was into coaching – I'd taken my coaching badge at the age of 19 with Bobby Moore – and he helped word get around that I was looking for a coaching job. QPR offered me a lot of money, but Bertie mentioned Hull City and said he'd been talking to Cliff Britton, asking if I'd be interested in joining as player-manager. My response was instantly: "Where the hell is Hull?" I said I'd think about it as I was getting back into the Arsenal team around then. Brian James – a journalist friend of mine – did a lot of leg work for me and thanks to him I got to know everything about Hull City. I knew about every player, board member, the groundsman. I then started to meet up with Harold Needler on a regular basis in London. From the first minute we got on like a house on fire. A great man. The patron saint of Hull. He was very similar to Dennis Hill-Wood at the Arsenal, who'd been like a second father to me when I arrived.

I was enchanted by Harold, and when he finally offered me the job after a few meetings, I couldn't say anything but yes. I'd just been married and I came home from training and said to Sandra: "How do you fancy going to live in Hull?" She said: "Where is it?" Thankfully it wasn't long before she was as enchanted by Harold Needler and his family as I was. When we first drove into Hull together it was a lovely sunny day, which is always very helpful! Matt Busby was the first person to ring me when I got the job. He said: "It's not for me to give you advice, Terry, but aim for the stars and maybe you'll hit the sky." I must confess that I thought: 'It's far enough away from London that if I mess up, they might not hear down there.'

John Kaye: Terry was strict when he had to be, and he liked you to listen. You had to play exactly how he wanted you to play. He was great at man management too. That's one of the biggest assets a manager could have in any walk of life – if you can man manage, you're half way to being successful.

Paul Denman: He wasn't everyone's favourite but Terry Neill brought something to City we hadn't seen before: quick, one-touch football. We played Peterborough away in a cup game on a beautiful summer's day, it was his first game in charge and we were incredible. Different level. He had class and we were lucky to have him for that short period.

So what did Terry make of his new surroundings?

Terry Neill: I knew everything about everyone by the time I'd joined. I got the tail end of a lot of talented players. Ian Butler and Ken Houghton were great talents but they weren't getting any younger. We needed a bit of regeneration. We'd qualified for the Watney Cup thanks to two guys – Chilton and Wagstaff. I knew that what they needed was someone like me – a bit of steel at the back. Ian McKechnie was in goal, and I'd been in digs with him when I first arrived at the Arsenal. He was a left winger then. I was still fit enough as a player, and I think shocked a few. I don't think they were quite ready for the strenuous pre-season I had planned. It shocked them even more when I was out front in the runs, but I had to lead by example.

I got Ron Goodman, who supplied the playing kit to Celtic, Manchester United, and everybody who was anybody at the time. We were playing in stripes, and I said to him: "Ron, what I want is just the amber, and right in the middle of the shirt I want a big tiger with big fangs." I talked the players through it. I wanted to intimidate the opposition. I wanted it to remind them of who we were. It might sound a bit gimmicky, but at away games we knew the home fans didn't like us, but we'd all go out together in one line – not in dribs and drabs – and stand on the halfway line together and wave at the crowd. We'd get abuse, but it would wind the opposition players and fans up. They'd want to kick ten bells out of us. That worked in our favour.

Don Revie used to ring me every Thursday afternoon. That was when managers would do their gossiping. Don was brilliant, as was his wife Elsie. She'd ring Sandra when Don rang me. They used to invite us over all the time. Don was a huge help to me as he knew I was new to management and he was always there for advice.

Terry's first task was to lead City in the pre-season Watney Cup tournament, which was a pre-season knock-out competition for the leading scorers in the Football League from the previous season. First up, in the quarter finals, were Peterborough.

Terry Neill: David Pleat was a good winger but he ended up in Row Z after about 20 minutes thanks to yours truly. Waggy got two, Chillo got two and I ended up putting a winger into the crowd.

In the semi-final at Boothferry Park against Manchester United, a 1-1 draw created a little bit of history, as the match went on to be decided by penalties, a first in England. City lost the shootout, though Denis Law became the first person to miss in such a shootout when his penalty was saved by Ian McKechnie. However, McKechnie missed the final spot-kick to see City lose 4-3.

Terry Neill: Bobby Charlton is a good friend of mine, and he did me a favour. He took the coin off the referee and didn't let me see it. He just looked at me and said: "It's you to take a penalty, Terry." So I took the first one. And I think that Alex Stepney, as a favour to an old pal, dived early, as I was thinking: 'This is my home debut in front of 34,000 people and I'm taking the first penalty in a shoot-out.' I just whacked it and it went in thanks to Alex. It had been a good start.

Going into the season, there was an element of knowing what to expect from City – thrilling attacking play interspersed with some questionable defending.

Ken Wagstaff: We had great players like Ken Houghton, Ian Butler, Chris Simpkin. We bought John Kaye in the end to play in the defence, but if we'd had him when he was at his prime we'd have got in the top flight no problem. We'd always win 5-4 and 4-3. We didn't have the defenders.

Robert Crampton: We used to always start with the same team, week in week out. You could name all the starting XIs at that point. It seemed like that team of the early 70s had played together for ever. At that point it was the second best era in the club's history, and Waggy and Chillo were comfortably First Division strikers.

City eventually hit their straps under Neill and were to become fixtures in the top three. The 1970/71 season, however, would be defined by two games played in the space of four days in early March. On March 6th, City played a sixth round FA Cup tie against Gordon Banks' Stoke City at Boothferry Park. Ken Wagstaff scored twice but City lost a controversial game 3-2.

Ken Wagstaff: It didn't matter who the goalie was to me. I sent Gordon Banks the wrong way twice. He wrote about it at the time, saying the only team he didn't want to play against was Hull City because of what we could do. I always knew where Chillo was going to head it. We just knew each other's game.

Ian Thomson: In the Stoke cup-tie in which we were cheated twice, what ought to have been a 3-2 win went down as a 3-2 defeat.

Robert Crampton: The first game I have any recollection of is the 1971 FA Cup sixth round match against Stoke City, when I was seven. In classic clichéd fashion, I was stood on an orange box so that I could see. We were 2-0 up and lost 3-2, which set the pattern for the next 40-odd years. We did the same in the FA Cup final in 2014. It was gravely disappointing, but also hugely exciting.

Terry Neill: I was close to the action. We switched off, which was unprofessional, and I take a lot of the blame for that as I was meant to be leading by example. I was raging about the referee's decisions though.

Then, on March 9th, came the Battle of Bramall Lane. City travelled to Sheffield United with both sides chasing promotion. An early goal for the Blades couldn't shake City, who scored through Chris Simpkin and Ken Wagstaff to win 2-1 and go joint top of Division Two with 11 games to play.

Ken Wagstaff: That's when we bought Ken Knighton. On his debut he tackled someone round the neck and then it got all nasty.

Frank and Margaret Beill: We could smell promotion to the First Division.

Chris Chilton: I was excited and nearly deaf because of the crowd. It looked easy for us, and it felt easy for us. But then afterwards it was a huge disappointment. Five or six players just felt that they'd done well enough for the season and that stopped us going up. It was one of the weak links of the team.

Terry Neill: It was a hard game. Their manager had a right go at me afterwards. A few managers had done that because my job as a player and a manager was to stop us from conceding goals, and I rubbed a few talented players up the wrong way. Bob Stokoe wanted to stick one on me at the end of a game at Boothferry Park. But at Bramall Lane it was a real battle. The players had taken on board all the things that I was trying to do. We were resilient and we stood up to everyone – home and away – that season.

Ken Houghton: I was dropped for Ken Knighton! Someone else was dropped for Bill Baxter. Terry wanted the hard men in to nullify Sheffield United and to be fair we got the result. But after that we didn't do anything. We lost to Oxford in the next game. Terry changed the side and it turned the tide. Sometimes it works in your favour and sometimes it doesn't.

City did indeed fall away, winning only four of those remaining 11 games to finish a disappointing fifth.

Tom Wilson: We were good enough to go up. We had Bill Baxter and a good, solid defence, we had Waggy and Chillo up front and the under-rated Ken Houghton in midfield. Ian Butler was still there. We should have gone up, but I think it was more bad luck than any tactical reason that cost us promotion.

Terry Neill: I don't know why we fizzled out. I'm happy to take the blame though, because when you're the leader the onus is on you. There have been a lot of things in my playing and managerial career that I reflect on from time to time and think: 'Why did I do that?' So I have my regrets, as much for Harold Needler as for me, but even at that time I was thinking: 'If we do get promotion, we're going to have to spend some serious money.' And I'm not sure whether we could have afforded it. For a start, the training facilities weren't good enough. It was a poor excuse for a training pitch at the back of Boothferry Park. The pitch was great – Stan was a brilliant groundsman – but he didn't have the time to sort out the training pitch. I saw John Cooper at Hull University. I'd seen the pitches and been so impressed with them, so I did a deal that we'd go and train there. That was brilliant for us.

That summer Cliff Britton left the club and Tommy Docherty joined as assistant manager. Optimism was high but soon City were facing a future without their all-time leading scorer. With 193 league goals and 222 in all competitions, Chris Chilton left for Coventry for a fee of £92,000.

Chris Chilton: I had no chance of leaving the club. I was told that. It was a case of don't bother even asking for a transfer as it will get slung out. Finally I went to Coventry but got injured and had to retire.

Terry Neill: Chris was such a great player and so brave. He deserved a big money move. I talked with Noel Cantwell, who was at Coventry and in a bit of a fix, and I wanted to do the right thing by someone like Chris and let him earn a few quid, which he thoroughly deserved.

Stuart Pearson took on Chillo's number nine shirt and scored three goals in the next three games. It was the formative stages of what was to be a terrific career that would see the striker play for Manchester United and England.

Terry Neill: The younger players at the club at the time needed a season or so to bed in, but I just had to play Stuart Pearson. I loved him. Not only could he play, he would pick a fight with his shadow. I knew it was time to get him in the first team. He was taking on the other reserve teams on his own. In the end, Bill Nicholson at Spurs was ringing me constantly about him. It went on for months and months.

John Kaye: Stuart Pearson really stood out. He was an outstanding player. His pace was electric, he was a great finisher and he had good ability on the ball. Then when he went to Manchester United he improved further.

Ian Farrow: For some reason I recall a shout from the crowd during a game just after Chris Chilton was transferred to Coventry. "Pearson! You'll never be a Chilton!" opined the supporter. Obviously Stuart Pearson went on to score in cup finals and for England.

Mark Robinson (Hull City fan and England women's cricket team coach): My first game was in 1973, against Portsmouth at home. We won 4-1 and Stuart Pearson got all four. My dad and grandad were Hull City fans, and it's in your blood for good and bad. Chris Galvin was my early hero. I always wanted to be Chris Galvin.

After the excellence of the previous season, however, City couldn't escape mid-table in the 1971/72 season. One positive came in the November, when a defender signed and went on to have a big impact on the club in several ways.

John Kaye: I'd played at West Brom for nine years but they got a new manager in. I'm a local lad, from Goole, and this move meant I'd be living back near home. City were doing well at the time, and Terry Neill bought me. I'd been at Hull City when I was 15 or 16 and played a few games for the A team. I didn't like the set-up. The people running the team at the time would bully you, and I didn't think that was necessary with young players. Bob Brocklebank was the Hull City manager at the time, and he'd come to my mother's house a couple of times a week to try to change my mind, but I wouldn't budge. I played for Goole Town for about three months when Scunthorpe signed me for £5,000. I was there for three years and they sold me for £45,000.

Kaye helped to shore up the City defence, but a disappointing season was played out, resulting in a 12th-placed finish, after City had spent part of the season in the relegation places. However, this was a young side that only looked set to improve.

Terry Neill: I think the fans understood we had to go through a bit of evolution. As well as Stuart Pearson we had John Hawley coming through and others such as Roger De Vries. Roy Greenwood was extremely talented. He was so skinny but a good trainer and tough, even though he wasn't physically robust. I just needed a bit of patience. That said, I was player-manager of Hull, doing loads of PR stuff for the club, scouting players, managing Northern Ireland. I was doing 1000 miles a week. Maybe that didn't help. Thank God I had Wilf Dixon and Tommy Docherty assisting me. They were terrific. Always surround yourself with people who know more than you do!

Meanwhile, a physio who was to become a cult figure made his first appearance in the dugout.

Jeff Radcliffe: I started in 1973 and Terry Neill was the manager. Tommy Docherty had just left. We were a good Second Division club.

For the rest of Terry Neill's tenure at the club, City trod an uneventful path, never looking likely to go up or down. Then, in the summer of 1974, Neill left to manage Tottenham.

Terry Neill: I do regret that I didn't get Hull promotion, particularly for Harold Needler. He was a gentleman. A class act. I loved my time at Hull City. I loved the people there. But I got an illegal phone call from Tottenham. Out of my respect for Harold Needler I said they had to speak to him. Harold said: "I think you're ready for a bigger stage, Terry." I told him I'd only go with his blessing. I then got lovely notes and telegrams from players when I went down to Spurs. It was a change at Tottenham though. A horrible bunch of directors

This left the question of who would replace him. Brian Clough – recently sacked by Leeds – was one of the names rumoured. However, the answer came from within the current staff.

John Kaye: Terry went to Tottenham and had put my case forward with Harold Needler. When they asked me I said I'd do it for a month and see how it went. That month went fantastically and I got Manager of the Month. I felt that the players were behind me so I decided to have a go at it. When I took over, we were about third or fourth from bottom, and for the majority of my time as manager we were in the top half.

Jeff Radcliffe: John was carved out of granite but was a good chap.

Kaye enjoyed a successful first season in 1974/75, with City finishing eighth, the club's highest finish since 1970/71. Division Two was won by Manchester United, led by Stuart Pearson, who they'd signed from City for a record £200,000. However, the Red Devils lost to the Tigers 2-0 at Boothferry Park in November.

Robert Crampton: I was at the Manchester United home game in 1974/75. They were the hooligan kings of England at that time, believe it or not, and their fans just tore through a succession of provincial English clubs with this reign of terror for a year. They mounted a massive pitch invasion, with their scarves tied round their wrists, looking like Bay City Rollers fans. They ran up to the South Stand shouting "pussy cats". I've had this experience since as a journalist watching riots and wars, where on the one hand you're really frightened, but it's also one of the most thrilling things you've ever seen. I remember the infamous South Stand having a look and thinking: 'We don't fancy this.'

It was around this time that an important piece of headwear was introduced to the Boothferry Park masses. Jeff Radcliffe's famous tam-o-shanter was to get its first airing.

Jeff Radcliffe: On a cold wet night in Halifax or Rochdale when it's freezing and raining you need a hat. I don't remember quite how I got it. I think my mother bought it for me and I just stuck with it. But I got known by it. Lawrie McMenemy would always greet me saying: "Ah, it's the man with the tartan hat!"

On July 24th, 1975, Harold Needler, 'the father of Hull City', passed away unexpectedly. Needler was more than simply an owner, a chairman, he was an avuncular figure who'd built City in his own image – a family club that knew its importance to its community. His death was widely mourned, and to this day very, very few people can match the great man's contribution to the black and amber cause.

Terry Neill: Harold was a quietly spoken man who knew and loved his football. It was an absolute privilege to have known Harold and his family. I only ever had a great relationship with him. I worked with him, not for him. I had the greatest admiration and love for him.

When he died I was on pre-season tour in Germany with Tottenham. When I heard the news I didn't even contact the Spurs directors. I just got the next flight I could back to Hull. Tommy Docherty joined me at the funeral service and said to me: "I'd go over the end of the earth for that man. He is the best chairman I've ever known." When I look back on my life, I feel I've been one of the most fortunate guys – even though I've worked hard – to have had people like Dennis Hill-Wood, Danny Blanchflower and Harold Needler guide me along the way.

John Kaye: Harold Needler wanted Hull City in the top flight and I think he'd have put more money in, but the tax man had something to do with it. There seemed to be issues with corporation tax at the time. That held him back a little, meaning he couldn't put the money in as he had when he bought the likes of Ken Wagstaff and Ken Houghton.

It left a massive gap at Hull City when he passed away. His son took over at the club, but he wasn't committed in the same way as his father had been. He got people in as directors who thought they knew a lot about football but knew nothing. That led to me falling out with them.

Terry Neill: Hull City went on a long slide after Harold passed away. He knew his football and the club missed his leadership. I loved him.

In the 1975/76 season, City were left facing life without the genius of Ken Wagstaff. His last game came in a home match against Chelsea – the opponent that had done so much to build his reputation in 1966 – in November 1975.

Ken Wagstaff: I went to Harley Street and they said my cruciate ligaments were in a mess so the club took the insurance and I retired. Then I went out to Australia and I was managing but I played a little bit.

City finished the season in 14th, with Alf Wood, Paul Fletcher and Dave Sunley struggling to fill Waggy's boots, and attendances dipping considerably below the 10,000 mark.

With Chillo long gone, Stuart Pearson starring for Manchester United, and now Waggy retired, the emphasis was very much on looking for the next generation of stars to move Hull City onwards and upwards. Jeff Wealands was an outstanding goalkeeper who was to spend much of his career in the top flight. Frank Banks, Roger De Vries, Peter Daniel and Stuart Croft were all very good defenders at this level, with Daniel receiving England under-21 call-ups along with midfielder Paul Haigh. Haigh was joined in midfield by the likes of Jimmy McGill, Chris Galvin and Mally Lord. However, even though John Hawley was coming through, it was goals that City were lacking.

John Kaye: I put a lot of kids in when I was a manager. The likes of Dave Stewart, Paul Haigh, Stuart Croft, Peter Daniels. When they were playing for us we'd got up to third or fourth, and had beaten Sunderland at home 3-1 in late 1974 with a load of young players. I made a mistake, however. I thought I was doing the right thing in resting a few of them as I thought they'd get tired. I should have left them in until they did get tired. But you do what you think is right at the time.

There was no youth policy at all when I took over. When I came in we had scouts all over the country. Steve McLaren came through like that, as did Eddie Blackburn and Stuart Croft. But then the directors complained that we'd spent too much on scouting and the like. I pointed out that the sale of Stuart Pearson paid for the scouting system for 20 years, so I don't know what they were complaining about.

City were to finish 14th in the 1976/77 season too. However, within the Tigers' ranks now was one of the most tigerish players of all time: Leeds and Scotland legend Billy Bremner.

John Kaye: Billy was a fantastic player. I'd played against him numerous times and I thought a player with his ability and enthusiasm would rub off on the younger players. It did to a certain extent, but Billy had a bad back and couldn't play as much as we needed him to. But it wasn't a difficult task to get him to Hull City. I knew him, and I knew he'd had a fall out at Leeds. That helped get him here.

Jeff Radcliffe: Billy Bremner was marvellous. When he had his medical his fitness was remarkable, his joints showed no sign of wear. He was very good around the place.

John Kaye had hoped to follow this up with other high-profile signings but was finding that Harold Needler's absence in the boardroom was hindering him.

John Kaye: I thought I was doing quite well. I sold Roy Greenwood to Sunderland for £100,000 or so, and I wanted to sign Frank Stapleton, who was 19 and at Arsenal back then, Alan Ball, who I used to room with, and Terry McDermott. I didn't get any of them. If Harold Needler had still been alive, he'd have said yes. Christopher Needler didn't have the same enthusiasm though.

I got Alan Warboys and Bruce Bannister here to do a job, which I thought they would do, and I would have got them to do that, but they didn't give me enough time. I wasn't with them long enough.

However, one arrival at Boothferry Park was very welcome indeed.

Ken Houghton: John Kaye became manager and I was the player-manager at Scarborough. John brought a team to play us, mainly kids, and after that he thought I could do a job looking after the apprentices – Garreth Roberts, Brian Marwood, Craig Norrie, Rob MacDonald, Garry Swann, we had quite a few good players. We blended them into a good side.

Christopher Needler stepped down as chairman before the 1977/78 season, with Bob Chapman taking the reins, and City started with a 3-0 win at home to Sunderland, thanks in part to a strike from new signing Bruce Bannister. By early October, however, John Kaye was sacked in spite of City still being in mid-table.

John Kaye: We weren't progressing enough. One of the directors would ring me before games telling me he'd looked in the Guinness Book of Records and had seen that a certain player had broken a scoring record. I'd have to explain that the player he was talking about had retired. But this director kept coming back, always with the same players' names trying to tell me who to sign. I got argumentative and that was an issue behind why they got rid of me.

Bobby Collins was given the manager's job – much to the surprise of the press and fans, who'd been expecting Billy Bremner to get it – but only succeeded in leading City into the relegation zone. He was sacked in February 1978, having had the job for only four months. Wilf McGuinness was given the job on a caretaker basis until in April, with City already effectively relegated, Ken Houghton was given the role full-time.

Ken Houghton: After John was sacked they had a load of quickfire managers and they didn't know who to turn to. I was the last one left who could take over. Andy Davidson was pushing for me to get the job, and they offered me it. Naturally I wasn't going to refuse, but I don't think I was ready for it. And the club was all but relegated at that point.

Jeff Radcliffe: After John went, Ken Houghton took over. Him and his assistant Wilf McGuiness were great to work with but the results didn't quite reflect that.

City finished bottom of Division Two but went into the next season with some renewed vigour, despite losing the services of Bremner, John Hawley, Dave Roberts, Peter Daniel and a handful of others. The excitement came because Sheffield United's star striker, Keith Edwards, had moved to Boothferry Park.

Keith Edwards: My first problem, coming from Sheffield, was figuring where Hull was. I met Ken Houghton in Pontefract and he was down to earth, not big on the compliments – and I was a bit disappointed with the fee. When I eventually got to Hull, having come from Sheffield United, it was a bit of a let down, without being too disrespectful. However, I loved the pitch, which was 10 times better than Bramall Lane. So it was a mixed feeling on moving. But it was my first ever move so it was bound to be a little bit strange. I'd been on £150 a week at Sheffield United and went to £190 a week at Hull, along with a loyalty bonus of £6000 at the end of the season, and as a young man just married with a child, such a pay rise was great. I was shocked that Sheffield United were prepared to sell me though.

Ken Houghton: I'd seen Keith a few times and I thought he would fit in brilliantly and score us goals. He didn't disappoint. He knew where the back of the net was. He was another Waggy.

Also breaking through were two legends in the making in Pete Skipper and Garreth Roberts.

Pete Skipper: I was playing at Schultz in a local league. We were one of the best amateur sides in the city. I'd had three games on trial at Carlisle, and did reasonably well there, but then Ken Houghton put an advert in the paper to ask if there was anyone local who thought they were good enough to play for City. The best ones would play in the reserves. Brian Redburn and Norman England from Schultz got in touch with City to ask that Paul Oberg and myself be given a couple of games. Things went okay. That was November 1978, and in February 1979 I was offered a full-time contract. I had just come out of my apprenticeship and I actually took a pay cut to go to City, but I was more than willing to do it. I made my debut in the March at Swansea in a 5-3 defeat on a Friday night. They had a very good side with John Toshack, Leighton James, Jeremy Charles and Ian Callaghan. I did okay for the rest of the season.

Garreth Roberts: I'd been at City for a season-and-a-half as an apprentice, with Ken Houghton and Chillo running that side of things. You couldn't ask for better than that for a start in your career. I made my debut when I was 18 at home to Bury, playing alongside Keith Edwards and Gordon Nisbet. It was a team in transition. We weren't that great, and that's when as a young lad you generally get your chance to make your debut. Ken had been promoted from the backroom staff to being the manager and had decided to put some of the young lads like me, Brian Marwood and Pete Skipper in the team. I think we finished mid-table in the end so it worked for him. But the club was struggling.

Keith Edwards: Garreth Roberts was a great midfield player and ended up being my best pal. We instantly hit it off. There was a bit of a drink culture in those days. I wasn't included in that, so me and Garreth would go off and play a few other sports. Garreth was a great help to me, and he was bright enough to see that I could knock a few goals in, so he'd play the ball through to me all the time. He passed to me all the time, and I didn't pass to anyone!

City started the season reasonably well, with the away support bolstered by the now highly visible 'City Psychos' coaches following the club everywhere, but with money short in supply and interest among the board seemingly low, an instant return to the second tier never seemed likely.

Ken Houghton: I don't think Chris Needler was that interested in the football side, which was fair enough. But if his dad had been there we'd have been given a bit more money. The board didn't have money to spend. It was a bit beg, steal and borrow when I was having to get sponsors, the kit and things like that. That's unheard of now, a manager doing that.

Keith Edwards: It was a really good season for me. I got my first goal at Tranmere and then knocked them in left, right and centre. The team's performance was disappointing but the consolation was that I was scoring goals and soon established myself. Twenty-four goals in a struggling team is a very good return.

After finishing eighth in the first season back in Division Three in 1978/79, hopes were high that City had something to build on in the following season. However, by New Year's Eve City had won just four league games, and Ken Houghton lost his job in the December.

Ken Houghton: If you're the manager and the team's not doing well, it's you that gets the push. It was results driven. I thought we were doing okay, and I fancied our chances the second season back in that division. We started off well but we had a run of four or five games where we didn't win and the axe came out very quickly. I knew we weren't quite good enough to go up, but the money wasn't there.

I enjoyed my time at Hull. I hadn't wanted to leave Rotherham, as they were my home town and are a lovely family club, but when I came to City it was more of a professional club and I really enjoyed myself. I felt I got on well with everybody, and every year since I got the sack I've been to watch with my son.

Former Wales manager Mike Smith replaced Houghton and was to be the man to take City into a new decade.

The 1970s had started with City being one of the most upwardly mobile football clubs outside the top flight. Harold Needler's benevolence, Cliff Britton and then Terry Neill's tactical acumen, and the brilliance of the likes of Waggy, Chillo, Ken Houghton, Ian Butler, Ray Henderson, Chris Simpkin and co made the Tigers the envy of many clubs. However, the decade had seen the club unravel, unable to replace Harold Needler's dedication in the boardroom and Waggy and Chilllo's exploits in front of goal. The club's financial problems were mounting too, the extent of which would only become known in the years to come. After a bright start the 1970s ended up being a disappointing decade for City in many ways, and the prospects for the 1980s did not look good.

1980s

A new decade started with a new manager in Mike Smith but a familiar problem on the pitch, as City were thrashed 5-1 at Plymouth. How were City players finding their new manager?

Garreth Roberts: Mike Smith was like a schoolteacher. He'd been at Wales and was managing in a different way to what any of the players were used to. He wanted to do strange things. One was the 'POMO line', which was 'the position of maximum opportunity'. He'd always be telling us to get the ball to the 'POMO line' but none of us knew what the hell it was. Eventually he told us he meant the far post.

Keith Edwards: Mike Smith was hit and miss. I didn't quite see eye to eye with him. He took me off once and I reacted immaturely and had a bit of a tantrum. As the crowd were walking past the dressing room after the game they were all banging on the walls shouting: "Smith out, Edwards in!" which was embarrassing.

Jeff Radcliffe: It was awful. Mike Smith was one for statistics. One pre-season he took us through to Carnegie College in Leeds for some fitness assessments. We did all these tests on the players, and Garreth Roberts' fitness level came back as 'man in the street'. Garreth could run forever! Mike put a training regime into place that had us running our socks off, even on a Friday before the game, and we'd just leave everything out there on the track. They were too knackered come the Saturday.

Indeed, Smith was to clash with one promising local lad.

Pete Skipper: Mike Smith came in after Ken Houghton had been sacked. My face didn't fit, so I went up to Darlington for two years. Some people at the club had been trying to get me to go to local non-league sides, which I didn't want to do.

Smith was to bring in Tony Norman, Nicky Deacy and Dale Roberts, and ushered out the likes of Paul Moss, Malcolm Lord, Ian Dobson, Trevor Phillips, Dave Hawker and Eddie Blackburn.

On May 3rd, 1980, Hull KR played Hull FC at Wembley in rugby league's Challenge Cup final. Both sides were regulars on Grandstand in the early 80s, and at a domestic level at least, rugby league was one of the most visible team sports in the country, with Eddie Waring's commentary a favourite of every impressionist of the time. The final was to give credence to a myth that was to follow Hull City around for the next 20 years – that Hull was a 'rugby town'. This was rarely backed up with any hard evidence. Indeed, over the next two decades football was to be the predominant sport in the city in some respects. Each year group in each junior or senior school in the city would have a football team, but not necessarily a rugby team. Hull's Sunday League football network was – with more than 20 leagues of 12 teams – considered to be the largest in the UK. Five-aside football was much more widely played in the city's leisure centres than touch rugby. Pubs would be much fuller for football games of national significance than their rugby counterparts (particularly from the 1990s onwards).

Historically, Hull City have bettered Hull FC's record home attendance of 28,798 more than 100 times and Hull KR's 22,282 more than 300 times. Hull City's average league attendance since the move to the KC Stadium up to and including the 2017/18 season has been 15,600 at its lowest and 24,800 at its highest (though this figure looks set to drop for the 2018/19 season). The respective figures for Hull FC are 10,600 and 14,600. Hull undoubtedly has a passion for rugby league – most people in the city have an allegiance of some sort to one of the two sides – but this has not necessarily been at the expense of the round-ball game. Hull – to its credit – is simply a sporting city with no footballing code able to claim any real supremacy. However, in May 1980, Hull City did feel like a local irrelevance.

Garreth Roberts: At that time football didn't have the status it has today and the media coverage wasn't half what it is now. I remember playing against Southend at home when Hull FC played Hull KR at Wembley in the Challenge Cup final and there was that classic sign left on the A63 saying: 'Would the last person out of Hull turn out the lights?' There were about 4,000 there and we did feel that we were under the radar locally at that point, but it didn't take us long to turn that around and within a year or two we were the top dogs. At that point maybe Hull did feel like a rugby town when City were in the doldrums and FC and Rovers were at the top of their game. You had maybe 30,000 sports lovers in the city and who'd get the support depended on who was top dog. If we were doing well we could get 12,000 or 13,000 or so and the rugby clubs would be getting 6,000. Whoever was winning or entertaining would get the bigger crowds.

Mark Robinson: In my youth the Hull City fans seemed to hate Hull FC more than anyone else, Leeds included. When City were about to go bust, the club decided to let Hull FC parade the Challenge Cup around the pitch to try to get a few more fans in. The Hull FC fans supported our opponents that day. It was an important game and when the opposition scored the Hull FC fans cheered them. So there was a big anti-rugby feeling. We felt like a minority as Hull City fans within the city around then.

The 1979/80 season ended with City finishing fifth from bottom in the Third Division. The club didn't feel particularly forward-looking or ambitious, but the core of an excellent side was already taking shape with Tony Norman, Brian Marwood, Steve McClaren and Garreth Roberts breaking through. Indeed, the latter was soon elevated to a captaincy role.

Garreth Roberts: Mike made me captain at 20 or 21, which was a bit of a poisoned chalice as one or two of the older lads weren't too pleased about it. I was proud to captain my home-town club though, and luckily that carried on for a number of years. I had to battle through the differences of opinions of an older dressing room on a daily basis though.

Keith Edwards was reliably knocking in goals for City in the 1980/81 season, but was lacking a suitable foil, particularly one with a physical presence. That was to be resolved in October 1980 with a signing from non-league football for the sum of £2,000. Billy Whitehurst was now a Tiger.

Billy Whitehurst: I was playing for Mexborough Town in the Midland League and got picked for a select side to play against Nottingham Forest. I scored but didn't think I played that well. There was due to be a series of select games against league sides, as we were quite a good standard, and this was the first. There was a scout there from Hull City who asked Mexborough's manager, Harry Lee, if I'd go and play for Hull reserves at Notts County. Harry asked me if I wanted to and I said yes, so I went and played in the reserves. I met up with Cyril Lea, and Chris Chilton was on the coaching staff. Chris was playing a few games for the reserves then so I got to play alongside him, which was great. That said, I wasn't too strong on my Hull City history at that point, so I didn't really know who he was. When I look back, it's great to think the first person I played up front with in a Hull City shirt was Chillo.

I scored a goal in that game, gave 100% and afterwards Mike Smith spoke to Harry Lee and said they wanted to sign me there and then. That was on the Tuesday night and I was in Hull on Thursday signing, and then I played for the first team on the Saturday against Gillingham. It was quite a culture shock for me. I think it came as a shock to some of my team mates too, as Keith Edwards and a few of the others didn't seem too impressed with my performance or how I went about things! Chillo called me a rough diamond. I think he was being kind. I was more like a rough brick.

Keith Edwards: We wondered about this edgy footballer who'd come in from being a bricklayer, but he was perfect for me. We didn't hit it off straight away, but once we did it was great.

Billy started a handful of games but his raw talent had not yet won over the Boothferry Park faithful. Luckily Billy had a kindred spirit among the coaching staff in Chris Chilton.

Billy Whitehurst: Chris worked hard with me but I found the transition hard. I was in digs down Calvert Lane with Brian Marwood and Gary Swann. That was fortunate for me as they were both model professionals. I went in and didn't know what was going off, but I got into their rhythm and I wouldn't have made it without that. The first 18 months in particular were difficult for me, I didn't play at all well. But Chris worked so hard with me, even after training and he really helped me with my touch, which was terrible. My second *and* third touch were a tackle. When I worked on that, I improved so much as a player. Chris was massive for getting me where I got to as a player.

Chris Chilton: When I was coaching Billy Whitehurst, I was committed to being a marvellous header of the football but Billy was useless at it. I think he just wanted to punch the ball in the goal. He was very aggressive. He maybe looked at me and saw someone who'd done it all and I got him under my wing and told him what I wanted him to do. He did the club proud in the end.

Keith Edwards: Chris Chilton was a wonderful coach, and I learned so much from him. He was a nice fella and an absolute pleasure to work with. You could see that he was a bloody good player in training too. Chris was a real positive for me.

Billy Whitehurst: My first goal came against Iain Hesford, who was playing for Blackpool. Alan Ball was their manager at the time. It was as if a monkey was taken off my back. Each week after that it seemed to get easier. I was playing with more freedom. I started to get a few cheers from the fans, particularly when they were calling my name out before a game, and that gives you confidence too. The crowd doesn't realise how much they can affect a player, even in the pre-match kickabout. A bit of encouragement makes a player feel 10 times bigger than what they are. When I was getting cheers from the Hull fans I felt like 10 men. I'd improved a lot though. I just turned the corner before my two-year contract was up, and they thought I was worth persevering with.

The 1980/81 season is not one that Hull City fans will look back upon with much affection. By mid-November, City had only won two games and were propping up the Third Division. The likes of Paul Haigh, Gordon Nisbet and Stuart Croft were sold. However, drawing Blyth Spartans in the second round of the FA Cup was to prove memorable for two reasons. First, it took a third game on a neutral Elland Road to settle the tie. Second, City fans were to get their first glimpse of the great Les Mutrie.

Les Mutrie: Blyth should have won every one of those games. We were a team full of what we would class as 'proper' footballers, with three current England non-league players, including myself. Even bearing in mind where Hull were in their league, we were very confident of beating them.

In the first game we hit the bar and the post and were generally running amok but Hull scored on the break through Keith Edwards. I equalised late in the game with a right-foot strike that gave Tony Norman no chance. That meant we were off to sunny Blyth for the midweek replay, which saw goals and drama galore.

It was a sell-out crowd, a great atmosphere and Hull were first off the mark through Edwards again. Then I went on a mazy midfield run past a few and the ball just sat up inviting a 30-yard strike, which flew into the net. This was followed by another run and long cross-field pass to Ray Young, who struck another 30-yarder screaming into the net. It was pandemonium. However, Hull equalised to take the match into extra time. That led to more high drama in a game that Blyth should have already won. I was fouled in the box and a penalty was given. I had been penalty taker in every team I played for from an early age, and I struck it hard and low to Tony Norman's left, who dived full length and saved it, and then saved the follow up as well. So a draw and off to Leeds for a second replay.

At Elland Road, Keith Edwards scored first. Then there was more extraordinary drama which saw Blyth awarded another penalty, which I hit into Row Z. Fortunately the ref noticed an encroachment and ordered it to be retaken, before which I could hear my manager screaming at me to ask if I was OK to take it, among various other expletives. I got the job done and scored, which meant extra time again. Hull got the winner, and then in a very disappointed dressing room my manager told me to get changed very quickly and come with him and the chairman. I was led to Christopher Needler and told of Hull's interest in signing me. The next morning I was picked up early by my chairman and driven to Boothferry Park. I sat there while Mr Turney, Blyth's chairman, organised a record fee for a non-league player, as well as my contract, and so the story began.

City were eventually knocked out of the FA Cup by First Division Tottenham, who won the third-round tie at White Hart Lane 2-0 in spite of a Tony Norman masterclass. However, Les Mutrie was now a City player. Keith Edwards was the focal point of the City attack, but Les was also being partnered up front with Billy Whitehurst, who by now was more settled into the ways of league football. The two were to hit it off, albeit not immediately.

Billy Whitehurst: We complemented each other. Les was very, very skilful. I played with some of the best players in the world – the likes of Paul Gascoigne – and I'm serious here: Les Mutrie's touch was as good as anyone I've played with. He had the ball on a string. It was a pity that he was lost in the non-league system for so long. Had he not been released as a kid he'd have gone on to be a top-class player in the higher leagues. But in those days it was always a physical battle between the centre-half and the centre-forward, and I was always happy to take on the brunt of that. I'd always take the knocks for the likes of Les and Keith Edwards.

Les Mutrie: I went from a very successful non-league side to one struggling bottom of their division. I also had to contend with the ardour of full-time training and trying to fill the boots of fan favourite and legendary goalscorer Keith Edwards, who was in dispute with the club and shortly to leave for Sheffield United. Mike Smith was a quiet boss who I was extremely grateful to. Unfortunately it was apparent that quite a few of the squad were either not up to scratch or were not putting in the effort to justify their substantial weekly wages, which was the reason for the malaise and the uncertainty surrounding the club, which resulted in relegation. I only scored five or so goals in that season, which led to the Hull Daily Mail reporter Simon Redfern giving an absolutely scathing opinion of my ability and that of my partner in crime Billy Whitehurst in his profile for the coming season. To what was a dwindling fan base, I scored 27 goals that next season, as I had the great pleasure of reminding Simon, which included 14 in nine games – still a record to this day.

What had been for a long time an inevitable relegation came with City finishing the 1980/81 season bottom of the Third Division. This meant fourth-tier football for the first time in the club's history, having only ever played in Division Three (North) at its previous low points. The 'Action Group' was formed towards the end of the season, and was to organise coffins to be led down Boothferry Road and ask Raich Carter to take over the club.

Another blow came early in the 1981/82 season as Keith Edwards left the club to return to Sheffield United.

Keith Edwards: Hull City needed the money. It was a very difficult time. My first spell at Hull City was ruined with relegation, a lack of finance – though I was always well paid – and problems on and off the pitch. I had my second daughter born in Hull, which was a bit difficult, and my wife wasn't convinced about settling in the city so we were looking to move back to Sheffield. Personally I did alright, and was linked with a lot of other clubs – which you enjoy as a young man – such as Newcastle and Middlesbrough. But Hull needed to get some money back.

City didn't quite set Division Four on fire at the beginning of the 1981/82 season, but Les Mutrie had most certainly settled into the life of a full-time pro by this point and was gaining admirers among the City faithful. Indeed, between a game against Tranmere on February 13th and a home match against Port Vale on March 20th, Les scored in nine consecutive league matches (hitting the back of the net 14 times), a club record.

Les Mutrie: Around this time I was perceived as the man to go in the big games as the team's main goalscorer, along with Big Billy, who was by now a firm favourite with the fans.

Another far more serious event was to take place in the February, however. Christopher Needler announced that his family could put no more money into Hull City. The club was losing a reported £9,000 a week. This led to Hull City becoming the first club in English football to go into receivership, on February 25th, 1982. First to go was manager Mike Smith along with assistant Cyril Lea. Bobby Brown and Chris Chilton took over managing the first team. Every player was placed on the transfer list.

Billy Whitehurst: I felt sorry for Mike Smith. The nucleus of that squad that went on to be so successful was down to him. Colin Appleton reaped the rewards of Mike's work to a certain extent.

For the players and fans, even though the club's form had picked up, it was a time of uncertainty and worry. Well, for most. Unsurprisingly very little worried Billy Whitehurst.

Billy Whitehurst: It wasn't a worrying time. We didn't worry about that. We were winning games. We were still getting paid, even though some of that was coming from the fans, which was tremendous. I thought they were great days. We had great camaraderie. We all got together and rolled our sleeves up. It brought us closer together. We were great mates in that team. We didn't have that in the teams I went to afterwards. The atmosphere wasn't the same.

Ian Farrow: The first time you go into receivership, especially when your club is the first to face that humiliation, it is shocking. When we heard the news me and my City-supporting buddy and best mate Dave decided we'd wear black ties to our respective office jobs. It was a sign of respect for the death of our club – we really did think they were going out of existence – and we also did it so people would ask why we were wearing black. We thought it would help publicise the predicament. We went to the pub after work and talked about how we'd spend our Saturdays when there was no City. At that time it made national headlines in the newspapers and it really did seem like it was the end.

Martin Batchelor: I remember receiving the Hull Daily Mail from my dad in 1982, with front page headline saying we'd gone into receivership. I thought we'd never get back from that.

Matt Rudd: Nineteen eighty-two was a bad one, as the money had run out and nobody seemed inclined to find any. Half the management team was made redundant, the players all went on the transfer list and the supporters cried on Bunkers and on North Road.

With Hull City in financial peril, all that the fans could do was hope a saviour would turn up from somewhere. Hull FC chairman Roy Waudby was widely reported to be on the verge of buying the club. However, it turned out that just up the A165 in Scarborough there was a man with money, ambition and a desire to get involved with the Tigers.

Don Robinson: I'd been running Scarborough – where we'd been to Wembley and won the FA Trophy a few times – and out of the blue Chris Needler and another director approached me about coming to Hull City because they were in trouble. I'd played a bit of rugby league for Hull KR and I was over the moon! I thought: 'Gee whizz!'

Jeff Radcliffe: Don was like a breath of fresh air. You never knew what was going to happen with him. He was good for the club, he did lots of publicity things, took us abroad. I always had a lot of time for Don.

Billy Whitehurst: The first time I ever met him, in a restaurant in Scarborough, he told me he'd take me in a phone box and knock 10 bells of shit out of me. It was all tongue-in-cheek though. Don Robinson was one of the best things to happen to Hull City. As a person he is really nice. He helped a lot of people with things away from football, me included. He was like a friend to us and he's a fantastic man. He did stuff that lower division teams just didn't do. Going to America was incredible. He had us all over the place, forever dressing up in different outfits promoting the club. At the time we felt like redcoats at Butlins, but when you look back on it they are great, great memories.

Garreth Roberts: Don was the catalyst to that five or six years of success. It was all because of him. If he hadn't come along the club would have dawdled along and we'd have gone nowhere. His enthusiasm, his bravado… everything he did was weird, scary, funny or all three at once. He was so vibrant and it rubbed off on the players. We thought he was completely nuts at times, but what a bloke… The stuff he was saying, such as us being the first team to play on the moon, was great and it got us noticed.

Billy Whitehurst: Don got Jack Charlton in to give us a talk not long after he'd started. I always remember Jack Charlton saying: "All of us like to dream, but Don Robinson makes his dreams come true." And that's what he did at Hull City. He took us out of the dark days.

Les Mutrie: Don Robinson was the glue that held everyone together, taking us on outings that were bonding sessions, organising family get-togethers, and the poor bloke tried his best to broker a truce between Colin Appleton and myself, to no avail. My abiding memory of Don was when I heard a knock on the back door at my club house on North Road after I'd complained there were no kitchen tops there. Don came along with his tool box, took off his coat and tie and spent the next few hours sweating like a pitbull until the job was done. He was a very likeable man.

Ian Bunton (Hull City fan): After many dark years at City, Don Robinson seemed to put the fun back into the game and club. His ideas may have been a bit odd at times, but he did help generate some success on the pitch, which had been lacking for many a year.

Neil Buckley: I didn't spend that much time with Don, as I was a junior pro in his time there, but I went with the first team to Port Aventura in Spain with him a couple of times. Don knew every celebrity out there. You'd have Joe Cocker, Sean Connery and people like that in the hotel, and Don knew every single one of them. On those trips he knew I was a young kid and he'd treat me wonderfully.

Martin Fish: Don was a one-off. He's a unique man. Procedures, companies acts and all the rest of it – he didn't want any of that. He worked on his wits. You'd rarely see him write anything down. He'd conduct board meetings and tell us what he was going to do, but then he left everyone else to get on with their particular functions. But you never knew what was going to come next. He was very charismatic. Christopher Needler found him difficult to deal with though. Chris was very straightforward and Don was a loose wire. But Chris knew Don was trying to do a decent job.

Pete Skipper: Don was very extrovert, but it was great for the football club. Whatever he did, publicity wise, got people interested. He did well by the players, he introduced a new bonus scheme for us where we got crowd bonuses if the attendance hit a certain level. He kept everyone involved. Everybody was happy.

Ian Thomson: I was very lucky to have had the job of looking after directors, visiting directors and their guests in the Boothferry Park boardroom between 1983 and 1993 and so got to know a succession of directors, managers, players and staff. Colin Appleton was very reserved, Brian Horton and Dennis Booth were tremendous, Eddie Gray a nice guy but quiet. As you might expect, Don Robinson was the absolute life and soul of the place, a real larger-than-life character. In the early Robinson days his vice-chairman was a guy called Clifford Waite, very old school and a real stickler, who actually ran things behind the scenes and was as responsible as Robinson for the strict financial controls that were in place at that time. I can still hear him chuntering and harrumphing when it got to 7pm and the party was still in full swing, with Don showing no sign of wanting to head off home to Scarborough.

Martin Fish: I remember one case where Don had been advised by the auditors that it was alright to loan money to players. I was involved on the financial side, and I noticed a few loans that had been made. I told Don and he said: "That's alright, the auditor said I can do that." I told him that there was nothing anywhere on paper as to when the players were going to repay these loans. Don said: "Leave that with me, but I doubt we'll get any of it back so we can write it off as a bad debt." I asked him if he'd okayed that with the auditors, and I didn't get a clear answer. One day he came to me and said: "I'd like you to try and get the money that Billy Whitehurst owes." It was nothing much at all but I called Billy to the office and asked him for a repayment. Billy told me that Don had told him it was a gift. We carried on for about half an hour. Billy was a big fella, and he got off his chair and leaned over to me and said: "Are you asking me to repay this?" I thought: 'I'm going to finish up in this filing cabinet, aren't I?' But I told him that I was, and I had a job to do. He turned to me and said: "You can tell Don Robinson to stick this money where the sun doesn't shine. But I might pay a bit of it because I admire your guts."

Don came in as part of an arrangement that saw the Needler family – largely through a trust set up by Harold's wife, Hilary – retain their involvement in both Hull City and Boothferry Park. However, as far as the day-to-day running of the club was concerned, it was Don Robinson's show, and with Mike Smith long gone City needed a manager. Colin Appleton had done an excellent job for Don Robinson at Scarborough, and he was given the opportunity to repeat that success at Boothferry Park.

Colin Appleton: I'd received a phone call from Don Robinson asking me to go and watch a Hull City game with him at Boothferry Park. At the time Hull City were struggling financially. I later heard that he'd paid £250,000 to become the club's majority shareholder and he asked me to join him at Hull as the new manager. He told me there were severe financial limitations and I wouldn't be offered a contract, but the chance to get back into management in full-time football was something I couldn't turn down.

Don Robinson: Colin had been at Scarborough as a player and manager, and had won the FA Cup as a player with Leicester. He'd done a very good job at Scarborough, very team minded and very good with the fans. He could spot what was wrong and put it right. It was great to get him to Hull.

Les Mutrie: Colin Appleton came in at a very difficult time, with the club having sacked Mike Smith and having just had to contend with receivership. Colin was renowned as a very defensive-minded manager for what was one of the most successful non-league sides of all time. They were a side I never scored against at Blyth so I knew what was coming.

Garreth Roberts: Colin Appleton was not a normal type of manager but he had a massive impact on the younger players. That was the type of player he needed – ones that would listen – because he could talk the hind legs off a donkey. You'd listen to him in a team meeting, which would last hours, and not really realise what he was talking about for days afterwards. When it clicked, however, you'd realise he was spot in. He was a good manager and he was the right foil to Don. Don was the Eric Morecambe to Colin's Ernie Wise. They were a great double act.

Jeff Radcliffe: Colin was a character – his team talks were interesting. I'd listen into them and you'd look around and see that the players didn't have a clue what was going on. He carried his office around in his jacket pocket!

Les Mutrie: Colin picked me regularly in the side until he realised I could not, at my age, track up and down the field and then show my skill and flair when given the chance, which is when he resorted to his back five, leaving out a forward, which was usually me. One of my favourite goals came around this time, though, against Sheffield United, where I took the ball from in the corner, beat two defenders in the box and curled it past the keeper.

An early move was made in the transfer market. The money the fans had raised when the club was in receivership was used to bring back a local lad who'd been sold to Darlington a few years prior.

Pete Skipper: I'd had two good seasons at Darlington. Going there really helped me. I'd been playing as a centre-half, which was where I wanted to play, instead of being pushed out to left-back. Chris Chilton and Bobby Brown were in temporary charge at City. They came up to Darlington with Hull City and we won 2-1. I played well and Chillo just asked me if I'd be interested in coming back. I told him I'd consider it but I was under contract at Darlington so I didn't think any more of it. Don Robinson took over, Colin Appleton took the manager's job, and I received a phone call asking if I fancied speaking to them. I did, and I agreed to come back to Hull. I think they paid £10,000, which the supporters had raised.

Colin Appleton: I kept virtually the same squad, with my only signing being Pete Skipper. He was a good, reliable pro and played in every match for two seasons, winning the supporters' player of the year award in 1982/83.

Slowly but surely the squad was being added to with players who were to stamp their mark on the club throughout the decade. Next in was Billy Askew.

Billy Askew: Colin Appleton would play me as more of a left-wing back at first, with Dennis Booth playing as a sweeper. Not many teams did that at that time, but it worked for us. I was very fit, so I could get up and down quite easily.

One of the early ideas Don Robinson embraced – along with adding red to the first team strip and announcing plans to transform Boothferry Park into a 'Hollywood Bowl'-style arena – was for the club to release a single to celebrate its recent renaissance. A couple of musically minded Hull City fans were called upon.

Mark Herman: Henry Priestman, who later went on to have big success with his band The Christians, and I have been friends and City fans since childhood. Back in 1982 he'd only recently ended his time with the best band that never made it – Yachts – and we were both despairing at City's plight – the club was in desperate financial trouble and players were not being paid. We decided to record a song with the aim of sales proceeds going to 'The Players' Pool', which had just been set up. For the sake of speed more than anything else we decided to use an existing tune of Henry's (Out of Touch, by Yachts), to which we'd add new lyrics. It was all thrown together very quickly, but very enjoyably, with the help of the (slightly bewildered) squad at that time, and of course new chairman Don Robinson. We were amazed by its success, knocking Duran Duran off the number one spot (in the Sydney Scarborough 'Underneath the City Hall, Hull' charts). For a while it replaced 'Tiger Rag' as the music which the team ran out to. Quite an accolade.

Garreth Roberts: We sang in the boardroom at Boothferry Park. It was great. Not many teams would do that outside a cup final. I still sing it to the wife now, getting the kids to do the "wo-oah" bits.

Pete Skipper: Do I have to admit to singing on it? Whatever I did wasn't in tune. It was a good laugh doing it though. When I got married for the second time my wife managed to get a copy of the single and it was played at our night do.

With Top of the Pops scandalously remaining untroubled by the City players' efforts, back on the pitch a squad was now assembled that many would identify with as being one of the club's best ever.

Billy Askew: The atmosphere in the squad was absolutely fantastic. If you look at the players who went on to great things: Billy Whitehurst went to Newcastle, Steve McClaren did brilliantly, Brian Marwood ended up at Arsenal and England, Tony Norman went to Sunderland and FA Cup finals, Pete Skipper was outstanding. Had Garreth not got his knee injury early on a big club would have come in for him, I'm sure of that. That said, he was Mr Hull City. These guys weren't ordinary players. They might have been playing at a lower league level, but they were capable of playing much, much higher. I probably could have moved before I did. We had a really good team and we could give anybody – and I mean anybody in the country – a game at Boothferry Park. No one liked coming there.

Pete Skipper: It was a younger side than when I'd been at City previously. Garreth was still about, Steve McClaren, Bobby McNeil and Garry Swann were coming through the youth team, Ian Davis was knocking on the door, and Brian Marwood and Les Mutrie were about. Big Billy had been coming on. It was a club that looked as though it was going to go places. We had players who'd rise during the important games.

Les Mutrie: The funniest character in the Hull City set-up, but also someone who would lend a shoulder to cry on, was Dennis Booth. He'd really help me when I was left out because the manager lost his nerve and insisted on defence, defence, defence.

Rich Lusmore (Hull City fan): Many of my heroes come from the era I still regard as my favourite watching the Tigers: the early 1980s. Included among them is every player who helped take City from receivership to redemption. They are true legends in black and amber. Among them I'd say strikers 'Sir' Les Mutrie and 'Big' Billy Whitehurst would be prominent in the list along with Tony Norman and Brian Marwood. As a man who often sided with the underdog, I'd also add Bobby McNeil to the list – often an easy target for the boo boys, but in my opinion he rarely let City down.

The results came on the pitch as Don Robinson and Colin Appleton made an immediate impact. City took up residence in the top four at an early stage of the season and never looked like relinquishing their position. Thrashings were routinely handed out at Boothferry Park, including a 7-0 win over Stockport.

Colin Appleton: In January 1983 we won 7-0 against Stockport, with Andy Flounders scoring a hat-trick. It was Hull City's biggest win in 18 years. Shortly afterwards Colchester United expressed an interest in me taking their vacant managerial position, but I wasn't interested. These were exciting times. After several years of decline, City were at last attracting big crowds. A top-of-the-table clash against Port Vale in March was watched by 15,615 fans.

In that Port Vale game a household name featured for the Tigers. Emlyn Hughes was known throughout the country as a genial team captain on the hugely popular Question of Sport, as well as being a former England skipper. Now he was playing for City on a short-term contract.

Colin Appleton: It was a pleasure to be able to work with such a great player, and he was also a lovely person with a real passion for the game. Prior to every match, while all the other players were warming up on the pitch, Emlyn did his warm up in the dressing room, something he had previously done during his time under Bill Shankly at Liverpool.

Promotion was finally achieved through a 0-0 draw at Chester on April 30th, with City finishing second in the league behind Wimbledon, on 90 points.

Garreth Roberts: We were promoted in 1982/83. Having Chillo there was great. He'd been there and done it, and you couldn't help but respect him. He was very forthright when compared with Colin. He added to that great combination.

Les Mutrie: The promotion year was a strange one for me. We had become a hard-to-beat, skilful, strong, determined side but I was becoming less and less a part of it – from the main man to a bit-part player. It was really difficult for a front man with a terrific goal ratio to take, especially when I was told my role had changed to chasing full-backs up and down the field, taking away all my energy when receiving the ball. My game suffered and the team reverted to a back five with yours truly left out due to the manager's core belief that the team would not be beaten. To be fair they very rarely were.

Billy Askew: I didn't always see eye to eye with Colin Appleton because I was a 'get it down and pass it' player but he wanted things done in a certain way, a way that I didn't always agree with. That led to me getting left out once or twice. But he knew his stuff, I can't deny that. Later on, when I got a bit older, I realised, yes, he was right. But when you're 22 or 23 and you're left out you don't see things like that.

Chris Chilton: I felt a real sense of pride in what that team of the 1980s achieved. It was heart-warming to see but it didn't make any difference to my wages!

City went into the 1983/84 season full of optimism. Steve Massey was added to the squad, with Stan McEwan joining later in the season. The first game saw City beat Burnley 4-1, with

Millwall beaten 5-0 in the fourth. City had only lost twice by late January. This run of form was turning heads, particularly where the manager was concerned.

Colin Appleton: As Christmas was approaching, I was surprised to hear from Don Robinson that Swansea, who were struggling at the bottom of Division Two, wanted to speak to me about becoming their new manager following the departure of John Toshack. Because I wasn't on a contract at Hull, I was within my rights to speak to other clubs, but I had a gentleman's agreement with Don that I would inform him of any developments, and I was also grateful to him for giving me my chance to get back into full-time management at Hull City. I spoke to Swansea chairman Doug Sharpe on the phone. I was offered the job with an increase in salary. My wife and I travelled to Swansea to have a look around, but after giving it much thought I decided to remain at Hull to try to finish off the job of guiding them into Division Two.

As well as City were doing in the league, for one fan favourite the end of his time at the club was nigh.

Les Mutrie: I should have taken much more notice when the gaffer spoke about me having a different role at the club. Upon being left out, words were said – I can't recall exactly what – and Don tried to intervene. I left on a successful loan to Doncaster only to be told by their manager Billy Bremner that he had better and younger than me, so it was back to Hull where an incident occurred in the players' car park shortly afterwards – all of my making, out of character, regrettable, but not to be retold!

I don't know if the boss felt threatened by me. I settled into a spell of reserve team football while waiting for a first-team recall while still organising hospital events, etc… for the first-team squad. I was also the lads' rep for pensions. I had at this time been asked to go on 'watching briefs' or to look and report on opponents, hence my belief I was being lined up for a different role. However, two events occurred to make my mind up that I had to leave. The club wanted me to go, and then I was left with no choice after a training day. During a training exercise I stopped to talk to our full-back Bobby McNeil, asking about a point of play. Colin saw it differently and got everybody in a tight circle and proceeded to lambast me in front of every single player at the club, including the youth team. That was the day I moved my boots out of the club. But I then knuckled down and scored a lot of goals in the reserves, keeping my nose clean, early to training, always wearing a club suit, shirt, tie, etc… After a while, someone said to me: "Les, the gaffer wants to see you." When I went into his office he uttered the immortal words: "I want you to go on a watching brief…" Enough said!

When I went to Hull City, I thought 'about time'. I had played well enough to be the England semi-pro target man and for years had been a prolific goalscorer for every team I played for. My only other pro club had been Carlisle, who released me after a year in which I broke my leg in my debut game. Once I settled into the daily routine and finally got settled with my family we took to life in Hull like ducks to water. I was playing well, scoring regularly, and was well liked by fans and team-mates. Hull gave me that chance, for which I remain profoundly grateful and retain proud memories of my time with the Tigers. My only downside was the way I left, amid the rumours that spread among some fans that I was a pill popper. I can assure everyone that the only pills I have ever taken were prescribed by the club doctor for my anxiety, and if anything they slowed me down!

Les Mutrie sadly passed away after giving the interview for this book, which was to prove his last. Getting to know Les, and his wonderful family, has been a high point of the whole project. He remains a hugely popular figure within Hull, as was shown by the outpourings of grief when news of his death was announced. Les lit up a particularly bleak time for Hull City with his skill and hard work, and his legendary status will remain undiminished as long as there is a Hull City.

On the pitch, City's form dipped a little, though they were still to thrash champions-elect Wimbledon 4-1 at Plough Lane. However, what had seemed at one point to be a nailed-on promotion was now uncertain. Everything led to a rearranged game at the end of the season at Burnley. All of the other games had been played and City – in fourth place – knew what they had to do to overtake Sheffield United in third place and the final promotion spot: win by three goals.

Garreth Roberts: In the initial game we were driving over the Pennines, and the players were trying to convince the bus driver to turn around because it was too dangerous because of the snow. We managed to get it called off but then found that quite a few supporters had got there and it wasn't that bad once you were over the top of the Pennines.

For the rearrangement, in those days you could play the last game of the season after everyone else had finished, so we knew what we had to do. We had to beat Burnley at Turf Moor by three goals. We started off like a house on fire, Brian Marwood got a couple, but I've still got a picture at home of me having a shot and beating the keeper but a lad called Vince Overton blocking it with his knee. That would have made it 3-0. We were slaughtering them.

Billy Whitehurst: It was surreal. There were as many Sheffield United fans there as there were Burnley. That night, we should have scored seven. We were magnificent, though I missed a couple of sitters. We battered them. It was incessant. It seemed inevitable that we'd beat them by three or four.

City went two goals up through Brian Marwood, the second coming after 65 minutes, but couldn't find a third to gain promotion. The defeat came with a sting in the tail: Colin Appleton had decided to take up the managerial vacancy at Swansea.

Colin Appleton: Before the game at Burnley I had again been contacted by Swansea chairman Doug Clarke, who once again offered me the chance to take over as their manager for the following season. I had made my mind up to take the job, and perhaps felt it was good to leave Hull City in a much stronger position than when I'd arrived at the club. I informed the players of my decision to leave the club at the end of the match. It had been a very difficult decision to make, but sometimes in life you have to take a chance when it comes along.

Garreth Roberts: It ended up being a bit of a damp squib. We knew the Sheffield United players were in the stands which just twisted the knife that bit further. Then when we finished we found out straight away that Colin had resigned and was off to Swansea. We were good enough to go up and we showed that the next season. We just couldn't finish the job off that season.

Billy Whitehurst: We came up short, and straight after the game Colin resigned. It was a sickening feeling. But it was character-building. We rolled our sleeves up after that.

Pete Skipper: We couldn't have done any more. We played as well as we could. Burnley didn't make it easy for us. We had enough chances to get the third goal but it just wouldn't go in. But you get promoted over the course of a season, not just the final game.

Jeff Radcliffe: Absolute despair. We just needed that extra goal. We battered them but couldn't quite get it. Then there was the bombshell of Colin Appleton saying he was going to Swansea.

Billy Askew: Colin left me out of that game, so at that particular time, when Colin walked in and said he was leaving, I wasn't that fussed. It was a selfish, personal point of view. I was gutted to not get promotion as I'd played a lot of games that season and done a lot to get us into that position and I wanted to play at a higher level. The dressing room was devastated as we'd missed out by a single goal. So for him to walk in and do that was a bit selfish from Colin's point of view. He could have waited. But it didn't bother me at the time. I didn't shed any tears.

Mark Robinson: I'd got to the original Burnley away game, but the Hull City players hadn't and it had been postponed. But then in the rearranged fixture we played like Brazil, went 2-0 up, but then never really looked like scoring again. I just felt disgust and hatred for Burnley as their fans were supporting Sheffield United and their players were playing for that 2-0.

City then lost the inaugural Associate Members Cup final 2-1 to Bournemouth. The final was due to have been played at Wembley – a venue City had never graced – but had to be moved because of damage done to the pitch by the Horse of the Year Show. It was held at Boothferry Park instead after the two finalists tossed a coin to decide on the venue. Every final afterwards was to be played at Wembley, save for the years the national stadium was being rebuilt, when it was moved to Cardiff's Millennium Stadium. Typical City…

The mood in the camp was a miserable one, but that was lifted by another of Don Robinson's madcap schemes. Managerless Hull City were to go on an end-of-season tour of the USA.

Don Robinson: We took the players to the USA to play in a tournament we'd invented called the Anglo-American Trophy. We played a couple of teams out there – Tampa Bay Rowdies and Fort Lauderdale Strikers – with Tampa Bay coming back to England. I'd got the airline Airco to sponsor the tournament too. We received a lot of publicity in the USA back then, as football was just taking off over there. Quite a few fans came with us – we filled the plane! Things like that really built team spirit.

Garreth Roberts: You don't normally go on a post-season tour and we were all fed up that we'd missed out on going up. It took us a bit of convincing to go there. We were out there for a long time too, 15 or 16 days. We played Tampa Bay Rowdies and Fort Lauderdale and you never forget experiences like that. The Tampa stadium was incredible and we went round Universal Studios, which normally takes you a day to get round, but Don made us wear bowler hats and weird cotton suits as well as carry umbrellas to attract the media from home and in the US. We were sweating like mad but we got round the tour in about 40 minutes!

Pete Skipper: Don tried to get us to wear bowler hats and umbrellas walking round Disneyland in 40-degree heat. Some of the lads did it, and some managed to bin them. You wouldn't have thought that Hull City were going to be playing in places like Fort Lauderdale or Tampa. But that was Don. He was fantastic for the club.

Billy Askew: It was a fantastic experience. Hull City just didn't do that sort of thing. It was all down to Don. He was a brilliant man. We played Tampa Bay Rowdies, Fort Lauderdale, it was brilliant. We had no manager, so Dennis Booth was in charge. Dennis hated running as a player, but now he was managing us he'd get us up at eight in the morning and run the knackers off us. Me and Billy Whitehurst would generally have got in at four in the morning and then we'd be out running at eight!

Mark Herman: I was at the National Film School but not particularly enjoying life as an animator there. I tried to convince them that actually my real talent and ambitions as a film-maker lay not in the field of animation but in that of documentary, and that I was desperately keen to make a film highlighting the social and cultural divide between young professionals in the US and northern England. When they asked how I intended to do this, and I told them the ideal illustration would be Hull City's forthcoming tour of Florida, their faint interest quickly turned into deep (and justified) suspicion. Surprisingly, though, they allowed me to go ahead and very soon we were having a whale of a time making 'A Kick In The Grass', joining Dennis Booth, Billy Whitehurst, Pete Skipper and all on holiday in the Sunshine State at taxpayers' expense. Madness. Memories of the Florida trip largely feature the unpredictable behaviour of one William Whitehurst, but sadly no, those particular ones can't be shared.

I remember when the Tampa Bay Rowdies came over to the UK for the first leg of the hastily invented 'Arrow Air Cup', I met with their PR woman to outline our plans for filming when we went over to Florida the following week. She told us that when we arrive at the airport: "The fannies will all be lined up waiting for you." After the initial heady moment of confusion, it was eventually explained to us that, disappointingly, 'fannies' are what the Americans call soccer supporters.

Midway through the tour, an extra guest was to join the party. It was Brian Horton. Jack Charlton, Colin Murphy and Chris Chilton had been rumoured to be the frontrunners for the vacant managerial post, but as the players were about to discover, Brian was now the club's player-manager.

Brian Horton: We'd just stayed up in Division 1 at Luton. I was 34 and had discussed my future with my manager, David Pleat, and my intention was to try to get into coaching, as a player-coach or player-manager. I'd had a few offers from different people – Bobby Moore at Southend, John Bond at Burnley – to be a player-coach; then out of the blue I got a phone call from Don Robinson saying: "I'd like to interview you for the Hull City manager's job." He told me to meet him at the Queen's Hotel at 9 o'clock the next morning. I went in, we had a cup of coffee and he said: "The job's yours if you want it" and we started to agree terms. It was all done within 10 minutes. The opportunity to go to somewhere like Hull City… it was a no-brainer.

Don Robinson: He was a great guy. I had to stop him playing in every game! He was a good 'un. He got us so near to the First Division.

Garreth Roberts: Brian came when we were on tour in Tampa. Billy Whitehurst had had a few beers, and then we found out that Brian had arrived and wanted to meet everybody. I was rooming with Billy at the time and it took three of us to get him into the shower to sober him up a bit. Brian was a combative midfield player so I was happy he was there. He could kill you with a look though.

Billy Whitehurst: No one knew Brian was coming. I was as drunk as a rat. We were summonsed to this meeting. We met Brian, and Don asked if anyone had any questions at the end of it. Mick Hollifield put his hand up and said: "Who's going out with Billy tonight?" Everyone burst out laughing as no one fancied it. It was an inauspicious first meeting, but I thought Brian was great. Having that team as his first managerial job was great for him, too. We had great players back to front.

Billy Askew: A week or so into the trip, Brian turned up. We'd been drinking all day at Clearwater Beach in Tampa, me, Billy, Skip, Steve McClaren and Mick Hollifield. When Billy walked in on that first meeting with Brian, I'm sure he had a pair of elephant ears and an elephant trunk on.

Pete Skipper: We'd been out in the afternoon before Brian arrived. We weren't expecting him. We were letting our hair down after a long season. We did the right things at the right time, but when we were allowed to enjoy ourselves we did.

And a name that was already well known at the club was now a full-time feature.

Tom Wilson: I went to Goole Town in 1971 after leaving Hull and was studying law. I also coached part-time at Hull City with Dave King. Dave recommended me to Brian Horton as a replacement for Chris Chilton on the full-time coaching staff, and the three of us started the school of excellence, which did very well.

City started well under Horton, in spite of star winger Brian Marwood being sold to Sheffield Wednesday, quickly cementing a place in the top three. The most famous win of the season – and one of the most remarkable in the club's history – came against Leyton Orient in mid-November when City found themselves 4-1 down with only 25 minutes of the match left. Steve Massey and Andy Flounders brought the score back to 4-3, before Stan McEwan equalised with 12 minutes remaining. On 88 minutes Andy Flounders prodded home to seal an incredible victory.

Brian Horton was to prove to be a master when it came to spotting a bargain. His reputation for finding players costing £40,000 or so and selling them on for multiple times that was nothing short of outstanding. The first player he brought into Hull City for such a sum was Hull-born Richard Jobson, who'd been playing for Watford.

Richard Jobson: My dad worked for BP in east Hull but he moved away to Burton upon Trent when I was five, so I don't have any recollections of being brought up there. I spent most of my younger days in Burton and then signed for Hull in 1985, but that was just coincidence. I didn't have any ties there. I met my wife there, and my three children were born there, so we're all born in Hull! The reserve team goalkeeper at Watford – Eric Steele – was good friends with Brian Horton and had mentioned that I could play right-back so that was where I started, with Skip and Stan McEwan at centre-back.

Mark Herman's film-making career was also taking off at this time. The success of his documenting of Hull City's trip to Florida was followed by a play, 'See You At Wembley, Frankie Walsh', which was based around a fictitious Hull City FA Cup semi-final involving Hull City. It ended up being shown on national TV.

Mark Herman: In the mid-1980s, Hull City were in the depths of the Football League and it was the virtual impossibility of them making it as far as the semi-finals of the FA Cup that made the plot plausible. It was quite reasonable, even for the most ardent fan, to use the date of the cup semi-finals to organise something else, even a wedding. Cup semi-final dates were 'free days'. I suppose it's indicative of Hull City's potential at the time that I only used the semi-finals rather than the final. The cup final would have been just too preposterous.

The one essential was that we captured a Hull City goal on film. Remember we're talking expensive film stock here, not like nowadays when you can shoot digitally and therefore constantly, we were going to have to turn over each time there looked like a promising attack, and with Hull City in those days they didn't occur that often. As far as I remember, Hull City had three home games during our shoot, so those days were built into the schedule in case of the (likely) event that City failed to score, or if they did, we failed to capture it. We budgeted for two extra cameras on the first game, against Sunderland. It was one of those rare occasions when Hull City delivered, Garreth Roberts scoring very early on in that first game, with all cameras fortunately turning. I remember walking in front of the Sunderland end to a chorus of: "You fat bastard", looking around expecting to see somebody larger than me in the vicinity, but seeing no one, and realising it was being directed at me.

On a separate day we had to shoot the scene of a supposedly massive victorious home crowd leaving a cup quarter-final, so with a budget of five bob and only about 10 extras that was not an easy task. We raided the club shop for use of scarves, hats, etc… but that didn't seem to have much of an effect. A lot of the extras had vaguely amber coloured paper table napkins tucked into their collars to pass for scarves. It was early on in the shoot and it felt like a disaster, and if anybody had said then that this film might win an award – it won a student Oscar – there'd have been a call to the men in white coats.

Roy North: It was Mark's student film, at the end of his course. We all did it for nothing but the BBC bought it so all the cast got BBC wages! It was good fun filming at the church at Bishop Burton.

A feature of the 1984/85 season was the goalscoring form of Billy Whitehurst, the man who couldn't trap a bag of sand when joining the club four years earlier. He was to score 24 goals in all competitions throughout the season, making him one of the most feared strikers – in more ways than one – outside of the top flight.

Billy Whitehurst: It had all come together. I was full of confidence. I didn't think I could do a thing wrong. Even when I was making mistakes it didn't bother me. All the comments these days about my playing days are about how hard I was and all that rubbish, but it's rare that people say I was a good player. I always reflect on a game against Manchester United when I was at Newcastle. We lost 3-2 but I got man of the match. I played against Paul McGrath, and Ron Atkinson said afterwards that I'd run him ragged. In the Newcastle Journal the next day, Bobby Charlton wrote: "I came tonight to watch Peter Beardsley and Paul Gascoigne, as well as the Manchester United team, but I think the best player on the pitch by far was Billy Whitehurst." That was one of the highlights of my career. My boyhood hero said I was the best player on the pitch against those players. That was great.

Garreth Roberts: Billy was my room-mate, and I was his dogsbody. We always got on really well though. If you put 100% into training and playing then he was your best mate. If you didn't, he wouldn't be happy. He liked a beer and he liked enjoying himself. You knew in training if he'd had a bit of a night as he'd put on these bin liners and put it underneath his training gear. When he took it off rivers of sweat would flood off him. And he was built well. There wasn't an ounce of fat on him. He knew how to play hard, but he worked hard as well. He was always the first pick in five-asides too! He made a great career out of football though. He gave it everything he had. He wouldn't let you stop until we had won. And that rubbed off everybody, but particularly the likes of me, Skip and Billy Askew. We just felt unbeatable at Boothferry Park because of it.

Pete Skipper: Training against Big Billy would depend on if he liked you. I always got on really well with him and I still do. I'd seen him do bad things to people in games and in training, but that was Billy. You couldn't change him and you wouldn't want to really. He's actually a really nice fella, but when he turns… you don't want to be on the receiving end.

The promotion that had been so close the previous season was to be achieved with a degree of comfort this time around. City looked terrific throughout Brian Horton's first season and with three games left travelled to Walsall to seal a move back up to Division Two, with Pete Skipper fittingly being the man to seal matters.

Pete Skipper: It was at the old Fellows Park, and we were battered by them, but we won. Tony Norman had one of those games, which he had quite frequently, where he saved everything. My goal came from a Billy Askew free-kick. He put it in from the left-hand side. I managed to get above the kid who was marking me just inside their box, and headed it towards the bottom corner. Ronnie Green, who was in their goal, dived over it and let it in.

It was a great occasion. The fans loved it and we got a great reception afterwards with fans on the pitch trying to nick your boots and so on. It was a fantastic achievement. Brian improved us. He brought in different ideas.

Brian Horton: We had a good squad and I added a couple of players such as Neil Williams and Michael Ring on free transfers, as well as myself. I changed the system slightly, partly to accommodate myself. We played 4-3-3 and it was very successful. To get promotion in my first year was fantastic.

Jeff Radcliffe: Brian Horton was an excellent manager. One of the best while I was there. Great to work with. Him and Dennis Booth were ideal. Brian was the hard man who'd give them a right bollocking after a game if things hadn't gone well, and then Dennis would come in and lighten things up. It was an excellent few years working with them.

Billy Askew: I think I played 50-something games that season, every league and cup game. I didn't always see eye to eye with Brian but he probably got the best out of me. I was starting to have a greater influence on the pitch as I got older.

Richard Jobson: There were a lot of big, strong characters there. They'd just missed out on promotion the season before, but everyone was pretty buoyant with how we were playing. Of the characters, Billy Whitehurst, Steve McClaren, Stan McEwan, Pete Skipper, Garreth Roberts and Tony Norman stood out – it was a terrific changing room.

Garreth Roberts: We always got promoted away from home! Garry Swann and myself were together at the end of the game and just said: "Good job well done." We deserved it. We were a very good team, and very strong at the back with Stan McEwan and Pete Skipper, and Tony Norman in goal. Tony was one hell of a goalkeeper and a great bloke.

City were back in Division Two. The club's final positions in the respective leagues being played in over the past three seasons were second, fourth and third, so there was strong momentum around the Tigers. This, combined with a number of astute signings throughout the season such as Garry Parker, Bobby Doyle and Frankie Bunn, led to City finishing the 1985/86 season in sixth, the club's highest finish since the 1970/71 season. The play-offs, which would eventually give the sixth-placed team a shot at promotion, were to be introduced a year later. Typical City...

Brian Horton: We had a good side. We reached the Northern Final of the Full Members Cup and finished sixth. It was a good season. I changed a few players round but we retained the nucleus of the team and we were getting good crowds. The place was flying. Don Robinson was fantastic with me. He never interfered with the football side of things – the selling or buying – he just let me run the football club. At a later time he asked me to be a director, the first and only player-manager-director in English football. He wanted me to run a football club. And I learned a lot from him on the business side. When you go into it fresh, as I'd done, you need to know lots and he taught me all about the finances. It was a great learning curve for me.

Garreth Roberts: At that time we just needed to put our hands in our pockets to add a couple of quality players to give us that push for the next season but it never quite happened. We had a few injuries the next season but finishing sixth that season was one of the best the club had ever done. The club and the board didn't have enough gumption in them to spend some money. But we ended up sixth the year before the play-offs came in. It was typical.

Tom Wilson: We had a great goalkeeper in Tony Norman. Garry Parker was a Paul Scholes-type player. He never wasted a ball. His vision was second to none. Richard Jobson was like a Rolls Royce, nothing was too difficult for him and he'd never break sweat. Brian would get annoyed with him when he scored because he'd never show any emotion. He played next to Pete Skipper, who was a completely different type of player – totally reliable, not the quickest but just terrific. I was given the task of looking after the back four at the time and they were great to work with.

Richard Jobson: I had a good understanding with Skip. He was a great player. He was left-footed, I was right-footed, so that worked nicely. We worked well together. Skip was a dominant centre-half and great in the air, and he could ping the ball about with his left foot. And we had a great goalkeeper behind us in Tony.

Pete Skipper: I was lucky to play with a number of great centre-back partners at Hull. I started off with Dale Roberts, and then Stan McEwan came in, so I could easily forge decent partnerships with players of that calibre. Jobbo came in as a right-back but then was moved into the centre of defence after Stan got injured. Jobbo was a class player. He gave himself so much time on the ball, never got flustered, and he was very good in the air but was happy to let me attack it and then would mop up anything I missed or anything that was flicked on. I missed quite a lot so I made him look good! He was good enough to have played for England.

Billy Askew: We were good players. When you're talking about players of that quality, the step up doesn't bother you. Even at that level, no one wanted to come to Boothferry Park. We'd give anybody a tough game. Brian kept on making great signings for not much money – Frankie Bunn, Richard Jobson, Garry Parker – and we were just a very good side. And Brian was still a very good player!

John Eyre: I grew up just off Boothferry Road, so Hull City was in my life as soon as I could walk and talk as I lived a stone's throw from the ground. When I was at City Boys I'd get a season pass and would get to be a ballboy, so I was always at Boothferry Park. My early heroes were Big Billy Whitehurst, Keith Edwards, Billy Askew and Garreth Roberts, who used to coach me when I was younger. I loved Alex Dyer too. That 1980s team was strong.

Jeff Radcliffe: We were very close to getting us into the top flight with players like Garry Parker and Richard Jobson. Another couple of players and we might have made it.

Rob Smith: I started part-time at the club at the beginning of the 1985/86 season as a young lad. Brian Horton was manager and we'd just been promoted. It was a dressing room full of characters. I was a bit naïve at the time, star-struck by them all, but you soon worked out who were the ones to keep an eye out for, who'd chuck you in the bath as soon as your back was turned. But when you look at the club then to how it ended up, it was almost Sunday League level. It was proper football, a million miles away from where football is today. The money wasn't there, the players were down-to-earth, grounded lads, who'd go for a pint after training, go home and come back the next day.

Ian Farrow: I always liked Andy Flounders and being a Hull lad, in many ways, he typified Hull City. Not perhaps the most stylish or exciting of players, and it would be difficult for me to argue that he was City's greatest ever player, but he is one of my favourites because he was a fully paid-up member of the first City sides I supported that had any quantifiable success. But I mainly appreciated him as a City player because he did what he was paid to do, which was to score goals, and he did so without much fuss, fanfare or transfer requests.

In the November of the 1985/86 season, City sold talismanic striker Billy Whitehurst to Newcastle for a fee of £232,000. It was a blow for the fans, who'd grown to love his all-action, whole-hearted displays.

Billy Whitehurst: There were a few teams in for me, but I wasn't that bothered about leaving Hull. I thought that if the club had kept me and maybe Brian Marwood, and brought in a couple more players, we'd have had every chance of getting into the old First Division. But I think Don was still looking at balancing the books, for all I love him, as he was first and foremost a businessman. We were well capable of getting promotion, as Wimbledon did. We were better than them at every stage that we went through the leagues together. But I think it would have been better for me to stay at Hull City and build from there.

In the 1986/87 season, while bringing through youngsters such as Nicky Brown, Neil Buckley, Leigh Jenkinson and Andy Payton, Brian Horton made a couple more signings that would serve the club fantastically well, with Alex Dyer joining from Blackpool for £27,500 and Charlie Palmer coming in from Derby for £30,000. It was clear that Horton had a real eye for a bargain.

Brian Horton: I bought Alex Dyer for £27,500 and sold him for a lot of money. Richard Jobson came for not much and they sold him for a fortune. Garry Parker came in for £60,000 and I sold him for £270,000. Frankie Bunn was the same.

One player in particular was standing out at this level though.

Brian Horton: Garry Parker was the one I regret selling. We shouldn't have sold him because we couldn't replace him.

Matt Rudd: Garry Parker was my first Hull City hero. I only saw him for six months but this was a super-skilled, visionary, intricate footballer who could supply wingers and centre forwards with killer, imaginative passes and was always the epitome of composure. I adored him so much that I became a minor Forest fan when he left and was thrilled when he got into the team and won a handful of domestic honours.

Nick Barmby: I knew quite a lot of the players. You had cult heroes like Big Billy Whitehurst, but my favourite was Garry Parker. He was an unbelievable player. I loved him the minute I saw him play football. Brian Clough doesn't just go buy someone willy-nilly. I loved Jobbo and Pete Skipper, Garreth Roberts, Billy Askew. It's unfortunate that because of the era in which I played for Hull City people tend to forget those players a little bit. Garreth Roberts was a fantastic captain, very loyal, and I was honoured to play in his testimonial for Spurs. The likes of Garreth and Pete Skipper continue to do good work in the community with the ex-Tigers and I'll always be respectful of those players, because I enjoyed watching them.

A 14th-placed finish in the 1986/87 season was a little disappointing given the successes of the previous season, but given the club's relatively meagre resources such a position was still respectable enough. Off the pitch, a name that was to become synonymous with the club in the 1990s officially joined the board.

Martin Fish: I'd been helping the club during the 1980s, mainly with the share register. When the Needler family had taken over the club, Harold Needler had offered the fans a deal whereby if they paid a pound they'd be offered four shares. There were an awful lot of people who took him up on that, some paying a pound, some paying a fiver. The share register was a nightmare, full of names and addresses that went on for 15 pages on foolscap paper. A lot of these people had died or moved away, and no one had really bothered with the register for a lot of years. I was an accountant and had said to Clifford Waite, who was on the board, if there's anything I can help with please let me know. He asked me to do the share register, so I agreed. I did all of that. It took a long, long time. And then in 1987 Don Robinson rang me and thanked me for the work I'd done and asked me to come on the board. I accepted and on I went. Little did I know how things were going to turn out...

Another member of the backroom staff whose input would prove to be crucial to Hull City over the next two-and-a-bit decades was also about to become a part of the club's fabric.

John Cooper: I first got involved with City in the early 1970s, when Terry Neill approached me to ask if City could come down to the university where I was based. Then, in 1987, Brian Horton was continuing this. Brian and I got on like a house on fire, and he said: "Why haven't we got facilities like this at Boothferry Park?" I had always been a City fan, and was going to watch the games, but I couldn't get involved with somebody else's playing surface. However, people would tell me how poor the surface at Boothferry Park was, and how good the pitches at the university were, so it all evolved from there.

I met Clifford Waite, Don Robinson's vice-chairman, and he sold me the head groundsman job. My two young sons were football mad and had been mascots at City. They were telling me I had to go. I was 40 at the time and I felt that it couldn't do me any harm. I joined, and couldn't believe the poor standards of the facilities that a professional football club could have! It was terrible. However, we managed to change that round with the help of quite a few people. The problem with getting Boothferry Park up to scratch was always going to be finance.

A player only a handful of fans had heard of made an exit in the summer of 1987 when the list of released YTS lads was announced. Dean Windass's Hull City career seemed over before it had ever really started.

Dean Windass: I wasn't one of the stars in that juniors team. There were players like Neil Buckley, Leigh Jenkinson, Mark Richardson, Mike Smith, Les Thompson, just a good crop of YTS players. I was technically very good, but I was very small. They'd give you the two years in those days to develop physically, and I've spoken to Brian Horton about it a lot since, and it was all because I was a late developer and my body hadn't grown. I was miles away from everyone else physically. It was a tough time for me. I was gutted. Every young kid wants to be a professional footballer, particularly with your home town club.

Brian Horton: It was a similar situation to what I had at that age. I was released from Walsall because I was too small, and Dean was the same. His football brain, his technical ability, was unbelievable but physically he couldn't get round the pitch. He would be the first to admit that. When Dean came out of school, the late Dave King, the youth team coach at the time who did a fantastic job with Freddy Cowell along with the likes of Jeff Barmby and Tom Wilson behind the scenes for next to nothing, took me into my office when he was bringing in a load of YTS lads and said: "I've got one place left, give it to Dean Windass." I said, OK, give him that two years, but at the end of it he wasn't mobile enough to be a first-year pro. I said to him: "Dean, it happened to me when I was 18, go and prove me wrong. You've got the ability." And our football careers are very similar. He would now say it was the right decision at that time, but I'm very pleased he proved me wrong.

Neil Buckley: I had a lot of man strength at a young age, and that meant I was ready quicker for first-team football. Deano didn't have that. At 20 he still looked like a 16-year-old lad. At 22 or so he looked like a man. He just took time. He was brave, he just needed that man strength. It still felt like a surprise when he wasn't taken on though, as he had such fantastic technical ability. His feet were incredible throughout all our time with Hull Schoolboys. He just had no strength and he was very small at the time.

Tom Wilson: Sadly Deano was released because he was too small. I tried to get him kept on as I was the youth team coach at the time and losing any player would break my heart. We got lots of players round then signed on – the likes of Andy Payton, Nicky Brown, Leigh Jenkinson, Neil Buckley – and Deano was the best of the lot. Even when we had him at the School of Excellence when he was 13, he was a pro back then – a dirty pro but a pro! He knew all the tricks. I remember discussing it with Brian for ages. It broke my heart when he was let go. But he was determined for that not to be the end of his career and ended up at North Ferriby, while his job in the building trade built him up a lot, and that made him the figure that he is today. I felt we could have kept him and nurtured him though.

Indeed, Dean was partially a victim of playing in a juniors team that was laden with youngsters who would go on to represent the club.

Neil Buckley: There were players who were terrific juniors but maybe didn't develop as pros as you'd have expected, and then vice versa – players who weren't great juniors but ended up being terrific pros, like Deano. Mike Smith was technically fantastic and he did make the first team, but like myself he never really kicked on. When he was 17 you thought he could go where he wanted to go in football. You thought that Les Thompson would easily get in the top leagues. He made a decent career for himself but never quite fulfilled that potential. Of that age group, Deano was probably the only one who became as good a footballer as he could possibly become. He was in and out the juniors team though, as was Leigh Jenkinson, who went to play in the Premier League for Coventry. The rest of us had the potential but never got there. Andy Payton was in the year group above, though, and he was always a brilliant striker. So was Nicky Brown, and then one season he just started playing at right-back and slotted in nicely. The lad I felt really sorry for was Steve Corkain. He just got better and better and then got a really bad injury that finished his pro career.

Indeed, of that age group, Neil was the first to be offered professional terms. How did a young lad feel going into a changing room so full of characters?

Neil Buckley: There were a lot of people to look up to. Pete Skipper was lovely to me, a proper gentleman, really honest and just a great player. Garreth Roberts and Billy Askew were always brilliant to be around. Billy Whitehurst was salt of the earth – a wonderful man – and really looked after you on and off the pitch. It was a privilege to play alongside them, even though I didn't think I was close to being ready. I signed a contract on my 18th birthday as Middlesbrough had come in for me and the club wanted to tie me down. I was only a second-year apprentice and all of a sudden I was a pro. I felt too young to be there. I felt out of place. The dressing room was full of quality. Bobby Doyle was brilliant; an amazing footballer and a great person. Charlie Palmer and Alex Dyer were wonderful; lovely people and great to have in the dressing room. And they wanted you, as a youngster, to do so well. Charlie was always offering advice, and Alex was a brilliant laugh. We seemed to have a load of players who'd signed for Luton and Watford and that helped with the team spirit. But all of those pros were great. There wasn't one who I didn't enjoy being around. Everyone was nothing but lovely, just honest lads, mostly off council estates like me, who'd made good.

City started the 1987/88 season in barnstorming fashion, losing only one match by early November. Indeed, the 0-0 draw against Bradford City at Boothferry Park on November 3rd was a top-of-the-table encounter. Many of the decade's legends – Tony Norman, Pete Skipper, Richard Jobson, Billy Askew, Garry Parker and Garreth Roberts – were at the top of their game. However, Parker was sold to Nottingham Forest in March 1988. To soften the blow, Horton signed young left-back Wayne Jacobs from Sheffield Wednesday, and a hero from a few seasons prior made a much-welcomed return.

Keith Edwards: I got a call when I was in Aberdeen. I hadn't settled there. There was talk of Sheffield United coming back for me. Rotherham fancied me but I didn't quite fancy that. Then out of the blue, late on, Hull City bid for me. I took a wage cut to go back to Hull – it wasn't a financial move for me. I'd liked Dennis Booth, and he was still there. But it meant that my family could go back to Sheffield and I could commute to Hull.

Garreth Roberts: Keith Edwards was by far and away the best striker I ever played with. What a finisher! He got the Golden Boot one year when we almost went down. He'd score goals in teams that weren't playing well or giving him chances. He'd be worth millions now.

Keith picked up where he'd left off, scoring goals left, right and centre. However, City were in a poor run of form. Going into a night match against Swindon Town on April 12th, the Tigers had recorded only one win since the start of the year, and that had come on January 3rd against Leeds United. The good start to the season meant there was no danger of City going down, but the 4-1 defeat that night was to have major repercussions.

Brian Horton: We couldn't go up, we couldn't go down, so I decided to put some of the kids in like Andy Payton, Nicky Brown and Leigh Jenkinson. It was probably too tough a game to put them in, but in the first half we played really well and were winning, but they got back into it before half-time and we ended up losing 4-1. There was a smattering of people that were unhappy in the crowd – as supporters are – who were shouting for me to be sacked. As I came off the pitch and went to my office, Don Robinson called me in and said: "I'm making a change and sacking you." I said: "Are you going to tell the players or shall I," and he said he would. He went and told them and apparently they had a right go at him as we had a good bond between us all. The reserves were doing well, the youth team was doing well, and we had money in the bank for a recruitment drive in the summer. The club was in a good state. The players had a go at Don so he came back to my office and asked me to reconsider. Well there was nothing to reconsider because he'd sacked me. I said: "You can't do that." He spoke to me again the following day and asked me to rethink but I said: "No, once something's happened like that there's no going back." It was sad, as I'd had five good years.

When the senior players found out about Horton's sacking, they explained to Robinson in no uncertain terms that he'd made a mistake.

Garreth Roberts: I wasn't in Brian's good books at that time, so from a personal point of view my initial reaction was: 'Well he's just dropped me so stuff him.' After the dust had settled, though, there were a four or five of us decided to go in and convince Don to change his mind. But you can't really go back on things like that.

We were going through a bad patch at the time, but Brian had done such a terrific job with us and there was no reason why he wouldn't have been able to turn it around.

Pete Skipper: The performance of the players was poor. We didn't do our job and let the manager, the club, the supporters and ourselves down. Don obviously heard a reaction to that in the stands and he acted on it. He hadn't really thought about it, and it was a massive shock. A few of the senior players – I was one of them – went to see Don afterwards and said to him that it wasn't the gaffer's fault, we'd had a bad run of injuries, and would he reconsider. To be fair to Don he went to Brian and said he'd been a bit hasty, asking to withdraw the sacking, but Brian said that he'd made his mind up to move on.

Richard Jobson: I was really disappointed. Brian had brought me to the club, and put a lot of faith in me. We'd had a few games without winning, but it still seemed an odd time to sack him as there was no danger of us going down as it was early April. Don came in the changing room and told us what he'd done, and that was the first we knew of it. The senior lads spoke up in his favour – they were quite vocal, telling Don he must be mad to sack him.

Keith Edwards: I was a bit of a Jonah for managers who'd brought me in. But it was a negative as soon as I'd signed. I did ask myself the question why the hell I bothered with Hull City as everything seemed to go pear-shaped when I was there!

The backroom staff were as shocked as the players.

Tom Wilson: We were staggered. We'd played at Bradford on the Saturday, and Brian, myself and Dennis were invited into Trevor Cherry's office – the opposition manager. We'd been booked to go to a League Manager's awards that evening along with Don when he burst into the room and said: "Everything's cancelled, get the players in tomorrow morning." Don was insistent and then we lost to Swindon on the Tuesday night. As we went off the pitch, I was the last off. As I passed the manager's door Brian grabbed me and pulled me in and said: "He's sacked me, Tom." I said: "You're joking!" I offered to go and have a word with Don straight away but Brian told me that there was no going back. He just asked me to get his wife from the boardroom. It was crowded, and I went in and the other directors seemed happy, as they hadn't heard anything. Apparently Don had stormed out of the director's box at the end of the game and made the decision on his own without consulting any of the other directors. There was no going back.

Jeff Radcliffe: We couldn't go up or down, and Brian was looking toward the next season and played fringe players like Leigh Jenkinson. Brian just wanted to see what the younger players could do. We got beat and Don lost his rag and sacked him. Within an hour he regretted it but the press had got hold of it and it couldn't be overturned. A sad night.

Tom Wilson: The players couldn't believe it. Don had told them the news. Brian was on his way and Dennis and I had to take over until the end of the season.

Indeed, Dennis Booth and Tom Wilson took over for the rest of the season. Many favoured Dennis for the job, while Peter Reid and Terry Yorath were reportedly interviewed. However, when the appointment came it was out of left field. Or Rochdale. Or both.

Tom Wilson: I was backing Dennis for the manager's job. We went to Marbella at the end of the season and I kept telling Don that Dennis was his man. He'd have done a decent job, but it wasn't to be. Weeks later I got a call from Dennis to tell me one of my Celtic mates had got the job: Eddie Gray.

Garreth Roberts: Eddie was a brilliant bloke. He'd just know everything about you, he'd know what your partner was called, what your kids were called. But he never really got mad and that was half the problem. He'd been a great player; everyone knew that and respected him, but there was a spark missing. He was one of the best players in practice matches and was as fit as anyone there. He just lacked a killer instinct.

Tom Wilson: Eddie wasn't a manager. Too nice a man. But he wouldn't suffer fools. At half-time he couldn't understand why the players hadn't been doing the kind of things that he could do, which was the problem the likes of Bobby Moore and Bobby Charlton had when they went into management. Eddie was the best in training, be it running, practice games, anything. He couldn't understand why players couldn't reach the heights that he could. The players were never convinced when he was talking to them too, which was sad really given how much knowledge he had, but just couldn't portray it.

Jeff Radcliffe: He is a super man, possibly too nice to be a manager. But what a fit chap. Always in the top three on cross-country runs. And what a touch he still had.

Eddie Gray went about assembling his own squad, though it was Dennis Booth that had signed centre-back Steve Terry just before the Scotsman was given the managerial role. With Richard Jobson at the top of his game and youngster Neil Buckley captaining the reserves there was perhaps one centre-back too many in the squad. This was to bring about the end of Pete Skipper's Hull City career.

Pete Skipper: I did myself little justice in the first few games of the season. The season was off to a poor start and I understood that Steve Terry was going to be playing, as we'd paid a lot of money for him. It was up to me to try and keep him out. That didn't happen. We were playing at Oldham and I was stood in the entrance. Joe Royle saw me and said: "Are you not playing?" I told him I was out of favour, and then a week or two later he came in for me. I went to speak to them and thought: 'Why not?' I was going to get regular football.

I was gutted when I left City. Eddie was a really good coach, and I look back and think we both made a bad decision, though I was 30 or 31 and needed to be playing football. But Hull's my home town club. I still work there on a matchday. I had a few tears in my eyes when I left.

55

It upset me. When I left Walsall I tried to speak to Terry Dolan to see if I could come training, but it fell on deaf ears. I had a decent career, but I'd have liked to have seen it out at Hull.

Off the pitch, two trends were emerging among a wider football fan base in England that was viewed by most in the press and Parliament as little more than a bunch of hooligans. The inflatables craze – started, it is claimed, by Manchester City fans waving inflatable bananas at away games – was short-lived. Fanzines, however, became more and more influential, and Hull City had two of the best in the country: 'Hull, Hell & Happiness' and 'On Cloud Seven'.

Andy Medcalf (City fan): The first Hull City fanzine – 'Hull, Hell & Happiness' – was an idea hatched many miles away from East Yorkshire, in deepest Staffordshire. The brainchild of myself, then an undergraduate at Stafford University, and Ian Websdale, an exiled Staffordshire-based Tiger. It finally came to life after I was given a placement at the BP gas terminal at Easington on the East Yorkshire coast. Here I came into contact with fellow City fan Rich Lusmore and – more importantly – access to the works photocopier!

The plan almost never got off the ground when Rich's boss discovered 100 or so sheets of amber paper flying through a hot copier one lunchtime. Thankfully he turned a blind eye and City fans' first contribution to subversive literature was born.

'Hull, Hell & Happiness' first appeared on September 28, 1988, in time for the home League Cup tie against Arsenal. Two-hundred and fifty copies were furtively flogged out of Jackson's carrier bags at the top of Bunkers, thus confirming the Hull public's appetite for independent writing about the way the club was being run. It would last 14 issues (the other 13 all produced professionally!) before coming to its end in 1992. As a joint football/music fanzine, 'Hull, Hell & Happiness' also organised gigs and even local music compilation cassettes – 'There's Something Stirring In King Billy's Bogs' selling out to critical local acclaim.

Later in the 1980s, 'Hull, Hell & Happiness' was joined by 'On Cloud Seven, titled from a now infamous quote from manager Colin Appleton. A third fanzine on the scene appeared in the autumn of 1990 when Rich Lusmore and fellow 'Hull, Hell & Happiness' co-editor Gary Hook launched 'From Hull To Eternity' along with a seemingly vast local T-shirt production line. It differed from the other two by being an A4-sized publication and lasted five issues, the last of which came out in the spring of 1992.

That summer, the 'Hull, Hell & Happiness' and 'From Hull To Eternity' editors came together again under the Blind Faith '92 umbrella, from which was launched the 'Look Back In Amber' fanzine, which first hit the streets that September – four years to the month since that first 'Hull, Hell & Happiness'.

'Look Back In Amber' would also last five issues (as well as having a two-page monthly feature in the Hull Daily Mail green Sportsmail) before making way for the next kid on the block out of the same stable, 'Tiger Rag', which was launched by myself, Geoff Bradley and Gary Hook in May 1994 and would stretch to 12 issues by its close in December 1996.

Alongside these 'core' publications, City fans were also able to buy several offshoots, from the sublime – Gary Hook's 'Last Train To Boothferry Halt', October 1993 – to the even less sublime and, frankly, plain bonkers 'Fearful Symmetry', a small number of sparky issues edited by the irrepressible Karl Vint.

Mike Scott (City fan): Back in the late 1980s, the wet-lipped eagerness of university-educated football fans was starting to see the hooligan excesses of the previous two decades diminish. Never believe that the government, Colin Moynihan and their appallingly repressive football membership scheme had anything to do with the demise of hooligan culture – that happened from within.

'On Cloud Seven' did nothing to tackle the snarling violence that infected football at the time, but it definitely had a high wet-lipped student quotient. Inspired by a verbal hiccup of Colin

Appleton when reappointed for a mercifully short second term at the City helm, 'On Cloud Seven' – edited by Gary Clipson, Catherine Redgwell, Steve Weatherill, Andy Wilson and myself – ran for three years and combined humour, travel advice, in-depth articles and general knob-head chicanery to form a monthly fanzine that was sold on the approaches to Boothferry Park. The fanzine has passé but the name lives on in a website maintained by one of the wet-lipped original editors, who maintains carefree biogs, career details and statistics for everyone that's ever played for City.

The first few months of Eddie Gray's tenure at Hull City were a bit stop-start. There were impressive wins – a 3-0 victory at home to Chelsea, and a 5-2 thrashing of Brighton, which saw Andy Payton underline his rich potential by scoring after a length-of-the-pitch run – but there were numerous dispiriting defeats too. Then, just after Christmas 1988, a move in the transfer market was made. Invoking much sadness, Tony Norman departed for Sunderland.

Billy Whitehurst: Tony Norman was as good a keeper as you could wish to have. He was unfortunate that he played in the same era as Neville Southall. But even then, as fantastic as Neville Southall was, I don't think he was necessarily any better than Tony Norman. Tony was world-class. He was a lovely kid too.

Coming in the opposite direction were goalkeeper Iain Hesford and a Hull City legend. Big Billy was welcomed back, and made his second debut in a home match against Ipswich Town on New Year's Eve.

Billy Whitehurst: Don got someone to spray 'Rambo Billy' and 'Welcome Back Big Billy' on the boards near the stands. It was a fairytale. I didn't play particularly well but the crowd were brilliant and I scored. They say never go back, but I had a great time.

Billy scored with a header in a 1-1 draw. However, absent from the starting line-up that day was Keith Edwards. Before long, the two veteran strikers were to be paired together again, and to devastating effect.

Keith Edwards: I'd missed two games because my mother had died on Christmas Day. I told Eddie and that's when I became quite close to him as it was a tough time for me. I broke down in front of Eddie and he handled the situation beautifully and it's something I'll never forget. I loved Eddie Gray. Loved the man.

While I was in the north-east, Eddie signed Billy Whitehurst. Coming back into the dressing room after that, Billy came straight up to me, said: "Sorry about your mam, nice to see you back." I had an understanding with him immediately. Garreth, myself and Billy were a real positive in that time and the three of us got on really well. It was a huge boost to me at the end of my career.

Billy Whitehurst: Keith Edwards was the best goalscorer I ever played with. I played with some good goalscorers – Peter Beardsley, John Aldridge, Tommy Tynan – but if I put my life on someone to finish a chance, it would be Keith. But I did 90% of his running for him! We're still good mates to this day. He's a lovely man.

Ian Bunton: If Billy Whitehurst was playing, you knew that something entertaining would happen in the match. He was the typical player you loved to be on your team, but would hate if you were the opposition. Keith Edwards seemed to be a perfect foil for him as well. He knew where the goal was and had the knack of being in the right place at the right time; a natural goalscorer's instinct.

With Keith and Billy reunited up front, and Billy Askew returning from injury in midfield, City went on a terrific run of form in both the league and the FA Cup. In the third round, Cardiff were beaten 2-1 at Ninian Park. In the fourth, a brilliant 2-1 victory at Valley Parade saw both Keith and Billy net, future Tiger Leigh Palin get sent off for the Bantams, and future City manager Terry Dolan receive his P45 from the West Yorkshire club in the immediate aftermath of the game.

Keith Edwards: I got through on the left-hand side. The keeper thought I was going far post so I drilled it near post. But Billy's goal was even better – left foot into the top corner. I hadn't seen it before and I've not seen it again! We always scored against Bradford. They hated playing against Bill.

When the draw for the fifth round was made on breakfast television the following Monday morning, there was only one team everyone wanted to face: Liverpool. This Liverpool side were astonishing, able to call upon talents such as Bruce Grobbelaar, Alan Hansen, Jan Molby, Steve McMahon, Ray Houghton, John Barnes, Peter Beardsley, John Aldridge and Ian Rush. When they'd beaten second-placed Nottingham Forest 5-0 the season before, Tom Finney had said they were the best club side of all time in England. Few argued. So when City pulled this all-conquering side out of the hat – at Boothferry Park, too – the whole of Hull seemed to come down with the much-clichéed 'cup fever'.

Keith Edwards: That week was fabulous. We were doing things in the town centre. The city was buzzing. It was fabulous to see. Going into the game, I was frightened of nothing, Billy offered great protection. I was looking forward to it immensely.

Neil Buckley: I didn't get much sleep the night before. They were possibly the best club side in the world at the time. I was nervous, not eating. I was only young, as were Nicky Brown and Wayne Jacobs, who were going to be in the back four with me. We were marking some of the greatest players in the world. I walked into the ground, and everyone wanted autographs and were patting me on the back. I loved that side of things.

Eddie Gray did a brilliant job to level us. He got inside your head and made you feel important, like you could cope with someone such as Peter Beardsley. We went out there thinking: 'It's 11 men against 11 men and we can do this.' We thought that if we stuck together and put our heads on when we had to, we had a chance. And so it proved.

Liverpool started off like a house on fire. After 10 minutes or so, the best City could hope for, it seemed, was to avoid embarrassment.

Garreth Roberts: They were one of the best teams in Europe, but we were on one hell of a run. It's one of those never-to-be-forgotten games against the likes of John Barnes, Peter Beardsley, Steve McMahon, John Aldridge… There was some trepidation before the game, hoping we wouldn't get a pasting, but as soon as the game started it was completely different. We were chasing shadows for the first 20 minutes though. I didn't know where Steve McMahon was and Beardsley was flying all over the place.

In the 15th minute, John Barnes glanced home a cross to put Liverpool 1-0 up.

Billy Whitehurst: I bet that was the only header John Barnes scored with in his life.

Against the run of play, Neil Buckley headed City's first real chance wide from a corner.

Neil Buckley: I should have scored at the far post. It was a poor effort to be honest. And what a memory that would have been!

Then something clicked. A few tricks by Billy Askew and Keith Edwards came off. Billy Whitehurst started to impose himself. Liverpool's defence was struggling to readjust after

Gary Gillespie had gone off injured. In the 34th minute City did the unthinkable. They equalised.

Billy Whitehurst: It came off my shin. The only reason it went in the back of the net was because Bruce Grobbelaar shit himself. He stopped, I slashed at it and it bobbled in. I went up to the Liverpool fans and put my fists up, thinking: 'We can beat these.'

The sublime went to the ridiculous 11 minutes later. On the stroke of half-time, Keith Edwards, the master goalscorer, made it 2-1 to City.

Keith Edwards: I had to score to make it eight consecutive games scored in, which was my personal record. Billy was at the far post and the ball came across the goal. Someone slipped and I heard screams for a penalty. I didn't want the penalty though because I had a chance to score and I knocked it in.

Garreth Roberts: I knocked a ball into the box, which Gary Ablett completely missed and we're back in the game. The crowd were unbelievable. Then Keith scored, and you didn't want half-time to come.

Matt Rudd: That was the only time I ever climbed out of the terracing (the Well, actually) to celebrate a goal on the (edge of the) pitch.

Half-time came. Like Cassius Clay fighting Henry Cooper in 1963, Liverpool were saved by the bell.

Tom Wilson: It was one of the best Liverpool teams of all time. And at half-time I was all for consolidating and maybe hit them on the break through Keith and Big Billy. But the feeling from Eddie was that we needed a third goal. I told him: "We're playing Liverpool not Torquay!"

Billy Askew: We were 6-1 to win. I put £50 on us, and we're winning 2-1 at half-time. So I was getting £400 crowd bonus, and I was close to winning another £300 at that point. And it was a lot of money back then!

Mark Robinson: I missed the Liverpool game in the FA Cup in 1989 as I was playing cricket in New Zealand. I woke up at 2am to listen to it on BBC World Service, and they commented on the first half but didn't do the second. So I spent the whole of the second half trying to find out what was happening as the last I'd known we were 2-1 up!

Neil Buckley: The noise at half-time was incredible. Eddie seemed in shock as much as we were. He was trying to keep a lid on it, telling us we were good enough to finish the job, but the noise throughout the whole of half-time from our fans was deafening. I'll remember it forever. And in some respects that did more harm to us from an expectation point of view than anything the Liverpool players did!

Sadly, Liverpool – reenergised by Kenny Dalglish's half-time team-talk – flew out of the traps. John Aldridge scored twice early in the second half to make it 3-2.

Neil Buckley: I think some of us younger lads were in awe of it all. I went out into the second half thinking: 'Come on, we can do this,' but a few of us were like rabbits in the headlights for those first 10 minutes. And that's what did the damage. When we settled again, we gave as good as we got.

Garreth Roberts: John Aldridge scuppered us. We played a lot better in the second half. We started to believe in ourselves.

City kept coming, and had one glorious chance for an equaliser.

Billy Whitehurst: I missed an open net. It went through my legs. I always blame Keith for it, because I ran in behind him. I would have bet my house on Keith scoring when the ball came in the area, but he swung at it and missed. I was so astounded that he missed it that I missed it too. So it was his fault!

Sadly, it wasn't to be. City had to contend with being the most gallant of losers in what was one of the most memorable games in a generation for City fans.

Richard Jobson: That's one of the games I remember the most. They were the team of that era. They won everything. The pitch wasn't at its best because of the weather, and that helped us a bit. Even at 2-1 though you were waiting for them to turn the screw. It would have been one of the all-time shocks of the FA Cup.

Neil Buckley: The best team won, but we gave them a game. It was wonderful. It was the pinnacle of my career. At the end, I was gone. I didn't even go out that night, and that was unknown. I was shattered emotionally.

Garreth Roberts: I'm pleased we did ourselves proud, but there was an opportunity there to turn them over.

Billy Askew: Such fantastic memories. I was playing against the best players in the country and I was as good as them! I still have the man-of-the-match crystal in my house. I just played my normal game. I maybe lacked a bit of consistency but on my day I could play as well as anyone. It was just a fantastic day. We came so close to beating not just a good Liverpool team, but one of the best of all time.

Matt Rudd: That we lost the game, eventually, feels less and less important the more time goes on.

Amid the disappointment, Keith Edwards could look with satisfaction on the fact that he'd scored in eight consecutive games. Indeed, that season he had scored against Manchester City, Arsenal, Chelsea and Liverpool. Do that today and you're instantly worth tens of millions. Keith, however, could only think of how grateful he was to his strike partner.

Keith Edwards: Whenever I get the opportunity to mention Billy, I always throw in that he was a much better footballer than people give him credit for. He was a leader, he looked after people, but the beauty of Bill was that it didn't matter if I scored every goal. He was unselfish and he'd just keep knocking them down to me and creating chances. My one disappointment at the end of that season was that I didn't create enough chances for Bill. He was great to play with. My 26 goals that season won me the Golden Boot. Ian Wright and Kerry Dixon were promoted with Palace and Chelsea and only scored 25 and 24. I class that as my finest achievement in football, at the age of 33, scoring those goals in the team that finished fourth bottom.

While City's form trailed off a little, Eddie Gray was given the money to break the club's transfer record twice in a day, with Ian McParland joining from Notts County for £155,000 and Peter Swan coming in from Leeds for £200,000.

Peter Swan: Eddie Gray was the main thing that attracted me to Hull City. He'd been my manager at Leeds and Howard Wilkinson had taken over. Straight away we'd clashed and I knew I had to move. I'd got on really well with Eddie, so when the opportunity came up to leave Elland Road, there was only one place I wanted to go.

Big Billy really stood out. I'd had to mark him a week before I'd joined in a Leeds v Hull game. He was giving me a bit of a battering and I was thinking: 'Come on Billy, cut me a bit of slack, I'm signing for you next week!' But even then I was thinking it would be great to play alongside him and share a dressing room with him. Him and Iain Hesford were fantastic together. They were like the Chuckle Brothers. We had some great players at that time, such as Richard Jobson, Andy Payton and Billy Askew. It was a dressing room full of characters.

Away from Boothferry Park, a serious level of excitement was being generated by a Hull-born schoolboy, largely recognised as the finest player of his age in the country.

Nick Barmby: I don't think I ever thought I was hot property. I just wanted to play football from an early age. I wanted to play at the top level; I had an ambition to play for England – I had an inbuilt thing where I thought I could really do it. But I just wanted to play, be it for school, Sunday League or Hull Boys. I loved playing for Hull Boys, the memories that I have, and I still see lads like Carl Lund, Gary Hobson and Neil Allison (before he moved to the other side of the world). We'd play away from home and then get dropped off at Boothferry Park where we'd be ballboys. I always had an ambition to play for Hull City but I was showing promise in the game and I was fortunate enough to go to Manchester United every summer to train with them, I trained with Arsenal, trained with Tottenham and went to Liverpool where I played in a practice game with Kenny Dalglish, who was my hero when I was 14. But even when I went to Lilleshall and then to London, I always had an ambition to play for my home-town club, and when I knew I could still play, not in my late 30s when my legs had gone. Les Mallory at City Boys and Mr Kay at Wyke were great to me, Frank Donoghue used to look after all the ball boys and was involved in Hull City until 2018. He's Hull City through and through. Thank you to them.

Even with the costly injection of new blood, the 1988/89 season petered out for City. From mid-February onwards, the club won one more game to finish fourth from bottom. At the end of the season, Eddie Gray was sacked, along with assistant Dennis Booth.

Martin Fish: Don wasn't too happy with Eddie Gray, though the results weren't too bad. He didn't like some of the training methods, the discipline, and Eddie wanted money for players that Don didn't have. There was no big bust up, but there were disagreements about non-football matters.

Billy Whitehurst: Losing against Liverpool burst our bubble for some reason, and we hardly won a game for the rest of the season. I think that's what got Eddie Gray the sack, which was a travesty. That moment in time when Eddie got sacked put Hull on a long-term downward spiral. He was a great manager.

Keith Edwards: If they'd kept Eddie Gray on we'd have progressed to be a much better side.

Neil Buckley: That was a mistake. He was wonderful to work with. He was an attacking manager, but he understood defenders. He'd say: "This is what I want you to do, and this is how you do it." He was great at talking you through things. Colin Appleton couldn't do that. Not many can. We were really coming on under Eddie. I think he'd have attracted some very good players, because a name like that does that. I was gutted when he left, for him, for the club, and for me as he was good for my game.

Eddie Gray needed replacing, and for a while it was widely expected that John Hollins would get the job. However, Don Robinson was to make a phone call to an old friend.

Colin Appleton: I'd enjoyed a season managing Bridlington Town, but just a few days after our East Riding Cup final win against Hull City's reserves I was surprised to receive a phone call from Don offering me the chance to return to the club as manager. I was delighted to be given the chance.

Martin Fish: Colin and Don both lived in Scarborough, and Don wanted to bring him back. It was just what Don would do. It was all done on a hunch. When Colin Appleton came back I asked where he'd come from, and Don said Colin had made a mistake going to Swansea a few years earlier and he wanted to let him atone for it.

Colin Appleton: There had been massive changes at the club in the five years since I was last there, and only three players remained: Billy Askew, Billy Whitehurst and Garreth Roberts. There was no money to bring in new players, so we began the 1989/90 campaign with the same squad that had just escaped relegation, with the only addition being Steve Doyle, who came in from Sunderland. I approached Oxford United to bring Steve McClaren back to Hull, but they wouldn't release him.

So how were the players and staff feeling about Colin's return?

Tom Wilson: He was a bizarre character. An eccentric. We'd do daft things in training and have daft meetings. Colin used to talk as if the game was too easy. The players didn't really get the message he was trying to portray, and his lengthy meetings would just lose and bore the players. He didn't go down well. Colin sacked me at one point. Before training one day he said: "I want you to leave. You shouldn't have won the reserves league last year as it raised too many expectations with the supporters over the youngsters." I couldn't believe it, I was sacked for being too good. With the training I had in law, I wrote out an A4 page of what had happened, asked Jeff Radcliffe and Freddy Cowell to sign it, and got myself reinstated.

Peter Swan: Eddie was trying to build for the following year, but Don made the decision. When I reported back for pre-season training, there was this bloke in the dressing room fitting all these panels and stuff like that. He never spoke to me or anything. I found out a week later that he was our new manager. I'd been the record signing a few months previous and he was now my new manager, but he never said a word to me. It was weird. The way he spoke, the way he trained us, he was a bit of a clown to me. I was just thinking: 'I can't play under this.' He maybe had too many big characters to handle.

Billy Askew: I was at home in the north-east and I was told to come back to Boothferry Park because they were going to announce the new manager. I loved Eddie Gray, he was my type of manager. He thought the world of me because he liked footballers, and I thought the world of him. I'd been devastated when he was sacked. Then Colin walked through the doors and I thought: 'Oh my God.' But I was older and more experienced so we got on really well. And he started to look to me as a senior player.

Peter Swan: Colin once told me that I was starting up front because Billy Whitehurst was injured. I walked down to the dressing room and Billy Whitehurst was sat there. He told me to get lost when I tried to get the number nine shirt. When Colin saw that, he just kept Billy as the number nine and put me on the bench. That just shows how weak he could be.

For one player, Colin's return was all too much.

Keith Edwards: Me and Colin Appleton didn't gel. He took over and Big Billy said to me: "Keith, he's a bit dour." I was disappointed Eddie had gone. I'd have stayed under Eddie.

Colin Appleton: I had to make some unpopular decisions, one of which I think played a part in costing me my job. I needed all the players pulling together to try to get us climbing up the league. Keith Edwards was a huge favourite with the fans, but at one training session he turned up late. I dropped him from the team, which didn't go down well with some of the supporters, and I don't think some of the directors agreed with my decision either.

Keith Edwards: I walked into the dressing room and Colin was fixing something on the ceiling. We had a meeting in the stand, and he said: "Footballers can't concentrate for more than 20 minutes, so this meeting won't last for more than 20 minutes." An hour and 45 minutes later, he was still babbling on about fuck all. I lost a bit of patience and reminded him of his silly comment about footballers not being able to concentrate. That meant we didn't hit it off. I didn't have a lot of time for him – he didn't respect me and I didn't respect him. Hull is a club I'm very, very fond of though.

Keith Edwards departed for Stockport, and it wasn't long until Colin Appleton was to follow him out of the exit door. City lost 2-0 at home to Brighton in late October, which marked 14 league games without a win that season. With the club firmly rooted in the relegation zone it was all too much for Don Robinson – who'd seen a number of fans turn against him over his decision to emblazon the much-hated word 'Humberside' across the kit when no shirt sponsor could be found – and he stepped down as chairman, to be replaced by Richard Chetham.

Don Robinson: It was the best time of my life. I loved Hull City and the people of Hull. I regard Hull as a second home, one of the warmest, friendliest places there is. I hadn't been the best rugby league player at Hull KR but hopefully I made more of a mark on Hull City. I'm proud of what we did at that time.

Martin Fish: In the end I think it got a bit much for Don. I'd only been on the board for two years and he came to me at half-time in a game and said: "I'm thinking of giving up, Martin. I think it's time for someone else to do it, do you fancy it?" I told him that I'd only been on the board for five minutes, and he had the Needler family to take into consideration, and Richard Chetham was married to a Needler, so he should come before me. Richard Chetham was asked, and he became chairman.

Chetham moved quickly to sack Colin Appleton. This meant that within days of becoming chairman he had to appoint a manager. Rumours linked the likes of Billy Bremner, Ray Wilkins, Ian Porterfield and Frank Stapleton to the job, but it went to a relative unknown: Crystal Palace assistant manager Stan Ternant.

Martin Fish: Richard Chetham interviewed Stan. He wanted his own man.

Tom Wilson: Stan offered me the role of assistant manager. He was also eccentric in his own way. I thought he was a fantastic coach – one of the best I've ever worked with – but some of the things he'd do got the players backs up. Some of his tactics just weren't right. He wanted it all to be done his way. He'd listen to you but not hear you. I enjoyed his coaching sessions but they didn't get through to the games we were playing. He fell out with Richard Chetham over something small, and I ended up acting as a go-between for them.

Peter Swan: I liked Stan. I got on with him. In my first meeting with him though, he'd turned up at the Bradford away game. Me and Billy were playing up front and 15 minutes into the game he came down to the dug out and brought me off. I was fuming. He wasn't even our manager at that point. I went to see him on the Monday morning and went crackers, had a massive blow out, but he didn't hold a grudge or anything. He explained to me that he thought it was right at the time but that he saw me as a good centre forward. Billy left for Sheffield United not long after and I had a really good spell up front.

Neil Buckley: I loved Stan, I just don't think he was a manager at that point. He was very approachable, and technically he was very good. He'd obviously been a very good player himself. He knew everybody in the game. I just think he was more like one of the lads, rather than someone who was running the lads. We went on one or two tours and he could stand his corner in the pubs as well as any man. He loved a drink and a laugh. I think he was still in that transition of crossing over from player to manager. Dennis Booth was similar to Stan. As good a number two as you'd meet but he was a coach – a bloody good coach – but not a manager. Stan was just too nice in my opinion.

City won that first game after Stan's appointment 3-2 thanks to a last-minute Ian McParland goal. Indeed, Stan oversaw a big improvement in City's fortunes, with the final three games of the decade – a home match against Port Vale and away matches at Wolverhampton and Plymouth – all resulting in 2-1 victories, to give some hope of avoiding what had looked to be an inevitable relegation at one point.

This provided an optimistic note on which to end a decade that had been good to Hull City. Starting in the bottom tier and with the club's very existence coming under threat at one point, Don Robinson provided colour and excitement to the club, and the likes of Brian Horton, Dennis Booth, Tom Wilson, Tony Norman, Pete Skipper, Richard Jobson, Wayne Jacobs, Brian Marwood, Billy Askew, Garreth Roberts, Steve McClaren, Garry Parker, Andy Payton, Les Mutrie, Billy Whitehurst and Keith Edwards would be very fondly remembered for decades to come. In spite of having had three managers in the past six months, the club could go into the 1990s in a positive mood. After all, what was the worst that could happen?

1990s

The 1990s were the decade that transformed English football like no other. The sport had been largely unloved in the 1980s, epitomised by hooliganism both at home and abroad, the tragedies at Bradford, Heysel and Hillsborough, dwindling crowds, disputes over television rights, attempts to introduce identity cards, and the ban from European club football.

The next decade kicked off with Italia 90, Nessun Dorma, New Order, the beautiful stadia, Gazza's tears, Waddle and Pearce's penalty misses. As the decade progressed, all-seater stadia were to become mandatory in the higher leagues, the Premier League would be launched along with Sky's exhaustive coverage. Nick Hornby wrote Fever Pitch, which took the style of writing that had been prevalent in the fanzines for a decade or so and moved it on to the best-sellers list. Euro 96 saw yet more glorious failure for England, only this time it was played out to the soundtrack of Baddiel and Skinner's seminal Three Lions. Players such as David Beckham, Ryan Giggs, Eric Cantona and Michael Owen became global superstars. Every pop star and politician was only too eager to jump on the football bandwagon and be seen in their club's hospitality suite. Football was the new rock n roll. It was everywhere, and its popularity surged and surged and surged.

Except in Hull.

As football rode on the crest of a wave throughout England, Hull City sank and sank and then sank some more. On the pitch, two relegations; off it, numerous brushes with liquidation, all played out in a crumbling stadium in front of a dwindling number of fans. The Premier League – its glitz, its glamour, its riches, its ubiquity – seemed to belong to a different sport, with Hull City largely living on a hand-to-mouth existence, save for a couple of false messiahs who only served to deepen the agony of those still bothering. The promise of the 1980s, the optimism under Don Robinson, had faded and the club embarked upon the worst decade in its history.

That said, it started promisingly. An early kick-off in the game between City and Sunderland on New Year's Day 1990 saw Andy Payton score the first goal of the decade in the entire Football League, with City running out 3-2 winners. Stan Ternant's revolution seemed to be working, as City won at Upton Park for the first time since 1934, with goals from Neil Buckley and Andy Payton sealing a 2-1 win. Victories came at Swindon, Sunderland and Ipswich as City finished 14th, comfortably avoiding a relegation that had looked certain as Colin Appleton searched in vain for a win at the start of the season. The Ternant-Chetham double act promised a brighter future.

However, one piece of business saw one of the biggest legends in the Hull City's history leave the club for the final time.

Billy Whitehurst: I didn't get on with Stan Ternant, who in his infinite wisdom decided to get rid of me to Sheffield United and bring in Dave Bamber, who I thought was a carthorse at that stage of his career. I couldn't understand the logic of it. I'd played what was arguably my best ever game for Hull City a week or two before at West Ham where we won 2-1. Dave Bassett had sent Wally Downes to watch the game, and afterwards he told me that I'd been the best player on the pitch. But it was a clash of personalities with Stan. He was a clever little twat as a manager. I think he thought he was Rocky Marciano. It was sad leaving somewhere where you love because of someone like him.

Jeff Radcliffe: Billy Whitehurst was a big basher, but he had a heart of gold – when he didn't have you pinned up against a wall. He trained like he played. The only one who could stand up to him was Pete Skipper. I remember him getting keepers carried off two weeks running. The next week he said: "I'm going for my hat-trick today."

Rob Smith: Billy Whitehurst was amazing. He still keeps in touch with my family after the friendship we formed. He viewed my mum as a mother figure at the club and he's never forgotten us. I still get calls from him checking how everyone is, and it means a lot to us. He never forgets anyone. He had a reputation, but the club chaplain at the time would always say what a big, big heart Billy had. He's a good guy.

Billy Whitehurst: My memories of Hull City will live with me for the rest of my life. Hull people, the supporters, were fantastic. I think Hull is the best city in England. Hull people are absolutely top, top drawer. I've lived all over the country, and the Hull people are so genuine and warm and friendly. They were great with me, even when I was shit, because I gave 110%. The fans and people of Hull were always fabulous. Please put that in the book. I can't emphasise that enough.

Not long after Big Billy had played his final game for the club, Little Billy was to follow, moving back up to the north-east to don the black and white of his beloved Newcastle United.

Billy Askew: I saw Stan Ternant years later, and he said: "I got you your dream move." He didn't know I'd already been tapped up. Colin Appleton, of all people, rang me at home and asked if I fancied a move. I was nearly 31 and I wondered: 'Where does he want me to go? Scunthorpe? Scarborough?' He went: "Newcastle." I nearly fell off my chair. I was always a Newcastle fan. So by the time Hull City told me Newcastle wanted me on deadline day, I already knew all about it. I hadn't been playing well under Stan, as the style didn't suit me, and he seemed happy to sell me.

Billy Whitehurst: Billy Askew was as good a left-sided midfielder as there was in any division we played in. I get more praise than Billy because I'd smash people about a bit, which I thought led to someone like Billy Askew getting overlooked. But Billy was so much better than me at football. He'd be the first name on the sheet every week.

Neil Buckley: Of all the players I ever played with, there was no one I loved playing alongside more than Billy Askew. You watched him and used to think: 'Why has he got all that natural ability and I haven't?' He was always one of the best players on the pitch. He could make the ball talk. He just had a gift. I think you have to be born with that.

Billy Askew: It was the best time of my life, without any shadow of a doubt. I'd been there eight years. They'd offered a new two-year contract – which Eddie Gray had mainly been behind – with a decent signing on fee and a testimonial. Then Newcastle came in. Hindsight's a wonderful thing, but moving to Newcastle was the worst thing that happened to me. I should have stayed at Hull. I loved living there, I loved playing for City. It was class. I loved that city.

In the summer of 1990 optimism prevailed around Boothferry Park. The signings of David Mail, Russ Wilcox and Tony Finnigan had fanzine 'Hull, Hell & Happiness' asking on its front page: 'Is THIS the season?' It wasn't. That was apparent by the third league game (and third defeat) when City had just sold star defender Richard Jobson to Oldham for £460,000 and subsequently lost 5-1 to Sheffield Wednesday.

Richard Jobson: Oldham came in for me. I think they'd had their eye on me for a few years but had never had the money to buy me. But the season before they'd had a lot of cup success, and they used that money to sign me. I wasn't particularly looking to leave, it was more Oldham pushing for the deal.

It did feel like I was leaving a club on a downward spiral, however. In my first full season there we'd finished sixth, and then it was mid-table and then relegation fights after Brian Horton left. Our stock in that division was reducing every season. That said, the only game we lost at home at Oldham that season was to Hull. But it felt like the club was deteriorating.

It's still one of the clubs whose results I look out for. I played more league games for Hull than any other, so I look back at that time with real fondness. And I think I still hold the record for the most consecutive games for an outfield player, about 160. But I have fantastic memories, particularly the games against Leeds. It was five really good years.

No Jobson, no hope. It was eight games into the league season before City recorded their first win – 3-2 at home to Port Vale – and though this was followed by a 1-0 win at Watford, the club's many frailties were laid bare at Upton Park in the next game when West Ham ran out 7-1 winners.

By the end of 1990 City had won just five league games and had taken root in the relegation zone. A 5-1 defeat at Portsmouth on New Year's Day saw Stan Ternant given his marching orders. Somewhat unfairly, he was to claim that he hadn't been given sufficient backing from the board. This heralded a change in the chairman's office, too.

Martin Fish: Richard Chetham had a heart scare and had to give up. At the board meeting he told us he'd been advised to give up any strenuous activity so he'd have to resign as chairman, and then said he was nominating me to replace him. Then he said: "All those in favour?" Every hand went up. I said: "Hold on a minute, don't I get a say in this?" So I then became chairman, largely because no one else wanted the job.

Richard had sacked Stan. It was his decision, and I was sorry to see Stan go. But Richard had given him a lot of money to buy players and he was getting fed up with a lack of results on the pitch.

In the first game after Ternant's sacking City feebly exited the FA Cup at home to Notts County.

Gary Clark: My lowest point supporting City was the FA Cup game versus Notts County at Boothferry Park in 1991. Chairman Richard Chetham had sacked manager Stan Ternant a couple of days earlier then left the club in absolute turmoil and County under Neil Warnock took us to the cleaners. It was embarrassing and we threw the towel in, losing 5-2. I was gutted, distraught, and I wondered if we would ever come back from it.

Martin Fish's first task was to bring in a new manager.

Martin Fish: Richard had started the process of bringing in Terry Dolan and I had to finish it off.

Terry Dolan: Leaving Rochdale wasn't straightforward. I'd been told by the Rochdale directors that if a job in a higher league came up they wouldn't stand in my way. When that opportunity arose they decided they wanted compensation for me. Eventually Hull City had to pay that. At that time, the move for me was an obvious one as I was moving up in the size of club I was managing.

When I joined I was made aware that there wouldn't be much money to spend. The Needler family had been bankrolling the club and had decided that enough was enough. I suspect that my record of doing well on a budget at Bradford City and Rochdale was a factor in my getting the job as they thought I wouldn't have to be spending fortunes.

Peter Swan: My mind was set on moving by the time Terry had joined. I knuckled down but it was to get the move. I didn't want to drop down a level, selfishly. But Terry was brilliant at handling that. I was happy to play for him again at York later in my career. I'll only ever say good things about him.

Neil Buckley: I knew from an early stage that my days were numbered under Terry. I was in a drinking culture within the club. Footballers just did that in those days. I worked hard in training but I played hard. I knew nothing of Terry. I was one of the more senior pros at this point and my first impression was that I wasn't going to get on here, which proved to be the case. He wasn't one of my favourite managers. I didn't like how he did business. I didn't rate him as a manager and I thought his style of football was poor.

It soon became apparent to both Martin Fish and Terry Dolan that they would be operating under a very restrictive budget.

Martin Fish: There was a monetary problem right from the off. Richard had introduced a lot of money, that I'd assumed was family money. Stan used that to buy a lot of players who were on big wages, but a lot of them weren't producing the goods. I asked Richard if this money was a gift or a loan, but he couldn't really say. He said he'd let me know. He then stepped down, very quickly, and I didn't really know how to allocate the money. I asked Richard and Christopher Needler. They told me it was a family matter, but I told them I still had to put it in the books. Richard came back and told me it was a loan. Shortly after Richard stood down, there were divorce proceedings between him and his wife. So then the money wasn't just a loan, they wanted it back as part of the divorce proceedings. That put me up against a wall from day one, as I thought that money was going to be written off or given to us. I had to find that money as well as bank overdrafts, Inland Revenue money and so on. This was to have a long-term impact on us not being able to buy players.

The club was still technically in the hands of the Needler family – namely Harold's son, Christopher – but how much interest was he taking in Hull City's fortunes?

Martin Fish: Christopher didn't get involved in the day-to-day running of the club. He was really taking on the family interests. His father had died in 1975 and he suddenly had all these business interests thrust on him. I think he found it hard work, understandably, as he was young when his father died. Hull City was one of these interests. Christopher was interested in football and had had a period as Hull City chairman. That ended in receivership and that seemed to leave a bitter taste for him. But he had to represent the family. He did take an interest in Hull City, but he didn't take an active interest because he had a lot of other family interests. Yes, he'd be going abroad and all the rest of it, but he was always on the Hull City board and would always attend board meetings.

Terry Dolan: I got on very well with Martin Fish and we were always very honest with each other. But Martin wasn't a particularly wealthy man. He certainly didn't have the financial clout that the Needlers had, and the Needlers had said enough was enough, they weren't spending any more money. The Needlers can't be criticised that much as they'd developed the club from the 1950s onwards. I don't think you could say that Christopher Needler didn't care about the club, because he did. All of the Needler family did. But Christopher wasn't the type who wanted to be the front man. He wanted to be in the background as much as possible.

Martin Fish: Christopher had control of the club through the famous non-voting shares which turned into voting shares in special situations such as liquidation, winding up, receivership. When there was a vote to be taken over such issues, then the non-voting shares became voting shares which would give Christopher complete control. A lot of people would say to me: "Why did you take Hull City on because you never really had control? You couldn't say what you could do." But somebody had to run the club. Christopher was always wanting to be kept involved and informed. He would come to matches and come to away games. But the whole situation did leave me in a corner. I was dealing with the Needlers' interests, trying to buy and sell players, dealing with the banks, dealing with the Inland Revenue and then dealing with the supporters. It really was chronic at times. Quite often I'd have to work through the night. It was a very hard situation and no one was willing to help. Sometimes I'd have to pay the wages out of my own bank account, and then be facing the High Court.

As Hull City's fortunes off the pitch looked increasingly bleak, the pitch itself was looking more like a billiard table. Indeed, throughout the 1990s, as the club wondered how it would be able to pay its electricity bills, never mind the players, the Boothferry Park baize was never anything less than immaculate. So how did groundsman John Cooper manage to produce as good a surface as could be found in the country?

John Cooper: By 1989/90 I'd put a plan together to transform – somehow – the playing surface at Boothferry Park. I brought in a friend who had a company in West Yorkshire. I told him I had an idea and asked him what he thought. The most important thing you can do with any playing surface is build a strong foundation, a core. I came up with a plan to redrain the whole playing surface. At that time City were beginning to struggle financially. When I joined the club I insisted on bringing a youngster from one of the local colleges to learn that trade. That was Mark Harrison, who was a very quick learner. We put a plan together and off we went.

A few years later I met an ex-Sunderland director, introduced to me by Stan Ternant. He said to me: "I've found a man who's as mad about sports surfaces as you!" I was introduced to Dixie Thompson, who had a product that he wanted to get into football. He had a bag of sand with him that had what was like a fibre mixed in with it. He showed me this stuff and told me it was the way forward. I was eager to learn about it, but also conscious of the fact that if I cocked up I had no hiding place. He was trialling it in the north-east, using a field as a car park where he laid this product on the surface. It absorbed moisture and held together.

I said to Dixie: "Look, the playing surface at Boothferry Park is a disgrace. I'm prepared to take a punt on this on certain guarantees. One – it doesn't cost us anything. Two – you provide the products. And three – you also provide the labour to put it in." I was trying to cover every angle of how we could transform the playing surface at that time, as the drainage system we put in was second to none.

We did it in 1991/92 and it took eight weeks to do the work. My lasting memory of it is when we'd finished the pitch looked like a sea of sand. This was just when the players were reporting back for pre-season training. Malcolm Shotton walked through the north-west gates at Boothferry Park and said: "Coops, what have you done?" For a minute I stopped and questioned myself. I had to be strong, and I just said: "Malcolm, it'll work, it needs time. By the time you play the first game you'll have a far better playing surface." Luckily we managed it and it went on from there.

Under Terry Dolan and Jeff Lee City improved defensively but – in spite of the goalscoring heroics of Andy Payton (25 goals) and Peter Swan (13 goals) – the club remained rooted to the bottom of the table and relegation was confirmed after a home defeat to Brighton in April.

Peter Swan: Andy and I scored more goals between us than the West Ham partnership that got promoted. It was tough for us to go down.

The relegation did allow Terry Dolan to blood some youngsters in the remaining games, one of whom was 17-year-old goalkeeper Steve Wilson, who started in the season's penultimate game – keeping a clean sheet in a 2-0 win at home to Plymouth – before helping the side to a shock 2-1 win at Newcastle, with another youngster, Dave Walmsley, scoring.

Steve Wilson: I'd been thinking of calling it a day about six months before I was called up. I know being a footballer is every kid's dream, but there's a lot of pressure on you, particularly as a goalkeeper, and the fitness side of things is hard work. We had to do jobs around the stadium too, so every day we wouldn't get home until after five o'clock because we'd be cleaning the stands, doing boots and so on.

I once went into Dale Roberts' office and asked for a chat, with me planning to tell him I was quitting. Just before I started he told me that we were a keeper down in the FA Youth Cup, and he was really looking forward to seeing what I could do. I may have been a bit cowardly, but instead of talking about quitting I just made out that I was checking that I'd be playing and told him how I was really looking forward to it. I walked out and never looked back.

It came as a shock when I was called into the first team. I'd only played a couple of reserve games beforehand and had had a good season for the juniors, then I'm travelling away as cover to a game versus West Brom to give me a bit of experience. We still weren't relegated by that point. But as soon as relegation was confirmed I was named in the squad. I still wasn't expecting to play. We went to Marina for a pre-match meal, which I'd never really known before so I had to borrow a suit jacket. When I turned up Terry told me I was playing against Plymouth. So I made my debut just after I turned 17. I must be one of the youngest keepers to have ever played for Hull City. I was honoured. I kept a clean sheet as well!

As promising as some of the youngsters were, City were skint and an instant return to the Second Division looked unlikely.

Terry Dolan: You're always optimistic. When you go down you hope to go back up as soon as possible. But because of the lack of finances we had to try to get as many good quality players as possible without spending money, so we were reliant on loan players to a large extent. The likes of Ray Wallace, Gary Lund, Ian Ormondroyd and Martin Carruthers really helped, but with loan players you know they're only temporary so you might not get the long-term buy-in.

At the end of the season the club announced plans for a new all-seater North Stand – the first of many ambitious plans made for Boothferry Park that never came close to fruition – as well as the list of players to be released. Among them – to the shock and disgust of many – was an all-time Hull City great, Garreth Roberts.

Garreth Roberts: It wasn't a great way to finish. I'd got an injury against Charlton, turning in the centre circle at Selhurst Park, and my knee just locked. I'd already had operations on it. There was confusion at the club over my rehab and I didn't feel I'd got what I'd deserved. I can still remember having the conversation with Terry Dolan in his office at that house down North Road when I was let go. I was pretty disgusted at how it ended with someone who'd been there 15 years. I got a letter that consisted of two lines essentially saying: 'Thanks very much but you're out,' as my contract was up. I felt left in the lurch. Terry then asked me on the Friday if I wanted to be the youth team manager, which I asked for the weekend to consider as I wanted to try to carry on playing but was waiting to find out if that was a possibility. I went back in after the weekend to say yes, but he told me he'd changed his mind and was giving the job to Mally Shotton, who had another year of his contract left but wasn't in the first team so would come a lot cheaper than me. So that made it even worse. It took me a long time to get over that.

Being a local lad and playing for the team I'd supported from the age of eight, going to games with my mum, it was a dream come true. To captain them to a couple of promotions, play 400 or so games and have such great team-mates… you couldn't ask for more.

Another player to leave – for £300,000 to Port Vale – was record signing Peter Swan.

Peter Swan: I look back on my time at Hull with massive affection. I was only a kid then. I wish now that I could have been a bit more grown up and enjoyed my time there more. I kept seeing my career as one stepping stone after another and a way to make more money. I look back at the goals I scored and wish I'd enjoyed them and the fans a lot more. I loved the Hull fans and they seemed to like me. I have a lot of strong feelings for Hull. I wish I'd been able to spend more time playing there and hadn't just seen it as a stepping stone.

It was now time for Terry Dolan to start building his own squad. This had to be done largely through free transfers such as Gareth Stoker, loan signings, or bringing youth team players through. However, one transfer deal that did get done was to have a huge impact on the club: Alan Fettis had been playing for Ards in the Northern Irish leagues, but was now to become a Tiger.

Alan Fettis: I was 20 years of age and had played Northern Irish league football for a couple of years. I'd been part-time and was just about to go into the civil service, but Bernard Ellison from Hull had watched me a couple of times and then asked me to go there on trial for a week. I wasn't keen as I'd had a few trials in England and was getting sent back, and I just wanted to settle down in Northern Ireland now I had a decent job. In the end I went to Hull for three days with another player called Andy Smith and it went pretty well. Both of us went into Terry Dolan's office after our third day and he offered us a two-year contract each. He said to go home and think about it, so I spoke to Smithy who said he wanted to stay in Northern Ireland, but I said: "I'm off!" My brother had been an apprentice at Mansfield a few years before under Jeff Lee and he always regretted coming back to Northern Ireland and not having a go at it, so I really wanted to give it my best shot. And it went alright!

Terry Dolan: Alan Fettis's brother had been at Mansfield with Jeff Lee and had been looking at players for us in Northern Ireland. We had a look at him, he cost us about £40,000 but it was money well spent!

Alan Fettis: I was trying to forge a career for myself, but going out onto the pitch at Boothferry Park, a place that I loved, felt right. I just wanted to give it everything I'd got.

The 1991/92 season got off to a mixed start. City beat Reading in the first game thanks to a Leigh Jenkinson goal, and then knocked newly minted Blackburn Rovers out of the League Cup. But – in spite of the continuing good form of Andy Payton – only one more league win came before mid-October. However, it was at this time when a signing was made to bring back a local lad who'd been released by City as a youngster and was making a name for himself at North Ferriby United.

Dean Windass: At first a lad called Andy McMillan had been training with City but never got a contract. He ended up going to York and him and his dad got me a trial there. I was there for about four months under Bobby Saxton. I did well. I'd started to grow a bit and get more physical. But Bobby came in and said they had to get players out to get players in and that they couldn't offer me a pro contract. Then I started playing for North Ferriby and Northwood in the Hull Sunday League. Pete Winham was the manager of Northwood and he was a scout at Sunderland. He said he would ask Dennis Smith if I could go for a trial – Ian Sampson had done the same a few years before and signed for them – so I went there for two weeks.

Terry Dolan: Jeff Lee and Bernard Ellison, the youth team coach, had been watching North Ferriby regularly and said I should have a look at Dean. When I actually did get him on trial, he trained on the Monday morning and within an hour I'd seen what he was capable of. It took us two or three days to offer him a contract.

Dean Windass: Terry knew I'd been at Sunderland, and he asked me to go to Hull. He asked me to come in on the Monday and apparently he'd made his mind up by the Monday afternoon – though I didn't know that. I played in the reserves on the Tuesday and scored from midfield, and then on the Wednesday I was offered a two-and-a-half-year contract. The rest is history.

Neil Buckley: Bringing Deano back gave Terry a career lift, but in my opinion there was a lot of luck involved. He was about to go to Sunderland, as he'd impressed there, and City came in at the 11th hour. I don't think Terry had even seen him play, so he took a chance and it came off, so fair play to him there.

Adam Lowthorpe: Dean was great. My uncle had run Ideal Standard football team, and I remembered seeing Dean play at that time. My uncle Tony was playing for North Ferriby too so I'd go see him, and obviously Deano was playing for them. I remember one pre-season game in which Ferriby beat Hull City you could tell that Dean was a good player. When he came back on trial you could see straight away he had such good quality. It was a mystery why he wasn't playing league football. Once he'd played a few games and realised he belonged at that level, he never looked back.

Neil Buckley: Deano had gone away and made his strength match his ability. There was no stopping him then. He was phenomenal. And he's a great guy. I've had some fantastic times with him. He's a larger-than-life character. He's brilliant. And he's much more intelligent than people think. He's the smartest dumbest get that I know!

Dean Windass: I felt at home immediately. I knew I was very good technically, and physically I was better as I was training every day. Terry threw me in straight away, making my debut against QPR in the League Cup. They were a top-flight team with the likes of Ray Wilkins and Les Ferdinand playing. We were beaten 5-1 but Terry told me I'd done well.

Roy North: I was sat next to Tom Wilson at a League Cup match at QPR and he was raving about Dean, telling me what a great lad he was and what a star he was going to be.

City continued to struggle on the pitch. A brief run of form in late October and early November – in which Darlington were beaten 5-2 and Shrewsbury 4-0 – came to an abrupt end when Andy Payton was sold to Middlesbrough for a reported £750,000. However, as on-pitch matters deteriorated, this meant that the club's fanzines gained a more prominent voice, and a player embracing this – as well as the local music scene – was Alan Fettis. Indeed, his popularity was such that one local band named themselves after the goalkeeper.

Alan Fettis: I went to the Welly Club to see them with Rich Lusmore, who ran one of the fanzines. They picked 'Fettis' for some reason – they seemed to think it was a great name, even though I've been trying to get rid of it for years! I've been in touch recently with Gary Hook from the fanzines and would speak to Andy Medcalf from Hull, Hell & Happiness. I used to do stuff for them at Easington United. People like that really helped me settle in at

Hull. It was a really good period of my life and something I owe a lot of people huge thanks for. I loved it in Spiders too. Down-to-earth people and decent music.

Between late November and early February City won just one league game, and back-to-back relegations seemed like a genuine possibility. This was a poor return from a squad that still had a great deal of quality and experience within its ranks.

Steve Wilson: We had a very experienced defence with people like Wayne Jacobs, Russ Wilcox, Dave Norton, Dave Mail and Neil Buckley and they really brought me through. That stood me in great stead for the long haul. Deano was a big character in the squad, and you had Leigh Jenkinson with his shuffle. We just had a good mixture of characters. Even though we didn't do too well in the league we had a real togetherness and we'd go and have a good laugh after the football was done with. We were all good mates, going out together, and we all looked after each other on the pitch.

Alan Fettis: Graeme Atkinson was an excellent, very under-rated player. He would be a player who would get in any team. Every manager or coach would want a player like him – reliable, skilful, he could run, he could score goals, he could tackle. He had so many good characteristics and a great personality. A really nice guy.

Martin Fish: The players weren't bothered so much about the material things. The team spirit we had in that time was incredible. The players would sometimes get their wages in coins as the bank had closed our account. David Mail – a good man who'd had a difficult time losing his wife just after he'd joined – was loaning us money to pay the wages at one point. There was great camaraderie, and that made you carry on. I thought if you could get the support of players like that, who might not have been the best but they were playing the best they could, then I had to keep going. We were so close knit. And there was always laughing and joking in the dressing room.

Towards the end of the season the club was finally represented at Wembley, too, as winger Leigh Jenkinson took part in a 100-metre race with seven other footballers to determine the fastest player in the Football League as part of the Rumbelows Sprint Challenge. Jenks finished eighth in the final as Swansea's 'Flying Postman', John Williams, won in a time of 11.49 seconds.

City finished the season strongly, winning eight of the last 15 games to finish 14th. In that summer Terry Dolan culled the team of the 1980s further to build his own side. Among those released were Leigh Palin, Malcolm Shotton, Nicky Brown and Neil Buckley.

Neil Buckley: I was released on the last day possible. If they'd let me know a month or so earlier I'd have been able to try to get myself something else sorted, and I don't think I was alone in receiving that sort of treatment. I know I was an average professional, and I know that letting me go wasn't a great loss, but he let someone like Leigh Palin go, who was a wonderful footballer – the best I ever played with – and other terrific players like Nicky Brown. And none of us ever got back into the pro game, which was frustrating and you wondered what was being said about us. Terry effectively seemed to replace Leigh Palin in the squad with Gareth Stoker. How can you do that? It may have been down to finances, but none of us were earning huge money.

The 1992/93 season was to be a tough one. The club's new tiger-stripe kit raised eyebrows and a few more were raised when City beat title favourites Stoke 1-0 at Boothferry Park in the first game of the season thanks to a Paul Hunter goal. City drew the next league game and then won three more on the trot before the struggles started. The Tigers lost nine of their next 11 games, drawing the other two, and were soon plunged into relegation trouble. Able to bolster the squad through the signing of Linton Brown – brought in with the £11,000 the fans had raised through the 'Put a Tiger in your Team' campaign – as well as loanees such as Martin Carruthers, Gary Lund and Nicky Mohan, Terry Dolan managed to enjoy a run of good form in December. However, even when things were going well on the pitch there were reminders off it of the club's perilous financial situation. The level of City's financial strife was made clear over Christmas 1992 when popular left-back Wayne Jacobs – who'd suffered a serious knee injury – was released by the club. The fans were not happy.

Martin Fish: That was a very difficult one. He had a long-term injury and it was all about money and costs. We couldn't afford to keep on paying the wages of a player who wasn't going to play for a very long time. He's a nice lad, and I've apologised to him over what happened. It was a financial thing, and he was OK about that.

Wayne's story had a happy ending as he went on to recover from his knee injury and play more than 300 games for Bradford, including a spell in the Premier League.

Elsewhere in 1992, a feature film by the name of Blame It On The Bellboy was released. It was written and directed by City fan Mark Herman, of See You At Wembley Frankie Walsh fame, and included a character by the name of 'Horton'. This was to start a run of Hull City references in Mark's films.

Mark Herman: I don't really remember exactly how this started. I suppose having done two student films, both heavily featuring Hull City, I thought I'd carry on the link and do my own sort of Hitchcock and have a sort of signature somewhere in every film. This can often irritate script editors or film financiers, but so far I've always managed to squeeze in at least a player's name. I remember the powers-that-be on Purely Belter shaking their heads sadly as I tried hopelessly to offer some valid artistic justification in changing the name of the original novel's psychopath to 'Brabin', and cast and crew being confused when I insisted on the right pronunciation, and not 'Braybin' as they constantly referred to him as. The Boy In The Striped Pyjamas was the trickiest one as all the characters have German names, and I thought 'Gruppenfuhrer Vindass' might be a bit too obvious. The full list is:

Blame It On The Bellboy – A character called 'Horton' after Brian.
Brassed Off – A character called 'Ormondroyd' after Ian.
Little Voice – A pigeon called 'Duane' after Duane Darby.
Purely Belter – A psychopath called 'Brabin' after Gary.
Hope Springs – The name Keith Edwards is on a wedding invitation.
The Boy In Striped Pyjamas – A character called 'Meinberg', German for 'My Hill'.

Away from the glitz of the film world, City spent the rest of the 1992/93 season embroiled in a relegation scrap that was to go right down to the wire. Going into the last game of the season City were still technically able to go down, three points ahead of Preston North End but with a superior goal difference. Even though City lost 3-1 to West Brom, Preston lost at Bolton to ensure that City lived to fight another season in the third tier.

Something special was needed to give the fans some hope, and something special came along at the start of the 1993/94 season. An injury crisis saw Linton Brown partnered up front with midfielder Dean Windass. Dean scored nine goals in five games – including hat-tricks against Cambridge and Bristol Rovers – and City won seven of their first 10 games of the season to be among the early pace-setters.

Dean Windass: I'd never played up front in my life. Chris Hargreaves and Steve Moran were injured. I was a good finisher in training with a natural eye for goal. Terry pulled me over and said: "We're playing Plymouth, you're going to have to go up front." I played up front, scored and never played in midfield again.

Terry Dolan: Dean ended up up front because we had a lack of strikers. Chris Hargreaves broke his leg pre-season, and we'd signed Linton Brown, but we had nobody else. Dean had such a quality that we didn't think twice about putting him up front. We asked him, and he'd only just really signed as a professional so he was happy to play anywhere.

Dean Windass: They brought Linton Brown in from non-league and me and him had a great partnership. We had to shop in the non-league because we didn't have any money. If City had had the money they probably wouldn't have been looking non-league, so it was a blessing for me really.

The last of those seven wins was an unforgettable game against Bradford City at Boothferry Park. Some 9,492 fans saw Dean Windass score and then get sent off within the opening minutes of the game. Bradford equalised but a Greg Abbott penalty and Linton Brown goal gave the Tigers a memorable victory. It was a particularly special afternoon for one Hull lad.

Adam Lowthorpe: Terry Dolan had pinned the team sheet on the dressing room wall for the reserve game on the Wednesday night and I wasn't in it, so my first thought was that I'd been dropped from the reserves. He then pulled me to one side and told me that Brian Mitchell wasn't fit for the Saturday and I would be playing. It took a couple of seconds to sink in, but then I realised he meant I was playing for the first team.

From there, he said that as far as the press were concerned we were saying Brian had a chance, but that I was definitely playing. For me it was great to have those few days to get my head around it. My dream had been to play for my hometown club and there was Terry telling me that this was going to happen.

I remember the senior pros being really good around that time such as Deano, Alan Fettis, Dave Norton and others. They'd really settle you down and help you understand what was coming. We knew there'd be a big crowd too.

Deano had said to me: "We'll give you an early touch", so he played it to me, but I'd been wandering around trying to get my head ready and I wasn't where Deano was expecting me to be, so my first touch was a tackle in front of the Kempton which ended up going out for a throw-in to us. I threw it down the line, it got flicked on to Linton Brown who outpaced Dean Richards and crossed it in for Deano to score after about 30 seconds. One abiding memory of that day, after Deano scored, was turning around and seeing a view from the centre circle of the South Stand just erupting. I remember freezing looking at it. I'd been stood there as a kid, and seeing it in raptures like that was amazing. Then Deano got sent off… But it was a brilliant day. I remember getting home afterwards and looking in the mirror and thinking: 'I've played for Hull City.' I knew that no matter what else happened to me, I'd played for Hull City.

Martin Fish had to make a number of tough decisions in his time at Hull City, but the decision to let Tom Wilson go in the autumn of 1993 was one of the most unpopular. Tom had been associated with the club for decades in a number of roles, and was widely liked and respected. However, his time at Hull City was brought to an end.

Tom Wilson: Terry Dolan came in with Jeff Lee. I had some of the young lads in the first team at that time and we'd teach them how to play football, passing the ball, bringing it out from the back and so on. We'd teach them different systems. Terry just dropped all of that, and said that the young players didn't mean anything to him. He didn't seem bothered about leaving a legacy for who followed him. I was kicked out of training. I felt like a spare part. It was embarrassing. I was offered the secretary's job, which got me out of things. Even then I'd travel with the team, and sometimes the players would come and sit with me on the coach to chat about the game. This seemed to make Terry and Jeff paranoid, as if I was talking about them – which I wasn't, I never said a bad word about them back then. I was then dishonourably made redundant. It was sad. I'd done a lot for the club as secretary, trying to make money for the club on top of everything else. I even sold the Hull City sign. We needed the money – I managed to get £11,000 for it from some guy in Nottingham.

Martin Fish: It was a difficult thing with Tom. The situation we had there was more of an inheritance from Richard Chetham's period as chairman as Tom had been given the assistant manager's job, but he didn't seem to want that any more. So Richard said: "I can hardly get rid of him, can you find him a place in the office?" I said: "The only thing I can think of is the secretary's job." However, he was still on an assistant manager's salary with a car attached. That was much more than what the secretary of a football club would generally be on. We had an issue there with the money side of things. Tom was a sensible fellow, but I told him we couldn't afford him. Eventually it got to the point where I said we'd have to let him go and take on some of the duties he'd been doing within my accountancy firm to save the club money. He was upset and wanted wrongful dismissal. It was an awkward time.

Neil Buckley: Tom Wilson is as big a gentleman in the game as you'll ever meet. He's honest and fair and always approachable. I can't think of a man in the game who I respect more. He did a lot for my career. He helped me and developed me, being a centre-back himself. A charming gentleman on and off the pitch. He cared. And that's massive. He cared about you as a footballer and as a person and also about your family. To me that's a gift when somebody does that. A wonderful man. He helped so many people along the way.

The rest of the season was the Dean Windass show, with Linton Brown playing a prominent supporting role. Amid all of this, City made national headlines when a wall collapsed as fans were celebrating a goal in an FA Cup tie at Runcorn. City spent the season on the fringes of the play-offs, with Windass's reputation going up a few notches on a weekly basis. When City beat Huddersfield 2-0 at Leeds Road in mid-March a play-off berth – and with it a shot at a first ever game at Wembley – looked nailed on. Alas, two wins in the final 11 games of the season brought a disappointing ninth-place finish, five points off Burnley in sixth. Dean Windass had notched 24 goals and for the first time in a long time Hull City looked upwardly mobile on the pitch, even if an outstanding Inland Revenue bill of more than £200,000 was hanging over the club.

Hopes were high of a play-off spot or better at the start of the 1994/95 season. A 4-0 defeat at Oxford in the opening game of the season dampened these hopes, as did the 2-0 defeat to Swansea at Boothferry Park a week later. City roared back, however, and after drawing the next game against Leyton Orient won nine of their next 13 games, and were back in the play-off spots. The side that beat Crewe Alexandra 7-1 in late October did so by out-footballing what was widely recognised as one of the most attractive sides to watch in the country. City's efforts even saw Terry Dolan win the division's Manager of the Month trophy. A more poignant moment was to come in October when the great Raich Carter passed away. His funeral procession stopped at Boothferry Park so that past and present players, as well as fans, could pay their last respects.

Dean Windass was leading the way as City gave the fans something to get excited about, but he was backed up by some terrific players at that level. Linton Brown was a pacey foil for Windass's guile, while Neil Mann's runs down the left wing made him a firm crowd favourite. The likes of Chris Lee, Greg Abbott, David Norton and Graeme Atkinson were firming up the midfield, with Richard Peacock, signed from non-league football, looking like a player with the world at his feet. Rob Dewhurst stood out in defence and he, along with David Mail, helped to bring on youngsters such as Adam Lowthorpe, Gary Hobson and Neil Allison. In goal, Steve Wilson was winning the battle of the number ones, which, in the December of that season, led to an unusual turn of events.

Alan Fettis: I'd damaged my thumb and was really struggling to play in goal, but I was able to train and would do so out-field. Every goalkeeper thinks they're a great outfield player and they always want to be centre-forwards for some reason. Numbers were very short and the squad was thin – we had a few injuries and suspensions. I was warming up Steve Wilson before the Oxford game and Neil Allison came up to me – he was a massive piss taker, you couldn't believe anything he'd say – and he said to me: "You're sub, Terry says you've got to go in and get changed." I thought he was joking so I carried on warming Willo up, but when I went in Terry said: "Right Fets, you're number 12, get your kit on."

With about 15 minutes to go Linton Brown started struggling with a back injury so Terry told me to warm up. I thought: 'This is taking the piss,' but that was it, I went on for Linton. I then just remember playing the ball out wide and running into the goalmouth. The ball came to me about six yards out, I aimed at a corner and the ball went into completely the opposite side of the goal that I'd been aiming for. I don't think Oxford's goalkeeper was best pleased, but it was fantastic. I think the attendance that day was three or four thousand, but everyone in Hull seems to have been there. If everyone who claims to have been there was actually there there'd have been a crowd of about 15,000!

Terry Dolan: Alan going up front was again through necessity. People these days wouldn't believe that a goalkeeper would score two goals that weren't a freak from a goal kick. It will probably never happen again given the size of squads now. The first game he came on as a sub, he was on the bench because he'd had an injury problem so he couldn't play as a goalkeeper. We were short of numbers and needed him as an outfield player, where he loved playing in five-asides. We knew it wasn't a stupid decision to make.

As maligned as the Dolan years have been in the intervening years, it's easy to forget what a good feeling there was around the club at that time, and how much fun it was. The off-field problems were mounting, but on the pitch the team and the fans were galvanised, with the starting line-up usually featuring half-a-dozen or so local lads. For two seasons on the trot, the play-offs looked to be a real possibility. However, in the 1994/95 season City couldn't quite hold on to a top-six spot – finishing eighth, seven points off the play-offs, in spite of loan signings Ian Ormondroyd and Warren Joyce bolstering the squad. However, Alan Fettis was to get another chance up front, and was to deliver another goal at Bloomfield Road, Blackpool.

Alan Fettis: I ran into the box, Gary Lund challenged the goalkeeper and I just smashed it as hard as I could. There was no guile or craft in that. I just kept my head down and smacked it as hard as I could.

Terry Dolan: At Blackpool, who were managed by Sam Allardyce then, he started the game and scored a late winner. When you think about the things that happened in that period – Alan's goals, beating Crewe 7-1, beating Whitby Town 8-4 after being 4-3 down in stoppage time of the 90 minutes – you just wouldn't believe that sort of thing these days.

With the Boothferry Park pitch still in pristine condition – a fact not lost on the wider football world – some money was saved by John Cooper's ingenuity.

John Cooper: In 1994 I managed to pick up an award for the playing surface. I was down in London for the presentation ceremony. I didn't think we'd win anything. We'd been nominated for our division – the old Third Division. We managed to pick up that award, and then we won the award for the four divisional winners. That opened a door as people wanted to know what we'd done. The idea then was to use that to our advantage. One company came in from Lancashire and said: "We like what you're doing, if you need any sponsorship we'd be interested." By that time we really needed the money. I told them that what I wanted to do was help the club financially, so I'd work with them but I wanted products at no cost to the club. In the 1994/95 season I managed to secure a deal with this company to sponsor literally every product we used – nets, corner flags, everything for one year. In return, I told them if they brought any clients to see Boothferry Park I'd sell their company for them. That worked a treat.

Our philosophy was quite simple: when fans walk into a stadium they've got time on their hands, so let's give them a show. Let's give them something that looks good. If you've got a great playing surface, not only is it attractive to the fans, it makes footballers want to play football. However, the stadium was in need of management, which I got involved with. In the wake of the Bradford, Heysel and Hillsborough disasters, the way stadiums needed to be run changed completely, with things like CCTV.

The financial issues were really starting to bite now, too, and in the 1995/96 season those problems were to come home to roost. By late October, City had won just one game. In a match at Wycombe, few were expecting much to get excited about, only for Dean Windass to score one of the greatest goals ever scored by a Hull City player with an astonishing 40-yard volley after collecting and controlling a goal kick.

Dean Windass: We were 2-0 down and I got the biggest bollocking of my life at half-time. There were a lot of rumours about me moving at the time, Norwich were meant to be interested, and Jeff Lee hammered me at half-time, slagging me off. Chris Lee scored the first, and then I did that. I looked towards the bench afterwards as if to say: 'I've proved you wrong.' Jeff came in at the end and said: "That's why I gave you a bollocking as that's the sort of thing I know you can do." But it was an unbelievable goal. The bollocking helped though. I was a player that would respond to that sort of thing. I didn't like being cuddled. I liked to be told what I was doing wrong.

Such goals only attracted more and more scouts to Boothferry Park to see the great man in action, and in December 1995, after months of speculation, Dean Windass departed to Aberdeen for a reported £700,000.

Dean Windass: Norwich came in for me. Martin O'Neill was their manager and Terry told me that they put an offer in. But City had a £250,000 Inland Revenue debt and they were going to close the gates at Boothferry Park, so they needed the money up front and Norwich weren't offering that. However, by that point I'd put my house up for sale and someone had bought it. I was worried I'd have nowhere to live over Christmas. Apparently Martin O'Neill then resigned because he couldn't sign me.

I was a young lad who'd never really left Hull. I wanted to play at a higher level. I was playing well and scoring goals. My dad used to say: "The better you play the more goals you score and the more money you earn." Then we were supposed to play in a reserve game as we'd been knocked out of the FA Cup and Terry was punishing all the first-team players by making them play in this. I was preparing one Thursday afternoon for this game, then I got the call to say I wasn't playing in it and City had agreed a fee of £600,000 plus add-ons with Aberdeen. The £600,000 basically saved the club, and North Ferriby got £60,000 so that helped them as well.

A month later, with the club still in a desperate financial situation, Alan Fettis was sold to Nottingham Forest for £250,000.

Alan Fettis: The club needed the money. They were in the mire. I was an international and I was ambitious and wanted to see how far I could take my career. People from Northern Ireland were saying I needed to play – as I was in and out of the Hull team because of things like contract disputes – if I wanted to play for the national team. Then the Nottingham Forest thing came up, which probably wasn't the best thing to do looking back. But you don't turn down a club like Nottingham Forest.

Rich Lusmore: Alan Fettis was not only an outstanding goalkeeper who also famously earned plaudits for his headline-making goals at the other end of the pitch, but he was a bloke only too willing to engage with supporters. A member of a City side that won't be remembered long in the annals of history, Fettis became a friend of the fanzines, giving interviews, modelling t-shirts and even turning up for gigs (including that of the band named after him). He even came down to an Easington United presentation do. A top man.

No Windass, no Fettis, no hope. Linton Brown was also sold to Swansea in March 1996 for £60,000. This left the 1995/96 season as possibly the most miserable in the club's history. City won just five league games to finish rock bottom of the Third Division, failing to win a league match throughout the whole of September, October and November. This led to the formation of the Tigers 2000 protest group, led by Angie Rowe. Meanwhile, the club was struggling to pay the bills, leaving the threat of administration or worse lingering over the club. Patience was also now wearing very thin with manager Terry Dolan, though he did retain the unwavering support of his chairman.

Martin Fish: Terry Dolan was very good at finding players who really didn't cost very much. We had a glut of goalkeepers who went on to be sold for good money. Linton Brown was picked up playing local football in the Driffield area, Dean Windass was at North Ferriby.

Dean Windass: Terry was my second dad. I used to get hammered for that by the players, who'd say: "Your dad's doing this for you, your dad's doing that for you." We still have a great relationship now. Terry changed my life. He was the one who gave me that chance. He said to me when I signed: "You've got a second chance now, don't blow it."

Terry Dolan: I'd like to think that most of the players that I'd dealt with would feel that they could trust me and that I trusted them. And that goes a long way in all walks of life but particularly football.

Steve Wilson: I found Terry Dolan really good. Terry was the nice, placid guy, and then Jeff Lee was fiery and would let you know if you weren't doing what was expected of you. They were well organised in what they wanted to do, the way they wanted to play.

Rob Smith: We had a lot of down-to-earth lads in the Dolan years, no prima donnas. I still have a lot of contact with those players. The club was always teetering financially, and we couldn't pay big wages, but the nucleus of that team was together for a couple of season and really seemed to bond. People would knock the management but there was a good team there for a couple of seasons. We just always had this financial threat there and the crowd base wasn't massive.

Dave Burns: I was working at Radio Humberside in the glory days of Martin Fish and Terry Dolan, both of whom I liked. But the club was in decline, there was very little investment, supporters groups were being formed and it just seemed to be wilting away. I was once banned by a naked Terry Dolan. I'd had what I thought was an off-the-record conversation with commercial manager Simon Cawkhill and I'd said that the club was a disgrace, the ground was falling apart and so on. He told Terry, and I was in the dressing room waiting for my weekly interview only for Terry to emerge out of the shower and tell me he wasn't talking to me and I was banned! But the club was in decline. Chris Needler wasn't going to put any money in and didn't seem to know what to do with the club, and nobody was coming forward to take it on. Not long after that I moved to Radio Sheffield.

Perhaps the lowest point in a season of low points came in the final game. Bradford City were coming to Boothferry Park needing a win to stay in play-off contention. With several thousand Bantams fans expected to make the journey along the M62, the South Stand was given to away fans. This led to a ramping up of protests against the club's owners and manager.

Terry Dolan: We were informed that on police advice that we had to give the South Stand to the Bradford fans. Martin got a lot of stick for that, as the fans thought it was his decision, but I can assure you that it wasn't. Bearing in mind my history with Bradford City, it wasn't nice the way in which it happened. It was around that time that there was talk the club was up for sale, and the supporters seemed to think that something had to happen. David Lloyd was already in the background, but it took a long time from the first murmurings of the club being up for sale to it actually happening, and during that period as we weren't being very successful on the pitch the protesting got even worse.

To add insult to injury, reports were coming through that the owners of Boothferry Park (i.e. the Needler family) had received a £5m bid for the land. If accepted, City would need a new home. Rumours spread about the club moving to the Costello athletics stadium, sharing the Boulevard with Hull FC or building their own 8,000-capacity stadium. Thankfully, Christopher Needler turned down the offer and the Tigers were to stay put.

Fans were further enraged when Terry Dolan – who had now become the first manager to lead the club to two relegations – was offered a new contract along with assistant Jeff Lee.

Martin Fish: Terry had found a number of decent players at very little cost to the club who would gain in value. His contract was coming up for renewal and I thought: 'Do I want a new manager to come in and change the team and me have to go through all this again?' We were getting some results and I thought Terry was doing a good job given the players he was bringing in, so I renewed his contract as I thought the players he was bringing in might help keep the club afloat. He signed on the same terms, no increase in salaries and so on.

There was a lot of controversy over him getting a percentage of the transfer fees, and that was true, but the wording of the clause meant that he had to sell a certain number of players for a certain value within a season, not the calendar year. A lot of supporters thought the contract stated it was in a calendar year and worked out that he'd sold various players to get a certain amount. But it didn't fall into the right periods for him to get the sums that fans were claiming. And Terry wasn't really a money man, he just wanted to try and do what he could for the club. I thought the fans and the media had picked up the wrong angle, particularly given that they didn't know what the clause said. I'm sure I didn't pay him a bonus at any point. If I did it was only a very small amount. The timings of the sales didn't fall within what was set out in the clause to warrant a payment.

To back Fish's opinion of Dolan's ability to identify players, a couple of signings were made in the summer of 1996 that were to be pivotal to the club in the years to come. Warren Joyce joined from Burnley for £30,000 – a sum he was to more than pay back a few years later – while another player was unearthed from the local non-league system, just as Dean Windass and Linton Brown had been.

Mark Greaves: It wasn't the smoothest of signings, as Scunthorpe, Sheffield Wednesday and a few others wanted to sign me based on what I'd done at Brigg, getting to Wembley and winning the FA Vase. Brigg wanted me to sign a contract close to the end of the season so they'd get some money when I moved, which was fair enough. I'd had a great time at Brigg. Neil Buckley was there and he helped me massively, teaching me a lot.

I knew Hull were interested so I didn't sign the contract offered, as I just wanted to go there. Brigg weren't happy when I signed for Hull though, as it was on a free transfer. John Kaye, Brigg's manager, went to see Terry Dolan about it and had a massive argument with him. I was happy to sign for my home-town club though.

I really struggled at first. The first few months were difficult on every level. In my first game, a friendly, I did my ankle ligaments so I was out for seven or eight weeks, meaning I was in rehab from almost day one. I made my full debut against Scunthorpe in October 1996, coming on for Neil Allison at half-time. It was 0-0 at that point, but they scored two late goals to win 2-0 and there was a pitch invasion from the Hull fans, chanting 'Dolan out! Fish out!' I'd gone from playing in front of 250 people to having pitch invasions! It was an eye-opener. The passion from the fans was extraordinary.

Around this time, yet more fan anger was aimed at Martin Fish when an 'exciting development' at the club was teasingly announced. Many speculated that a sale was finally in the offing. There was widespread disappointment when Fish announced that the East Stand at Boothferry Park was going to be redeveloped, with a series of grants covering the costs.

Martin Fish: I made that press announcement about the East Stand at the time when Christopher Needler had, unbeknown to me, made a statement to the press to say that the Needler family were looking to get out of the club. So that put the kybosh on the East Stand thing, which I'd already got the press conference sorted for. Christopher had made these comments literally one day earlier. I subsequently said to Christopher: "I wish you hadn't said that, as it made the announcement a damp squib." So we had to forget that and go on, which ultimately led to David Lloyd coming in.

Locally the club were now something of a joke, and nationally they were an irrelevance.

Mark Robinson: The Yorkshire cricket lads tended to support the Sheffield teams more than anyone else. But I never got any stick in cricket for being a Hull City fan when I was playing because we were largely rubbish and therefore deemed irrelevant.

Robert Crampton: The club were a bit of a joke throughout the decade. I'd moved to London by this point, but we'd always have our Boxing Day outing to see City, and I'd go whenever I was back in Hull, but at that point you didn't go expecting anything to happen. You were expecting them to lose. The football was dreadful, the stadium was appalling, the whole thing was falling apart. You were going out of habit, out of loyalty, but also because there was a sense of comedy to it. I remember us conceding an own goal in one game and everyone in the stands just falling about laughing. It was like we'd given up.

With the club now in the bottom division, the fan protests through the Tigers 2000 group reached fever pitch. The targets of this ire were Christopher Needler, Martin Fish and Terry Dolan, but with Needler frequently absent by this point, Fish and Dolan – being the most visible of the trio – were to bear the brunt of this anger.

Martin Fish: I intended to ride through it as best as I could. I had to stand my ground and explain what I was doing. But the protests caused an enormous amount of work and caused great difficulties for my family. My family were a little split up at the time, as my son was working abroad and my daughter was at the Royal College of Music in London and fell ill, which forced my wife down there to deal with it. That led to her staying down there for three years when I was chairman, from 1992 to 1995. But obviously I was trying to get down there every weekend to see them. So I'd go straight from games to London on a Saturday, but would be back on Sunday as I had an accountancy practice to run as well as the club. The hours I did were incredible. I'd be at the club most days but not all day as I had to keep the staff at the accountancy practice in jobs.

My daughter and wife came back in 1995, but that was when Tigers 2000 was getting into full action. So that was difficult. We had all sorts of protests. Protestors sent fresh cod heads in the post to every opposition chairman just before we were going to play in an away game. I alerted the chairmen as to what was going on, and Jimmy Hill, who was then the chairman of Fulham, said: "They're not very friendly supporters in Hull. Why only send the head, I wanted the rest of the fish!" There were lots of things like that, but I got a lot of support from my fellow chairmen.

The worst thing I encountered, though, was when an open-top double-decker bus was driven outside our house with a loudspeaker chanting: "Fish out." The people in the neighbourhood couldn't believe what was happening. My wife was about to go out to the shops and was trapped in the garage for the time the bus was there. That was a very bad moment.

Terry Dolan: The protests didn't make life easy. The big problem was that we were relegated twice, gates had dropped, money was getting tighter. People don't realise that we had three winding up orders and myself, Jeff and the backroom staff take a little bit of credit that we were able to sign the likes of Dean Windass, Alan Fettis and Roy Carroll, who were valued highly and kept the club going from a financial point of view. I don't think people realised how serious it was at that stage. A lot of the protests were against the directors and then later against me, as things weren't getting any better on the pitch. It wasn't easy but I had thick skin. It wasn't nice for my family though.

Martin Fish: I was always hopeful that something would pull the club through whenever we were on the brink. If I'd thought that we were going to go out of existence, I wouldn't have stayed as long. I wouldn't have used my own resources to keep the club going if I thought it wasn't going to survive. I also knew that, as a chartered accountant with a practice in the city, I didn't want a liquidated football club on my hands. So I stuck it out, and obviously it took a while to find someone.

So how were the protests affecting the players and backroom staff?

Adam Lowthorpe: I don't think the off-field stuff affected the players. I understood the frustrations of the fans. I remember Rod Wallace playing for us on loan while we were pushing for promotion and his club wanted £30,000, which wasn't a lot even in those days. We couldn't afford him even though he was helping us push towards the play-offs, and that's when I realised just how little money there was in the club. I genuinely think that every player who played for Hull City at that time gave it everything they had. Even from a playing point of view, though, it felt that the soul of the club was being sucked out more and more as time went on. There were two or three occasions where I felt that I was going to be a part of Hull City's final ever football match, and that's not a pleasant thought.

Rob Smith: I was doing commercial stuff – the backroom staff was less than a dozen people in total – and I'd worked in most positions. We didn't have a marketing manager in those days. In those final two years under Fish and Dolan, when the protests increased, the people inside the club really stuck together. There was a lot of loyalty there to Hull City. People really had the club at heart. I remember turning up to the office in the summer for something or other and could smell something awful. I found dog mess and maggots that had been posted through the letterbox. The reception and the offices were crawling with bluebottles. I stood there wondering: 'What the hell do I do here,' so I just got a vacuum cleaner out and started clearing everything up. The fan base might not have been massive, but the frustration among the fans was. And they just wanted success. That's fans for you. I felt that a lot of the criticism was unfair though, and that people at the club were trying to do their best.

Jeff Radcliffe: Terry Dolan was a smashing bloke. The club were really struggling. The abuse he, Jeff Lee and Martin Fish received was not deserved. Martin wasn't a very wealthy man and was doing his best.

Steve Wilson: The off-field stuff didn't affect me at all. I think players can look for excuses – they still do today – when they're not playing well. For me at the time, the only thing that did bother me was whether I'd be getting paid, which we generally did. I don't think it really affected the other players too. In some respects I think it helped with the squad camaraderie. I think that helped us pull through a few difficult times.

Mark Robinson: As a professional sportsman I just have total empathy with players trying their best. I'm sympathetic to any player because I know what it's like to try your best and it not come off. It's the same for managers. Abuse can sometimes be too easy. Every time you go out on the pitch you put your career on the line.

A rare high point on the pitch at this point was the form of young Northern Irish goalkeeper Roy Carroll. Roy only played for Hull City 50 times before he was sold to Wigan for £350,000, who were to later sell him to Manchester United for £2.5m. Such a high-flying career wasn't evident from the off, however.

Terry Dolan: We brought in Roy as a 16-year-old and in his first training session we did a shooting practice. He was stopping everything, but with his knees, elbows, feet. I remember saying to Jeff Lee: "If we can get him to use his hands properly we've got one hell of a keeper here." Eventually that's what happened.

In November 1996, the antipathy towards Hull City was shown when the club recorded its lowest ever league attendance – 1,775 – in a midweek home match against Torquay (after, it should be added, Tigers 2000 had called for a boycott of the match). A week later came a crazy FA Cup first round replay at Boothferry Park against Whitby Town. The first game had finished 0-0. The second was to produce 12 goals, with City 4-3 down with seconds of normal time left only to win 8-4 after extra time.

James Richardson (Hull City fan): The Whitby FA Cup replay remains one of the best-worst games I've seen. Twelve goals, 120 minutes, a double hat-trick (sextrick?) from Duane Darby, including a last-minute 'worldie' volleyed equaliser that made it 4-4 and featured on Match of the Day's goal of the month, and some of the most shambolic defending imaginable.

Throughout this time there were frequent rumours that City were on the verge of being sold. Local entrepreneurs such as the Healeys, Lord White and even the Hart brothers would be mentioned, but nothing happened. Had anyone made a serious bid for the club?

Martin Fish: Don Robinson came in towards the end, when we were close to finalising the David Lloyd deal, and said: "I have got some money and I'm prepared to buy the club but I need the non-voting shares from Christopher Needler." I said to Don that I'd put it to Christopher – and it should be added that Christopher and Don had really stopped speaking to each other by this time – but Chris said: "No, I can't have Don coming in again, and the family will not let me part with the shares because of the tradition." That created a big fall out and Don just fell away after that. Other than that there were no serious buyers that came in. The odd enquiry, but no one who was seriously interested until David Lloyd.

City ended a forgettable first season back in the bottom tier finishing 17th, their lowest ever position in the Football League pyramid. The club and fans remained at odds, a fact demonstrated when Warren Joyce celebrated a goal against Brighton in front of some empty terracing as a show of support for his beleaguered boss Terry Dolan.

Then, in the summer of 1997, something stirred. A takeover was announced by former Hull FC full-back Tim Wilby on behalf of former tennis pro and now leisure entrepreneur David Lloyd. Lloyd was to be the new owner of Hull City and Hull Sharks (née FC), who the consortium had taken control of a few months earlier. So how did the deal come about?

Martin Fish: David Lloyd had these tennis clubs that had made a lot of money. But he was tied in with an Irish group. One of the people they knew very well was Tim Wilby. Tim was a former Hull FC player, and David took over that club and put Tim in charge. He then seemed to think it would be a good idea to get the football club linked with the rugby club, so that's how the approach was made. There'd been various Irish connections that I didn't get involved with, which was all to do with raising the money to pay for the club. I told David that I wanted x amount, and he hoo-ha'ed and then we got around a table in a London hotel and I said – tongue in cheek – this is the deal, x million, you're going to have to take it or leave it as time is getting short for us. He said: "Well you haven't got anyone else interested." I replied: "How do you know I haven't?" So I told him if he wanted the club, then he should put his money where his mouth was and get the deal done.

However, I told him there was the condition of deal: I wanted x amount of the money paid in to my solicitor's account as I wanted to pay the creditors off. That included the Inland Revenue, the bank overdraft, other loans and so on. He said: "That's unusual, we'd normally pay those off." I said: "Don't take this the wrong way, it's not that I don't trust you, but I want to be able to say to the people of Hull that at the end of the day that the club was clear of debt, and this is the only way I can do that." I didn't want to touch any of the money, just for us to agree which creditors needed to be paid and we'd get the solicitors to pay them. He looked at me and said: "Are there any more conditions?" I told him there weren't, and he said: "Thank god for that! I will do the deal, Martin, but I'm not having any more conditions. Anything else and I walk away."

After that we could get drafting and signing. I wanted it done that way because I'd taken so much stick, up against the wall from day one with the debts, and I wanted to be able to walk away and say that the debts had been paid. It also meant that my accountancy clients could see that I'd done a decent job. Later on he said that he'd admired what I'd done even if he couldn't understand it initially.

This was to be the last act of a chairmanship that had been eventful to say the least. And while Martin Fish had plenty of critics among the club's fans, his popularity among the players and remaining staff was high.

Dean Windass: Martin Fish was a lovely guy. I'd just got married and had my first son. I had a mortgage. When I signed my second contract with City I was getting a £15,000 signing-on fee but I wasn't getting the second £5,000 until July, and I needed some money. I asked Martin what I could do, and he lent me £1,000 out of his own bank account until that money came through. Supporters don't see that. Martin's a great man.

Ian Thomson: Martin Fish always treated me very well when I worked looking after the directors at Boothferry Park on matchdays, which made me (and still makes me) particularly sad in the light of the mismanagement of the club which was to ensue on his watch.

Steve Wilson: Martin Fish did a terrific job. To keep the club afloat in the way he did – he wasn't a millionaire or anything like that – was extraordinary. If it wasn't for him, Hull City would have gone under a long time ago.

John Cooper: Along with Adam Pearson, Martin Fish was the best chairman I worked with. He was a gentle man and a gentleman. He allowed me to use the skills that I had to the best of my ability. He didn't interfere with anything. He supported me, encouraged me, and I did the same for him, as that was at a time when things were starting to go wrong. The Needler family were taking more and more of a back seat, especially Christopher, and Martin was left holding the baby. I cannot stress enough how close everyone was at that time just to make sure the club survived. It was an important part of my professional life working with those people, because I learnt a lot about camaraderie and where that can get you.

With Martin Fish no longer running the club, Terry Dolan was heading for the exit door.

Terry Dolan: It was strange to say the least. David Lloyd was one of a few names mentioned but we knew that something was going to happen. To be fair to Martin he kept me informed as to the progress of any takeover but it went on far too long and didn't help with any continuity at the club.

To demonstrate how stupid it was, the Lloyd camp kept putting things out that they'd bought the club. Tim Wilby sat in my office to tell me that my services were no longer required. I never met David Lloyd once, despite him negotiating to buy the club for nine months. New people coming in invariably want their own people, so I had it in the back of my mind that my days were numbered. But I wanted to be fair to the club and be fair to Martin, so I didn't want to leave during the season. But to show how amateur the new people were in their dealing with people, Tim Wilby met with me in the office on North Road. It took 30 seconds for him to tell me the new regime didn't want me. That was on a Saturday morning. But they hadn't signed forms to take over the club at that stage. It was all over the Hull Daily Mail about my sacking with carefully engineered photos of me leaving my office, but Martin said to me I had to go in on the Monday when pre-season training started as the new lot hadn't taken over the club yet and I'd be in breach of contract if I didn't go in. So having been reported as having been sacked, along with Jeff Lee, we then spent the next five days training the players because no one had taken over. It wasn't until the following Friday that the new regime signed the takeover forms. How many managers have had to do that?

I look back with pride at the good young players we produced: Roy Carroll, Dean Windass and Alan Fettis were sold on at a huge profit. There were some interesting times. Whatever group of players we had, during that period although the football may not have been brilliant and we didn't have much success, we had a group of players who'd work for each other and would stick together. From a management point of view I didn't have any success, which disappoints me, but we did our best. People might say our best wasn't good enough and if that's the case then unfortunately there's not much more we could have done about that. From an experience point of view it didn't do me any harm. I also think it will be a long time before Hull City have another manager who's there for six-and-a-half years.

Alan Fettis: Terry took a lot of hits, but I always thought very highly of him. Now that I'm a coach, from the outside looking in, I see that he did a marvellous job. He made a lot of money for the club and barely spent anything. And there were times when Deano was there – and Dean was phenomenal – alongside the likes of Linton Brown, Rob Dewhurst, Richard Peacock, Neil Mann, Jimmy Graham and Greg Abbott that were great. Terry identified those players and was brilliant at building a team. And we had some fantastic times. We were on a pittance in football terms, but there was such camaraderie within the team, coupled with some talented players, and we got on a few decent runs and did some decent things.

With Fish and Dolan – along with Christopher Needler – now no longer involved in the club, Hull City fans were looking forward with genuine optimism. The new regime was given a rapturous welcome. A meeting with the new owner at Hull City Hall was packed out. David Lloyd had what seemed to be the perfect combination of a business brain and a sporting background. Tim Wilby – albeit on a smaller scale – could claim similar. Expectations went to fever pitch when a new player-manager was announced. Mark Hateley had 32 England caps and was a legend at AC Milan and Rangers. Now he was Hull City's manager.

Mark Hateley: I thought the potential was enormous. It was a great football club with great support – that was the main thing that attracted me. All great football clubs are wrapped up with the supporters, and none more so than Hull City. I came from a footballing family, and when I'd watch my dad Hull City were a very, very well-supported football club with a legendary playing surface and a great football stadium. It ticked all the boxes for me. It was an opportunity that I thought was a good one.

So how were those within the club reacting to the new regime?

Rob Smith: It was a totally different ball game to Fish and Dolan. You had the David Lloyd name, which was pretty big news for the club. I didn't know much about Tim Wilby but met him when he arrived, and everybody seemed like fairly flash businessmen. Mark Hateley came with a football pedigree and I was thinking: 'This is amazing.' It was all so high profile, like a whirlwind.

Steve Wilson: All the players were buzzing at first. You knew that if they were going to be spending money your place might be under threat, but that helped in training in pre-season. Everyone was trying harder. There were rumours about company cars and things like that – which obviously we'd never had – but that didn't come through. We brought a fitness coach in, which we'd never had before. To start with everything seemed a bit more professional and we were hopeful and optimistic. We all wanted to be on that ride.

Adam Lowthorpe: We'd been struggling on for a while and the players were looking forward to a change in management. Terry and Jeff had been there for a while, and while they were popular with some they were not popular with others. But there was genuine excitement in a big personality like Mark Hateley coming in.

It was with great anticipation that City travelled to Field Mill, Mansfield, for the opening game of the 1997/98 season. About 2,000 City fans turned up to see the opening act of this brave new era, but on the pitch little seemed to have changed. City put in an insipid display, losing 2-0.

Mark Hateley: I'd expected that level of support. I know football clubs and traditions, and that level of support and passion was exactly what I expected from Hull City. It stayed right the way through. I felt the supporters supported me right the way through my time at the football club.

Off the pitch was where the ambition seemed to lie. The plan was for Hull City and Hull Sharks to share a newly built 20,000-capacity 'super stadium' located on land donated by the council, and for Hull City to play at the Boulevard while it was being built, with Boothferry Park being sold and developed for non-sporting use. These plans were not going down well with some of the long-serving backroom staff, however, who didn't see how such a move would serve the club's best interests.

Rob Smith: Underneath all of the early excitement you had this awful undercurrent of what was going on with the amalgamation with Hull Sharks. It was the darkest time of all the 20-odd years I was there. You just didn't know what was happening with both clubs. I was shipped down to the Boulevard very quickly, which left me trying to do the Hull City stuff almost undercover as they just didn't seem bothered about the football stuff as the emphasis was on the rugby. I was not a rugby fan, a rugby person, and football was in my blood. It was awful to contemplate where it was all going and what was going to happen to Hull City. We never really knew what was happening. It was horrible. A dark era.

John Cooper: Lloyd and co moved in after they'd bought Hull Sharks. Tim Wilby became chairman at first, and he was a strange guy. When David Lloyd came in we were told that

Hull City would be moving to the Boulevard. I was tasked with turning the Boulevard into a football stadium. At the time I'd got to know the directors of Hull Sharks. They were concerned that, while we were doing the required work at the Boulevard, Hull Sharks were going to be playing at Boothferry Park. There were certain games played at Boothferry Park in that era during the rugby league play-offs. In that time the Boothferry Park playing surface was probably at its best ever. We'd put a plan together for the Boulevard, however the plan was never going to meet the criteria laid down under the regulations of the Football League.

Rob Smith: I never thought David Lloyd had an interest in Hull City. His lack of knowledge of the club was frightening. Whether he was ill-informed on getting involved, I don't know, but you can't help but wonder how a businessman of his nature got involved with something that he didn't seem to have the passion for or an understanding of what he'd bought. You saw the history of the club almost being dumped in a skip in the car park. There was no passion or feeling for what the club stood for. It was probably just a plan to merge and move into a stadium together and make money from the sale of one of the grounds. It was very demoralising.

It was all too much for one long-serving, much-loved member of the backroom team.

Jeff Radcliffe: It was the regime. I'd have cracked up if I'd stayed any longer under that regime. They were trying to change things to cut costs, hiring physios on a match-by-match basis for games on the south coast. I told them where to stick it in the end. It was sad.

Ian Thomson: I doubt if any non-playing member of staff has been such a loyal and valuable servant of Hull City as Jeff Radcliffe.

After the defeat at Mansfield on the opening day, City continued to struggle, winning just one of the first 10 matches of the season, a memorable 7-4 thrashing of Swansea. Even though the Tigers knocked top-flight opposition out of the League Cup – beating Crystal Palace on away goals over two legs – it was clear that things weren't quite right on the pitch.

Steve Wilson: Mark Hateley came as a name, a spearhead. Assistant manager Billy Kirkwood was brilliant – a lovely guy whose training was very good. But Mark wasn't the right man for the job. He was inexperienced. One pre-season he'd been injured and barely playing, but picked himself for the first game of the season. It meant we played in a totally different style as everyone just kept lumping it up to him. We'd had a decent pre-season, we had a decent squad, we had Scott Thomson in goal… But Mark was just a figurehead to attract people to the club. It just didn't work with him as a manager.

Adam Lowthorpe: Mark made some mistakes. He told the press early on that he had to remember that the players he had now weren't at the same standard of those he was used to. We knew we weren't Brian Laudrup but you don't want to read that from your manager in the local paper. What used to happen was the juniors would train together, then the first team squad of about 16 would train together, and then the rest of the lads would be left in limbo. There were six to eight of us training by ourselves. Darren Beckford came to us on trial and he couldn't believe how people were being treated. It was a real low point. There didn't seem to be much purpose to what we were doing.

Mark Greaves: I have huge respect for Mark Hateley as a player, but as a manager we didn't see eye to eye. He didn't seem to fancy me as a player, though I probably wasn't at my strongest at that point. He brought his own centre-halves in, and I didn't have a good time. I didn't feel Mark was suited to Hull City. I felt he felt that he was a little bit above what Hull City were. He'd get frustrated with players at League 2 level because they couldn't do what he was used to. I didn't feel he helped me as much as other managers did.

With a boost needed on the pitch, Mark Hateley used his vast array of contacts to bring in a box-office name. Arsenal legend David Rocastle joined City on loan.

Mark Hateley: I knew Rocky from way back. He was a neighbour of mine in Ascot when I played for QPR. I knew what his predicament was at Chelsea, where he wasn't getting a game, and I phoned him up and he just wanted to come and play for us. He knew the club, he knew what great support we had, he knew the pitch was the best in the league. That's what footballers want to come for. We had Steve Nicol training at the club as well at the time, who was also fantastic.

Adam Lowthorpe: Rocky had magic ability, on a different level to the rest of us, even the likes of Glyn Hodges who we had at the time.

I was a 20-year-old kid, he was an ex-England international. I was sub and he'd been playing. Late in the game he went down injured and was hobbling, so the gaffer said to me: "Get warmed up." I stripped off ready and came on for Rocky as the opposition had a goal kick. The keeper kicked the ball and the whistle went for full-time. I didn't think much of it but when I came off a few of the lads were taking the mickey that I'd only been on for a few seconds. Then on the Monday morning at training, Rocky said: "Adam, can I have a word?" I said yes, but was thinking: 'What can this be about?' He then said: "I'm really sorry. I didn't mean to disrespect you. If I'd known that was how long was left I'd have stayed on." I hadn't even thought about it, but this was an England international who'd obviously thought about that throughout the weekend… That says everything about him and his outlook on life.

Steve Wilson: He was a true gent and a top professional. He wasn't a big-time Charlie – just one of the lads. He was brilliant with the younger players too. His touch and vision was second to none. When he sadly passed away you saw loads of lovely tributes to him, and every one of them was bang on.

Mark Greaves: He was as good as it gets. The man was inspirational. I know when people pass away young, people speak highly of them because of that, but that's not why people speak highly of David Rocastle. He was just so well respected, had such incredible ability, all while he was struggling with his knee. When he was training his knee was ballooning, yet he always had a smile on his face. He was so unassuming. You see big pros coming to clubs flashing their wealth about, but there was none of that with David. You couldn't get near him in the five-asides in training too. As a man – not just a footballer – he was inspirational.

Neil Mann: I can recall thinking: 'How have we managed to get him?' I was injured a fair bit (nothing new) when David arrived and we already knew that he was a top player, but straight away we found out that he was a top-class bloke who was happy to be playing with us at Hull. It's fair to say that at that time we were streets apart from Arsenal and the other teams he'd been used to, but he didn't once say anything and soon became one of the lads. I've a great memory of us travelling back from Newcastle after we played them in the League Cup and asking him about the night that Arsenal beat Liverpool 2-0 to win the league. For the next couple of hours we listened to his stories of that night and the rest of his career. A top bloke.

Tragically David was to pass away at the age of 33 after being diagnosed with non-Hodgkin's lymphoma. The football world mourned the passing of one of the game's good guys. No one who saw him at Hull City will ever forget him.

David Rocastle's influence helped the club's form improve a little, and with Doncaster Rovers already looking nailed on for the relegation spot into non-league football there seemed to be no danger of City going down, though an FA Cup exit to a non-league side for the first time in the club's history – with Hednesford Town winning 2-0 at Boothferry Park – gave warning to how desperate times were. Meanwhile, the off-pitch turmoil continued. Tim

Wilby – the key figure behind the deal that had brought David Lloyd to Hull – had resigned and was eventually replaced by Michael Appleton.

Mark Hateley: The plans that were set out in front of me before we started were changed drastically, so we had to approach the way we took the team forward in a different direction. I was promised a certain amount of money to spend on providing a team fitting of the supporters that would be capable of pushing for a promotion and moving through the leagues. After a couple of weeks of moving into the job, the goalposts were moved. We then had to work out a different strategy that would take a lot longer, but we needed the experience of a few seasoned pros to bring on the younger players we were going to look to build on, players from the academy. That was the reason why the likes of David Rocastle, Glyn Hodges and Steve Nicol were at the club – to bring on the youngsters. They were key to what we were trying to do.

The youngsters that Hateley was talking of – Patrick Dickinson, Adam Lowthorpe, Paul Fewings, Gavin Gordon, Lee Ellington – were coping admirably in a team that was finding wins hard to come by. And in one of the more memorable games of that season – a 5-4 defeat at Rotherham in late December – another member of the juniors was blooded.

Mike Edwards: I was training with the youth team on the Friday, and Billy Kirkwood asked me what I was doing on the Saturday. I told him that the youth team had a game and he said: "Do you fancy playing for us?" meaning the first team. I said: "Yes!" He told me I was playing left-back and that I should meet them at the bus at the ground at half 10, and that we were playing Rotherham. It came out of the blue, but that helped me.

What a game it was! It was packed, round Christmas time, and when we got to 5-1 down I was thinking: 'Oh my god!' But then Glyn Hodges picked up the ball on the right-hand side of the box and bent one into the top corner to make it 5-2. Our fans were brilliant from then, chanting "we only need three more", then when we scored again "we only need two more". Sadly we couldn't quite get them. But to have a debut like that, with nine goals and the crowd in great form, was brilliant.

The bleaker the backdrop, the more prominent a club's fanzines tend to become. And with a permanent state of despair already settling in around the Lloyd regime, a new Hull City fanzine was born.

Les Motherby (Hull City fan): I was an avid collector of City fanzines, from 'On Cloud Seven', 'Hull Hell & Happiness', 'From Hull to Eternity', 'Last Train to Boothferry Halt', the fabulously surreal 'Fearful Symmetry' to 'Tiger Rag'. With David Lloyd in charge of Hull City and merging the business side of the club with Hull Sharks, there was lots to talk about but Tiger Rag seemed to be gone for good. I was stood on the South Stand terrace talking to a few fans I knew and said: "There really needs to be a new City fanzine." I wasn't meaning that I'd write one, but a voice behind me said: "I'll help you," and that voice belonged to Andy Dalton. I didn't know him, but I did recognise him from waiting outside YEB for Simon Gray buses to away games. Within a few weeks we were sat in his house working on a paper fanzine and a rudimentary website hosted by Angelfire, while his mother provided an ongoing supply of refreshments.

On February 21st, 1998, the first issue of 'Amber Nectar' went on sale before the Scunthorpe United game, with City third bottom in Division Three and fans driven to 'thank God for Doncaster Rovers'. It was an amateurish first effort in truth, but it was an arch to build upon. Incredibly 'Amber Nectar' is still publishing 20 years later, albeit not in hardcopy format, but we recognised from the off that the internet was our future and nowadays Twitter posts and podcast broadcasts make up a significant part of our output. That 20 years has been eventful though, with numerous protests against dodgy owners: the tennis ball protest at Bolton which inspired David Lloyd to put the club up for sale was our idea, and we've been active in the politics of the club since then. Andy's work protesting against West Yorkshire Police's decision to impose travel restrictions on City fans travelling to Huddersfield was amazing, and contributed to West Yorkshire Police admitting their football policing tactics were over the top. It's a source of great pride that we were able to play a role in defeating the vandalism of the club's identity by opposing the dreadful Hull Tigers name change. I doubt 'Amber Nectar' will be around in another 20 years, but I think we can look on the impact we've had on the cultural landscape of Hull City AFC with satisfaction.

On the pitch, even with the likes of Glyn Hodges firing, the results wouldn't come. City took up root third from bottom in the table, above the two basket cases of clubs at the time: Brighton and Doncaster. But Hateley did make some moves in the transfer market, with his links in Scotland being used to bring in two useful attacking options in Brian McGinty and Steven Boyack, while the highly rated David Brown joined from Manchester United for the rest of the season.

David Brown: I'd been at Manchester United for about four years, and it can be a difficult place to be, as even though I was playing for the reserves and training with the first team, I saw a few lads a few years older than me who weren't really getting anywhere. I wanted to play competitive football so I spoke to Sir Alex and a few others about what to do. At the end of the 1997/98 season I decided to go out on loan. Warren Joyce was a coach at Manchester United at the time with the under 16s, so there was a connection there, and Mark Hateley showed an interest in me coming on loan. So that was it really. I went on loan for the rest of the season, went back to Old Trafford to discuss what I was going to do. I could have stayed there for another year but I had an offer from Hull to make the deal permanent, and that's what I did.

Doncaster Rovers were enduring one of the worst Football League campaigns of all time. Deeply rooted at the bottom of the league, the relegation spot to the Conference was never in doubt, much to the relief of Hull City and Brighton fans. Before what is now an infamous game between the Tigers and Doncaster in early April, the home side had lost eight games on the trot. City somehow managed to lose to a last-minute goal at Belle Vue, however. The game seemed to represent an all-time low for the Tigers.

David Brown: It was an eye-opener in terms of going to Hull City. I'd been in an environment at Manchester United where you go in and everything's done for you. On the first day I came to Hull City, Dexter Tucker booted the ball at me in training and bust my nose. I remember walking into the dressing room at Boothferry Park. If you got in early enough you could get some decent training kit, but if you didn't there were two shopping trolleys from the supermarket full of crusty old horrible kit that was full of holes. It was a massive culture shock. There were also various disputes between the fans and the owners at that time, so it wasn't a great atmosphere, but as a player you just get on with it.

I remember the Doncaster game, because of their fans going on the pitch and dropping drawing pins all over the centre circle. I'd never seen anything like that. After the game, Mark Hateley was kicking tables and throwing tea cups about. At that time, there were a few players who didn't quite gel with Mark and his style, and that was very evident, particularly during my loan spell.

Ian Thomson: The 1-0 defeat at Doncaster was on my 38th birthday. That Doncaster side were by some margin the most ill-equipped side for league football that I have ever seen, and the Doncaster club itself was in desperate straits: their own fans even staged a sit-down protest during the game and the programme receipts were used to buy the half-time food for the away fans' kiosk, yet we contrived to lose to them. At the end of the game the City fans sang: "You're not fit to wear the shirt." Whether or not you condone fans berating their own team in that fashion, it was in fact the truth. I trudged away from Belle Vue after that Doncaster game at a loss to see where City could go from there.

The Doncaster game seemed to rally City, who then ended the season strongly, winning three of the last five games, as well as drawing 2-2 at Brighton and losing by the odd goal in seven at Colchester. That put a slightly more positive sheen on what had been a hugely disappointing season. Nothing could alter the fact, however, that the 22nd-placed finish was the worst in the club's history.

Mark Hateley: I thought we'd really stepped up and got to where I thought we should be with the development of the squad. Steven Boyack and Brian McGinty were good pros. McGinty had good energy and good legs, and Boyack was a sweet player and was only going to get better if we could get him in permanently. Those sorts of players would be able to come on. At the end of that first season I felt we'd really taken a step forward and it was exciting going into the summer.

A number of players were released at the end of the season as Hateley looked to refresh the squad, while star striker Duane Darby refused to sign a new contract and left on what was then termed as a 'Bosman free'. Of all of the names on the released list, it was that of Adam Lowthorpe that was the most upsetting for the City fans.

Adam Lowthorpe: I'd missed a pre-season tour of Scotland through injury and when we came back Lloyd and Hateley told me and a few others that our contracts were up at the end of the season and they were going to release us. I think Hateley had been promised that he could sign who he wanted, and he thought: 'I'm going to sign better players than we have now, anybody who's out of contract will go so I can get new bodies in.' That's how he would treat a lot of players from the off, but then pretty quickly he needed those same players.

There were a few injuries and I got back in the squad and did alright, stayed in and around the squad, scoring a couple of goals. But I was still out of contract and was always going to be released. Four or five games before the end of the season, Warren Joyce pulled me over and said: "Has the gaffer had a word with you?" I said "no", and he said: "I can't see him releasing you while you're playing like this." As it turned out I did get released and then Warren was manager not long after. The one thing I was pleased about was that I scored in front of the South Stand against Leyton Orient. Looking back now, that is the definite high point for me.

The soul of the club was being sucked away though, and there weren't many big personalities in the dressing room. It was just a depressing place to be.

Steve Wilson: Adam was solid, dependable, and was unlucky that a new coach came in at the wrong time for him. He never let us down, and he'd always give his all.

The wild optimism of the summer of 1997 was not repeated in 1998. David Lloyd was struggling to sell Boothferry Park due to a long-term tenancy clause owned by sitting tenants Kwik Save. He'd also fallen out with the council too. Moving City from Boothferry Park to the Boulevard was thought to be on the cards, too.

John Cooper: I spent a lot of time at the Boulevard trying to do a job but protracting it as I couldn't see the sense in moving the football club there when Boothferry Park was better. It was just that David Lloyd seemed to think he'd make more money by selling Boothferry Park off. I was down at the Boulevard and we were doing a load of work to turn it round, but we were losing a battle with the weather. It was the height of summer in 1997 and I said to the Boulevard groundsman to stop what he was doing as we were losing the playing surface.

There wasn't enough water. And that was the best thing that happened, as that took us into the 1997/98 season.

David Lloyd was meeting the sponsors at Boothferry Park one day at the start of the season. I said to the groundstaff that I wanted the playing surface to look the best it's ever looked. We presented an immaculate pitch to David. I knew that, being an ex-tennis player who'd played at Wimbledon, he would have to walk on the playing surface. That was the plan. I stayed out of the way, but when David came and walked out I immediately walked out to him and asked the question: "Why do you want to move to the Boulevard when we've got this?" He said: "I'm not going." That threw me completely because I wasn't expecting it. That's how Hull City managed to stay at Boothferry Park. A lot of people put a lot of hard work into that, though. People wanted to stay at Boothferry Park. We had a band of brothers and that's what got us through that period.

City fans were now aware that if any progress was to be made, it was going to be slow. The manager seemed to grasp this reality too.

Mark Hateley: I knew it was going to be a slow journey. We weren't going to be buying and buying and buying because the money wasn't there. It was always going to be a campaign where we had to be patient again, waiting for the young lads to push on. I just wanted us to pick up on how we'd finished the last season and step up to the next level midway through my second season.

Something that was a little tantalising for City fans was the talk of a 'super stadium' to be used by Hull City and Hull Sharks. This had been one of the prospects that had enticed David Lloyd to Hull in the first place. The local council had made positive moves, at first by promising land for the site of the new building, and then through potentially being involved in the funding. However, with David Lloyd's behaviour antagonising many City fans, this dream seemed to be a long way from becoming a reality. Still, a seed had been planted...

Tom McVie (councillor on Hull City council): All three professional clubs in the city were having problems in the late 1990s and there'd already been discussions over a new stadium with David Lloyd when he was running Hull Sharks and Hull City. So there'd been discussions going on around 1996/97/98. Getting the money together was difficult. Hull City had wanted to build a stadium of their own, which was fine, but it became clear reasonably quickly that that was not going to happen.

The 1998/99 season started disastrously. City lost the first game 3-1 at Rotherham and the next 2-1 at home to Darlington. The first win arrived at home to Peterborough in late August, but it soon became apparent that David Lloyd had gone cold on his vision for the club. A fan protest – involving tennis balls being thrown on the pitch to hold up play in a League Cup match at Bolton – brought the club's plight some national exposure, with Lloyd having described the people of Hull as "crap" and "living in the dark ages". He had also been linked in the media with buying crisis-hit and homeless Wimbledon and bringing them to Hull, though at this point – after the tennis ball protest – it is believed that Lloyd just wanted out of Hull by whatever means possible. By the time of the home match against Cardiff on October 9th, he was threatening to pull the plug on Hull City altogether, claiming that he didn't have to put the club into administration as it was his debt. Then came this chilling sentence: "It will be the end of professional football in the city." The match was billed as the club's last ever.

David Brown: From a professional point of view you always say that that sort of thing doesn't affect you, but in the back of your mind it does. There was lots of unrest, and the Cardiff game was meant to be the club's last ever, and that sort of environment isn't a nice one to be in. There were times we weren't getting paid either, which makes life a bit of a battle. I only met David Lloyd once in the whole time I was there, so I don't think his heart was really in it.

Mike Edwards: Being young I didn't realise anything was wrong. Some of the older pros might have, but I just loved it. I did have the likes of Warren Joyce guiding me through things. I really looked up to Warren.

Mark Greaves: I was hardly playing in the end for Mark Hateley, but we didn't feel like a club with everyone going in the same direction. We had a lot of players with big reputations who weren't producing. We'd train at five or six training grounds too, including the university and Costello – we had no base.

Mark Hateley: It completely affected the footballing side of things. David Lloyd's business model didn't seem to work the way he thought it would, and that's just the way it was. His ideal plan was to move to a new stadium and take the club forward that way, and that didn't materialise. That was his vision and it never really got off the ground. After that he seemed to fall out of love with the whole idea. It really did affect the way we were performing. For a lot of away trips we'd be travelling on the day of the game, even for long, long journeys – getting off the bus, playing the game, getting back on and coming home. That's impossible to do. It was a disappointment the way it ended up. I thought we were having a really good go at it with the funds that were available to us. I must give credit to the supporters for sticking with it and enjoying the better side of the games we played in in the beginning, when the chairman was fresh and his ideas were big in his mind.

Mark Greaves: With David Lloyd, it was a nightmare from start to finish from a footballing point of view. Everyone was excited when he took over and was going to spend money. We knew Hull City were capable of playing in the top flight and thought that David Lloyd would be the man to do it, but it just didn't happen.

One man heavily involved in the efforts to save the club was the editor of another recently launched fanzine, 'City Independent'.

Ian Farrow: The David Lloyd days were the club's lowest point, probably because of all the complications, plus the fact that football fans, especially City ones, were by then a lot more savvy, and therefore knew all the ramifications of these complications, which were terrifying. At so many points in those days it did appear to be the absolute end. As fans we felt that even if the club survived relegation on the field, and we were particularly poor under Hateley, we just couldn't imagine the club surviving in any real form off it. We had no ground, were on the brink of liquidation, and there seemed little chance of obtaining a Football League licence.

Lloyd had fallen out with Hull City Council, which meant they were not going to help fund his dream of a new stadium complex or even offer a cut-price site to redevelop. Even worse for Lloyd and Hull City they were also not going to help facilitate a lower scale 'leisure city' at Boothferry Park by offering Kwik-Save an alternative site to move their supermarket. Lloyd hadn't done his homework and like a lover spurned would prove to be intransigent with anyone he deemed even partly responsible. He'd removed Tim Wilby, who had originally sold David Lloyd and his 'vision' to the fans, and we now had Michael Appleton, who didn't seem to give a toss about fans (football or rugby) or players. Duane Darby once told us he had seriously considered crashing his car into the chief executive while spotting him as he drove out of the City car park.

City were knocked out of the FA Cup by a non-league side for the first time in their history; they were near the bottom of the entire Football League in Lloyd's first season and absolute bottom in his next. Unfortunately Mark Hateley seemed more bothered about the local nightlife than playing for or managing Hull City. The future didn't seem bright, especially when Lloyd spat the first of his many dummies out by saying he was not funding any new stadium or offering funds for any new players.

It was then he said that Hull was crap, the place was living in the dark ages, had cold showers and holes in our tennis nets. He added that he was prepared to sell the club for a £1. Luckily a friend had his number. I rang him from outside Three Tuns after another defeat. Surprisingly I got through! I introduced myself, weathered a barrage of swear words and made my very reasonable offer of £2 as a starting negotiation to see what he would say. I said I could bring the cash round immediately. I listened while he ranted and raved about wanting to make Hull a town where people wanted to live in and people wanted to be associated with. His voice got higher and his words came faster as he said the situation wasn't funny and that he'd done all he could and came with the best intentions but people in Hull were frightened and thick. He eventually told me that my lawyers would have to meet his and he still wanted his £5m and asked could I pay the players' wages? Obviously the call had got a lot further than I imagined but we had already talked to Bournemouth, who had successfully facilitated a supporters buy out and I told him this. He put the phone down. It was engaged each time we called after that.

We could see no way out. Who in their right mind for the right reasons could and would deal with Lloyd? He seemed unstable not only in his rantings to me but to the press. How could City survive? The club had no assets and Lloyd was soon dummy-spitting again and threatening to pull out of the club totally, accept his losses, and close the club. Meanwhile off the field, even if we survived the season, what about next season? No one would sign for us. Would Boothferry Park pass league regulations? Would Lloyd let us play there? A month before the end of his first season Lloyd was aiming further afield as he launched another pacifier by suggesting that homeless Premier League Wimbledon could play at Boothferry Park under the name Hull Dons or some such. Which league this club would play in was another question. Then there was a proposal that this new club, or either Hull City or Wimbledon, plus Hull Sharks would play there while Lloyd recouped some money by selling the Boothferry Park land even with the Kwik-Save lease. There was then talk of the amalgamated clubs playing in Dublin. This was how ludicrously surreal it got.

With the club seemingly on the brink of extinction, City travelled to Seamer Road, Scarborough, to play in a bottom-of-the-table battle. City had lost seven consecutive games but managed to win 2-1, with the player-manager netting the winner amid jubilant scenes.

Mark Hateley: I've always been a fans' player and I have always wanted to play how the fans expect you to play – being brave, putting yourself on the line and wanting to win at all costs. When you look at the gates that came to watch us, people saw we were making something worth watching.

David Lloyd now seemed to be intent on alienating everyone within the club. In a radio interview he claimed that he'd been the "only person in the history of Hull who's put his hand in his pocket and paid the bills". Harold Needler and Don Robinson, to name but two, might have had something to say about that. He also told the press that Mark Hateley was earning £250,000 a year including bonuses, a figure the manager disputed. Reports were coming through that Don Robinson was back in for the club, while Irish businessman Kevin Phelan claimed to have agreed a deal to have purchased it. Both came to nothing.

City were close to breaking point by November 1998. Then, as had been rumoured, news came through that the club had been sold. Former Scunthorpe chairman Tom Belton had formed a consortium with some Sheffield-based businessmen to bring an end to the regime of the now-hated David Lloyd (though Lloyd would ominously retain ownership of Boothferry Park). City fans rejoiced, doing their best to overlook the fact that one of the consortium – Stephen Hinchliffe – was serving a Department of Trade and Industry ban from acting as a director of a company due to the collapse of his Facia retail empire.

John Cooper: Tom Belton was a farmer from Lincolnshire. He was trying to diversify into making money outside of farming, so he used to organise pigeon shoots. At one of these he came across Stephen Hinchliffe and Nick Buchanan. They were part of a party that came to his land and they were looking to buy a football club. Tom was an ex-Scunthorpe United chairman and a good friend of Martin Fish. Hinchliffe and Buchanan looked at what was on the market and used Tom to broker the deal to get Hull City. A more strange couple of people you'd never want to meet.

Rob Smith: A load of staff were summoned up to Boothferry Park and Tom was revealed and told us who he was and what was going on. A load of us had to move from the Boulevard to Boothferry Park and there was no room for us anywhere. But we all had to introduce ourselves to Tom and explain who we were and what we did. No one seemed to really know anything about the backroom staff. The regime clearly had plans to bring staff in from Sheffield though. We only really saw Tom, out of the people in the incoming consortium, at that point. He was a very down-to-earth guy. You wouldn't really pin him as a football person. Very unassuming, constantly smoking, but the fans loved him.

Mark Hateley had come to Hull City with high hopes and good intentions, but regardless of any broken promises over funding, his style of management had not worked. City were bottom of the bottom division and staring at non-league football for the first time in the club's history. Within a week of their arrival the new owners had relieved Mark of his duties.

Mark Hateley: I really enjoyed my time there. I loved being in Hull. I loved being with the players that we had. The goalposts moving early on didn't put me off – there's always a way to win. I thought we acclimatised to the circumstances put before us. I was proud of the fact that we changed tack in midstream and we played some fantastic stuff with some great players coming through. Unfortunately we weren't allowed to see it through to completion. That's the only disappointment for me. I though the job was a decent job though, given the circumstances we had.

David Brown: I was quite sad really, because Mark Hateley's a legend. I used to watch him on TV and he'd played for some of the biggest clubs out there. And when he wanted to sign me that was great. He was coming towards the end of his career, but even though I was only with him for a short period I learnt a lot from him in terms of how to be a better striker. I liked him. Management is harsh and at the time it was difficult for him to be a manager under a chairman who was limiting him so much in terms of who he could sign and so on, so he couldn't put his stamp on the team. There were players who didn't like him and didn't want to play for him, but from my point of view I liked him and I was happy with him. I was sad when he was sacked.

Rob Smith: Mark will have been promised the earth when he joined the club and that never transpired. He had standards, he had a reputation in football, and coming to Hull probably wasn't his best move. I think it must be the last thing on his CV. He was probably too flash for the team we had at the time. I think he was a good guy, I just don't think he had the weapons at his disposal.

City were managerless and six points adrift at the bottom of the Football League. After sacking Hateley, Belton wasted no time in appointing Warren Joyce – already a highly rated coach in Manchester United's youth academy – in the role of caretaker player-manager with John McGovern as his assistant. The decision was a popular one within the squad.

David Brown: Joycey was in his mid-30s at the time, coming towards the end of his career, and he was the club captain so he had that respect among the team. I'd known him from a coaching point of view at Manchester United too, so there was a relationship already there. I was happy he got the job.

Mark Greaves: We got more stability as soon as Warren took over. I felt that he liked me as a player. He signed Justin and Brabs – without them we'd have been relegated. I think all fans could see that. They would get better performances from the people around them too. They were inspirational, like Ian Ashbee would be in later years. Warren got us back to basics and had us bullying teams. We had a lot of big lads. I felt as though I'd learned to defend properly at professional level under Warren. If you did well he'd get you in his office and tell you that, and as a young player that can be needed.

Mike Edwards: I'd played a load of games but then Mark Hateley had left me out of the side for six or seven weeks and Joycey had kept me going throughout all of that. I spent endless hours training on my own round then, doing whatever I could to get back in the team. Then Joycey came in as manager and he put his trust in me to start playing again. Maybe one or two of the older pros weren't too happy, but I was getting my chance. We were six points adrift, but fair play to Warren, he knew the types of players we needed to get in. And the dressing room changed from not having full-on unity to having a spirit in it where we were fighting all together.

Steve Wilson: Warren was a popular choice among the squad. Whenever he played he gave 100% and his knowledge of the game was second to none. He was the players' choice. Sometimes the players have a bit of power and we all wanted him. We all put everything into every game under him. And he brought in people who were used to battling through games and grinding out results.

Mike Edwards: Joycey used to moan that I was too laid back before games. He'd come in the dressing room and start kicking me in the shins to get me going! Once I got on the pitch I'd do a job though.

However, the new manager knew he had his work cut out forming a squad equipped for the task in hand.

Warren Joyce: I'd been in the dressing room so I knew there were some players who weren't as professional as they should be. I knew who was going out for a drink and was more bothered about that side of things than they were about their football. We didn't have much money so we had to look at players who weren't really wanted by their clubs. But then I was offering people contracts with the reality that we could be a non-league club the year after, all while persuading them to come for no money. I couldn't offer any of these players a rosy future. All I could say is that we're not in the greatest of circumstances at the minute, but you can come and fight and if we stay in the league the club will grow and you can be part of that growth in the future. So I was looking for a particular type of character. I went around and assembled a group of guys who maybe few others wanted but I knew from playing against them that they were tough, they were fit, they were aggressive and they were horrible to play against. It was needs must to get us out of that situation.

Amid all of the off-pitch chaos, City were becoming more and more marooned at the bottom of the fourth tier, losing 3-1 to Exeter, drawing two matches, losing at home to Leyton Orient and then, embarrassingly, going down 2-0 to nine-man Brighton.

James Richardson: As I started going to City during the 1990s, and became curiously accustomed to bleakness as the club seemingly lurched from one crisis to another, the home defeat to Brighton in the Great Escape season felt horrific to me. Even with Hateley and Lloyd's removal from the dressing room and boardroom I had so little hope and being comfortably beaten in 2-0 by a nine-man team was just as dispiriting to me as the Doncaster defeat the previous season. And this time we didn't have another basket case of a club to cushion us from relegation and probable oblivion.

As the club looked to be a lost cause on the pitch, more details began to emerge regarding the consortium that had taken over. Tom Belton was the front man, with the main players in the rest of the consortium being Stephen Hinchliffe and Nick Buchanan. Hinchliffe used his Sheffield United connections to bring in experienced football administrator Andy Daykin.

Andy Daykin: I didn't know Nick Buchanan at all when I went to Hull but I had worked with Stephen at Sheffield United, where he'd been a director in the early 90s. At that time he was to all intents and purposes a wealthy guy. I thought he was still a wealthy guy at this time, but as it turned out he probably wasn't.

Rob Smith: Hinchliffe and Buchanan appeared within a couple of weeks. I remember seeing their shadows in the office and thinking: 'Just keep your head down.' I was also wondering who the hell they were. I soon got to know them, and to be fair my memories of that time are not bad ones. It was fun to work with them.

Andy Daykin: I was aware of Stephen's ban, but I was just trying my best to generate funds into the club so it didn't affect me. It wasn't a problem. If there was a problem then perhaps it was that Stephen would try to influence matters – even though he didn't have a right to – because he owned the shares. That was not necessarily appropriate all the time but that was the nature of the beast.

The new owners released some money to Warren Joyce. Craig Dudley was brought in on loan from Notts County, and John McGovern was added to the coaching staff. They were soon followed by left midfielder Gareth Williams and a man who would become a Hull City legend: Justin Whittle.

Justin Whittle: Brian Little had just taken over at Stoke after we'd been relegated and the fans had voted me player of the season. That was the 1996/97 season. I'd been in and out the team and I had another year on my contract, but I got a phone call from Brian telling me that Hull City wanted to speak to me. He told me he'd given Hull City permission and it was up to me. I thought that as I wasn't playing very much I might as well see what they had to say. So I put the phone down and figured that I'd better look where Hull is, and see what division they were in and how many points they had. When I saw, I just went: 'Hmmnnn... bottom of the league, by about six points.'

But I just wanted to play football so I spoke to John McGovern. I ummed and ahhed a bit, but to be fair to John he said Lou Macari had recommended me and that they were trying to build a team. I spoke to my agent, went down to Hull and trained. It was a big decision to move from a team that had recently been in the Championship to go to League 2. I'd had four great years at Stoke, and I'm from Derby which isn't too far away from Stoke so I could live in my home town. But I thought that Hull City needed the help so I might as well sign.

Two players signed that day, me and a Gareth Williams, who'd been playing for Scarborough. However, Gareth lived down the road from me in Derby so it meant we could car share. My wife said she'd go along with it all, and we'd only just had our first child – Olivia – so there were no obstacles in my way as she hadn't started school or anything. I moved to Brough at the end of that season and I've been here ever since.

The impact was instant. City beat Carlisle at home with a last-minute goal from Dudley.

Justin Whittle: I drove into the wrong bit of Boothferry Park at first, near the gym. Eventually someone in a burger van directed me to the players' entrance near that house that the club owned. It reminded me of Stoke's old place, the Victoria Ground, with the housing and a similar set of fans, hard-working people who turned out to support their club. But when I first stepped out on the pitch, all I could think was: 'Why is there a supermarket in the stand?'

Craig Dudley was on loan from Notts County – Big Sam was mates with Warren Joyce and was helping him out – and it was a tough game against Carlisle. We only scored in the last minute, but the atmosphere was great. The Kempton Stand seemed packed.

Ian Farrow: City were playing fellow strugglers Carlisle United. It was an awful game, I suppose not helped by the fact that it poured down throughout the match. It later transpired that the ref was going to abandon the game but John Cooper told him the groundstaff could get the pitch fit to play for the second half. The ref agreed to let him try and all credit must go to Cooper and his staff that they did get the match to continue. Thankfully they did because after all the scores from other grounds had come in, Craig Dudley headed home to earn three valuable points, which at the time seemed vitally important and did give us a fighting chance of staying up.

A further boost came in the second round of the FA Cup. Luton Town were flying high in the division above City, so when the Tigers won 2-1 it came as a huge shock, but also gave notice of a new resilience within the squad. The goals came from Rob Dewhurst and youngster Ben Morley.

Justin Whittle: Games like that gave us great confidence. Ben Morley was only young, but he was fast, keen and energetic. We deserved to win that game. That said, Steve Davis nutmegged me for their goal. But I felt that the new players in the team were bringing a bit of a resurgence with them. At that time the bonus you got for playing and winning made a huge difference to your wages too, so everyone wanted to play. We had great support that day.

Further signings were made as Warren Joyce looked to build a side capable of fighting tooth and nail for survival. Silky winger Richard Peacock was allowed to join Lincoln, with defenders Jon Whitney and Jason Perry moving in the opposite direction.

Jon Whitney: Myself and Jason Perry got an inquiry. I was settled in Lincoln, really fond of the team, but I'd just come out of the starting 11 and I just wanted to play. I couldn't just sit on the bench. It felt like the right move for me, with the club being six points adrift at the bottom. I liked what they wanted me for. Warren really sold it to me. That was a deciding factor. When you speak to a manager and you get that feeling in your stomach for somebody, you just know it's the right move. And the challenge was mouthwatering. It was an incredible opportunity for me to do what I do best, which is fight fires. I made up my mind within a day. I travelled up with Jason Perry and I just loved the old-style stadium and the feel for the place. And it turned out to be one of the most memorable periods in my career.

I wasn't the most technically gifted of players but I more than made up for that with my desire and passion and my winning mentality. I was able to cope with the situation we were in. People call it pressure but to me it's not pressure, you've just got to give your all.

The first thing I noticed in Boothferry Park was the old wood cladding on the walls of the changing room, because it reminded me of growing up on a council estate as a kid. My dad had put those exact panel boards on our front room, so there were a few home comforts.

One of the things that stood out was how intense the training was. It was what Warren wanted – he'd done his homework on the type of characters he wanted to bring in. When you'd see the likes of Justin, Greavesy, Mikey Edwards and later on Brabs in training, you saw we were all winners and that brought an even greater intensity to it. And it's no coincidence that we carried that over into matchdays. I just couldn't see many teams living with us on the physical side of things. But we also had quality in the team with lads like David Brown, who was a really exciting striker.

It still wasn't coming together, however. After the Luton victory City lost four successive league games to Torquay, Swansea, Chester and Shrewsbury to stay six points adrift at the bottom of the league. The Luton victory, however, had led to a plum FA Cup tie against Aston Villa. The match pitted the team top of the Premier League against the team at rock bottom of the Football League in 92nd. And while City lost 3-0, they were in no way disgraced.

Justin Whittle: That game helped us build momentum. Warren was bringing in the players that he needed. He brought in the right characters at the right time. We might not have been the best footballing team, but that wasn't what we needed at that time. We needed hard workers who'd give 100% no matter what. We had players like David Brown and David D'Auria who could produce a moment of brilliance but we had players who'd bully the opposition off the park. Teams knew we wouldn't let them settle.

After the Aston Villa game Warren Joyce dipped into the transfer market to add two midfielders to the squad. Both were to have a big impact on the club, one in the short term, the other over a much longer period. First in was Mark Bonner, signed on loan from Cardiff.

Mark Bonner: I had been injured at Cardiff and I couldn't get back into the first team so I decided to go out on loan to get a few games under my belt. I spoke to Warren and he told me to come up to Hull.

Next was Gary Brabin. The Hull Daily Mail reported upon his signing that Brabin had previously worked as a nightclub bouncer. Such information meant that before Brabin had kicked a ball – or an opponent – the crowd were besotted.

Gary Brabin: Warren came to a Blackpool reserve game. I was playing in League 1 but hadn't seen eye to eye with the Blackpool manager. There'd been a bit of interest in me, both for a loan or permanent move. I didn't want to leave Blackpool but Warren came in and told me about what was happening in Hull. He told me about a couple of players they'd signed, who I thought were decent. I looked at the situation and thought Hull looked in trouble. I said I'd think about it, but I didn't sign. I ended up going on loan to Lincoln, who were in League 1. I had three weeks there and during that time I'd spoken to Hull a couple more times about a permanent deal and I had another look. Hull had played Aston Villa in the FA Cup and it looked like they just kept getting beat by the odd goal in their league games. There were also another couple of players who'd come in who I thought were good signings. I'd been speaking to Lincoln about going there permanently too, but I just liked what I saw in Hull. I liked the people. I liked Warren and Tom Belton. I decided to sign and it was the best thing I did. I loved it from minute one. The rest is history.

David Brown: Justin Whittle and Gary Brabin as characters are like chalk and cheese, but they both had a massive impact. On the pitch they're both warriors, but off it totally different characters. At the time we needed characters who perhaps weren't scared to come in and tell a few home truths to a few players who hadn't been pulling their fingers out, particularly under Mark Hateley. The likes of Brabs, Jon Whitney and Jason Perry were animals on and off the pitch. It raised everybody's game. The intensity in training, when I look back at some of the challenges that were flying in, they'd be considered X-rated these days. We needed that little bit of bite though. We needed outsiders to come in and challenge the way things were. Some had come in from decent clubs, had been decent professionals, and that helped too, as things had gotten a little bit sloppy in regard to people's attitudes towards training. Brabs, Justin, Jon Whitney, Jason Perry, Colin Alcide – they made a real impact.

Justin Whittle: Brabs was actually quite skilful. He was a bruiser and would get stuck in, but he could play a bit. And he scored some very important goals for us. But when you've got a player like that in your team it's great. When Brabs decided he was going for a ball, no one else would bother going for it – team-mates or opposition. When you heard him call for the ball there'd be a ten-yard circle of emptiness around him as you'd wonder if you'd be getting back up again if you challenged him. He was feared. Some good teams would come to Boothferry Park with young, skilful players, but they all knew about Brabs and would be very wary of him.

Mike Edwards: Brabs and Justin took the pressure off us. They helped the dressing room to relax. They didn't seem phased by the enormity of the task. They worked hard, putting everything on the line in every game. They were good leaders in the dressing room and great to learn off. Jon Whitney was another. They brought us all together and we had some cracking times on the bus coming back from games.

Mark Bonner: I'd played at Blackpool with Gary for quite a few years, as we were both from near Southport, so it was nice having him there. He's a colourful character, I think it's safe to say. He gives everything, and motivates everyone, and the fans appreciate that.

Steve Wilson: You felt safe wherever you went with Brabs, let's put it that way. On the pitch you knew you could go that little bit further than you usually would because you had Brabs behind you. Nothing was going to happen when Brabs was around. Wherever we went Brabs looked after us all. He was a great laugh too, but he'd let you know if you weren't pulling your weight.

Where the turning point of the 1998/99 season – or the beginning of the Great Escape, as it would come to be known – lies is the topic of much debate. But most would plump for the match at home to Rotherham on January 9th. Within 10 minutes of the kick-off Gary Brabin had attempted to tackle a player with his head while laying prostrate on the ground. On 35 minutes, Mark Bonner scored the game's only goal.

Gary Brabin: I felt an instant rapport but I'm the type of player who fans take to because I'm whole-hearted. It was extra-special at Hull though, because during that period we turned around a poor position quite quickly. Also I was quite influential in some of the goals we scored, and I scored a few too. It just seemed right at the time. I was loving my football.

Mark Bonner: I had a good track record against Rotherham – I never seemed to lose against them and I had scored a few goals. Nobody expected Hull to win so there was no pressure or expectation, which was a nice feeling. That said, the boys were confident and Warren was always chirpy. The training had been really sharp too. It wasn't the type of thing you usually get in a team that isn't doing well. Everyone was bubbly and putting in loads of effort. You wouldn't have thought the team was struggling.

For my goal the ball was cleared, I picked it up towards the edge of the box and it may have taken a little deflection to go in. It was a great team effort from the guys though, and Warren was a great manager and leader.

A fortnight later, in their next game, City put on a terrific footballing display, beating Hartlepool 4-0 at Boothferry Park with David Brown and Brian McGinty getting two goals each, all before half-time. The confidence and belief were building.

David Brown: From a players' point of view you always have a belief that you're going to go out and win your next game, even if you're on a 10-game losing streak. But a game like that gives you a bit of spark and confidence, which you need. The way we played in that first half was pretty similar to how we'd played in a few games before that, but things hadn't quite gone for us. It's not very often that you're 4-0 up at half-time and that was one of those days where we went out and it seemed that everything we tried was working. From a confidence point of view it was brilliant.

Jon Whitney: We felt like it was knitting together. Up until that point Warren hadn't quite known his best team, he was still making changes. But we never over-reacted when we lost and we never got too carried away when we won. Joycey was good on that. Up until that point we'd been really confident without getting results. We kept our belief, we kept up our work ethic, and we ended up getting those two wins. Teams were starting to fear us by that point too. Not many teams wanted to play us.

In the next match, away at Peterborough, two players stood out. Goalkeeper Andy Oakes had been hugely impressive since signing from non-league Winsford United a few weeks earlier.

Ian Farrow: Andy Oakes was a bow-legged chicken. Every catch from every cross seemed pre-destined to see him snapped in two. Yet it never happened. He caught with confidence and commanded his box better than most other keepers. The only time he did get injured was early in a game away at Peterborough. He remained on the pitch despite limping badly with an injured leg that meant he couldn't take kicks. Yet he still managed to give a superb performance, including two or three excellent saves, and he conceded only once and so played a very major part in our 1-1 draw, clinching a vital point as we fought to avoid relegation.

The other stand-out player was left-back Jon Whitney, who was quickly becoming a cult hero, and who was to score a screamer of a goal from a considerable – if debatable – distance as City claimed a crucial point.

Jon Whitney: It's just instinctive. I wasn't there to get a shot on goal, I was there to stop them getting a breakaway. The opportunity came. It bobbled up very nicely. I'd always fancied myself with my left foot a little bit and I just let fly. I still show my kids it on YouTube and they show their mates at school. It's the best goal I scored, out of the 15 or so I got in my career. It was a great goal and it's nice that it's remembered. But even I exaggerate how far out it was when I recount it; I've got it up to about 40 or 45 yards now. Realistically I think it was about 30.

In 1999 Brentford were the polar opposite to Hull City as a football club. Well-run and progressive, the Bees had not lost at home all season and had just signed Hermann Hreidarsson for a divisional record of £750,000. They were at the top of the league, City were bottom, but after the recent upturn in form Scarborough were within striking distance for the Tigers. Almost 2,000 City fans packed into Griffin Park's low-roofed terraces and made a wall of noise that only standing areas can produce. Inspired by this, City put in a quite incredible performance to win 2-0, with new signing Colin Alcide scoring the opener and David Brown sealing matters 10 minutes from the end.

David Brown: It was a close game, and I scored in front of the Hull fans with a side-foot volley after Gareth Williams had put me in, then I did some dodgy celebration. Getting that second goal gave us a bit of comfort. To go down there and do that was very, very good.

Gary Brabin: I remember little bits about games. I upset their keeper early in the game from a corner which I thought rattled them a little bit. I aggressively collided with the keeper and the centre-half and they were knocked by that. That desire and passion we had going into games would put teams on the back foot.

Justin Whittle: That was a great game. I was marking Leo Fortune-West, who was their danger man and a good few inches taller than me. He was more my kind of player to play against though, as I knew he wasn't going to run me or twist and turn. I have always liked physical games, I liked battles. We defended a lot but scored two very good goals. They were claiming that Colin was offside for his opener but he never was.

We'd been told that Brabs had had an issue with someone in the Brentford team while he was at Blackpool, where someone had said something to him and he'd dragged the lad out of the dressing room, which led to him being banned for a while. The lad in question was still at Brentford, but had wisely stuck up for Brabs when the FA had hauled him up, so it was all okay there that day. Brabs played well that game. It's a game that sticks in the mind.

Mark Greaves: We were very comfortable in a game against a side who hadn't lost at home all season. They'd bought Hermann Hreidarsson for £750,000 too, which at that level was an incredible amount of money. We'd progressed so quickly as a side. We wouldn't have got anything there in September or October. The away fans of City were always louder than the home fans and we really felt that at Brentford. We took loads of fans and it felt like such a turning point. It gave us great confidence and we really kicked on then.

News filtered through that Scarborough were losing heavily at home to Cambridge. City were off the bottom of the table. There was still work to be done, but it was apparent that there was something special within the squad.

After the euphoria of Brentford, City were brought back down to earth, losing their first ever televised league game 3-0 to Rochdale. Away wins at Darlington and Halifax helped to keep City out of the relegation spot, though the home form remained patchy. Then came Leyton Orient away. Orient were another upwardly mobile team within the division, destined for a play-off spot, but as had been the case with City's last visit to the capital, a raucous crowd roared the Tigers on to an unlikely win. The 2-1 victory was sealed late on by David Brown but was inspired by something of a collector's item – a Gary Brabin overhead kick.

Gary Brabin: I think David Brown set me up and it seemed the only way I could connect with the ball, so I scored with an overhead kick. But for all people remember individual games I just remember that period as a block. And I loved every second of it. It wasn't just the goals or specific games, it was the whole of that period. Everything in that period seemed essential – pivotal in the club's fortunes.

Justin Whittle: At Orient it was similar to the Brentford game. Brownie scored some very important goals. He could really finish. Skill-wise he was way ahead of most players in our team. I'd have always had him in my team. We all knew that if we did the hard work to set Brownie up, nine times out of 10 he'd finish it. We really needed that sort of player.

Gary Brabin: I'm the type of person who believes in myself. I try to be a positive person and I'd never have gone to the club had I not genuinely believed that we'd stay up. I really felt that. I went into a mode; other people will go out after a game and celebrate a win but I wasn't that type of person. I don't get too up and I don't get too down. I remember a lot of people getting excited over certain games but I knew my work wasn't done. I hadn't finished the job I came to do so I couldn't celebrate for all I was loving every minute of it. I wanted to take responsibility and I thrived on that.

Jon Whitney: We always celebrated our wins! The atmosphere on the bus on the way home from those games was what people would call 'old school'. I think that old school can be the right school. It was important to keep those team dynamics. We all did everything for the team. There were no individuals in that squad that Joycey had built. I know the goalscorers would get the accolades but it was a complete team effort.

A 1-0 win at home to Plymouth courtesy of another Brabin goal came, followed by another single-goal victory at Southend – with David D'Auria netting – in a performance that impressed the manager.

Warren Joyce: Southend was the game that clinched it for me. They were going quite well and we really looked like a team then. At that time we were comfortable. Everyone knew their roles. We were solid. That really sticks in my mind. There was an unbelievable atmosphere from the travelling support that night. It's not a short trip, but the people who went to help the lads on that day, every one of them deserves every credit for helping secure the future of the club.

This sent City into a crucial game at Boothferry Park against Scarborough in confident mood. The division looked comforting for City now, with Scarborough propping it up and the likes of Hartlepool and Carlisle being dragged into the battle for survival. Relegation was still a possibility, however, and '13,949' fans packed into Boothferry Park for what was to be one of the last great occasions at the old ground.

Mike Edwards: We were laughing about the official attendance. We knew the capacity was 13,000 and something and when we went out we knew there were more than that there. I used to go when I was a kid, and I remember Don Robinson going round the pitch on his horse. The ground felt fullish back then, but it was rammed that day. There wasn't a space anywhere. That's what football's about.

Andy Daykin: We got a severe rollocking from what is now called the Safety Advisory Group as there were too many people in the stadium.

Warren Joyce: Boothferry Park was a fantastic stadium, atmosphere wise, and the crowd that day were magnificent. Just going out there on the pitch was incredible. You really wanted to be a part of a Hull side that would get that sort of crowd every week.

City ended up drawing 1-1, with Jamie Hoyland equalising Gary Brabin's opener. The point was of much more use to City than it was the Seasiders, however.

Warren Joyce: We might not have won that day but we could afford to draw. The hard work had been done building up to it.

Mark Greaves: I was gutted in that game because we didn't keep a clean sheet. I loved the game and it was the biggest crowd I'd played in front of at Boothferry Park, but we were so much better than Scarborough. I was massively proud though as I knew we wouldn't be relegated after that.

Gary Brabin: I remember the fans spilling onto the pitch. It was such a great spirit and togetherness.

Justin Whittle: Even the Best Stand was bouncing that day. I wasn't playing and was watching from there, and all the pigeon crap was landing on my head.

Jon Whitney: We didn't fear that we'd go down at that point, but we knew that if we didn't lose that game then we'd be more or less safe. It was a bit edgy in front of that packed house. But that game really stands out for me. It was incredible to play in front of that crowd. It was a throwback to the stadium's golden era. When I first signed for Huddersfield they were still at the old Leeds Road, and that was similar, but I never saw it as packed out as Boothferry Park that day. It was incredible. It was more or less a party atmosphere. We were all revelling in what it was about. I remember looking around the stands, taking a few deep breaths and thinking: 'This is what football's about. This is what we do it for. Me running on the streets playing as a kid, kicking a can around, wanting to be Kenny Dalglish, it all happened because you wanted a day like this, playing in front of a packed house at Boothferry Park.'

Mike Edwards: We knew we couldn't get beat, but we knew we could pretty much put relegation to bed if we won the game, so it was frustrating from that point of view. The atmosphere was amazing. It was a great game to be part of.

The trust within the squad at this point was so strong that they were even performing medical procedures on each other.

Mark Greaves: I broke my nose! Brabs tried to put it back into place afterwards – and it's still bent now! He told me that it would be fine by the following Monday and I took his word for it and didn't bother going to hospital. At least I looked more like a proper centre-half then. I'd been too good looking before that!

Gary Brabin: He was a vain get! Not the prettiest but he had nice hair. But yes, I remember getting his nose – after a lot of persuasion – and straightening it for him.

City took four points from their next two games. Colin Alcide earned a draw at Cardiff, and then scored a last-minute winner at home to Exeter to seal three points. Alcide hadn't had the easiest of times at City since signing from Lincoln a few months earlier, but was now proving his worth.

Gary Brabin: The fans didn't take to Colin at first but I remember coming out and defending him and it seemed the fans were brilliant with him after that. It maybe needed someone like me to support Colin. He went from strength to strength after that, as he had such great backing. I knew what it was like to get that brilliant backing from the Hull City supporters because it drove me on. I'd certainly put Colin in the under-rated bracket. He gave us something really different, a key player who never got the recognition and praise he deserved.

While relegation never really looked likely after the Exeter victory, City went into the season's penultimate game – at home to Torquay – knowing a win would make survival a mathematical certainty. David Brown scored past Neville Southall in the 31st minute to clinch the victory and seal the Great Escape. The fans spent what seemed like the whole of the second half chanting the main score from the film on the terraces.

David Brown: It was just an instinctive thing. I've looked back and I scored a lot of goals for Hull City similar to that one – cutting in from the left and scoring with a right-footed shot into the bottom corner. I think Colin Alcide flicked on an Oakes goal kick, and I just managed to get in behind. I half expected Neville Southall to come out and clear it but he decided to stay on his line and that allowed me to take a couple of touches and pick my spot. As a right-footer going in from that angle it's one of your preferred finishes as the target becomes bigger. It was nice to score in front of the Hull fans in the South Stand. The relief of scoring that goal and knowing that potentially it was the goal that would seal the Great Escape was a good feeling. I didn't look at it that way when I was celebrating the goal, but on reflection it was an important one!

Justin Whittle: For any team, no matter the level, you just don't want to be relegated. I'd had it with Stoke and it's not a nice feeling. We'd worked hard to try to do as well as we could, to the best of our ability. If we'd gone down it wouldn't have been through lack of effort. We all gave 100% and we finally got there, so we could breathe a sign of relief. But once we got going we knew we had a chance. It was quite easy in the end but it was a great achievement. Form-wise, we'd have been near the top from that second half of the season.

When you bring a new team together it can take a year or two to gel, but we had to do it in a matter of weeks. We had to perform instantly and that's a huge credit to Warren and John McGovern, as well as Tom Belton, who'd helped him get those players in. It was also to the credit of the fans, who'd given us fantastic support. They'd been turning up no matter what, and we'd been lifting them.

Jon Whitney: Through my career I've had promotions, but the fondest memories for me are staying up in relegation fights. Hull was the best one for me, but I did it at Lincoln and Walsall too. The party atmosphere and the feeling afterwards by far outweighs the feeling when you get promotion. I think it's a sense of relief; to know that we now couldn't go down mathematically and we'd achieved what I was brought in to do. We'd been brought in to do a job, to keep Hull City in the Football League. We did that, and it's something that I'm immensely proud of. But I think the whole club, and particularly the fans from that time, should be really proud of themselves. You will never know what would have happened to Hull City had they gone down. We've seen it with many clubs that there's no guarantee that you'll come back up.

Andy Daykin: When I started Hull were six points adrift at the bottom of the division, so I thought: 'This will be a challenge.' Then the club bought Gary Brabin and I would say he was the strongest influence behind the club escaping relegation.

Mark Greaves: I'm a Hull lad, and I was living in First Lane Hessle at that point. There was a bus stop outside my house and a lot of fans knew I lived there. If we'd been relegated I was worried about my windows, so I was relieved when we stayed up! Had we been relegated, would we have come back up? It's very hard to get out of the Conference. I felt that I'd contributed to the football club that season and I felt more proud of that than I ever had done.

Mike Edwards: That year is up there with anything I've done in football. It was such a great year and a massive achievement. We might not have won a medal at the end of it but for the fans and ourselves it was an unbelievable turnaround. Joycey got the right chemistry there.

Jon Whitney: People like myself, Brabs and Justin are like missionaries in a way. We came in and helped save a sinking ship. Teams just didn't want to come and play us, especially with that home support, which was the best I'd played under. We had that 'click'. You could see it in training, and we loved coming into training. Joycey would just allow us to be who we were, though he kept it under some controlled chaos, because there were some big, big characters in that team. That said, there were no egos, and we were keen to let the younger players come through and have their say. As long as they had the work ethic and there was a mutual respect, a mutual humility, that was the important thing. The main reason we did what we did, however, is because we didn't see ourselves as any different to the fans. I like to sit with a beer and a smile on my face and think back to those games. The fans sensed what we were about to do and responded to our energy.

Warren Joyce: There was a real sense of satisfaction. You were proud of what the players had achieved and I was delighted for the fans. I knew what a good place Hull was and how great the fans were. I was then thinking about trying to build the club up and progress in the future. With little money we'd put together a side that was very competitive and they were good people to be around. They did everything for the fans, everything for the cause. It was terrific to be involved with them.

For a fan base starved of success as far as promotions or cup finals went, this survival was the best that a generation of City supporters had known. Such an escape had seemed nigh on impossible in late December, but just four defeats in 22 games, including 11 clean sheets, told the story of a team with tremendous self belief, meticulous organisation and incredible togetherness. City fans could watch on as Scarborough were relegated by the last kick of the season, with loanee goalkeeper Jimmy Glass scoring a famous winner for Carlisle against Plymouth. Scarborough were never to be seen again in the Football League. Would that fate have met Hull City? Who knows? But we should forever be extremely grateful to Warren

Joyce, John McGovern, Gary Brabin, Justin Whittle, Jon Whitney, Mark Greaves, Mike Edwards, David Brown and co that we never had to find out.

The optimism generated by the Great Escape was tempered by the removal of Tom Belton as chairman along with original consortium member David Bennett. Tom had been a popular figure with the City fan base, being named 'supporter of the year' by the official supporters club. This brought Nick Buchanan and, ominously, 'vice-president' Stephen Hinchliffe to the fore, something the football authorities were taking note of.

Rob Smith: Tom Belton going was a bit of a mystery. There one day and then removed from office the next, and Hinch and Buchanan were moving more and more into the spotlight. Tom possibly felt a bit undermined by that, as he was the club spokesman and would go have a beer with the fans. But I don't know why he was removed. It was a shock, but when you've worked at Hull City over a number of years you get used to shocks like that.

John Cooper: I got to know Tom quite well. He was uncomfortable with how things were going, and then the Sheffield guys got rid of him. It's a Saturday I'll never forget. Tom rang me at home and said: "I've been ousted, but my private papers are at Boothferry Park." I knew every little nook and cranny at Boothferry Park because of certain issues we'd been having long before the lock-out problems we were to have with David Lloyd. With the help of a few others we managed to get him into the ground and get his paperwork out and away before anyone knew anything. After that period, the club went downhill quite rapidly.

Rob Smith: You had a lot of ex-Sheffield United staff, and they were brilliant at bringing the staff together. Work became enjoyable. They'd been great at rallying people and we'd all pull together, doing things like decorating the hospitality lounges the week before the season started. Dayks would turn up with a load of paintbrushes and then go and buy fish and chips for everybody, because that was all the club could afford. Everybody would muck in. I appreciate that from an outsider's point of view the reputation of the owners was worrying, but it really was enjoyable for us working there. The Sheffield guys had a football pedigree as well, they were football people, and that was great after working under David Lloyd and his people. Andy Daykin in particular knew everyone in football. He was a top guy and he still has a lot of friendships from his time in Hull.

Off the pitch, and seemingly irrelevant to Hull City, that summer saw Hull City Council's telephone network floated on the stock exchange. No one could have known, but this move was to have huge implications for Hull City's future prospects.

Tom McVie: We had the money from the Kingston Communication shares, with which we did a lot of things around the city – central heating in council houses, improving street lights, and such like – but it became clear that neither Hull City nor Hull Sharks were going to be able to solve the problems they had with their stadia on their own. I'd been going to Boothferry Park and the Boulevard since 1956 so I didn't need telling how dreadful the conditions had become.

Indeed, talk of a 'super stadium' was still ongoing.

Andy Daykin: I represented the club on the development board, someone else represented Hull Sharks and there was a representative from Hull KR as it was going to host both rugby clubs at that stage.

On the pitch, Warren Joyce had signed the likes of Jason Harris, Jon Schofield, Lee Bracey and Steve Morgan, while Andy Oakes was sold to Derby for just shy of £500,000. But the stand-out player coming in was undoubtedly Hull-born forward John Eyre from Scunthorpe.

John Eyre: I was doing really well at Scunthorpe. We were near the top of the league and looking like we might go up automatically. David D'Auria was a friend of mine and had moved from Scunthorpe to Hull the season before. I'd kept in touch with him and he told me that Warren was interested in signing me. My contract was up at Scunthorpe and they were really dithering about me signing a new deal, even though we were riding high and I was scoring goals. Because I knew that Hull were interested I just let my contract run out, and I eventually had a really good meeting with Warren and I signed there and then. So even though Scunthorpe were promoted from what is now League 2, I stayed in that division! It had been a dream for me to go back and play for my home-town club, and the way Warren was doing things it seemed like the club was being turned around. There was talk of a new stadium and I wanted to be part of a Hull team that would be a force again.

When you're playing for your home-town team there's that extra buzz. I think it means a lot to the supporters too, to see someone who's from their city, who they can relate to, who they maybe played against as a schoolboy; it gives you an extra spur. To achieve something for your home town is extra special.

There was a widespread assumption among some fans and parts of the media that City would simply pick up where they had left off when the 1999/2000 season started. But surviving relegation is one thing, winning promotion another. City lost four and drew one of their first five league games. Was too much being expected?

Warren Joyce: I was keen to build from the previous season, to progress from that, and I was thinking of a longer term plan. Tom Belton leaving was a blow to me personally, though, and also for the club in my opinion. It was being portrayed financially that we were going to have a go, but the reality was that there was little or no money to spend and the players that were brought in were on really low wages, with the exception of John Eyre. The rest were on low money and were just added to what we had as squad members. Then there was a tax bill to be paid so we had to sell Andy Oakes, who'd done brilliantly for us, to save the club. That was a one-off hit. The bill was somewhere around £660,000 and we sold Andy Oakes for something approaching that. If we hadn't done that you were – again – looking at the prospect of there being no Hull City. So while the fans were expecting a promotion push, I was signing lads like Jon Schofield on very, very little wages with no signing on fee, but who were desperate to come. I felt the fans' hopes were being built on something that wasn't a reality. I couldn't say anything at the time, even when I left, as I didn't want to tittle-tattle. Any stories being spread around about building up the club at that time certainly weren't based on reality.

David Brown: Expectations were maybe a little bit too high. Our form in the second half of the Great Escape season before was brilliant and Joycey had been able to sign a couple of players, but it's a tough league with quite a few tough teams. So that over-optimism and the fact that some of Joycey's signings didn't quite come off affected us.

Mark Greaves: I always felt we needed a better option up front – someone to play alongside Browny or John Eyre. Defensively we were strong but we needed tweaking a bit going forward, as it never seemed to work. Jason Harris didn't score as many as we'd hoped. We nearly signed Marco Gabbiadini, and he went on to score loads of goals for Darlington. If we'd got him, we'd have kicked on.

Jon Whitney: Expectancy is a big thing. Suddenly the fans aren't as patient and that can affect the atmosphere and the players, particularly the more technical ones. There wasn't quite the same positivity. There was an expectancy that we'd just carry on with the form we'd shown the season before, but it never really happens that way. It was a totally different situation. It was always going to be a season for stability, and we saw that. It takes time to build a promotion team.

Steve Wilson: Lee Bracey came in. I don't think he was a good goalkeeper. I think he was Warren's worst signing. I think I would have started as first choice in the first game, but I did my medial ligament in a pre-season friendly at Goole. As soon as I was fit I was in the first team, but then I did the same injury again, which meant I missed the Liverpool games.

The Liverpool games were a high point of the season. In the League Cup City were beaten 5-1 by the Merseysiders at Boothferry Park, but in the second leg at Anfield managed to claw the game back to 2-2 after going 2-0 down and having Lee Bracey sent off (something he was making a habit of). After that, however, City went another seven league matches without a win. The team needed a bit of flair. That was to arrive in November from Jamaica in the form of midfielder Theo Whitmore and defender Ian Goodison.

Andy Daykin: We were playing away at Barnet when it was announced that they were signing, and Theo was quite a player. The only thing in my mind was where the money was going to come from. I think there was a belief that after that game against Scarborough at Boothferry Park, when the crowd was probably greater than the capacity, that it was easy: all we'd have to do was win matches and we'd fill the stadium and bring all this revenue in. The Great Escape had raised everybody's expectations and they were flattened very quickly. Needless to say the crowds didn't come in and the revenue fell accordingly.

Warren Joyce: We managed to get the two Jamaicans for very little money. The deals were that there was no fee to their club, but their clubs in Jamaica would get 75% of any fee we sold them for. I didn't mind that because we wouldn't have to sell them, but if we did we'd be getting what was effectively 25% on zero layout. We couldn't afford to pay a penny for them. They ended up being good players. Theo had a move to Bolton lined up, but he was in a car crash in Jamaica and he went off the boil after that. Even with those deals, though, we weren't really building the club. It might have looked like we were but that wasn't the case.

Frank and Margaret Beill: What the heck were they doing playing for a club in Hull City's position? Ian Goodison was probably the coolest central defender who ever played for Hull City.

To make room in the squad, one of the heroes of the Great Escape, David D'Auria, was to leave for Chesterfield.

Justin Whittle: David D'Auria was a terrific player. He got stuck in and he had ability. I was sad when we sold him. He rarely gets mentioned in the Great Escape heroes but he should.

However, though the spirit within the club was good, the results wouldn't come consistently. City took up root in the lower to middle reaches of the table and never looked like shifting.

Gary Brabin: There were several factors behind us not kicking on. We were a little bit disappointed as we thought we were going to go for it financially. We thought there was going to be a lot of money put behind the club to kick on from what we'd done, but it never really happened. I remember speaking to Warren about players who were going to come to the club, but we couldn't quite afford them and we ended up getting players who probably weren't as good – some were, some weren't, and others were a bit of a gamble like Theo Whitmore and Ian Goodison. People seemed to be sitting back and letting nature take its course. Also, things weren't as transparent as they were when I first went. The people who put their neck on the line were the people who you were dealing with at first. The next year all of a sudden it had changed – less transparency, less financial backing; it wasn't as positive behind the scenes as it had been. We all sensed that too. Everyone seemed to want to change what we had because we weren't in danger any more. Warren wasn't backed and more people had come to the forefront to offer an opinion.

Mike Edwards: We were hugely optimistic that we'd kick on. We had to make an adjustment though, this season, as we were no longer scrapping for our lives trying to stay up. The adjustment was coming but you can't just do it in a season. You need time to build a promotion-winning team.

An FA Cup game in the December against Chelsea, in which City lost 6-1, gave the season a little bit of sparkle, but in truth it was a fittingly flat end to the most miserable of decades. When City beat Mansfield 2-0 at Boothferry Park to close out the 1990s, there was a feeling of 'good riddance' to 10 years of famine as far as success was concerned. The feelgood factor from the Great Escape had dissipated and worries were becoming increasingly vocal regarding the owners of the club. The much-discussed 'super stadium' seemed to consist entirely of hot air as long as City had owners that the now cash-rich council were reluctant to deal with. 'More of the same' was all that seemed to lie ahead. All that the 2000s would serve up would be yet more underachievement and disappointment, wouldn't they?

January 2000 to May 2000

When Big Ben ushered in the new millennium, it also signalled the end of a decade (some would say century) of underachievement by Hull City AFC. EGD Wright, Matt Bell, Billy Bly, Raich, Viggo, Jock, Waggy, Chillo, Ken Houghton, Ian Butler, Stuart Pearson, Keith Edwards, Big Billy, Little Billy, Skip, Tony Norman, Jobbo, Garreth et al had been a privilege to witness in a Hull City shirt, but none of them had taken the club to the promised land of the top flight of English football. None of them had taken us to Wembley.

Anyone proclaiming at that point that within the next decade City would be packing out a brand new 25,000-capacity all-seater stadium, would be taken over by a visionary such as Adam Pearson, would be steered to the Championship by a former England manager, would see Nick Barmby come home, would see yet more heroics in a City shirt from Dean Windass, would see Jay-Jay Okocha in a City shirt, would play at Wembley for the first time, would get to the Premier League for the first time courtesy of a goal from a 39-year-old local hero, would win at Arsenal, Tottenham, Newcastle, would stand joint top of the Premier League on points, would stave off a relegation that the national press had seen as a formality... Well, let's just say they'd have been given a wide berth.

On January 3rd, 2000, City travelled to Brisbane Road, Leyton, to play out a tepid 0-0 draw in rainy, cold conditions. It was a match that barely registered with anyone beyond the 5,169 fans in attendance. City's starting line-up that day – Nick Culkin, Steve Harper, Steve Swales, Mark Greaves, Justin Whittle, Steve Morgan, Warren Joyce, Gary Brabin, Adam Bolder, David Brown and John Eyre – contained a number of players still held high in many City fans' affections, but it was a world away from the multi-million-pound signings and internationals that would close the decade out at the Reebok Stadium, Bolton, on December 29th, 2009. Indeed, the match was so low-key that it is difficult finding anyone – fan or player – who has any memory of it other than a few hardy, committed souls.

Mark Greaves: I'm usually really good with remembering matches, but I can't remember a thing about that game.

Frank and Margaret Beill: The main recollection of that day is speaking to manager Warren Joyce before the match. We were surprised with how expensive the tickets were. He provided our family with a couple of complimentary tickets for the game. Warren is a genuinely good guy.

Ian Thomson: I have vivid recollections of that day at Orient, but not because of the football. My then wife had informed me the day before that she was divorcing me, and I remember telling my friends about it in the pub. So not exactly an auspicious start to the new millennium.

Ian Farrow: We were beginning to realise that the heroics of the Great Escape season were not going to transfer into a promotion season this time around. However, we had just signed Whitmore and Goodison and this promised to add glamour to our campaign. On-loan keeper Nick Culkin gave an outstanding and commanding performance and although he gave away a penalty in the first half, he subsequently saved the kick. A 0-0 draw was typical of our season. We didn't win enough games.

Gary Clark: I treated the wife to a city break in London over that particular bank holiday, where City just happened to be away at Orient. The match was dreadful and the 100 or so away fans sat in one corner of the tin-pot stand on the wooden benches were dodging the rain bouncing and dripping from the corrugated tin roof and the cascading water spluttering out of the broken-down pipes and rusting guttering, but we fought out a 0-0 draw.

The season never picked up. The achievements of the Great Escape became ever more distant. Through February and March, City won just two games – and drew five 0-0 – taking up root in the lower-middle half of the table. Then something clicked. In early April City travelled to Brunton Park and beat Carlisle 4-0, with two goals from the hitherto disappointing Jason Harris, one from Steve Morgan, and a Richard Prokas own goal. Goals from Jon Whitney and David Brown then saw City beat Leyton Orient 2-0 at Boothferry Park. A 1-0 win at Mansfield, thanks to a David Brown strike, followed. Finally it seemed that Warren Joyce had discovered an attacking mojo. It therefore came as a surprise when he was duly sacked in mid-April.

Warren Joyce: We'd won three games on the trot. I didn't get any explanation. My father had just died and I thought to myself: 'He wouldn't put up with the bullshit of working with some of these people.' I had my own private issues as things weren't right. There were things going on at the club that to me were not honest or true. But I wasn't looking to make excuses and I've kept my mouth shut about it until this interview.

David Brown: We were mid-table. Was the board expecting too much? Should we have accepted that we needed a season to consolidate? Maybe on reflection that would have been a better way to look at things. Those particular owners weren't the ones who'd appointed Warren too. I'd travel in with Joycey from the north-west, so while we weren't privy to the private meetings that were going on we did know quite a lot about what was happening and we knew it wasn't easy for Warren, given the unreasonable behaviour of the board at times and their expectations of him. It was harsh. They weren't the most constructive board and that was evident when they didn't stay around long after that sacking. Joycey is always straight with people and I don't think they appreciated that. When we'd played Aston Villa away, various members of the board were trying to come in the dressing room at half-time and we were thinking: 'What are you doing?' Joycey had to tell them to get out at the time. So they'd clashed a few times when Joycey's attitude seemed to be: 'Let me manage the football team and you manage the football club.'

Frank and Margaret Beill: Warren Joyce was the one who saved us from dropping out of the Football League. He deserved much better treatment from the owners.

Jon Whitney: Warren is still a good friend of mine. It's never nice when a manager loses his job, and as players you've all got to take a bit of responsibility. It was a shock. I understand that that's just football, but I think the decision was made a little bit too soon. But there was stuff going on off the pitch as well. Warren will possibly be the most fondly remembered manager in Hull City's history based on what he did, and the most important manager. And he's not just a good manager, he's a really good, honest bloke.

Gary Brabin: I was devastated. I thought it was poor. We'd just won a load of games. There'd been a lot of politics that were coming to the fore involving a lot of people who were nowhere to be seen when we had our backs to the wall fighting relegation. That had an effect on the club. It was disappointing. It was like people wanted to rip it all up and start again.

Mark Greaves: I was gutted. As a person and as a footballer I had huge admiration for him. He was so honest and was such a good pro. He was probably the biggest influence on my career.

John Eyre: I had a really bad elbow injury that put me out for a long time. I was out from January until the end of the season and Warren was sacked in that time. We had so many players who could play, and we had a big squad, but I don't think that Warren found the right formula. We did it at times – and we had a strong physical unit – but I don't think he ever found his best 11, which can be hard when you've got a squad that size. I still felt Warren was unlucky to be sacked though. I was with Neil Mann when we found out – we were both injured – and we were devastated. Given a bit more time I think he'd have found the right formula and been successful for Hull City.

Mike Edwards: I was devastated. He'd looked after me my whole career. He was a father figure to me. I had such huge respect for him.

Steve Wilson: That following season everyone was expecting us to get promoted but it doesn't work like that. I felt really sorry for Joycey. It was sad to see. We had an OK pre-season, we went to Newquay and we really bonded. But expectations were a bit too high.

Justin Whittle: The expectation was high and we signed quite a few players. Sometimes it doesn't happen immediately and you have to be given time. I feel that Buchanan and Hinchliffe should have stuck with Warren a bit longer as he'd have found the right balance and the right players. Football's difficult and it's hard to achieve anything instantly. It was sad. Warren was a player's manager. Everyone respected him. You never heard anyone bad-mouthing him, even the players not in the team. Then you're left thinking about who the new manager will be and whether you'll be in his thoughts.

Jon Whitney: When Joycey played he was a catalyst for us. His energy just drove the rest of us on. We saw him as our general. He led from the front. The fans might think of him more now as a manager, but as a player he had real quality.

The usual frenzy of speculation descended upon Boothferry Park with regards to the identity of the new manager, but when Brian Little was announced as Warren Joyce's successor it was seen as something of a coup. He'd been managing in the Premier League relatively recently with Aston Villa and was still a big name in football. So how did City get him?

Andy Daykin: Gary Megson was interviewed, and later on Neil Warnock was after a job at Hull City. I was present when Brian Little was interviewed at the Hilton at East Midlands

Airport. It was a major coup. He wanted the job and took it seriously. The guy we were really after, though, was Steve Cotterill at Cheltenham.

Brian Little: A friend of my financial adviser had spoken to someone at Hull and they'd asked if I'd be interested in going there. I'd just split up with my wife and I'd just met the woman that is now my wife, and we said that it might do me good to get away from the Midlands for a little while and start a new challenge, a little like I'd done at Darlington a few years before. It was a break for me, something different.

I went up and met the board and said yes. Everything just suited my situation, though I wasn't to know how difficult it was going to get pretty much within the first few weeks.

David Brown: Brian Little was brilliant for me. From a PR point of view Brian is one of the best; he's got a lovely smile, he gets on with all the reporters and so on. When he came in I played every game, sometimes dropping into midfield. I was happy. His training was always good, and the club was a bubbly place to be.

Mark Greaves: Brian was very good as a manager, a lot more gentle than Warren. He would never shout but he had something special when he spoke. He had an aura about him. I enjoyed everything about him at Hull City as a manager.

Gary Brabin: I liked Brian, but I knew as soon as he came in that he'd want to bring in all of his own people. He was honest with me, which I respected, but I was still gutted. I understand that that happens. I knew the writing was on the wall as soon as he arrived. I ended up playing a lot of games at centre-half after he'd taken over, which I didn't mind but I felt less effective. I didn't feel as wanted by the management even though the fans were still great. I felt like my time at the club was coming to an end. That was disappointing as I'd signed a lengthy contract at the club and I'd turned down some good, good offers from clubs like Stoke and Preston, who were in higher divisions. I wanted to commit to Hull though as I was excited about what the future held. And it never quite lived up to that. I was never quite given the role I'd wanted after that.

John Eyre: I was thinking what a coup it was to get him. He'd done well at Villa and was a big name in football. It seemed like a fantastic appointment. He was a great guy, too. A top man. Maybe too nice at times. Sometimes as a manager you need to have a bit of steeliness, an aloofness, but when I look back at my managers in my career Brian was the nicest I played under. I was sad to see Warren go but it was a good appointment.

Justin Whittle was the only member of the squad to have played under Little, though he had been sold by him to City. So how did he feel about the appointment?

Justin Whittle: I could have stayed at Stoke. The Stoke fans had let Brian know that they weren't happy with him for selling me and I think he knew that it might not have been the best decision at that time. But I never had a problem with Brian and we got on well. When he first came in, if I was fit I'd be playing.

When Brian Little was appointed City only had two games of the season left. In the first – a 1-0 win at Plymouth – caretaker Billy Russell was still sat in the dugout. In the second, Little took full control and watched on as his new team lost 3-0 at home to Hartlepool.

Brian Little: I joined just before the last game of the season. I watched the game from the dugout but I wasn't really managing. We lost 3-0 to a good Hartlepool side, and it was a hard game to watch. I saw a lot of things to work on and it gave me some indication of what the task might be. When you go into a club that's struggling you might have some good players, you might have lads doing well, but there's invariably something wrong with the mix. I felt that way at Hull. The team wasn't gelling, the system had been different to what I wanted to do. I wanted to play with three centre-backs. I thought we could be competitive that way.

We'd conceded too many goals and we weren't scoring as many as we should have done despite having decent possession. My first task was making Hull City a hard side to beat. Watching that first game, I knew I wanted a bigger goalkeeper. I wanted another centre-back. Mostly it was about the set-up of the team and how we would approach games. We had to be harder to play against.

As the season ended, the previous summer's marquee signing could only reflect upon a frustrating return to his home town.

John Eyre: I had three major injuries in my career – a broken elbow, medial ligaments and a ruptured ankle ligament. They all happened at Hull within the space of about 12 months. That meant my seasons there were quite disrupted.

City ended the season in 14th position, and Neil Whitworth, Jon Schofield, Jon French, Steve Morgan, Stephen Hawes, Mike Quigley and Matt Baker were released. However, heading into the 2001/02 season there were murmurings of problems off the pitch. Concerns had been raised about Stephen Hinchliffe's involvement in the club, and issues such as the redesign of the club crest (the work of his son, James) and the purchase of a team coach from a company owned by Hinchliffe only added to the consternation. But the manager was a big name, and that alone was enough to create an air of optimism around Boothferry Park in May 2000, however misplaced it would soon prove to be.

2000/01 season

Even though City still had a box-office manager in Brian Little, the core of the Great Escape squad and mercurial talents such as Theo Whitmore and Ian Goodison, any optimism going into the 2000/01 season was soon quelled. It had become apparent that the board – already under suspicion from a lot of Hull City fans given Stephen Hinchliffe's DTI ban from being a company director – did not have the money to take the club forward. Or pay the rent on the club's ground. Or pay the players. This became apparent when the club was locked out of Boothferry Park by former owner David Lloyd in the pre-season. Lloyd called the bailiffs over unpaid rent of more than £100,000 and the gates were padlocked. Not long after, a transfer embargo was imposed on the club as a result of the PFA being called in to pay the players' wages. This came after promising youngster Adam Bolder had been sold to Derby for £90,000 to pay off a tax bill.

Andy Daykin: In financial terms we'd not known who on the board actually had any money to put in. There was a lot of talk of money but it never seemed to appear. I used to commute from Sheffield to Hull and would go in a gym at the end of Clive Sullivan Way. A woman called Bronwyn who worked at the club rang me and told me we couldn't get in to Boothferry Park. I said I'd be there in a couple of minutes and realised that we'd actually been locked out of the ground.

A chap had turned up in the car park to buy a season ticket for the next year. We'd taken the staff into the supermarket for a cup of coffee and this chap started playing hell, saying: "I'm here to buy my season ticket, I've been dropped off and I'm not being picked up for ages, what am I going to do?" We told him to have a cup of coffee with us, give us the money for his season ticket and then when we got back in the ground we'd send him his season ticket. He gave us his money! I wouldn't have given cash to someone in those circumstances. That was the spirit of the place though. Although there was a very small staff, everybody did seem to care.

John Cooper: I'd been expecting something. Emotional intelligence tells you certain things. I knew something wasn't quite right. I'd been at a funeral of a very dear friend near Market Weighton. I got a call to say the locks had been changed. I was generally looked upon as the older head who'd know what to do in these situations. I said: "The best thing to do is go away. We'll meet up and I'll get back to the ground." I drove back with my wife, and parked on Boothferry Road. The media were all over the place. It looked like a pre-planned operation to lock the ground. I set up a little office at home where I could liaise with people and we'd meet up at a pub near Hessle. We met as a group there and discussed what we were going to do. All I could do was keep people informed from home.

It was close season, and we were locked out. You can't tell nature to close down though. Everything on the pitch was still growing. With two other people I hatched a plan to keep an eye on the security company who were checking the ground twice a day. I then knew when they were not there. At Boothferry Halt there was a little warren of runs, so that was our route into the ground. We managed to keep the pitch in reasonable order. We knew that the landlords wouldn't want to lose too much money.

I got a call from home from one of the club directors, Philip Webster, to say we could get back into the ground. He asked me to be at the ground first thing on the Saturday morning to let people into the ground. Unbeknown to me, the person I was meeting was a serving female police officer – Philip Webster's girlfriend. On the morning the media knew what was going on. I had some paperwork that had been sent to me and I had to hand over this paperwork and then get the keys back. That wasn't to be the case, however. I had a word with the media to explain what I hoped was going to happen. But the only keys that were handed over by this police officer – who turned up in a marked police car in full uniform – were for the offices, not the stadium. The media wanted to be in the ground to see the pitch and so on. I just had to tell them they'd sent us the wrong keys. We managed to get back in and get the season going, but it was a very, very difficult time for the staff because we weren't being paid. We stuck together though.

Brian Little: I was wondering what I'd let myself in for. I was invited to a board meeting early doors and it was held in a pub on the banks on the Humber. I am not a big drinker and within two hours they'd had a few bottles of wine and had moved on… It was quite daunting for me. I just left and went home. There was something about the board that I liked though. There was a rogueishness about some of them and they were good to me, they liked me. They knew that I knew football and they let me get on with it. I could have said: "I'm not doing this," but I just laughed and thought: 'Well they're going to let me get on with the football side of things so I'll just get on with it.' There were a few strange days though. There were several occasions where some of the board liked to enjoy themselves and I'd be sat there shaking my head at what was going on, but with a bit of a grin on my face. There was a niceness to them while all this was going on. It was a challenge but quite funny.

Andy Daykin: I remember a Friday night before the start of the season all the staff coming in to paint the directors' suite for us. There was no thought of taking any money for it. The staff were fabulous under very difficult circumstances.

Despite being under investigation from the footballing authorities and the police, City managed to do some transfer business in the summer, bringing in centre-back David Brightwell, midfielder Phil Brumwell and the experienced Lee Philpott. There was also a surprise returnee.

Mike Edwards: In pre-season, we'd gone away but because of the rules in his contract, Joycey turned up! He was always so fit, and he ran all over every single player that was there. Brian was class with him though. There was no animosity.

Blackpool in mid-August may have been many people's idea of fun, but for Hull City it was the location of a pretty grim start to the season. In spite of Mike Edwards quickly equalising Brett Ormerod's opener, City were to lose 3-1.

Mark Greaves: In the opening game at Blackpool Brett Ormerod crossed the ball and it ended up in the back of the net. That summed up our start to that season. And it happened in the next game too – Plymouth at home in a 1-1 draw. As a defender getting beaten by a cross is hard to take. But under Brian I felt there'd be a time when we would get things going. You felt that as a manager he was learning the league.

That may have been the case, but the start to the season was pretty worrying. After the Blackpool game defeat and the Plymouth draw, City were to draw or lose their next five games, waiting until mid-September to register their first three points of the season, beating Shrewsbury 1-0 thanks to a David Brown goal. An important bit of business was done around this time, too.

City had had the sublime and the ridiculous keeping goal in recent seasons. Scott Thomson and current incumbent Lee Bracey hadn't inspired much confidence, and recent memories of the likes of Alan Fettis, Roy Carroll and Andy Oakes only served to highlight their deficiencies. The ever-dependable Steve Wilson was still at the club, but in late September Brian Little moved to bring in the experience of Paul Musselwhite after the former Port Vale number one had completed a short spell at Sheffield Wednesday.

Paul Musselwhite: There were still a lot of strong characters in that changing room, and we had a well-known manager. The likes of Gary Brabin, Justin Whittle and Jon Whitney stood out in there. I'd moved back to Scunthorpe and would travel in with Jon Whitney and Jason Perry. When I joined we were below mid-table. A squad that was as good as that in League 2 should have been doing better.

Musselwhite's signing seemed to settle the team, with the next eight games bringing three wins, four draws and a solitary defeat at home to Brighton. By the time City had beaten local rivals Scunthorpe 1-0 at Glanford Park in early December, thanks to a David Brightwell goal, the club stood eighth in the league.

1. **Chesterfield P20 W13 D6 L1 Pts45**
2. **Brighton P20 W13 D3 L4 Pts42**
3. **Rochdale P19 W10 D6 L3 Pts36**
4. **Orient P20 W10 D6 L4 Pts36**
5. **Cardiff P19 W9 D8 L2 Pts35**
6. **Cheltenham P20 W10 D4 L6 Pts34**
7. **Scunthorpe P20 W9 D4 L7 Pts31**
8. **Hull City P20 W7 D9 L4 Pts30**

Sadly, City were to pick up only two points in the next six games, sinking to 13th position in the league, though in this time a new strike partnership was formed.

Brian Little: Rodney Rowe had been recommended by my brother Alan, who was doing some chief scouting work for me and had worked with Rodney previously.

There was a period in my coaching career when I was younger that saw me at Stockport County a lot. There were just things about Kevin Francis. I wanted a big man, small man partnership. I knew what a handful Kevin was, even though he was clumsy at times. People didn't want to play against him. It helped to change the dynamics of the team. I didn't realise he was going to be as effective as he would be. It surprised me how well he did for us. He led from the front, he defended from the front, and he was outstanding for us. When he tackled, he really tackled. Opposition players wouldn't get up easily after he tackled them. As a manager you love having a player who defends from the front like that.

Kevin Francis: I was injured while in my second stint at Stockport County. I went down to Peterborough to work with Barry Fry to get fit. From there Noel Blake took me to Exeter on a month-to-month contract and this also helped me with my fitness and got me some games. Exeter offered me a contract and this caught the attention of Brian Little, who then also made me a contract offer which I accepted. Little did I know a short time later Hull would run into financial problems and not be able to pay the players. To be honest I would probably still have signed for Hull had I known.

Rodney Rowe: Brian Little had approached me quite a few times while I was at Gillingham. We'd just been promoted to the Championship, and I wanted to stay at that level. But I was coming back up to Huddersfield to my family every week, and I'd been getting the papers and seeing all the issues that Hull had been having with the ground closing and stuff like that. So I'd been thinking, even though I'm not playing for Gillingham I'm not sure about going there. But Brian kept reassuring me, and I thought: 'I want to be back up north, why not?' Getting to work with Brian was a big thing for me. He'd made such an effort to get me there. But then within the first week of me signing all the stuff off the pitch started to unravel. Everything happens for a reason though, and in the end I couldn't have scripted it all any better.

Kevin Francis: The people of Hull were working class, proud and dedicated from my observations. I knew the club had the potential to be big from the battles I had against them when I was at Stockport. During one game I was getting horrendous abuse from a Hull fan while I was playing for Stockport. I picked up the ball on the left wing, in front of the main stand, I cut inside on my right and bent the ball in the top corner. I then turned to where the fan was sitting to give him some abuse and everyone around was pointing at his empty seat. The cheeky bugger didn't stay to witness the best part of the game. Props to the fans around the empty seat though, as they applauded the goal.

Rodney Rowe: Kev's an absolute gentleman: One-hundred per cent. But in training and on the football field he's an absolute beast. Anyone who's played against him or with him will tell you that. I have never, ever backed out of a challenge, but Kev told me that he'd do all the ugly stuff and I could do the rest. And that's just how it was with us. It gave me a real confidence. Then we had lads like Gary Brabin and Justin Whittle who you knew would win any battle too. We also had Theo Whitmore and Ian Goodison, and in training and on the pitch they were utter quality. You just couldn't fault them.

Kevin Francis: Rodney Rowe was a great foil for me. He was strong, quick, hard-working and a prolific finisher. We developed an amazing understanding in a short space of time.

Frank and Margaret Beill: Although big Kevin Francis was only with City for a short period, he brought something new. Before he arrived a big boot out of defence was inevitably followed by the ball coming straight back again from the opposition. The difference was that he won the ball and it stayed at the other end of the pitch!

Kevin Francis: I am an acquired taste but I pride myself on my work ethic. I worked in an everyday job before I became a professional footballer so I always felt privileged to be a pro. I never took this blessing for granted and I think that is something the fans could see. I could sense the fans liked me but I felt it was due to the team pulling together to help them through the tough time the club was going through. I always felt the Hull fans were welcoming and I wanted to work harder and do better for them to secure the club's future.

Rodney and Kevin made their debuts in a goalless draw at home to Macclesfield. It was the third of a five-game run in which City failed to trouble the scoresheet. The fifth of these games came in mid-January when City lost 1-0 at home to Blackpool. The season was fizzling out, with City in 13th place, nine points off a play-off spot.

11. **Barnet P25 W9 D6 L10 Pts33**
12. **Kidderminster P24 W8 D9 L7 Pts33**
13. **Hull City P26 W7 D11 L8 Pts32**
14. **Plymouth P23 W8 D6 L9 Pts30**
15. **Mansfield P25 W7 D9 L9 Pts30**

However, as worrying as this form was, the situation off the pitch was much more frightening, as it became apparent that the club couldn't afford to pay the players. There was, quite simply, no money. On February 6th Hull City were put into administration, owing the Inland Revenue a reported £500,000 and losing tens of thousands of pounds a week. Yet again, the club were behind with the rent for Boothferry Park, too. Nick Buchanan immediately resigned as chairman and most of his Sheffield-based colleagues went with him.

Andy Daykin: I had to leave the club within days. I was advised by the administrator that my services wouldn't be required, so I went and joined Barnsley. Ironically Nick Buchanan was an insolvency practitioner, so he knew that the writing was on the wall and had instructed a company in Sheffield called the BMA Partnership to act in the club's interests in terms of seeing it potentially into administration. A Leeds company became the administrator. But I have great affection for Hull. I genuinely loved my time there. From a commercial point of view everyone was great.

As it was becoming evident that the players wouldn't be paid, the club started putting a few results together. David Brown and Kevin Francis scored as City drew 2-2 at Kidderminster, then another Francis goal gave City a 1-0 win at Cheltenham. In the first game after the administrators had been called in, against Leyton Orient on February 10th, City played what was being billed as potentially the club's final ever game. At a winding up order at the High Court on February 7th, City had been given a 14-day stay of execution, but David Lloyd had again locked the gates, claiming he was owed £45,000 in rent arrears. Grimsby Town had even been approached about playing the game at Blundell Park.

John Cooper: Keeping the club running was my job. I didn't look at it any other way. I was paid to do a job, and it was a job I loved. With that camaraderie we had, if any of the backroom staff could help any of the others in any way, shape or form, that's what we did. There wasn't one bad apple at that time. And we needed that when we were locked out.

Rob Smith: We'd been locked out, Hinchliffe and Buchanan were nowhere to be seen, but John Cooper and the rest of the staff took on extra responsibilities as there were only about six of us left.

Thanks to the efforts of a skeleton backroom staff, the game was allowed to be played at Boothferry Park. In a raucous, emotional atmosphere Rodney Rowe scored in the 69th minute after being put through one on one with the Orient goalkeeper to give City a 1-0 win.

Rodney Rowe: We'd always been told that the club was going to be safe, but we'd been told it so many times we started to think that maybe it wasn't as safe as people were trying to tell us. I never took survival for granted. For the sake of myself and my family, I knew I just had to keep putting in the performances on the pitch and trying to get the wins under our belt. For my goal against Orient I just bundled over a defender and thought to myself: 'Just smash it.' I didn't even think about where the ball might end up. Usually I'd pick my spot. At the old Boothferry Park, the old-style standing was still there. I just remember setting off to celebrate and all that was on my mind was making sure I went off the right set of fans. The fans in the Kempton stand had always been particularly great with me and I really wanted to celebrate with them. It was really special for me. During that time it was special to be able to say thank you to those fans. The support we got in every single game – home and away – was unbelievable. The away support was absolutely amazing.

City won their next three games – 2-0 at Shrewsbury, with Rowe and Francis on the scoresheet to underline what a potent attack they had formed; 2-1 at home to Mansfield, with Francis and Rowe again getting a goal apiece; and 2-1 at home to Barnet, with a John Eyre double showing that the club had firepower beyond the two more recent signings. Brian Little won the Manager of the Month award – rarely has it been more deserved – and in the blink of an eye City were up to eighth.

1. **Chesterfield P35 W22 D11 L2 Pts77**
2. **Cardiff P32 W17 D10 L5 Pts61**
3. **Brighton P31 W19 D4 L8 Pts61**
4. **Hartlepool P33 W16 D9 L8 Pts57**
5. **Orient P31 W15 D9 L7 Pts54**
6. **Blackpool P32 W15 D4 L13 Pts49**
7. **Rochdale P30 W13 D10 L7 Pts49**
8. **Hull City P32 W12 D12 L8 Pts48**

The form was all the more incredible given that the players weren't being paid and the club was, it seemed, surviving on a week-to-week basis, with the administrators having the unenviable task of unweaving the club's tangled web of debt.

Brian Little: It brought us together. I had to deal with the players living a long way away in different ways, letting them train less with the team. We had a team bus, which had been bought by Stephen Hinchliffe, and it kept breaking down. But we had a laugh about that and we'd plan our journey around stopping at all the service stations on the way to an away game as we knew the bus would break down and we had to do something like top the radiator up. The players were having to bring their own food in Tupperware boxes. We'd plan it out painstakingly. On the mornings of games all the players would be asking each other what they'd brought to eat and showing each other their Tupperware boxes – Justin's stuff was always immaculate from his time in the army. It was comic stuff, but it got everyone focused on what we were doing. No one moaned, no one refused to do it. Everybody helped everybody out.

Everything was planned for. We planned for the disruption. We were open about the difficulties, we didn't hide from them. On the way back from games, I'd get dropped off at Elloughton on the A63. My wife, Lizzie, would be waiting in her pyjamas in our car and would then go on dropping off all the lads like Justin who lived round that area. We'd just laugh and joke about it, and after a while it just became matter of fact. And all the preparation stuff helped focus everyone's mind. But if we hadn't prepared for everything we'd have ended up looking like Fred Karno's circus. The players were magnificent. They wanted to play, they accepted the fact that we wouldn't be staying in hotels as a rule. We would stay at the odd hotel, but if we stayed at one they'd demand payment beforehand... Even if we did that it would be quite basic. Eggs on toast for breakfast, that sort of thing. It could have been embarrassing for a professional football team, but we just had a good laugh about it.

Gary Brabin: My vision on it was that the club had changed, all these people were coming in and offering an opinion, then the money dried up. It was backs against the wall again then, those people disappeared and we felt quite isolated as players. Some of us hadn't been paid for five-and-a-half months, including over Christmas. We were all entitled to free transfers and the lads could easily leave. We were asking the PFA to help but that wasn't easy. It was all about the character of the lads.

I held a meeting with the players – as the lads were saying they couldn't afford the mortgages – and I said look, we can't afford to come in every day, but let's just play for the club. And if that means playing for the club for nothing then that's what we'll do. And all the lads were in agreement with that. We then had a meeting with the management where we said: "You can't expect us to come in here every day for nothing but we want to play for the club." I think Brian – although he didn't want to hear that – respected it and understood that. And that coincided with our best form. We agreed to come in for one training session a week and apart from that we just played games. It was like we were back though. All of a sudden the interfering stopped as people seemed to think the club was a mess again and that we weren't worth the bother. A lot of us had had offers and one or two left but the lads who stayed rallied together and we went on a fantastic run.

Rodney Rowe: It got to the point where some players were having bank managers telling them they couldn't go any more overdrawn and stuff like that. Some lads couldn't afford petrol for their cars and were struggling to buy food for their families. At the start of it all we were just training as usual every day, but on the way home from training one day I got a phone call from Gary Brabin and he told me that we couldn't carry on coming in every day, and as one of the new players could I have a word with the manager. I said: "Hang on a minute, I can't do that. Can't Justin do it, or you?" Gary just said: "No, he doesn't like me at the minute", so I said I'd do it. I rang Brian and tried to explain we weren't trying to skive off or anything. Brian turned around and he said that we'd just train on the Fridays and we could just keep ticking over the rest of the time unless we had a midweek game. That's how it went when we weren't getting paid. The lads knew that other clubs could take us, but we also knew we'd sort everything out. And that uplifted everybody. And then the fans donations, which maybe meant we'd get the odd £50 here and there, helped us buy shopping and pay mortgages. Whatever we got, it really helped. I can never show the fans enough appreciation for what they did. I'll never forget it. They were so generous.

Kevin Francis: The administration period was not ideal, especially after I'd been out injured for a while and was having to battle back. Not getting paid added to the stress, but Brian was fantastic and told us all to have pride in what we do. At the time of signing I told Brian that I was getting paid for doing something I would gladly do for free; Brian told me: "Now's your chance!" Regardless of the off-field turmoil, on the field is where you can forget your troubles and create a distraction by lifting the club, the fans and yourself.

Justin Whittle: If the fans saw us giving it a go and showing willing, they'd stay behind us. It was hard for some players because money was tight but we could survive for so long and the PFA helped out as well, as did the fans clubbing together, which was massive. We could have lost a lot of players – as other teams were allowed to come in for us – but we only lost two or three. We kept the nucleus of the team. And it was just a matter of time, hopefully, before we would get something sorted.

The players just wanted to play. Unless we were being offered stacks of money somewhere else, the vast majority of us were going to stay. No one ever told us that there was no chance of the club surviving so we all stuck around, and we had a good, solid team with the likes of Kevin Francis and Rodney Rowe up front.

John Eyre: The off-pitch stuff maybe does affect things during the week, but we had a lot of strong characters – Gary Brabin, Justin Whittle, Jon Whitney, Jason Perry – and when you go out on the pitch, they wouldn't let you get distracted. We were very defensively strong, and we found ways to score goals. But that was very much down to the character of the players.

Mike Edwards: I had a possibility to move on, and being under 24 I was classed as an asset so I'd have had to demand a fee, but I spoke to Brian and he convinced me that a backer would come in and after that he'd sign me up to a new contract. He told me that he wanted me to be a big part of the plans he had, and that just sold me. I wanted to be successful with Hull City.

Mark Greaves: The off-field problems were good in some ways. It united us as a team, with us all not getting paid. Brian Little was great then. He told the players coming in from places like Manchester to only come in a couple of times a week if they wanted, and told us if anyone was really struggling financially that he'd help them out. You could sense he felt for us. He couldn't do enough for us. And that united us. It was humbling though, with the fans having whip-rounds and the like. But it galvanised us.

Also, the players were given a creditors list, and that meant we could see what money everyone was on. I was gutted at how much less I was earning than some of the players.

Mike Edwards: The local lads trained twice a week and the lads who travelled trained once a week as they couldn't afford the petrol. I always thought you were meant to train to get better and win games, but we were training a heck of a lot less and winning more!

Paul Musselwhite: I'd signed in the September and it was pretty clear soon after that the club was having financial problems. I'd seen it on the news that there'd been a few problems before I signed but it wasn't really discussed when I joined as I thought the club had got through the problems, but by the end of January, when we were first told that we weren't going to get paid, you realised they weren't. We then found out the club was going into administration. Brian would tell us to come in a couple of times a week. He was great at that time. And all of a sudden we went on a run where we couldn't seem to lose. Before we went into administration we were in the lower half of the league and when we came out of administration we were pretty much in the play-offs.

David Brown: Brian was very good at concentrating on what we needed to do as players, creating an atmosphere where we could come in and not worry about the stuff happening off the pitch. From that point of view he was good. I think it was a petrol crisis at that time too, so he was good from that side of things in being understanding on people's travel arrangements, apart from on match days. He'd often insist that those of us coming from the north-west would come to Hull to get on a coach to go back to the north-west as he wanted us all travelling together, so that could be a nightmare. We went to Halifax over Christmas one year, and we had to get up at 7am to drive past Halifax to get to Hull to drive back to Halifax! Little things like that weren't ideal. But Brian really created a happy dressing room.

Rob Smith: Brian Little was a reassuring presence in that time, letting us all know it would be OK. We'd teetered on going into administration many times in my time at the club, but we'd always seem to avoid it. I never believed the club would go under at that point. I'd have left if I thought it was going to happen. My mentality was: 'We'll find a way through this and if we have to work without pay, so be it.' We all stuck with it, and the hardcore fans rallied round too.

John Eyre: Brian was coming in at times and telling us that people had been to his door handing him money for the players. When the fans are doing that sort of thing, you can't do anything but put 100% in on a Saturday. So many fantastic gestures which were massively appreciated by everyone.

All of Hull City's players were free to leave the club, and a handful – David Brightwell, Clint Marcelle and Steve Harper – did. But when the chips were down, the big characters were needed, and characters don't come much bigger than Jon Whitney. The Great Escape hero had barely featured under Brian Little, but his services were now to be called upon.

Jon Whitney: I wasn't Brian Little's type of player. I understood that. I probably had too much to say, and I think he wanted more of a technical player. That wasn't really me. I carried on the same, trained in the same way – which was liked by some but not by others, because I'd put in a few challenges that might have been a bit too strong. But that's just me. One thing I could never be faulted for was my effort and attitude in training. I never sulked. I just wanted to be ready when the chance came. And when the chance came it was great.

With the club on the brink, as it had spent much of the past decade, there was little hope among fans at the meetings at venues such as the 147 Club on Spring Bank, where the usual suspects among the supporter groups – so energised in the Fish and Lloyd eras – seemed to think the Hinchliffe/Buchanan regime was too much for any club to take. Hull City was a corpse awaiting cremation, no longer the 'sleeping giant' it had been talked of in years before. Few were talking about City's 'potential' now, just its estimated debt of nearly £2m. The discussions of the past few years of a 'super stadium' – derided by so many in the city – now seemed pie in the sky. The very idea of a local club filling a 20,000-capacity stadium on a regular basis seemed unlikely to say the least. Who would bother with such a basket case of a club? Who in their right mind? Well...

On February 21st it was announced that City had found an anonymous buyer. Creditors and shareholders were asked to vote on a creditors voluntary arrangement, which saw the Tigers sold for £360,000. Who was the buyer? Rumours spread that Tom Belton had come back in with a new consortium, and that Don Robinson was making an attempt to buy the club again. The buyer wasn't anonymous for long. On March 12th, it was revealed that Adam Pearson – a commercial director at Premier League Leeds United – had rescued the club, and he was the sole owner of a new company that would trade under the name of The Hull City AFC (Tigers) Ltd. And he was to go about systematically rebuilding it from day one. For now, however, we were just happy to have a team to support at all.

Dave Burns: I came back to Radio Humberside the week of a creditors' meeting at the Willerby Manor Hotel, when the club could have gone under. My first job was to report on that meeting, where the club was saved by somebody, but we didn't know who. Ian Blakey, who was a bit of a power-broker, came out of the meeting saying that he thought they had somebody, but no name was mentioned. Then Adam Pearson emerged a few days later to say that he was the man.

Adam Pearson: Leeds were flying but already you could see they were going in a different direction. Although the board were very ambitious there were areas of the club that were giving rise for concern. The opportunity came up to be my own boss at Hull – and it was too good an opportunity to pass up. Also I was backed by Peter Wilkinson, who was a prominent Leeds businessman, which helped get the funding right for the club. So when I did the deal with the administrator at such a good price, and I also had the benefit of conversations with the council and Pat Doyle about the new stadium, the opportunity was too great to turn down. It did look a strange move but I genuinely believed that we could push Hull City forward, finally.

Brian Little: Adam and I got on really well to start with. He'd been impressed with what had gone on. I'd spoken to a couple of possible people to take over the club – Adam and a group from the US who were very interested. But Adam was great. We went from having nothing to Adam saying to me: "Right, what do you want?" He came into my office early on and said: "What sort of car do you want?" I just said: "What? What do you mean car? I've not had anything like that!" Then we started to make transfers and spend a bit of money. Adam's determination was there to be seen. If he wanted something, he wanted to get it straight away. In some respects it was harder going from one extreme to the other, as the ground was still in a mess, we had no training facilities. We'd had nothing, and then we went to having things, just not the things that we needed. It was a slightly different mentality to adopt but we managed to hang on.

John Cooper: The first time I met Adam, I was a creditor. I'd bought certain things to keep Hull City going out of my own money. So I, like everyone else, turned up at the hotel in North Ferriby, and there he was. He wasn't just a breath of fresh air, he was a hurricane. He was bouncy, he knew what he wanted, he had vision. And his vision was the important thing.

Rob Smith: After the turmoil, going at 200mph all the time, we then had the uncertainty of a mystery owner coming in. Adam's name just appeared out of nowhere and a knight in shining armour arrived and the club's transformation went to another level almost immediately.

Dave Burns: I was impressed with Adam from the off. He'd communicate. You could see he had a plan and the passion. He was willing to involve people. He had the council on board. He was maybe a little impatient but he was switched on. I just thought: 'This fella is going to take the club somewhere.' His heart and his head were in the right place.

Mark Greaves: When Adam Pearson took over, I was offered a new contract, and having seen the creditors' list I had loads of power as I knew what everybody was on! I didn't get anything near Brabs' wages but I got a good deal.

Mike Edwards: Adam was brilliant. He came in and spoke well and ambitiously. We didn't realise how much money was available but I went in for my first ever contract negotiations. I just wanted to make sure I'd be a footballer for another three years, I wasn't really bothered about the money at that stage. But myself, Mark Greaves and one or two others penned new deals, which Brian had promised us.

Kevin Francis: Adam was a great relief and boosted the club and players alike. He had the club's best interests at heart.

Mark Greaves: Adam is a good man. I have a lot of respect for him, as do a lot of people in the game. He was more professional than the previous regime. You knew he had an idea and a direction. He spoke to us like a visionary and we believed in him. He was the most influential person to come into Hull City in my time at the club.

Paul Musselwhite: I regarded Hull as a big club but they'd been in the bottom division for a while. When you're involved in football, over the years you realise that if the club has the biggest crowds in the division going to watch it, they should probably be near the top of the league. So something had been going wrong behind the scenes and it just needed someone who was going to come in and put some money in. Once the supporters realised that Adam was someone who wanted to take the club forward, the momentum just seemed to build.

John Eyre: You got the feeling that we became a different club overnight. We'd stuck in there, and then this money came in and we were getting players on loan and signing permanently who were improving the team. That original optimism when I first joined the club was there again.

Justin Whittle: We got all our money back! We were over the moon. With the money I'd got from the fans, I went out and bought a load of balls and got all the players to sign them so we could kick them into the crowd for the next game. That was just to say thank you. It was easier than going round and giving them a little bit back each! But Adam coming in gave us all a big lift because we knew we were going to survive and our personal financial worries had ended. But maybe a lot of the travellers had been playing better by not having to drive in and train every day.

Gary Brabin: We were taken over, and were paid by Adam Pearson. With that, Brian got us back in training every day. I remember saying to Brian: "What are you doing? Why spoil what we're doing? We're feeling good, we're in a good run, why spoil it, why change it?" He insisted on getting us back in but I wanted to keep things as they'd been as we were in such good form.

Adam Pearson wasted no time in moving into the transfer market. Winger Rob Matthews and forward Gary Fletcher came in, the latter on loan. Best of all was another loanee, Andy Holt, a left-back playing at Oldham in League 1.

Andy Holt: I was at Oldham and they asked me if I fancied going on loan anywhere. Aberdeen had made an approach so I listened to them and quite fancied playing in the Scottish Premier League, but then I was told that Hull had shown an interest. I didn't really know the circumstances, and Hull were a league below Oldham, but I thought I'd give it a go. I turned up and the lads were a bit sarcastic, saying that the club were splashing money about now, but I warmed to them really quickly. They seemed like a really good set of lads, considering all the trouble they'd been through.

Brian Little: In the first training session where we had Andy Holt, the ball was on the half-way line and I said: "Kevin, go stand in the box." He looked at me funny. I said: "Okay, Andy, show them," and he launched a ball from the half-way line into the box and everybody went: "Wow." It was a bit one-dimensional but you could cause some real problems with it. We played football but we also had an option of where if the ball went out of play we could instantly put the opposition under pressure, and Kevin was the focal point of that.

Just as Hull City were at the start of a huge transformation for the better, the same was to be said of Radio Humberside's sports coverage. The station had lost all credibility with football fans in the region. Nicknamed 'Radio Rugby' by many, the sports desk seemed to make no bones about which sport was its priority. Full-match commentaries on Hull City, Scunthorpe or Grimsby were rare, and if a kick-off veered slightly from 3pm on Saturday or a Tuesday evening, finding out how your club was doing on the airwaves was a near impossibility. To top it all off, the sports anchorman – Dave Gibbins – would generally seem more interested in discussing the fortunes of the club he supported, Arsenal, and would frequently antagonise the fans of the local football clubs.

Just as Adam Pearson had come in to fix something that was badly broken, Dave Burns – who had had a stint at the station in the mid-1990s reporting on City – was brought back to knock Radio Humberside into shape, something he wasted no time in doing.

Dave Burns: I had done four years at Radio Sheffield and flirted with national radio, but I preferred the local stuff. The then head of Radio Humberside said to me: "We'd really like you to come back, we're in a bit of a mess, the reputation's not great. Will you come in and head up the sports team?"

The Sheffield experience had been fantastic for me. I got to present 'Praise or Grumble', which is the world's oldest phone-in. They had expert summarisers, so I'd work with the likes of Billy Bremner, Mick McCarthy, Keith Edwards and Mel Sterland. I knew how passionate the football fans of South Yorkshire were, and I thought: 'Why can't I do that when I come back to Humberside?' I came back full of ideas, getting the expert summarisers, having the phone-ins on a Saturday evening. For the very first forum, the very first call we got came from a City fan. City had won, and this guy was eulogising about City and his closing words were: "Burnsy, I'm so excited I'm off for four Yorkshire puddings and a wank." There's no delay, and I was thinking: 'Oh god, the boss will never allow another phone-in.' Somehow we got through it. On reflection I wish I'd told him that most people just go for gravy as an accompaniment. From then on we got it up and running, and I wanted the programme to be like going to the match with your mates, where you'd talk about the serious and the less serious stuff. We wanted to involve the fans and get under the skin of all the clubs. And I think largely it's worked.

On the pitch, after five successive victories, City had lost to second-placed Cardiff before beating Halifax, losing to Brighton and then drawing at Plymouth. The home game against Exeter on March 17th, the first at Boothferry Park since Adam Pearson had taken over, felt like the ushering in of a new era. More than 7,500 fans watched as Andy Holt made his debut.

Andy Holt: The first game I played was Exeter at home. I'd been playing in the league above at Oldham, getting 4,000 fans or so, so naively I expected fewer than that at Boothferry Park. There was more than 7,000 there! I was thinking: 'This is incredible.' I hadn't realised the enormity of the club and the fan base. It was brilliant. We won and I thought: 'I'm really looking forward to playing here.'

City beat Exeter 2-1 thanks to an own goal and a Rodney Rowe penalty, and retained their grip on the final play-off spot. This was followed by a 3-2 win at home to Rochdale, with goals coming from Gary Brabin, Mike Edwards and Rodney Rowe. The table looked good and the spirit in the squad reflected that.

1. **Chesterfield P38 W23 D12 L3 Pts81**
2. **Cardiff P37 W20 D11 L6 Pts71**
3. **Brighton P36 W22 D5 L9 Pts71**
4. **Hartlepool P39 W18 D13 L8 Pts67**
5. **Orient P38 W16 D12 L10 Pts60**
6. **Blackpool P38 W18 D5 L15 Pts59**
7. **Hull City P38 W15 D13 L10 Pts58**

Adam Pearson: We had a fantastic spirit, with people like Jon Whitney, Gary Brabin, Kevin Francis and Lee Philpott, who were all extremely good characters and had come together as a group, kept the team up and then were moving up and putting together quite a run for a team that was travelling in a cobbled-together bus and had no training facilities and six practice balls. It was quite a scary situation – like walking into the worst-funded village team – but they had a marked spirit and determination that was going to take them places. Brian Little was clever in that he allowed that spirit and those strong personalities within the team to move it forward.

Andy Holt: I got on really well with Kevin Francis. We were staying in the same hotel and we had a lot in common, as I was from Stockport and he'd played there for so long. Gary Brabin was an absolute monster of a guy in size, but such a lovely lad. Other people would often tell you stories about Brabs, and you'd definitely believe them. You had Jon Whitney in there, who was a big character. But what I loved about the club was the way the big characters – who you were delighted to have on your team – would help the youngsters like me out.

Justin Whittle: We still had a few lads about from the Great Escape so we still had that terrific, hard-working attitude, as well as some good players added later. We shouldn't have been thinking of making the play-offs, but we stuck together.

Andy Holt: We'd go into the changing room and the big characters would be shouting and geeing us up, but as soon as Brian Little came in nobody said a word. He just had this instant respect. It was impressive. He'd never shout or raise his voice. If we were drawing a game 0-0 that we should have been winning, he'd come in at half-time and say: "Lads, don't be embarrassed about it being 0-0," and everyone would just instantly feel calmer. He had an amazing way of controlling a dressing room without really doing anything. I've not seen that many times in football.

Off the pitch, a more significant development was moving along. The much talked about 'super stadium' was gaining traction, thanks in no small part to Hull City now having an owner who was both trustworthy and ambitious.

Tom McVie: I'm certain that Adam Pearson would not have come here had it not been for the plans around the stadium. Getting together with such a partner – who was clearly up for the job and wanted the best for the club and the city – just made it so much easier. He signed a commitment to Hull City using the stadium and that made it much easier. It's okay building a stadium but if you haven't got any clubs wanting to use it then you're snookered! I can't speak highly enough of Adam Pearson.

Paddy Doyle was clear, as were the rest of us, about getting it built. Lots of people were telling us it would be a white elephant but it never has been and it's not cost the council a penny since it was built.

John Cooper: I knew long before Adam came in that the council wanted to build a stadium. I was involved with various meetings about a prospective super stadium, particularly under Hinchliffe and Buchanan. The problem was that the council didn't trust the club's owners at that time. But the council were adamant in their hope that the right person or people would come in to run the stadium.

Meanwhile, Adam Pearson was putting together a backroom team that matched his ambition, though at that point the backdrop still had something of a basic feel to it.

Brendon Smurthwaite: Adam had taken over in the March of 2001 and I joined not long after. Rob Smith got me in to work on the website. We were still at Boothferry Park working in the broom cupboard, on dial-up connections. Adam was outside in a Portakabin. It was hardly glamorous. There was no real media person at the club at that point. I used to look after the press box on a match day, and those steps up to the press box at Boothferry Park were terrifying.

A draw away at Torquay, in which Andy Holt scored his first goal for the club, was followed by a home derby against Scunthorpe. More than 10,000 packed into a crumbling Boothferry Park to witness a classic 2-1 win for City, with both goals being memorable for very different reasons. On 28 minutes, Jon Whitney scored from a corner. The goal was unremarkable, the celebration wasn't, as the uncompromising full-back simply glowered at the away fans.

Jon Whitney: I just knew that if I peeled around the back off a corner, I'd have a chance. We'd worked on it in training. It worked out really well and I got the header and scored. For the celebration, I didn't go too close to the Scunthorpe fans, but I did just enough to incite them, so you couldn't really put any charges my way over it. But you could see in my face that I really enjoyed that so much. I did think about running into them, but then I figured that that was just asking for trouble. I played it safe! But of course I want to wind the away fans up – that's football, and they give you enough stick so I just gave some back. Opposition fans generally weren't very keen on me, and that was a good thing as I saw it.

Scunthorpe equalised just before half-time with a terrific free-kick from an annoyingly good left back called Andy Dawson. Remember that name. Speaking of left-backs scoring terrific free-kicks...

Andy Holt: It felt like a real derby. I'd not played in anything as intense as that. I remember the goal and game really clearly. I'd been practising free-kicks in training, and we were awarded one that seemed very inviting. I was stood over the ball with John Eyre and told him I fancied it, and managed to bend the ball around the wall with pace. When it went in I was just shouting and screaming, running somewhere – I don't know where – then everyone jumping on top of me. Within a few games of me playing I just felt part of this amazing team spirit. Everyone was running through brick walls for each other. I loved it.

As City were closing the game out, Scunthorpe were inexplicably awarded a penalty by inexperienced referee Mark Clattenburg. Happily, Lee Hodges hit the post and a memorable victory was secured. City moved up to sixth.

The week after, on Easter Saturday, City went to Hartlepool – the scene of many a dispiriting defeat for the Tigers – and won 1-0 thanks to a John Eyre goal. On Easter Monday, City drew disappointingly with York – with Rob Matthews having a goal ruled out as the referee blew the half-time whistle just as his volley was about to cross the line. No matter, not much could shake this Hull City side. An away match at Darlington then brought a 2-0 win through an own goal and another from John Eyre.

1. **Chesterfield P43 W24 D14 L5 Pts86**
2. **Brighton P42 W26 D7 L9 Pts85**
3. **Cardiff P43 W22 D13 L8 Pts79**
4. **Hartlepool P44 W19 D14 L11 Pts71**
5. **Orient P44 W19 D14 L11 Pts71**
6. **Hull City P43 W18 D15 L10 Pts69**
7. **Scunthorpe P44 W18 D11 L15 Pts65**

In sixth, but within striking distance of the teams in fourth and fifth due to the game in hand. However, the table doesn't tell the full story. Chesterfield had been top of the league for the entire season, but had been charged with nine breaches of league rules, mostly based around the acquisition of players and the manner in which they were paid. On April 12th, the Football League had announced a nine-point penalty when most had been expecting something far more severe, including an automatic relegation. An appeal had been lodged – by the Football League's own hierarchy – due to the leniency of the punishment. Should the Chesterfield point deduction be increased, then fourth would effectively become third. City were potentially playing for automatic promotion. As fate would have it, the next visitors to Boothferry Park were Chesterfield.

Andy Holt: I was surprised in some ways at the confidence of the lads – maybe because of what they'd been through – in that they felt they had nothing to fear. And the Chesterfield game just showed that. It seemed very comfortable. In our own minds we felt like we were expected to win every game.

City fans were baying for blood given that they – rightly – suspected Chesterfield were going to get away with cheating their way to promotion. Brown paper envelopes were waved at Spireites players as the home fans at Boothferry Park whipped up a febrile atmosphere. When Mike Edwards scored after five minutes the volume went up to 11.

Mike Edwards: We knew they had a possibility of an extended points deduction. We knew if we could beat them we'd stand a chance of catching them. It was a great crowd. With us having Big Kev, it was great. I scored a few goals round then just gambling off him as he'd take out a couple of defenders and get a knock down or I could just nip in front. But that goal was one of my better goals as I took a couple of touches before I tapped it in.

Ian Breckin equalised on 16 minutes, but six minutes later 'Big Kev' intervened to cement a lasting place in Hull City fans' affections.

Kevin Francis: It felt like a high-pressure game but for no apparent reason. It was like we had to prove something against a side who were also in the hunt for promotion. We had a great start to the game with an early goal. We seemed to ease off and gave them the opportunity to equalise. Yours truly scored a textbook header after some fantastic service from Rob Matthews, and the atmosphere felt electric.

A tense match ensued with Ryan Williams on the visitors' right wing causing all sorts of problems. Then, in the 79th minute, Rodney Rowe won a penalty after being pulled back on the edge of the box. He'd already scored three penalties in his short time at Hull City. Actually, make that four.

Rodney Rowe: I'd taken penalties at York. I was always confident I'd score them. I knew the game was massive but I also knew I'd score. It was at the right end too and that felt really good.

Mark Greaves: People always tell me how brilliant Ryan Williams was in that game, yet we won 3-1! He did alright but we battered them! We had chance after chance. We felt we could go up automatically at that point, as we were waiting and hoping for a bigger points deduction for Chesterfield. We were on the crest of a wave. Maybe we'd peaked too early though.

Paul Musselwhite: In the build up Chesterfield were rumoured to be losing a certain number of points. We were in a position to go straight up if we beat them and they had a few more points deducted. It was a massive game. They'd been top most of the season and beat us 1-0 in one of my first games. But we hammered them. When we came off afterwards all we could think about was what their points deduction was going to be.

James Richardson: Basking in the sunshine on the Bunkers terrace as City swatted aside the skullduggerous Spireites. Kempton waving brown envelopes at any Chesterfield player that dared come near provided some pantomime to a soap opera season that'd looked like it was heading toward the happiest of endings, and this was my personal peak. I adored Kevin Francis and his goal in that game was awesome.

City were up to fifth and all eyes were on the Football League ruling.

1. **Brighton P43 W27 D7 L9 Pts88**
2. **Chesterfield P44 W24 D14 L5 Pts86**
3. **Cardiff P45 W23 D13 L9 Pts82**
4. **Hartlepool P45 W20 D14 L11 Pts74**
5. **Hull City P44 W19 D15 L10 Pts72**

On May 1st, just before City played a midweek match at Southend, it was announced that Chesterfield's initial 'punishment' of a nine-point deduction would stand. This would put them on 75 points and therefore unlikely to be caught by City. This was confirmed when City drew 1-1 at Roots Hall.

Mike Edwards: We went into the Southend game knowing we had to win, and they scored from a freak goal that was a mishit cross. But then I scored again, which got us the point and guaranteed the play-offs, though I didn't fully realise that at the time. I was gutted as I knew if we'd won we'd have had a chance of automatic promotion. When I look back now, though,

I don't think we were fully set for going up. I don't know if the foundations were fully there. I don't think we'd have kicked on.

A much-changed City side drew the final game of the season 0-0 at Carlisle, which resulted in a sixth-place finish and a play-off semi-final against Leyton Orient.

Jon Whitney: Play-offs are great but you'd much rather do it automatically. First, you get your summer earlier, and two, you can plan earlier. There's less risk too. We knew we were a match for anybody and we really believed that we could go up automatically.

Rodney Rowe: The play-offs just became a reality for us. The belief just continued through every game. We weren't a bad side. We could compete with anyone. No opponent worried us. We felt other teams should fear us.

City played the first leg at home. Some 13,310 packed into Boothferry Park for one of the last great occasions at the old ground. A tight game needed something special to break the deadlock. On 64 minutes John Eyre was brought on as a substitute; on 67 minutes he provided that something special.

John Eyre: I was really disappointed not to start the game. I'd played in the games leading up to it, but I'd had a back problem earlier in the week in training, though I'd still trained. Brian decided to keep me on the bench, however. Maybe it was a tactic of his to get me revved up. I came on in the 60th minute, and not long after I think a corner came out to me on the edge of the box. I remember one of their players tried to close me down, I just cut inside and hit it. I struck it very well and then what a great feeling to see it go in the corner. I just ran off and celebrated. I think I scored 98 goals in my career but that goal was the biggest buzz of all of them. It was amazing. I just ran to the Kempton and everyone was spilling on to the pitch. And I'd proved my point that I should have started.

Despite exerting most of the pressure, City couldn't find the killer second and would travel to Brisbane Road with a 1-0 advantage.

Brian Little: We should have won the game by more. That's my over-riding feeling. We should have won by two or three goals to nil. We played really well and were a little bit unlucky. The fact that they were still in the tie in the second leg gave them the upper hand in some respects. I've been in a few play-offs and if you're the away team in the first leg, you need to get to the second leg thinking you've got a good chance. I went home after the game feeling disappointed – not defeatist – I just knew we needed another one. They were still in the game.

Mark Greaves: We had so much pressure in that game. I hit the bar late on, and if we'd have gone 2-0 up, I just didn't see Leyton Orient beating us by three at their place. We could have shut up shop and held them out quite comfortably. But 1-0 left us vulnerable.

Andy Holt: We just expected to win. And we won. We felt we were on a roll. There was such an air of confidence in the team. I hadn't experienced a defeat with Hull City yet. It just felt like our year. It felt like a natural thing to just go on and win promotion.

Kevin Francis: I remember it being a packed house and the crowd was very vocal and passionate. We could feel it on the pitch and it gave us the motivation to bring home a well-deserved victory.

Justin Whittle: It was a brilliant atmosphere but it was going to be tough in the second leg.

Paul Musselwhite: That game was fantastic. I'd played at Boothferry Park when it had been pretty full for other teams, but people had said that when it was really full the atmosphere was fantastic, and that was the case that day. We played really well and won 1-0. We thought we'd set ourselves up to get through to the final.

The win was welcomed, but an injury to Ian Goodison – who'd formed an almost impenetrable partnership at centre-back with Justin Whittle – was a big cause for concern.

Ian Farrow: There is a conspiracy theory to suggest that Orient deliberately targeted Ian Goodison to get him injured for the second leg so they wouldn't have to try to get past the Jamaican Bobby Moore. Losing Goodison alongside Whittle also negated the fluidity of a team and our formation.

Mark Greaves: Ian Goodison getting injured didn't help. In the second leg I had to go to centre-back – I'd played in midfield in the home leg – and that affected us as we lost Ian's strength in defence, and my energy in midfield. Away from home that might have served us better.

Ian Goodison's injury wasn't the only concern in the camp.

Gary Brabin: Brian got us back in training every day and it really took a toll. In the Orient away game I was sat in a hotel and you could see the lads were shattered. I remember sitting with an experienced player like Mark Atkins, and looking at him and saying: "You look fucked." He said: "I am." I was never the kind of player who wanted to admit it but I remember thinking: 'I'm fucked too.' You could just see that we'd hit a brick wall. I think it was going from one training session a week to every day. We'd been so confident going into the play-offs but the week before them you could see we were drained. If we'd kept on going as we'd been – maybe if Adam hadn't paid us for another month or so – we'd have gone up.

Regardless, City were one game away from a play-off final, something the club hadn't been anywhere near since their introduction in the 1980s. Even though the final would be played at Cardiff's Millennium Stadium – as part of the first batch of games being played there while Wembley was being rebuilt – the excitement levels were high.

Gary Clark: A very unlikely appearance in a play-off final beckoned. Could we do it? Midweek in London, late spring, perfect for football and City fans turned up in their thousands. We were everywhere, drinking on the high street outside pubs, stopping the rush-hour traffic and even playing football in the street. I saw my first City smoke bomb/flare that day, a sure sign that we had arrived, we were now nearly big time. I never saw an Orient fan until we neared the turnstiles and a little gang of them were rushing around frantically ringing up mates screeching down mobiles: "There's facking thousands of 'em." I loved it.

Brian Little: I felt we could do something, but we just needed that other goal. The semi-finals of the play-offs are the hardest games you can play in. Both sides are hugely motivated.

City were dealt a blow in a tight first half when Andy Holt – an inspirational form since signing – was the victim of a cynical foul.

Andy Holt: I was playing against a full-back called Matt Joseph and felt like I'd done well against him in the first leg. Then in the first half he mullered me, two-footing me on the ankle. In today's game it would have been a red card. I knew straight away my ankle had gone. After the game I was on crutches.

Gary Clark: Orient did a job on us and quickly knobbled Andy Holt, who did everything for us in those days – long thrown-ins, free kicks, corners, the lot. No Holt, no chance.

Just as City were eyeing getting into half-time on level terms, disaster struck.

Justin Whittle: We'd been doing so well, approaching half-time holding them out. Just before half-time we broke away and Big Kev stood on the ball and it went to Matty Lockwood. He had a left foot like a wand, their centre-forward got in between me and Greavsy and it's 1-0 at half-time. This came after Andy Holt had had to go off. We were at bare bones as it was.

Steve Watts' goal had been a hammer blow. And City never really got going in the second half. In left-back Matty Lockwood, Orient had probably the best player in the league. His class was to prove decisive.

Paul Musselwhite: In the second half we got peppered a bit, and then Matty Lockwood – who was well known for having the most powerful shot in the lower divisions – picked one up from about 30 yards and smashed it straight into the top corner. In my career it's one of the best goals I've let in.

Justin Whittle: That second half, with us going up the slope, was terrible. Matty Lockwood's goal deflated us. We'd tried so hard but we ran out of steam a little bit. We should never have made the play-offs all things considered but it would have been nice to get to the final.

Mark Greaves: In the second half it was like the Alamo. It was defend, defend, defend. But to score from that distance past a keeper of the quality of Paul Musselwhite – as Matt Lockwood did – was some achievement. It just wasn't to be.

Rodney Rowe: In the first leg I did okay but Johnny Eyre did really well when he came on and it was right of the manager to start with him, but I was fuming. During the game, I just thought we should have done better. The fans were angry and rightly so. When I came on I was running around like a crazed man. We had to get in the final.

Jon Whitney: I thought we'd done enough to go there and make it difficult but it wasn't to be. They got momentum after their equaliser and then a wonder strike like that… there's not much you can do about it. It was a disappointing finish.

An away goal to take the match into extra time never really looked like coming, even after Orient had Watts sent off on 85 minutes. A season that had at times defied belief was to end in crushing disappointment.

Rodney Rowe: I remember the fans' faces. It hurt. I was like that myself. It took me weeks and weeks to get over that result. I was furious. A few fans had a go at a few of the players when we stopped off on the way back, and I could really understand that, because the performance was a shambles by all of us. We'd let them down. We hadn't played to anything like the best of our ability. It was horrible. The manager spoke on the coach, but I couldn't take any of it in. I was so upset.

Paul Musselwhite: It was disappointing as we hadn't done ourselves justice on the night when you think of how we'd done in the second half of the season.

Adam Pearson: After the home leg we thought we were going to go up, but we never turned up at all at Orient. The night was like an old-fashioned football night marred by hooliganism in the east end of London, very rough. It was a real eye-opener for me.

Andy Holt: It was always going to be tough at 1-0 after the first leg. At the end of the game it was just surreal. But the gaffer was as cool as ever. He told us how we'd had a fantastic season, we should go away and come back and start the next season on the front foot. It was a great season, it just didn't end well. A lot of people were saying it was too soon to get promoted, but I don't agree with that. We were ready. We were a massive club.

John Eyre: They had some very good players, and were similar to us in that they didn't concede many goals but had a little spark that could create things at the other end. It was always going to be tight. Once they got the goal, home advantage just did it for them. But we didn't perform on the night. We'd come from nowhere but we had one of those evenings where things just didn't work out, even though we gave it our all. Very disappointing. From one extreme the week before, to what was one of my worst times in football.

Mark Greaves: On the coach journey home I was gutted. It took me a long time to get over it. That was a sour summer for me.

Kevin Francis: A bad day at the office...

The coming summer was to see a huge overhaul of the squad, but one player whose exit was swiftly confirmed was long-serving goalkeeper Steve Wilson, who had been out on loan at Macclesfield and was to make the move permanent.

Steve Wilson: Brian didn't really speak to me. I was a bit disappointed with the way I was handled after spending 11 years there. I didn't get a testimonial even though I asked for one. No one told me to my face that I was being released, I just got a letter through the post. We had our first annual dinner after getting in the play-offs, where I thought they might give me a little farewell after the time I was there. So I was disappointed. Though Brian did then sign me when he was at Tranmere! He had also signed Muzzy at City, who was a terrific keeper.

I look back on my time at Hull with great pride. The average life span of a professional footballer in the lower leagues is perhaps two or three years. So to have 11 years at your home-town club is a great source of pride. That taught me all about the game, about organisation, about respect for people, about performing in front of big crowds. I have a lot of fond memories about drinking on the bus, the bingo we'd play, the quizzes we'd do.

Mike Scott: Emphatically Bransholme's number one, Steve Wilson was a locally born goalkeeper that dedicated himself to the Tigers for the whole of the 1990s, playing his final half-season in 2000 before a move to Macclesfield. An athletic shot stopper and an agile blocker of advancing strikers, Wilson clearly had a decent skillset. But he wasn't the tallest, was among the slightest and was sometimes nervous and error-prone. He was loved unconditionally by City fans, even after he left the club. But we needed better in the 2000s and we got better.

In Adam Pearson, Hull City had an ambitious and, by the division's standards, wealthy owner. The club had a big name manager in Brian Little. After the disappointment had died down, all eyes turned to the coming season. Surely Hull City couldn't fail this time.

2001/02 season

It had been the summer of long knives. Players that had been integral to the club's success a few weeks previous were told they were not wanted, and contracts were paid up. Brian Little was given a transfer budget beyond the wildest dreams of most lower league managers. He went on a spending spree that was to bring in a whole new team and then some. But was it too much, too soon?

Adam Pearson: I came in and saw us get to the play-offs and I slightly underestimated the spirit and the work ethic that was in the team. And by giving Brian all the money I gave him that summer to buy a new team, we lost a lot of that spirit. Brabin, Whitney, Eyre – all those guys had a great work ethic, determination, aggression and we should have kept them as they're exactly when you need in League 2, and we replaced them with possibly technically better footballers, but footballers who didn't have that determination, and ultimately that cost Brian his job because in the recruitment that we did – although it produced some good players – we made a lot of mistakes. We never replaced Brabs in midfield or someone like Jon Whitney at left-back and eventually that cost us and we had to start again, eventually, under Peter Taylor.

Brian Little: Ryan Williams had played terrifically well against us. I'd seen David Beresford play well. I'd been thinking: 'We're going to be a different team next year. We're going to be that team that goes out to win games rather than being a hard side to beat.' I tried to change the whole dimension of the team again. Whether that was wrong or not – well I didn't keep my job so it obviously was wrong. I wanted to change the dynamics of the team. It's easy after the event though. I thought the two wingers would open teams up. It was a new way to play. We were quicker, younger, more mobile.

There was a platform put down there by some but you have to move on from that, and you're not going to get everything right as a manager. Nicky Mohan and Ben Petty had both played for me before. I was looking to progress, but with Adam he wanted everything yesterday! There was an urgency coming from the top and perhaps I got sucked into it. I don't regret what we did though.

Justin Whittle: It felt like too much. I was thinking: 'Am I going to be next out?' I've always thought: 'Bring in who you want, and if I have to work harder to stay in the team then so be it.' If you think that the players coming in are better than you then you might as well just leave anyway. Players are always going to try to replace you but if you're performing well you stay in the team.

Andy Holt: It was like we'd won the lottery and gone crazy. When they saw how much money we were spending a lot of agents would have been straight on the phone trying to get their lads to Hull. More of the characters could have stayed on though. Lads like Gary Brabin and Jon Whitney didn't give a crap about the money. They'd go out and run through a brick wall for you regardless.

Paul Musselwhite: Though I understand that Adam Pearson came in with ambitious goals, I felt that on the back of what that squad had achieved in that second half of the season there were way too many changes to the squad. The squad was already a very good squad for that division. We maybe needed four or five players added to what we had. But the chairman and Brian took a long-term view, and the players they brought in were mostly younger. We needed goalscorers at the time but the situation we found ourselves in was quite strange.

Mark Greaves: I was surprised by all the moves. I think Brian would even admit now that he let a few diamonds go and signed one or two lads who didn't produce. He signed some great players like Gary Alexander and Lawrie Dudfield, who did fantastically in that first season. But we signed too many. We'd kept 20-something clean sheets the season before. There was no need to change it that much. Nicky Mohan was a fantastic player but we didn't need any more centre-halves. We had a squad of 25 or 26 which was like a Premier League squad but that creates a lot of unhappiness as only 11 can start on a Saturday. No one there was there to be a squad player.

Rodney Rowe: You have to move on. You were never sure who might be coming in but you knew it was going to be a battle. It kept you on your toes. If it was better for the team you just had to accept it. The club had to move forward, though a lot of people were disappointed.

Rob Smith: I got married that summer. I went away on honeymoon and came back to a completely new team. It was then when I realised we had serious money to spend. I was thinking: 'This is going to be the best time ever.'

These changes saw 11 players head out of the club and 13 arrive. The departures – or players who were told they were free to leave – included some predictable names. Jason Harris, Lee Bracey, Steve Swales, Jason Perry and Jamie Wood hadn't featured prominently in the first team for quite some time, while Steve Wilson's exit was merely rubber-stamped. The other five players, however, were popular figures within the squad and with fans. Gary Brabin, John Eyre, David Brown and Jon Whitney were all shown the door, while Kevin Francis was told that his contract was not to be renewed.

There is a school of thought that says Gary Brabin is the most important player in Hull City's history. The players who were behind the Great Escape will generally point to Brabin as the rock around which that incredible achievement was built. Brabs' refusal to accept defeat, his drive and his ability to scare the opposition were all integral to Hull City avoiding what had looked to be an inevitable drop into non-league football. And what might have become of the club then? While his form had wavered slightly the season after the Great Escape, when the chips were down – when the club was seemingly on the brink of extinction – Brabs was back in his element. The play-off run had Gary Brabin at its heart, and he remained a big fan favourite. Except now he was told he was surplus to requirements.

Gary Brabin: I was gutted. I was devastated. I like and respect Adam Pearson and I like Brian Little, but at that time I didn't. I wanted Adam to understand what I'd given up to be at Hull, what the club had meant to me. I think he was being sincere when he said he didn't want me to go but the manager wanted it. I didn't want to go. I remember going into the car park after and feeling that my heart had been ripped out. I had a couple of options but I didn't want to sign for another club. I just wasn't ready to commit to another club when I felt the way I did about Hull City. It took me a few weeks to recover and it was a few months before I could play for anyone else. I'd committed to a three-year contract at this club but everything changed so quickly. A lot of other players were going too.

Brian Little: I've spoken to Brabs a few times since and I was convinced he was wanting to move closer to home. He insists that he wasn't. I was convinced he'd told me a club near his home wanted him but I might be wrong.

David Brown: Gary was a key player for us. Whenever you went out on that pitch he'd be brutal. I remember the Macclesfield game where it turned into an all-out scrap – Brabs would step over the line every now and then. When he went on the pitch you had a bit of extra belief because you knew that if anything kicked off in the game you had Brabs on your side and he'd sort it out. He was brilliant. And when he came in he really helped to galvanise us, as he's such a character off the pitch. He was a raving lunatic back then!

Rodney Rowe: Ability wise Gary Brabin wasn't the best, but for what he did on the pitch – letting the opposition know they couldn't get away with anything – it was amazing to have him on your side.

Jon Whitney: I'd heard a lot of stories about Brabs before I played alongside him. He was quite notorious in football. But he's one of the most genuinely nice people I've ever met. He'd do anything for you. And to sit in those changing rooms or stand in that tunnel and know you were going out there with Brabs in your team, that can't help but give you a huge lift, even for players such as myself who didn't need much to get motivated. Brabs stands out for me. I loved it when he'd take stick from the opposition fans about his weight, score a goal and stick his top over his head. When the opposition saw that sort of thing, they'd see that we didn't fear them.

Gary Brabin: I'm so proud of what we did during my time at the club. My little boy was four when I took him to Goodison Park to see Everton play Hull City in the Premier League. I know it sounds corny but I was so proud sitting in the stands. My boy loves Everton, he knows all about them and knows I support them, but I was also telling him about Hull City. In fact I spoke more about Hull than I did about Everton. I was sitting there telling this little lad wearing an Everton scarf all about his dad's exploits at Hull, showing him my goals on YouTube back when I had hair. He was probably bored stupid, but I was just so, so proud of my role at the club. I was so proud when the club went on to have so much success.

Justin Whittle ended up staying for years and I would have loved to have had that. But he was so whole-hearted. My strength was my weakness. I was a strong character that the club needed when it was at rock bottom, but then when new people come in they can fear those strong characters. Brian Little would admit perhaps that I was too strong a personality for what he liked to work with, even though we get on really well now. Though I tell him that he broke my heart. But I'm not bitter. Just proud.

Local lad John Eyre had been unlucky with injuries during his time at Hull City, but had still been a fan favourite and had also weighed in with some important goals, none more so than his winner in the first leg of the play-offs against Orient. His departure was difficult to take on many levels.

John Eyre: Adam pulled me in the day after the play-off semi-final. I was thinking that, having had a strong season and having scored in the play-offs, he was going to offer me a new contract. I had a year left on what I had. But he just said to me that Brian didn't see me as part of his plans. Adam told me that he didn't see the reason behind it but he had to back his manager. He gave me an offer to pay up my contract, and he told me I was free to find someone else. I was flabbergasted. I felt my injuries were behind me, I felt strong and really ready to go into a new season firing. I was devastated. They offered contracts to Neil Mann and Mark Greaves at that time, and I just couldn't understand why I was having to leave.

It took me a few weeks to get my head around it. I spoke to my wife at the time, and I said: "They can't force me out, I've got a year left, I don't want to leave so I'm going to stick it out." I intended to go into pre-season and prove to them that I should be playing. It had turned out they'd done it to a few players, however. At the time it looked like an attempt to get rid of the voices in the dressing room, those who were maybe a little opinionated, the strong characters. I wasn't a disruption in any way, but I felt like Brian wanted players he could control better.

I went back pre-season and I was flying. Brian kept bringing in these new players and I was looking at them thinking: 'I'm better than these, I can get back in this team.' After about two or three weeks, Brian pulled me in and said: "Andy Ritchie at Oldham has been on to me. They want you." Brian told me that if I didn't go he wasn't going to play me, no matter what. I'd spent four years at Oldham alongside Andy, and my old youth team coach there was now the assistant manager. They were the only team I'd have left Hull for.

I went down to Oldham and made it as hard as possible for them to sign me. I told them I needed a load of scans, my back was bad, and so on, but they wanted to do the deal. It wasn't about money, but they offered me more than I was on and they were in a higher division. I just turned round and said to the people close to me: "I don't want to, but I'm going to have to just go and do it." But for my first six months at Oldham I wasn't the same player I had been because I was still so disappointed that I'd had to move. I was just gutted. I could see what was happening. I really liked Adam and would have liked to work with him. You could see the new stadium was going to happen. What I should have done was stick it out. Oldham played Hull in the FA Cup and we were one of the first teams to beat them at Boothferry Park that season. I played okay, and after that things seemed to go downhill for Hull.

I look back and I think: 'He didn't need to do it that way.' Maybe we did need a David Beresford or Gary Alexander to add quality to the squad, but it didn't need overhauling like that. I felt for him to get rid of me and the others then was a crazy decision. Those two years for Hull were the most enjoyable in my career. You can't beat playing for your home-town club and it was taken away from me. I wish I'd stuck around and made it hard for Brian not to play me.

David Brown was another hero of the Great Escape – his goal against Torquay sealed City's survival – who was told his time at the club was up.

David Brown: At the time Brian seemed to want to go in a few different directions. Some of the more aggressive players that had kept us in the league were being phased out. I was still quite young at the time and I was happy to stay at Hull, but at that particular time there were changes going on. Looking back at it now it was quite sad in the way it ended. I'd gone three seasons playing regularly with a half-decent scoring record in a team that wasn't particularly attacking. I was optimistic about the future. My agent had spoken to Brian Little, as I had, because I had one year left on my contract. I was ready to commit to longer and Brian seemed happy with that. He told me to speak to the chairman, and my agent went to Adam Pearson and he was told that the club was going to pay me up. That side of it was sad. I felt I was an integral part of that era of the club's history.

Then I had to go back at pre-season training. Brian had signed a lot of players, paid a lot of money, and I had to train on my own. I didn't really think it was fair, and I spoke to Brian about it, asking what was going on. He told me that the chairman had told him I'd asked to leave, so I told him that that wasn't true and that there'd been some mixed messages somewhere over that summer. But then he'd already signed a number of players in my position. I felt at that point that I had no choice but to negotiate my way out of Hull. I didn't think there was a place for me there, and a few other players were in the same boat.

When I reflect on my career, I look back at my time at Hull with a bit of pride. The club were six points adrift at the bottom that Great Escape season, so to turn that around and save the club was amazing. You look at Hull and Scarborough, and what's happened since… you've never seen Scarborough. When clubs go into that Conference it can take years to get out. Some, like Scarborough, go under. You never know what would have happened to Hull City if we'd gone down that season. So I look at the Great Escape as a great achievement. That allowed the club to build from that point onwards. I loved it up there, loved playing for Hull City, and I'd have committed for a lot longer, but football's football.

Mike Hall (Hull City fan): When City signed strikers David Brown and Jamie Wood on loan from Manchester United in 1998, it was Brown who garnered the most intrigue, largely because he'd been signed by Manchester United in controversial circumstances while at Oldham. But how good was he? Pretty good, it turned out. While he maybe never quite reached his full potential, he brought an intelligence and movement to our forward play that was eventually rewarded with a full-time contract. He was never wildly prolific, but goals against Chelsea and Liverpool in cup competitions in his first season with the club perhaps hinted at the player Manchester United thought they'd signed. He made more than 100 appearances for City before leaving in 2001, and was a largely effective, intelligent player, whose presence in those fallow years hinted at brighter times to come.

Few players have gained cult status as rapidly in Hull City's history as Kevin Francis did. His popularity in the city endures to this day, but he had sadly played the last of his 22 games in the black and amber.

Kevin Francis: I was dismayed. I received emails from the Tiger-chat email group thanking me for what I'd done for the club and I still have them. My wife and I have looked at them many times over the years and they bring back many happy memories.

As a player you hope to make your name at one club, and if you are lucky you get to play for good managers, clubs and fans. I have been fortunate to do this for Danny Bergara at Stockport and Barry Fry at Birmingham. However, Hull and Brian Little was a place I felt could have been my home earlier in my career. Brian was a manager that I respected and enjoyed playing for. My time at Hull was a great chapter in my career and the experience was capped by being named in Hull City's Top 100 Players of the Century… Fucking awesome!

On my car keys I still proudly display my Hull City key ring that was gifted to me at the ceremony to celebrate being named in the Top 100 players. We also had my Hull City shirt framed and it hangs proudly on the wall in my home.

Paul Musselwhite: I played against Kevin Francis a lot when I was at Port Vale and he was at Stockport. I'd always thought that Kev was just a big unit who'd only score with his head. When I played with him at Hull I realised that he was an excellent team player. And I was much happier to have him on my side than be playing against him! A lot of teams were scared of him at that level as he didn't mind putting himself about. But the supporters loved him, and rightly so.

Jon Whitney's departure was also rued by many fans, who loved his never-say-die attitude, best encapsulated by his menacing stare at the Scunthorpe fans when celebrating his goal against the Iron.

Jon Whitney: I remember the pre-season. I was flying and was looking forward to kicking on after the previous season, so I was surprised when I was called in. It was Adam Pearson who called me in and told me that Brian didn't want to move forward with me and they wanted to pay up my contract. I didn't argue. Once that's happened and the manager's made it clear you're not in his plans, I have no problem with that. I have no problem with Brian, and I've had to do the same as a manager. In hindsight Brian will have things that he'd do differently, but he did it for the right reasons and the club were upfront with me. I have no problem with that. It's part of football. It came as a shock, it was something you didn't want, but you have to accept it and move on. I never played a professional game after that.

People talk about the 12th man, but from the first game I played in the Hull City fans were an extra man for us. It's why I still have such a fondness for the club. That sort of connection is quite rare. A lot of footballers will never have that. For me to be one of the heroes in the 'Heroes and Villains' series on Amber Nectar – my article is something I read a lot – always puts a massive smile on my face. I have it in a scrapbook!

I remember my time at Hull with a wry smile on my face. When I think about my time there I get the same feeling as I would get when I'd made a crunching tackle, got the ball and sent the winger into Row Z. There's a real feeling of accomplishment. I have so many memories that come flushing though. My heart rate starts to increase when I think about that time! Because of the people who I played with, and the fans, that chapter of my playing career is the fondest I ever had. It was an incredible achievement to get the Great Escape, and it was an achievement that goes down to a manager, a backroom staff, a group of players and a set of fans that were as one. It was a selfless kind of energy we had, and that was powerful, built on hard work and desire with a positive attitude. We refused to be beaten. I'm so proud of what Hull have achieved since.

James Richardson: In a team packed with so many players that had the perfect characteristics to be cult heroes, Jon Whitney was in the background to many, but not to me. He wasn't as fashionable or as talented as Whittle or Brabin, but his style of play; hard and delivered with an extra kick for good measure. In the most affectionate way possible, it felt like he was a relic from a bygone era and was the epitome of the unflinching, never-say-die attitude exhibited by the Great Escape squad. His spectacular moments were few but memorable. The Hot Shot Hamish-esque strike that nearly uprooted the goal at Peterborough and his cold, dead-eyed celebration in front of the North Stand after netting in the Humber derby was enough to moisten the underwear of the entire Scunthorpe support with fear. What a man!

In total, 13 players signed for Hull City that summer. They were goalkeeper Matt Glennon, defenders Ben Petty, Matt Bloomer, Nicky Mohan and Michael Price (with Andy Holt having his loan move made permanent), midfielders David Lee, Ryan Williams, David Beresford, Scott Kerr and Julian Johnsson, and forwards Gary Alexander and Lawrie Dudfield. The latter arrived for £250,000, breaking a club record that had stood since 1989 when Peter Swan signed from Leeds United for £200,000.

Lawrie Dudfield: I'm a bit of a football geek but I knew nothing about Hull City. It was a leap into the unknown. I'd been on holiday for a week and I got a phone call from Leicester asking where I'd been because Hull City had bid £250,000 for me. I thought they were joking, but they told me it was a club record. I wanted to play first-team football and not go back to the loans I'd been doing, so once I knew about the bid I couldn't wait to get up there and sign. Before this I'd wanted to sign for Chesterfield because they'd just been promoted and I'd enjoyed a spell on loan there. But once Hull City came in for me and I met Adam Pearson and Brian Little, and saw their vision, it was a no-brainer. Brian had the wow factor and was a lovely guy, whereas Adam had an unbelievable vision of where he wanted the club to go – which he more than achieved. Adam was a doer, and was outstanding to me in every way from the first moment I met him. Everything he promised he delivered on.

The fee didn't bother me. In fact I liked it. It never went to my head – my family would never have let that happen – and I saw it as an honour and a privilege. Initially I thrived on that.

Dave Burns: Lawrie Dudfield cost me my TV career. He was the record signing and the BBC were trying to get us to do TV as well as radio. When Lawrie signed I was shooting loads of stuff on a camera, and Lawrie was doing everything we'd asked. I thought I had some good stuff, but when I went back to the office I found out that I'd put a cleaning tape in the camera so there was nothing there. I felt so sorry for Lawrie as I'd wasted so much of his time.

That wasn't the only element of Lawrie's first day on the job that was to prove mildly traumatic. The club photographer wanted to get an image to mark the transfer record being shattered in such a way.

Lawrie Dudfield: I'm a normal, down-to-earth guy, but the photographer wanted me to lay on the pitch in an over-sized Hull City shirt like a male model among a dozen or so footballs that were arranged to make a pound sign. It was the most unnatural looking photograph you'll ever see, and it still gets dragged out on Twitter from time to time. Signing for Hull City was such an amazing experience, and that's all I've got to remember it by!

Joining Lawrie up front to form a forward line that had fans salivating was Gary Alexander, who arrived from Swindon Town for a six-figure sum.

Gary Alexander: From what I could make out Swindon were in financial trouble and hadn't paid a bill to West Ham from when they signed me. Hull City made a bid to cover that money plus a little bit more. I hadn't been at Swindon long and hadn't had the best of times there but I'd been keen to stay there and rectify that. I had good people around me who told me what was happening about Hull and I liked what I heard. All the people being linked with the club were decent young players and I wanted to be a part of that and take on that challenge.

The plan was for Lawrie and Gary to be supplied by right winger Ryan Williams – who'd signed from Chesterfield for £150,000 after impressing in the game at Boothferry Park a few months earlier – and David Beresford, a left winger who signed on a free transfer from Huddersfield. It was a forward line that had many naming Hull City as their favourites to gain promotion from the division. But the mood in the squad still wasn't quite right.

Lawrie Dudfield: There were 13 or so new signings coming into a squad that had done well. In hindsight I think most people would accept that only a few new signings were needed. You had massive characters on the way out. Lads like Gary Brabin, John Eyre, Jon Whitney and David Brown stayed with us but knew they were leaving and just negotiating a pay-off. But the 13 new signings had all been living in the same hotel so we'd all got to know each other, even though we didn't know the squad we were coming into.

My first experience was walking into the training ground at the university and everyone was a bit stand-offish, the dozen or so new players on one side and the five or six existing squad players on the other, and the first person to say anything was Mark Greaves – one of my best friends in football now, and a lovely guy – who had a shirt he needed signing. He got all his mates from the previous season to sign it and then threw it on a table in front of the new signings and said: "There you go lads, we might as well get the reserves to sign it as well." If you know Greavesy, you'll know he has an extremely dry sense of humour, but at the time we were thinking: 'Who is this guy? What an idiot!' It took a few weeks for us to start to bond.

After that, a few of the big characters from the previous season moved on, and everything just seemed really optimistic, largely thanks to Brian Little and Adam Pearson. That year was all about 'great expectations', and all we thought about was going up. We thought we were easily going to go up.

Once the squad took shape, the club embarked upon a decent pre-season campaign and travelled down to Exeter for the opening game of the season in good spirits. And the optimism was to prove to be well founded, with City winning 3-1. Theo Whitmore and Mark Greaves got the ball rolling before the victory was sealed by the club's new record signing.

Lawrie Dudfield: That day is one of my best memories in football. I didn't have a great pre-season and then on the opening day it just went right. In the first half I nicked the ball off a defender, ran down the line and put a cross in which I got a lot of confidence from. For my goal I remember the throw-in coming in, taking a touch and spinning to put the ball towards the bottom right-hand corner. I thought my first effort was in but the keeper saved it but then a poor clearance came straight to me and I volleyed it in.

I just remember feeling ecstatic, first because we were winning the game and I was convinced we'd go on to win it, and second, to score on your debut bodes well. It was nice to show everyone what I could do. As I walked off the pitch at the end, Kevan Smith, the assistant manager, said to me: "Fucking hell, Duds, you've been leaving stuff out of pre-season! We were wondering what we were getting and then we got that today!" Brian surrounded himself with great people like Kevan, who were funny and kept the pressure off.

Mike Edwards: We started off flying. I'd played against Ryan Williams when he was at Chesterfield so I knew his game, and in the pre-season games we'd had a great balance on that right-hand side. We lost him early in the game against Exeter and Theo Whitmore came on. Theo was a great guy and had unbelievable skill, but he wasn't an out-and-out right-winger. And we didn't really have a replacement for Ryan in the squad.

Mark Greaves: That side was huge. I think our average height in that game was about 6 foot 2, and that included Ryan Williams who was about 5 foot 4. When Ryan went off injured for Theo Whitmore every player was above six foot. Even despite that start, we didn't feel united. And you had lads like Brabs and Browny still around the club training on the periphery, even though they'd officially left. They were unhappy and us old lads felt a sense of loyalty to them. None of that helped.

The much-missed Steve 'Ozzy' Winfield takes part in the half-time penalty competition

City drew the next two games 0-0 – at home to Plymouth and away to Carlisle – before a memorable game at home to a Kidderminster side managed by Jan Molby.

Gary Alexander: I scored a header from a cross from David Beresford. They equalised, then Justin was sent off for a tackle, then we went up the other end and scored. Every time I scored at Boothferry Park it was special.

Justin Whittle: I won the ball!

Mark Greaves: I broke my leg in the game against Kidderminster. When I was being stretchered off I already knew I'd broken my leg. It was 1-1 when I got injured, and I was in such a daze I thought I was getting an amazing reception from the crowd as I was being carried off the pitch. I didn't realise we'd just scored a last-minute winner! I was thinking: 'The crowd love me,' and putting my hand up to acknowledge the reception I was getting.

This game was followed up by a comprehensive thrashing of York City. The 4-0 scoreline flattered the visitors, with Nicky Mohan, Lawrie Dudfield and Gary Alexander putting City three up before a brilliant David Lee free-kick capped a wonderful afternoon. A 0-0 draw at Macclesfield was followed by a 3-1 win at home to Rochdale in which Gary Alexander scored his fifth and sixth goals of the season, and Lawrie Dudfield his third. It was still only mid-September, but the partnership was looking hugely promising.

Gary Alexander: I knew I could score goals – even though I hadn't scored as many as I would have liked at Swindon – and Lawrie was highly rated too. It usually takes time to form a new partnership but we clicked pretty quickly and started scoring a lot of goals between us. If I didn't score Lawrie would, and if Lawrie didn't I would. We had a good understanding.

Lawrie Dudfield: There was no reason behind why we hit it off. We were mates and living together at the hotel but were total opposites in many ways. Gary was a brash-talking Londoner, quite loud, and I was quite quiet, just keeping my head down. But we didn't really work on our partnership. It was probably just that Gary was an out-and-out goalscorer whereas my game was about running the channels and hopefully adding a bit of flair. And I think Brian had seen that and wanted to link us up because of it. It was one of those dream things where it just worked.

Mark Greaves: If you'd have put a price on Lawrie's head in that first few months, it would have been a few bob. He looked fantastic.

Even some mischievous rumours on the Boothferry Park terraces regarding their personal lives and partners couldn't shake the strike duo's bond.

Gary Alexander: I've heard of the rumours about me and Lawrie Dudfield and we would always just laugh about it, wondering where it would come from. Lawrie remains a good friend to me to this day.

After beating Rochdale so soundly, Swansea were then put to the sword at Boothferry Park by two goals to one, with Lawrie Dudfield and Faroe Islands captain Julian Johnsson scoring. The league table looked as had been expected at the start of the season.

1. **Shrewsbury P9 W6 D1 L2 Pts19**
2. **Hull City P8 W5 D3 L0 Pts18**
3. **Luton Town P9 W5 D3 L1 Pts18**
4. **Darlington P9 W5 D2 L2 Pts17**
5. **Plymouth P9 W5 D2 L2 Pts17**

However, despite the decent league position, concerns about the make up of the squad were lingering. And those doubts were to be realised in a night match at Mansfield when the home side, inspired by Chris Greenacre, tore City apart in a 4-2 win that, if anything, was kind on the Tigers.

Adam Pearson: I felt we'd become soft and I felt it was my fault because we'd put all this money in and had set ourselves up as the league's Billy Bigtimes and the players didn't show enough respect to the club or to the league to get us out of there. I didn't think we were working hard enough, on the training ground or on the pitch. I remember going to Field Mill and watching a really bright, young home-grown team rip us apart and it could have been any scoreline. Then exactly the same happened at Hartlepool. I thought we'd pulled together a squad that could get results at home but didn't have that Brabin, that Whitney mentality to eke out victories away and that was a worry.

Andy Holt: There were so many new players and they didn't quite understand the expectations. That Mansfield game was a particularly horrible one. But the whole season was stop-start.

Gary Alexander: It's a tough league and while me and Lawrie had gelled we were only a unit of two so it's easier for us than it is for the units of four in the defence and the midfield. We had a lot of new players and getting that gelling all over the park is difficult.

Justin Whittle: We lacked experience. We had some great players technically but we didn't gel one bit. We had too many majors but not enough soldiers. Mansfield were a very good young team, and they were 3-0 up after a few minutes and we're wondering: 'What's going on here?' We got going eventually but it was too late. That gave us a dose of reality. We realised that we couldn't just turn up and expect to win. You had to put the effort in. We had two flying wingers in David Beresford and Ryan Williams providing for Lawrie Dudfield and Gary Alexander but it didn't happen throughout the whole of the team. We knew something wasn't right. That was to happen again at Hartlepool.

City recovered from this battering to beat Halifax 3-0 at fortress Boothferry Park, with loanee Michael Reddy scoring two and Dudfield one. An away draw at Shrewsbury – in which Gary Alexander scored yet another – kept City in second, before an emotional game loomed: Gary Brabin was coming back to Hull as captain of Torquay United.

Gary Brabin: I'd signed for Torquay on a great deal. They'd made me captain and we'd started really well, in the promotion positions, and we went to Boothferry Park to play Hull. The reception I got… I felt like a gladiator walking into an arena. The fans were fantastic. The hairs were standing up on the back of my neck – they still do when I tell the story – I just loved it. All the Torquay players were looking at me thinking: 'Fucking hell.' Torquay were a young side that I'd been brought in to galvanise. Hull were now a rich club.

It was 0-0, I'm enjoying the game and we get an injury to a key player. The manager wanted to put a young kid on and I was saying: "He's not ready, put a more experienced player on." There was 10 to 15 minutes left and this young lad is at fault for Hull City's goal. My head had gone. It had fallen off. I was running and it was a bit reckless – there was no intent to injure but I was wound up – and went in on Julian Johnsson. I flew in and was sent off. My head was still gone. And I couldn't have been sent off any further from the tunnel. And as good as I'd felt before the game because of the reception I'd got, the boos and the jeers when I was walking off the pitch – which felt like an eternity – was the lowest point of my career. I was absolutely gutted. I felt ashamed.

I had to do an interview after the game up in the stands with one of the local newspapers for Torquay, and at the bottom of the steps Brian Little had all these Sky cameras around him. I was looking round thinking: 'This club's going forward,' and I was gutted that I couldn't be part of it. I felt cheated. I felt I should have been part of it. It was that that made me go into coaching and managing. After that interview, after looking round and analysing Brian and Hull City, that was the day I realised that I wasn't going to be a Premier League footballer. I thought: 'What am I doing living away from home in Torquay?' I didn't want to be a player who just plays for the sake of playing and picks up his wages. I told the Torquay manager and chairman that I wanted to go home and play and coach football locally. They didn't want me to go, they resisted for a couple of weeks, then I was sent off again – I was so frustrated and unhappy – and in the end they agreed to let me go. I came home, signed for Chester and started to educate myself towards doing my coaching badges.

City won the game 1-0 thanks to another Michael Reddy goal. The worries of the Mansfield game seemed to have been banished as the table looked very nice indeed.

1. **Rochdale P11 W7 D2 L2 Pts23**
2. **Hull City P10 W6 D3 L1 Pts21**
3. **Luton Town P11 W6 D3 L2 Pts21**
4. **Plymouth P11 W6 D3 L2 Pts21**
5. **Shrewsbury P11 W6 D2 L3 Pts20**

After the Torquay win, City's run of decent form continued. A 3-3 draw at Rushden came after City had been 3-1 down after 26 minutes, and the equaliser saw Rodney Rowe score his first goal of the season. City drew at home to Orient and then beat Darlington at Feethams. This was followed by what was probably City's best attacking performance of the season, as Cheltenham – managed by the highly rated Steve Cotterill – were beaten 5-1 at Boothferry Park thanks to goals from Lawrie Dudfield, Gary Alexander, Theo Whitmore, David Beresford and an own goal.

Lawrie Dudfield: When we played Cheltenham and beat them 5-1, that was one of my most enjoyable games for Hull City. In that game I got the ball on the halfway line, sped down the wing and put a cross into the box from which Gary scored. Brian said to me after the game:

"Did you know Gary was in there?" and I said no, I just knew that was where he was going to be. He was a natural goalscorer and that was how it worked.

This emphatic victory left City third in the league with a game in hand over their rivals.

1. **Plymouth P17 W11 D4 L2 Pts37**
2. **Rochdale P17 W10 D4 L3 Pts34**
3. **Hull City P16 W9 D6 L1 Pts33**
4. **Luton Town P17 W3 D4 L2 Pts33**
5. **Mansfield P17 W9 D4 L4 Pts31**

In all competitions Gary Alexander had 15 goals and Lawrie Dudfield had six by the time Hull City travelled to Victoria Park, Hartlepool, to take on the side bottom of the division. But the team's frailties were about to be laid bare as they had been at Mansfield six weeks prior, with Hartlepool running out 4-0 winners.

Brian Little: I was thinking this wouldn't have happened to us before this season, as we had an unbelievable mentality.

A problem was that we had all the money but we didn't have things like the training facilities. When you've got nothing and everybody knows you've got nothing, it's a doddle. But when you're spending all this money, the players were expecting more, expecting better. That made the mentality side of things a little bit harder. We didn't have the whole package at that point, and that helped create a few stumbling blocks along the way. It was a period we had to come through. If you get a better job, you expect better things to come to you. We'd given people better jobs but we weren't giving them the full package.

I'd spoken to Adam about the poor form and we tried a few things. We tried making a training facility at the back of the ground, where we'd be on our own, but we couldn't use it for long enough, which was shortening training sessions. That was making the job harder for me. There were lots of little things getting in the way. I kept telling Adam that everything needed a bit more time.

Often you see in English football a team starting the season well but people saying: "Yes, but wait until it gets to December and January," and we were perhaps that type of team. On reflection we could maybe have done with a Kevin Francis or perhaps a Gary Brabin. When it got cold and mucky we maybe didn't have the right personnel out there. You could perhaps say: "Yes, they're a good team, but there might be a period in the season where if they lose a couple they might lose a couple more."

Lawrie Dudfield: What became obvious to us quite early was that we were struggling on the road. We were great at home, we just struggled away from Boothferry Park. We couldn't play the same expansive football as we were playing at home for some reason. And Brian realised that. But a team with the likes of Ryan Williams down one wing, David Beresford down the other and Theo Whitmore in midfield isn't going to be particularly defensive-minded. Our only defensive midfielder was Julian Johnsson, who was still finding his feet in the English game.

Even though the Hartlepool defeat was only City's second in the league – and it was now November – there was a sense of despondency around the club. And City never really got going again that season. December and January were miserable months, with the club's freescoring displays becoming less frequent, and the goals still flying in at the other end.

Mark Greaves: When I came back we played Kidderminster away, and lost 3-0. You felt that the writing was perhaps on the wall for Brian at that point.

Paul Musselwhite: We started the season well and had been top of the table or in the play-offs for most of it. The club had signed a number of assets, and in the first half of the season it went well. But when it started to go wrong we missed a few of the players that had been released. We lacked seasoned pros in League 2 at that time.

Mike Edwards: Everything seemed to be going great at first. The training side was hard. Coming up to Christmas we couldn't train on the grass at the university as it was so wet, and we ended up on Astroturf. We had 30-odd players at the time and our fitness seemed to trail away as you'd not be moving too much on Astroturf. We just seemed to dwindle away. It was frustrating as we'd been in the play-off positions.

In mid-January, after City had failed to win any of their previous six league and cup games, second-to-bottom Carlisle visited Boothferry Park. City had dropped down to sixth by this point, but would still have expected to beat the Cumbrians. However, the 1-0 Carlisle victory was inspired by a young loanee from Newcastle running the game from midfield. His name? Stuart Green.

Stuart Green: I remember that game like it was yesterday. I was always told Hull away is a fixture everyone in the lower leagues looks for. I remember it being a night game and I was thinking: 'This is somewhere I could be.' It was a great atmosphere. Hull were a massive club and I came away from that night thinking: 'I would love to play for that club.' I knew I'd be going out on loan from Newcastle again, and I wanted to do better than Carlisle. I remember sitting on the Carlisle team coach thinking: 'I want to be there next season,' and luckily for me it came true.

City recovered slightly after that defeat. Exeter, Shrewsbury and Rushden were beaten at Boothferry Park, in addition to a 1-1 draw with Hartlepool, and on the road things picked up a little. City lost at Southend and York, but won 1-0 at Halifax thanks to a Julian Johnsson goal, and gained a draw at Torquay. This left City fifth in the table, 15 points off top-of-the-table Plymouth.

1. **Plymouth P33 W21 D7 L5 Pts70**
2. **Luton Town P33 W18 D6 L9 Pts60**
3. **Mansfield P32 W18 D6 L8 Pts60**
4. **Rochdale P33 W15 D11 L7 Pts56**
5. **Hull City P34 W15 D10 L9 Pts55**

Then came a Friday night home game against 15th-placed Macclesfield. Steve Wilson – the man who Brian Little had released a year or so previous – was to keep a clean sheet for the visitors, but it was Rickie Lambert who did the damage, scoring to inflict a 1-0 defeat on a miserable City side who had Ryan Williams sent off. It was to prove too much for the club's ambitious new chairman.

Adam Pearson: It was the first time we'd come across Rickie Lambert. He scored a load against us and he was unplayable. His name kept coming up with moves to the club for many years, because technically he was such a good player. That night he battered us and I realised we were going backwards. I took the very difficult decision to let Brian go as we were just going nowhere.

Brian Little: We had a bad run prior to me leaving, but I didn't think it was bad enough for me to lose my job.

I thought we did alright in the game but we lost. What wound Adam up was that after the game – which was a Friday night – that I'd said: "I'll see you Monday morning," to the lads. I spoke to Adam on the Monday and he asked me why I didn't have them in over the weekend.

I asked him what he'd have wanted me to do, and he told me he'd have wanted me to run them into the ground. I told him that that's a bit archaic for me. I didn't see the point of it. And that was the final straw and he told me that he didn't want me there anymore. I was gutted as I was really happy there. I still think we'd have got out of it. I didn't think we'd done badly on the Friday. But basically I felt I was relieved of my duties because I hadn't had them in over the weekend. Adam had invested a lot of money, but the dynamics had changed. I didn't argue or fight, as he'd made his mind up. Still to this day I'm gutted. When I went there I was relating to having watched Hull playing in the old Division 2 and always liking the support, always thinking it was a good club to be at. And it was, even during the tough times financially. But I have nothing but fond memories of my time at Hull. Lizzie and I's first son was born in Cottingham a few days after I was sacked.

Gary Alexander: I was devastated. I got on really well with Brian. He was a cracking manager. Everything he did I enjoyed and he had some good people around him who I got on really well with. It came as a shock as we could still get in the play-offs. But obviously Adam Pearson had put a lot of money in and expected better. It's part and parcel of the game but it was gutting news for us as we had faith in what Brian was trying to achieve and I'm sure he would have got there.

Rob Smith: I wouldn't be critical of that move to sign all of those players, as everyone thought it was a good thing at the time. We all thought we were going to see exciting football played by fresh young talent. But the league we were in needed a Gary Brabin. You needed to kick your way out of that league to an extent. That may have been a bit of naivety in the club, but it was understandable naivety. And you learn from your mistakes.

Andy Holt: I'd learned that it was part and parcel of football, but Brian was a real gentleman both on and off the field. Whether it was the right thing to do, I don't know, but I hadn't put as much money into the club as Adam Pearson. If he'd seen three or four months into the future, though, he might have stuck with Brian.

Justin Whittle: Brian was popular among the players. We had a lot of skilful players and Gary Alexander was a brilliant finisher, but a lot of players didn't have the impact we were expecting and that cost Brian his job. The chairman had splashed out a lot money to bring these players in and we should have been doing better.

Lawrie Dudfield: It was difficult for me personally. Brian brought me in and I loved him. We had an inkling that things weren't going well off the pitch, and I've heard many, many times that Brian would have kept his job had he not given us the weekend off after that Friday night game. How true that is I don't know. I got a phone call a day or two later from the local paper asking for a quote about him being sacked. That was the first I knew of it. I was distraught. I don't think I ever had a manager like him again. He whole-heartedly believed in me and gave me a confidence that I don't think I had anywhere else in my career. I'll always be thankful to him. We all knew it was us that had let him down, particularly losing those home games.

Brian is a real players' manager. The players loved him and you wanted to play for him. He had been there and done it so had our respect, but he was also a nice guy, impossible not to like. Even if you weren't in the team you couldn't dislike him.

Mark Greaves: Because Brian was such a good man I was slightly surprised, but looking at where we were in the league and how ambitious Adam was – knowing he had to fill this big new stadium we were going to get – it perhaps wasn't surprising. It was disappointing though. I had a lot of respect for Brian.

Paul Musselwhite: I was sad to see Brian go. And it was a shock. We were sixth in the league but had been on a poor run. And it was big news. Brian was a big name. It was a surprise to all of us. And it wasn't just Brian, it was his assistants Dave Moore and Kevan Smith. I'd known Dave for years so I was sad to see him go too. Brian still came in and had a chat with the lads, but that was it.

Mike Edwards: I always think you should give a manager to the end of the season in those circumstances and have a look then. To get promoted out of the lower leagues you need consistency. I think we'd have kicked on again under Brian that season, but the change in manager upset the applecart too much. Fair play to Adam, he wanted success straight away and I could never knock him as he was always brilliant with me. It must have been a tough decision to make as Brian was loved by everyone. On the day he left, I'd been sent off a few weeks previous against Scunthorpe and had to appear before the FA to see if my three-game ban was going to be extended. Brian had said that he'd come with me and speak up for me. He was sacked the day before my hearing and came into the changing room the next day to tell us he was going. During all of this he was looking at me weird, because I was in a suit as I was due to drive up to Manchester later in the day. Then it twigged and he said: "Oh Mike, I'm so sorry I'm not going to be able to make it in with you today. I've got another problem I need to address." I got an extra two-game ban then too!

Dave Burns: Brian Little was an absolute gent. He was a terrific man. I'm sorry it didn't quite work out for him, and Adam was maybe a bit impatient. He wanted to get the club moving and that maybe put managers under pressure.

1. **Plymouth P34 W22 D7 L5 Pts73**
2. **Luton Town P34 W19 D6 L9 Pts63**
3. **Mansfield P33 W18 D6 L9 Pts60**
4. **Scunthorpe P35 W15 D11 L9 Pts56**
5. **Rochdale P34 W15 D11 L8 Pts56**
6. **Hull City P35 W15 D10 L10 Pts55**
7. **Shrewsbury P35 W15 D9 L11 Pts54**

With Brian Little sacked, youth team coach Billy Russell was made caretaker manager until a replacement was appointed. In his first game – another Friday night match at Swansea – City lost 1-0, but then came a Tuesday night match against the Mansfield side that had inflicted the first wound on Brian Little's revamped Hull City side. And there was almost a return for the very player who embodied the battling spirit that the club stood accused of lacking.

Gary Brabin: I got a phone call from Adam Pearson to tell me that Brian Little had been sacked. He asked me to go back as a player. I was captaining Chester, helping to keep them up in a similar way to what we'd done at Hull City in the Great Escape. I told him I'd walk back to Hull to play for the club. There was a game that evening in which they were beaten in an away match. Billy Russell had been the caretaker manager. Adam told me that he'd phone me back. I was excited, couldn't sleep. I phoned Adam a couple of days later after hearing nothing and he told me that Billy Russell didn't want to do it. I'd felt I'd been destined to go back but it never happened.

Lawrie Dudfield: As soon as Brian went out the door there was a change in atmosphere at the club. Billy Russell came in and did fine, but there was still an air of disappointment everywhere.

The Mansfield game proved to be the club's best performance in many months, with a 4-1 victory coming courtesy of goals from Lee Philpott, Gary Bradshaw, newly signed loanee David Norris and Julian Johnsson. So was there any chance of Billy Russell's caretaker role being made permanent?

Adam Pearson: I wasn't tempted to appoint Billy Russell full-time but perhaps I should have been. Perhaps I got sidelined into looking for somebody who had that big-time experience and personality and presence to take us forward. But ultimately Billy turned out to be a fantastic servant to the club, but in the backroom and at Academy level. He had all the assets to be a manager – hard-working, diligent, honest.

Mark Greaves: Billy had been around from when I'd been a youth connected with City. I didn't expect him to get the job – I felt a big name would come in – but I wouldn't have minded seeing Billy get it. He knew the game, he'd learnt the ropes. The youth team lads liked him and he brought a few through like Mike Edwards and Gary Bradshaw. That 4-1 win was great though. I think David Norris scored with his first touch.

That win kept City in sixth but it was to prove to be the last victory of the season. A disappointing 1-0 defeat at home to Scunthorpe followed, then defeats against Oxford, Darlington and Cheltenham with a draw against Orient mixed in with them. City had slumped to 11th position, eight points off the play-offs with four games to play. In this time rumours had been circulating about the identity of Adam Pearson's first managerial appointment. And when the announcement came, it was indeed a big name.

Adam Pearson: At that point, I knew I wanted Jan Molby because of what he'd done at Kidderminster, but it wasn't nailed on and I was also looking at Ronnie Moore. In the end I plumped for Jan. It was certainly an entertaining six months, but I did Jan no favours at all by bringing him in at the back end of that season when the team wasn't good enough. He inherited a whole bunch of players who couldn't handle it. And unfortunately it got Jan off to a really bad start at the end of the season, and it meant he was under pressure right from the first game the next season.

Gary Alexander: When you get connected with a name like Jan Molby it's exciting as he was one of the best footballers in the country when I was growing up watching Liverpool.

Lawrie Dudfield: Jan was the exact opposite of Brian Little in every way. My initial reaction was: 'Bloody hell, I'm going to play for a football legend! How lucky am I?' I was thinking what a great appointment. The first time I met him he was very cocksure, and had the arrogance about him of someone who'd played at the top level and won things. The first thing he said to me was: "You and Gary Alexander are pretty much the only players who are going to stay here beyond the summer. I will be making changes. This is not my team." It was great that he rated me, but on the down side I knew that some of my mates were going to be going.

Jan couldn't make an immediate impact on the pitch, however. In his first game City lost 4-0 at home to Luton, with Steve Howard scoring a hat-trick. Defeats at Rochdale and Bristol Rovers followed, with the final game of the season being drawn 1-1 at home to Lincoln. City finished in 11th, having spent much of the first two-thirds of the season in the promotion or play-off places. In the end, the Tigers finished 10 points off a play-off spot and 41 points behind champions Plymouth.

Lawrie Dudfield: I don't remember much of the games Jan managed at the end of that season, but I scored a few goals. Personally things were OK on that level, but from a very early stage I'd come to despise Jan's assistant, Gary Barnett. I'm a people person, and Gary Barnett was the type who'd go behind your back. I couldn't trust him. An assistant has to have the players onside and be that middleman, but Gary wasn't that middleman, he'd just go straight to Jan. Kevan Smith had been brilliant, we trusted him, but none of the boys liked Gary Barnett.

Another summer of change loomed, and as the season ended a few players were to say goodbye to the club. The most high-profile departures were Jamaicans Theo Whitmore and Ian Goodison.

Mark Greaves: Theo was held in high regard by the fans of Hull City but how he didn't play at a higher level I do not know. He was phenomenal. He was 6 foot 3, quick, and had the best feet you could ever imagine. In training he'd be first pick from everyone in five-asides. He'd start walking before you picked him because it was so obvious he'd get chosen first.

Craig Sargent (Hull City fan): I loved Theo Whitmore, of course, but Ian Goodison had Theo's swagger combined with a willingness to get down and dirty when it mattered. I never heard or saw him interviewed so for me he seemed to have an aura of otherworldliness about him. He was consistently fantastic at a time when City were just starting their renaissance. A classy, international defender didn't seem out of place at all at the time. I also loved the fact that he kept playing in England for what seemed like for ever after he left us.

Mark Greaves: We'd do a thing in training where it would be four or five forwards versus four or five defenders. You'd each get a number and you'd be directly up against your opposite number among the attackers. If you came up against Theo in those it was a nightmare. He'd twist you all over the place and make you look silly. At the end of one season we watched the highlights of the year at our end-of-season do. Pretty much all of it just seemed to be Theo beating people for fun. I have no idea how he never played higher than Tranmere and Hull City. I played with a lot of former and future Premier League players in my career, but no one came near Theo for pure ability and skill.

Brian Little: How Theo Whitmore didn't play at a higher level I just don't know.

Rodney Rowe was a massively popular player at Boothferry Park, and he had the best chant at the club, but he was also to make his departure.

Rodney Rowe: It was weird for me in a way, as I'd had a poor pre-season but I was thinking that I had a year left on my contract, but no one seemed to be talking to me. I'd seen how much they'd paid for some good forwards and at first they were on fire. I just thought that I'd keep biding my time. But then I got injured. I knew I'd get an opportunity at some point. In an away match at Rushden and Diamonds in a 3-3 draw I came on and scored. Me and the chairman spoke afterwards. He said: "Do you want to stay at this club?" and I was like: "What?" He seemed to think I was trying to leave, which I wasn't at all. That was so far from the truth. I spoke with Brian Little who said we'd sort something out, and then over time he got the sack. Jan Molby came in and wanted to bring his own players in, and let me go, for which I don't hold any grudges.

I had an amazing time at Hull. I am truly grateful to everyone there. The fans were amazing. That time we didn't get paid, seeing staff in tears and stuff, we fought through it. I've been thankful at every club I've played for but with Hull it was just a real, real pleasure. I regret I couldn't get the fans a promotion. I would have loved to have played at the new stadium too.

Neil Mann's injuries also caught up with him, and he was forced to retire as a player, though he was to take up a role coaching the youngsters. Neil was universally recognised as one of the good guys, and the end of his playing days was widely mourned.

Andy Holt: I loved Neil Mann. He was just a really nice guy. He was never sure if he was going to get a contract all the time as sadly he got a lot of injuries, but he was a big character in those teams and was never scared of speaking his mind.

Rodney Rowe: He used to put so much training into work every single day. Such a lovely lad, and I felt so sorry for him with his injuries.

James Richardson: As a youngster, I adored Neil Mann's thrilling, buccaneering runs. In a low-flair Dolan team, he was a standout alongside Deano. Such a pity he had misfortune with injuries as he could've easily graced the teams that bridged Boothferry Park to the KC.

Julian Johnsson returned to the Faroe Islands after his wife failed to settle in England, while David Beresford, Richard Sneekes, Rob Matthews, Ben Morley and Adrian Cacares were also released. For the rest of the bloated squad, a journey into the unknown awaited. The new stadium was going to be opened the next season, but more importantly no one knew what Jan Molby's plans were with regards to the playing side of things. The next season was going to be memorable alright, but would it be for the right reasons?

2002-03 season

The summer of 2001 had seen City's transfer record smashed, more than half a million pounds spent, a new team (and then some) incoming and a mass exodus. One year on and the club had regressed. There wasn't to be the profligate spending of 12 months previous, but Jan Molby was still given a war chest that would be the envy of every other manager in League 2.

The team built by Brian Little had been capable of some mesmerising football, but was nigh on incapable of eking out 1-0 wins at the Macclesfields and Hartlepools of this world. Too few players wanted to do the ugly stuff. This was a fact not lost on Jan Molby as he embarked upon building 'his' team. Greg Strong and John Anderson were no-nonsense centre-backs plying their trade north of the border at Motherwell and Livingstone, respectively. Shaun Smith was a cultured left-back with a hard tackle. Richie Appleby was a skilful midfielder but came with a reputation from Kidderminster of not shirking the tough stuff. He was to be joined in midfield by some bloke coming in from Cambridge called 'Ashbee'. All of this business was on free transfers. A loanee was brought in in Stuart Green from Newcastle United, who'd impressed when playing at Boothferry Park for Carlisle some months earlier. The marquee signing, however, was left-winger Stuart Elliott from Motherwell. The Northern Ireland international came in for what was to prove a bargain £230,000.

Meanwhile, the new stadium was mere months away from opening. These players were tasked with giving Boothferry Park a fitting send off and ushering in a new era at the club.

Ian Ashbee was a hard-tackling central midfielder, respected in the lower leagues but largely unheard of beyond that level. His contract at Cambridge had been run down, and three teams were in for him. He chose Hull. Nothing seemed untoward. No one expected much from the new signing. Yet it was to be as important a bit of business as the club had done in its history. We just didn't know that yet.

Ian Ashbee: Barnet and Oxford were in for me. I went down to see Oxford and the day after went to see Hull City. Jan Molby told me he'd seen me play and wanted me to sign and asked if I'd go see him, so I said no problem. I knew him a little bit from when he was Kidderminster manager as I had a friend playing for them and I'd played against them a few times. I went up to Boothferry Park, saw the Kwik Save there, but once I was sold the new ground and saw what was happening it was a no-brainer. I signed within a couple of days.

Lawrie Dudfield: When he first came into the dressing room, Ian Ashbee wasn't the Ian Ashbee that you saw eight years later. Ash was just a League 2 journeyman, one of us. He wasn't necessarily even brought in as a first-team regular, though what he went on to achieve was absolutely outstanding. But he was a relatively unknown, untried, inconsistent footballer at that stage. He'd always had an inner confidence. Jan brought in an unheard of player who became one of the greatest in the club's history and he deserves a lot of praise for that.

Ian Ashbee wasn't even brought in as captain. That honour went to a more high-profile signing: Greg Strong, a centre-back who had been playing for Motherwell.

Greg Strong: Things were going well at Motherwell after I'd signed for them from Bolton, but two years in we went into administration and 24 players had their contracts terminated. I was in a position that I'd not been in before, in that I was out of contract. I got a few phone calls, both from British clubs and countries such as Sweden and the Netherlands. I wasn't in a rush to choose at first as my head was spinning, but Hull City contacted me after a couple of weeks. My initial thoughts were that I didn't want to go to League 2, but I took some advice when I was very young that I stand by, and that's no matter what happens, always listen to people, always hear them out because you never know.

In the summer I had a trip to Hull to meet Jan Molby and Adam Pearson. I'd played at Boothferry Park in the past, so I knew it was a good pitch and a decent crowd, but when Adam told me of his plans and took me in his car to what was to become the new and beautiful KC Stadium I realised that it was a club that was going somewhere. I remember leaving and ringing my wife and telling her: "It looks like we're moving to Hull!"

I grew up watching Jan play, and I was a Liverpool fan so I was a bit in awe of him. When the contract side of things was agreed, he said: "I want you to be my captain." To me, that was just wow! The club ticked so many boxes.

Joining Strong in in swapping Fir Park for Boothferry Park was Stuart Elliott.

Stuart Elliott: Motherwell had gone into administration and I was one of their assets. There'd been speculation that a lot of Championship and League 1 clubs were in for me, but it turned out that Hull City had bid £230,000, and Motherwell accepted that. I asked Jan Molby when it was that he'd watched me, and he said he was commentating at a Denmark v Northern Ireland game in Copenhagen and had fancied me as a player at the time. He'd decided then that he was going to try to sign me if he ever got the chance. After that Adam Pearson made it happen.

Greg Strong: Jan called me in. He was looking for a left-sided wide player and asked me about Stuart, and told him he had great potential. He did his own due diligence and ended up making an offer. Throughout the process me and Stuart were speaking a lot, and he was asking all about Hull. I like to think I had a key part in Stuart coming.

Lawrie Dudfield: With Stuart Elliott, he was a really quiet lad, deeply religious, didn't socialise much, but you could just see his ability on the football pitch straight away. He had real quality. Greg Strong had said to Jan to get him as he was flying at Motherwell. Jan took that gamble but Greg's contribution was massive because he did so much to get Stuart Elliott here. I think Stuart took some convincing from Greg to come down too.

Joining Ian Ashbee in the middle of the park would be Stuart Green.

Stuart Green: I was talking to an agent who was friendly with Adam Pearson who told me it was on the cards – even before Jan Molby was manager – but Jan liked me from his time at Kidderminster. Then they came in for me on a season-long loan and I was delighted. They took me to the new stadium and I knew it was the place for me. I couldn't wait to get started. I knew that that Hull team had to be better, and I knew they were going to be better.

Making up a tasty looking midfield – eventually – was Dean Keates.

Dean Keates: I'd been without a job for a few weeks. I'd broken into the team at Walsall – my home-town club – at an early age but then let go. I went to Hull a couple of weeks before the season started and spoke with Jan who said he was carrying a bit of bulk in the squad. In the end I came up just to train and worked out a pay-as-you-play agreement until some of the players could be shifted. This was on the understanding that when those players moved on I'd then get a contract. It was all done with a handshake with Jan and Adam Pearson, which they honoured.

Jan Molby now had a core of his own players in place, and his team was taking shape. However, there were already some issues arising in pre-season.

Lawrie Dudfield: Jan was very vocal. His approach was totally different to Brian's. We were in the pool at 7am every day at training. I think that was because Jan was like an eel through the water. He could swim all day.

Mark Greaves: Jan came in and I was playing at first, so I had no problems. But that summer I went away and I wasn't sure whether he fancied me. Then he signed John Anderson and Greg Strong. I knew we had Justin and Mike Edwards, so I wondered where I was standing. I thought that if I was going to play I'd play right-back – and I didn't want to play right-back for anybody as I was probably the worst right-back in Hull City's history – or in centre midfield. I felt I was a much better centre-half than I was a midfielder though. At that point of my career I wanted to be a centre-half and I felt me and Justin had earned the right to be considered as good a centre-half partnership as there was in that league, without wanting to sound big-headed.

Paul Musselwhite: Again, in the summer there was a massive influx of players. That didn't do us any favours. It's always difficult when you have that turnover. We still had a lot of players from the summer before and the manager was making it clear that he was going to bring in a load of players that he wanted as well.

Lawrie Dudfield: We knew we were in trouble when the manager signed a player that had played for him previously and we asked what he's like, expecting a positive answer. His answer was "a nob". Somebody saying that is not a good start.

Mike Edwards: I knew Jan was a great player, but pre-season was completely different. We'd do three-session days. We'd be in at 7am in the morning to go swimming. That was amusing as a couple of the boys couldn't swim! We'd then go have breakfast, do football-based stuff in the morning and then do the running stuff in the afternoon. That came as a shock to the system to a lot of us.

Stuart Green: Promotion was all we spoke about. We had to get promoted with those players. You've got to give Jan credit for the players that he signed. He brought in a legend in Ian Ashbee, someone who was scoring goals left, right and centre in Stuart Elliott, and he brought in myself, and I think I was alright.

Gary Alexander: There were rumours that Jan was trying to sell me. He would deny it but why were other clubs saying they'd been allowed to talk to me? He'd deny that to my face, but if he didn't want me I'd rather have been told the truth.

Andy Holt: Jan was weird. I've known managers get jobs and careers based on their name, and with Jan you'd train with him and he could pass the ball in a way you wouldn't believe. But when it came to matches – and I've seen this a lot of times in football – the good coaches aren't necessarily good man managers. I don't think Jan found it easy to communicate with us, and the only way he could communicate in the end was through stories of what he'd done in his career. He didn't seem to find speaking one on one very easy. I don't know that the players warmed to him at any point. It was maybe a bit too much of a big job for him too.

Lawrie Dudfield: Despite bringing these future greats in, they hadn't done anything yet, and they didn't know us and we didn't know them. There didn't seem to be the great expectations that we'd had the year before. Jan didn't want anyone to feel confident. He'd rather hammer you into the ground. That was his style. I quite liked him as a guy, but he seemed to get frustrated that we didn't have the ability he'd had as a player. He'd do stuff in training that no League 2 player could do. I remember one day him stopping training, sitting everybody down and going mental at us, saying how what we were doing wasn't good enough, saying how he was 10 stone overweight, 40-something and still the best player at the club. To be fair, he probably was. He did the same again the next day. He liked people to know that he was Jan Molby, the successful Liverpool player. There was no harmony.

Justin Whittle: Jan wanted to bring his own players in, which he did. A lot of them did very well. But we trained so hard in pre-season and that led to us not doing well in the first few games. The fitness team he'd brought in kept saying we weren't fit enough so we'd be back on the bleep tests and the like. We were fit enough – we were doing what they wanted us to do – but it left us knackered. Jan changed formation too, going 4-3-3. Some players struggled to adapt to it. We had gifted players such as Stuart Green and Stuart Elliott but it still wasn't working.

So how was the chairman viewing the club's progress under Molby?

Adam Pearson: On a personal level Jan was a great guy and I really liked him. He had a fantastic personality and he's a lovely bloke with a lovely family. What he'd done at Kidderminster was brilliant but I put him under pressure.

The season started at home to Southend. City got off to a great start, with new signings Stuart Green and Stuart Elliott giving City a 2-1 lead going into the closing stages. However, Ian Ashbee was sent off in the 85th minute and then in injury time disaster struck.

Ian Ashbee: Boothferry Park's pitch was beautiful and though the ground was dated you'd still get a brilliant atmosphere. I used to love Boothferry Park. I've looked back at my debut many a time and thought: 'What was I trying to do?' I'd had a touch on the ball and it got away from me and I launched myself into Ian Selley, so I was sent off. I was thinking that it was over there and then. I was sat in the changing room on my own thinking: 'Hold on, boys, hold on,' because normally you get away with a sending off if your team wins. They scored in the last minute and I got a bit of a roasting from Jan.

Stuart Green: That first game summed up our season. We were so much better than the other team on the ball but we couldn't defend. I woke up that morning thinking: 'I've got to score today.' I felt good, and to score that early was great for me. They were out the game. We were 2-1 up and me and Lawrie Dudfield clashed heads and they got the ball and went and scored.

Stuart Elliott: I went from ecstasy to depression in one game. It was amazing scoring that goal, but the late equaliser just knocked us back on our heels. It was difficult for us to pick up the pieces from that. It was a great day and the fans were going crazy after I'd scored. I'll never forget how the fans welcomed me from the minute I arrived at the club. It was just a disappointment we couldn't get that win.

Greg Strong: I remember pre-season going fantastic. We knitted very quickly. I think a dozen or so players signed but we all just got on fantastically. The last pre-season game we had was a game against Middlesbrough and we performed well to draw 2-2. We were all excited for the season to start, but there was a real sense of disappointment after the opening game. I'd got injured and had to leave the pitch after I'd given away the corner that they scored from, so I just remember a sense of frustration. I think we were expecting to steamroller over the top of them and it just didn't happen.

Still, Ian Ashbee had made an impression on at least one City fan.

Ian Farrow: We knew the determined player we had from his opening game for us. There was immediately a never-say-die attitude and a give all for the shirt he was wearing from the very start. He was sent off on his home debut against Southend for a lunging tackle to try and win the ball back after losing it near the half-way line. He was still arguably our man of the match in that game.

And the match marked the start of an association with the club that was – to put it mildly – to see some sights!

Dave Richardson: That was the first game I photographed at Boothferry Park. It led to a 14-year stint as one of the club's official photographers. The best job in the world!

The second league game of the season came three days later, with Bristol Rovers playing at home. No cats were kicked, but Bristol forward Paul Tait was by new captain Greg Strong. Strong was sent off, though City managed to come away with a creditable 1-1 draw thanks to a late equaliser from recently recruited loanee Simon Johnson. However, it was two games, two points, and two new signings sent off.

Greg Strong: They were quite direct, playing Paul Tait up front. I'd played at Wigan with him as a young lad and had a few scrapes, particularly in youth football when he was at Everton and I was still at Wigan. I don't think we performed particularly well. Paul had run into the back of me and I thought it was deliberate given the history we had, so I lashed out, which for an experienced player was a ridiculous reaction, and deservedly I was sent off.

Mike Edwards: At the beginning of the season I was starting. In the second game of the season, away at Bristol Rovers, Greg Strong was sent off, we were losing at half-time and Jan was calling us cheats in the dressing room. He lost the plot. We were down to 10 men digging in. I've been called everything in my career, but being called a cheat is something I'd never do to anyone else. From that day he lost the dressing room. I still wanted to play, it didn't bother me, and we drew that game, but then I was cast aside. My wife was working in Liverpool at the time and I had a chance to go to Tranmere as Jan wanted me off the books. I was gutted but I realised it was maybe time to move on.

Around this time the local media was taking an interest in Stuart Elliott, whose strong Christian faith made him stand out among his fellow footballers.

Stuart Elliott: It's never easy as a Christian in that environment as you're a fish swimming against the tide. But once the boys saw that I wasn't just talking the talk, I was walking it out in my life over many years, rather than rebel against me they were always very complimentary and wanted to know about my Christian faith.

Greg Strong had been identified as a key signing by many upon joining City. He would – it was predicted – add grit to a side that had been sorely lacking such a quality the season before. In his second game he was sent off. In his third he was taken off at half-time (Stuart Green had been sent off on 41 minutes – three in three for City that season). The man Jan Molby had chosen as his captain had already played his last league match for Hull City, in which City lost 3-1 at Exeter.

Greg Strong: It was a bitty game. They were very direct and the game was scrappy, with very little quality. We underperformed as a team and were losing at half-time. Justin Whittle had been out of the team, and replaced me. He was a trusted presence and the supporters felt like we needed him. I have no animosity. I was brought off, probably rightly, but I wasn't the only one who underperformed. It hurt because I was the captain but you just have to get on with it. It was a long old trip back home though.

Of course, this left a vacancy where the captaincy was concerned. Ian Ashbee was given the role. It's fair to say he made it his own.

Ian Ashbee: I'd been captain at Derby's youth team, even as a first-year apprentice playing with the second-year apprentices, and we won the league that year. I'd also been captain at Cambridge, so I was used to it. People had seen something in me, recognising that I had a captain's role within me. I think it was between John Anderson and myself and Jan went with me. I don't think anyone got it off me after that.

The Exeter defeat was followed by a disappointing 1-1 draw at home to Bury (though City did finish the match with 11 men for the first time in the season). Then came a calamitous game at Hartlepool.

Lawrie Dudfield: I'd been in and out of the team, and had had differences with Jan. Around the time of the Hartlepool away game, my partner had had an ectopic pregnancy and was rushed to hospital. Obviously she lost the baby. Jan asked me if I was OK to play and I said yes. Before the game he pulled me to one side. A good manager would have said stuff about this being your opportunity to forget about the off-field stuff for a little bit, but Jan told me that if I used it as an excuse, he didn't want to hear about it. That message could have been dealt with in a much better way. I lost a lot of respect for him that day. I could perhaps have been bigger and said I wasn't going to play, but I was 21 years old and wanted to play football, and I'd never been through things like that before. To me that summed up what Jan was like as a person. He didn't have that human side.

Mark Greaves: In my very last game at Hartlepool under Jan Molby I was a sub and didn't get on. Afterwards, Adam Pearson came into the dressing room took his jacket off, rolled up his sleeves and chatted to the lads. No shouting, no screaming, just asking what was going wrong. You could see how badly he wanted us to do well. The players were more gutted for him as we'd let him down. We felt more sorry for Adam than Jan. You could see the passion in him.

Mark Herman: I think one of my worst moments watching City was early on in Jan Molby's 'reign', a 2-0 defeat at Hartlepool, his ninth consecutive winless game after taking the helm. City played like they'd never met each other, which, considering the amount of ludicrous loan signings at the time, was probably true. As the Hartlepool bench were never off their feet, pumping constant and urgent encouragement to their players, Molby sat back, arms folded, immobile and clueless on ours and I remember thinking this must be as bad as I could ever remember. Hard to believe then that it was only another six seasons before my very favourite game...

The end was nigh, sadly, for Mark Greaves, a player who had never given less than 100% for the Hull City cause, who had never let the club down, and who had been as committed to the club and its fans off the pitch as he had been on it. Letting a player such as Greavsey leave so easily and unnecessarily was hard to stomach.

Mark Greaves: When we came in, first day of the season, I looked at the team numbers and I was number 23. It wasn't a David Beckham thing where I'd picked a cool number, it meant I was 23rd choice. I was not happy. I went to see Jan and told him I wasn't happy and he told me that I had to fight for my place and I might still start the season. I actually ended up doing that in centre-midfield but I felt I was just a number then. I knew Oxford wanted me – Mark Atkins rang me in the summer to try to negotiate a deal with me – but I had two years left on my contract at Hull. It did leave me wondering if someone at Hull had let Oxford know I was available though. I told them I didn't want to move. A few weeks into the season I told Jan that I wanted to go somewhere and play centre-half. There were a few clubs coming in for me. It was a horrible thing to have to do though, the hardest thing I've ever done. I don't regret it in many ways as I had the strength to do it, but I did regret it when I heard the news about Jan a few weeks later. It was tough to take.

I spoke to Adam who tried to convince me to go on loan for a month. I asked him what the point of that would be, and he said I should go and get some games under my belt. I told him that I'd just be in the same position when I came back but he wouldn't give up trying to convince me to go out on loan. Then Jan got sacked three weeks later! It just wasn't meant to be. But I'm proud to have played 200 games for my home-town club.

Ian Farrow: There's something about locally born players that make me proud, but with some supporters it is a hindrance to be a local lad. Hull lads often have to try extra hard to win certain supporters over or else they end up victims of the boo-boys.

Unfortunately for Greaves he played in the City side that was going out of the league under Mark Hateley. For his first two years at City, Greaves competed for a place in the starting side with the likes of Rob Dewhurst, Tony Brien and Ian Wright. When he got the call he was sometimes told to play as part of a back four, in other games he was one of three centre backs, and other occasions given a midfield role. But when Warren Joyce took over from Mark Hateley, the new manager rebuilt his side but had enough faith in Greaves to keep picking him and Greaves grew into one of the best footballing centre halves in the lower leagues. He played a crucial role in our Great Escape season and was named supporters player of the season the following year. A fantastic turnaround for the player. A year later, and after the appointment of Brian Little, Greaves starred in the side that took City to the play-offs. Changes at the club and injury meant that Greaves was transferred to Boston having only ever played in the bottom division for City. However, we all know he could and should have played at a much higher level with us.

A 1-1 draw at home to Leyton Orient left City with four points from six games and still seeking a first win of the season.

Adam Pearson: We were coasting at home against Southend and we drew 2-2, and then we went to Bristol Rovers and Greg Strong was sent-off and all of a sudden we were under pressure – after just two games. Then we went on a really bad run, we couldn't buy a win. Jan kept bringing in good players like Dean Keates and we weren't that far away, but Jan was losing, we weren't improving and we needed a change of approach to the players, because the players were good. Jan never quite got the back four sorted out. We kept conceding stupid goals. But he built the nucleus of that team.

Ian Ashbee: Jan knew what he wanted, but the level of quality that we had – not meaning any disrespect to anyone – wasn't what he was used to. He'd join in training and he was still the best player. Now I know a bit more about the game and I've matured a bit I realise that you have to tell players things, you have to deal with them and show them formations and he never did that. He expected us to go out and understand things without him telling you. You have to show individuals things and he'd just tell you without ever showing you. So it just never quite materialised.

City won their next game – 2-1 at Cambridge, with Justin Whittle and Shaun Smith scoring – but never really got going under Jan. Going into October, City had won two, drawn six and lost three, leaving them 16th in the table. Next up were the team City had taken Jan from – Kidderminster. A dreadful 1-0 defeat at Aggborough was calamitous in a number of ways.

Andy Holt: Jan came in the changing room afterwards and was completely downhearted, talking about all the Kidderminster players and how they were lads that he'd signed.

Mike Edwards: I wasn't meant to play but Nathan Peat had been late for a meeting and was dropped so I was brought in. The move to Tranmere was still a possibility but I played anyway, and that's when I did my knee. I heard it pop and I'd done my cruciate ligament. I went in for an operation and was told my cruciate was OK, but I was still out for a couple of months.

16. **Macclesfield P12 W4 D1 L7 Pts13**
17. **Darlington P12 W3 D4 L5 Pts13**
18. **Hull City P12 W2 D6 L4 Pts12**
19. **Leyton Orient P12 W3 D3 L6 Pts12**
20. **Shrewsbury P12 W3 D3 L6 Pts12**

The issues that had dogged Brian Little's final season as City manager showed no sign of being alleviated under Jan Molby. The defence was just as poor and the attack was faltering. Adam Pearson had spent big by the division's standards for two summers on the trot and only had a mid-table side to show for it. With this in mind, Jan Molby was sacked.

Adam Pearson: He was a difficult chap to sack. Most managers just want to move on and sort out the settlement figure. Jan definitely did not want to leave. He didn't think he'd been given a chance – and he certainly hadn't been given long enough, that is for sure – but I couldn't afford to carry on another season without going up.

Dean Keates: There was a very big squad and Jan had told a lot of people that they weren't part of his plans. This meant there was a divide in the changing room – the players who he'd brought in or who were part of his plans, and then the players who he'd left to one side. As changing rooms go it wasn't a great place to be as there were a lot of unhappy people.

Greg Strong: We had the belief because of our strong pre-season, and we knew we had good players and we thought it was going to be fine. I picked up an injury during my suspension, and during that process Jan lost his job. Jan probably over-criticised the players in the press a little bit too much and that drained some of that belief and togetherness. What's said behind closed doors is fine, but with the stuff said in the press a few players seemed to think they were hung out to dry a little bit.

Lawrie Dudfield: Ultimately he didn't get long in that position, maybe 17 games, but it just wasn't working. For all of his good signings there were some bad ones. Greg Strong is a great bloke but it didn't work out, and Richie Appleby didn't seem to want to play football. It just never really happened.

Paul Musselwhite: It was a difficult start. The club had a lot of very good players to choose from and we were near the bottom of League 2. I only played in Jan's last couple of games, so for me I'd been standing and watching these defeats. I was one of the more experienced players in the squad and you always think you're going to make a difference if you play, but convincing the manager of that isn't easy. But we had a lot of players who were disillusioned with not playing.

Ian Ashbee: A lot of players didn't warm to Jan because he didn't want them. We weren't winning enough games of football and bits and bobs got back to people like Adam Pearson that Jan wasn't as good as had been originally thought. I think Adam always wanted Peter Taylor anyway. But my philosophy is that you give everything you've got for each individual manager, and if you're liked then fair enough, and if you're not then you just crack on with it. I don't think Jan was liked by many because he was quite outspoken and would talk to a few people as though they just weren't good enough, largely because he was such a good player himself. I do sympathise with him in a way on that, but it was a very short reign.

I think Jan needed that little bit of time. He needed that transitional period to get the old players out of the changing room as they can cause you problems. But Adam Pearson was impatient and wanted results.

Stuart Elliott: There's a fine line between success and failure. You saw later that Jan signed quality players, it just didn't seem to work out for him, he didn't get the rub of the green. Jan was also unfortunate with injuries. During my first few months at the club I ended up with a medial ligament injury and so he lost a striker there. I was just sad in the end that I couldn't contribute more during his time at the club, especially after he'd shown such faith in me.

Stuart Green: The problem was that we couldn't defend. We looked great going forward. I felt sorry for Jan. After that Kidderminster game we all knew that was probably going to be Jan's last game. I remember being in tears in the car on the way back to Cumbria. I was devastated because he'd put so much faith in me. He was great for my game. He put so many new things into my game. He should go down in Hull City's history, though, for making the signings that he made.

Gary Alexander: Did I gel with Jan? No. Things were going on behind the scenes that I didn't agree with and we had our clashes, so it didn't really work out.

Paul Musselwhite: When you watched the old Liverpool teams they'd just go out and play, and I think Jan thought we could do that. But we needed a lot more organisation, a lot more structure, to how we played. Not many teams at that level would have been able to just go out and play.

Justin Whittle: Adam decided that Jan wasn't the man for the job. Jan expected us all to be like him but we were never going to be as good as he was. In training he'd expect us to be able to do what he could do or his old Liverpool team-mates could do. We had good players but not superstars.

Lawrie Dudfield: I wasn't celebrating that he'd been sacked, but I think you'd have struggled to find anybody in that dressing room who was disappointed, including the players that he'd signed. Once you have that management style, and lose the players, he didn't have another side to him – a human side – to turn it around. He didn't get a response from the players and that's what cost him his job.

Rob Smith: Jan as an individual was quite old-school and very obliging to muck in and do anything for the good of the club. He'd make sure he was about for the sponsors. He was brilliant for the club when it came to that side of things and he was a likeable guy. Maybe Hull wasn't the best move for him, and Adam wanted something to show for his investment. With the move to the stadium coming up we didn't have time on our side.

Dave Burns: Jan was a top bloke. Charming and great to interview. He'd been a top, top player and he was a top, top bloke. He still has a chat when we see him. I don't know why it wasn't happening. If he was a poor man-manager I didn't pick that up at the time. I remember before one game, in an away match, I was working with former City player Dave Roberts and he made a comment about City's warm-up not looking organised, not on it, a bit shambolic. Adam had a go at us in the next home match programme, saying you wouldn't get that in the big football cities such as Leeds and Newcastle from the BBC. Then within a few games he'd sacked Jan.

This left Adam Pearson looking to make his second managerial appointment in six months. Rumours circulated that Steve Coppell and Ronnie Moore had been interviewed, but within days Peter Taylor was the only candidate anyone was talking about, and he was duly appointed. Just two years prior, after doing so well managing England U21s, Peter had been made the temporary England manager, and had made David Beckham captain for the first time. He was introduced to the Boothferry Park faithful as the club's new manager on October 12th before a home game against Rochdale, and then watched from the stands as Billy Russell's side won 3-0.

Adam Pearson: The rumours about Steve Coppell and Ronnie Moore were accurate but Peter Taylor just came from left field. He had a great track record, particularly at Gillingham and Brighton where he'd got promotion, and I met him and he's a very charming guy, very honest, and a good coach. Players wanted to play for him. It was a nice match. It felt right. He was from the south-east, but I think he grew to like it in Hull.

He brought Colin Murphy and Steve Butler with him. Colin was very important for Peter. When Peter was in the south, Colin kept an eye on things. He had a great experience of the lower league, very eccentric, but in a good way. How he'd survive in these politically correct days I don't know. He knew football though, and he played me very well. He was a good foil for Peter.

Peter Taylor: I'd left Brighton after getting promotion so I was out of work. My agent had already mentioned Hull City to me as a possibility, even before I went to Brighton, so I knew a little bit about the club and how big it was, and the level of its potential. My assistant that I took to Hull – Colin Murphy – knew more about Hull than I did, and then when I got the call from Adam Pearson to ask if I could meet him in London I spoke to Colin again about the club's size and potential and we all agreed that it was worth going for.

I'd met Colin Murphy when he was at Luton. Then when I went to Southend from Hendon, Southend couldn't agree the fee as Hendon were holding out for too much money and Southend were threatening to pull out of the deal, which would have meant I couldn't manage Southend. Colin was due some money from Southend but said to the chairman: "Don't worry about my money, put it towards bringing Peter here," and I thought: 'What an incredible thing to do. I don't even know this bloke!' Then when I went to Leicester I took Colin to be my assistant, so that's why I brought him to Hull. The reason why I brought Colin to Hull and Leicester was his contacts within the game. A lot of our signings came from Colin.

Stuart Green: We knew pretty early on that it was going to be Peter Taylor, within a couple of days of Jan getting sacked. And with Pete having the record he did, we were excited. I was gutted for Jan, we were gutted with each other because we'd underperformed, but when you heard Peter Taylor was coming in you got renewed optimism.

Dean Keates: Peter came in with a massive reputation and was full of enthusiasm. He was fresh, he had new ideas and he used a lot of sports science, which I'd never really seen much of before. He brought Colin Murphy, who had massive experience in football. And the fitness levels changed too. It was a big change.

Brendon Smurthwaite: Within about a week Peter Taylor was sick of the David Beckham/captaincy question.

Ian Ashbee: I had an instant respect for him. He'd been England manager and given David Beckham his first taste of captaincy. We played at Boothferry Park against Rochdale knowing he was watching and you're always wondering does he want me, does he not want me? But luckily enough he wanted somebody who was like me, and he'd seen something in me that he wanted to make captain and take the club forward.

Stuart Elliott: Peter made an instant impact. I knew he was a no-nonsense manager and a fantastic coach, and within a few weeks he'd gone through drill after drill after drill. He knew exactly what he was looking for and he was certainly organised. I knew we were going to do well. But with any new manager coming in he wanted to bring in his own players and build a new squad. He did that brilliantly. I don't think he was quite convinced about me at the start though, because it took me a few months after my injury to get going. But once I started scoring I just couldn't stop. In the end I like to think I was one of his best players.

Justin Whittle: I'd had many managers so it wasn't a problem for me. I just wanted to do my best to stay in the team. Peter inherited some good players, he just had to get us playing well enough together. He brought in the likes of Damien Delaney, who he seemed to consider as a midfielder at first but soon saw that he slotted in nicely next to me.

Paul Musselwhite: It was a surprise when he came in, but when you think that the club had managed to attract someone like Brian Little you could see we were a draw.

Stuart Green: He's a top-class coach. The training was superb. It was sharp, high intensity, perfect for my game. He didn't really say a lot but from an early stage we could tell that we were going to be a lot more organised, and we knew we were going to win a lot more games – games that we'd have lost before.

Lawrie Dudfield: I made my Premier League debut for Leicester under Martin O'Neill at the end of the 2000/01 season. I played a couple of games and was travelling with the squad quite a bit. I really thought it was a breakthrough for me, but Martin got the Celtic job and Peter Taylor was appointed there. I was ecstatic given his reputation for working with young players and I was establishing a good reputation at the club. Then he signed a load of players like Ade Akinbiyi, and in our first pre-season game Ade scored a worldy, then Stan Collymore got the second, but I got the third. I was buzzing, but didn't play another minute for him pre-season. I wasn't in the squad, didn't travel anywhere. I was doing really well in the reserves, but he wouldn't put me in and was instead picking these players he'd signed from Ireland. After I'd scored a couple of goals for the reserves and still couldn't get in the squad I went in the next Monday and knocked on his door, because I was steaming. I said: "What do I need to do?" He replied: "Well we'd signed Kevin Ellison and wanted to give him a taste of the first team." I just thought: 'What message does that send out?' and I knew then it was over. So I went out on loan.

That said, I always got on with Peter as a person and still do – he's a lovely guy – but him as a manager and me as a player just didn't work. I wasn't his kind of player. So when he took over I toed the official line of being excited, but when I got the phone call to tell me he'd got the job I was knew I had to find another club. I knew that I'd be out of the door and that's pretty much what happened. I played a few games for him but not many.

Peter brought in a physio by the name of Simon Maltby, who was to play a crucial role in the club's success over the coming years.

Simon Maltby: I knew Peter and Colin, and there was a good atmosphere among the staff and the players. Peter didn't seem to have the players he wanted there at the time, and there were some who weren't involved. On the medical side of things there was nothing in place at all at that point. No protocols, no strategies to develop the medical side of things. Everything was very basic. I was quite shocked at that. It felt like we were starting from scratch.

Adam Pearson was great when it came to developing the medical side of things. He was supportive throughout my whole time there. Peter was the same.

So what did Taylor make of his new team on first viewing?

Peter Taylor: My first view of the team was a game against Rochdale at Boothferry Park, which they won and they looked pretty decent on that day, but it was obvious once I got more familiar with things that they weren't as consistent as they should have been, which happens with League 2 players. That's where we needed players with a bit more knowhow, a bit more end product and a bit more consistency, so they are the things that we started to look for.

Things got even better in Peter Taylor's first official match in charge at Torquay. City ran riot, winning 4-1 with goals from Ian Ashbee, Phil Jevons, John Anderson and Stuart Green. Ashbee's goal in particular was quite astonishing.

Ian Ashbee: Travelling down to Torquay, not many clubs were getting points down there at the time. It was Peter's first game, and we started quite well with everyone wanting to impress the new manager. The ball had gone down the right, a cross came in and was cleared towards me. I could hear John Anderson shouting "No!" and somebody told me after that Peter Taylor was also shouting "No!" too as the ball was coming to me through the air. But I just thought I'd hit it, and as I connected on the volley Adam Pearson and all the backroom staff were behind the goal and I can still see them on the videos all jumping up and the ball nestling in the top corner. I still smile every time I look at it or think about it because it was such a prominent period for Hull City and we were on a rollercoaster from then onwards. We were moving in the right direction with a respected manager in Peter Taylor.

Peter Taylor: The game started off with Torquay playing well but Ash scored a brilliant goal just before half time, which set us up. On that day we showed the potential that the team had. We counter-attacked well and it was as good as an away performance as you'd get at that time from us. I just felt straight away that I was looking forward to working with Ian Ashbee. I'd seen him play before and I knew a bit about him, and I just thought he could be a decent, important player. And I think it's fair to say he was!

Stuart Green: That was an unbelievable game. Everything went for us. Every person on the pitch did their job. That was a perfect performance. The problem was we couldn't keep it going.

Peter Taylor: My early views of the squad were good and bad, but the clues were there as to why they'd been 18th in League 2, as nobody knew what standard they were going to perform to when they turned up.

Making his Hull City debut in the Torquay game was an Irishman signed from Leicester. Peter Taylor returned to his old club to make Damien Delaney a Tiger in a move that was to prove pivotal for both club and player.

Damien Delaney: I'd been out on loan and playing in Leicester's reserve team and I wanted to play first-team football. I'd been on loan at Mansfield and they wanted to extend it for another month. I was just about to do that when Peter called and asked if I'd be interested in coming to Hull. I didn't even ask where it was, what division they were in, I just didn't care.

It was a permanent move for me and I just wanted to go and get playing. That's the only way you're going to improve. I got in my car and drove up to Hull.

I drove to the car park at Boothferry Park and sat there with that Kwik Save staring at me. Boothferry Park was a bit dilapidated at the time, and I was thinking to myself: 'Maybe I should have asked a few more questions before agreeing to come,' but then I met Adam Pearson and he whisked me away from Boothferry Park as quickly as possible and we drove to the KC Stadium. He told me we'd be moving there in a few months and would be looking to go through the divisions. That was it for me. I saw the ambition and Peter explained that he'd be signing lots of young players from Premier League academies and lads with a point to prove. I thought I fitted into that category perfectly and I signed that day. I never looked back.

Peter Taylor: Damien was full of potential. I'd signed him at Leicester City for £50,000 and then thankfully when I came to Hull he wasn't in Leicester's plans so I signed him for £50,000 again. To me it was two good bits of business. He could run up and down all day, he's a lovely size, a good left foot, a good lad who we knew. To me it was a no-brainer. He needed matches and to get to used to the English game, so it was perfect for him as well.

Adam Pearson: Colin Murphy loved Damien, because he could play anywhere. And he was underrated. He had a massive engine too.

Colin Murphy: Damien Delaney had been at Cork, and then at Leicester when I'd been there. He was about 6 foot 3, a great defender, he could do everything.

Justin Whittle: He went straight into the first team but I don't know why the fans got on his back at first. Sometimes it just happens. But I think the fans saw we had something good going on when he consistently played as a left-sided centre-half. He was very good to play alongside.

City didn't quite kick on from this bright start under Taylor. A 1-1 draw at home to Rushden and Diamonds was followed by another 1-1 draw at Shrewsbury. Then came a terrific 2-0 home win over Scunthorpe – the last great game at Boothferry Park – in which Michael Branch scored on 85 minutes and Gary Alexander sealed the game in injury time. However, this was followed by a disappointing 1-1 draw at Lincoln and a horrific 3-0 defeat at home to Macclesfield in the FA Cup.

Peter Taylor made another signing not long after this defeat, taking defender Marc Joseph from Peterborough.

Marc Joseph: Peter Taylor had been coaching at Peterborough, where I'd been playing, prior to getting the Hull job. When he moved to Hull he showed an interest in me, and even though it meant dropping down a league I had a chat with Ash and he reassured me it was a good move for me as the club was going places.

I preferred playing centre-half but seemed to play full-back – right or left – the majority of the time. I liked the physical side of things you get at centre-half, but I knew it would be difficult getting that centre-half position at Hull given you were up against he likes of Damien Delaney and, later on, Leon Cort, so I just took my chance wherever I was playing.

Taylor was slowly building his team, but what kind of player was he looking for?

Peter Taylor: I was looking for people who could handle the situation at Hull City. I was very fortunate to meet top managers in my life such as Sir Alex Ferguson, and he told me how he signed people who weren't just good players, but players who could handle Manchester United. He told me that Hull City players have got to handle the league that they are in and they've got to be able to handle the crowd expectations. So every time that we identified a player it wasn't just because of his ability. We felt that if he didn't have the strength of character and couldn't handle 20,000 people telling him he's useless, then he's not for us.

On November 23rd, City played at home to Boston United, winning 1-0. Damien Delaney scored his first goal for City, and though we weren't to know at this point, it was to be the last goal that Hull City would score at Boothferry Park.

Damien Delaney: The ball just popped out to me and I hit a cross which just happened to drop in at the far post.

Marc Joseph made his debut in a 0-0 draw at Wrexham, but in truth all that was on the fans' minds was the forthcoming final ever game at Boothferry Park and the move to the KC Stadium. On Saturday, December 14th, Hull City bade farewell to the old ground. Darlington were the visitors, and, inspired by a terrific goalkeeping display by Michael Ingram, ruined the party by winning 1-0.

Adam Pearson: It was typical of the club's recent history that we got beat at the last game at Boothferry Park. It was bound to happen. It was all set up, 10,000 fans in there, fantastic occasion, and we get beat by Darlington. We'd nearly signed Michael Ingram a couple of times but he was unbeatable that day.

Michael Ingham: I was just a young lad on loan from Sunderland. It was my third game in the spell. We knew it would be a good atmosphere, a full house, and we knew we'd have to be switched on. I just had to block out the noise and get on with the task, but it was difficult because the noise the Hull fans made that day was something else.

Stuart Green: The occasion was unbelievable. It wasn't a League 2 game. The atmosphere was amazing. There was a lot going on on the pitch and off it, and Darlington weren't a bad team. It was frustrating because we wanted to go out on a high. I was devastated, as I loved Boothferry Park. I only had six months there but the fans took to me and the pitch was perfect. I was devastated when we left. That place is so special to me.

Michael Ingham: I don't remember any specific saves. We were backs to the wall. Me and Stuart Elliott had had a little competition throughout our careers, going back to when I was at Cliftonville and Stuart was at Glentoran and we played in a few finals. We'd always have a little battle. I'd kept a clean sheet for York at Boothferry Park on my debut for them, so I was feeling good about the game.

Our left-back – Simon Betts – scored and after that we just defended the box for what felt like 180 minutes. The relief when the final whistle went was huge, but then I had to get off the pitch as quickly as possible because there was a pitch invasion. Half-an-hour later I'd been recalled from my loan by Sunderland!

Nick Turner (Hull City fan and author): The final game against Darlington was a not entirely unpredictable Boothferry mix of raw emotion and disappointing anti-climax against modest opponents, ensuring the farewell party was turned into a low-key wake by the final whistle, with fans lingering on the pitch at the end unsure of what emotion they were supposed to be feeling. It certainly wasn't the defiant or raucous finale that had been anticipated.

In truth, the match was a bit of a sideshow to what was an emotional day for many. Former players were given a last lap of honour, and Boothferry Park – which still had as good a playing surface as anywhere in the country, lit up by England's only sextet of free-standing floodlights – bowed out. Tears were shed by some, but not all.

Adam Pearson: I was delighted to move from Boothferry Park. I enjoyed it because it was a hostile environment and the playing surface was good, but I didn't think we'd be able to take the club forward from that base. We had to get rid of all the ghosts and shackles holding the club down, and unfortunately that ground was doing that. It was a proper football ground but I remember the rust falling on my head when the ball hit the roof. We'd never have been able to take City into the Championship from that ground.

Peter Taylor: When I was introduced to the crowd before the Rochdale game at Boothferry Park I absolutely loved it. The atmosphere was brilliant. I played there many times and I felt as though it was a proper football ground full of history with a great atmosphere. It's a shame you have to move from places like that, but it's the modern game. We knew we were moving to a brilliant stadium as well. We knew if we got things right at the new stadium things could really take off there. It was one of those things you just have to accept. We did carry on training there though, and that was good for us.

Nick Turner: Boothferry Park had become a patched-up, semi-derelict shadow of its former well-appointed self. It looked tacky, painted in gaudy colours and plastered with cheap advertising in areas of the ground that were once crowded with fans. It was something of an understatement to say it had seen better days. There was a palpable and deeply entrenched air of decline. Visiting lower league teams must have been inspired to raise their game at this big old stadium, and even further encouraged when they saw what straits the club were in. Harold Needler's 1960s dream of a modern 60,000 capacity Hull City ground had long since faded into distant memory, to the point where younger fans were completely oblivious to the style and ambition that once were hallmarks of the place.

Its location was very much out on a limb at one end of Hull, the western side most convenient for visiting fans and located in the outer limits of interwar suburbia. The sense of being deeply rooted in the district and the wider city was not as strong as it may have been for other football clubs, who had been playing at their original homes for far longer. In that regard, and in the absence of a complete and cripplingly expensive makeover, a move elsewhere (ideally nearer town) was the best option to get City back up the leagues.

John Cooper: Boothferry Park had a heart. It was opened in 1946 and everyone had grown up with it. It was like your best friend, and you don't ditch your best friend if you can help it. It was unfortunate that the ground suffered from a lack of investment over a long period, long before Martin Fish was chairman. Professional football isn't always as professional as you think it's going to be, and that was certainly the case with Boothferry Park.

Stuart Elliott: There was a lot of emotion. I was glad to be part of such a historic day because I knew how much Boothferry Park meant to the Hull City fans.

Tom Wilson: I had been there as a player, coach, secretary. I'd played there numerous times with Millwall and always loved it. I just loved the atmosphere. But I did a lot of check-ups with health and safety in my time as secretary and the ground was just falling apart.

Dave Burns: Going up to the press box on those steps on an icy day was not great. In the press box you'd wonder how soon David Bond would get wound up by the opposition reporter for the BBC. It was so enclosed.

Bernard Noble: We'd had so many problems in the 1990s, but it was still a shame that we had to leave Boothferry Park as everybody loved it. But football changes.

Billy Whitehurst: Boothferry Park had its own atmosphere. You could feel something when there was nobody in it. Of all the places I played in only Roker Park had that feel to it.

Ian Bunton: It sort of summed up a lot of my earlier years following City; a big anti-climax. I'd watched in all four stands, and it did feel like the end of an era. Time has now passed though, and I can still look back on being there with a nostalgic smile.

Chris Chilton: When I look back on my career, I can't help but think back to seeing those queues outside the North and East Stands at Boothferry Park an hour before kick-off just to see us play.

Raich Carter Junior: It was strange. It wasn't as bad as we'd thought it would be. What eased it was seeing how good the KC was. Boothferry Park, by the end, was a shack. Obviously I have lots of good memories there, I knew all the staff, and now and again when I smell a certain cigar brand it takes me back there. I miss that walk from Three Tuns to the South Stand too.

Mark Robinson: I loved the old Kempton with the away fans so close to you. When the home fans had the Kempton we had a great atmosphere. But that last game seemed to sum up our time at Boothferry Park. Loads of promise and excitement but we lost 1-0 to Darlington on a wet afternoon. It was sad as it was part of my life, part of my childhood, with my dad taking me to all those fallen dreams and broken promises, but it was still just what you did. I'd try to get there as early as I could to go behind the goal and then switch sides at half-time.

Ken Houghton: It was sad. We went round the pitch and it was very emotional. None of the old players wanted the club to move, but it's progress.

Frank and Margaret Beill: We were pleased to see the back of the place. As Frank left the ground after the end of the final game he spoke to Dan Pratt, who was the fans' liaison officer at the time, and told him that there had been more disappointments in that place than anywhere else in his life!

Ken Wagstaff: What they should have done was buy all those neighbouring houses and then do Boothferry Park up. It had its own train station, training ground the lot.

Roy North: It was really sad. I'd worked quite a few times at Hull Truck over the years and I'd take my bike up to Boothferry Park after we'd left and I saw it decaying. It was a really special place for me. I used to go and watch the players training. You could sneak in and watch them train. Sometimes – in the 1950s – they'd be playing in the car park and they'd let you join in with them. We had a nice lad called Linaker – a right winger – who was great with us and would let us join in and always pass to us. As a 12-year-old that was great fun!

Gary Clark: I walked out of Boothferry Park for the last time and I didn't look back. Another Hull City anti-climax to which we had gotten used to during the past 25 years or so. I wanted to store away the memories when the place was packed to the rafters, when it was in its pomp, among the best stadiums in the land. A stadium ripe for First Division football, but sadly a stadium that had been neglected, unloved and seen far better days. Thanks for the memories.

Justin Whittle: The atmosphere was different at Boothferry Park – better than the KC (apart from the Swansea 1-0 win) – and the pitch was terrific, so it was difficult to leave. I'd mostly had great times there, playing the likes of Liverpool and Chelsea, against players such as Michael Owen, Ruud Gullit and Gianfranco Zola.

Robert Crampton: It was dangerous. Football fans are often conservative, and there seemed to be a hardcore of fans who didn't want us to move from Boothferry Park, but bits would fall off the roof during games. It seemed like a tragedy waiting to happen. I was pleased when we moved.

Craig Sargent: I started following City in 1986 and like anyone those first memories are the strongest. The floodlights; the club shop under the South Stand; the little chalk board with the attendance on as you walked out from under the West Stand. However, my generation had never really known success there. I loved Boothferry Park but can't honestly say I lamented leaving. The future seemed bright and the dirge of a final game against Darlington seemed the perfect death rattle for the tired old lady. However, give me one chance to go and sit in the South Stand seats circa 1986 and I would bite your hand off!

Garreth Roberts: Playing at Boothferry Park was just incredible. It's only when you pack it in that you realise what you've been involved in. We were all invited back, which was nice, but it was sad to see the state of the ground. The toilets underneath the West Stand, even when I was an apprentice and had to clean them, were an absolute disgrace.

James Richardson: The Darlington match came approximately 10 years and two days after my first City game vs Exeter at Boothferry Park. I didn't go regularly to City until a few years after that match but the old place was where I grew up. I spent time there with my dad, my grandad, my mates. Upon the final whistle in the Darlington game, my dad and I filtered onto the pitch and took it all in. We talked about some isolated memories but generally there was more optimism than sadness. The KC Stadium felt too good to an opportunity to miss out on and, for the first time in my supporting life, it felt like the club was really looking forward rather than backwards. I went to the final reserve game that was played at Boothferry Park. As I was wandering across the Kwik Save car park, it dawned on me that this really was the last time I'd be able walk up to a game, clunk through the West Stand turnstiles and, potentially, have to brush rust from my hair, and that got me.

Ian Farrow: I was sad. It was where I was brought up watching City. It was where my grandad took my mother to watch City. It was where my mother took me to watch City. It was where, during my formative years, I learned to love the crowds, the sounds and the excitement and the camaraderie of being a Hull City fan. It was where I first met a lot of long-term friends and acquaintances. However, it ended, quite aptly, as it had nearly always been, in a big disappointment. 'City Independent' produced a souvenir edition of 50% more than our usual print run and they sold out immediately. Unfortunately, it was a damp, dull day and typically City lost to Darlington. This made us realise that it was time to move on. Boothferry Park may have had great memories for us but it hadn't been a successful ground. There may have been a thousand and one memories linked to Boothferry Park but it was certainly time to move on.

Ian Thomson: I was completely relaxed about leaving Boothferry Park. I had some fine memories, obviously, but just as many – in fact more – bad ones: 'Fer Ark' (which summed up the place, certainly in the latter days) was a veritable monument to underachievement. Look what we've done since we moved.

Jeff Radcliffe: I was obviously sad, but times move on and the new stadium has brought in a new era with fantastic facilities. When I started I was the physio, and I maybe had an option of using an orthopaedic surgeon. Now there's an army of physios, psychiatrists, dieticians and so on and so forth.

John Kaye: I was there on the final day. It was a shame, but what's happened since has given the whole city a boost and the crowds have come back.

John Cooper: The Darlington game was emotional. I was first there in the morning and one of the last to leave on the night. But that said, my head was already in the KC. We'd already moved certain things there. We were having an opening day there the day after the Darlington game, but there was only a certain few of the staff had been there at that point. It still belonged to the company that were building it. It wasn't handed over until December 18th,

2002. There was that much going on, you just didn't have time to sit and ponder. We still used Boothferry Park for a while after. The reserves played there, so it wasn't an instantaneous death. But it was sad to see all the hard work that had been put into certain areas of the stadium – and by that I mean the pitch as the most important part – just gone. I can vividly remember standing at Boothferry Park in a completely empty stadium and thinking: 'You can still hear the crowd.'

Martin Batchelor: I have lots of wonderful memories but the place was falling down, almost three-sided and when the ball landed on the Best Stand roof everyone underneath was showered in rust. It was time for it to go

Roy Bly: I used to spend so much time down there with my father – particularly when he was injured! – so it was sad to see it come to an end. I'd always hoped Hull City would develop the stadium like Newcastle and Everton. It was a shame but we'd had two or three owners that had let the club and the ground spiral down, and people have to move on, and you can't argue against the KC!

Matt Rudd: I wasn't upset or full of regret, aside from my not being able to attend the final game. Moving to the KC has done everything we hoped it would do, and more. The only thing I would change is the way Boothferry Park was allowed to rot for months and years after it became surplus to requirements. It deserved better.

Mike Hall: My overriding emotion was definitely sadness at the final whistle, but somehow a drab 1-0 defeat beneath a drab, grey sky seemed quite apt for a ground that had been in decline for too long. I think I was very ready for the move to the new stadium though. Throughout the 1990s I'd felt as though City had missed an opportunity to jump on board the boom years –particularly after Euro 96 – and this represented the best chance of us finally doing that. Looking back I think I'd maybe come to resent Boothferry Park a little for that, and seen it as holding us back, and maybe I shouldn't have.

Rich Lusmore: I'm one of those sad old soaks for whom Hull City will always be synonymous with Boothferry Park. And before I get accused of remembering the past through rose-tinted spectacles, yes I know it was a dump. I never got to see the ground in its pomp and/or anywhere near full (I was too young for the Waggy-Chillo glory days). I can also remember thinking how pitiful it looked when Kempton was first closed, leaving a three-sided ground (for some reason it never felt that bad during the North Stand demolition). But Boothferry Park had an atmosphere (even with only 4,000 in there) that I'm afraid to say has rarely been replicated at the KC. And when I have seen it reasonably packed – the 4-1 win over Sheffield United in 1983 and a league cup tie against Southampton around the same time spring to mind – the place really did rock. I know this leaves me at risk of accusations of having a certain 'dinosaur' mentality but those days in the Kempton with away fans just the other side of a thin dividing wall generated a noise at City matches I've rarely experienced since. Ironically, despite all this, I didn't go to the final game against Darlo, preferring instead to retain my own memories of the ground rather than see it ended at some else's behest. And despite my love of Boothferry Park, I didn't disagree with the decision to move. Instead, I was simply relieved that the move had been engineered by people with the interests of the club at heart. And of course it was one that obviously proved beneficial for the club.

Dave Burns: On the last day, my abiding memory was me wanting to do something to reflect on the end of an era. I like to mix music with football clips, and as the last piece of audio as we closed the programme was Cast's Walkaway with bits of commentary involving people like Waggy and Raich. I was getting messages from people saying that they were crying in their car while they were driving.

John Cooper: A family once asked me if they could scatter a loved one's ashes at Boothferry Park. It wasn't a problem, as Boothferry Park was a home for people, it wasn't just a football ground. I hadn't thought who'd scatter the ashes though. It ended up being me. It was something we started and let's just say that I worked with a lot of undertakers, particularly from the mid-1990s onwards. Quite a few people had their ashes scattered there and we carried that on at the new stadium because it's an important thing. It's the people that matter. It's the fans that matter. Us staff, we're only custodians.

Keith Edwards: These days I drive an articulated lorry delivering insulation to new housing estates. I got a job one day saying 'Hull – Boothferry Road'. I couldn't believe it. I did my old journey from Sheffield to Hull, turn right at the traffic lights, then a sharp left straight through where the stand used to be. I sat where the halfway line used to be, thinking: 'Where has that time gone?' I had a nice little daydream about the goals I'd scored on this patch of land. I was soon brought back to earth by a forklift driver shouting: "Oi, pal, get your arse out of there!"

Out with the old, in with the new. Regardless of the emotional ties to Boothferry Park, the KC was awaiting. And it looked incredible. It was not the kind of stadium the people of Hull were used to. And on December 18th, 2002, it would host a friendly against Sunderland to usher in a new era. But would everything be ready in time?

Adam Pearson: We had a really good atmosphere at the club and the council got it built so quickly. There was none of the messing around that there was at Brighton. We had a great opening night against Sunderland and we kicked straight on.

Tom McVie: The national stadium at Wembley was built with a massive, massive overspend, and we said we'd spend £47m on the KC and we spent £46m, and it was built on time too, under budget! That shows what local politicians can do!

John Cooper: It was built within a year. It had some flaws at the time but it was what both clubs needed. The stadium saved both clubs. We couldn't have lived at Boothferry Park for much longer, and it was the same at the Boulevard for Hull FC.

Peter Taylor: I felt it was the start of something special, and so did the staff. I was really pleased with the staff that we had – Colin Murphy, Steve Butler, Mark Prudhoe, Simon Maltby, Billy Russell, Phil Hough – all good people, so to me the spirit in the camp was terrific. I felt we could have a party and everybody would be invited. And that's how I felt about the move to the KC because we were all saying: "Look at our fans, look what a big club this is. We've got a real chance here of getting it right." I knew that if we made sensible decisions we were going to be successful. We were confident about our ability, we just had to pick the right people, make sure we had the right squad, work out what we needed, who'd score the goals, who'd stop them. We'd been a sleeping giant but we were awake. It was an enjoyable place to come into every day as we felt like we had something special in our grasp.

Tom McVie: We took a lot of advice from Bob Murray – the then Sunderland chairman. We wanted to make it unique, but we were let down badly by Sport England, for which I'll never forgive them. But whatever the size of it – and it can be expanded – it had to be unique but it had to be part of the new generation stadia. Many of those built 20 years or so ago were just four stands in a line, whereas the KC is a bowl which guarantees you a good view. It had to be top of the shop. I still have a certificate from the 'British Construction Awards 2002 Best Practice category highly commended – the KC Stadium, Hull' it was that good. We beat Manchester City's stadium in one of those awards.

Brendon Smurthwaite: When we moved stadia, everything about the club garnered more interest and we needed a full-time media person. The interest in the club was phenomenal, even on a national scale. People realised there was a story here. People were seeing a sleeping giant coming alive.

Ian Farrow: As a fanzine editor I'd been invited into the KC at various times during its construction. Each time it was amazing to think Hull City, the club we'd supported through some thick and a lot of thin, were to be playing in such a grand, modern arena. We had been to various new stadia such as Bolton's but this was better with it elliptical design, well-spaced seats in our (and the rugby club's) colours, bars and food outlets. Most importantly it was ours (well the council's) and not owned by one megalomaniac who could kick us out at will.

Tom McVie: Pat Doyle, the then leader of the council, is the man who first and foremost has to be credited with the existence of the KC Stadium. He's the one who talked to the council and decided we needed to build a stadium that would stop the problems we'd been having.

We needed a lot of hits out of this. We talked endlessly about it being part of a regeneration project for west Hull, creating jobs, bringing state-of-the-art sports facilities to the city, but clearly we wanted a situation where the clubs couldn't suddenly find they'd had their grounds' gates padlocked because they hadn't paid their bills. It became apparent that the only way we could do that was if we built a stadium, we ran it and we hired it out to the clubs.

Nick Turner: Less than 24 hours after the Darlington defeat, a preview session was held at the KC Stadium, and on a drizzly December Sunday afternoon of Stygian gloom, an awed public being permitted to file in and walk around the pitch perimeter under the watchful eyes of hi-viz clad stewards. The pristine green turf glistened in the steady rain under the KC's fancy lilac illumination as curious fans murmured in quiet amazement at the stunning quality and size of their new home.

The immediate surrounds were still a work in progress, but over the railway line lay a relic of pre-Boothferry Park days – the ruins of the original Anlaby Road ground with the steps of the old Spion Kop and its retaining wall still visible among the trees and undergrowth.

By chance or design, the Tigers had come home to their original lair; a central and historical sports ground in a familiar part of town. This time it would be a state-of-the-art facility in a perfect location. No soulless out-of-town retail park or unfamiliar surroundings, but nestled centrally on the very land where we made our Division 2 debut back in 1905.

Tom McVie: When you go in the KC, when you look around at the platforms for the people with disabilities or in wheelchairs, at Boothferry Park you were right at the bottom of a stand in a little tin box. At the KC, the platforms are at the same level as the directors' boxes. That's the kind of thing we'd carefully thought about it. Other places weren't doing that at the time. It's asymmetric, it can be extended, it was a one-off. It still gets voted as one of the favourite away grounds of Football League clubs.

Rob Smith: It was a good opportunity for us all to raise our game. We'd been stuck in a rut a little in our jobs under previous regimes but Adam changed that around. He had the vision and the stadium was part of that. He involved us all at an early stage and really took our advice. We all felt part of that move. We were still a very small staff, but that helped to bring out the best in everybody. Preparing for that move, and having to upsell what wasn't always good football to get sponsorships and get the supporter base up – it almost doubled in that first half-season at the KC – was a challenge. There were times when you wouldn't invite your worst enemy to Boothferry Park, which was sad, and I was one of the last to leave the offices there, but we were in a totally new world.

Dave Burns: One of the first things I'd done with Adam was a phone-in at the Guildhall just after the council had announced the plans for the stadium. Everyone was really excited. I'd been along to the site as it was being built and asked Adam to put the press box right on halfway. He did that, but I didn't realise he was going to put the box right at the top of the stand. You'd moan about the steps at Boothferry Park, but you needed a sherpa to get you to the top of those steps at the KC. It was great though. I love it as a stadium. With its curves it still looks sexy.

Ken Wagstaff: I had a part in opening it. It was freezing! They had a bed in the middle of the pitch, and Burnsy was sleeping in it, dreaming that he was playing football with me. Then I came on the pitch with angel's wings on and we pass each other the ball and run down the pitch. I was meant to pass him the ball so that he could score but when I got to the penalty area I shot and scored. He called me a few names! When I go now, they still ask me if I've brought my boots.

Dave Burns: I got to do the opening night along with the Fine Young Cannibals. I'd designed a dream sequence where I was lying in a double bed, when I pop out from the bed and dribble a ball through a group of school kids in football kits. At the end there's Waggy with a pair of angel wings waiting in the penalty box. I always say I scored the first goal at the KC, but there was nobody there to see it. I was really proud of that!

Tom Wilson: It was moving on, advancing. Adam got me back involved. I'd been scouting for Brian Horton – I scouted for him everywhere. Adam Pearson saw me at Boothferry Park and asked me to come and do the sponsors hosting. At first I did it on my own and then when we moved to the KC I got a load of other lads involved.

Dave Richardson: I'd been to the KC a few times during its construction but it was difficult to appreciate just how good it was until the place was complete. Was this fabulous stadium for us? Modern facilities, great views and an ill-thought-out photographers' room. Whoever thought of siting it in a small room off the West Stand Upper concourse clearly hadn't carried a bag full off camera gear up a few flights of stairs! We later got moved to the corridor underneath the South Stand which had sub-Arctic temperatures in winter! It wasn't until we were in the Premier League that we got the great facilities they have now.

Frank and Margaret Beill: As members of the Fan Liaison Committee we had been on a conducted tour of the stadium while building work was still in progress. Before the first game with Sunderland we met other supporters in the ground who had tears in their eyes. Boothferry Park had been allowed to become a slum by previous owners who were only interested in its real estate value, if they had any interest at all. The KC was a great improvement on what had gone before but our personal impression was that it was a good rugby league ground but not big enough for an association football club with ambition.

Mike Hall: Now, with the benefit of 15 years of hindsight, I see the move from Boothferry Park to the KC Stadium as four days in which the club was reborn. It began feeling like a different club entirely from that opening friendly against Sunderland and I loved that – I still do – but I would go quite a long way to spend one more afternoon or evening stood on the South Stand terrace or Kempton at Boothferry Park.

James Richardson: I'd keenly watched the KC being built as I lived 10 minutes away from West Park, and watching cranes hoisting the West Stand together only heightened my anticipation to ridiculous levels for its opening. It matched them and more. I think the open day got a lot of the novelty and tourist feeling out of my system although I did spend a lot of time during the early games marvelling over the blue lit halo that was emitting around the bowl. I had some concerns over how long it would take to bed in and feel homely, although those passed pretty quickly. I was more overwhelmed with how beautiful the stadium was and how we really had no excuses not to push on anymore.

Lawrie Dudfield: It was brilliant. I talk about the KC with a heavy heart, and I go back a lot now, but the football fanatic in me loved Boothferry Park. The pitch was amazing, the atmosphere – such as in that 4-0 win against York City – was incredible. The big stadia lose that sort of thing. So I was torn. It was amazing to play in that stadium, and you knew the club was going somewhere.

On the day of the Sunderland game, it seemed strange that a friendly – with the Raich Carter Trophy at stake – could generate such excitement. But this was no ordinary friendly.

Dave Burns: They asked me to get involved in the committee for the opening night, and then I was invited to host it. I was honoured and privileged to do that. One of the things I wanted to do, which never happened, was to dig the centre spot up from Boothferry Park and walk it down Anlaby Road with a load of fans in a torch-light parade to the KC, and then have it lifted up to the top of the West Stand. We'd then have someone in an amber and black lamé suit come down on a zipwire to deliver the centre spot from Boothferry Park to the centre of the KC. It would have had a great sense of theatre, but for health and safety reasons it never happened.

Raich Carter Junior: It made the family really proud and when I got on the pitch at the end of present the trophy – it meant a lot to us. They also named a suite after him. There's a picture of him on a mural on the West Stand. I'm just sorry my dad never got to play there.

John Cooper: I hadn't had time to think in the run up to the Sunderland and Hartlepool games. I was on autopilot. I had to put any feelings I might have had to one side. It was a long time after that it sunk in that we had lost Boothferry Park and we had this great new stadium. It was probably only when Boothferry Park was demolished when it fully hit me. The time was a strange one for me. It was exciting though, as it wasn't just the move, it was the way the move was done. The city wanted it to happen.

Rob Smith: I would go down during the building and stand in West Park looking at this thing going up, almost in disbelief. We'd had so many years of lean times, and I was just thinking: 'This is amazing, I'm part of this.' Everything was going to be 10 times the size of what we were operating in at Boothferry Park. But obviously we couldn't get in there until it was finished, and we only got the keys a few days before the Sunderland game. So my memories of the Sunderland game are of not knowing where anything was. I was trying to take key sponsors on a tour before the game, and I kept getting lost as I just didn't know where anything was. But we'd moved to another planet. This was where Hull City deserved to be.

Dave Burns: We'd run a competition for a fan to kick the game off against Sunderland and it was won by a former World War Two commando named Frank Barrett who'd seen City play at the Circle. We thought he was the right person to link the past, the present and the future to kick off the game. If I remember correctly, Alex Burgess, who was commentating the game, started things off by shouting: "Give it some welly, Frank." It was a lovely night.

Mike White (Hull City fan and Radio Humberside reporter): As a City fan growing up, I had mixed feelings going into the KC. I'm a traditionalist, and I had a real soft spot for Boothferry Park – I was a regular in the South Stand seats – but there was something appealing about moving to something new. And you got a sense that it could really do something for the city. It gave the whole place a feelgood vibe. I was working at Kingston Communications at the time, and before the game there was a buzz and excitement among all the staff about going there. You sensed good times ahead, though I don't think we suspected quite how good…

Gary Clark: My biggest dilemma was where to go for a drink before the game. It had been Silver Cod for as long as I could remember, so where would you see old mates? Where was everyone else meeting? Word on the street was that we should give Polar Bear a try on Spring

Bank and slowly the bar filled up with all the usual faces, much to the annoyance of the handful or regulars who were a bit put out.

In goal for Sunderland was a familiar face to City fans, one who'd done so much to ruin the occasion at Boothferry Park a few days prior.

Michael Ingham: I made a little bit of history playing in both games. I sometimes come across Hull fans and like to let them know that.

Ian Farrow: As we walked in that first time for a friendly against Sunderland we realised – with the lights symbolically shining bright – that Hull City now had ambition, and had decided to compete in the modern football world. I vaguely recall Steve Melton's goal but remember most of all how bright the floodlights shone without being intrusive, how the crowd, from our seats perched up high, looked more uniformed, and how the whole place looked so much bigger but still neatly enclosed. The clean and modern toilets made it seem like a visit to the theatre. Even after all these years I'm still in awe of being at the stadium. Moving to the KC was the starting point of the greatest era in Hull City's history.

Gary Clark: Into the ground, all brand new this, new experience and so on, then the first glimpse of the West Stand from the East Stand concourse…Wow ! Incredible. Words failed me, the stadium looked 100% better then I imagined, and because of my Hull upbringing I fully expected anything that Hull City Council had built to be on the disappointing side, but this was truly magnificent. Our new home, a new future, and a bright one at that.

Michael Ingham: It was a night match, and just driving into the stadium it was so impressive. It's got quite a long tunnel, so you don't really see the pitch until quite late. We were laughing though, because the guest of honour was Sunderland chairman, Bob Murray, and he was walking along us in a line shaking our hands. It was all a bit strange. We never really saw him in Sunderland!

I just remember Steve Melton going round me in a one on one to score. But it was great for me to play at Boothferry Park one day and at the KC Stadium a few days afterwards.

Tom McVie: I remember the open day in early December. I just remember seeing people walking around open mouthed. Looking around at the Sunderland match, I just felt a real sense of pride, that local people had done this, local companies.

Mike Scott: My abiding memory was two-fold. First, the thrill of leaving the E5 vomitory and entering the arena for the first time. The impossible brightness of the lights (which by today's standards would be akin to holding up lit matches) and the greeniest green of the pitch. It felt modern and coherent and welcoming – all the things that Boothferry Park had stopped being some years before. Second, the fireworks display that heralded the exhibition match against Sunderland, which was programmed to mimic the "clap, clap, clap-clap-clap, clap-clap-clap-clap, City!" chant. It blew me away! Sarah Whatmore was quite a sight, too…

Ian Thomson: I was sitting there watching the Sunderland friendly and thinking, over and over again: 'Bloody hell, this is our ground!'

Adam Lowthorpe: I never believed it was going to happen. We'd heard all these plans so much. The move got everybody in the city more interested in sport. It gave us a kick-start. The participation rates in junior football rocketed around that time and have carried on going since. And the number of Hull City shirts you get around the city compared with what it was 20 years ago was staggering.

Chris Chilton: I was in awe when I first saw the KC. It was massive.

Nick Barmby: It's a difficult one because of the history and tradition of Boothferry Park. But you look at Derby with the Baseball Ground and other clubs such as Arsenal. Yes everyone should always remember their history, but the minute we went into the KC the momentum just snowballed. A lot of people have commented to me, ex-players, they've loved the KC and think it's a fantastic stadium. When the KC's buzzing there are not a lot of places that are better.

Ken Houghton: When they opened the KC I thought it was terrific. Boothferry Park was one of the best playing surfaces in the country but when you came to the KC it was brilliant. You felt as if you were in a proper stadium. It would have been nice to have played on it.

Gary Alexander: I'd been at Hull City through the period of the KC being built and we'd spend a lot of time down there. I'm disappointed I didn't get to stay longer in terms of playing there. It's a fantastic stadium and the club were a Premier League side in the making.

Marc Joseph: I loved it. There weren't that many of those new-build stadia at the time. It was needed for the city and we loved playing there. It brought everyone together and it was something we could be proud of.

Ian Ashbee: The club was ready to move forward. The fan base was incredible. Getting 15,000 fans in League 2 is ridiculous. To have that fan base and to be able to move to a stadium like that can only help. I think for a few people the stadium was too big and they inevitably fell along the wayside. But I think it was a massive thing for Peter Taylor too. It was great. I embraced it.

Damien Delaney: It was fantastic. A lot of those lads had come to Hull from playing reserve team football or playing in the lower leagues in front of empty or old stadiums. For us to be able to say "this is our home"... I felt really proud. This was our stadium and 15,000-plus every week in what is now League 2 – that was unheard of, and probably still is to this day. You could just tell that the city was fully behind it. Adam Pearson had done a great job of selling the club, he'd brought in a big-name manager. We had a lot of young, hungry players with a point to prove.

Garreth Roberts: Moving to the KC and Adam Pearson doing such a good job was the catalyst to Hull City's success. I'd have loved to have played there. What a stadium. It's great for families too, which Boothferry Park wasn't, as much as I loved it.

Rob Harmer (Hull City fan): I thought it felt slightly surreal, hard to believe that it was actually our stadium. It was such a departure from Boothferry Park and initially it almost felt like being at an away game. As with anyone moving to a new home, it doesn't take long before things start to feel familiar and Boothferry Park now seems like a lifetime away.

Mark Robinson: Even now it has a wow factor for me, particularly when you think back to Boothferry Park and the rust coming down from the roof and the broken toilets.

Peter Taylor: I just thought about how incredibly lucky we were. We used to chuckle about it, even going to away games saying to each other: "Look at how many Hull City shirts are about." And then in home matches our average in the KC was something like 18,000 in League 2. Unbelievable.

Martin Batchelor: A stadium fit for progress, good enough for the Premier League let alone the bottom division. Finally a sign that City were going the right way.

John Cooper: I found those early games difficult as the KC didn't have the atmosphere that Boothferry Park had had. It didn't have the low roofing or anything like that. It was different.

People had to come to terms with it and get used to it. Also, I was tasked with putting concerts on as I was the stadium manager. I'd never put a concert on in my life, and there I was arranging shows by people like Elton John and Westlife!

Tom McVie: The impact on Hull has been profound. It's brought pride to the city, it's fulfilled many of the objectives we had to start with. A lot of people have jobs connected to the stadium, directly and indirectly. It holds major conferences and exhibitions. The sports facilities are second to none. We achieved what we wanted with our original objectives, it's a beautiful stadium to watch sport in, it's a beautiful stadium to watch concerts in, and it's guaranteed the successful futures of Hull City and Hull FC. I've no idea where the two clubs would have been had the stadium not been built. Was it worth it? Yes, it was.

The first game 'proper' at the KC was at home to Hartlepool on Boxing Day, with future World Cup final referee Howard Webb officiating. There was to be no party-pooping this time. City announced the permanent signing of Stuart Green before kick-off, and the midfielder sealed the 2-0 win. It was Dean Keates, however, who had the honour of scoring the stadium's first league goal.

Dean Keates: It was Boxing Day and my dad had come up to watch his first Hull City game. Walking out on to the pitch and taking in that atmosphere showed that it was a special place. It was an unbelievable experience. You could really see the potential within the city.

Rich Lusmore: To see more than 22,000 inside a ground for a Hull City home game was something I'd never before witnessed. It felt like we'd finally arrived back in the big time.

Robert Crampton: I thought: 'This is brilliant.' I took my five-year-old son. I couldn't have, in all conscience, taken him to Boothferry Park. That would have made me an irresponsible parent! We won and it felt like there was a bit of glamour. I remember the on-pitch announcer going up to the Hartlepool fans and going: "Hartlepool! This is Hull City!" and them all laughing, but there was still something about it. Some drama, 20,000-odd fans. It was my son's first game – who fell asleep when the ref blew his whistle and didn't wake up until half-time. But bearing in mind that the lock-out by David Lloyd had been two years ago, it was great. It felt like we were on the move. My kids were five and three at the time, and that sort of thing makes you think a lot about your identity. They were living in north London near Arsenal's ground, and I was thinking: 'Do I make them Hull City fans?' And I'm proud to say that they are both now proud Hull City fans.

Paul Musselwhite: It was fantastic. I feel very lucky to have played in the last game at Boothferry Park and the first game at the KC. That's something I like to be associated with. They were career high points for me. The Sunderland game was a fantastic night, but the Hartlepool game was just amazing. You could see it was a massive turning point in the club's history. People had had visions to do it before, but Adam Pearson made it happen.

The first goal came on 21 minutes.

Dean Keates: I made a run into the right-hand side of the box, Gary Alexander played the ball to me and I ended up one-on-one with a very good friend of mine, Chris Westwood, who I'd played with at Walsall and then was to later at Peterborough, Wycombe and Wrexham. I checked back inside to go for a curler with my left foot. Chris blocked that, so switched back to my right foot. Being left-footed, I didn't think I'd be able to get much power behind my right foot. I then thought I'd try a little dink and fortunately it came off and went in the top corner. It will live long in the memory of the stadium and it was an unbelievable experience that I'll take to the grave with me.

Stuart Green sealed the 2-0 victory in the 75th minute.

Stuart Green: My mum came to that game, and she didn't watch me much. It was such a special day for me. Hartlepool were a good team, but everybody clicked into gear. I just thought to myself: 'I have to score.' An incredible day and an incredible game for me, because of the fact that I scored a goal and the way in which I took it. We were on a high. We were starting to think we could push for play-offs.

So, a brand new stadium worthy of a much higher level of football, a former England manager at the helm, and a 2-0 win in front of a crowd of 22,319. What could stop City now? As had been the case for the past season-and-a-half, City couldn't back up the big games with further victories. In the club's next game a 1-1 draw was played out at York, then came a 1-0 defeat at Bury. A poor Bristol Rovers side were beaten 1-0 in a tepid game at the KC – with Gary Alexander scoring what would be his last goal for the club – before Exeter drew 2-2 at the new stadium, with City's goals coming from Stuart Elliott. A dreadful performance then saw City lose 2-0 at Leyton Orient, after which rumours spread like wildfire about unrest among the players and a number of fallings out with Peter Taylor. City had won one, drawn two and lost two since the Hartlepool game. The fans, however, were given a boost when one of the club's most popular players of the past decade or so, goalkeeper Alan Fettis, was re-signed from York City.

Alan Fettis: York went into administration. We'd been like that for three months and the club were trying to offload players and cut costs. We hadn't been paid for months and it was a difficult time. Then I got a phone call saying: "Would you like to go to Hull?" To be honest, initially I said no. As much as I had really fond memories there, and would still look out for the club's results, I just thought you shouldn't go back. Then I thought that it was a completely different club, as they were now at the KC, so I thought I should give it a go. We sorted out the contract but looking back it was the wrong decision.

One 1990s legend had returned and rumours were rife that another was on the way. That was partly because the legend himself – Dean Windass – was behind them.

Dave Burns: Deano was desperate to come back. I was at some ground or other and got a message in my cans saying that the next caller is Dean. I asked him what he wanted to talk about. "City, Burnsy, City," came the reply. Then he said: "It's Deano! I'm at Stamford Bridge, I've been playing at Chelsea and I'm on the Middlesbrough team coach. I wanna come back, tell Peter Taylor to sign me!" He was playing in the Premier League at Chelsea ringing me up telling me he wanted to play League 2 football. I always thought Peter Taylor should have signed Deano, but I got the impression that he thought Deano was probably more trouble than he was worth. But Deano's a pussycat.

Meanwhile, Gary Alexander had decided to return to London, and signed for Leyton Orient.

Gary Alexander: I had to get back to London. I'd just had a little boy and I'd not long split up with his mum. It became difficult for me living in Hull on my own knowing my son was in London, where I was nowhere near him. Some of the stories you'd hear at the time from me leaving Hull City were pretty horrendous – I couldn't work out where they'd come from – but if I'm being honest I was going off the rails a little bit having had a relationship break up and not being able to see my boy when I wanted. It was a difficult time. There was no bust up though.

Lawrie Dudfield: Gary went on to have an exceptional career, and he earned that. He'd score goals whenever he went. He was a very, very good striker.

City were both Deano-less and hopeless. A 0-0 home draw against a York side in financial peril was followed by an abysmal display in Essex against Southend, a club close to Peter Taylor's heart. Alan Fettis was making his second debut, and City lost 3-0 to 10 men, with big money signings Stuart Green, Stuart Elliott and Andy Holt all taken off at half-time, to be replaced by John Anderson, Steve Burton and Danny Webb.

Peter Taylor: That game hurt. I would never take an individual off to get a response from others, so if I took off Stuart Green, Stuart Elliott and Andy Holt at half-time it was because I didn't think they were performing. The way I felt, if we could have used six substitutes that day I'd have done it. That game showed our problem. We didn't know how we were going to play. If you want to be successful the players have got to be able to look around the team and know that they'd be OK because of who was alongside them. As a manager I've got to then look at the group of players and think: 'Well I know what I'm going to get today.' With those players, you didn't know what you were going to get. You'd hope you'd get a performance, and at times I'd think of them as '18-handicappers' where all of a sudden you'd go on the golf course and they'd hit a brilliant shot, but then they'd slice their next shot. I wanted more consistent golfers, because I wanted to know at 3pm on a Saturday what I was going to get out of them.

Alan Fettis: It was cold in Southend. We'd gone down the day before and we couldn't train as there was snow everywhere. The weather made it seem so disorganised. The game isn't one that sticks in my head, but it wasn't one of the best. And I never really got off the ground after that. I regret it. I wish it could have been better as I could have been part of something that Peter Taylor was taking forwards.

Stuart Green: At Southend the weather was bad and we didn't train for a couple of days before hand. I had to train the day before. If I didn't train the day before I would struggle. We hadn't been winning many games and I felt sluggish. Pete made a couple of important changes, changing the keeper and dropping John Anderson. I got a dead leg early on and I just never had a good game at Roots Hall. At half-time Pete just came in, made three changes, and what happened after was pretty unbelievable. We were disappointed. Looking back at it now, you could see how desperate Pete was to beat a former club.

Dean Keates: There was no consistency. It was all very bitty, and you couldn't put your finger on why. It just didn't happen for us.

Peter Taylor: That was the lowest I was at Hull City. I live near Southend and they'd been my team. That's where Adam Pearson was magnificent. He knew how low I was and he came to me and just said: "Don't worry, we'll get it sorted out." That's how brilliant a chairman he is. He could have easily said: "Well Jan Molby didn't work and now Peter Taylor isn't working," and made another change.

Lawrie Dudfield: We were 3-0 down at half-time and Peter had had enough. He was just saying: "I can't change things, I can't get things working my way, that's it I'm off." Thankfully that never happened. Adam Pearson must have turned it around. That game was a big turning point in Peter's leadership. He came back from that and a lot of people wouldn't.

Adam Pearson: I felt we'd always get there but it was a personal frustration. I just couldn't understand why it wouldn't click. I'm not sure that Peter completely trusted Stuart Elliott at that point, though that developed over the coming months.

The game – and the half-time substitutions – were to have a huge impact on the immediate future of one of City's star players. Stuart Green had been welcomed on to the pitch like a gladiator six weeks earlier in the first game at the KC. Now he wanted out, and wanted to move to Carlisle.

Stuart Green: It was the biggest mistake I made in my career. I was a young man and I needed someone to point me in the right direction. Me and a few others were left out of the game the week after Southend and got given the weekend off. I came home to Cumbria, where I was half-an-hour away from Brunton Park, so I went along to watch the game and see some friends. I'd just signed a three-and-a-half-year contact at Hull so I had no intention of leaving. I was invited into the Carlisle directors box so went in – you just don't do that! – and that filtered back to Hull and they weren't happy. One thing led to another, I wasn't training with the squad, and I should have dealt with it a lot differently, but Carlisle came in for me and by that point I wanted to go. I just wanted to get away from Hull, to calm down, as I wasn't enjoying it. So I left. Within a week I was wishing I'd just ridden it out and played a couple of games in the reserves.

Peter Taylor: I left Stuart Green out of the team after Southend. On the Saturday afternoon he didn't come to the Hull game against Lincoln. Then I'm told he wants to go to Carlisle, so I told him he could go. If you're showing an interest in Carlisle and you don't want to be at the KC Stadium then a) you're mad, and b) if that's what you want to be then off you go. Then a week later I found out from my wife that he'd taken my daughter out on a date. So not only did I want to kill him because they'd both broken the rules – my daughter more than Stuart, to be fair – I'm thinking: 'Oh no, all the supporters are going to be thinking that I've got rid of him because he's gone out with my daughter when I didn't even know about it!'

Adam Pearson: There were things going on in Stuart Green's life that meant he had to leave. Stuart was a good player who'd lost his way, and it was a bit symptomatic of the whole team at that point.

Things were to get worse still. After the Southend debacle, Lincoln became the first team to inflict defeat upon City at the KC courtesy of a 1-0 win. Scunthorpe then beat City 3-1 at Glanford Park, before another disappointing result came, a 1-1 draw at home to Cambridge. Off the pitch everything was in place for City to succeed, but on the pitch the club was seemingly going nowhere.

Adam Pearson: I just felt we were going to go and take the league by storm, but it never really happened that season. We were beaten at home 1-0 by Lincoln and Dean Keates hit the inside of the post, the ball rolled along the line and it hit the other side of the post and came back out. I remember thinking: 'I'm never going to crack this.' I went home to my local pub and drank every optic across the bar that night.

Justin Whittle: There were some echoes with what had happened under Brian and Jan. We weren't playing well and the move to the KC seemed to lift the away teams as much as it lifted us. Everyone wanted to beat us in a stadium like that, the best in the division. It took us a while to get it right. I'd been at Stoke when we moved from the Victoria Ground to the Brittania and we went down that first season, so it does happen elsewhere. Thankfully Adam Pearson had learned by that point not to be too hasty when it came to firing managers. You can buy as many players as you want but it doesn't mean that you're instantly going to get a great team.

A couple of away wins managed to inject a little bit of optimism into the club. Carlisle were hammered 5-1 at Brunton Park, a victory inspired by new loan signing Jonathan Walters. Macclesfield were then beaten 1-0 thanks to a Stuart Elliott goal. However, this upturn in events was followed by a disappointing 0-0 draw at home to Oxford, a 4-2 defeat at Rushden, and a 1-1 draw at home to Torquay. Goals from loanee Jon Otsemobor and Dean Keates saw City to a 2-0 win over struggling Shrewsbury at the KC, then Peter Taylor moved into the transfer market again. Big Ben Burgess was coming to the KC.

Ben Burgess: It was Peter Taylor who convinced me. He was such a good manager and I'd always liked the way his teams played. He really wanted me too. When he showed me the KC

I just thought: 'Wow, what are these doing in League 2?' It was incredible. It was a Premier League club in League 2.

Peter Taylor: He was a terrific footballer. The perfect centre-forward for League 1 or League 2 and probably the Championship because of his size and the ability he had. He was a good target man for us. He wanted to score goals but he wasn't selfish to the point where he wouldn't help his partner score goals as well. Just a tremendous centre-forward and a lovely lad who wanted to be a team player.

Ben wasn't just a goalscorer, and he was a confident boy. It wouldn't affect Ben if he missed a penalty. They're the little things we looked at when we recruited.

Ben's debut didn't go to plan, however, with Wrexham winning 2-1 at the KC.

Ben Burgess: I won a penalty and Dean Keates missed it. I really enjoyed it even though we lost. The nucleus of the team was there, but Peter Taylor had made it clear to me that this wouldn't be the team for the next season.

The nucleus of a very good team was forming, however. Stuart Elliott and Ian Ashbee were established as certain starters at this stage, and Damien Delaney, Marc Joseph and Ben Burgess were all becoming accustomed to their new surroundings. However, the squad was still bloated from the excessive transfer activity of the past two summers, leaving many good players at a loose end.

Greg Strong: Peter had brought in Damien Delaney who was left-sided, 6 foot 3 and a centre-half so I thought the writing was on the wall to some extent, but I never stopped trying. I went in every day and worked my hardest. I hardly missed a reserve game and put myself in a position where I could be selected. At times I think Peter got fed up of me knocking on the door and saying: "Any chance?" But as you get older you understand these things a little bit more, that every manager has his own beliefs and preferences. You just have to say: "I'm not for him."

Mike Edwards: I upset Peter a little bit because I would turn up for training on a Thursday. He'd say: "What are you doing here?" and I'd say: "I need to get my fitness back". He'd say: "You're just making the numbers up," but I wanted to train with the team and get seen. I couldn't get into the team though.

Damien Delaney: It was a transition period. Peter kept saying: "Next year will be our year." He was putting the building blocks in place so that when we came back for pre-season there was nothing left to be done. There were a few players there who Peter was looking to move on, and that just meant there was an adjustment period. We were lucky to have that half-season, as the city and the fans saw what was going on and stayed behind us and were patient. That said, we knew if we didn't start the next season very well that patience would be tested.

Marc Joseph: It was a case of the manager just getting his own players in. No disrespect to the players that were there, but Peter Taylor had his own ideas and brought in lots and lots of young, talented players who've since gone on to do very, very well at a very high level.

Around this time Damien Delaney was getting a bit of stick from some sections of the City fan base. This wasn't helped by the fact that he was filling in in a number of different positions.

Damien Delaney: Moving positions never really bothered me. All I wanted to do was play. As long as I was playing I was happy. You can't beat that as a professional. Half the time Peter wouldn't even tell me where I'd be playing, he'd just announce the team and he'd know I wouldn't be bothered. I'd still run around, put my all in. I may not have done very well in some of the positions I played, but I always tried my hardest.

City's form improved in the final few games of the season. Boston were beaten 1-0 at York Street through a Stuart Elliott goal, and the Ulsterman was to score twice more, with Walters getting one, as City beat Bournemouth 3-1 at the KC. A 2-0 defeat at Darlington followed, but then came a piece of history in a home match against Kidderminster. Ben Burgess scored the KC Stadium's first hat-trick.

Ben Burgess: When I'd scored my third goal, Jonathan Walters ran up to me and said: "That's the worst hat-trick I've ever seen." It wasn't great. One was a tackle, one was a penalty and one was a header from 25 yards. It was my first career hat-trick and they were my first goals for Hull so it was nice to break my duck.

City won 4-1, with Walters getting the other. The penultimate game of the season saw City lose 2-1 at Rochdale, with Burgess getting another. However, Peter Taylor's mind was already firmly fixed on his plans for the 2003/04 season, and one player in particular had realised that he wanted to be part of them.

Stuart Green: Peter Taylor rang me one morning on the way into training and said: "What's happening?" I said: "I want to come back, and if I could play for Hull now I would. I realise I've made a mistake." Pete told me to come back pre-season and work my socks off to get into the team. That was all I wanted. I think Pete saw it as a bit like signing a new player too.

There was only one game left of the season, but it was to be one of huge significance for City's opponents, Swansea, who needed to win to stay in the Football League. The Welsh side duly won, 4-2, but that only tells part of the story. Swansea's fans were continually invading the pitch, and referee Scott Mathieson seemed completely intimidated by the home crowd, meaning the Swans got a number of highly contentious decisions going their way.

Dean Keates: The rest is history for Swansea, but there were a few decisions that the ref let go to make sure he could get out of Swansea and get back home safely. Their fans were full of passion, but there were a few decisions that didn't go our way…

Another summer loomed and another squad shake-up was on the cards. For two players in particular, that brought with it an air of uncertainty.

Andy Holt: Peter was a fantastic coach. He knew his stuff and was precise on everything. At the end of that season, even though I had another year on my contract, Peter pulled me in and said: "You're not for me, go and find yourself another club." I went away in the summer, Peter had given me the name of an agent to help me find a new club and a couple of teams down south came in for me. I'd just had a baby so I didn't want to move all that way away. Then Northampton showed an interest, offering a two-year contract. I thought that was fantastic. Only then it turned out I had to complete a trial period first. I rang Peter and told him I was being messed about. He told me to give him five minutes. He rang me back and told me to come back to Hull. He told me to stay in Hull and train with the club. I'd got really fit and started playing for the reserves, then got back into the first-team squad and then started a few games. Peter told me I'd really changed his opinion of me and how much he respected that and how I was back in his plans.

Dean Keates: I thought I'd done well though I'd done my ankle in a game at York. I'd always been an honest, hard-working player. I sat down with Peter at the end of the season and he told me that he thought I'd done OK and told me what was then expected of me and that I was part of his plans.

As for the new captain, was the underwhelming season just passed causing any regrets about his choice of club 12 months prior?

Ian Ashbee: I still knew I'd made the right move. The club was still a sleeping giant waiting to happen. We just needed to get out of that bottom division. That season was a transitional one, getting rid of Jan, and then Peter building a squad that had players from Brian Little's reign and Jan's reign. Peter had to get his own players in. I think the fans accepted that and took it on board. At the start of the next season it would be a different story though.

A bloated squad needed pruning, and Lawrie Dudfield, who'd signed for a record fee in a blaze of glory, was allowed to leave on a free.

Lawrie Dudfield: I was gutted. I'd just had my bathroom redecorated! It cost four grand! But I was disappointed. I could have stayed there but I was becoming disillusioned with football as a whole. I was on good money, but I just wanted to play.

My first six months at the club were amazing, by far and away the best of my career, but then there were also some major disappointments. I've learned since that my time at Hull City was the start of a new era at the club, and a lot of people seem to relate to that time. Football is a bubble now and you can't get near players. But back then we'd go into bars with fans and go into the community and I loved that. For some reason the Hull City fans took to me, and with my daughter living in Hull I've constantly been coming back. Hull showed me the best time of my career. You hear all these bad things about Hull as a city, but I always defend it. I love it. It's my home from home. I feel lucky to be associated with the club.

Mike Scott: Lawrie Dudfield forged an immediate and fruitful striking partnership with Gary Alexander when he joined City from Leicester in 2001 to spearhead Brian Little's attempted charge out of the fourth tier. Barrel-chested and lightning quick, Dudfield was a reliable scorer and a nippy foil to Alexander's brazen power. Early in his second season he suffered a serious injury and never regained a regular first team slot as Peter Taylor took the helm and refreshed his striker choices. Like so many before him, Dudfield's short spell in Hull saw him develop a strong affinity for the club, and he still attends ex-Tiger functions to this day.

Perhaps the saddest departure of all was that of youth team product Mike Edwards.

Mike Edwards: I knew I had to move. I spoke with my family and my dad had spoken to Adam who'd asked about me getting my contract terminated so I could maybe go elsewhere. I had a meeting with Peter, and I'd played the last six weeks in the reserves at centre-half. I thought I'd been doing well. I had a meeting with Adam Pearson to sort out leaving terms, but Peter pulled me in for a meeting, which surprised me, and he said: "When I've seen you play right-back in the reserves, you've been brilliant defensively but going forward I need more from a full-back." He kept going on about me playing right-back, which was the final nail in the coffin for me. I said to him: "I've been playing centre-half in the reserves, so you've obviously not been coming to watch." He didn't know what to say then, so I said: "It's fine, thanks for your time, but if I'm not in your plans don't worry about it. I don't need excuses." Then I saw Adam, who was gutted. I had a lot of time for Adam for all he'd done. He didn't want me to go but I told him that I had to. Being a young lad in my hometown team I thought football was such a big world, but it was only when I moved it's much smaller than you realise. I learned a lot more since I left that bubble. But I was devastated to have to go.

Lawrie Dudfield: Mike's my best friend in football. He was a young lad coming through into the first team. Normally the fans get behind a local lad coming through but Mike had a tough time with the fans. He was playing right back a lot and his distribution wasn't as good as it was to eventually become. He had to leave in the end but was still playing in his late 30s. He's still the last Hull City youth player to make 100 appearances for the club, and that's a sad but amazing statistic. But he got better and better as he went along. I don't think he gets the credit he deserves. He's an unsung hero at Hull.

Matt Rudd: Mike Edwards was a good defender and it remains a great regret of mine that a local boy who had developed and learned so readily in difficult circumstances was allowed to leave by Peter Taylor, who'd never really seen him play, just before the good times started to come.

Rodney Rowe: Mike Edwards never stopped smiling. It was a real pleasure to play alongside him.

Two seasons that had promised so much had come to nothing. A third such season was not an option.

2003/04 season

Promotion campaign under Adam Pearson, take four.

The 2001 play-off run had come to an end at Brisbane Road, Orient. Brian Little had brought in a whole new team and then some the season after, and paid with his job when the results didn't come in 2002. His replacement, Jan Molby, had been given yet more money to spend but was soon on his way, only for Peter Taylor to struggle to elevate Hull City beyond mid-table in the basement division for the rest of the 2002/03 season.

At the beginning of the 2003/04 season, the stadium, the fan base, the chairman and the manager all belonged at a much higher level, but football doesn't work like that; promotions have to be earned by the men out on the pitch. Peter Taylor now had his team. Everything was in place. Another failure wasn't an option.

Adam Pearson: The recruitment that summer by Peter and Colin changed everything. The wallet was pretty much empty then. There was nothing more. It wasn't quite the last throw of the dice, as we'd have kept going, but we'd have had to scale it back.

While Ben Burgess was one piece of the goal-scoring jigsaw, a foil for him had not yet been found. It turned out he'd been lurking at Meadow Lane all along...

Danny Allsopp: My agent at the time was banging on that Hull City were interested and I had to come up and check out the club. I really just drove up to keep him happy as I had no intention of dropping to League 2. Then I met Adam Pearson and Peter Taylor and saw the new stadium. I called my wife on the way home to tell her we were moving to Hull. I was inspired and excited about the potential and to possibly be a part of something special.

Peter Taylor: Danny Allsopp had goals on his CV. It was as simple as that.

Stuart Elliott's goal threat from the left was already evident, but no one had really convinced on the right side of midfield. That was another problem remedied that summer.

Jason Price: It was Ben Burgess that got me to Hull. I'd been at Tranmere, but the contract they offered me was pretty crap. I'd played with Ben at Brentford a couple of seasons before, and we'd kept in contact. He told me that Peter Taylor was looking for a right-sided player and put my name forward. Peter Taylor phoned me up and told me he was looking for a right-back, so I told him I could play there – as I had done for Swansea, though I was a right midfielder at the time – as I wanted to sign for Hull. We met up and had a chat, and I ended up more or less signing there and then.

Peter Taylor: I spoke to Steve Coppell about Jason Price and he told me not to hesitate, go and sign him. He said at times he won't look a great player but he'll end up scoring. We knew he'd work up and down on the right-hand side and he made up a front four that we knew could score goals. Pricey was a big success for us.

Club legends don't often arrive on a free transfer from Scunthorpe United. That summer Andy Dawson came to the KC on a free transfer from Scunthorpe United.

Andy Dawson: The previous summer I'd been offered a contract by a few clubs, but I was 22 and I couldn't leave Scunthorpe without a fee being involved, so I signed a week-to-week contract in my last year, which, looking back, I don't know why! We had a baby due in the summer and I was an injury away from my career finishing and financially being nowhere. I'd had four-and-a-half great years at Scunthorpe though, and I knew it was time for me to move on and experience different things in my career.

A couple of clubs from higher leagues had shown an interest that summer previous – Norwich, who'd just lost in the Championship play-offs, and Bradford – but ITV Digital had gone bust and they weren't willing to pay a fee. I'm a great believer that things happen for a reason. Some interest had come from Hull City earlier on that season. Not long after that I met with Peter Taylor, went round the KC, and though Hull City and Scunthorpe were in the same league – with Scunthorpe having been in the play-offs and Hull City only finishing mid-table – seeing the size of the club, the stadium, the infrastructure, the city, it was a club that I believed would go places. To play at the KC was what you want to do as a footballer, playing in front of 17,000 or 18,000 fans in League 2. It was a massive opportunity.

Adam Pearson and Peter Taylor had sold it to me and told me that they wanted to progress. It had been 18 years since they'd been promoted and that was just the kind of challenge I liked. It was a club ready to take off – I didn't quite expect it to take off to the extent that it did five years later – and it was a great, great place to have the opportunity to play football.

Peter Taylor: With Andy Dawson, I went to see Scunthorpe play Cambridge away and everybody thought I was looking at another player, but I was looking at Daws because I knew he was a free transfer and we wanted a left-footer at a left-back. We just knew with him. It was an easy decision. We were lucky that he was playing and living so close to Hull. Adam Pearson was delighted with that one.

Adam Pearson: A fantastic signing, one of the best signings for Hull City ever. A great lad and a top player. We brought in players that summer who were going to be integral to the club.

Stuart Green had made up with Peter Taylor and returned to Hull City after his dalliance with Carlisle the season before. But how was he feeling?

Stuart Green: I was nervous all summer thinking about how the fans and my team-mates were going to react, but I was just looking forward to getting back to normal.

Joining Allsopp, Price and Dawson were right-back Alton Thelwell – who'd played several games for Tottenham Hotspur and even been capped by England under-21s – and utility defender Richard Hinds. And it didn't take long for the team's spirit to develop.

Ian Ashbee: You could see quality coming through. Colin Murphy was important for me. You have to get recruitment right and bringing in the likes of Damien Delaney and Ben Burgess before, and then the likes of Daws and Danny Allsopp, was paramount to the good things that were to happen to the football club. It felt like a different place. There was a different vibe with a hunger around the place. There was a pressure on the football club and pressure on the players and when I first arrived they couldn't really deal with it. But those players, we got it together; we were young, fit and enthusiastic and it felt right. And that was credit to Colin Murphy and Peter Taylor.

Ben Burgess: It was clear that promotion was expected. That was why I signed. I knew if we could get promoted we wouldn't stop. Adam Pearson was a fantastic chairman. He was so ambitious and good with the players and so honest, better than any chairman I've ever known.

Paul Musselwhite: From my point of view I'd seen three summers on the trot where managers would bring in new teams. We'd had a lot of players – including myself – that should have got us higher in the league. But Peter is an experienced manager and brought in some excellent players; you could see he was taking the club in the right direction.

Stuart Elliott: Peter knew he had to put his own stamp on the club, and that's what he did. You had this mix where you had goals that could come from all over, combined with a very solid, well-organised back line. Peter knew that if you were going to win promotion you needed more than just your centre-forwards scoring, you needed goals from midfield and on the wings too. Ash was always solid sitting in midfield and allowed Jason Price, Stuart Green and myself to get the goals that we needed.

Ben Burgess: Me and Danny Allsopp just hit it off straight away and Jason Price was living with me because I knew him from Brentford. Next door to us were Alton Thelwell and Damien Delaney.

Damien Delaney: We were a close-knit group. Me, Alton Thelwell, Jason Price and Ben Burgess all lived in the same apartment block in Beverley. We hung around with each other every minute of every day. We were always in each other's flats. It was almost like a boys' club that we had going. We socialised every weekend together, going out or playing computer games. We had an incredible bond and a great chemistry. It was like the perfect storm.

Dean Keates: The previous year there seemed to be a divide in the changing room, but this year there was a really good feeling in there, with some good lads brought in such as Big Ben and Pricey, who helped change the mood. If you've got a good changing room it helps. If you're all pulling together it gives you an opportunity. In the end the changing room got what it deserved and the fans got what they deserved.

Marc Joseph: You could tell in training that we had good players everywhere. You knew that if you gave someone the ball they would find a way of doing something with it. And we were close as a group. We had a bond as many of us had moved our families to Hull. We wanted to be part of the city as it evolved.

Jason Price: When you join a team, you might know one or two on arrival and you gradually get to know everyone else, but because there were so many new signings at the time, about a third of the team were in the same boat. There were no cliques. Everybody just clicked.

Simon Maltby: All of the new staff Peter had brought in seemed to add a greater professionalism to things. We'd all worked at reasonable levels. I'd worked with England, as had Peter, so we knew what we were doing. But there was a real buzz that season, from the pre-season onwards.

Damien Delaney: Once you'd met Adam Pearson you knew that he wasn't the kind of person to string you along and tell you things you wanted to hear for the sake of it. We knew we were building to something. But we felt the energy from the city as a whole – the energy and enthusiasm. Every time you went out you'd hear stories of all the old players and how great they were, and I just kept thinking: 'Yeah, we could actually do something special.' We just needed to get players in with the right mentality, but Peter Taylor knew exactly what he was doing and exactly what he wanted. When you get a collective mindset among a group of people, you can move mountains.

Stuart Green: Damien Delaney had settled in. Jason Price came in and we looked at him in training and we were all wondering how he was going to fit in, but he was unbelievable. He'd get goals but his all-round contribution was brilliant. People like that just moved us on to the next level.

Ben Burgess: Pre-season didn't start great. We lost to Grimsby and we were dreadful. But Peter had a few words, then we played Leeds at home and battered them 2-0. We then thought: 'Oh wow, we could do something this season.'

On August 9th, Darlington – the side that had won the last ever game at Boothferry Park eight months earlier – got the campaign under way with a visit to the KC. They were, quite simply, blown away.

Peter Taylor: In pre-season there was a good feeling around the place. Hopefully the supporters were confident about the management, the management were certainly confident about the players and the players had a good spirit and they believed in themselves. Everybody was enjoying it. Then all of a sudden you play the first game of the season and you start to feel a bit of pressure. We were thinking: 'Let's show them what we've got,' and we did. And all the new signings scored that day, which gives you even more confidence.

Ben Burgess: League 2 isn't the hardest league to get out of but it's so much harder if you're a big club because the expectation is there and everyone wants to beat you. All anyone would talk about in that division was Hull City and the players and money we had. It's hard to play with that expectation but we handled it well that season. It was good to start off with a win. They pulled it back to 1-1 but we were in control. It was good to see the goals spread around.

Danny Allsopp: The first game of the season was typically in searing heat and we all felt a weight of expectation to perform. We'd had a great pre-season and it gave us confidence that we'd over-run Darlington in the second half, which we did. All but one of the goals were scored by debutants and I was happy with how I played. I put away a nice one which helped to settle me in to the club.

Jason Price: I scored, I set one up… it was like a party game. We just knew we were going to win. We had better players than Darlington. And having a crowd of that size in League 2 was like having a 12th man. At home, before we kicked a ball we knew everything was 60/40 in our favour because of the crowd.

Stuart Elliott: We had so much confidence in each other. We had big characters with Ian Ashbee always driving the team forward, keeping us on our toes. We had a mixture of youth and experience, we knew it was going to be hard for anyone to beat us. That proved true in the first game of the season and we went on from there.

Brendon Smurthwaite: Colin Murphy always said that if you get eight out of 10 signings right, you'll always be in a job. Any less and you'll probably get the sack. And that year we got the signings right. There were goals all over the team.

Mike Hall: We'd had a couple of false starts since Adam Pearson took over, and the previous season had seen Peter Taylor steady things after Jan Molby's departure, but he was not quite able to complete a turnaround. The summer saw a few astute signings rather than wholesale changes, and in that game it was apparent to me what some well-thought-out recruitment and a decent pre-season could do. We won 4-1 in front of a big crowd and never really looked back. Finally the club seemed to have the attributes to head in the right direction.

Rich Lusmore: A 4-1 win on a day when we found out the East Stand wasn't the best place to watch football from in August if you didn't have a pair of shades or Factor 50 on – phew, what a scorcher!

Gary Clark: I took my father to the opening game of the season against Darlington. I wanted him to see the new stadium more than anything and also experience the 'new' day out. He was very much a Boothferry Park man although he hadn't been to a live football game for more than 20 years. He'd taken me to my first ever game versus Everton in the FA Cup at Boothferry Park in 1964 so I was really paying him back. We sat on the half-way line with the sun shining directly in our faces. By half-time he was like a boiled beetroot and gasping for breath. Then he collapsed and along with the help of the stewards we carried him out of the ground and into a waiting taxi and rushed him home. I missed all the second half and the goals, and he hasn't set foot in the KC since!

Ian Ashbee: It felt like we'd arrived. We were saying "we're here" and it felt like we were moving forward.

Spirits were high, as were expectations, for the next game at the Kassam Stadium against Oxford. However, after playing such sparkling football the Saturday previous, City were bullied into a 2-1 defeat by a thuggish Oxford side managed by Ian Atkins, who was to oafishly comment in the press afterwards that he'd have Hull City 10 points clear at the top of the table if he was the club's manager.

Ian Ashbee: We lacked a physical edge and Peter Taylor addressed that correctly. You've got to have more than one person running around in midfield; you've got to have 11 players that might not be big in stature but are big in other senses, that have got fire in their bellies. You need that fire to take anything forward. I did sense – and I think Peter sensed it too – that although we had players who were big in stature maybe they weren't big enough to take the challenge on at that time. It was difficult as everyone was expecting us to run riot in the league, with Peter Taylor being manager and us getting a lot of press, and there was pressure on. We had to deal with that.

Expectations were further dampened in the next game. Stuart Elliott, Jason Price and Danny Allsopp all scored for City, but a 3-3 home draw against Cheltenham – whose goals came from a nine-minute hat-trick from Damian Spencer in the first half – was not a result that a promotion-chasing side would be happy with. With the defence proving leaky, a familiar and popular face was recalled for the trip to Cambridge, whose Dave Kitson was considered the most dangerous forward in the league. A clean sheet was duly earned.

Justin Whittle: The manager knew what he got with me and I think that's why he brought me in. And it was nice because I got on well with Peter and Colin Murphy. Peter was always great with me. If the fans felt there was any sort of resentment from Peter towards me, I'd disagree. We got on really well.

City beat Cambridge 2-0 thanks to goals from Jason Price and Danny Allsopp. Boston were then beaten at the KC courtesy of a late winner from Stuart Green after Stuart Elliott had given City the lead.

The next game was to be televised, away at a newly promoted Doncaster side who'd made a surprisingly strong start to the campaign. Two debuts were to be made – loanee keeper Michel Kuipers, who'd served as a chef in the Dutch marines, and a left-back who'd had to exercise a fair bit of patience.

Andy Dawson: I'd been injured in pre-season doing a block tackle with Damien Delaney, a challenge in which we didn't communicate with each other. I was out for eight or nine weeks, watching the games and it was hard work as I couldn't wait to start playing. I remember the home game against Darlington, thinking that it should be me out there. But that only made me hungrier and increased my desire. At Doncaster it was great to get back – live on Sky on a Monday night. I'd been waiting to make my debut since July 1, but it was quite a dull game to be honest.

The 'dull game' finished 0-0. This was followed by a quite remarkable game at home to Southend.

Andy Dawson: I couldn't wait to make my debut at the KC, but it was an up-and-down game. We went 1-0 down, got back into it through Danny Allsopp, and then I scored with a free-kick, which was great for a home debut – a dream come true. At 3-1 we were comfortable. It went to 3-2 and then I gave away a penalty. It was a really daft one – a shirt pull that was nothing. Thankfully Michel Kuipers saved the day keeping out not only the penalty but getting up and making a brilliant save from the rebound that I remember to this day.

The Southend game marked the fifth goal that Danny Allsopp had scored, and it was only mid-September. His strike partner, Ben Burgess, was to score in the next two matches – a 1-1 draw at Orient and a 2-0 win at Rochdale, with Stuart Green getting the other. The partnership was blossoming nicely.

Danny Allsopp: The season started really well and I felt like I was in great form. It was one of the most enjoyable times of my career. I was scoring regularly and enjoying our style. Peter Taylor was a good manager to play for and I was lucky to have him there. He knew what he wanted and he is a good man.

I also had Ben Burgess up front with me, which was brilliant. Ben was probably the first time in my life that I found a strike partner who was as genuinely happy as I was if I scored a goal, and I felt the same way when he scored. We seemed to have a natural understanding of what the other was going to do, so it was a lot of fun playing together.

For quite some time early that season he was getting a bit of rough treatment from some of the supporters, which was tough, but it wasn't too long before I think they learned to appreciate his quality and he scored some great goals too.

Dave Richardson: Sitting near the goal, the sight of Allsopp and Burgess thundering down the pitch, bearing down on the goal, made my hair stand on end. God knows what it did to defenders

Gary Clark: Ben Burgess and Danny Allsopp were big players for us when we needed them the most. Cool and brave in front of goal, very Chris Chilton-like, and that is praise indeed.

Another addition was made to the squad that September. A young midfielder had been winning rave reviews while playing for non-league Alfreton Town. Naturally Colin Murphy was one step ahead of everyone else.

Ryan France: A year before I joined Hull I'd been on trial at Coventry. I was two years into a three-year course at university. Gary McAllister wanted to sign me there and then but I didn't want to quit university with one year to go. I look back and think I must have been mad! But I did alright with Hull. I had a two-year deal on the table but I couldn't chuck away all that education.

A year went by and Hull City came in for me; Colin Murphy came to watch me a few times. After a week's training they offered me a two-year contract and I'd got my degree so I thought it was the right time, and I took the plunge. Definitely the right decision.

Peter Taylor: Colin was really keen on Ryan France. He said: "There's a boy at Alfreton, could be a right-back, could be a right winger, good in the air, got everything." If you put a good case about a player to Adam Pearson, he'd say "do it" and we did that with Ryan.

Adam Pearson: Ryan France – what a signing he was! He could play anywhere on the right-hand side, a really good footballer.

Ryan France: I'd had a different introduction to football to most, being turned away from Sheffield Wednesday as a 16 year old, so I was in awe all the time. Playing in front of 16,000 fans was a dream come true. I didn't take a day for granted. Peter Taylor and Colin Murphy were fantastic. I look at the training ground at the time – at Brantingham – and it wasn't great, but I didn't know any different so to me it was brilliant. We had so much togetherness it was scary.

Ryan was to get a rapid introduction to league football in a home game against Kidderminster. The match was to be the first act of three in a week that was to announce Hull City as a force in the division.

Ryan France: I just sit here today thinking: 'Did I actually do that?' That week flew by so fast. I signed on Tuesday 23rd September, and didn't expect to be in the squad. I was named on the bench. I just thought Peter Taylor would let me experience being involved in pro football. At Alfreton you could hear every shout from the fans. It was different at the KC!

Andy Dawson: That was the marker that we put down in the league, winning 6-1 at home, with our strikers scoring goals, and we were moving up the table. I scored with a strike from the edge of the box that had come back out to me. We were playing in front of 18,000 fans. That was what any footballer wants to do.

Ryan France: Andy Dawson put a shot in the stanchion from about 35 yards and I was thinking to myself: 'Have I got to do that as well, because I can't do that!'

Ben Burgess: When you've got that confidence you feel invincible. We thrashed Kidderminster and I even scored with an overhead kick.

Ryan France: In the second half, Peter said go get warmed up. It hit home that I was going to make my debut. I wasn't nervous until then, when I thought: 'It's happening.' I didn't know what to expect so I went out and played how I normally played. Then I made a run; I went one way, the defender went the other, Andy Holt put a great ball in and it just landed at my feet. Then I'm in the six-yard box sliding the ball into the net. It was just like: 'What?!? What's happening?' I didn't quite know what I was doing. I just stood there with my hands in the air. I should have worked on my celebration a little bit. I was just thinking: 'Oh my god, what's happening? I'm finally a footballer!' Not that I was going to stop trying to learn or better myself.

Peter Taylor and Colin Murphy managed me so well. I was sub again the next game. They were saying: "You've not made it yet," and Pricey was doing well on the wing. I got more and more time and started more games towards the end of the season. I was just developing myself and trying to be more consistent.

1. **Swansea P10 W7 D1 L2 Pts22**
2. **Hull City P10 W6 D3 L1 Pts21**
3. **Oxford P10 W5 D4 L1 Pts19**
4. **Torquay P10 W5 D3 L2 Pts18**
5. **Yeovil P10 W6 D0 L4 Pts 18**

Swatting aside the likes of Kidderminster was one thing. Next up were Swansea, who were the only team above City in the league. There was a buzz around the city, and the first real landmark night at the KC was upon us.

Stuart Elliott: Peter Taylor phoned me because I'd had the flu and was ill in bed a few hours before the game started. Peter asked if I was OK to play, and I wasn't really but I pulled myself out of my sick bed to play that night. The supporters didn't know that, and it was a cold, cold night, so I needed to muster all the strength that I had. But the atmosphere was electric. I didn't want to miss it.

Adam Pearson: I'd gone outside in the evening as I heard we were having crowd problems, and there were 24,000 inside and must have been 5,000 outside. I was getting lambasted and I thought: 'What do they want?' We get slated for not being successful and then when we're successful we can't get everyone in!

Tom McVie: The place was throbbing, packed out. The kick-off was delayed to get people in the ground. I thought: 'This is why we built this.' It was such a fantastic atmosphere.

Ben Burgess: I remember that Swansea game because it was being bigged up all week. The stadium was full, it was really exciting. Swansea are a big club. Just thinking about it now gives me goosebumps.

Andy Dawson: That game was amazing. An awesome atmosphere. A full house in League 2 in a stadium that holds 25,000. What a night! And it was another marker where everybody was saying: "What a big club this is." We were getting Premier League attendances.

Paul Musselwhite: It was fantastic to play in. There was a lot of talk at the time of the new grounds being built not having a great atmosphere, but when you get the KC like that it was fantastic. It was as good an atmosphere as I played in in Hull.

The game was to be decided by a solitary goal. In truth, such was the goalscoring ability of City's 'front four', it could have come from any of them. However, when Andy Dawson swung in a corner in the 27th minute, there was a reliable forehead waiting.

Stuart Elliott: The corner came in and I got the bullet header in, and my cold seemed to go all of a sudden! Those are great nights, and memories I'll never forget.

Jason Price: We were practising near-post corners in the run-up to the game because Peter had seen they had nobody on the edge of the six-yard box. And Stuart was the best header of a ball outside the Premier League. Obviously it worked out. It was nice to get one over on my old club as well.

Adam Pearson: Stuart Elliott's header that night was as hard as any shot. He just smashed it in. I'd never heard a Hull City ground like that that night. It was a fantastic occasion, with both Swansea and ourselves on this inexorable march to the Premier League.

Swansea were a good team, already containing players that would take them from the bottom division to the Premier League. One of them, Leon Britton, was considered to be as good a midfielder as League 2 had to offer. However, Ian Ashbee gave his finest performance for Hull City to date and won the midfield battle, with Britton barely getting a kick.

Ian Ashbee: I was never the best technically, but many a time I've come up against players such as Leon Britton that are a lot better technically than I'll ever be, but the one thing I'll do is make people stop. I'll stop those players on that day, not single-handedly, but I'll go out thinking: 'I'll make sure I'm better than you,' and if I can affect this, this and this then I will do. I'd do that without being noticed. And that was what I was about. I did everything under the radar.

The 1-0 win was sealed, and a packed KC Stadium saluted a Hull City team that were – for the first time in a long time – top of the league.

Andy Dawson: To us as players – and no doubt the fans – everyone was leaving the stadium that night going: "Wow, things are on the up, things are feeling good!" Everyone had a spark about them. That's when we believed we were going to go up. There were so many positives to take from it.

City fans had become accustomed to Stuart Elliott's amazing aerial ability – he was only 5 foot 10 – but now, under the tactical prowess of Peter Taylor, it was becoming apparent just how potent a weapon it was. But how did he float?

Stuart Elliott: It was just a God-given ability. I wasn't a big guy, but I had springs on my feet. It was also about timing. If a defender went up a little bit early I'd go up a little bit later. I'd get my timing right and almost always get that flick-on or that header at the back post. I was just blessed with that ability.

Saturday: Kidderminster destroyed by six goals to one. Tuesday: top-of-the-table Swansea given a demonstration of what a real promotion side looked like. Saturday: a trip to Sixfields

Stadium, Northampton, to play a team that had been title favourites with some bookmakers at the start of the season, but who had endured a poor start to the season and had just appointed Colin Calderwood as manager to replace the sacked Martin Wilkinson.

Peter Taylor: In the division that we were playing in, with the players that we had, if they performed 8 out of 10 then there was a very good chance we'd score goals. I was just confident that our spirit and our organisation was going to get stronger and stronger. We'd do most things the same most weeks. We were into our routines and wouldn't take anything for granted. After a big win we wouldn't stop. The players responded to that.

And how. Northampton couldn't live with City, and goals from Stuart Elliott, Danny Allsopp, Jason Price, Ben Burgess and Jamie Forrester saw City saunter to a 5-1 win.

Ian Thomson: I landed at Manchester Airport that morning after a week on business in Chicago and drove straight to Northampton. Any feelings of fatigue or jet-lag were blasted to high heaven thanks to a truly sumptuous City performance against a team who were no mugs – indeed, they beat us in the return fixture at the KC late in the season – and it was the first time I had seen us score five away.

Ben Burgess: Northampton had spent a lot of money and were one of the favourites to go up and we demolished them. I missed a penalty – the sub keeper went the wrong way and saved it with his feet – the only penalty I missed in my career. I was massively disappointed but I scored in the end and it didn't matter too much.

Four consecutive wins was to become five as Carlisle visited the KC on a Sunday afternoon. City won 2-1 thanks to goals from Ben Burgess and Jamie Forrester. It was increasingly apparent that – after two seasons of disappointment – City had 'clicked'. The togetherness in the squad was tangible. Peter Taylor, it seemed, had found the perfect blend.

Jason Price: I was the DJ and would mess around. To psyche myself up for a football match I have to mess around. If I think about the game too much I get nervous. So I needed to do things to stop me from thinking about a game too much. That's why I'd do things in the changing room to have a laugh and cheer everybody up. I was a one-off!

We had a Beverley group and a Brough group. I was in the Beverley group with Ben Burgess, Damien Delaney, Alton Thelwell and a couple of others. Most of the rest of the team lived in Brough. We'd have great banter in the changing rooms. The Beverley boys would change together, as would the Brough boys, and it was just constant banter. We'd all see who could sing the loudest out of the two groups. It was great having silly games like that.

Justin Whittle: We had a better mixture of quality players then, but players who'd also get stuck in when you needed it. Damien had found his position at centre-half and players like Ryan France had come in, who was a very good player, while Danny Allsopp and Ben Burgess hit it off immediately up front.

Marc Joseph: There were so many games where we'd turn up and Peter would tell us how much he hated the other manager, or there was an opposition player who'd annoyed him, or just someone we were coming up against that he didn't like. That instilled in us a bigger desire to perform and make sure we didn't get beat.

Andy Holt: That team had such an air of confidence. We had a fantastic stadium, a fantastic crowd, and we all knew we should be at a higher level. Colin Murphy was a funny guy, but even in League 2 he was talking about many of the players going on to play in the Premier League, which many of them did. There was so much confidence there. I'd generally come on in left midfield in a defensive role to shore games up, coming on for Stuart Elliott. I scored a couple of goals and felt really involved.

Marc Joseph: Damien was very good in the air, physically strong, and his fitness levels were one of the highest in the club. He was tough for the opposition to get past. In our partnership I hope that I brought a little bit of experience and was a bit more old school. I wouldn't take defeat easily, wouldn't accept below-par performances. Me and Ash had played together for a long time, from being schoolboys at Derby, and we both had the same mentality, and I think that helped build a backbone in the team which helped the younger players.

Although one player was still trying to regain his mojo.

Stuart Green: I wasn't happy with how I played in League 2. When I came back my game changed dramatically. I'd gone from a free-flowing midfielder to a lot more reserved player, spending more time on the half-way line than I ever had, but I had to do that to stay in the team. I had to be more of a team player.

After a 1-1 draw at Torquay, thanks to a late Stuart Elliott goal, and a 0-0 draw at Bury, Lincoln City – so often a niggly, annoying opponent for City in the 1990s – came to the KC. The 3-0 result flattered the visitors, and the scoring was opened by a popular source.

Andy Holt: The Lincoln game was a memorable one. I scored the first goal and got man of the match. After I'd been brought off I was taken straight for drugs testing. My son, then-wife and father-in-law were there but I couldn't go and celebrate with everyone as I couldn't do a wee. It took me two hours and when I finally got out of the room, the stadium was dead. Even the cleaning staff had gone home. All I had to celebrate with was a pissed-off son, wife and father-in-law.

Danny Allsopp and Stuart Green rounded off the win as City moved into November four points clear at the top of the league. However, November was to see City play six times in all competitions and fail to win a single game. A 2-2 draw at home to 10-men Macclesfield, with Richard Hinds and Danny Allsopp scoring, opened the month, with City then going out of the Football League Trophy to Scunthorpe and the FA Cup to Cheltenham within the space of a few days. There was worse to come, however, in the shape of a horrible 3-1 defeat at Huddersfield.

Andy Dawson: From a players' perspective, when you looked round that changing room you had Danny Allsopp, Ben Burgess, Stuart Green, Ash, Stuey Elliott, Damien Delaney. Obviously we didn't know then what we know now, but we did know we had a squad that was far better than League 2. Yes we lost games but deep down we knew what the fans, the manager and the chairman expected, and we knew what we expected as players. Games like that one at Huddersfield were a negative, as we wanted to win every game, but we as players knew that the reality of football means it doesn't work like that. What we did really well that season was we'd come out of a bad patch and win three, four, five games on the bounce. That's what good teams do, and that's what we did.

Justin Whittle: In the away match at Huddersfield I was on the bench and we started conceding goals. The fans started chanting my name, and Peter Taylor turned to me and said: "You don't say a word!"

A disappointing 0-0 draw at home to Yeovil followed, and then a 2-1 defeat at Bristol Rovers. Finally, the six-match winless streak was ended with a 2-0 home win against Bury, with Ben Burgess and Jason Price scoring. This was followed by a 1-1 draw at Scunthorpe and a 1-0 home defeat to Mansfield. City had gone from top of the league to fifth in the space of less than two months, were now five points off leaders Doncaster, and had played one game more than the rest of the top five.

The last of those games against Mansfield had been notable for one reason, however: It marked the debut of one Glyn Oliver Myhill, though everyone knew him as 'Boaz'. Little did we know that a little bit of Hull City history had been made.

Adam Pearson: Colin kept going over to watch Stockport and kept saying Boaz was a bit overweight, not good enough on crosses and a few other bits, but then one day he came back and just said: "He's brilliant." Eventually we agreed to pay £50,000 for him.

Boaz Myhill: It was strange. I was on loan at Stockport at the time. I was quite keen to leave Aston Villa and Stockport's manager, Sammy McIlroy, had asked me to go there. I was going to sign permanently at first, then all of a sudden they changed it to a three-month loan. I'd played a couple of games and then Hull City agreed a fee with Villa and I was on my way to the KC. It was a bit awkward being at Stockport because I'd gone from saying "I'll sign permanently" to saying "I want to go to Hull." The first game I was there for I was ill, so I was sat in the Jarvis Hotel in Willerby just itching to play. But I was just so excited to be leaving Aston Villa – which I'd wanted to do for a couple of years – and get an opportunity at a club that was going places.

Peter Taylor: You've got to set your standards as high as you can. Alan Fettis and Paul Musselwhite were terrific pros and it was very difficult to tell them that they wouldn't be the number one as they are good lads. Mussy was a gentle giant, a lovely fella, but I felt that him and Alan were at the end of their careers rather than the beginning and I felt that I wanted a young goalkeeper that could handle the situation at Hull. I knew Paul Barron, who was the goalkeeping coach for a while at Aston Villa, and he knew Boaz inside out. He told me to sign him. I went to watch him out on loan and I thought: 'Yes, that'll do.' Because not only was he a good goalkeeper, he was young, athletic, a great kicker; everything about him fitted the bill. And in Aston Villa's eyes he was probably too young for the first team so they wanted £50,000 for him. We told Adam and he backed me. If I'd have been the manager of Southend and wanted to buy a goalkeeper for £50,000, they wouldn't be able to afford it. I knew how lucky I was at Hull but you've got to take advantage of that.

Boaz Myhill: First of all, when you turned up at the KC Stadium you knew that the club was going places. The manager was a well-respected name, they had a strong squad and they were already doing well in the league; it was a no-brainer. I was excited and nervous as I'd gone from being a youth team player to a first-team player.

Alan Fettis: I only saw bits and pieces of him at the time but he's a very good goalkeeper who hasn't looked back. So fair play to him. I'd done the same when I went in as a young kid coming in and Iain Hesford left.

Paul Musselwhite: I said he'd play in the Premier League at an early point of seeing him. I'd had a few challengers for my position in my time at Hull, and seen them off, but when I saw Bo I just knew he had a good chance of really doing good things. He was a bit like myself in that he was very laid back, but you could just see that he was a very, very good goalkeeper.

Andy Dawson: I didn't know Bo but I'd heard people in football say what a good keeper he was. I knew Paul Musselwhite really well and we had Alan Fettis still – two keepers that had loads of experience – but the manager and the chairman saw something in Bo that saw him become an international footballer and play in the Premier League for the majority of his career. He was a good, good keeper. And fair play to the manager because he showed faith in a young lad when he had an international keeper in Alan Fettis and someone as reliable as Mussy. A great addition to the squad though, and one that did brilliantly for Hull City.

Damien Delaney: The manager signed people with something to prove. We'd been at bigger clubs and it hadn't worked out, and we'd been waiting for our chance. We were determined to take it. We had a mindset that we weren't going to let it slip, and if we didn't go up it wasn't going to be for the want of trying.

Boaz's signing meant a final farewell to one of the most popular players to have ever worn the Hull City jersey.

Alan Fettis: I had disagreements with Peter Taylor but he was trying to do something with the football club and he achieved that. He was fine, I just wasn't part of his plans, particularly after he'd signed Boaz. But I have no problem with Peter Taylor at all. I was annoyed that it ended the way it did, but never mind.

Going into the Christmas fixtures, City had won just two in 10 league games. Hardly promotion form. However, a Boxing Day win at York courtesy of goals from Ben Burgess and Jamie Forrester helped shift things back into gear. Then came Doncaster Rovers at home, and a night that would belong to Jason Price.

Jason Price: We were playing a team coming up from non-league so we didn't really know how they'd play. We knew they'd be tough though. They had that togetherness you get in non-league football.

Andy Dawson: Another full house. Doncaster were top and we were fourth still behind Oxford and Mansfield. It was a massive time for us. We'd gone to York and won, and Doncaster were another local derby and had become fierce rivals. Pricey was another player who could score goals, and he was a great character and a great lad. I'd played against him when he was at Swansea and I was at Scunthorpe and he was always one of those lads where you didn't really know what he was like, apart from being a tough opponent. But when he came into the changing room he was a great character, always had a smile on his face, always had something to say.

Jason Price was to score a hat-trick in unforgettable style as Doncaster were swept aside.

Jason Price: I remember each goal exactly as it happened. We'd done a lot of set plays, and I scored the first from a set play off a header. I made a run for the near post, the keeper came for it but I was brave for once in my life and flicked it on and it went in. I took my top off after that one – which I'd never do now! For my second goal they tried to play me offside, and I'd done a bit of a handball, the ball fell on my left foot and Andy Warrington in their goal showed me his right-hand post. I just went for it, shut my eyes, swung my left leg and it went in the bottom corner. I was lucky for the third – I took a long throw to Ben who volleyed it, but the keeper saved it. I'd followed the throw-in in and to this day the boys reckon it was an own goal because I volleyed it and it hit the keeper and went in. It was an unbelievable feeling to score three in front of a crowd that size. I felt like a god.

Andy Dawson: The last goal, someone played it across and he volleyed it into the corner. What a goal! And it was another great occasion, another marker where everybody's saying: "These are about to hit form."

Peter Taylor: I don't remember much of the individual goals, but I remember that night very well. Pricey was a funny lad, in that he'd make you laugh. He used to take the mickey out of me, in front of me too! He was a good lad and a popular lad, and that was a very popular hat-trick among the players. At times Pricey could look an awful player but he could look very good too. And he scored some great goals. He was a success for us without doubt. All the staff were so pleased for him that night.

Ben Burgess: The local derbies were great. Doncaster were going well. I missed a few chances that day so Pricey got me out of jail. We had that sort of team; if you weren't doing so well you had Pricey down the right, Stuart Elliott down the left, Danny scoring goals. We had matchwinners all over the place.

Adam Pearson: Pricey was a fantastic character and scored a lot of goals. He was great for that league and the players loved him. I was still completely paranoid that we were going to throw it away though!

Ian Ashbee: We were getting stronger. Peter Taylor was relentless in the systems that we played. He was relentless in how we set up. On a Tuesday or Wednesday we'd do team play. It would be laborious for the lads – who'd maybe want headers and volleys or circles – but Peter knew what he wanted and that's what we'd do. At any point in that season we were getting better at what was required from us and where he wanted us to be. That was coming to fruition. It did feel that we were solid and workmanlike but we had goals for sure. Someone like Jason Price can go and score a hat-trick because he knows he's got people sat there protecting him when he goes forward.

Jason Price: Every time someone mentions that game, I always feel like I'm Carl Froch when I mention the attendance. I tell them I scored a hat-trick in front of 20-odd thousand. The match ball is still in a cabinet in my mother's house.

1. **Oxford P24 W14 D9 L1 Pts51**
2. **Doncaster P24 W15 D4 L5 Pts49**
3. **Hull City P25 W13 D8 L4 Pts47**
4. **Mansfield P24 W14 D4 L6 Pts46**
5. **Yeovil P24 W14 D1 L9 Pts43**

The Doncaster game acted as the catalyst for a winning streak, with a Stuart Elliott opening 2004 in style at the KC to clinch a 2-0 win over Cambridge. Another Stuart Elliott goal was to be the difference in the next game, a 1-0 win at Darlington. Next up was another big game at the KC, as Oxford United – joint top of the table on points with City – faced the Tigers for the first time since they'd bullied their way to victory in August at the Kassam Stadium. This was a defeat that needed to be avenged, with regards to both the final scoreline and the physical manner in which it had been achieved.

Peter Taylor: I like my teams to play football and I also like them to be able to handle themselves, but in the right way, not feigning injury and things like that, but I'm up for us being stronger and tougher than the other teams. And I think that night showed the balance of the team we had was right. We had players like Marc Joseph and Ian Ashbee who could really look after themselves. Even someone like Ben Burgess wouldn't seek people out or do anything nasty, but he was very strong and could really look after himself. Stuart Elliott was the loveliest person in the world, but you wouldn't relish challenging him in the air. Pricey was tough, as was Alton Thelwell. We weren't just a pretty team of nice footballers – we could handle most situations. If Oxford bullied us a bit earlier in the season, we'd have mentioned that to make sure it wouldn't happen again.

Ian Ashbee: We'd become a stronger, tougher team. I'd agree with that a million per cent. Peter Taylor gave us confidence. In that first game against Oxford we were battered. That wasn't what Peter Taylor was about and it certainly wasn't what I was about. I don't mind losing to a bit of skill and being played off the park, but one thing you can't lose to is a team having a bit more endeavour and a bit more fight inside them than you have. That was addressed in the changing room. We were self-managed to an extent, and we were getting better. Winning that game was an eye-opener as it showed we'd come on in leaps and bounds.

City won the game 4-2, with Ben Burgess (who scored one goal and was heavily involved in the Crosby own goal) and Danny Allsopp (who scored two), again proving what a potent partnership they were.

Andy Dawson: We were the top two teams, and we all knew the importance of the game, particularly at that time of year when you need to start beating the teams that are around you; it gives you massive confidence. We put a lot of pressure on ourselves because we knew that if we lost they'd start building points on us. We played really well, and after we beat Oxford the other teams will have started looking at us and really worrying as we had such good, good players. Another good night at the KC… we'd had a lot of them already!

Ben Burgess: They'd beaten us away from home – the first game we'd lost – and they'd been very fortunate. We were fired up. After that they fell away and didn't even make the play-offs. Those big games at the KC were fantastic occasions. Danny Allsopp had been injured for a while and that was his first game back. It gave me and the rest of the team a lift. Me and Danny just hit it off on and off the pitch and it showed. It was nice to have him back as we had that telepathic understanding.

Danny Allsopp: I remember the game against Oxford in particular as well because the centre-back was roughing me up which I found always gave me extra motivation. I ended up with six stitches but got a couple of goals and the three points!

The result saw Ian Atkins' thuggish, graceless Oxford side move down to third. This game seemed to break them, however, and they ended up finishing ninth. A stint in non-league football was then to await before Oxford could get back up towards third-tier football more than a decade later. Ha!

1. **Hull City P28 W16 D8 L4 Pts56**
2. **Doncaster P27 W17 D4 L6 Pts55**
3. **Oxford P27 W14 D11 L2 Pts53**
4. **Mansfield P26 W15 D4 L7 Pts49**
5. **Yeovil P26 W15 D1 L10 Pts46**

The injury that Danny Allsopp had been suffering with had been problematic, and was proving to be a worry for the prolific striker.

Danny Allsopp: Just when I felt like things were going perfectly and I think we were close to the top of the league, I remember scoring a goal against Macclesfield and having a strange feeling in my lower abdomen and groin. I can't remember how it progressed but it soon grew into a feeling like I was being stabbed every time I tried to exert myself, doing something like sprinting. Otherwise I was fine and I was desperate to not let it stop me. I tried to play an away game but I couldn't run properly. It was one of the most frustrating times of my career as I was desperate to play. And it wasn't like a normal type of injury. No one seemed to be able to tell me what it was so I felt a paranoia that some people may have thought I was making it up. It cost me a big part of that season until we got on top of it and it settled down so I could get back into it.

One player who was on his way out of the KC was Dean Keates, the man who had scored the first league goal at the new stadium. Keates had never let City down, but was struggling to break into a midfield that comprised Ian Ashbee, Stuart Green, Jason Price and Stuart Elliott, with Ryan France generally considered to be the next cab off the rank. It was a sad goodbye for a fan favourite, however.

Dean Keates: In the 2003/04 season I was being played more in the away games and being left out for the home games. It was a frustrating period for me. I didn't really feel like I was getting a fair crack, and certain promises that were made weren't fulfilled. Before I left I chatted with Adam Pearson and there were certain guarantees that were made, that Adam said he'd honour, but in the end I felt it was best that I headed back down to the Midlands to a club where I'd be playing, given that I was still only 25.

Mike Scott: Nuggety. A term surely devised for this diminutive but influential Midlands midfielder. Acquired by Jan Molby in August 2002 but used mainly by the Dane's successor Peter Taylor for the next season and a bit, Keates battled his way past Fourth Division opponents and made Tigers history when he thumped in City's first League goal at their new home on Boxing Day 2002.

Filling the squad vacancy left by Dean Keates was a familiar face to Peter Taylor, that of midfielder Junior Lewis.

Junior Lewis: I just knew what Peter wanted and the way I played suited him. He always wanted me to get us playing. It was easy under him because he only ever wanted me to do what I was good at. He knew I could deal with pressure. I was a player who'd always want the ball. Peter knew I would keep wanting the ball no matter what kind of game I was having or what the fans were saying. I've been cheered by fans and I've been booed by them but it has never made the slightest difference to my game. I was a banker for Peter. Very rarely did I give the ball away, particularly in our third or the middle third.

Peter Taylor: A lot of people give me a bit of jip about Junior Lewis because I've signed him so many times. But if people were to see what he did at the clubs that I've been at... At Gillingham, when we beat Wigan at Wembley in the play-off final, he played three positions that day and was magnificent in every one of them. Alan Brazil – working for Sky at that time – made him man of the match. What Junior was was a team player – he wanted the ball even if he was playing terrible, and his team-mates respected that a lot.

I went to Leicester after Gillingham and lost Neil Lennon, so I brought Junior in on loan. In that month we beat both Liverpool and Chelsea 2-0 at home. The Liverpool manager told me Junior had played like Patrick Vieira, and all the fans were saying: "You've got to sign him." Then he was filling in everywhere. He was never signed to be a first-team player, just a squad player.

I lost my job at Leicester and went to Brighton and Hove Albion. Brighton were quite a direct team – I signed Junior, put him in the middle of the park and we were then suddenly playing football. He was the difference.

As much as Junior gets a lot of stick, and I get a little bit of stick, he got six promotions. Some players go their entire careers without winning a thing. One of the problems with Junior was that he's gangly; he doesn't look right. But if people looked at what he actually did, they'd respect him a little bit more.

Buoyed by the home win against Oxford, City won their next two games, a 2-0 win at Cheltenham courtesy of the Burgess/Allsopp double act, and a 2-1 home win against York City, with Jonathan Walters – who'd joined the club permanently – and Danny Allsopp doing the damage. City's run of seven consecutive league victories put the club three points clear at the top, and nine points clear of Mansfield in fourth. The winning streak was ended by a 1-1 draw at Carlisle in which Stuart Green scored an equaliser to silence the home crowd that had been abusing him for coming back to Hull City. Although we weren't to know it, the game would also represent the last time we'd see Justin Whittle representing Hull City.

Justin Whittle: I have no real memory of leaving the pitch at Carlisle. I'm told I was the last player off the pitch, but I was always the last off the pitch as I liked to applaud the fans.

City's form was then to take a worrying dip. A counter-attacking masterclass helped Torquay to a shock 1-0 victory at the KC and defeats at Lincoln and Mansfield followed. So what better way to get back on track than a local derby against Scunthorpe? A Ben Burgess brace got City's season back up and running in a 2-1 win.

Ben Burgess: Me and Jonathan Walters were up front that day. Yet another great occasion at the KC. Walters won the ball back and it came to me. I don't know why I went to chip it with my weaker right foot but it went in, then literally straight after that the ball went out to Stuart Elliott and I did a diving header and scored. I just wanted the ball to come to me. It was one of those games where everything just went well!

Orient were then clinically swatted aside at the KC a few days later as Burgess, Elliott and France gave City a 3-0 win. After this came a game that hadn't promised to be memorable. City in second took on Rochdale in 20th at the KC. However, the match was to feature one of the great KC Stadium goals. City were drawing 0-0, and down to 10 men through injury, with just over 10 minutes remaining. Cometh the hour, cometh Damien Delaney.

Damien Delaney: I think because of us being down to nine or 10 men I was pretty much playing left-wing back for some reason as we'd had to change our shape and play three at the back. The game seemed to be fizzling out and the ball came to me. I started running with it and everything seemed to open up in front of me. By the time I got to hit it I was so tired, so drained, I just threw a leg at it. Luckily the ball bobbled correctly and I caught it flush.

I ran off, and though I'd always thought I'd never do it, I took my shirt off for some reason and threw it away. Everyone was celebrating, even Boaz had come up to join in, then when it died down Ian Ashbee took my shirt, tucked it into his shirt and ran up to the halfway line. I was stood in the Rochdale end of the pitch, topless, trying to find my shirt, asking if anyone had seen it. It was really embarrassing. It was about 30 seconds panicking and Ash was shouting to me: "Get back, get back!" I was shouting back: "I haven't got a shirt! I can't find it!" Then Ash pulled my shirt out and all I could think was: 'You bastard!'

Peter Taylor: Damien scored a few good goals for us and he showed exactly what he could be that day. We knew he was capable of it. I always felt he could be a left midfielder with his skills. It just shows the confidence of that team; when it was 10 against 11 we still believed we could win that match. You'd have seen a lot of smiles among the staff for that goal, because Damien was a very popular member of the squad.

Ben Burgess: I just felt such relief. Boy, did we need that! It came from nowhere. He just didn't stop. Then he hit it and all I could think was: 'Thank god for that!' When things weren't going well for the forwards we'd have a centre-half running the length of the field and scoring a wonder goal. It just shows the magic of that season.

1. **Doncaster P38 W22 D9 L7 Pts75**
2. **Hull City P37 W21 D9 L7 Pts72**
3. **Huddersfield P38 W20 D9 L9 Pts69**
4. **Torquay P38 W19 D10 L9 Pts67**
5. **Oxford P38 W17 D15 L6 Pts66**

March had started with a grisly defeat at Mansfield, but three wins on the trot had seen City stay in second position. Up next, however, was a big test. No team had particularly enjoyed playing at Boston's tight York Street ground, but the match was to prove that City had steel to go with their silk. The 2-1 win, with goals coming from Stuart Elliott and Danny Allsopp, was a particularly satisfying one.

Stuart Elliott: It was a difficult game. Boston had a tight ground and the pitch wasn't great. I was more of a flair player rather than one who'd dig the ball out and put in hard tackles, so it was a difficult game for me, but I always knew that if an opportunity came along or a chance or a set piece I could contribute, and my free-kick in that game was a fair way out – about 30 yards! I just said I fancied it and kept my head down. Seeing it hit the back of the net was fantastic.

Danny Allsopp: I usually only remember bits and pieces over the years from coaches' pre-match talks as you hear so many, but I can remember like yesterday Peter Taylor's at the match at Boston. He said that if we could get the three points there we would get promoted. It was so close! We again had great support from the travelling supporters and it was huge to get that win. The Hull City supporters really embraced me in my time there so it felt great to celebrate scoring in that game with them.

Stuart Green: Boston weren't a bad team, and it was a horrible place to go, but we got over the line and played some good stuff. Nobody liked to play there and we did a tough job. The season previous we'd have rolled over in that game. It was a major win for us.

A 1-1 draw at Kidderminster, with Ben Burgess getting on the scoresheet, followed the win at Boston, only for City to then lose at home to a much-improved Northampton side at the KC Stadium on Easter Saturday. Swansea – City's next opponents on Easter Monday – had gone into freefall after their excellent start to the season, but a trip to the Vetch Field was always a daunting prospect. However, City needed to get back on track.

Andy Dawson: Swansea was one of my first games back after four or five weeks out. I'd been wondering if I was going to get a game even as we travelled down to Swansea. Peter Taylor pulled me into a room and asked me if I was fit to play. Looking back now, I'd hardly trained but I wanted to play so I said yes. It was a massively tense game at a pressure time of the season. You put pressure on yourself, the fans are putting pressure on you as they want you to achieve – and rightly so – and you know what the main goal is.

Ben Burgess: I really wanted to win because of the game the season before, in the last game of the season. Swansea beat us at the Vetch Field to stay in the league in the most farcical game I've ever played in. The referee was a joke. It really annoyed me as we should have got something from that. They should have been relegated.

City went one up through Danny Allsopp only for Andy Robinson to equalise on the stroke of half-time. This led to what could be described as an 'interesting' half-time atmosphere in the away changing room.

Ian Ashbee: Marc Joseph was having a go at somebody and I've basically told him to shut his mouth. I told him that Lee Trundle was tearing him a new arsehole, and I told him to sort himself out before he started having a go at anyone else. We had a bit of a tussle, fighting on the floor. I've cocked my right hand to whack Marc, but then big Paul Musselwhite grabbed my hand so Marc landed one on me because Mussy had my hand! I freed myself up from Mussy and it went into a brawl. These things happen. It's not the first time and it won't be the last time. It was just heat of the moment.

Marc Joseph: It was nothing more than a bit of passion. Me and Ash have known each other since we were 14 or 15. We knew we had to perform and again we were senior players – captain and vice-captain – and we both didn't want to lose and we felt that performances weren't as good as they should be. We didn't quite come to blows, we just made our feelings known to each other. We were just passionate about not losing. Me and Ash lived three doors away from each other and were always round at each other's houses. It was never anything more than just a heated disagreement in a changing room that didn't have much space.

Junior Lewis: It happens in football now and again. Ash and Marc Joseph were best of friends in football, and they'd clashed over a goal we'd conceded. I just said: "Oh boys, come on." But sometimes it's good to let them get on with it as it gets the team going again, but I did break it up. They came out of the changing rooms cuddling and it got us going and we ended up winning the game. The bust-up kick-started that and got us into gear. It did us good.

Andy Dawson: They were the big things that made us what we were: it mattered. It wasn't OK to be drawing 1-1, it was about playing well and everyone doing things right. That was why we were successful, not just in that season but in the years to come, as everyone demanded so much from each other. If people weren't doing their job right people were told. And with the emotions running wild, things did get a bit excitable. They were the reasons why we ended up being successful.

Stuart Green: At half-time, that's where the big characters came together, and that's what gets you promoted as a team. A few fists were thrown about!

Danny Allsopp: We were very fired up and it probably boiled over a bit at half time in that game. I can only vaguely remember that Ian Ashbee, who was a fantastic leader in the team, and Marc Joseph started arguing about something which then led to it getting a little bit physical. I can't remember it escalating too much before they were separated. They were mates so I'm sure we laughed about it after the game. It was just a heat of the moment thing and it was because they both wanted to win so badly.

Peter Taylor: Marc and Ash were there wanting to kill each other. I think Junior Lewis and Alton Thelwell were in the mix as well pulling people away, but Marc and Ash knew each other from Cambridge. The whole changing room was stunned as it was a real smash-up, so I stood up and said: "I've got nothing to say, I can't believe what's happened, err… let's go out and show 'em." It was one hell of a bust-up, but a good team spirit is one in which you can show your feelings.

The bust-up did the trick. City gained a famous and much-needed 3-2 victory, with Ben Burgess scoring twice in the second half, his second being the winner in the 87th minute.

Ben Burgess: They pulled it back to 2-2 then right at the end Jonathan Walters put a cross in, I managed to get ahead of the defender. We had so many fans there – we seemed to have more than the home side at some places – and seeing them all celebrate, as I'd scored right in front of them, was just brilliant.

Brendon Smurthwaite: The winner was offside! We were sat in the press box, which was just behind the directors' box where Adam was sat. Just to the left of that were the hardcore Swansea fans. It was a weird set-up. When we scored the winner, Adam stood up and celebrated, leading to one of the Swansea fans shouting: "Sit down you English bastard or I'll sit you down." Adam sat down quickly. Me and John Fieldhouse walked out after the game back to the car and saw a mob coming towards us. I hid my Hull City tie and just about got away with it.

Adam Pearson: I was getting a lot of abuse from the Swansea fans in that game, so when we won I was really giving it loads with the celebration, and all their fans were trying to get over the walls to the directors' box. Then when I got outside some of them were waiting for me there, so I had to leg it to the hotel to get away from them. A great game though! Ben and Danny up front were fantastic.

Danny Allsopp: The victory at Swansea was a big one for us. We were well up for it. They'd been challengers for promotion as well so we expected it to be tough. We were a very close-knit team that season. Most of us lived close together around Hull, we socialised a lot together and I felt like we were all mates. I felt like we all knew the importance and responsibility of the team being successful.

A couple of tough away matches awaited in which a victory and other results going City's way could have seen the club promoted, with Macclesfield first up. A 1-1 draw ensued, however, and City's goal came from an unexpected source.

Marc Joseph: I still get stick about that goal to this day from Ben Burgess, who I see through work around Blackpool. He mocks me for pulling my shorts up around my chest after I'd scored. I didn't score many goals, but it was getting towards the end of the season and any goals we scored were important ones. It wasn't the one that got us promoted but it got us one point closer to where we wanted to be.

1. **Doncaster P43 W25 D10 L8 Pts85 (plus 39)**
2. **Hull City P42 W23 D11 L8 Pts80 (plus 34)**
3. **Huddersfield P42 W22 D10 L10 Pts76 (plus 17)**
4. **Torquay P43 W21 D11 L11 Pts74 (plus 21)**
5. **Lincoln P43 W19 D16 L8 Pts73 (plus 24)**

Next up it was Southend, City's game in hand. A win would have all but given City promotion, given Torquay in fourth's inferior goal difference. However, a 2-2 draw was the result, with City coming back from behind twice and scoring through Junior Lewis and Ian Ashbee.

Junior Lewis: I was just surprised I was allowed in the box!

1. **Doncaster P43 W25 D10 L8 Pts85 (plus 39)**
2. **Hull City P43 W23 D12 L8 Pts81 (plus 34)**
3. **Huddersfield P43 W23 D10 L10 Pts79 (plus 18)**
4. **Torquay P43 W21 D11 L11 Pts74 (plus 21)**
5. **Lincoln P43 W19 D16 L8 Pts73 (plus 24)**

Promotion was again at stake in the home match against third-placed Huddersfield. A win and City were up. Defeat for Torquay at Cheltenham along with a defeat or draw for Lincoln and City were up. Torquay were to win 3-1, which left it down to City. However, a frustrating 0-0 draw ensued, though the game was to be overshadowed by a serious injury to top scorer Ben Burgess. The injury would keep the big-hearted striker out of action for a whole year.

Ben Burgess: I was desperate to win. I tried to get to the ball ahead of Paul Rachubka, didn't, then I just remember the worst pain. I needed an injection in my bum to get rid of the pain then I was told I'd done my cruciate. I'm still crippled in my knee. It just happens in football. I'm just thankful I managed to squeeze out a few more years from football.

Danny Allsopp: It was terrible when Ben got injured so seriously at the end of the season. It was obvious out on the pitch that it was a bad one. I was really gutted for him. He'd really proven his worth and shown everyone what he could do, and he'd been a huge part of the team's performances and mine over the whole season. I guess these things are bad luck and part of the game but it was obviously terrible for him and I knew that I wouldn't have him out there with me as well.

1. **Doncaster P44 W26 D10 L8 Pts88 (plus 41)**
2. **Hull City P44 W23 D13 L8 Pts82 (plus 34)**
3. **Huddersfield P44 W23 D11 L10 Pts80 (plus 18)**
4. **Torquay P44 W22 D11 L11 Pts77 (plus 23)**
5. **Lincoln P44 W19 D17 L8 Pts74 (plus 24)**

With Lincoln now out of the picture and Doncaster already promoted, the final two automatic promotion spots were between Hull City, Huddersfield Town and Torquay United. On May 1st, 2004, Hull City were away to seventh-placed Yeovil, Huddersfield at home to sixth-placed Mansfield, and Torquay were at home to 16th-placed Kidderminster. Essentially, City had to match Torquay's result, or hope that Torquay could only draw in the event of a loss at Yeovil, to gain a promotion that had seemed so close after the victory at Swansea but just wouldn't come. Only five teams had beaten Yeovil at Huish Park that season, so nerves were understandably frayed among the supporters. For the players, there was an element of calmness in the days running up to the big game.

Damien Delaney: There'd been a lot of big games that year, but once we started going down that back stretch, as great as the fans were, you'd get this sense of nervousness and uneasiness from them as they'd had so many lows over the years. It was like a lot of them were expecting us to throw it away. Whenever we were out on a night, people seemed nervous asking: "Are we going to do it?" I would be thinking: 'Why are you asking me that? Of course we're going to do it.' We had that ultimate confidence. I was wondering why everyone was so anxious. It was going to happen.

Brendon Smurthwaite: I went to Yeovil on the Friday, and it took us seven-and-a-half hours to get there. The bloke who checked us in at the hotel did everything: he'd check you in then go to serve you at the bar, then run off to serve you food. The next morning Peter Taylor and Damien Delaney came in and the guy said to Peter: "You know that every visiting team that has stayed here has lost, don't you?" Peter didn't say anything. It seemed like an omen.

Peter Taylor: We stayed away at a hotel near Yeovil. I was down with the staff for breakfast. Adam came in and I remember saying to him: "Adam, we're going to get promotion today," and he replied: "Well, I hope you're right!" I was very confident. It was a tough game, and Yeovil were a good team with Gary Johnson as their manager. At Gillingham and Brighton I'd never had a promotion on home soil, so I was just confident because of that.

Andy Dawson: I remember the emotions going into the game. I was rooming with Jamie Forrester at the time and we were just speaking saying: "If we win tomorrow, we go up" and all these emotions were building, just asking yourself: 'What if…?' You have to go out and do it though.

Ian Thomson: I remember it like it was yesterday, and probably always will. We had gone into each of the three previous games with a chance of clinching automatic promotion if we had won, and ended up drawing each of them. Yeovil had play-off aspirations and many tipped us to bottle the game.

Danny Allsopp: I'm sure we wanted to secure promotion at home but it turned out we had to do it at Yeovil. I think they'd been up there in the table so we knew it wouldn't be easy as they were near the play-offs.

Stuart Green: We were limping over the line. We'd looked like a team that was nervous in the previous games. We had a good training session the day before… lively, bubbly, but the hotel was horrific. We'd always stayed in nice hotels but it was horrible. We woke up and went for a walk, and there was just a feeling we were going to do it.

Ian Ashbee: The games before were becoming a bit of an issue. We'd had our chances and I was confident it was coming but there was a little bit of a wobble. Going away from home probably did help us with our nerves, and Yeovil is an arduous journey. There are always nerves, and you need them, but there were two games of the season left and so we were thinking it was a do-or-die game as we didn't want it going down to the last game of the season.

Stuart Elliott: It was another difficult game. People don't understand how difficult it can be to get over the line, with the emotions that you go through. You can't play your normal game and we weren't putting in the performances in that we had been in the early part of the season, which was understandable because of the nerves, but the Yeovil game was one that by hook or by crook we had to get over the line.

The away terraces at Huish Park were packed to the brim, as was the Gemtec Arena back at the KC Stadium, which was screening the game.

Marc Joseph: When we came out for the warm-up and saw the number of Hull fans that were there we knew it would be a high-pressure game, and it just emphasised what an important day it was for the club and the city of Hull. We knew that people were back home watching on the big screen. It was a massive, massive game for us. We needed to perform.

Nerves were settled when City were awarded a penalty in the 11th minute.

Danny Allsopp: I remember going down for a penalty which gave us the lead. I didn't have to take a dive, but when we really needed a win I couldn't believe my luck when the defender just wouldn't let me go when I'd beat him in the box!

Stuart Green: Yeovil played some great football – they were a good football team. I remember Danny Allsopp going down to win the penalty, and I just started running towards the ball. I put the ball down and turned around to the bench. Pete would always sit down with the rest of the bench for penalties but they hadn't. I knew I was going to score, I knew where I was going to put it, but I remember looking at the bench thinking: 'Some of you think I'm going to miss,' and I turned round and couldn't have hit it any better. That end behind the goal just erupted. That settled us down.

A 1-0 lead at half-time was not enough to banish the nerves among the players or the fans, particularly given that Torquay had taken the lead against Kidderminster just before half-time. Then, for the first 25 minutes or so of the second half, Yeovil were undoubtedly on top. An equaliser looked likely, and came from a set piece when 6 foot 7 centre-back Hugo Rodrigues towered over the City defence to score from a free-kick in the 64th minute.

Andy Dawson: It was a massive pressure game. There were all the fans in the Gemtec, all the fans at Yeovil, a great start to the game. I was thinking: 'Come on, just let the game finish now.' Then I gave a free-kick away and the big lad scored for them.

Ian Thomson: We got off to the best possible start and it could have been even better when Allsopp hit the post, but when they equalised the tension was unbearable, even though a draw might still have been enough.

'Typical City' was going through the minds of every Hull City fan. Typical City is the notion that if anything can be screwed up, Hull City will find a way to screw it up, no matter how difficult it may seem to do so. Typical City is failing to go up to the top flight by a single point in the 1909/10 season. Typical City is managing to alienate Raich Carter when he looked to be leading the club to untold glory. Typical City is failing to capitalise on the Battle of Bramall Lane in 1971. Typical City is reaching the final of the Associate Members' Cup in 1984, the year before it started to be played at Wembley. Typical City is finishing sixth in the old Second Division in 1986, the season before the play-offs were introduced. Typical City is being 2-1 up against the great Liverpool side of 1989 only to lose 3-2. Typical City is the optimism of David Lloyd and Mark Hateley coming to the club in 1997 only for it all to end in tears. Typical City is Adam Pearson coming in, spending oodles of money and getting the KC Stadium built, and having nothing to show for it on the pitch.

Our captain, our leader, our inspiration, Ian Ashbee, didn't give a toss about 'Typical City'. Ian Ashbee scored a goal in the 76th minute that would end 19 years of agony. Ian Ashbee's Hull City career could have ended that afternoon and he'd still have been a Hull City legend. Little did we know he was only getting started.

Ian Ashbee: I think Ryan France went down the right, crossed it and they cleared it. The ball bounced to me on the edge of the box – Peter Taylor would drill it into us to get the second balls and keep the play alive – and I kneed it to Junior Lewis. I don't know what he was doing but it hit his leg and fell back to me, and my momentum took me forward and it was just sat there. I just thought: 'I'm going to bend this in the top corner,' and to be fair, what I thought about then actually happened, which was not normal for me; I bent it in the top corner. Then it was just a feeling that you can't replicate. At that point, to think about the history of the football club – I was living in the town centre around the people so I understood what it meant to them – that sent a feeling of elation going through my body that was special.

Andy Dawson: He doesn't get many, but he'd scored one previous to that at Southend. When he got them they were good, good goals. We got there in the end.

Stuart Elliott: Ian Ashbee talked about that goal for years to come. But it was a tremendous goal. Right in the top corner.

Ian Farrow: Oh what a goal! What a memory! I can picture it now and, of course, savour it whenever it is mentioned. A glorious goal. A glorious moment. The goal came out of the blue, and what do you do except go absolutely deliriously ape-shit crazy? We were behind the goal and I got carried forward, and then back. It was just a mass of people all losing their minds. If football is a drug then at such times it is the most beautiful of drugs where you lose yourself; nothing else matters and you love everybody and everything.

Ian Thomson: It came out of the blue. It was at the far end from the City support, of course, and there was that moment you often experience from the other end when you aren't quite sure – for maybe half a second – whether it has gone in, especially as we were to the right of the City goal and not, therefore, behind the trajectory of the shot. I remember desperately trying not to lose my cigar out of my mouth as the City support celebrated wildly. I also remember trying very hard not to think about the consequences of that goal: the previous 19 years had taught me neither to expect nor hope for anything where City were concerned. The emotion kicked in as the clock ticked into injury time and it became clear that Yeovil were not going to equalise again.

Marc Joseph: It was nail-biting. It wasn't easy, but Ash scoring the winner was just meant to be. And what a goal it was! We just had a feeling of being invincible. We had such good players, and we felt if we got our noses in front we would see the game out.

Mike Hall: It wasn't just the quality of the goal that makes it stand out – that goal was more than the culmination of that season's work. It exorcised the ghosts of the previous 19 promotion-less years, and marked the catalyst for our rise up the divisions, with its scorer at the heart of it all.

Damien Delaney: The game seemed to be going nowhere, then Ash scored that beauty and the rest was brilliant. That was one of the best days of my career. It was a great day for everyone and well deserved.

Ryan France: We'd had a couple of games to win promotion before then and we were saying: "This is getting serious now lads, we need to bloody win!" The games before Yeovil we were thinking: 'We've got another game, don't worry,' but we got to Yeovil and it was like: 'Lads, this is it.' Every one of us stood up that day. It was more like how we'd been playing earlier in the season, turning up to teams thinking: 'We're going to batter you.'

Ben Burgess: I didn't go to Yeovil as I was on crutches. I was driving to Hull while the game was on – I had an automatic, luckily – and was listening to the game, then when Ash scored I was bouncing up and down in my car. Where did that come from? He's someone who doesn't score goals, but he was there at the right time.

Ian Bunton: Having spent most of that season watching City with my dad, he didn't want to travel to Yeovil, so we watched the screening in the Gemtec Arena at the KC. When the goal went in I can just recall trying to make sure my old man wasn't injured in the melee of beer throwing and jubilation that ensued. Once it died down I can recall thinking: 'Bloody hell, watching all that mediocre football for all those years was finally worth it.' Hull City were on the brink of promotion, and things were starting to look good. As a friend has said to me on numerous occasions: "It's where it all began."

Martin Batchelor: We needed a win and for the winning goal to come from Ash was the icing on the cake. An unbelievable shot at the far end from us on the open terrace. When the ball hit the back of the net we went crackers. You can't beat terraces for celebrations like that! I'm sure they could hear us back in Hull, even without the live beam-back.

Andy Dawson: It was a long 15 minutes though. It felt like half an hour.

The final whistle eventually went and the celebrations could begin. And how…

Adam Pearson: Everything was right about that set up. Yeovil were very gracious and knew how important it was to us. I wanted to stay out of the way of the celebrations as it was down to Peter and Colin and the team, so I stayed in the background, but I was emotional about it as it had taken a long time to get it going. We'd been a bit flash and hired a helicopter to get back for a concert by Blue so I left quickly. I regret it to this day that I didn't get involved more with the celebrations. But I didn't want to be seen on the pitch and I didn't want to take anything away from the manager or players. Maybe I should have enjoyed it more.

Peter Taylor: I felt we deserved it on the day. It was a brilliant goal from Ash. That was the difference. The feeling was fantastic. One of the first people I saw was Adam and I was so pleased for him because he'd put so much money into the club. It was just a lovely feeling that finally Hull City had got a promotion they should have got a few years ago. It was even better the days after when you saw the fans watching the game at the arena at the KC. I've still got the DVD at home and I love watching it. It just gives you so much pride knowing you've done a decent job and that people have got so much satisfaction out of it.

Ian Ashbee: I would have preferred to do it at home in front of all the fans, as it had been such a long, arduous journey getting there. There are many fans who'd been trawling around the country for years and years and put the hard yards in. Even seeing the scenes afterwards at the Gemtec Arena and the beers going everywhere, it was really, really good. It was a special time for me and for the football club.

Stuart Elliott: When the final whistle went I just remember looking at the Hull City fans behind the goal going crazy. It was the start of big things for us as a club.

Stuart Green: I'd come off, but I was thinking that the ref wasn't going to blow up. We were ready to run to our fans. It was a long, hard season. Such a battle. All of us had an injury, we were all shattered and we couldn't wait for it to be over. We knew what it meant to the fans.

Ryan France: Running up to all the fans, giving my shirt away to a young lad: they were just great scenes. A proud, proud moment. I'd been a big part of a professional football team that was about to break records.

Jason Price: I had a dodgy amber and black wig on. The wig was an afro though, so it just looked like I'd dyed my normal hair!

Boaz Myhill: I always had the belief we could do it. Promotion is an unbelievable experience. I was delighted just to get first-team football but to get promoted was just unbelievable.

Danny Allsopp: The win was a huge relief and hugely satisfying for us. We knew we'd achieved something significant for the club.

Simon Maltby: There'd been very few down points that season, we had a good set of lads, the interaction between the backroom staff and players was really good. That success hadn't happened by chance. It was no accident that we had a good set of players, good staff. It all just came together.

Dave Burns: I was quite chilled about it because I knew it was coming. There was a sense of destiny about it and I knew it would happen. The club was going somewhere. I felt that all the way through Adam's time there, as he knew what he wanted and how he was going to achieve it. And I was so pleased for Ash. He was a top man.

Ian Thomson: It was profound happiness, yes, but more than that it felt like the end of the most horrible nightmare imaginable; we had fought through and come out of the other end after all the years of real misery, and it was that which for me brought a tear to the eye.

Brendon Smurthwaite: That season, and Yeovil in particular, was my favourite time at the club. It was the start. People realised something was happening. Sky had never bothered with us before, but Soccer Saturday started turning up.

Jason Price: The team we had on paper was too good for League 2. We knew we had round pegs for round holes. There were no bad eggs in the team. We knew what jobs we had to do, and we all enjoyed training. If somebody went out we'd all go out.

John Cooper: The day that Hull City beat Yeovil away, by the time the game had finished we'd opened the gates for the Blue concert. But it was such a wonderful feeling. You knew the club was on the up. You knew something was happening. You knew by the way Adam Pearson was that he wouldn't allow us to go backwards. That period was a big growth spurt for the club. Foundations are so important to build a house on, and that's what Adam did.

Ian Thomson: Despite so many memories that, at the start of the decade, would have been beyond our wildest dreams, Yeovil was the day when the rot was stopped, the boil lanced. From the very instant Ash's shot hit the back of the Yeovil net, Hull City ceased to be a laughing stock.

Brendon Smurthwaite: The press box held about four people, so you were sat with a laptop on your knee. At the end of the game I had to walk around the edge of the pitch to get to the dressing room side. When I got there I opened the door and Jamie Forrester covered me in champagne. I knew I was driving John Holmes' car back to Hull to get to the concert at the KC by Blue. Adam and a few others were going by air. I was stuck to the leather seats in my champagne-soaked suit for the whole journey. It was still a brilliant day though.

Rob Smith: I missed the Yeovil game. I stayed at the KC to organise that concert for bloody Blue. Afterwards I thought: 'I've worked here 19 years and never had a promotion and now I've missed one!' I probably put the job first, and when everyone got back that night from the game I started to really regret my decision.

Justin Whittle: Peter had said I'd have played if I'd got fit and I was desperate to be playing, but my back was taking a long time to heal. So I wasn't there, and my biggest memory that season is the 1-0 win against Swansea, when I was marking Lee Trundle and the fans were amazing all night long.

Marc Joseph: I've still got photos around my house of the guys spraying champagne everywhere. It was a feeling of 'job done'. We knew we were heading in the right direction.

Mike Scott: The 2-1 win at Yeovil had everything; a hot sunny weekend in a faraway, hitherto unvisited town; a packed away terrace with all the people you expect to be there, there; a seesaw 90 minutes where promotion was claimed, snatched away and reclaimed; and a fabulous goal from a true City hero that led to that special kind of mayhem and cavorting joy that only football can stimulate. City had been so poor for so long, fans had forgotten what a smattering of success felt like. That day in Somerset we celebrated deep into the night, blissfully unaware that this was the start of something unimaginable. That night, promotion to the third tier was all our dreams come true.

With a player who'd done so much to get Hull City in that position – Ben Burgess – sadly absent from the celebrations, one team-mate made sure he wasn't to be forgotten.

Damien Delaney: I lived opposite Ben. We were like family, along with Alton and Pricey. No one ever locked their doors and we were in and out of each other's apartments. We'd become really close. We knew the extent of the injury. We knew he'd miss most of the following season. We really did feel for him, and I just wrote on a t-shirt in marker pen before the game as we thought we'd do something for him. That said, I always look at that picture of us celebrating at the end of the game when everyone's in their City shirts and I'm in just there in this tatty white t-shirt with writing scrawled all over it.

Ben Burgess: It was a nice gesture, but I'll always regret that I wasn't there.

Promotion achieved, which meant that the final game of the season, at home to Bristol Rovers, was a party. A 3-0 win was a fitting end to a wonderful season.

Ian Thomson: On the final day Damien Delaney's goal against Bristol Rovers was quite magnificent. Starting the break from defence, the timing of the run, the cut-back and the glorious cross-shot across the keeper all contributed to produce a goal of real quality befitting of such a carnival afternoon.

Jason Price: My hamstring went again in that game. My mum and dad had come up. I was sub, came on, scored, but as soon as I scored I felt my hamstring go and I just thought: 'Oh no!' Peter Taylor wasn't the best person to tell that you had to come off just after he'd brought you on!

Andy Dawson: When I signed and the fixtures came out, I remember saying to my wife that my dream was getting promoted and me having that last game of the season going out in front of the crowds with us already up. I'd never had anything like that in my career. Everything up until that point had always been the play-offs. So playing in front of a big crowd like that, already up, was a great day for me. Everything that I'd spoken about at the beginning of the season had happened.

And the celebrations were to continue with an open-top bus tour of the city.

Jason Price: When we went on the open-top bus there wasn't a 10-second gap where there was nobody. It was that busy on the streets, there were so many people out to congratulate us, it was unbelievable. The reception – considering it was a promotion from League 2 – was incredible. You were just constantly waving at people.

Danny Allsopp: It was amazing the reception we got in Hull with the parade and all the celebrations. It was one of the few moments in my career, with all the ups and downs, when I was really happy knowing that we'd achieved something special.

The promotion celebrations were tinged with an element of sadness for a number of City fans, as it had become apparent that we'd seen Justin Whittle, a hero of the Great Escape and beyond, in a Hull City shirt for the last time.

Justin Whittle: I had the option of another year, but new defenders were going to be coming in. I'd have loved to have stayed in many ways, but I was 33 and I didn't want to be a bit-part player. I didn't know if I'd get another contract at the end of that season too if I hadn't played much. Grimsby had just got relegated and asked me to go there. I was there four years and ended up playing 150 or so games. I wouldn't have played that much had I stayed at Hull.

Peter Taylor: It was a tough decision. I knew Justin was popular with the supporters, but he was also popular with me. I liked him a lot. But I could only then think: 'Is he the type of centre-half I want?' I thought Justin was an army-type centre half. If there's a battle going on, Justin Whittle's going to win it without a doubt. But I didn't think he fully understood how to play the football that I wanted the team to play. Not that I expect my centre-halves to play stupid football, but I wanted them to play some football and I felt as though I could get a bit better. If I'd been managing someone like Scunthorpe at that time and not a Hull City I'd have kept him. I was just looking at what we needed. As a man and as a professional he was fantastic. I've seen him since and he's still the same. It was tough for him and it was tough for me as I knew he was a fan's favourite – the last thing I wanted to do was fall out with the fans – but it was an honest selection decision. I felt as though he wasn't the type of centre-half that I wanted and I felt as though I could do better. It was a tough decision, and I know it was unlucky for Justin but I hope he understands it.

Justin Whittle: Whatever decision I've made in life I've always enjoyed it. I had four great years at Stoke, six fantastic years at Hull City and then four great years at Grimsby. But I moved to Hull and I'm still here now. I love it here, love the fans. Football is all about the fans. I wasn't the most skilful of players but I always gave 100%.

David Brown: Justin was the quietest man you could meet off the pitch, but he could be an animal on it. However, in games, he'd just laugh at really inopportune or inappropriate times, sometimes after we'd just conceded a goal. We'd call him Dr Hibbert after the doctor on The Simpsons who'd laugh when he was telling patients that they're going to die. He'd just giggle all the time. You couldn't help but like him.

Greg Strong: Justin Whittle was technically not a good footballer – I don't think he'd mind me saying that – but he had heart and passion and he loved that club. He'd put his body on the line for it. It wasn't pretty at times, but you couldn't help but take your hat off to him. He was a leader in the way he played, and people followed him. He was as brave as a lion.

Stuart Elliott: Justin Whittle was Hull City through and through and an absolute gentleman. He was another leader in that team.

Andy Holt was another saying goodbye to the club.

Andy Holt: I'd been told in the November by my agent that I was going to get a new two-year contract, which I was delighted with, but then it all dragged on and for the last four or five games of the season I wasn't even in the squad, so I was thinking: 'This doesn't look good!' Then at the end of the season I was told that I wasn't being offered a contract. I was gutted. I loved the place. And I felt I could have given more in League 1 and beyond, but that's just the way football is.

Mike Hall: When Andy Holt joined City on loan in 2001 he immediately brought quality to our left-hand side. He also offered much-needed versatility as he was comfortable on the wing or at full-back, had a dangerous long throw and could take an excellent free-kick (notably a brilliant winning goal in front of the South Stand against Scunthorpe in City's unlikely run to the play-offs in 2001). Unfortunately, his loan spell ultimately turned out to be his peak at the club. When he was signed the following summer for a then eye-watering £150,000, it was a real statement of intent from Adam Pearson. While Holt perhaps never quite lived up to the promise of his loan spell, his signing was significant in that it demonstrated where the club was trying to go – in terms of targeting talented young players and being prepared to spend real money to get them.

Paul Musselwhite, a goalkeeper who'd never let Hull City down, was also to leave.

Paul Musselwhite: Peter and I had a few heated discussions at the time. I was 35 and I said what I thought to him, and though I'd had a good time at Hull I felt there were a few disappointments towards the end, when I was left out when I felt I didn't deserve it. But I look back on my time at Hull City as one of the most enjoyable parts of my career. It was eventful over the four years and I met a lot of new players in that time. I wouldn't like to think how many players came through the door and left in such a short period. But I have nothing but fond memories of my time at Hull. One of my first conversations with Brian Little when I joined had been about getting Hull promoted, so it was nice four years later to leave having been part of a promotion, as I'd played quite a few games that season. And I had a good record under Peter Taylor, as I try to remind him when I see him! I enjoyed playing for him but he was looking long term at the club's future.

Justin Whittle: I loved having Paul Musselwhite behind me. He pulled off a save in a game against Scunny at home that I still can't work out.

Ian Farrow: Paul Musselwhite was signed by Brian Little but his period in goal was the foundation for our rise through the leagues. He was the 'keeper as City reached the play-off semi-finals in 2001. Musselwhite organised the defence, gave confidence at the back and pulled off many a memorable save in his time with us. We all loved Paul Musselwhite and it was only the arrival of a young upstart called Boaz Myhill that saw him drop into a supporting role.

Along with Jamie Forrester and John Anderson, Greg Strong finally said goodbye to Hull after a move that had promised so much but had ultimately not worked out.

Greg Strong: My family enjoyed ourselves there. We lived in South Cave which is a lovely area, and we met a lot of nice, genuine people. You don't make that many true friends in football as you're moving so much, but I made a lot of good friends at Hull City. There were a lot of good people in and around the club. Even though it was frustrating not being a full part of it, seeing the club grow and be successful was really nice. It was good to see all that hard work, all those plans, come off.

The third tier of English football is hardly the promised land, but to Hull City that summer represented a long-awaited symbol of progression. The next season would see the club come up against the likes of Sheffield Wednesday, Barnsley and Bradford, local rivals who had seemed a million miles ahead of City in recent years when plying their trade in the Premier League. We were at their level now. And we were to more than match them.

2004/05 season

The last time Hull City had played a match in the third tier of English football had been May 4th, 1996. That was the infamous Bradford City game, in which the away fans had been given the South Stand of a crumbling Boothferry Park, the protests against Terry Dolan, Martin Fish and Christopher Needler had reached fever pitch, and Bradford fans frequently invaded the pitch, contained only by mounted police. Nine years and two months later, the Hull City preparing for the opening game against Bournemouth could not have stood in starker contrast to that mess of a club. The KC still looked too good for the level of football it was hosting. Peter Taylor was the division's most high-profile manager, Adam Pearson its most ambitious chairman. The squad was packed with talent, but perhaps lacked a little experience. That gap was soon to be plugged, however, in a move that was beyond the fans' wildest dreams.

Nick Barmby was something of a celebrity in Hull before he had made his teens. A footballing prodigy, the son of former City player Jeff, Nick had had managers from all the top clubs in the country knocking on his Bricknell Avenue door in the 1980s when he was still attending Kelvin Hall school. Though he was representing Hull City Boys at this stage, the senior club was starting a spiral that would lead to afternoons such as that against Bradford. Nick was destined for better things, and via the Lilleshall School of Excellence and England Schoolboys, he signed for Tottenham, somewhat unexpectedly as he'd been training alongside the likes of Ryan Giggs at Manchester United. The day after that grim afternoon in which Hull City lost 3-2 to a play-off-bound Bradford, Nick lined up for Middlesbrough – the club he'd joined for £5.25m from Spurs – at Old Trafford.

Nick joined Everton for £5.75m at the end of that season, and then crossed Stanley Park for a sum of £6m to ply his trade with Liverpool. After a successful spell at Anfield, in which he won numerous trophies, Nick moved to Leeds. A series of injuries and loan moves had limited his impact at Elland Road, leading to rumours that he was unhappy at the club. He was also frequently seen at the KC watching both his beloved Hull FC and Hull City. In retrospect it seems like the perfect fit, but when the first murmurings of the prodigal son making a glorious return emerged, most City fans assumed that it was pie in the sky. Nick had played for England in the famous 5-1 stuffing of Germany less than four years previous. Surely he could do better than League 1. Surely. Well, actually…

Nick Barmby: I was at Leeds but I was still coming to some Hull City games. I didn't really know Adam Pearson at Leeds but I got to know him at Hull and he just said: "I'd love to get you back here one day," and I said: "I'd love to come back." I'd had a few good offers but the timing was right, I wanted to come back, I wanted to make an impact and put something back in the city. I sat down with Peter Taylor and established that he wanted me – because I would never come back if the manager didn't want me, and it wasn't a publicity stunt – so we sat down and we made things happen.

Adam Pearson: With Nick Barmby, his agent had told me that Nick wanted to play for Hull City and I thought 'no chance'. Nick was on 20 times what we were paying and what he'd eventually be on. He was still in the prime of his career, still only 28. I thought he wasn't happy at Leeds, and he wanted to come home. He made the negotiations very easy. He wasn't the highest paid player at the club, came for not a lot. I don't think Peter expected him to sign and was surprised when he did. But in the dressing room and on the pitch he was a model pro. His preparation, training, application and honesty throughout everything was exceptional. He was a proper professional. It was a great statement of intent. And it certainly wasn't for financial reasons that he came here. What marks Nick out is his humility. He has none of the airs and graces of players with half his talent.

Peter Taylor: If you're ever after a player of that ability, you have to make sure that they want to come to the club for the right reasons. I knew Nick had Hull connections, I knew he was a good lad and I knew about his ability, but what I loved about him before he signed was that he wanted to make sure that I wanted him. He didn't want me to be appeasing Adam because he was a big name – which isn't my style anyway. I only want a player if he's going to be of use to the team, if he's going to join in and be a part of what we're trying to achieve. And I loved him because he said: "I want to know if you want me." He wanted to be sure. That's why it was perfect.

Andy Dawson: When we started back Nick just introduced himself. He'd been an England international and spent his career in the Premier League but he just came in and fitted in seamlessly. He's a down-to-earth guy who came to get Hull City promoted again and see the club progress. He was a top, top player, he helped us all out, and it opened the eyes of the rest of us as we knew the club really meant business and wanted to get promoted again. He was a great character who was an example to us all every day in training.

Boaz Myhill: I remember watching Nick Barmby running up the hills at Brantingham and being starstruck, thinking: 'Wow, it's Nick Barmby off the telly.' It was a big coup for us, as I'm sure he could have gone to clubs higher up in the Football League. We all knew that when he was at Leeds the season before he'd come and watch us, so there'd been whispers, but when it did happen it was unbelievable.

Stuart Elliott: Nick was a massive influence in both the club's and my success. With one pass he'd open up a defence, which was perfect for my game making runs behind the defender. So with Nick having such great control, and being a first-class player, he could see a pass. Peter Taylor would tell me to make late runs and Nick would just thread it through the defenders.

Simon Maltby: Nick's a really good pro. He lived life right and trained hard. He was of the mentality that if you trained hard you'd then play to that level. Some footballers think that you just do it on a Saturday, but that's not my opinion. If you train hard you'll reproduce it on a Saturday to better effect. And he was always in early to get his prep done. When you see someone who's played to the level that Nick had doing things properly, then it rubs off on other people. It makes them think: 'If I do things properly then I might achieve more in my career.' He was always a pleasure to work with.

Ryan France: The impact Nick Barmby had matched the intention we had as a team. We weren't resting on our laurels. We wanted to go even further. So bringing in Barmby – what a statement that was. He wasn't past it. I watched Nick a lot – he was the ultimate professional.

He came and gave it his all. He wasn't doing it for the money, he was doing it for the club. It was great to see. You only had to be in his company for five minutes and you were doing things differently. He never stopped on the pitch. Even when the gaffers were talking, he'd be stretching. He was always on the move. He was the best player I've played with because he was always on the next page. You always knew if you made a run, he'd find you. He was the difference for us that season.

Colin Murphy: Nick Barmby was incredible in everything he did. You could see why he'd won so many England caps.

Junior Lewis: He was a great signing. A really good lad. I'd known him for years, as we're the same age, and he was great with the youngsters. We all learnt off him.

Peter Taylor: It was an easy signing based on what I knew about him regarding his ability and as a person. Of course you want to be sure that he was going to be fit, but he was a first-class signing and a first-class lad. But with that, with him being used to playing in the Premier League, that could make it hard to substitute him every now and then. He didn't like it. But that just showed his desire.

Mike White: Nick is top drawer as a bloke, very approachable and friendly. When you look now at what that signing did for the club, it just raised the profile. When City were struggling in the 1990s, and Nick was playing for Spurs, you never really felt a player of that calibre was going to end up as a City player. We'd had a glimpse of that sort of thing with Emlyn Hughes and David Rocastle. But once it sunk in you were like: 'OK, the hometown kid's come home, this can only mean good things.' And getting him here showed a real level of ambition and intent, and it showed what Adam Pearson and Peter Taylor had to offer. Home-town club or not, they had to have something there to get a player of Nick's standing down to that level.

Mark Robinson: I remember playing cricket on Teskey King school and seeing my dad running across the field from our home on Inglemire Lane shouting: "We've signed Billy Bremner! We've signed Billy Bremner!" Nick Barmby had that kind of effect on the club and the city. It was a legend coming to play for Hull City, and that sort of thing never really happened to us.

Brendon Smurthwaite: I'd never met Nick, even though he'd been in the stadium a few times. I didn't know how to be with him, so when Adam said I had to chat with him for the club magazine, I was a bit scared. Everything was taking ages, and I gave him the option to finish it all another time but he just said: "No, crack on with it now." It was at that point where I realised what a normal, down-to-earth bloke he was. Some players don't want to do all of that, but Nick was more than happy to do whatever you asked.

When he did all the promo stuff on signing, we didn't have the right size shirt for him, so he was appearing on stuff like Look North in a shirt three sizes too big for him. But he didn't throw a strop or anything. Again, it made people wonder what was going on at Hull City. Nick was hugely influential at the club, on the pitch and off it. His professionalism really affected the younger players.

Peter Taylor: Two minutes into his debut in a pre-season friendly at Canvey Island, Nick flicked the ball over a defender's head and scored a great goal. We all just looked at each other and said: "Blimey! What a player."

The recruitment wasn't done there. The departures of Alan Fettis and Paul Musselwhite meant that Boaz Myhill was the only senior goalkeeper within the club's ranks. That was soon remedied with the signing of a goalkeeper who Colin Murphy had spotted at Burton Albion, and who would go on to play out one of the great football stories.

Matt Duke: Colin Murphy had watched me playing for Burton, then I'd played for Hull in a friendly at Alfreton. They liked what they saw and signed me. It was all done and dusted pretty quickly. It came out of the blue a little bit but I was just grateful for the opportunity and couldn't wait to get started.

Peter Taylor: Matt Duke was one that Colin had found: Burton Albion, 20 grand. He was terrific. What a good signing.

Boaz Myhill: The signing of Dukey was brilliant. He ended up being there for years and did a really good job. He's still a really good friend. You couldn't write the story of the stuff that happened to Matt Duke, but it just went to show what a strong character he was. It was a great signing personally for me and for the club.

Matt Duke: I didn't feel I had to be better than Boaz, I just wanted to go in and learn and take the opportunity of being back in the professional game. I knew Ryan France, which was nice as I could relate to him and travel in with him. The stadium was fantastic and it was just a great club to be at.

The departure of Justin Whittle to Grimsby meant that competition was needed for Damien Delaney and Marc Joseph at centre-back. That came in the shape of Southend's Leon Cort.

Leon Cort: A few teams were in for me – Scunthorpe and Oldham were the ones I knew about – but my brother Carl had played under Peter Taylor and I knew him from that. Carl told me that Peter liked me as a player, so when I knew he'd come in for me I knew I had to go. Also, Hull were going in the right direction as a football club so I just had to take that opportunity.

Peter Taylor: With Leon Cort we knew that he'd win every header, he'd win most of his battles, we knew he wasn't the most confident on the ball so we had to help in in those areas – which we did. When he first joined the club he didn't want to touch the ball, but when he left he could handle it very well. He was a good signing.

Leon Cort: It was a sleeping giant. Everyone knew that Hull City were the team to join at that time, with the stadium, the fan base, the players… When I'd played against them at Southend they were always tough, with players like Ben Burgess, Stuart Green, Ian Ashbee, Marc Joseph, all those leaders in the team had always caused a problem for us.

The midfield was also bolstered with a couple of signings. One –that of Junior Lewis – was completing what seemed like a formality given his time on loan at the club the previous season. The other was Preston's Michael Keane.

Junior Lewis: I had a few offers but I felt comfortable at Hull. I didn't want to play for a new manager who didn't know me. Peter knew what I was about, my strengths and weaknesses. And Hull were a huge club, going places, and I wanted to be a part of that. It wasn't a hard decision to make. Even then I felt that as long as we kept the same players and added a few signings we could go up again.

Michael Keane: I joined Hull City because they were a big club with fantastic support and a club that wanted to progress up the leagues, while Peter Taylor was was a big name and big manager. The characters at the club were Ian Ashbee, Aaron Wilbraham, Stuart Green, Damien Delaney and Jason Price, a great bunch of lads.

Other additions came in the form of Stockport's Aaron Wilbraham, brought in essentially as a 'big man' centre forward to fill the boots temporarily vacated by the injured Ben Burgess. Another was West Brom centre-forward Delroy Facey, who had tasted the Premier League with Bolton Wanderers. That aside, the core of the rest of the squad was retained and looking to build on the momentum gathered from the promotion from League 2.

Marc Joseph: In pre-season, me and Ash had trained really hard together, doing some boxing training and going up into the hills to do running exercises. I was fitter than I'd ever been going into that season. Peter was asked by the press before the first game if Damien and Leon would be the first-choice centre-backs, and he told them not to rule me out, which I took as a compliment and an acknowledgment of how hard I'd been working. Seeing players from your position come in isn't always easy but it makes you work that bit harder. But if it meant playing right-back or left-back or sweeper then that's what you'd do for the team. I just wanted to be involved. At a club like Hull you have to take your chance when it comes.

Matt Duke: Ash was the captain and was just fantastic. On the pitch he'd tell people if they weren't doing well. He kept people on their toes. Then Nick provided the experience. Because he'd been a top professional and played for the teams he had, his application was top drawer and he kept us all on our toes too. He led by example. You could see why he'd been at the top. Everything he did he did to the best of his ability.

Nick Barmby: I'd been fortunate enough to play at unbelievable training grounds with great facilities, and we were at Hull Ionians sharing with Hull FC, but that didn't bother me one bit. It was a bit of an eye-opener though. We had to bring our kit home and wash it. The missus wasn't too happy! The lads were fantastic right from day one. I'd seen them play a lot in League 2, and I got to know lads like Andy Dawson straight away, who's still a big friend. The dressing room was really good.

Damien Delaney: There was a bit of wondering about how we'd do at that level as we were playing against better clubs and in better stadiums. You'd be hearing that certain clubs were paying certain amounts of money for players and thinking: 'This is serious.' But that spirit and will we all had was still there. So many players had a point to prove in their careers, and the promotion from League 2 hadn't really proved it for us. It was just a stepping stone to where we felt we should be. Once the 2003/04 season had finished there were no crazy celebrations. We all went on our holidays, came back for pre-season and the attitude was very much one of: 'That's one stepping stone out of the way. To prove our point we have to go a lot further.' We needed to get to the Championship. That was the main aim.

Jason Price: Because we were so close-knit in League 2, when the new players came in I was a bit: 'What? Why have we changed? We don't need new players.' Obviously we did need them, but as a player you'd just think that way, as we had such a good group.

Stuart Elliott: I felt we were equipped to do well. You have to test yourself to know how it's going to go, but after those first couple of games I knew I wasn't going to be overawed. I knew that Peter had managed at a much higher level, and a lot of the boys had played at that level, so we weren't going to be fazed. We knew we were going to be challenging again given the camaraderie we had, the experience, and the goals in that team. After a couple of games we knew we wouldn't just be in the middle of the table.

Stuart Green: We were used to winning games but even we didn't think we were going to go up again. Our results in pre-season were quite negative but we had a good pre-season fitness wise. We were pretty sharp and ready to go.

Ryan France: It helped me having a pre-season with a pro club as it's completely different. We had a bit of an iffy start but once we'd got to know the new signings it was just like the season before where we just turned up and thought: 'I don't care who you put against us on the pitch, we're going to beat you.'

Rob Smith: Off the field we always felt we were a step ahead. We always felt we were operating like a club from a higher division. So when we got promoted it was so much easier, because we'd set such high standards. We wanted the best publications, the best hospitality offering, and people would come in and even compare us favourably to the likes of Manchester United and Liverpool. So when we went up on the pitch, it was just reaching par with what we were doing off the pitch.

Junior Lewis: Sometimes when you get promoted bigger clubs come in for your better players, but we didn't lose anyone. Peter Taylor did really well to keep everyone.

Awaiting Hull City in the first game were a Bournemouth side that had been challenging for the League 1 play-offs the season previous. It was a tough start for City, and more than 17,500 fans packed into the KC hoping that the momentum from the previous season would be carried over. On the pitch, two debutants were looking to make their mark.

Nick Barmby: We'd started pre-season a bit iffy. I'd played three friendlies at the KC, which was great, but playing in a league game at the KC was a proud moment for me and my family; it was another ambition I'd always wanted to fulfil.

I don't think some people grasp what a different feeling it is playing for your home-town club, your club. I always used to look at Steven Gerrard walking out at Anfield and you could see the pride in his eyes, and in the way he played. I'm not saying that anyone not affiliated with a city doesn't necessarily play the right way, but it's different. Anyone who has played for their home-town club will know what I'm talking about.

Leon Cort: It was a great day. I don't think my Hull City career started as well as I would have liked as I had some quite poor games in the early part of that season, and in that game I was really nervous coming into a settled team with a group of players that had already gelled and trusted each other. As a new guy coming in I didn't want to upset the apple cart. That was my main concern.

The game itself was a strange one. A penalty converted by Stuart Green secured the three points, but the victory could and should have been more comfortable.

Stuart Green: Pete always drummed into us, always win your first game. I scored the penalty but it was a strange day for me as we struggled a bit and I took another penalty and missed. Instead of getting in the car delighted I was thinking I could have had two. But it set us up nicely for that long trip to Torquay.

That long trip to Torquay saw City playing at Plainmoor – the venue of Peter Taylor's first game in charge of Hull City – on a Tuesday night. If the Bournemouth performance had been a little disjointed, the fluidity that City fans were more accustomed to was back on show in an attacking display that had opposition manager Leroy Rosenior opining post-match that he couldn't see any side stopping City from scoring all season.

Stuart Green: I scored early on then Stuart Elliott got a couple. Even after that second game we were looking at the table thinking: 'This is a great start,' but we never spoke of promotion. But we did have a winning mentality.

Adam Pearson: We knew we could cope at that level. We expected to be in and around the play-offs. But when we went to Torquay in our second game and won 3-0 with Stuart Green scoring a terrific goal and Stuart Elliott scoring two it was brilliant. I was worried where we were going to get the goals from but then we walked into this Stuart Elliott phenomenon where he couldn't stop scoring, with a whole range of efforts with his left foot or head and all of them were fantastic goals.

Peter Taylor: I wasn't thinking about promotion after a couple of games, but I knew we had momentum, as any team that wins promotion has. We still had goal scorers and I felt that there wasn't a massive difference in the two divisions. So I felt that with good organisation and confident players we could have a good season.

Two wins from two, and off to Vale Park for a showdown with Port Vale. A huge City following saw an entertaining game in which the Tigers lost out by the odd goal in five, with the winner coming in stoppage time. However, they also witnessed Nick Barmby's first league goal for City.

Nick Barmby: It was a relief to get off the mark. I'd gone clean through in the last few minutes of the Bournemouth game and I'd tried to be clever and put it through the goalkeeper's legs, but he read me. I was gutted because it would have been nice to score on my debut, as I've been fortunate enough to do a few times in my career. At Port Vale the ball just came to me and I hit it. It was a proud moment.

The first defeat of the season, then, but for a City side still getting used to League 1 there was no sense of panic.

Ian Ashbee: It was a case of 'let's see how we start'. Peter Taylor was an experienced manager, we were getting stronger individually and collectively. We had power, we had pace, we had strength. We were confident but we just wanted to get the first six to eight games under our belts and see where we were then. Colin Murphy had been around a long, long time and there were patterns that he knew about that no one else would even mention; how many games you need to win, how many points you need to get, how much you have to do away from home, blah, blah, blah, and he'd drill that into you at the training ground. He was an old-school man, driving his car around Brantingham so he could get the exact number of metres of the runs we used to do, so we were as fit as butchers' dogs. The step up wasn't a massive step up. Maybe if you get four chances you need to put one of them away, whereas in League 2 sometimes those chances can be missed. But once we had a good start we were confident in what we were doing.

Andy Dawson: It took longer to realise we were one of the better teams in the league than it had done the previous year. We wanted to get promoted but there were a lot of big teams in there like Barnsley, Bradford and Sheffield Wednesday who'd been in the Premier League not many years before. But the start we had was just carrying on the momentum from the previous year, where we were used to winning.

Boaz Myhill: I don't remember noticing a massive difference in standard. I was a bit nervous as Dukey had been signed and I was wondering if I'd be playing, and the Bournemouth game was the first time that I'd ever played in the first game of a season at any club, so that was big for me. I probably didn't really appreciate how exciting it all was.

Jason Price: We carried over the togetherness. The new boys took to us really well and we took to them really well. They knew what our objectives were – to get promotion – and they knew they'd have to fit in, as we were so close-knit. And we were just going from strength to strength. It was the craziest two seasons I had in football. The confidence was through the roof. You'd look at the crowds we were getting at home and scratch your head, thinking: 'We're lower league here.'

The defeat at Port Vale was followed by a straightforward 2-0 win at home to Oldham courtesy of goals from Stuart Green and Danny Allsopp, then an exit from the League Cup on penalties at Wrexham. Next came one of the tougher looking games of the season, an away fixture at Barnsley, who had been a Premier League side only a few years previous.

The home side took the lead, only to see Stuart Elliott equalise with a header from a corner. Then, with two minutes remaining, the ball fell to new signing Michael Keane on the edge of the box. A low shot hit the back of the net and pandemonium ensued in the away end.

Michael Keane: I'd scored on debuts before, most notably my first-team debut for Preston. I remember the support was relentless and I was always keen to make sure people knew who I was on the pitch.

Four wins out of five and City were flying. However, as a reminder against any complacency, an off-colour City were then beaten by a single goal at the KC by a Bradford side (including Dean Windass), and then, with Peter Taylor absent on England U21 duty, Huddersfield awaited. At the McAlpine Stadium, City were deservedly stuffed 4-0. In particular, new signing Leon Cort looked to be struggling.

Leon Cort: It's hard to put my finger on what was going wrong for me and us defensively, other than trotting out the cliché: 'Things take time.' Some players hit the ground running, others take a few months. At Hull you maybe didn't have that much time to settle in as the squad was strong and the finances were there, so there'd be people who could come in and replace you. To be fair to Peter Taylor he knew I could do the job and he gave me a chance to prove myself, which I had to do! I still don't know why it wasn't working out at that stage because I was surrounded by quality players and quality fans. The Huddersfield defeat was a real low point as they were not better than us so it was just very frustrating.

City weren't particularly convincing beating Blackpool 2-1 at the KC in the next match, as both Stuart Green and Stuart Elliott scored their fifth goals of the season, and were then to travel to London Road – something of a graveyard for the club in previous years – to take on Peterborough. The 3-2 victory that followed carried a significance beyond the three points, as the scorer of City's second goal – to give his team a 2-1 lead – would testify.

Leon Cort: That game was huge for me. I still talk to Michael Keane about it. It was a really big moment for me, as given my performances up to that point that season I knew I had to do something. I knew I was a goalscoring centre-back, so when Michael whipped that corner in and I scored it was an unbelievable feeling. I knew what I had to offer Hull and I knew the fans were getting frustrated and wondering who they'd signed, thinking that there must have been better options out there, but I knew I was the right option. I just needed that chance to show them that I could be the player they were expecting. To be fair to the fans, though, they never, ever got on my back. But I needed that goal and performance to propel myself.

City's other two goals came courtesy of Stuart Elliott, who surely couldn't keep up this goalscoring run…

Stuart Elliott: The team was playing very well, we knew at home we could beat anybody, but then away from home we became a very difficult team to beat. We had a great solid base at the back and in midfield. And when sides were really attacking us it played into our hands as we had goals all over the team and when we broke we'd often end up scoring. At Peterborough I just knew if I got a chance I'd put it in the back of the net. For the first goal Ash took a quick free-kick, the defence was sleeping and I nipped in to score, then in the second half I got in at the back post with one of my more typical goals. My confidence was soaring after that game. Every time I stepped on the pitch I felt like I was going to score.

Adam Pearson: You couldn't read Stuart Elliott a lot, but he scored goals. He was the difference between being a mid-table team and a promotion team, though we had a great team spirit and a manager who knew what he was doing. We got the recruitment right again.

As had happened after the Barnsley victory, City went on to show that they were still some way from being the finished product as a 0-0 draw at home to bottom-of-the-table Stockport and a tepid 2-0 loss at Hartlepool were to demonstrate. Injuries and a lack of form among the centre-forwards limited Peter Taylor's striking options for the upcoming game against Chesterfield. That said, his solution to this problem would raise the eyebrows of both the players and the fans.

Junior Lewis: We were in training on the Monday and Peter picked a team that had me up front. I didn't think much of it, just thinking I was filling a gap in training. But Peter knew that I used to play up front. I'd made my league debut as a winger. Even Ben Burgess would call me 'Da Costa' because of my dribbling skills! All week I stayed up front in training because we had a few injuries and a lack of forwards who were holding the ball up. On the Thursday Peter told me I was playing up front against Chesterfield. When I told the guys I was playing up front they just kept saying: "Shut up!"

Stuart Green: It was a Sunday lunchtime so it was a bit weird, and Chesterfield should have beaten us. Junior Lewis played up front and at the time we were all thinking: 'How are we going to get a goal here?' But it was Junior who set me up for the goal. He used his awkward body to get me the chance. We had a lot of games that season where we'd creep over the line and get a point or all three not playing well at all, and we didn't play well at all in that game. It proved we had the players in the squad to get us goals even when we weren't playing well.

Junior Lewis: I remember hearing the crowd when the team was announced. They were shocked. But according to my team-mates and my manager – the most important people – I played well. Nick Barmby told me I'd played like Teddy Sheringham! I just held the ball up and that's what Peter wanted. For the goal I saw Greeny making a run and I just slid it in to him to the side and he finished it.

The joy of that victory, which had seen Ian Ashbee sent off, was short lived as Bristol City eased past City the next Saturday at Ashton Gate with a 3-1 victory. This was followed by a first ever meeting between Hull City and MK Dons, who had callously stolen Wimbledon's league status a few seasons prior. Stuart Green scored in the first minute, only for MK Dons to take a 2-1 lead going into injury time. Michael Keane equalised, and then in the 96th minute Stuart Green sealed a memorable victory.

Stuart Green: That League 1 season is my favourite season. I was becoming more like the player that I used to be. I was fitter than I'd ever been and I was getting in the box more. I'd scored in the first minute but it turned into a crazy game. When you're in form and playing well, things go for you. I remember the ball falling down onto my right foot on the edge of the box, I couldn't have hit it any better – it went in the bottom corner. Running off into the crowd… that's a special, special game for me.

In scoring in the first and 96th minutes, Stuart Green broke what is believed to be an English football league record for the longest length of time between two goals by an individual player in a single match.

1. Luton P14, W10, D2, L2, Pts32
2. Brentford P14, W8, D3, L3, Pts 27
3. Bradford P14, W8, D1, L5, Pts 25
4. Hull City P14, W8, D1, L5, Pts 25
5. Bournemouth P14, W7, D3, L4, Pts 24
6. Tranmere P13, W6, D5, L2, Pts 23

The Luton Town game at the KC on October 23rd had loomed large on the calendar for a few weeks. Luton were top of the table, unbeaten until the Saturday previous and managed by a cocksure Mike Newell. It was the perfect test of City's promotion credentials.

Leon Cort: On the Friday you could feel the tension in the city. Everyone was getting ready for that game.

Peter Taylor: If you're playing the team top of the league it helps you as a manager. We had a good enough squad and team, and if we got it right we'd give anyone a game.

Stuart Elliott: I knew it was massive game with Luton doing so well, and I was in the sort of form where everything I touched was going in. My first goal was ridiculous. To be honest, it was supposed to be a cross, and I hit it from 25 yards out and it ended up in the top corner. Everyone was saying I had gold dust in my boots. For the second, it was a deflection, but it was a great win for us and it boosted the confidence right throughout the team.

Stuart Green: Peter Taylor never let us take our foot off the gas and he never gave us an inch, even in training. That match is an example of what happens when you've got a manager pushing you. When we thought we'd made it, he'd find a fault and push us even more. He has to take a lot of credit for that day.

A lot of fans didn't agree but he changed the team a lot. I didn't agree with it sometimes. He had a knack of picking a team to beat an opponent. That's what he was good at. He wouldn't always pick the best team, he'd look at the opposition and pick a team to beat them.

Leon Cort: On the day they couldn't live with us. They won the league in the end, but one on one that day they struggled with us. Every single player was up for it and the fans were brilliant. Everything went to plan.

Marc Joseph: We were creating so many chances and we knew that we could always be on the front foot with people like Stuart Elliott scoring like he did. We knew that we were one step ahead of most teams in that league. Confidence was sky high.

Ryan France: We raised our game and it was a massive statement, but as a team it gave us confidence. We'd made a step up. Luton were top of the league and we smashed them. Not only did we beat them 3-0 but they hardly touched the ball. It was like a cup game where they were a league below us. They must have gone back thinking: 'These are serious contenders.'

Nick Barmby: The MK Dons and Luton Town games were the catalyst. The lads started to believe that they could not only compete in this league, but have a big, big chance of going up. MK Dons were a decent side, and Luton were top of the league and to beat them 3-0 – and it was a convincing win – playing in front of full crowds at the KC, even the fans started to believe that we could achieve the dream of back-to-back promotions. The belief in the camp was amazing.

Having bagged a brace in the 3-0 win against Luton – with Delroy Facey getting the other – Stuart Elliott's goal tally moved up to nine, impressive for a left winger. After a 2-2 draw at Wrexham, with the goals coming from Leon Cort and Delroy Facey, Elliott was again to find himself on the scoresheet in a home game against Walsall. But the most notable goal of the game came from Nick Barmby, coming as it did after a mere seven seconds of play.

Nick Barmby: Peter Taylor's attention to detail was really good and he loved his set pieces. He loved doing different things. He had this kick-off that the two on the ball would put it back to Damien Delaney, who'd look to the left but swing his foot and hit it right to the winger. If the opposition had done their homework they'd know what was going to happen.

But Walsall, under Paul Merson, obviously hadn't seen us play, so it worked for the first time. Damo hit a great ball, Stuart Green got a great touch and cross, I caught it nicely but I think it took a bit of a deflection and deviated away from the goalie. But yes, it was a good start and it settled us down as Walsall were a good side with Merse pulling the strings. Then Junior Lewis scored the second, which was a rarity.

That 3-1 victory was followed by a grim 4-2 defeat in the snow at Swindon. But City's bouncebackability was on show in the next game against Brentford, and yet again it was Stuart Elliott running the show. And he wasn't just scoring goals, he was scoring what were increasingly being described as 'worldies'. His first saw him leap, salmon-like, to head home a hopeful punt into the box from Marc Joseph. His second was an astonishing opportunistic volley from about 30 yards out.

Alfie Potts Harmer (Hull City fan): It seemed like Stuart Elliott could score from anywhere at that time, and that goal showed the confidence he was playing with. I've convinced myself in my head that he hit it from the half-way line, but the video footage seems to suggest otherwise...

Peter Taylor: Stuart believed in himself, and always believed that he could get a goal. Stuart is one of the nicest people you could ever wish to meet and he wouldn't be too down on himself if he wasn't playing well. He'd just get on with it. He'd be thinking: 'I'll score in a minute.' The record he had in League 1 was phenomenal.

Boaz Myhill: He was unbelievable that season. Many of the lads, when he was shooting, would be ready to shout at him not to and then you'd look round and it was in the back of the net. Every team needs a talisman, a player that scores goals, and that was Stuart for us. He was unplayable at times. Good with his head defensively, as well as in attack.

Nick Barmby: We had some technically great players – Ryan France, Jason Price, Stuart Green – but Stuart Elliott was an off-the-cuff player. Off-the-cuff players are very, very dangerous because you don't know what they're going to do. In the air he was second to none – one of the best headers of a ball I've ever seen – brave, he had a great left foot, he very rarely passed the ball into the net, it was always smashed, and that year they were going in from all angles – crosses that he claimed were 'shots', one from the halfway line, but the confidence was flowing through. He missed two months of the season with a fractured cheekbone and still scored 29 goals. That's unbelievable.

When the fixtures had been announced in June, most City fans immediately looked to see when the Sheffield Wednesday away game was. It fell on a Wednesday evening, December 8th, and, in short it was one of the most incredible nights in the club's history.

Adam Pearson: My best night in football, ever. That performance that night was incredible. We had 7000 fans at kick off and they were still coming in at half-time. We didn't have any shorts that they'd let us play in so I'd had to go to JJB to buy these ridiculous shorts. Twenty pairs of extra-large white shorts! We wore them with black and amber and went out on to Hillsborough looking a bit like a dog's dinner, but we just played brilliantly.

Peter Taylor: I couldn't believe the noise at kick-off time. What an atmosphere. An unbelievable night and an unbelievable atmosphere. We took so many supporters, it was incredible. You could tell that we were still hungry, not just the players but the supporters. I still speak about that night. I'll never forget it.

Ian Ashbee: I heard one of the stewards say he'd never seen the away end at Hillsborough as full as it was, and I thought: 'Wow, this is something special.' It was a local derby, a full house, a big football club steeped in tradition, so to go there and show them what we were about, it was a great evening. That was laying a marker down.

Ryan France: Sheffield Wednesday is the game that I enjoyed the most as a footballer. It's my home club. The atmosphere that night was the best I've ever played in, from both sets of supporters. Hearing the Sheffield Wednesday song before the game, going out to that with the hairs on the back on my neck standing on end. All my mates were in the ground. Hillsborough's pitch always plays well. The thousands of Hull fans that were there were absolutely amazing and made the difference in the end.

Dave Burns: I was trying to get the kick-off delayed. We were getting calls from fans saying that there was loads of traffic and people were struggling to get in the ground. We tried to say to the club that they had to do something. I don't know if it was us that got the kick-off delayed, but as usual I was being big and gobby and taking the credit for it.

Rich Lusmore: That night at Hillsborough was pretty special. My last visit to the ground had been to see a City side with Iain Hesford in goal get hammered 5-1. To be alongside some 8,000 other City fans and turn a ground such as Hillsborough into a virtual home for the night was something else.

Damien Delaney: Sheffield Wednesday remains my favourite ground to play in in England because of that night. There was a nice bit of mist, dew on the grass, and that stadium when it's full is epic. To fill that two-tiered stand, I just came out of the tunnel and thought 'oh my god'. Then afterwards you'd hear that there were people who couldn't get in and that they'd opened another part of the stand. That was absolutely fantastic.

Andy Dawson: Wow! There must have been 8,000 City fans there. A night game at Hillsborough with 29,000 there. As a footballer, they are the occasions you want to be involved in.

Michael Keane: It was unbelievable. I remember coming out and our away support was the best away support you could ever see; it was absolutely packed.

Nick Barmby: We'd warmed up and there was a delayed kick-off. I'd played at Sheffield Wednesday many times, almost every season for maybe 15 years, and the atmosphere has always been good but I'd never seen the away end that full – and that night it wasn't only the away end that was full, but in the corner and another little bit opposite the tunnel. I came out and I looked around and thought: 'Wow, this is proper English football.' There'd been quite a few of the lads who hadn't played before a crowd like that and could have been rabbits in headlights – but when we went 1-0 down the response was incredible. We showed a lot of steel and character that night, but the 12th man was the crowd. We were desperate to do well in front of all those people. They said there were six or seven thousand people there, but there was more than that.

Boaz Myhill: To this day, that game is the best atmosphere I've played in. I talk about it all the time. It was electric. Their early goal and the fact that it was new to so many of our fans just made it all the more exciting. Hillsborough is an unbelievable stadium to play in. I'll never forget it. It was a great game to be involved in.

Steve Lee (Hull City fan): A few of us drove up from London knowing there were a fair few expected from Hull. What we saw when we arrived at the Leppings Lane end was absolute chaos – hordes of City fans desperately trying to get into the ground but only two turnstiles open. Amazingly it seemed Wednesday had learned nothing from their own disaster. Things started to get nasty when the match kicked off with thousands still outside unable to get in; even worse when we heard the obvious roar celebrating a goal. Was that for us or them? At last, two other 'cash only' turnstiles taking were opened. Whichever youth opportunity coves were manning them must've made a killing because – of course – they had no change and by that time people were so desperate to get in they didn't bother waiting for it. Once inside it was clear that the only available space was in the wedge in the corner next to Sheffield's finest, who were so intent on issuing throat-cutting gestures they were completely missing the mullering their team was receiving on the pitch.

Leon Cort: These games just bring a smile to my face. These are memories that no one can ever take away from me. Walking out in that stadium in front of 29,000 people, feeling that hostility in a proper derby, was brilliant. But it started pretty disastrously and we had to pick ourselves up and bounce back from that.

Sheffield Wednesday's early goal didn't seem to affect the City players – who continued to tear into their opposition – nor the fans, who continued to create an ear-splitting wall of sound. Then a City corner was met by Damien Delaney and hit a stray arm belonging to a Wednesday player.

Michael Keane: We won a penalty and everyone seemed to be shying away, so I said give me that ball and I'll stick this in. I never got nervous in stuff like that, I just always had confidence in my own ability and I was always bubbly character. I was an ex-team mate of Wednesday keeper David Lucas. It never entered my head that he'd know where I was sticking it, but the power and accuracy gave him no chance anyway. I was very happy to see it hit the back of the net though! A big goal. I had big guts on the field no matter where I played. When the supporters were singing my name, that is best feeling in the world. The Hull City away support was outstanding.

Adam Pearson: After they went 1-0 up we absolutely battered them. It was a fantastic football night under the lights at a traditional, great ground with the best support I'd ever witnessed from Hull City.

All-square at 1-1, with City establishing a foothold in the game. Then, Delroy Facey broke down the left and squared the ball into the box. Stuart Elliott scuffed a shot but waiting in predatory mode of few yards from goal in front of a rabid and expectant gathering of City fans was Nick Barmby.

Nick Barmby: It was a tap-in, but a tap-in that you can easily miss when it's coming to you that slow. All I thought was: 'Here it comes.' It was bobbling and I just had to keep it down, but it was great to score in front of the City fans.

The fans went wild. But that goal was a mere hors d'oeuvre. What was to come minutes later was gourmet football. It started with Michael Keane sending the ball skywards to just outside the Sheffield Wednesday penalty area. Under it were Ryan France and Sheffield Wednesday defender Paul Heckingbottom. It was no contest as France leapt like a salmon to direct the ball in the direction of Nick Barmby, who was advancing into the Owls' box.

Ryan France: Heading's always been a strong point for me. I had the timing. I had a good leap. Boaz would always know he could hit me on the right or Stuart Elliott on the left, and the players around us would expect us to win the flick-on. Nick Barmby did that. I saw his run. I flicked it into his path.

Nick Barmby: There are people who flick a ball on and it can go anywhere. Ryan France had seen me, got up and headed it into my path, which not many people can do.

The flick-on still left Barmby with a lot to do. The ball came over his shoulder and required a volley of the most astonishing technique to find the back of the net. Nick Barmby had the most astonishing of techniques. Nick Barmby found the back of the net.

Nick Barmby: As I've seen it come over my left shoulder I've hit it and it's one of those things. If it goes in everyone says it's a great goal, if it doesn't it's a Row Z job. It's just instinctive. With any footballer, even those playing Sunday League, if a ball comes to you on the volley, you're hitting it. I was just trying to guide it into the net.

Ryan France: I wouldn't say I put it on a plate for him – he still had a lot to do – but boy did he finish it. What a finish! I just thanked him for doing it because it made my flick-on look even better!

Adam Pearson: Nick was outstanding. The whole of that Leppings Lane end just went wild when he scored. And it was proper football support. The best atmosphere ever. I think there were 8000 City fans there in the end. They were still coming in halfway down the side at half time, paying cash on the gate. Everything was out of control, which is scary at Hillsborough.

Andy Dawson: What a goal. Top drawer. He was the difference in terms of that league. There wasn't another League 1 player could do that. And right in front of the Hull City fans. I'm not sure about his celebration though!

Mike Hall: Barmby's second would have graced a much higher level than the third tier. The game marked the moment when it felt back-to-back promotions weren't beyond us.

Steve Lee: Barmby's over-the-shoulder volley was a thing of beauty and you could tell by his celebrations that not only did it mean something special to him as a local boy, but it was now obvious that something very special was happening at our club and back-to-back promotions were very much on.

City were deservedly 3-1 up at half-time. In truth, the 'one' flattered Wednesday. In the second half, Jon-Paul McGovern pulled a goal back for the home side, causing some consternation among a still-vociferous City following. However, sub Danny Allsopp ran clear in the dying minutes to give the final scoreline a margin that City's superiority had warranted. The game will never be forgotten by those lucky enough to have been at Hillsborough that night.

Nick Barmby: At 3-2 they got back into it and Danny Allsopp went through to score an important goal. It was the best away following I'd seen domestically for a long while. To score a couple of goals in front of them was something I'll never forget. To win that game was a massive statement of intent.

Andy Dawson: An absolutely fantastic night. Two big clubs. When we beat them, that was the night we knew we could go up again. When you go to Hillsborough and take that many fans, you're showing not just the clubs in your league but those in the leagues above that this is a big, big club and one that's going to go places. A great, great night with a great performance.

Marc Joseph: That was such a big derby for City. I'd never played at Hillsborough before and it just felt like a massive game and one in which we were coming up against a very good side with very talented players. Barmbs made sure we knew how important games like that were for the people of Hull and we got what we deserved out of it. To this day, when people ask me about big games that I played in, that one is the first I talk about.

Brendon Smurthwaite: When you saw that support, and the way the game unfolded, it was incredible. Ryan France still talks about his role in Barmby's second endlessly. But the club was no longer a joke. People had to take us seriously. That result said that we weren't just there to compete in that league, we were there to go up again. And that season just seemed to go: win, win, win…

Junior Lewis: That was massive. Some players crumble under that pressure in that atmosphere. You've got to make sure your nerves don't get the better of you. You've got to be mentally strong. We were just that.

Leon Cort: It was just an unbelievable night. You can't buy experiences like that, though I've still got the DVD of the match! It was fantastic to be involved in. Being involved in games like that and then seeing what Hull have done since, you feel you're part of the team that started that climb up the ladder. I feel privileged to have been a part of it.

James Richardson: The 4-2 win at Hillsborough felt at the time, and later did transpire to be, a marker for me that City were truly upwardly mobile and once again belonged on that stage. It rubber-stamped for me that we were going places after so many false dawns.

Rob Harmer: Outside of the play-off final, my favourite City game of that decade would have to be beating Sheffield Wednesday 4-2. Nick Barmby was unplayable that night and the delayed kick-off due to the enormous travelling support all added to the feeling that the club was really going places.

Steve Lee: Officially there were 7,000 City fans but we know it was probably more than 9,000 on probably the most memorable away game since 1971's Battle of Bramall Lane. And 4-2 totally flattered our massive hosts. Lovely.

Adam Pearson: That performance made us as a football club. That was everybody understanding that Hull City were back as a football club. That was the night. In the history of this football club, that is a special night.

Amid the euphoria of the victory at Hillsborough, the player who had sealed the win was struggling. Danny Allsopp's goals had been crucial to the previous season's promotion campaign, and he was weighing in this season too, all be it in a reduced role. This, alongside other issues, was taking its toll.

Danny Allsopp: That season was a bit of a low point of my career personally. I guess I was a young guy miles from home and looking back I probably needed a bit more guidance from someone who could straighten out my head. We'd made a few signings during the off-season and I was nervous about my injury from the season before coming back so I didn't go as hard in pre-season as I'd have liked. I wasn't in the best form and so when I was left out after scoring my first goal of the season I over-reacted immaturely. I did score a few more after that, in particular in the big derby win at Hillsborough, but I'd decided I wanted to go back to Australia with my family. I don't regret how things turned out because the club has gone on to many more great things and I continued on too, but I regret my actions at the time. But you can't go back, unfortunately.

If there had been a criticism of City so far that season, it would have been that they'd failed to back up their big victories with another win. After the delirium of Hillsborough came a trip to Layer Road, Colchester, where one of the most highly rated young managers in the Football League – Phil Parkinson – was fashioning a side that was proving very difficult to beat. There were no worries this time for City, however, as Ryan France put City ahead after getting on the end of a brilliant team counter attack.

Ryan France: We were defending a corner then it was bang, bang, Stuart Elliott, and the ball came across to me. I touched it out in front of me, went past the left-back and smashed it from 25 yards into the bottom corner. My shot surprised the Colchester defence. We'd hit them on the counter attack and I took the shot on early as well so the keeper wasn't expecting it.

Stuart Elliott – who else? – added a second, and despite a few late jitters City hung on for a 2-1 victory.

Unsurprisingly, perhaps, given the promotion the season before and the form the team were in, the mood within the City camp was buoyant.

Brendon Smurthwaite: The spirit across the whole club was incredible. The players would hang around with you after training. They'd hang around with the office staff. We'd be visiting the fans all the time, in hospitals, out in the villages in East Yorkshire. There was a real connection with the club and the local people, and there wasn't a single player who you didn't want to do these events with. They were all just normal people and nothing was ever a problem for them. They made everything easy for everyone. There was the odd quiet character but no one who was awkward. I would have worked for nothing: that's how much fun it was. And I wasn't the only one who'd say that. A lot of that came from Adam, but Peter was keen on them playing a part in the local community too.

Simon Maltby: We were an even better side that year, as we'd made some good additions, the lads were more used to playing with each other, and Stuart Elliott was on fire. At times we looked unbeatable. When you were in the dressing room before a game you'd get a sense about what was to come. That season you just couldn't see us getting beaten pretty much every week, home or away.

Brendon Smurthwaite: Stuart Green would do a great impression of Colin Murphy. Colin would get off at Woodall services after a game and would constantly be asking the driver: "How long to Woodall, Gavin?" Gav would tell him and every time he'd answer: "Good, I've got a pint of John Smiths at home with my name on it." As soon as Col had got off, Greeny would stand at the front of the coach doing affectionate Colin Murphy impressions on the microphone. Murph was amazing, though he couldn't be in football now, as he didn't say the right things. But he knew everything about everything when it came to football. There wasn't a player he hadn't heard of. Though he always used to call Damien Delaney 'Damon'.

1. **Luton P21, W14, D3, L4, Pts45**
2. **Hull City P21, W13, D2, L6, Pts 41**
3. **Tranmere P21, W12, D5, L4, Pts 41**
4. **Bournemouth P21, W10, D4, L7, Pts 34**
5. **Brentford P21, W10, D4, L7, Pts 34**

Luton had recovered from their battering at the KC to pull clear at the top of League 1. The other automatic spot seemed to be shaping up to be a battle between Hull City and Tranmere Rovers, the next visitors to the KC. A tight first half was noteable for Tranmere losing two goalkeepers after clashes with Stuart Elliott and Delroy Facey. More importantly, a long-range Ian Ashbee strike separated the two sides.

Ian Farrow: Despite having Theo Whitmore and Ian Goodison in their squad Tranmere proved to be a physical and direct side, with hard tackles and long punts forward the order of their play. As I remember it wasn't a particularly thrilling first half and both teams seemed to cancel each other out.

Ian Ashbee: Left-foot, edge of the box, got the ball rolling. It was great to score against a good side.

As the players emerged from the tunnel at half-time, it became clear that a desperate Tranmere side had resorted to unusual measures to resolve their goalkeeping issue, with a familiar face to City fans donning the gloves.

Ian Farrow: Much to our surprise, and an appreciative round of applause from the City fans, Theo Whitmore came on and went in goal for the visitors. Apparently, the Jamaican had volunteered to do so. This may have been because he would have done anything to get on the pitch against his old club, or because he still had an affection for City and thought he'd help us out by letting goal after goal in. It certainly wasn't because he was any good.

Stuart Elliott: I knew Theo wasn't really at the races, and Tranmere were disheartened, but I didn't care who was in goal, I just wanted to get my hat-trick. I didn't get a lot of hat-tricks in my career – there were a lot of braces – but that was one I'll never forget. It was a tremendous game to be part of.

Nick Barmby: It was surreal really. The Tranmere lads were having a go at Stuart Elliott for taking out the goalie – but Stuey didn't have a bad bone in his body and wasn't like that – so we had to explain that to them. But seeing Theo Whitmore facing that penalty did make me laugh. It was a statement of intent to win 6-1 in a full KC. We just couldn't wait for Saturdays to come around. They couldn't come around quick enough. Especially home games and we always knew that the away following would be terrific.

Ian Farrow: It shouldn't have been easy. It shouldn't have been funny. In the end it was both and that's what made it memorable.

A hat-trick for Stuart Elliott, with Barmby and Allsopp also adding to Ian Ashbee's first-half strike saw City win their fourth league game in succession. And they weren't finished there, as Blackpool were to discover on Boxing Day.

Peter Taylor: I remember us playing Blackpool away in December in horrible conditions and Stuart Elliott was having a stinker. We were talking about taking him off but I said to Colin Murphy: "You can't take him off because he'll score in a minute." And he did! That was what Stuart Elliott did. Stuart was in a league of his own when it came to playing rubbish and getting a goal, and Jason Price wasn't far behind him at times! But that was the importance of knowing your players. A lot of managers that didn't know Stuart would take him off. But he was going to score, no matter how he was playing.

Three days later, Doncaster came to the KC. It was the first game between the clubs since the South Yorkshire side had beaten City to the League 2 title, and then hired a plane to fly over the KC sporting a banner gloating about this fact. Tempers were running high and a near-capacity KC Stadium saw another classic.

Danny Allsopp gave City the lead, only for Dave Mulligan to equalise on the stroke of half-time. Then, with about 10 minutes to go, Jermaine McSporran seemed to kick out at Nick Barmby as he was lying on the floor. Barmby reacted and saw red, as did McSporran.

Nick Barmby: It was a spiteful game, a Yorkshire derby, and I just reacted to a challenge and we squared up. It was handbags, I'd pushed my head into his head, it wasn't a headbutt but I shouldn't have done it. I was disappointed in myself. I missed three games for it.

With both teams down to 10 men, an aggrieved home crowd was baying for blood. There was one man in the mood to deliver it...

Stuart Elliott: It was a defining match for us. I was really tired and it looked like both teams were settling for a 1-1 draw. But I was always one for anticipating and their defender had done a weak header and I'd started off on my run anticipating that. I remember going past one defender and coming in one on one with the keeper. All I could hear in the background was all of the seats in the KC Stadium clanging at the same time as 20,000 people stood up to see me come up against the keeper. Jon Walters wanted me to square it to him at the time but there was only one place I was going to put it. It was sheer joy and sheer exhaustion at the same time. I had nothing left in my legs after that.

Nick Barmby: Thank you Stuart Elliott!

The New Year was to start with another Yorkshire derby at the KC. This one, however, with Huddersfield as the visitors, was to see a worrying development for City.

Stuart Elliott: I was high on confidence and it was another wet, typical winters day. I'd scored a great goal after Delroy Facey had put me through from a tight angle on the left-hand side. I'd cut in and put it through the keeper's legs, which showed the confidence that I had. And then, on the crest of a wave, where I was buzzing in every game, all of a sudden I go up at the back post to defend a corner and Efe Sodje's elbow smashed into the side of my face. I went down and felt my cheekbone and it felt like a Coke can that had been dented. I knew immediately that it wasn't good and that I'd be out for a while.

I often say I scored 29 goals that season and that was with two months out. Imagine what I'd have got without that break! It was extraordinary and disappointing at the same time as I was loving every minute of every game.

Mike Hall: Stuart Elliott's goalscoring was so consistent, so reliable, that when he was injured it felt as though the whole momentum of the season could fall away.

Happily Aaron Wilbraham scored the winner from a Stev Angus cross, but City faced up to two months without their goalscoring talisman. That said, the winning momentum was to carry through to Edgeley Park, Stockport, two days later as City were to win their eighth consecutive game, and their ninth in all competitions.

Peter Taylor: At times I kept playing Roland Edge away from home and Andy Dawson at home. When we played Stockport that day I knew it was going to be a real kick-up on that horrible pitch, so I didn't pick many footballers, so to speak. But we won the game, so it worked. They're the little things that you feel satisfied with as a manager.

While the league had been City's meat and drink that season, FA Cup victories against Morecambe and Macclesfield had seen the club advance to the third round of the competition. When Colchester came out of the hat to visit the KC, it felt like an anti-climax. However, the Essex team were to more than match the Tigers, winning 2-0. Impressive for the away side was an energetic forward who we'd soon be seeing a lot more of...

Craig Fagan: As a player, in that league, Hull City had the best stadium and were the biggest club, so the motivation to go there and perform that day was easy. During that season you'd watch the highlights and see how many fans were at the stadium and it was somewhere where I thought I could play. That FA Cup game was bizarre for me though. I got kicked to bits by Damien Delaney and Leon Cort, but I played well, scored and got loads of abuse from the fans; not bad abuse but weird abuse. Even though they were booing me it felt positive as I felt that they liked and enjoyed the way I played, if that doesn't sound too weird. It was a nice feeling. And it was so loud compared with other stadiums. It was like playing in the Premier League. It felt like real football. After that I found out Hull were interested, so I had to just keep on trying to do well.

An Elliott-less January was proving to be a struggle for City, and after the Colchester defeat came a disappointing 2-2 draw at home to Peterborough, then a 1-0 defeat at Doncaster where Ian Ashbee was sent off. This led to a match against Chesterfield in sub-Arctic conditions, in a 1-1 that was to prove memorable for one under-appreciated City player.

Junior Lewis: It was freezing! A cold, dark night. I think Leon Cort headed it across and I got the rebound. At the time I wasn't playing great and the fans were a bit on my back. I was getting a few boos. That didn't bother me as I was always mentally strong. But that goal was important as it seemed to turn the fans around. I played pretty well in that game and then everything seemed fine with the fans.

As good a point as that was, it didn't stir a revival in City. Bristol City drew 1-1 at the KC, and then a late Ahmet Brkovic goal saw Luton pull away at the top of the division as City lost 1-0 at Kenilworth Road. A 2-1 win at home to Wrexham in mid-February ended a six-match winless streak, as Danny Allsopp scored his final goals in a Hull City shirt. A 1-1 draw on a freezing night at MK Dons courtesy of a Delroy Facey goal and a comfortable 2-0 win at home to Colchester saw City regain a foothold in the League 1 promotion places, but Peter Taylor was still of the mindset that reinforcements were needed. This led to Craig Fagan making the move he'd hoped for from Colchester, and left-winger Kevin Ellison joining from Chester City.

Craig Fagan: I got the call from my agent, and then it was awkward as Colchester didn't want me to leave, and then there was interest from Doncaster. I was advised that Doncaster might have been better for me but I just wanted to go to Hull. For me, one of the main factors was that Nick Barmby was there. To play with someone like him… if he thought Hull were good enough for him to be there at that time, that was good enough for me. I just wanted to be involved in that. I also knew that Hull were taking the better players from that level. It was all positive. There were no negatives.

Peter Taylor: We needed a left-footer with Stuart Elliott being injured, and Kevin Ellison was the closest we could get to Stuart, as we knew that he'd score every now and then. That was where I was lucky managing Hull City as someone like Adam Pearson helps you in those situations. With Craig Fagan, we felt that we needed more options and ammunition up front. Fages was £150,000 from Colchester. He'd pretty much beaten us on his own in the FA Cup match a few weeks earlier. I knew you could play him up front on his own, I knew you could play him out wide. With my long-term hat on, I told Adam that at worst you'd sell him further down the road for more money. He was a really hard-working player. He was also moody, because he wanted to be successful, but if a player gets the hump because things aren't going too well, that's not a terrible thing.

Stuart Green: Our squad was more suited to League 1. You got a lot more freedom to play football. We had big players who in League 2 would be wasted because the standard wasn't good enough. Then Pete signed Craig Fagan. I remember playing against him for Colchester and he was outstanding. The day he came, that sealed the promotion because he was fantastic.

Leon Cort: The players Peter Taylor signed were just terrific. We needed that number nine and it was brilliant to have Craig Fagan in that team.

Andy Dawson: We'd played against him for Colchester. As players, we knew who were the better players in that league, and Fages had done really well against us. He was sub in his first game, and you just got those feelings that one, the manager was bringing top players in, two, they can't get in the team, and three, they'll come on and seal a game for us. The players Peter Taylor signed were top quality. They came in and contributed, and scored goals. We were strong everywhere.

Fagan and Ellison's first task was to ensure that Tranmere Rovers didn't gain ground on their new club in a crunch game at Prenton Park.

1. **Luton P35, W21, D9, L5, Pts72**
2. **Hull City P34, W20, D6, L8, Pts66**
3. **Tranmere P34, W12, D5, L4, Pts62**
4. **Sheffield Weds P35, W16, D11, L8, Pts59**
5. **Hartlepool P33, W18, D4, L11, Pts58**

Ryan Taylor put Tranmere 1-0 up after seven minutes with a free-kick. However, Hull City had a renewed vigour, as Tranmere were to find out.

Peter Taylor: If you're an experienced manager you'll have had good and bad times, and that's why you've got to appreciate the good times. When things work – Murph used to say if we get seven out of 10 decisions right we'll stay in work – it's great, and the majority of the players we signed were successful, and the club didn't lose out on them. When we played Tranmere, Craig and Kevin being a success straight away was a real positive and it gave everyone a boost. I remember Kevin Ellison that day having a real pop at John McMahon, who was on the Tranmere staff, and I thought to myself: 'We've signed a tough one here, he can look after himself.' I've signed both players since.

Craig Fagan: I understood why I wasn't going to start the game as they'd done so well without me. I knew it was going to be tough to get in the team. And it was a massive surprise to me to see how big the club was as the game was beamed back from the KC Stadium. I'd never seen or heard of that before.

Kevin Ellison equalised just before half-time, leaving the game finely balanced. As well as the new boys, City also had former Tranmere player Jason Price in the ranks, and it was to be the Welshman who was to give City the lead.

Jason Price: I wanted to score as I got booed all game for leaving them. They wanted to half my wages though!

Then, in the 60th minute, Craig Fagan entered the fray as he replaced Nick Barmby.

Craig Fagan: I knew I could come on and influence the game. When I came on I just felt confident that I was going to score. When I was played through and was one on one I just managed to cut in and hit it in the bottom corner. The relief to score was still massive though. I'd got that first goal out of the way, and I knew it was an important goal in helping gain promotion. It helped me settle in too, which was important as I'd never had the situation before where a club had spent a bit of money on me. The lads then accepted me a bit more, it made all of that easier.

Hull City fans: Three-one, with your keepers on.

Nick Barmby: Tranmere was a massive result. We withstood a lot of pressure that day and Craig Fagan scored on debut. When Fages came in he gave us a fresh impetus, he gave us that enthusiasm. He was a great signing by Peter Taylor. It was easy playing up front with him. If you put the ball in channel you knew he'd be running on to it. He'd chase lost causes, and he really stretched teams, which meant I could get on the ball coming off the front man. He was exciting to play with.

Back-to-back home victories against Hartlepool and Torquay saw City reassert themselves as one of the division's form teams. A fit again Stuart Elliott scored in both games to confirm his return to form too. Then it was a mid-March trip down to sunny Dorset to take on play-off chasing Bournemouth.

Ryan France put City 1-0 up after 26 minutes, and from there on in it was one-way traffic, with Stuart Elliott in goalscoring mood and the home side reduced to 10 men just after half-time when Shaun Maher was sent off.

Stuart Elliott: Not to be too cocky, but we knew we were a better team than these guys. We had big characters, an inspirational captain in Ian Ashbee, and then goals everywhere – with Craig Fagan added to the mix. You just looked around and it gave you confidence. The first goal I scored that day was just pure instinct, and the second I didn't have to think about – I just caught it on the volley – and we knew we were going to get promoted after that.

Three-nil up, and then City's army of travelling fans were treated to a collector's item: a goal from a Damien Delaney free-kick!

Damien Delaney: I was the only left-footer in the team and Peter Taylor had said he wanted me there as an option. I think I even took a couple of corners at one point as Peter wanted them inswinging. I was as bemused as everyone else. But if the manager asks you to do it, you do it. I wasn't the main part of the free-kick. I was just meant to run over it and then head to the edge of the box. But Peter had said to Barmbs: "If it's on, just roll it to Damien." So I ran over it and didn't think much, then I saw that Barmbs had rolled it to me and thought: 'Oh my god, he's actually played it to me!' Then it was just a case of getting it in the mixer where the bodies were, hoping one of our players would get on the end of it. Luckily it missed everyone and crept in at the back post.

Nick Barmby: It was March and it most have been 20-odd degrees. It was crazy. Even Damo scored. I said to him, you run over it and I'll put you in at an angle and shoot. It worked, and after he'd scored you just couldn't catch him. He just kept running.

Ian Ashbee: Bournemouth isn't a great place to go away. The journey takes it out of your legs. To go there and win 4-0, that's another marker. The fans who'd done the hard yards hadn't seen us do that sort of thing before and we kept doing it against good clubs that season.

Mike Hall: Back-to-back promotions seemed a real possibility at this point, but nothing could prepare me for the perfection of this day. An unseasonably sunny and warm March afternoon on the south coast saw us clinically take the hosts apart, leading to a joyous all-round away day weekender that I'm sure I'll remember long after such occasions are far behind me.

Craig Sargent: The sun was shining, City were ace, and all was well with the world. Quite possibly the perfect away day. Early train into Bournemouth just in time for a few beers and a game of crazy golf. City were unplayable that day and if my memory serves me correctly, 4-0 flattered the hosts.

A memorable day, then, though for one player it was to linger in the memory for all the wrong reasons.

Boaz Myhill: I faced an FA charge after the game at Bournemouth. Someone had thrown a bottle of cider on the pitch at me, and then we scored a couple of goals so I turned around and gave the fans a bit of stick, as you do. Then I ended up in a room in the Huddersfield train station speaking to four guys in suits who I'd never met before trying explain it. That was my abiding memory from that game!

1. **Luton P38, W23, D10, L5, Pts79**
2. **Hull City P38, W24, D6, L8, Pts78**
3. **Tranmere P37, W19, D11, L7, Pts68**
4. **Sheffield Weds P38, W18, D12, L8, Pts66**
5. **Hartlepool P37, W19, D4, L14, Pts61**

A departure was also announced later in March as Michael Keane – who'd scored some crucial goals in the first half of the season – left the club. He'd played in 25 games in total, scoring five times.

Michael Keane: I wasn't happy to be a bit-part player. I'm a passion player and I've got to be playing as I enjoy it better when I'm out there. Anyone that knows me knows it's not ever about money with me, it's about hard work and winning. I wasn't happy as I wasn't first choice on the team sheet. I couldn't stand being on the bench collecting wages I didn't feel I was earning. I had to play all the time and I wasn't, but I had a great record at Hull City.

City were to stutter through Easter, snatching a 2-2 draw at home to Port Vale thanks only to a last-minute Craig Fagan penalty, and losing 1-0 at Oldham. Barnsley were then put to the sword at the KC through goals from Leon Cort and Craig Fagan. Promotion seemed within reach, and while it couldn't be achieved in City's next match – a Sunday fixture at Valley Parade – a win against a Bradford side including a certain Dean Windass would make Championship football the next season a near inevitability.

The game carried extra significance for many long-time Hull City fans. The handing over of one of Valley Parade's home stands to the 6,000 or so travelling Hull City fans helped to put to rest the ghost of that fateful 1996 game at Boothferry Park against the Bantams. The 2-0 victory that ensued was the cherry on the cake.

Nick Barmby: The atmosphere was electric. Deano playing for Bradford gave it a bit of extra spice, as he was getting a bit of stick from our fans. The pitch wasn't great but Stuart Elliott scored early which settled us down, then I managed to score in front of the City fans, and I have a photo at home of me celebrating with them that I'll always treasure. But after that game, we were as good as up.

Ian Ashbee: Dean Windass slapped me in the face in that game. Deano being a Hull lad, he wanted to win, and there'd been a bit of banter and I went to try and smash him to let him know I was there. He was too old and wise though, and he jumped out of the way and smacked me in the face. We were both constantly trying to go at it, even in the tunnel.

Junior Lewis: Me and Ash had great games, really strong. We just dominated. They didn't get a sniff. And Dean Windass kept giving me stick about being Peter Taylor's love child!

Damien Delaney: We came away thinking we had it nailed. Dean Windass was chirping away for the whole game. I was looking at him thinking: 'Aren't you supposed to be a Hull lad?' It was a great game though. A real experience.

Peter Taylor: I just remember that atmosphere. I was very confident after that game that we'd get promoted. That day we looked a bloody good team. Barmby sealed it late on but we were comfortable. We had Ash and Junior in the middle of the park and they were such a good partnership.

Marc Joseph: When you get to the end of the season, every point, or hopefully three points, you get is so vital. We could see and almost touch promotion but we knew a good performance was needed. Valley Parade was a lucky ground for me, and the big pitch there really suited us. I know that saying that the fans are a 12th man is a bit of a cliché but in games like that, it's true. They really pushed us. We knew we needed to perform.

Junior Lewis: You look at all those big games, then you look at all the players who went on to bigger things. They'd proved then that they could play in the big games. There weren't many big games where we crumbled or looked nervy. In the big games we were straight at it. Those players have gone on to play in the Premier League: Walters, Ash, Leon, Fages, Daws, Delaney, Boaz. We were never fazed by anything and it was great to see so many of those lads get their rewards. It was a really good team.

Dean Windass had obviously made his mark on the Hull City players that day, both figuratively and literally. And yet the rumours of him making a return to the city of his birth would not go away. Was it even a possibility?

Dean Windass: I don't think that Peter Taylor liked me. I heard from some people that I was too big a character for him in the changing room. I was very opinionated, but I was a winner. I wanted to win. But that's a manager's prerogative. I would speak to Adam Pearson on the phone when I was scoring goals for Bradford – I scored 60 goals in three seasons – as every time City went through a dry patch in front of goal I got linked with them. It was always on my mind that I'd love to go back to City and finish my career there, no matter what capacity or what division.

And so to a home match against Swindon Town. City knew that they just had to match Tranmere's result in their home match against Blackpool and Championship football would be coming to the KC.

1. **Luton P42, W26, D10, L6, Pts88**
2. **Hull City P42, W26, D7, L9, Pts85**
3. **Tranmere P42, W21, D12, L9, Pts75**
4. **Hartlepool P43, W21, D7, L15, Pts70**
5. **Brentford P41, W20, D9, L12, Pts69**

As much as promotion may have looked a formality, the day wasn't to be quite as straightforward as had been hoped.

Stuart Elliott: The nerves were jangling all around the stadium and I think that affected us on the pitch. You've worked so hard – and the night before the boys will have been picturing the celebrations – and you could see the anxiety in us because we were struggling to get the result that we wanted.

Boaz Myhill: The way things were, we were such a well-supported club at that level and the passion of the fans was a big factor behind our success. But sometimes, towards the end of the two promotion seasons, it maybe ramped the pressure up a bit too much and we ended up stumbling over the line.

Andy Dawson: I missed a sitter that day. It was the same feelings as the Yeovil game in the run-up; if we win this one we're up. After about 20 minutes someone laid the ball to the edge of the box. I made my run and the ball came towards me. I was just thinking: 'Get your touch right,' I had a good first touch, and then I missed the target. I was thinking: 'Oh no, I've missed my chance. That was my opportunity to score the goal that might have taken us up.' We were just waiting for someone to score.

With Tranmere still drawing 0-0 in their match against Blackpool, in the 90th minute of the match at the KC, City were awarded a penalty after Leon Cort was fouled by Rhys Evans.

Craig Fagan stepped up hoping to make Hull City history as Ian Ashbee had done 12 months prior...

Craig Fagan: I changed my mind at the last minute, which I'd never done before. The rest is history...

Stuart Elliott: I'd had a tussle with Craig because I'd scored a few penalties and I told him that I wanted it. He grabbed the ball and I didn't want to get into a tizzy with him, so I let him have it. I would have loved to have taken it, but it didn't matter in the end.

Peter Taylor: I wanted to win the match more than anything. I'm not sure that Fages should have been the penalty taker. It does sound silly, but when Craig missed the penalty I was thinking: 'We're not up yet,' even though it seemed done and dusted. But I wanted to win to get promotion as that would have been the icing on the cake.

Andy Dawson: You fancied Fages all day. We'd had a penalty late on in a game a few weeks previous against Port Vale and he'd scored it, so we fancied him to score a last-minute penalty to get us promoted. I've seen the replay – my sons watch the DVDs of the promotion seasons a lot – and after the penalty miss you can see we're all gutted then almost straight away we're celebrating.

City were celebrating because, although Craig Fagan had missed the penalty, news came in that the final whistle had been blown at Prenton Park with neither side being able to break the deadlock. City secured the point and a second promotion in two seasons was achieved.

Stuart Elliott: It was a bit of an anti-climax. As professionals we wanted to end it with a win. But the bigger picture was we'd been promoted again and everyone was absolutely delighted.

Junior Lewis: It was a bit dull in a way. It was a brilliant feeling but promotion is always better when you win the game. That said, a promotion's a promotion, and I had six of them in my career!

Leon Cort: We felt we were always going to do it, but you just never know what might happen. Towards the end, when I won the penalty, which Craig Fagan missed, we were all wondering 'oh no, what's going on elsewhere' but we felt like we'd done enough.

Ian Ashbee: It was destined to happen. It was special to do the back-to-backs though. Getting promoted is special because of the number of games you have to do it across. Cup finals are maybe done on five games or so, but achieving something over 40-odd games – that is something special. We were on a roll. Everything we touched we turned into gold.

Jason Price: It was a bit weird as we'd had to wait on other news in the other game. I remember doing the lap of honour. I love my laps of honours. I had seven of them in my career.

Andy Dawson: Another great season. We'd achieved again what we'd set out to do at the start, and we'd made it a lot easier than we'd managed the previous year. I didn't believe it would be that comfortable. But getting two promotions in two years: it's very, very rare that that happens.

Marc Joseph: You don't feel it's real. You've worked so hard, and we knew that a draw might be OK, but we really wanted the win. The pressure on you to get over the line takes its toll and it gets very emotional. It was a feeling of relief and pride. We set off together, worked together and all crossed the line together. That's a big emotional experience.

Craig Fagan: I loved every minute of that season. It was such a great feeling having so much confidence in that team, knowing that even if we weren't playing well we could nick a goal and win games ugly. We had such togetherness. Personally, I thrived off the fact that the lads had confidence in me to score goals, and I loved working my nuts off for them.

Nick Barmby: I remember sitting with Adam Pearson when I signed, having a coffee together, and I said: "One day we'll be in the Premier League." It wasn't an off-the-wall comment, you could genuinely feel something at the club. I thought it might take a bit of time but I just knew we'd get in the Premier League. And when we went up that day against Swindon, I went up to him and said: "We've only got one more." The feeling of going up at home was fantastic, with all the kids and families on the pitch.

Ryan France: I was stretchered off, taken to hospital and missed all the celebrations. I was fuming. They wouldn't let me back in the ground. I was saying: "I'm a player, I've got my kit on", but they wouldn't let me back in. By the time I got back in all the celebrations were done so I missed the stuff on the pitch. But I'd had four back-to-back promotions if you include non-league.

Stuart Green: It was tough watching. We limped over the line in the end, but it was an easier promotion than in the bottom division. The fans believed in us. To do back-to-back promotions was a massive achievement and it was a squad effort.

Peter Taylor: I look back now and think: 'Blimey, I think that might have been easier than the first one.' There was less pressure on is that season, which was why it was a little bit easier.

There were still three games to play, and City stood a chance of catching Luton at the top of the table. However, a 3-0 defeat to Walsall in the next game courtesy of a Julian Joachim hat-trick made that seem unlikely. The next game, at home to play-off chasing Sheffield Wednesday, was notable for another reason. Coming off the bench that day was one Ben Burgess.

Ben Burgess: I had a tear in my eye. It was amazing. I'd been out for a year and it was a phenomenal feeling to know that the fans hadn't forgotten me. All that hard work had finally paid off. It was just nice to be one of the team again. I need to be involved and getting back among the lads was great.

Simon Maltby: Ben had a very serious knee injury – career threatening. He's a top lad and he worked relentlessly to get back. He'd had setbacks, and his knee was never to be 100% perfect again. But he battled through. From an outcome side of things, to battle back from that injury and go on to play in regularly in the Championship is something that Ben should be exceptionally proud of. A lot of players wouldn't have come back from that. Ben's attitude and mental strength and commitment to playing for Hull City was second to none. He was great to rehab as when you told him to do something, he'd do it 100% day in, day out, even during the low points.

As heartening as it was to see Ben back in action, City lost the game 2-1.

Peter Taylor: I was raving after that game, even though it didn't really matter, because we didn't meet the standards I'd set.

Another defeat in the final game of the season – 2-1 away to Brentford – meant that City had lost their final three games. The tepid close to the season meant City finished 12 points behind title rival Luton, a gap that didn't reflect the closeness in quality of the two squads.

1. **Luton P46, W29, D11, L6, Pts98**
2. **Hull City P46, W26, D8, L12, Pts86**
3. **Tranmere P46, W22, D13, L11, Pts79**
4. **Brentford P46, W22, D9, L15, Pts75**
5. **Sheffield Weds P46, W19, D15, L12, Pts72**
6. **Hartlepool P46, W21, D8, L17, Pts71**

Adam Pearson: We didn't finish that season right, and that carried on into the season after. We drew 0-0 against Swindon and then lost three. It was a disappointing end to what had been a fantastic season. Maybe I took that too strongly in the end because maybe the players just thought they'd done enough and that was it, but I wanted us to go on and win the league.

One player who'd enjoyed an annus mirabilis was Stuart Elliott, with 29 goals in 40 games. Speculation was already rife as to whether City would be able to keep hold of the red-hot Ulsterman.

Stuart Elliott: Had I not got that cheekbone injury, there was talk of Sunderland and Newcastle signing me in the January. Mick McCarthy, then Sunderland's manager, was watching me at the Huddersfield game. Maybe a move could have happened then, but it coincided with me fracturing my cheekbone so the interest went away. At the end of the season, we'd moved up to the Championship and Adam Pearson wanted me to sign again and I knew the club was going up another level and I was more than happy to do that, as my family were settled in Hull. I loved the city, so why would I want to move?

So Stuart was staying. There were, however, some sad goodbyes to be said. Danny Allsopp had decided to move back to Australia. In his 67 games for City, he'd scored 22 goals.

Danny Allsopp: I was extremely fortunate to have had the chance to be a part of that special time at Hull City. The supporters were brilliant with me and I think it was one of the most amazing times in my life to be a part of that era and that team, a great bunch of blokes, in that city. It was magic!

Peter Taylor: Danny was a powerful, running centre-forward. He was terrific for Hull City. If anything I'd have liked him to have a bit more confidence, as I felt as though he was such a lovely lad I don't think he realised just how good he could be. But he's another one who could be playing not brilliantly but he'd get you a goal, and his goal record was good.

Brendon Smurthwaite: Danny was a lovely, unassuming, nice guy who did a great job for the club. He wasn't a drinker and was a family man, but if you want a measure of the man, I was on the committee for Andy Dawson's testimonial. We were doing a legends game before the main game, and Danny messaged me and said: "Do you think Andy would mind if I came over and played in this game?" He came over for two weeks from Australia just for Andy. I just remember thinking: 'What a thing to do.'

Junior Lewis, who'd played just 55 games for Hull City, scoring three goals, had still managed to play a full part in two promotions. It was time for him to move on, however.

Junior Lewis: It was a massive experience to play for a massive club with fantastic fans. It was just brilliant. The staff and the players were great. I made a lot of good friends there. But seeing those younger players go on to bigger and better things was the best thing. It just shows you what great signings Peter Taylor made. It was really pleasing to see. I'm very proud to have played for Hull City.

Peter's signings – getting very good, hungry youngsters in – were the key. They were coming to a good club to put themselves on the map. But they wanted to go on to bigger and better things, and Peter managed to keep them and let them do that at Hull City.

Nick Barmby: Peter Taylor doesn't sign anyone who he doesn't think is a good player, and Junior Lewis did as much as anyone else in that season.

Mike Scott: Blessed with a highly developed pointing gene, Junior Lewis directed midfield traffic for Peter Taylor's double promotion squad of 2004 to 2005. Christened Karl Lewis, Junior wasn't blessed with the same fast-twitch fibres as his sprinter namesake – but neither was he such an ardent fan of anabolic steroids, so every cloud…

Lewis was a regular adornment to Peter Taylor's squads of that era, having previously played him at Gillingham and Leicester – and for some that fact alone, coupled with Taylor's attractive managerial track record, would be enough. Operating at the base of midfield and providing cover to full backs that bombed forward, Junior wasn't a midfielder that hurled himself into Herculean crash tackles, crucifying his cruciates and annihilating his anteriors as he went. He favoured the subtler arts of closing down space and blocking off through balls, picturing the game around him rather than trying to tear it down, before making simple passes to players more capable than he. This approach pleased midfield aficionados but drew ire from that uniquely Hull City brand of supporter that favours blood and thunder over all else.

Fans and team-mates were also sad to see Jonathan Walters leaving the club after playing 52 times for City in scoring eight goals in his two spells at Hull. However, his career was to reach satisfyingly impressive heights in the coming years.

Matt Duke: Jon didn't get as much footballing time as he perhaps deserved as he was a great player. It just didn't work for him at Hull. But when you see what he's done since it's great.

Michael Keane: Jon Walters couldn't get in the team, though we had a very strong squad to be fair. But look at what he went on to do!

Delroy Facey, Aaron Wilbraham, Richard Hinds, Clayton Donaldson and Nathan Peat were also to leave the club in the summer. As for the rest, the Championship was awaiting…

2005/06 season

It had been 14 years and two months since Hull City had last played a game in English football's second tier. Since that game – a 2-1 victory at Newcastle's St James' Park – the club had undergone numerous crises and false dawns. The scrimping and saving under the tenure of Martin Fish had meant that something as simple as a higher-than-expected tax bill would put the club's future under a very real threat. David Lloyd's petulance brought dark days, and those days were to get darker still under Stephen Hinchliffe and Nick Buchanan as the club battled for its league status on the pitch and its numerous creditors off it. Even under Adam Pearson, two summers that saw profligate spending under the reigns of Brian Little and Jan Molby couldn't seem to inspire the club to anything higher than mid-table in the fourth tier.

Now, in the blink of an eye, the club was preparing to mix it with 23 other Premier League wannabes. Hull City had been a big fish in Leagues 1 and 2 in the past two seasons. It was now back to being the bait. Only Crewe Alexandra had a record signing of a smaller sum than Hull City's. Crystal Palace, Norwich City and Southampton had been relegated from the Premier League the season before. The likes of Ipswich Town, Derby County, Leicester City and Wolverhampton Wanderers had been top-flight clubs in the seasons before that.

Then there was Leeds United.

Leeds were the team 60 miles down the M62. Leeds were the team that drew an unacceptable percentage of their fan base from East Yorkshire. Leeds were the team that were contesting a Champions League semi-final five years previous, when Hull City were fighting for their very survival. Leeds were the team that Adam Pearson had left to resurrect Hull City. Leeds were the team that considered themselves the pride of Yorkshire. Leeds were the first team that every Hull City fan looked for when the fixtures were announced. Leeds were the team to beat.

Leeds would have to wait, however. The matches against the West Yorkshire club were scheduled for New Year's Eve and April Fool's Day. In the meantime, there was business to be done.

There was to be no marquee signing this summer in the way that Nick Barmby had been 12 months earlier. Instead, young but largely unknown players were brought in: forward Stephen McPhee from Portuguese side Biera-Mar for a club record £400,000, Danny Coles from Bristol City for £200,000, Driffield-born midfielder Curtis Woodhouse for £25,000 from Peterborough, right-back Mark Lynch from Sunderland on a free, central midfielder Keith Andrews from Wolverhampton also on a free, and Portuguese goalkeeper Sergio Liete. Jon Welsh also came in from Liverpool, initially on loan, as part of a swap deal for highly rated youngster Paul Anderson.

Adam Pearson: Danny Coles was highly rated and we thought he was going to be a good player, but he got a bad injury. Mark Lynch got injured straight away. Steve McPhee did too. And we also signed Keith Andrews. I thought at the time they were all good signings but for one reason or another they didn't work out. Almost all of them got injuries and then struggled to kick on. That led me to feel that the whole progress and movement of the club had stagnated at that point.

Peter Taylor: It was just a case of 'what players can we get, what can we afford' because players want bigger wages in the Championship. Adam wanted to run us as a business, and rightly so, so we weren't paying top Championship wages. The players we got we thought would be good enough, but maybe needed a bit of time.

For the players who had two promotions to their names in two seasons, however, the challenge ahead was an exciting one.

Ian Ashbee: We went from being a big club in League 1 to a small club in the Championship overnight. But there was no pressure on us in that league. There were some big clubs that had spent a lot of money, or that had had years in the Premier League. For us going into that, the pressure was off. You'd hear fans and the like saying that we'd have to get rid of a few people, and I'm sure my name would be mentioned a few times, saying I wouldn't be good enough to make it at that level. But it's interesting what that can do as a motivational tool.

Andy Dawson: When I signed, I felt that getting to the Championship would be an amazing achievement for me as a player. There seemed to be a massive jump between the bottom two leagues and the Championship. Once you get to the Championship you're not far from the Premier League. So when we got there I was questioning myself, thinking: 'Can I do this?' I'd spent my career in League 1 and League 2 so getting promoted the previous year didn't bother me. I knew I could play in League 1 and get promoted out of that. But the Championship was a different question that I asked of myself. I remember playing QPR in the first game and I was thinking: 'Wow, we're in the big leagues now, playing against the big boys that had been in the Premier League.' It was difficult and we had a different outlook to that that we'd had the previous two years, but we coped alright with it. We never really signed any big hitters. When you sign Nick Barmby in League 1 you're going: 'Wow, we have to get promoted.' We didn't have that. We knew that consolidation was the order of the day and as players we knew we had to stay up. We had our ups and downs – it wasn't going to be like the previous two years where you win six or seven games on the bounce, because you're playing top clubs. There are no easy games.

Stuart Elliott: We knew the Championship would be difficult, but I think with back-to-back promotions the fans were realistic in their expectations.

Brendon Smurthwaite: It felt massive. It felt very serious. People were intrigued by Hull City and what would happen next. There was so much interest in that opening game against QPR. People saw it as an ongoing story and this was just the next step. Peter Taylor gets a bit of stick for how he approached that season because it was a bit functional. But having got there the last thing you wanted to do was fall out of it.

Boaz Myhill: It was the same for me every year where I was a mixture of excited and nervous, but when the game was starting I just wanted to do my best. It was a rollercoaster really. The steady progression had ramped up the excitement every season.

City's first game came against QPR at the KC, a tough, rough introduction back to second-tier football as Ian Holloway's side gave a performance that was somewhat at odds with the manager's likeable demeanour. Mark Lynch's debut lasted four minutes when he was taken off for a knee injury after a poor 'challenge' by Paul Furlong. Encouragingly, after undergoing such a physical going over, City emerged with a 0-0 draw.

Damien Delaney: There was a real step up. You were playing against established people who everyone had heard of. Marc Bircham, Danny Shittu, Paul Furlong, they were all established Championship players. It was quicker, there was more physicality. But it was another stepping stone for us. And we managed to hold on to the spirit that had seen us through the two promotions.

Jason Price: The play was a little bit slower and we got punished a lot more than in League 1. All the time you're thinking: 'I don't want to make a mistake,' whereas in League 1 and League 2 you can make mistakes and nine times out of 10 it's not going to be punished. In the Championship you had a load of players on big money, ex-Premier League strikers, and you don't want to be giving stuff away because you get punished.

Leon Cort: As time had gone on at Hull, my confidence had been rising and rising. You were facing better quality in the Championship, but in that first game against QPR I felt as comfortable as I had in any game in League 1. I was playing against seasoned professionals like Paul Furlong but I felt comfortable and confident. It wasn't like when I first joined Hull and I was nervous and didn't want to let anybody down. I felt like I deserved to be there.

Peter Taylor: The thing that I learned from that start in the Championship was to not give the opposition too much respect. I spoke to Ian Holloway after the first game of the season against QPR. He said that we'd be able to handle that level, so I just wanted to get in there and not give the other teams too much respect.

The second game of the season threw up familiar opposition and a ground with happy memories. There was to be no 4-2 victory at Hillsborough this season, but Nick Barmby again proved to be a thorn in Sheffield Wednesday's side, scoring City's equaliser in a 1-1 draw.

Nick Barmby: You tend to get grounds that you just score at. West Ham had been one, and Sheffield Wednesday was another. Craig Fagan had seen me make the run and it had gone over his head and I caught it nice on the volley.

Stuart Green: It was a big leap moving up a level. The difference between that and the previous season was we lacked belief. We could have won that game, and we were shattered putting everything into not getting beat. The performance against Sheffield Wednesday on the Tuesday was unbelievable though, when you saw Nick Barmby at his true best. But then the few games after that we found it tough. We struggled.

Wolves were to hand City a lesson in the next game at Molineux, with a 1-0 win flattering the Tigers. City were three games into the season and still awaiting a win when Brighton visited the KC in a game that was to provide not just three very welcome points, but also a goal that brought a smile to the face of everyone associated with the club.

Ben Burgess: I was sub in the Brighton game. I came on and someone played me through on goal. Craig Fagan was screaming at me to pass it to the side, but I shot, hit the post but got that bit of luck and it came back to me to tap in. It was just sheer relief that I'd actually done something, actually scored. My first goal back was an amazing feeling. Then my knee went again… It was frustrating but Hull was such a good club and had such a good chairman in Adam Pearson you never worried you'd be forgotten. They looked after you and got you the best medical attention.

A first home win was a relief, and it was soon to be followed by an away win too. A 1-0 victory at Home Park, Plymouth, was to prove memorable for two City players, albeit for very different reasons.

Marc Joseph: The Plymouth guy had taken a couple of dives. He had the ball in the corner, I took it off him and passed it to somebody in the middle of the park. Then as their guy ran past me I just stuck my arm out and I caught him in the face. I spoke to Peter afterwards and he knew it wasn't malicious. But the guy went to the ground holding his face and I was sent off.

Stuart Elliott: That was one of my favourite goals for Hull City. It was always difficult away at Plymouth and I wasn't having a good game, as Peter was letting me know from the sideline. But Peter always knew I was likely to come up with a goal, even if I wasn't playing well. I remember running with the ball and it was a sticky pitch and the ball was getting stuck under my feet. I wasn't getting any momentum so I thought I'd try to chip the keeper from about 35 yards, and it turned out that I'd chipped him perfectly.

Marc Joseph: That was my lowest point at Hull City, particularly because the next game was at home to Leicester. That's my home team and I'd never played against them in a competitive match. I'd been psyching myself up for that one and was getting all my family there and that was taken away from me from that one situation. I was very disappointed with how it happened but I had the backing of the manager. I think the fact that Stuart Elliott scored a worldy bailed me out though. I was sat at the exec bar watching the rest of the game with some of their fans. When Stuey scored I was the only one cheering. That was one of the last games I played for Hull and it wasn't how I wanted to go out.

Marc Joseph did indeed miss the Leicester game, but another player with links to the Foxes was not to be denied.

Damien Delaney: It was a sweet moment for me. When I left Leicester they were Premier League and I was moving down to League 2, so it was a nice milestone to play against them.

City drew the game at the KC 1-1 thanks to a Craig Fagan volley after the Tigers had hit the post three times. This meant the first six games had seen two wins, three draws and one defeat. So far, so impressive. But how were the players faring in their new surroundings?

Craig Fagan: I felt OK. That season was a learning curve for everybody. It showed in the first couple of games. The mistakes we'd get away with in League 1 would get punished in the Championship. The centre-forwards were better, we were creating fewer chances as the defenders were better. But in that first season in the Championship, I think we handled it well.

Nick Barmby: You go through the leagues but for me it's psychological as to whether you can play at the next level, and some players grasp that quicker than others, but I don't think anyone was lagging behind. Look at Andy Dawson: he got better in League 1, then even better in the Championship.

For all the club's progress on the pitch, the captain was nowhere to be seen on it. Rumours were spreading about a long-term knee injury, one that was possibly going to lead to an early retirement from the game. Things weren't quite that bad, but City fans had seen the last of Ian Ashbee for the season.

Ian Ashbee: I think I'd had an injury and something was niggling away at me. I went in and we had a look at it in a routine check. It was early signs of wear and tear, which is what the ostreochondral defect is, and they scraped it to get rid of the old bone and generate new bone. I think it seemed treatable and manageable at the time though. It was tough. I could have come back a bit earlier, but because we were having a consolidatory season we just thought it best to get it 100% before I started playing again.

Adam Pearson: Ian had become part of the furniture at Hull as a leader and had obviously done a great job in getting us through the leagues with his determination and leadership. The injury was a blow to the club and we struggled to replace him. Keith Andrews was earmarked to replace him and although he did develop into a leader, at that point he wasn't that kind of player and we definitely missed Ash.

Stuart Green: At times Ash would be a nightmare to play with, because he demanded so much from you, but he got the best out of you. We had Keith Andrews, who was very good for us, but to lose Ash was massive.

Andy Dawson: Ash was a big character. He was the one demanding from you when things weren't right, and even when they were right. He wanted better and was demanding more, and you need that. We still had big characters like Barmbs, but Ash was going to be a big miss as somebody who'd led the club to promotions the previous two years.

Reality was to bite over the next three games, with a 2-0 defeat at Selhurst Park followed by consecutive home defeats to Stoke and Luton. Going into the next game, away to Coventry, few were giving City much chance. The Sky Blues were unbeaten at their new home and still looked very much like a Premier League club on loan to the Championship. However, despite having Mark Lynch sent off after 70 minutes, a brace from John Welsh gave City an important and memorable 2-0 victory.

Matt Rudd: I loved John Welsh's individual goal at Coventry in 2005 because not only was it sublime, it also took about half-an-hour from the moment the ball left his foot for it to actually nestle in the net – and then utter bedlam.

The win at the Ricoh Arena left City 13th in the league, but then the going got tough. The next 11 games were to bring just one victory. That came at home to Derby – whose new manager Phil Brown looked on. Stuart Elliott put City ahead only for Inigo Iniakez to equalise with a penalty. Then, in the 84th minute after a foul on loanee Chris Brown, substitute Stuart Green stepped up and scored the decisive goal from the spot.

Stuart Green: That was a game where we played a very good side. We still lacked belief but we got over the line. We were always in the bottom eight or so and that's where we deserved to be. On a personal note I struggled in the first half of the season, mainly with my fitness. I picked up after Christmas but it was a tough season.

The Derby match was played on October 22nd. It would be December 3rd before City would win another game – with new signing Billy Paynter joining Craig Fagan on the scoresheet in a 2-0 home win against Cardiff. Then came a fourth game against Sheffield Wednesday in just over 12 months, and a win courtesy of a late winner from a popular source.

Jason Price: I'd come on as sub as Peter wanted somebody big up top. On the corner nobody picked me up. I was stood there, one of the biggest players in our team apart from Corty and Delaney, and I was moving round and no one was interested. So I thought I'd just trot between the penalty spot and six yard box. The corner went near post, and I knew Delaney was going to flick it, and I knew the ball was coming towards me. I wouldn't have got to it if I hadn't anticipated it like that as it was coming to me so quickly. I hit it sweet as a nut into the roof of the net, the keeper had no chance, and I was stunned at myself. I ran off and I remember Fages trying to rugby tackle me and I was trying to get away from him. It was a good moment in my career.

These back-to-back victories were followed by an away defeat at Brighton's ramshackle Withdean 'Stadium' and a 2-2 draw at Crewe. Ipswich were then beaten 2-0 at the KC thanks in no small part to a masterclass from a rapidly improving Craig Fagan. Then came the much-anticipated visit to Elland Road for a first league meeting with Leeds in 15 years. Sadly, City looked second best throughout and Leeds ran out 2-0 winners. Still, there was always the home tie to look forward to. And Premier League Aston Villa were visiting the KC in the FA Cup third round, a game notable for two reasons: It was the first time that City had been featured in a live game on terrestrial TV, and it was the first time that Boaz Myhill would play against the side he had left to come to the KC.

Boaz Myhill: I'd have let me go when I was 19 or 20 to be honest, so there was no bitterness there.

In truth, Villa's 1-0 win flattered City, and there were more pressing matters in the league. Also, some bits of transfer business were to be done, and some sad farewells were to be made.

First, Jason Price – a hugely popular figure both on and off the pitch over the past two-and-a-half seasons – was allowed to join Doncaster.

Jason Price: In the games before I left, I'd played against Sheffield Wednesday – in which I scored the winner; Ipswich at home in which I was man of the match; Sheffield United – in which I scored the best goal I've ever scored, with my left foot into the top corner; and I'd played really well at Stoke. I had a trapped nerve in my calf at the time, but I didn't know what it was. It was like I'd pulled my calf. We went to an away game and I was due to be sub, but I had to tell Peter Taylor I couldn't play because of my calf. He had the right hump, which was fair enough, and then a couple of weeks after that I had a phone call from my agent telling me that Peter Taylor had said I could speak to other teams and that Doncaster wanted me. That summer I'd had a meeting with Peter Jackson to sign for Huddersfield, which I turned down because I wanted to play in the Championship and see what my level was.

Mike Hall: I always appreciated the fact that Jason Price was aware of his limitations, and though he could never get close to, say, Stuart Elliott's exploits, he had a key role to play in those first two promotions. His hat-trick against Doncaster Rovers in 2003 was one of the most enjoyable – and well-deserved – I've ever had the pleasure of seeing. I think Peter Taylor once remarked that Pricey was simply pleased to make it as a Championship player. I'm pleased he managed that with us, and that he played such a big role in getting us there.

Ian Farrow: Jason Price always excelled in matches, and playing from the right wing complemented what Stuart Elliott was doing from the left. He didn't score as many goals as Elliott but was a very important part of our early success. He could defend better than Elliot when called upon but also, like the Ulsterman, had pace and could shoot with either foot. Unfortunately, football doesn't have enough characters and Pricey is one of the last of that almost extinct breed. More importantly, he played a big part in a high-scoring, successful City and scored some very important goals during a very important period in our history. He will be best remembered for the explosive and vital hat-trick against promotion rivals Doncaster. Those goals, and Price himself, will probably only ever be a small footnote in Hull City's history, but that history would be poorer without the big-haired and big-hearted Jason Price.

Jason Price: It was the best all-round two years of my life – where I lived, where I played, the friends I made. It all just came together.

Another hero of the back-to-back promotions was also to leave, with Marc Joseph joining Blackpool.

Marc Joseph: I knew my limitations and that I might have been a victim of our success as I wouldn't get as many games in the Championship. It was just unfortunate that it didn't end how I wanted things to end.

When anyone asks me what my best time playing football was, my answer is always when I was at Hull. I achieved things at a few other clubs but my three years at Hull and the development you could see throughout the whole city was amazing. I class Hull City as one of my teams, a team that I support.

Mike Hall: Perhaps with the benefit of hindsight we can look back on Marc Joseph's time with City with a bit more kindness than many were willing to afford him at the time. He was clearly a favourite of manager Peter Taylor, which aroused suspicion in itself as Taylor had a reputation for picking certain players he trusted over apparently more talented options. That Joseph was frequently favoured over a genuine hero of the era – Justin Whittle – was never going to work in his favour. You could see what Peter Taylor was hoping to achieve. In Joseph, he had a defender who perhaps possessed more ability on the ball and in his range of passing, but not, crucially, one able to defend as well as Whittle. In an era where mere survival had only recently been the norm, defending – raw, honest, committed defending – was what fans required above all else of their centre backs. That Joseph played almost 100 games for City says much about Taylor's faith in him. Perhaps now, as we look back on the two promotions his spell at the club coincided with, we can say that that success was partly because of Marc Joseph, and not in spite of him.

With two big characters leaving the dressing room, Peter Taylor busied himself by bringing in more firepower up front. Darryl Duffy joined for a reported £250,000 from Falkirk, while a very big character arrived from Macclesfield.

Jon Parkin: I didn't know a great deal about the club. I knew they'd gone through the leagues. But as soon as they got in touch with Macclesfield I was over the moon and wanted to join straight away as it was a jump from League 2 to the Championship and it was an hour and 15 minutes from my house. It was a perfect move for me.

Adam Pearson: Colin really fancied him. We were looking at him, Lee Trundle and one or two others. Jon was a risk but he was a hell of a talent. And he certainty brightened us up.

Peter Taylor: We needed another centre forward and we needed a presence. The choice was between Jon and Rory Fallon and in the end we went with Jon. He was Yorkshire based, we knew about his goal record, we knew about his weight issues, his feet were really good, and we were very pleased with our signing.

Colin Murphy: Jon Parkin was a big lad but I knew he'd be able to cut it at a higher level.

Andy Dawson: He came in and scored on his debut. A big character and a huge talent. Some of the goals he scored were incredible. He was just right at that time for the club because he got us over the line and took us forward that little bit more.

Craig Fagan: Off the pitch he was a character! The first day he turned up with no wash bag, no socks and pants. We said: "Where's your stuff?" He said: "I've only got my boots." In his first game I was rooming with him and I was thinking: 'What the hell's going on here.' As soon as we got in the room he stripped off naked and started watching TV. He wasn't the greatest of athletes but he was strong and he could nick a goal. We had an understanding that he'd hold the ball up and take a battering and I'd do the running in behind him and chasing down, so we complemented each other nicely.

Ryan France: I like characters around football. You need characters in the dressing room as you're there every day. You've got to be professional on the Saturday but who says you can't have a bit of fun on the way? And Jon Parkin was certainly that bit of fun.

Dave Burns: I got some good players for City! I claim credit for Jon Parkin. I'd seen him play in a Friday night game at Grimsby and he had scored the most astonishing goal. I'd said to Adam: "Get a scout to see him."

Jon Parkin: Ash was lively, more so when he got back from injury, and we had a great card school with me, Dukey and Sam Collins. A lot of the players had come up from the lower leagues which meant there were no egos. Even former England internationals like Nick Barmby were just nice blokes. There were no arseholes, and that helps when you're down at the bottom and fighting for your lives.

Parkin's debut came at home to Crystal Palace. City made a terrible start but were soon back in the game.

Jon Parkin: We were 2-0 down after about 15 minutes, but getting that goal back was a big relief for me. I'd scored lots of goals in League 2 and I'd played in the Championship for Barnsley at centre-half, but I'd had some thoughts of whether I'd be able to do it at that level so it was nice to get off the mark, even though we got beat. It meant I could think to myself: 'I might be alright in this league.'

Losing to Palace meant that City had lost three games on the trot and were edging worryingly close to the relegation zone. A trip to Stoke is rarely what is needed in such circumstances, but in the end City's 3-0 victory wasn't even the most remarkable thing about the game, as Boaz Myhill added to his burgeoning reputation with two penalty saves.

Boaz Myhill: Paul Gallacher took the first one and Luke Chadwick the second. The first save was much better than the second, as having had to dive to my right for the first I thought maybe he'd put it down the middle for the second and I got lucky. Saving two penalties in a game is something you don't expect to happen really.

Leon Cort: Boaz Myhill was fantastic. You always knew he was going to push on to greater heights. But even in those big games, even if we went a couple of goals down we still always felt as though we could get back into it. That is a great feeling to have in any team.

Matt Rudd: We won 3-0, with Myhill saving two penalties and Stoke fans beating each other up in frustration. Days like that don't come round often.

One of City's three goals was scored by Jon Parkin, already affectionately nicknamed 'The Beast', who was taking to Championship football like a duck to water.

Jon Parkin: Those early goals put my fears to bed at that level. I'd been wondering if I'd be able to do it two levels higher than I was used to, but the goals are still the same size.

17. **Hull City P30, W8, D9, L13, Pts 33**
18. **Derby P30, W6, D14, L10, Pts 32**
19. **Plymouth P28, W7, D11, L10, Pts 32**
20. **Sheffield Weds P30, W9, D3, L14, Pts 30**
21. **Brighton P30, W5, D13, L12, Pts 28**
22. **Leicester P29, W5, D11, L13, Pts 26**
23. **Millwall P30, W5, D11, L14, Pts 26**
24. **Crewe P30, W4, D10, L16, Pts 22**

The Parkin-inspired surge saw City in a lower-mid table position, seven points clear of relegation. However, the inconsistency wouldn't go away, with Coventry winning 2-1 at the KC and then City winning 3-2 at Luton. Draws at home to Norwich and away to Millwall were followed by defeat at Cardiff. Then Wolves visited the KC for what would be a family affair. In the Hull City defence was Leon Cort; in the Wolves attack was brother Carl.

Leon Cort: There was a good build-up to the game with us talking on the phone, winding each other up. It was really good to play in. When I scored in that game, hitting the top corner, I was really buzzing. Obviously Carl scored the winner in the 90th minute to make it 3-2 but it was still just really great to play in. It was nice playing against my brother because I never did at any other point in my career.

The Wolves game was followed by another 3-2 defeat in a match at Leicester that saw Joey Gudjonsson score from the halfway line. Again, City seemed to be at risk of becoming embroiled in a relegation scrap, all of which added to the importance of the next two games, with lowly Plymouth and then Crewe visiting the KC. Plymouth were beaten 1-0 courtesy of a Craig Fagan goal, and Crewe were beaten by the same scoreline as Stuart Green got what was to be a vital winner. City were 11 points clear of relegation with seven games to play.

Stuart Green: That was a game where we were nailed on to stay up if we won. It was a poor game. The ball came over, I hit it with the outside of my right foot and generated enough power for it to go in. That was the biggest three points in our season at that time.

The first of those seven was at Portman Road, where City drew 1-1 with Ipswich thanks to a Leon Cort header. Then, with another season in the Championship all but secured, Leeds visited the KC, and they were about to be 'Beasted'.

Jon Parkin: I forgot my boots! I used to travel in with Ryan France, Matt Duke and Sam Collins and I must have been in a rush and forgot my boots. I made a couple of phone calls and ended up borrowing some from Kevin Ellison. It was a scorching day, an early kick off. We should have gone 1-0 up with my goal that was disallowed. Before half-time I had another couple of half chances but at half-time we were still thinking that we had a good chance. If we won the game we'd pretty much be safe, so we just knew we needed to play like we did in the first half in the second so we could have a bit of a celebration that night.

Craig Fagan: This felt like a real step up as a game, the type you dream about playing in as a young lad. It just felt unbelievable winning that. I loved playing in atmospheres like that, where there's extra needle in the tackles.

Jon Parkin: Greeny's put the ball in, looped it a little bit, and I thought: 'I've a great chance here,' and got up early over Gary Kelly, leant on him a little bit, headed it and it went in. That was one of the most I've ever celebrated. It was a Yorkshire derby, a full house, we knew we'd be safe. It was euphoria.

Peter Taylor: I'll never forgot Jon Parkin's goal. I said to Adam Pearson a few days prior, we're going to beat Leeds 1-0 this week. And then Jon got the goal and it was great. The atmosphere was terrific.

Leon Cort: Another Yorkshire derby and another really good game. They were a good team at the time. I was up against Rob Hulse that day, and he smashed me with an elbow and busted my eye socket but I didn't want to come off in such a massive, massive game. Even though I was a Londoner I loved the Yorkshire derbies; really good games, really fiery.

Damien Delaney: The Hull fans have always had a huge hang-up on Leeds. Even when we played them in a couple of pre-season friendlies you could tell that we were viewed as the poor relations at that time. We felt like outsiders. To play them in a competitive game, given the disparity in the two clubs' positions not long back, was huge. I still have a picture at home of the stadium that day with the score underneath it. I just remember what the game meant to the Hull fans. I was so nervous that day, as it meant so much not just to the fans but to the city as a whole.

That was a good Leeds team. They still had players left over from their Premier League glory years. To beat them on a level surface was my abiding memory of my time at Hull City. Because it meant so much to the fans, that's the game I remember the most from my time at the club.

Adam Pearson: It was fantastic. For us to beat Leeds when four or five years before we'd been four leagues apart was a tremendous feeling for me personally and for the club. And it was a great goal from Jon.

Another Yorkshire derby followed as City travelled to Bramall Lane to take on second-placed Sheffield United in what would be a memorable match, even though at one point the Blades were 2-0 up and cruising.

Rob Harmer: A rather odd favourite of mine (because we lost 3-2) is Sheffield United in 2006. We'd beaten Leeds the week before and went into that game with great deal of optimism, despite Sheffield United being regarded by many as a Premier League team in waiting. I'm not sure quite what made it so enjoyable. Perhaps it was the fact that we looked the better team for much of the game. Perhaps it was running an automatic promotion team so close, or perhaps it was just the fun we had abusing Paddy Kenny. Kenny had taken out Stuart Green for a cast-iron penalty that wasn't given and had been winding up the City faithful all game, by holding up his fingers to remind us of the score. He went quiet when Darryl Duffy equalised, then went on to get clattered twice, latterly by his own player, and great joy was taken in the pantomime villain getting his comeuppance.

City were to end the season strongly, with only one defeat in the final nine games. One of a run of four draws to close out the campaign saw City draw 1-1 at Derby, a game in which one of the great forgotten goals of the decade was scored.

Stuart Green: There wasn't much to play for in the game. I was on the left of midfield. The ball was bouncing around and I always liked a side volley. I just wanted to get as much power behind it as I could and it went straight in the top corner. It's one of the best goals I've scored in my life. I didn't score a load of goals, but the ones that I did were quite special.

City ended the season in 18th position on 52 points, 10 points clear of the relegation zone, scoring 49 goals and conceding 55. That year hadn't been anywhere near as remarkable as the two promotions that had preceded it, yet there was still a feeling of 'job well done' about the club.

Peter Taylor: I still feel that us finishing 18th and staying up was as good an achievement as the promotions, because few of the players had played regular Championship football before. It worked out as an OK season.

Brendon Smurthwaite: Relegation would have been a massive setback on and off the field. We'd altered the infrastructure off the field – we needed a media room, the press box was enlarged – and it would have been sad to go back from doing all of that. Pete got a bit of stick with people asking if it was time for a change, but he had started that journey to the Premier League.

Leon Cort: When I think back to it, we ended the season comfortably. We didn't seem out of our depth. We had to work a little bit harder but I felt we didn't let anybody down.

Damien Delaney: The gap between League 1 and the Championship was huge, whereas between League 1 and League 2 there was a difference but it was more manageable. All of a sudden you were going into a completely different ball park. A lot of teams had just come out of the Premier League and still had a lot of Premier League players in their team. It was a huge step up for us and 18th was a good return.

Peter Taylor: The way we finished that season, if we'd have stuck together we'd done a little bit better the following year. We'd have been more consistent.

Stuart Elliott: There was a burden of expectation in some respects given what had happened the season before, but I'm a left-sided midfielder and the Championship was a massive step-up. There was real quality there. I still think I ended up the top scorer that season. It was a difficult season, but I still enjoyed it. The club was still making great strides.

Damien Delaney: We were still maybe a little behind off the pitch. The stadium was fantastic but the training ground was still a couple of years off catching up. We knew that we needed to consolidate for a couple of years before the club could push on again.

Ryan France: The previous season there had been a step up in quality but we were good enough to cope with it. But up to the Championship it was another step so it was just a consolidation season. We didn't have enough to push on that season. We did well to stay in the Championship though. It's a tough league.

Nick Barmby: Peter would say: "If Luton can be up there in the Championship, why can't we?" His ambition was as strong as ever. But the main thing was staying in the Championship.

Stuart Green: It was a tough year, and my fitness was shocking for the first six months. I wasn't playing regularly. I lacked a bit of belief against the big clubs and we spent a lot of time defending. We were looking forward to seeing what we could do the year after.

As the final whistle in the final match of the season at Vicarage Road blew, the post-season managerial merry-go-round was already swinging into action, with Alan Curbishley announcing that he was going to leave Charlton Athletic. This was to have major repercussions for Peter Taylor and Hull City.

Peter Taylor: First, I thought I was going to go to Charlton. Alan Curbishley was leaving, and someone had told me that Charlton wanted me. As much as I loved doing what I'd done at Hull City – and we'd just bought a house in North Ferriby, which we loved – all of a sudden the Charlton situation happened. I was thinking: 'I've got a chance to be in the Premier League again,' and I'd only had a year-and-a-half at that level with Leicester, so I showed an interest. I thought that was going to happen and Adam was aware of that a little bit.

Then it didn't happen as they went with Iain Dowie, and that's when Adam got the call from Crystal Palace asking for permission to talk to me. Because I'd had the thing with Charlton, and then spoke to Palace, that was the only time me and Adam didn't have the greatest relationship. He was getting frustrated with it, and I don't blame him one bit as he wanted to be planning for the following season, while also perhaps thinking about the compensation he'd be getting. But he wanted to know what was going on, so we had our only ding-dong over the phone with him saying to me: "Well if you don't want to be here…" but it was never a case of that. It was never a case of me not wanting to be at Hull. So in the end I thought: 'I might as well go to Palace.'

I felt as if the relationship had split a little bit, though not too much. But had the Charlton job not been a possibility the whole thing wouldn't have happened. If it had just been Palace coming in directly, I'm very confident I would have said no.

At Hull City I had a chairman that I got on with and I trusted. I also ran the team. Whatever I said football-wise would then happen. And going to Crystal Palace there was Simon Jordan… Colin Murphy said to me: "Do you know what you're doing?" I weighed all those things up, and it wasn't an easy decision.

Adam Pearson: At that point we were a moderate Championship club with moderate ambitions and Palace were had huge ambitions through their chairman, Simon Jordan. Palace was Peter's club; he was from south-east London and had been a successful player there. With all those things, I thought that if Palace came calling for him he wouldn't be able to say no. Simon was a totally different chairman to myself and got far more involved in the football side of things, so I knew that Peter might struggle but at that point I think it was the right move for Peter and the right move for Hull City because we'd reached the point where we were all getting a bit stagnant. It needed a new injection. It was the right move for Peter to take.

Andy Dawson: We'd had three amazing years, and as players we never saw it coming. He phoned us and explained his reasons for moving to Palace. He was a club legend there. Unfortunately that's part and parcel of being a footballer. You have to get on with it and be professional. But I have huge respect for him and what he achieved at Hull City was immense. Getting promoted twice is really difficult. Not many teams do it. He was a great fella and he was great for me as an individual, and he had a great impact on my career. One, for him to show the trust in me to bring me there, and two, to keep with me through that progression and keep improving me.

Ben Burgess: There'd been rumours for a while that he wanted to move down south. All good things come to an end, but it was disappointing.

Ian Ashbee: I'd experienced a lot of ups with Peter. Not that it would have made a difference, but I felt that I wasn't there for him at the end and that made it tough to see him go. But that's how football works. And I thought he was going to come and get me at Palace!

Damien Delaney: That's just football. There's no point in getting upset about it. If he wanted to achieve something different or go somewhere else then that's up to him. I was still at Hull City and I still just wanted to get the club up to the Premier League.

Stuart Elliott: I was disappointed but Peter seemed to feel he'd taken us as far as he could. I'd had a lot of success under him but that's football. We missed him but we had to get on with things. We thanked him for what he'd done and he encouraged us to do the best we could possibly do in our careers. I have nothing but fond memories of Peter Taylor. We had so many great players – lads like Stuart Green, Boaz Myhill, Ben Burgess, Jason Price – but the gel that brought it all together was Peter Taylor. He deserves tremendous credit. He did a phenomenal job.

Ryan France: It was a blow. I was upset because he'd brought me in. I'd have run through a brick wall for Peter Taylor and Colin Murphy. But things change. Peter had got an opportunity to go back down south. He lived half his time in Hull, half back down south and that had been difficult for him. And it was a great opportunity at Palace. You couldn't begrudge him it.

Craig Fagan: It was a strange one. You were just left wondering what was going on. Will Peter want to take me with him? Who's coming in and are they going to fancy me as a player? I was disappointed that he'd left, but then you have to focus on yourself and make sure you're playing well for the next manager that comes in. What we'd done in the past under Peter Taylor counted for nothing now.

Nick Barmby: I got on with Peter – he's one of the best managers I've worked under in terms of knowledge of the game – and I was disappointed, but that's football. Palace was his team.

Leon Cort: Nobody was happy. It was like a family member leaving. At that time Hull was a family-oriented club. Everyone felt together. When Peter left it felt like it was all breaking up, and we started to worry about who was coming in. I was disappointed.

Boaz Myhill: At the time he tried to sign me for Palace but I chose to stay. He said he could understand why and I just thanked him for what he'd done for me. When I signed for Hull City he said: "I want you to come, we're looking to come up through the leagues then maybe people will say in a few years what a good job I've done." I just remember saying to him: "You've done an unbelievable job and good luck at Crystal Palace." It was strange when he left as he was the manager that gave me the chance to play for Hull City and you don't know what's going to happen next, but it's the same every year in football. Situations change and you just learn to roll with the punches.

Simon Maltby: Peter offered to take me to Palace, offering me a job on a lot more money. I thought about it over the summer and decided to stay at Hull. I felt an allegiance to the club and to Adam Pearson. I thought there was more to come from Hull too, though I wasn't thinking it would necessarily be the Premier League. In the end it was the right decision, even if at that time you'd have thought that Palace were the more likely to go up to the Premier League. Peter was fine with me though, and I went to work with him twice after that.

Phil Buckingham: It was my first big story since getting the City job at the Hull Daily Mail. I think Peter just wanted out; he wanted a different challenge. For all everything was in place at Hull City I think there was a part of him that yearned to be back down south, and given his connections with Crystal Palace it was just a fairytale job for him. That's no reflection on Hull City, just what he might be able to achieve with Crystal Palace and the emotional connection he had with them. It was an alluring prospect for him.

Mike White: You still felt that there was more to come so it came as a bit of a surprise when Peter left.

So it was farewell to the man who had finally resurrected Hull City, a man who had led the club to back-to-back promotions and left City with a firm footing in the second tier. While the mood was one of sadness, there was a lot to be thankful for towards a manager whose prickly persona in the media was often at odds with how people would find him in person.

Brendon Smurthwaite: Pete was quite funny. He had his famous Norman Wisdom impression and he had his fallouts with the media. He used to ring me and say: "Tell John Fieldhouse he's banned," and I used the think: 'Not again.' But a lot of people forget about who they've worked with in football quite quickly, especially the backroom staff, but I know I could ring Pete tomorrow and ask him for a favour and he'd do it without a second's hesitation.

Rob Smith: I always got on well with Peter. He'd do anything that was good for Hull City. He'd turn up to anything to help the club. He wasn't necessarily outgoing at these things, as he would be in a football setting, but he'd do anything to help Hull City. He was someone who appreciated honesty, and was a great character to have around.

Peter Swan: I used to have fallouts with Peter Taylor over what I'd written or what I'd said, but he was so professional in everything he did. Sometimes the glove just fits for a certain manager with a certain club at a certain time, and Hull City and Peter Taylor were the perfect fit back then.

Dave Burns: I had the odd falling out with Peter Taylor, and Brendon Smurthwaite used to ring me up doing a really good Peter Taylor impression saying: "I've got the hump with you, Burnsy." But he was a top man and a really good manager. I have a lot of time for him. His set-piece routines were incredible. He had his teams so well organised. He got it right. Leaving the club was a mistake on his behalf and I think he regrets it to this day. Premier League football with Hull City could have been his.

Phil Buckingham: There's an unusual contradiction with Peter, where he puts in a steely front but he's a very genuine guy. The players who played under him had total respect for him. And as my first manager to deal with at City he was brilliant. Maybe on a quiet Tuesday when you had an empty back page you could always count on Peter. If you rang him and he couldn't answer he'd ring you back within the hour, and he knew what you wanted, he gave you a story. He was very old school. You don't get that very much anymore. But Peter was always fantastic with me. He maybe saw I was a young lad a little bit out of my depth and he was gentle with me, though I got the odd bollocking off him!

Lawrie Dudfield: I played against Palace for Notts County in the League Cup when Peter was the manager there. I scored a great goal and played really well. At the end of the match he put his arm around me and was just lovely. He brought me into his office later, introduced me to everyone and gave me the match ball, saying I'd deserved it. People assume we don't get on because he sold me twice, but he's a really lovely bloke. It just wasn't meant to be. I'm pleased he ultimately did really well at Hull and he deserves a lot of credit for that.

Brendon Smurthwaite: When he left I think the time might have been right for the club, but I think Pete regrets it. It was shame as he'd overseen such brilliant things. He is a lovely bloke though, and he wasn't the distant person that some people felt he was.

And how does the man himself reflect upon his three-and-a-half seasons in East Yorkshire?

Peter Taylor: Somebody asked me recently what was my proudest moment in football and I just answered: "Hull City." They seemed confused given that I'd managed England, but I told them that I didn't care. Hull City were 18th in League 2, a sleeping giant that we woke up in the respect that we got them to the Championship and people were enjoying themselves. There was a fantastic feeling around the area. It's a proud, proud feeling. I love to look at supporters enjoying their clubs and I know that I helped bring that to Hull City. That is the best work that I've done, without a doubt. No matter what happens to me in the future, nobody will ever take away Hull City.

One thing that Colin and myself are very proud of is not just the promotions that we got at Hull, but the players that we sold. When you look at how much they brought in compared with what we paid for them it's frightening! Leon Cort – nothing to £1.25m. Myhill – £50,000 to £1.5m. Not only were we successful we made a few bob too. A lot of that was down to Colin Murphy.

Following Peter to south London was player of the season Leon Cort. Leon had made a huge impression at the KC since his move from Southend, so even though City received a record £1.25m for him, his departure was a sad one.

Leon Cort: I was at home and got a call from Peter saying: "Leon, would you be interested in coming back to London." I said "yes", so he asked if he put in a bid at Palace if I'd be interested. I felt like I couldn't turn it down given the fee, and that's how it came off. It almost didn't come off as Simon Jordan was worried about the price tag, but Peter convinced him that I was a goalscoring centre-back so that sealed it.

Hull City was where I feel my career got started. Southend got me noticed but Hull really pushed my career on. If I'd gone anywhere else – if I'd gone to Oldham – I don't believe that I'd have pushed on in the way I did. My time at Hull City was the pivotal moment of my career. It set me in the right direction. When I go to the KC even today people come up to me, recognise me and ask how I'm doing. That's just really nice.

Matt Rudd: Leon Cort was a towering defender, the kind that never misses a header, never shirks a challenge, never gets caught out of position and, as an excellent bonus, never gets booked. For two seasons the City defence was a safe, strong and often impenetrable thing for his presence, and the fact that he also regularly plundered in a goal or two from getting on the end of set-pieces meant he was beyond vital as City stepped up under Peter Taylor. No wonder the manager came in for him with a big wodge of cash when he left for Palace.

Most of the rest of the squad were having to consider life at Hull City without Peter Taylor for the first time. A season in the Championship had been comfortably negotiated, but the landscape had changed and most were looking to the new season with a mixture of excitement and trepidation. Both emotions, it would turn out, would be experienced in the coming 12 months, and then some…

2006/07 season

A first season back in the second tier may have been a qualified success, but City had lost the services of the manager who'd hauled the club back to that level. This left a mood of both anxiety and anticipation among the fans. The Tigers were still considered an upwardly mobile club – albeit one lacking the financial might to match the recently relegated clubs from the Premier League – and the names of numerous potential managers were being bandied about.

The hottest property in Football League management circles at that point was Phil Parkinson, who, along with assistant Geraint Williams, had just delivered an unlikely promotion from League 1 for unfashionable Colchester. Parkinson had been linked with every vacant job in the Championship in the past few months, and it seemed that it would take something extra special to entice him away from Layer Road. None of that deterred Adam Pearson.

Phil Parkinson: We'd been promoted at Colchester and I'd been asked to speak to several clubs. The Colchester chairman kind of blocked that but then it got to the end of the summer and I decided it was time for me to leave and I spoke to a couple of clubs. Then I met Adam Pearson and was offered the Hull City job.

Adam Pearson: There was only one contender for the job. I paid ridiculous compensation for Phil – more than £400,000 – which put huge pressure on him from me. But he had a fantastic track record. We'd played Colchester and been battered. I thought: 'If he can do that there, what can he do here?' But I couldn't get him in. Their chairman was threatening an injunction. Phil sent the fitness coordinator in ahead of him and he immediately alienated every player in the club. They just didn't take to him, particularly the senior pros, and that got Phil off to a difficult start.

Phil Parkinson: The protracted nature of the move did hinder my plans. The Colchester chairman made life very, very difficult, which was a real shame considering what I'd done for the club. The problem was, being a young manager I'd naively signed a contract that didn't have a clear exit strategy. As much as the chairman had always said he'd be fair if something came up, when it came down to it, it turned out to be the exact opposite. It made life very difficult and it was a shame because I'd had such a good time at Colchester and committed three-and-a-half years of my life to the club. It was messy, but sometimes that happens.

Brendon Smurthwaite: Adam knew what he wanted to do. Nobody at the time thought we were doing the wrong thing. Phil came in with different ways of doing things, his backroom staff were very different to what we'd had. We had Frank Barlow, who was a lovely bloke. And Phil was alright to work with. After his arrival presser we went off on a pre-season trip to Spain. We got on the coach at the stadium to go to Doncaster airport and he was just so excited, and really positive about the squad that he had.

Craig Fagan: I didn't know the ins and outs of the deal to start off with, but I was assuming that he'd come with his number two, Geraint Williams, as they'd worked together ever since Phil went to Colchester. I only knew the two of them together and they were great as a pair, complementing each other well. So when Phil came in on his own it was a bit strange for me. I'd never seen him work on his own before. The lads were so used to Peter Taylor's methods and Phil maybe tried to change some things – in the right way – too quickly. They weren't bad things he was trying to do but it was all too quick. It was a shock for everyone and we didn't seem to cope.

Phil Parkinson: Tommy Stewart went down early to sort out fitness stuff. Peter Taylor had left and some of the staff had left with him, so I had to get someone down there. But he was happy with the fitness. The players had done alright, and they'd done really well to stay in the Championship the year before. I was just picking up the reins.

Phil Buckingham: I wouldn't say it had got flat for Hull City, but that group of players had come so far, and I think it did need a bit of an overhaul. A lot needed doing to take it to the next level. Phil Parkinson saw that and tried to do that, he just tried to do too much too soon.

With Leon Cort departing to Crystal Palace for £1.25m, Parkinson had some money at his disposal. It wasn't to be immediately apparent, but he was to bring in some bargains.

Adam Pearson: Phil got £1.25m from the Leon Cort sale, and invested it fantastically. His recruitment, similar to Jan Molby before, set up the team. He brought in Michael Turner, Dean Marney, Sam Ricketts and then Nicky Forster and Michael Bridges, all for Leon Cort. Fantastic business. Jon Parkin really should have kicked on with us but that summer he came back very unfit.

Phil Parkinson: Michael Turner in particular was a player I'd known for a long time and I felt he had great character and great potential. Him, Dean Marney and Sam Ricketts were three good young players who were only going to get better. However, the Championship was relatively new to them all and it's a tough division. It took them a while to adapt. While they were trying to adapt, I needed to get results. Sometimes as a manager you buy players with longevity in mind, and maybe I could have done with more of the Danny Mills-type signings – those who were comfortable and experienced at that level – to guide those players in those first few months of the season.

The most eye-catching signing was that of Dean Marney from Tottenham. The central midfielder had announced himself in the Premier League with a spectacular brace against Everton in 2005. He hadn't quite kicked on at White Hart Lane after that and had spent part of the previous season out on loan at Norwich. Even still, when City paid £500,000 for him – in a deal that could have gone up to £1m with add-ons – quite a few eyebrows were raised.

Dean Marney: I was at Tottenham training with the first team, but I couldn't see a real opportunity there as we'd signed Jermaine Jenas and Edgar Davids. I felt I was wasting my time a little bit. I'd been offered a three-year deal at Spurs but once I found out that Hull were interested and that I had a chance of some first-team football I turned them down. It was a big step for me, as I still lived at home with my parents, so I was leaving home to go to a new club, and then there was the pressure with the price tag even though I'd not played much first-team football.

Joining Dean was another Londoner, Michael Turner. The big centre-back had been a trainee at Charlton, and had even spent some time on loan at Inter Milan as a teenager, before settling in Brentford's defence where he was very highly rated. As with Marney his signing looked a real coup at £350,000.

Michael Turner: I knew of the interest earlier in that summer, just after Phil Parkinson was appointed. I was keen as I'd been playing in League 1 and the Championship was a progression. I looked at Hull City as a club and the stadium was impressive; I'd seen the success they'd had getting from League 2 into the Championship and it was something I wanted to be a part of. I knew the club had the potential to get to the Premier League.

Another big signing was Sam Ricketts, a right-back coaxed from Swansea for £300,000. The nephew of former National Hunt champion jockey John Francome, Ricketts had taken an eventful route into professional football, via Telford United after being released by Oxford, but was already a Wales international (as well as having represented England C) and looked a good bet to solve a problem position that City had had for a number of years.

Sam Ricketts: I'd come out of non-league and spent two seasons at Swansea. In my first year we'd been promoted from League 2 and in my second we'd been beaten in the League 1 play-off final. That summer I had a release clause in my contract if someone bid a certain figure. There was a bit of interest, including from Hull, and I was keen to go into the Championship. When I joined I said that I didn't want to leave Swansea for any reason other than going to a higher division. I felt that Hull were a couple of years ahead of Swansea. Very similar clubs, similar set-ups, passionately supported by their cities. If you're from Hull you support Hull, and the same applies at Swansea. I got a good feeling about Hull when I was at Swansea. There was a new ground, the club was trying to achieve something. It was an exciting time. When Hull put the bid in I came up and spoke to Phil Parkinson who showed me around. There was no hesitation in signing.

Dave Burns: I'd seen Sam Ricketts playing for Swansea against Grimsby or Scunny, and I'd told Adam to get somebody to see him. A while after, Adam rang me and asked me about which full-back I'd been talking about and I told him it was Sam Ricketts. Not long after they signed him. I didn't get any money for it though!

Sam Ricketts: I found it quite hard at first as I hardly knew anyone in the squad. I just partially knew Keith Andrews, then after a week or so he went off to MK Dons, but apart from him I didn't know anyone. It was hard to settle in at first. In the hotel at the time were myself, Dean Marney and Michael Turner, all new signings, so I became close with those two quickest out of anyone and I went on to become really good friends with them. Me and Turns were room-mates for the entire time we were at the club together. But at first it was hard as I was keeping myself to myself and gradually getting to know people as the season went on.

Marney, Turner and Ricketts were joined in the squad by David Livermore, who'd joined Leeds 10 days earlier from Millwall only for manager Kevin Blackwell to sign two more central midfielders and decide that Livermore was surplus to requirements.

City's first game of the season was an away match to newly relegated West Brom, who were the favourites to top the division. It was a chastening start for Phil Parkinson but there were signs of promise too.

Ian Farrow: City were thoroughly battered in the first half. We were stood behind the goal and the home team just attacked in what seemed wave after wave. I remember twice Turner went racing out from his central defensive position trying to cover, after a West Brom player had stormed down the wing past Sam Ricketts. Twice Turner slid in. Twice the West Brom player skipped past him and crossed. Twice Turner was left on his arse and out of position. Luckily City somehow managed to desperately scramble the ball away. At that point I was thinking Turner was more Nicky Mohan than a potential future England centre-back. Stuart Elliott was substituted after about 20 minutes having not touched the ball. He was our top scorer from the previous two seasons but wasn't the best man when you are permanently on the back foot defending. The game just passed him by. Sadly, for a player who had served us so well, it proved to be the beginning of the end.

Michael Turner: West Brom had just been relegated and had some really strong players. John Hartson was a real handful that day. It was a real eye-opener. In the end that day we were unlucky not to come away with anything. We had a goal disallowed and had some really bad decisions go against us. I was pleased to get my debut out of the way and was looking forward to more games.

Ian Farrow: With about 10 minutes to go, John Welsh got the ball at the edge of the box, jinked his way into the area and was brought down. Right in front of us it was an obvious penalty. Not given. The home team went straight back up field and John Hartson scored his second. A 2-0 defeat. We went away disappointed. We didn't really deserve anything from the game but with a little luck, or a better ref, we could have snatched a draw.

Phil Parkinson: I felt that overall the squad I inherited had had a season in the Championship in which there was still some momentum behind them after the promotion from League 1. After that, the second season is always tough. It needed improving more than I was able to do. They were a very honest group of players and we tried to set the team up in a positive way to get results early. But when you don't get results early it can affect confidence a little bit, and until you sneak that first win everybody's a bit down. But I was learning about the players all the time, and the ones I brought in were learning too.

Losing 2-0 away to West Brom having had a number of refereeing decisions go against you is no cause for panic. The next game was at home to Barnsley, widely expected to struggle that season. All worries from the Hawthorns were banished as Jon Parkin put City two up after nine minutes.

Jon Parkin: I've got a lot of friends and family in Barnsley. We got off to an incredible start and I'd managed to score both goals, but then the wheels fell off. For the second goal I broke Nick Colgan's nose. I saw him out in Barnsley three weeks later, so I could point out to him how much his nose had swollen up.

However, what happened next gave huge cause for concern. Barnsley pulled one back just before half-time and were then to score twice in the second half to run out 3-2 winners.

Adam Pearson: In Dean Marney's first game at the KC against Barnsley, I thought we'd signed Zico, he was that good. And we played so well at first in that game to go 2-0 up and then missed a sitter to make it three and ended up losing 3-2 and the pressure came on to Phil from the start.

Ian Farrow: The game started better than expected. Two attacks and we were 2-0 up after about 10 minutes. If anything this put more passion in the Barnsley players and our players were looking lethargic and as if they had done enough. Did the manager tell them to defend the two-goal lead or did the players just deliberately sit back? Whatever, we were terrible for the next 75 minutes. Barnsley got one back just before half-time and dominated the second period.

Dave Burns: They were 2-0 up against Barnsley and they sat off and lost 3-2. It suggested to me that Phil wasn't quite ready for the job at the time.

Michael Turner: We just got off to a really bad start. Losing the first game is never great but we had an opportunity in the second game at home. We were looking forward to the local derby and got off to a great start against Barnsley, but losing that game in that manner was just such a bad start. We just didn't kick on really.

Brendon Smurthwaite: Had that Barnsley game gone the other way, things might have been different. Maybe it was too big a job for Phil at the time.

Ian Farrow: Was this the game that destroyed Parkinson? He seemed to lose confidence in his team selections and his footballing ideals. The penalty decision at West Brom could have changed the result in the first game. Something snapped and went wrong in the second. But was that fate? Where would history have taken City if we had drawn those first two games as, with a little luck, we could have done?

City were to lose the next game – also at home – 2-1 to Derby, and Phil Parkinson's dream move was already turning into a nightmare. It was to get worse too. A 0-0 draw at Ipswich got City off the mark points-wise, but this was followed up by a horrible performance at home to Coventry which saw the visitors win 1-0 with a late goal. Concerned, Phil Parkinson brought in two experienced forwards – Nicky Forster and Michael Bridges, for £250,000 and £350,000, respectively – but needed to make room in the squad. This led to the departure of two bona fide heroes from the back-to-back promotions.

Ben Burgess: We had a few strikers. I scored in the League Cup but Phil Parkinson wanted to get rid of me to get Nicky Forster in. That was the end. It was disappointing as I'd had such a good time but the club had completely changed by the time I'd left. I wanted a fresh start. If I hadn't been injured, who knows…

Simon Maltby: I had so much admiration for Ben. For mental strength you just had to. I'm not sure I would have been able to do what he did.

Danny Allsopp: I would still consider Ben one of my good mates even if we are on the other side of the world. He gave me a picture of us when I left which I have up in my house!

Robert Crampton: I always loved Ben Burgess. He reminded me of Bob Latchford in the 1970s, because he'd always manage to score with any part of his body other than his foot. He was my kind of player.

Steve Lee: I always loved the way Ben Burgess played the game. He scored plenty of goals himself but must've been a dream for Danny Allsopp to play alongside. He was tall and a great target man but also had a lovely touch and always seemed to be aware of who and what was around him. I remember being at the north end of the East Stand – don't know who we were playing – and directly behind him as he bent the ball around a couple of defenders and into the far corner. It really was a thing of Geovanni-esque beauty.

Ben signed for Blackpool and was nearly joined by Stuart Green, who instead opted to join his old boss at Crystal Palace.

Stuart Green: It was strange. The last game of the 2005/06 season Adam was talking about a new contract and I said I'd love to stay. But at the end-of-season meetings I got the impression from Peter that things weren't the same. He wasn't as happy as he'd been previously. I went away on holiday thinking things weren't right. I didn't hear anything about my new contract but I still had a year left. Then we heard Pete was talking to Charlton, which wasn't a surprise because I'd seen his body language – he wasn't looking forward to the next season. It was a little bit flat. But as soon as Palace came in I knew it was a club close to his heart, and I thought that he thought he'd taken Hull as far as he could.

I loved playing for Hull City and didn't want to go, but when I was on holiday my dad said the newspapers were reporting that I was free to leave. So I came back off holiday, and Adam confirmed that. I was shocked because there wasn't a new manager at that stage. I was devastated, but it was true and my Hull days were finished. I felt I had more to offer the season after. I tried to cling on to it but it wasn't going to happen. I was on my way to Blackpool – I didn't want to go there but Phil Parkinson was never going to play me so I had to leave – but Pete rang me and said: "It's a cheap deal, do you want to come?" If Crystal Palace come knocking you go!

Andy Dawson: When my sons watch the DVDs of those back-to-back promotion seasons, it makes you realise what a good player Stuart Green was. Technically he was top, top drawer. Some of the goals he scored – you forget how great they were. And he scored a lot of important goals too. A top player. He was one for me, looking back, that could have played at a much higher level. He was a massive part of why we got to where we got to. He was a player that could win a match on his own. I have huge respect for him.

Leon Cort: Stuart deserved more accolades in terms of what he did in his forward play. I know he got frustrated because he was subbed a lot, but I felt like he was an important player for us in being that attacking midfielder who'd run beyond the strikers. He did that brilliantly.

Stuart Green: It feels like it was yesterday. I'm so honoured to have played for an incredible football club with incredible support and to achieve what we achieved in the time I was there. It set it up for the club's future success. We played our part in something incredible. They were the best days of my life.

Keith Andrews and Mark Lynch were also let go as Phil Parkinson further shaped the squad that he wanted. However, the defeats kept coming. After an international break, City travelled to St Andrews to take on Birmingham. The 2-1 defeat was not a surprise, but the game had huge significance in other ways: Ian Ashbee returned to action a year after his last game for the club.

Ian Ashbee: In some respects it was a bit too early for me. Birmingham had been my club so I was excited and my family were there. But in my head I was thinking that I wasn't quite right. Then I thought: 'Will you ever be right? You have to get out and start playing.' We lost the game 2-1 and I remember thinking that there were a few good signs on that day. But it's strange coming back after a long time out. I was just concentrating on making sure my knee was alright and that I didn't do anything stupid.

Simon Maltby: Ash was similar to Ben Burgess in the way that he worked his socks off to get back to playing again. Like Ben he had a real career-threatening injury. Those injuries have finished other players. And it's one thing coming back, it's another thing coming back and playing at a higher level. Both Ben and Ash came back from serious injury to play at a higher level of football. That's some achievement. Ash is resilient, strong, and he keeps on going and going and going. But he was spot on. He listened to me, trusted me, and did what I asked of him.

20. **Colchester P6, W2, D0, L4, Pts 6**
21. **Sunderland P6, W2, D0, L4, Pts 6**
22. **QPR P6, W1, D3, L2, Pts 6**
23. **Derby P6, W1, D2, L3, Pts 5**
24. **Hull City P6, W0, D1, L5, Pts 1**

A win was needed, by hook or by crook. And it was to come at the Walkers Stadium. A commendably raucous City following – even during the half-time interval – seemed to lift the players, and inspired Michael Bridges to score a terrific goal from outside the box in the 58th minute to claim a 1-0 win.

Phil Parkinson: I felt the supporters were always very fair to me, in spite of the fact that we didn't start very well. They knew that it was always going to be tough. But it was great to get that win, and it was a terrific goal from Michael Bridges. I always felt we were in every game and that we were competitors.

Next up the Sky cameras came to the KC to witness a home game against Sheffield Wednesday. City had never won when being televised – and this was the ninth attempt having lost to Middlesbrough, Rochdale, Liverpool, Bradford, Burnley, Luton and Aston Villa, with the only point coming from a 0-0 draw with Doncaster – so it didn't augur well. However, Jon Parkin was in good form, and City had bolstered the defence with the loan signing of Danny Mills, who'd won the last of his 19 England caps just two years prior. After four minutes Mills was wrongly adjudged to have handled in the area and City went one down to the resulting penalty. However, thanks to Parkin's intervention, City were to hold the advantage within the next 15 minutes.

Jon Parkin: It was Danny Mills' first game and he gave away a penalty in the first 10 minutes so we were all just thinking: 'Oh no!' Then the first goal I scored was a header similar to my goal against Leeds. With the second it got cleared from a corner and Daws put it back in and I managed to turn and volley it in. I had to have a little look to see if I was offside though.

City saw out a 2-1 win. But just as it looked like things were turning round for Phil Parkinson, City didn't win any of their next six league games. The pressure was mounting on the young manager. But how were the players seeing it?

Ian Ashbee: I like Phil but I think the club was too big for him. There were too many big characters, the fan base was too big. I remember chatting with Adam Pearson quite a bit at the time, when Paul Simpson at Preston was a big candidate, but Adam went with Phil. Phil tried to change a few things and struggled a bit. It seemed a bit 'rabbit in the headlights' at times. He'd come from Colchester and there was a gulf there. It was too much at that point. He's obviously a good manager, it just wasn't the right time for him.

Andy Dawson: The form of the three big signings – Turns, Dean Marney and Sam Ricketts – summed up the first three months of the season. It's hard to explain. That three months was like a non-event. No one shone, we hardly won any games, the signings were great signings but it just took time for them to flourish, as it did all of us.

Ben Burgess: He was young and tried to change too many things. When you're following a manager who's been successful you have to do things slowly, but he tried to change too many things too quickly.

Ryan France: He came in and tried to change too much. They came in and tried telling people like Nick Barmby and Ian Ashbee – players who hadn't just become professional footballers overnight – that they needed to do things in a different way. I was okay, I just thought I'd just do whatever, but even I was thinking: 'You can't say that, you can't do that.' For one reason or another Hull City and the players there didn't gel with Phil Parkinson and the backroom staff. Phil had his own ways and we adapted to it a bit, but you can't just change it overnight and the results showed that.

Boaz Myhill: He was a different character to Peter Taylor, a lot more quiet. He brought in a sports scientist who had a lot to do with training, and he signed some good players like Sam Ricketts and Michael Turner, which he deserves credit for.

Damien Delaney: When Peter Taylor left everyone took a deep breath and there was maybe an element of the club stagnating a little bit. There were a lot of changes at that time; the manager, coaches, players, people coming in who maybe didn't get what the club was about, or maybe people coming in thinking they were signing for an established Championship team, which we weren't at that point. We weren't fantastic but we had an effective way of doing things and some people wanted to do things in a different way. It all just got a bit fuzzy. We had a lot of people on a lot of different pages.

Sam Ricketts: I don't know why we didn't get going under Phil. As a person he's really nice and the staff with him were good. The biggest thing to do as a new manager coming in is to get results. That buys you respect from everyone at the club and that's maybe why I struggled to settle at first and the same could apply to him as a manager. Good results bring confidence and momentum and we really struggled with that.

Simon Maltby: Phil was good to me. He was different to what I was used to, but he was complimentary about what I did. Unfortunately, for whatever reason, he struggled from the start. Football isn't a perfect science. There's not a model in place to follow as such. We had a good pre-season and couldn't get going in the season proper. He just couldn't recover from that bad start.

Phil Buckingham: I got a feeling that things weren't quite right at an early stage. He'd brought in Frank Barlow as his assistant and he could be quite a divisive character. His fitness coach was ex-army and Phil Parkinson trusted him implicitly, but he seemed to rub everyone up the wrong way. So there was a divide very quickly. It sounds absurd now, but Michael Turner, Sam Ricketts and Dean Marney weren't ripping up any trees either. He tried too much too soon. Phil Parkinson was desperate to stamp his mark on Hull City rather than refining it slowly. He tried to rip everything up. He needed the senior figures at the club on his side and it felt like he didn't have that.

After a defeat to Preston in late October, Adam Pearson decided to take action. First-team coach Frank Barlow was relieved of his duties and a replacement was sought. The move – which barely registered with City fans at the time – was to have a huge impact on the club's future, although for the time being the new coach was just happy to be back in work.

Adam Pearson: It was all a bit intense at the training ground and there'd been attempts to change the whole culture of the club overnight. The lads weren't having that and we needed someone to lift their spirits. Phil Brown came in and did exactly that. He was fantastic.

Phil Parkinson: I'd had discussions with Adam. We had Colin Murphy at the club, who was a senior figure, and we had Frank Barlow as well who was older. Adam was pushing to change things round, and asked me to look out for a younger coach. I knew Browny well so I brought him in.

Phil Brown: I was sitting at home pulling together a CV – I was the type of person who never thought he'd be out of the game –following my time at Derby County. I got a phone call from Adam Pearson, who said he'd had a conversation with Phil Parkinson, and told me that Phil would be interested in talking to me. I said: "Thanks very much, Adam. I know who you are, but until I get that phone call from Phil Parkinson I'll continue to sit here twiddling my thumbs." Within a couple of hours Phil phoned me, we made arrangements to meet at a hotel in North Ferriby, and he then said that he'd like me to take some coaching sessions as first-team coach of the football club. It wasn't ideal as I wanted to continue in management, but it got me back into the game, and got me back on the training ground, which I considered to be one of my strengths and was the biggest thing I'd been missing in my seven or eight months out of work.

Ian Ashbee: Phil was exactly what was needed at the time – someone a bit outspoken with fresh ideas. He was as keen as mustard and training sessions were excellent. He might not have been everybody's cup of tea, but I'm not into being everybody's cup of tea. I'm into winning games of football and being successful and not having a list of mates as long as my arm. Phil was good for what was required.

Michael Turner: It was a strange one. A few of us were wondering that with Frank Barlow leaving and Phil Parkinson struggling: 'Is this our new manager here?' He took a few sessions and was really hands-on with the players.

Ryan France: I liked Frank Barlow. He was a nice bloke, so I was sorry to see him go. But Phil Brown from the off was second to none. His coaching sessions were really good, really interactive, but stuff that was still relevant to football.

Sam Ricketts: From the very first day Phil was very keen to get the team spirit sorted, very thorough in his training methods. You could see from the first day that he had aspirations to be a manager again. You could tell from the first day that he had belief in himself and a hunger to be successful.

Andy Dawson: Phil's impact was brilliant. He was just a massive character. Obviously things weren't going well at the time, we were bottom three, and he gave us a massive boost. He made us feel good about ourselves, he was bright and bubbly, he brought that spark back for me as an individual. The proof's in the pudding for what he did for the team as well, because all of a sudden players started playing again and showing what they were good at. Michael Turner was top drawer under Phil Brown, Dean Marney started scoring goals and breaking from midfield, Sam Ricketts showed that he's a top player. All of a sudden, Phil just made us feel good about ourselves.

Stuart Elliott: He was very passionate, a great coach and very organised, no-nonsense, and he really believed in the players. He also brought a competitive edge to the club.

Boaz Myhill: Phil Brown was always very optimistic, very positive. Everything was always the very best it could be, and that has an effect on people. He changed a lot of careers.

Dave Richardson: Phil Brown was an exceptional coach. I remember covering his first training session. He was so good that I stopped taking photos and just stood and listened.

Simon Maltby: Phil was very energetic. His sessions were really good, and the lads really enjoyed them. We were struggling, everything was a bit dour. That was affecting everyone throughout the club, going as far as the fans. But Phil brought in an energy and exuberance to the place. The place was on its knees a little bit and he tried to pick that up.

Damien Delaney: I quite liked him. He had great enthusiasm, good energy, and he had a spring in his step. His appointment definitely helped to pick the club back up again and get it moving.

Phil Buckingham: Phil Parkinson tried to salvage the situation with Phil Brown coming, but as is often the case with these things, you're bringing in an assistant who gives the club a contingency plan should they decide to get rid of you.

Phil Brown: Warm-ups were something that bored the living daylights out of me as a player, coach and manager, so I'd always get the balls out from the off. So the first 15 minutes of my first training session was doing ball work. I witnessed a level of quality that was so high that I stopped the session and said: "What the fuck are you doing at the bottom of the league?" It was quite astonishing. I was seeing a level of performance on the training ground that they needed to transfer to a Saturday. That is the art and the key of a good manager and a good coach. But they were obviously playing in a very uptight way, very tense, and we had to alleviate that and relax them, which we thought we did.

Something that had stuck out in my head was when Steve McClaren joined Manchester United, he asked Sir Alex Ferguson what he wanted him to do with the players. Sir Alex simply told him: "Keep a smile on their faces." That's what I needed to do at Hull City: get a smile on the players' faces, because they were very good.

Sadly, the improvements on the training ground weren't immediately evident as City lost to a late winner at home to fellow strugglers Sunderland.

20. **Sheffield Weds P14, W3, D5, L6, Pts 14**
21. **Leeds P14, W4, D1, L9, Pts 13**
22. **Barnsley P14, W3, D3, L8, Pts 12**
23. **Southend P14, W2, D4, L8, Pts 10**
24. **Hull City P14, W2, D3, L9, Pts 9**

Fourteen games into the season and the situation was desperate. The next game, away to Southend, offered City the chance to get off the foot of the table, though there was little in the club's recent form to suggest that three points would be forthcoming. However, City – who had Ian Ashbee sent off on 57 minutes with the score at 2-2 – ran out 3-2 winners, with goals from Jon Parkin and Stuart Elliott coming before Craig Fagan's winner in the 65th minute.

Phil Parkinson: The Southend game was an interesting one as I was signing for my house the next day and I was moving my family up to Yorkshire, so it was good to get a win on a Tuesday night. Looking back at the games – Colchester away apart – I felt we were very competitive. We won at Southend, went to Southampton and drew, went to Norwich and drew. It was always going to be a bit of a struggle down in the lower reaches of the division with the players we had, but I felt we were holding our own all the time.

Craig Fagan: That was when Phil Brown had come in and it was a massive turning point. We'd changed our system and gone to a 4-3-3 and I was playing on the right or the left of the three. It was much more positive. Browny came in and changed a lot of things. He made us more positive. We weren't having the best of seasons but he gave that bit of confidence to some of the lads who were doubting themselves. That was a great result.

As invigorating as the win was, the frustration at the club's situation had boiled over for one player.

Ian Ashbee: My sending off was frustration. Players aren't stupid, they can see what's evolving in front of them. They can see when something's not right. For me, I held Hull City close to my heart – I still do and I always will do – and if I think that things are not right I'll be outspoken. But there was frustration in it. I was still growing as a man and growing as a footballer and stupidly let myself down and the club down.

The Southend victory set off a mini revival. City then gained a creditable draw at Southampton before beating Wolves 2-0 at the KC with goals from Craig Fagan and Stuart Elliott. The next game saw Stoke win 2-0 in Hull, but City then claimed a draw at Carrow

Road against Norwich thanks to a last-minute Michael Turner header. Eight points from five games represented an improvement in form.

But then came Colchester. On a cold Tuesday night, Phil Parkinson returned to the ground where he'd made his name, managerially speaking. It was also to be the setting of the game that would all but break him as Hull City's manager.

Phil Parkinson: We'd played Norwich on the Saturday and stayed down there in a hotel in Essex. The night before the game Ian Ashbee's wife went into labour, and in those types of games Ian Ashbee is the kind of player you don't want to lose as he was a real leader. I also knew that going back to Layer Road, the fans would be upset with me for leaving. I knew how tight that ground could be and I knew what to expect. We were overpowered on the night and unfortunately were well beaten. It's not often I can say that teams I've managed have folded, but on that night that's what we did. The Colchester team was a good side though, and to them and the crowd it was a cup final. But it was one of the lowest points of my managerial career. It's all a learning curve though. We just weren't strong enough in this kind of environment, which you don't often get in the Championship.

Sam Ricketts: I remember the Colchester away game, feeling that we'd let him down as players as we listened to the jubilant home fans after the game. That was a real low point for me as a player. We felt that we owed Phil a debt after playing in a game like that.

City had lost 5-1 at Layer Road, with Chris Iwelumo scoring four times. The following Saturday, Southampton came to the KC and delivered what would be the final nail in Phil Parkinson's coffin with a 4-2 win.

Phil Parkinson: I think the Colchester game was the key one that got me sacked. I've spoken to Adam since and I kind of figure that he wishes he'd been able to give me longer as looking back it was a bit hasty. I got on well with Adam but I think he had potential investors looking at the club and he wanted to make sure the club was going to be in the Championship and he had to do what he had to do. After the Colchester game I'd stayed down south in a hotel in the town to drive to watch Southampton play the next night. I saw this young left-back called Gareth Bale – only 17 or 18 at the time – and thought 'there's no way he can produce a performance like that again', but a few days later he proved me wrong! We were up against a team that had better quality than us, and it proved to be my last game in charge.

Boaz Myhill: I have spoken a lot to Gareth Bale when we've been together with Wales and he told me that up until he went into the football hemisphere of greatness, the free-kick he scored in that game was his favourite goal.

- 20. **Leicester P21, W5, D7, L9, Pts 22**
- 21. **Barnsley P21, W6, D4, L11, Pts 22**
- 22. **Leeds P21, W6, D2, L13, Pts 20**
- 23. **Hull City P21, W4, D5, L12, Pts 17**
- 24. **Southend P21, W2, D6, L13, Pts 12**

Days after the Southampton defeat, Phil Parkinson – a manager who had promised so much – was sacked after a mere 21 league games, 159 days after he'd been appointed. Rumours were rife that some players had rebelled against Parkinson's methods.

Adam Pearson: There was no player rebellion. That just does not happen. I did not consult with any of the players about Phil Parkinson's sacking.

I think that now Phil would handle it all quite well but back then he really struggled with it. The amount of money I'd paid for him didn't help, the amount of time I'd given him didn't help. I still think getting rid of him was the right decision, but he was, and is, a good man.

Phil Parkinson: The players were great. My management style is very different to Peter Taylor's in terms of the training, so that took a while to adapt to. I just wanted to change the approach. But the players were great and the supporters were good with me as well. You're always going to get an element of disgruntlement, but they were very fair along the way and I enjoyed staying in North Ferriby and meeting the Hull fans when I was walking around, and having a chat with them. They were terrific. The players had been on a great journey through the divisions and I was confident that I'd go there and continue that progress, and I like to feel that I helped in the progress with the players I brought in.

Phil Brown: I took it personally. I was brought in to keep Phil Parkinson in the job, to take the pressure off him. Initially I thought I'd managed all of that. That fateful day was a reflection of the 5-1 defeat at Colchester and that home defeat to Southampton. I was brought in to save Phil's job and he eventually lost it. If anybody knows me, I'm not one to point fingers; I look in the mirror. I looked in the mirror and saw someone who hadn't succeeded.

Ian Ashbee: I think people thought Phil was a decent man, though there were individuals within the changing room who didn't get on with him as well as they should have done. Phil was never going to be right for the job and you know Adam Pearson is going to be trying to find that sort of thing out and he got moved on sharpish.

Sam Ricketts: It came as a shock because it was so early in the season. You think a new manager is going to get time to bring through his ideas and bring new players in.

Stuart Elliott: Phil was a lovely guy. It was just difficult for him to get going. He was always good with me, and very understanding with regards to my exercise-induced asthma and tried to get me a lot of help. He didn't see the best of me – I knew that my body was suffering – but I'll always have fond memories of him.

Michael Turner: It was a huge disappointment for me, with Phil having signed me. I felt that I'd let him down.

Craig Fagan: Phil is a good coach. The fit just wasn't quite right.

Sean Rush: I'll always be grateful to Phil Parkinson. He was intense. Everything had worked for him at Reading and Colchester, but now he was working with more senior pros and he never really had a plan B. The groundings that he put in place, though, were what led to our success. So he played a massive part in that.

Andy Dawson: He'd been hugely successful at Colchester but it just didn't happen for me as an individual while he was in charge, and obviously it didn't happen for him as a manager. It happens in football sometimes.

Dave Burns: I liked Phil. But the picture that sums up the Phil Parkinson era is the big blue ice bath bin on its side, totally abandoned. I think the players were resistant to some of his methods. And there were some strong players in that squad. I also suspect that Phil was a bit too conservative and the job was too big for him at that time. And maybe some of the players were too big for him.

Boaz Myhill: I don't know why we couldn't get going under Phil Parkinson. Sometimes things just don't work. At a different time it might have worked for him. It didn't start well, we didn't have a good run of results, but everything happens for a reason.

Nick Barmby: Adam wanted his man and the job he did at Colchester was fantastic. I got injured pretty early and missed a lot of pre-season. But it didn't quite work out for Phil. Sometimes clubs fit and sometimes they don't. I got on alright with Phil Parkinson, I never had a beef with him. Even though sometimes I didn't play, I'd never spit my dummy out. I'd just try to show him that I'd be the best in training.

Craig Fagan: You're disappointed in yourself when that happens, asking if you've done enough. At the end of the day it's someone losing their job, and they've got families to provide for. But in truth there was an air of positivity from my point of view in the fact that the way we'd played under Phil Brown meant he could come in and do a good job for the team. He was positive and wasn't so worried about defensive stuff. He wanted to get us on the front foot and give the opposition problems. Once he took charge we got decent results when we needed them. That he'd been there for a while and knew how to get the best out of everybody helped massively.

Brendon Smurthwaite: We'd not really done sports science before then, and all of a sudden it was all caffeine tablets and the like. And if the players don't quite buy into that you've got a problem. I don't think Adam wanted to sack him, but I don't think he had a choice. If you could go back in time you'd probably make the same appointment as he was the manager who everybody wanted. I was sad it didn't work out though. He was a nice bloke.

Dean Marney: That's just how it is sometimes. He had his ways of doing things, and he's proved to be a very good manager, but it just didn't quite work out for him. He maybe tried to change too much too soon and certain players didn't buy into that. It was difficult as I was one of his signings, so when it wasn't going well for him I felt a lot more pressure on myself. It would have been nice to see him get a little bit more time but that's the way football is now.

Jon Parkin: He had his own ideas but he tried to implement them too quickly. He came in and started changing everything. If you introduce things slowly you can maybe see how they work, and that gets people on board and buying into it. The fitness coach came in and was giving everyone supplements. Some lads just don't want stuff like that. He'd been successful at Colchester, it was just a case of bringing in too many ideas too quickly without giving the lads chance to buy into it all.

Phil Buckingham: Phil Parkinson has shown he's an excellent manager, it just didn't work. Sometimes your face doesn't fit, and it felt that was the case quite early with Phil. Sacking him hurt Adam Pearson. He was absolutely convinced he had the right man. The compensation he'd paid was nearly £500,000. Adam was utterly convinced he was the next big thing in English football. I think Adam still thought he could take the club on to the next level when he appointed Phil, but that season convinced him otherwise.

Phil Parkinson: I went away and was disappointed, but you always do the job to the best of your ability. I was always very thorough in the players I brought in and it was good to watch their progress and watch the journey Hull went on.

If I could do it again I'd have brought in more ready-made Championship players, and instead of paying out transfer fees I'd have looked to a few players on frees who were coming to the end of their careers but were comfortable at that level just to guide the younger players we'd brought in. I should have looked to protect myself in the short term. But Adam and myself were looking further forward. As a manager you've got to try to buy players that will be an asset to the club going forward. But with that particular squad we could have done to get a few players in similar to what we did with Danny Mills, who was so comfortable at that level. That may have helped me in that initial period.

With a vacant seat in the manager's office, Phil Brown was given the job on a caretaker basis while Adam Pearson assessed his options. Phil was popular with the players, and while his first game – away at Plymouth – was lost 1-0, in his second game at home to early pace-setters Cardiff, the club played an attacking brand of football not seen at that level from a Hull City side for a long time, winning 4-1. After that, there was little need to look elsewhere.

Phil Brown: When I was given the opportunity to manage the club in a caretaker role I found it difficult at first as I was still holding myself responsible for Phil losing his job. But then there's the old statement: 'The king is dead, long live the king,' and I had to dust myself down and get on with it. It was a great opportunity to get back into management and I had to quickly move on.

Adam Pearson: Gary Megson was in the frame for the job but Phil came in, lifted the spirits, was fantastic on the training ground and got everybody playing again. He was really hungry and everybody was enjoying it and we kept winning. When we beat Cardiff there was no way we could let Phil go. And he did the job for buttons until the end of the season.

Ian Ashbee: I think some people may be a bit dubious about Phil getting the job, but then we'd heard the rumours about Gary Megson being close to getting it and we knew his training was meant to be difficult, so it was all over the place really. Adam knew what he was doing though, and got it right.

Andy Dawson: I think there was an offer where kids could get in for a fiver in the Cardiff game and reading Phil's press he was just really bigging the occasion up. The first thing he'd done in his first game – away at Plymouth – in his team talk was talk about us all as individuals. All of a sudden, even though we were still at the bottom of the table, we were walking out of the room feeling 10-foot tall, purely because of what he'd said, and I think that showed in the performances from then until the end of the season.

Everybody wanted Phil to get the job. At the time there was no better man for me personally and for us as a squad to get us out of the mess we were in, because his man-management was second to none. He demanded from us all and you could see the energy in his performances. He had character and as a team we performed in that way.

Nick Barmby: When he first came in his enthusiasm was fantastic. Morale wasn't the best at the time. I'd never come across Phil before, and his enthusiasm was infectious for everyone – not just the lads who were playing but also the lads on the sidelines. When he eventually got the job the lads really responded to him.

Ryan France: Phil got the job and you were thinking: 'What a great appointment!' The lads took to him so why change something that's not broken? He got the lads on his side. We'd have gone through a brick wall for him as there was that kind of trust there.

Jon Parkin: At the time everyone got on with Browny. He was a bit of a character. At that point I got on really well with him and liked him. I was happy he got the job.

Michael Turner: He dropped me! That was disappointing. I managed to get back into the side but it was a tough season all round. He did shore things up at the back a little bit. He's very hands on, takes all the training sessions. We were better defensively in that initial period.

Sean Rush: Phil Brown believed in everything I did and delivered and let me get on with my ideas. I had a good working relationship with him. He came and took on what Parky had brought in, but he came with a smile, and the lads weren't used to that. He'd do daft things like play 'Simon Says' in training, but the lads loved it. He's a showman, but on the green stuff he was terrific.

Sam Ricketts: Phil wanted to work really hard on the defensive side of the game and simplify it too. It helped settle me down a little bit, and that got better as we put in a few better performances and got a few wins. As the season went on my confidence grew, as did that of the team. Things were getting through to players and you could see the way Phil wanted us to play. It was a very simple style, but exactly what was needed at the time to get the results that we needed.

The 4-1 win against Cardiff was an important one in so many ways, with goals coming from Damien Delaney, Craig Fagan, Michael Bridges and, at last, Dean Marney.

Phil Brown: Any manager will tell you that the DNA of a team is about you as a person, as an individual. They were Phil Parkinson's team and I had to quickly get my DNA and stamp that on the team. I think my style – without being disrespectful to Phil – was a little bit more open, more expansive and perhaps more entertaining. You tend to lose that entertainment when you're a manager under pressure.

Dean Marney: It was a huge game as it brought back everyone's confidence. It was what I needed as well. I never looked upon myself as a goalscoring midfielder but it's always nice to get that release and have something for the fans to celebrate.

Phil Buckingham: Phil's first game was Plymouth away, which was a pretty nondescript 1-0 defeat. The week after, for the Cardiff game, Adam Pearson made it cheap tickets. It was a big gate and that gave the club some lift-off. A 4-1 win and all of a sudden people were thinking: 'We're not such a bad team after all.'

The Cardiff game was followed by an encouraging 0-0 draw at Elland Road, and then a flat 2-1 defeat at home to Leicester on Boxing Day. Just as it seemed that Phil Brown's honeymoon effect was wearing off, three successive victories came the club's way. Burnley were beaten 2-0 at the KC, with Marney scoring his second City goal and Craig Fagan sealing the game from the penalty spot. Sheffield Wednesday were then beaten – again – at

Hillsborough, with the damage being done by Nick Barmby – again – who scored both goals. Then came QPR at home…

City had climbed to 21st – one place above the relegation zone –with QPR in 20th. City needed to win. However, with 10 minutes to go the away side were 1-0 up. Not only that, the west London side had resorted to the worst of football's dark arts; diving, time-wasting, feigning injury, constant haranguing of the referee. Stuart Elliott had been diagnosed with a respiratory condition earlier that season, which had reduced his effectiveness. However, he could still score goals, he could still float in the air, and he could still win games. Phil Brown brought him on for David Livermore.

Stuart Elliott: Phil knew that I was an asset coming off the bench because of my aerial prowess and my ability to get behind defenders and poach a goal. He said: "Go on and get yourself in the box and get something for us." I obliged! Dean Marney put in a cross and I managed to get across the defender, and I was delighted.

A point rescued. Vital within the context of the season, given that it kept QPR within striking range, and vital within the context of the match, given that it meant this dirty, horrible QPR side probably wouldn't win. Lee Cook – the chief provocateur of QPR's unpleasantness – was sent off on 87 minutes, and then, in the 90th minute, Stuart Elliott confirmed his legendary status at Hull City (not that it needed any confirming).

Stuart Elliott: Five minutes after my equaliser, we get a corner, I got my head on it and it went in off the post. It was an amazing feeling seeing the stadium erupt as I'd seen so many times before. I remember running over and celebrating and there seemed to be about 20 players launching themselves on me. I could barely breathe under the weight of it all.

Rob Harmer: QPR had spent the entire game falling over, feigning injury, time-wasting and generally attempting to give football a bad name. We were 1-0 down when Stuart Elliot came on in the 80th minute and scored a brace. Justice had been done and never had a team deserved to lose a game more than QPR did that afternoon and it was fitting that an honest player like Elliott should be the one to put them to the sword.

Stuart Elliott: In those days Phil was really good with me but during that season I sensed that perhaps my time at the club was coming to an end, although I was still playing good football and scoring some good goals.

    20. **QPR P28, W8, D6, L14, Pts 30**
    21. **Hull City P28, W8, D6, L14, Pts 30**
    22. **Barnsley P28, W7, D5, L16, Pts 26**
    23. **Leeds P27, W7, D3, L17, Pts 24**
    24. **Southend P28, W5, D9, L14, Pts 24**

One player who hadn't been in the team that beat QPR was Craig Fagan. The striker's excellent form had been attracting the attention of a number of scouts, and when Derby made a £750,000 bid early in January, the move was made.

Craig Fagan: They were pushing for promotion, and it was a good opportunity for Hull to make some money. I wasn't dying to leave or demanding to go, it was a mutual thing. It was a positive for me as I had a chance to play in the Premier League.

The three wins in the league had been broken up by a draw against Premier League Middlesbrough in the third round of the FA Cup. In an unforgettable replay, Boro won 4-3, but City – 3-0 down at one point – gave them a real scare. To add to the surreal nature of the game, Andy Dawson scored twice – once with a header – to add to a Jon Parkin goal.

Andy Dawson: Middlesbrough were a Premier League team but we believed we could go there and win because of the form we'd been in. That just goes to show what Phil did for us. We gave them a really good game, and it was great for me as that's a local club as I'm from up there. For my header, Dean Marney crossed it, I don't know what I was doing up there but I glanced a header home. All of a sudden we were in the game, we were having chances. Unfortunately we didn't quite get there in the end, but it was a great night, and a night that gave us all a bit of belief that we could stay up.

Around this time, unbeknown to the fans, Adam Pearson was contacted by an Essex-based consortium to query whether he'd be willing to sell the club. Was it something Adam was considering?

Adam Pearson: I wasn't going to sell the club until Russell Bartlett made an offer for it.

With City now four points clear of third-from-bottom Barnsley, there was an air of optimism around the club. That mood was to go up a few notches when a move was made to finally bring a legend home.

Dean Windass: I got a phone call from Colin Todd telling me that Bradford couldn't pay January or February wages, and it looked like they'd be going into administration. He also said they thought they could get £350,000 for me on a loan deal. I was given the choice of Roy Keane's Sunderland or Phil Brown's Hull City. Well it was a no-brainer. I said to Julian Roach, the chairman at Bradford: "You know where I want to go. I want to go back home."

Phil Brown: Where managers are concerned, there's an unwritten rule where you do value the owner's opinion and his input with regards to making big decisions such as bringing someone like Dean Windass back to his home-town club. Adam Pearson told me it was a win-win situation to bring Dean back, as we already had Nicky Barmby at the club and adding Dean to that would help to get the fans back onside as they'd have local produce playing for the club. I thought that was important, as I always say that any manager has to understand not just the players, but also the supporters, as the guy that stands on the terrace will only stand there if he gets value for money. I always thought that Hull City people were hard-working and weren't going to throw money at the club willy-nilly unless they were getting value, and a way to do that was offering them local lads in the team. It wasn't gimmicky though, as Dean still had to produce. And, if you look at his stats from when he was at Bradford, he was still producing. It became a no-brainer. So with the support of Adam Pearson, I met with Dean Windass at Medici in North Ferriby, and he brought along his wife, and it was a family thing; we were bringing the Windasses back to the area. It was a great move.

Adam Pearson: Phil was the only guy brave enough to bring Dean Windass back.

Dean Windass: It all happened within the space of 48 hours. Nicky Barmby had snapped his Achilles. He'd been playing just behind the front men and Phil asked me if I could play there. I wasn't as mobile as I'd been, but I'd scored 12 goals for Bradford that season and when I met Phil and Colin Murphy at Medici, Phil asked me how many goals I'd get between signing and the end of the season. I told him that over the past three seasons I'd scored 60 goals, so I was due to get eight goals to get me to my 20 and keep Hull City in the Championship.

Ian Ashbee: Adam had been trying to get Dean Windass back under Peter Taylor, but Peter didn't want him. But it would have been the right thing to do even under Peter Taylor. I think Peter was worried about what Dean might do to the changing room being an older pro and a local lad, but Phil Brown wasn't about that. And rightly so. If you think someone is going to make a positive impact in the changing room or on the team, then you sign them. That's what I'd say as a manager. The changing room was strong, and regardless, Dean isn't the sort of lad who's going to come in and try to take over. There were strong characters in there like

Damien Delaney, Daws, Nick Barmby, so you weren't going to have someone come in and start to run the changing room, especially when we'd had a core of people who'd been there a number of years. Regardless of that, Deano didn't do anything to the changing room other than add to it.

Andy Dawson: I'd had a few run-ins with Deano previously in terms of playing against him. He's a winner. He'd do everything he could to win on a Saturday afternoon. When he played for Bradford we'd had a few tussles. But Deano's a great character. When he came into the dressing room he was such a great presence. And he's a top, top man. I got on really well with him. And he could score goals, really important ones. Once he had a chance, you knew it was in the back of the net.

Boaz Myhill: You meet big personalities, but Deano was larger than life. He took a bit of getting used to as I'd never met anyone like him before. There's no denying what an unbelievable job he did for the club.

Jon Parkin: Anyone who knows Dean knows what he's like. He was very lively in the changing room straight away. He's a local lad and a bit of a hero, but you could tell he'd be able to contribute, even at 37. If he got chances he'd still score goals.

Damien Delaney: Dean's Dean. He's loud and opinionated, but he's good to have around. He knew he was coming back to a football team that had enjoyed some success. It was a completely different team to the one he'd left all those years ago. Obviously the fans held him in high regard. To have Dean and Nick Barmby in the same team was a dream for all Hull City fans.

Nick Barmby: When I used to train with City as a kid, Dean would be there, so I've known him for most of my life. I think it was inevitable he was going to come back. Phil brought him in in a win-win situation – he's a goalscorer and he's from Hull – it wasn't just a publicity stunt. He hit the ground running. He made us better. He can hold the ball up, he brings people into the game, but in the box he's got an eye for goal and we needed that. He certainly brought goals. The rest is history!

Elsewhere in the squad, two players were going to be out of action for City for quite a while. First, Ryan France suffered a horrible injury.

Ryan France: I ruptured my cruciate knee ligament in my left knee. At the time I was devastated as I was playing really well. I was enjoying my football. Phil Brown kept encouraging me and I'd become an established player. I was annoyed I'd been stretchered off – upset with myself thinking: 'What a wimp' – but had the orthoscopy. I was thinking four to six weeks and was then told seven to nine months. It was a kick to the knackers.

Meanwhile Jon Parkin was told he could leave to join fellow Championship side Stoke City on loan. The move, however, proved to be an acrimonious one.

Jon Parkin: The manager said that I wasn't going to feature and Stoke had come in for me. I hadn't been playing for a bit so I said I'd go out there. I played on the Saturday for Stoke and a couple of the Hull lads phoned me and said that Phil Brown had been asked in a radio interview why he'd let me go when Hull were in a relegation fight, and he'd said words to the effect of: "I need players who are committed to this football club and want to work hard." I phoned Phil on the Monday morning asking him about the interview. He said: "I never said that", and I told him that I knew for a fact that he had as two different people had told me. I told him that it was out of order and said that if that's what he thought it wasn't the case. I said: "If that's what you think you don't say it on the radio like that, using it as a reason to justify letting me go." He told me that he'd listen to the radio interview and get back to me.

Phil Brown: Jon wasn't setting the right standards that I could believe in. That was the reason we fell out. Sometimes tough love is the only way forward. I felt the supporters needed to see that I was setting a certain standard. When Jon went on loan Dean Windass effectively replaced him. I couldn't play them up front together as we wouldn't have had the movement or pace. We needed to have more of a threat up top, and for me moving from Jon to Dean was moving in the right direction.

On the pitch City went through a difficult patch. Dean Windass's second debut saw Ian Ashbee score to secure a 1-1 draw at Crystal Palace, but home defeats to Leeds and West Brom followed. Next up were Derby at Pride Park. Derby had set the division alight in the first half of the season but had stuttered since. Could Phil Brown get anything in his first game back at the club that had sacked him a year previous? Derby went one up, only for City to equalise through a terrific Andy Dawson free-kick. Which begged the question, why wasn't he taking more of them?

Andy Dawson: I was maybe too honest. I'd only ever take a free-kick if I really believed I could score. I do think players now take every free-kick on the pitch, no matter where it is, but there were certain areas where I believed that I could score a goal.

A late David Livermore equaliser – coming after some excellent work by new on-loan acquisition Ray Parlour – secured City an encouraging 2-2 draw. Encouraging was the last word that could be used to describe the next game, however, as City headed to fellow strugglers Barnsley for a midweek fixture. If anything the 3-0 drubbing dished out by the home side flattered City, and the game was given an extra level of notoriety when – after being berated by City fans – captain Ian Ashbee shrugged his shoulders towards them after the final whistle. Online forums went into meltdown, with speculation rife as to why Ash had done this, with some – ridiculously – doubting the skipper's dedication to the cause.

Ian Ashbee: I think it was just one person right at the front saying something or doing something. I was making a gesture towards an individual who'd probably had too many beers on the bus on the way down. I know what I'm about, and I think most people knew what I'm about. The gesture wasn't done to a group of people, just to one person getting a bit overzealous in what he was saying. And if our lads are getting hammered, I'll try to take that on my back. If I can get all the pressure on to me, I've got no problem doing that. That would have been in my head, taking things away from everyone else getting booed so it was only me getting hammered.

Phil Brown: The Barnsley game was a real low for me. It was a derby match, and we had a following of three or four thousand there. At the end of the game you had to run the gauntlet and walk past our away fans to get off the pitch. They weren't best pleased and rightly so. You have to understand that as a player, as a manager, as a coach, once you pull the shirt on you have to wear it with pride, and we didn't that day.

Andy Dawson: We believed we would stay up: We'd got players like Ray Parlour and Dean Windass by that point who just lifted everyone. Yes, there were bad nights and bad days but we believed we would stay up. I bet our form was that of a top 10 team after Christmas. We needed that, otherwise we'd have gone down. Yes, we lost, but Phil made it clear that it wasn't alright to lose games of football, so when we did lose we got told about it, and we knew we couldn't lose the next one.

    20. **Barnsley P34, W10, D5, L19, Pts 35**
    21. **QPR P33, W9, D7, L17, Pts 34**
    22. **Hull City P33, W8, D8, L17, Pts 32**
    23. **Southend P34, W7, D10, L17, Pts 31**
    24. **Leeds P33, W9, D4, L20, Pts 31**

A 2-0 victory over third-placed Birmingham at the KC followed, with Dean Windass scoring his first goals for the club since his return. However, two more defeats followed. The 2-0 loss at the Ricoh Arena to Coventry didn't set any alarm bells ringing. The 5-2 defeat at home to Ipswich, however, made relegation seem more likely than unlikely. Ipswich were not one of the division's high-flyers – they were 17th before kick-off – and City had won one game in the last eight. This latest defeat saw them fall back into the relegation places.

A home win against Preston – 2-0 with goals from Nicky Forster and David Livermore – settled the nerves a little before a night match at Kenilworth Road to take on a Luton side in freefall.

The first half of the season had not gone well for Michael Turner. The new signing looked out of his depth, and in truth many Hull City fans had written him off. However, since being partnered at the back with Damien Delaney at the turn of the year, a run of excellent form had seen many City fans reassessing their initial judgements. They were to be given further pause for thought when he scored a quite magnificent edge-of-the-box volley to add to a David Livermore goal, which saw City clinch a vital 2-1 win against the Hatters.

Michael Turner: Me and my wife had moved to East Yorkshire and it was a totally new lifestyle for us, leaving our families and friends behind. It was always going to be tough and I found it difficult. Things weren't going my way. But then I settled down in the area and got more experience at that level.

There was a bit of pressure on us with Luton struggling as well. It's always a tough game at their place. With the goal, David Livermore took the free-kick – it wasn't a very good one – I just made a run and luckily the ball came to me and my first thought was to hit it. It went in and I won goal of the season. We went on to win that game, and that gave us a lift going into the remaining games.

After a 2-0 defeat at Sunderland it was back to the KC to take on a Southend side that had been rooted to the bottom of the table for much of the season, but were now putting together what looked like a run of form that could pull them clear of danger. However, a confident City performance saw a 4-0 thrashing handed out, with Sam Ricketts getting what would prove to be his only goal for Hull City. Dean Windass did the rest with a clinical hat-trick.

Dean Windass: In training I said to the lads: "Get the ball into the box and I'll be there." I was very fit but I wasn't as mobile as I'd once been so I wasn't going to be running the channels. So every time Sam Ricketts or Andy Dawson got in the wide areas, I was in the box. I had an instinct of where the ball was going to go, where it would drop. That Southend game was a great example of that.

The victory saw City rise to a season high of 18th position, five points clear of the relegation spots. But then came Easter, which was comprised of a home match against Norwich and a trip to Molineux to face Wolves. A spirited City side were perhaps unlucky to lose 2-1 to Norwich at the KC, with Andy Dawson scoring against the team he'd so nearly joined. The 3-1 defeat at Wolverhampton, however, was morale sapping, as City were 3-0 down after 47 minutes. The Tigers looked utterly hopeless, with on-loan Ricardo Vaz Te putting in one of the most half-hearted performances in living memory. A disappointing 1-1 draw at home to Colchester the following Saturday saw City right back in the relegation mix.

20. **Barnsley P43, W14, D5, L24, Pts 47**
21. **Hull City P43, W12, D9, L22, Pts 45**
22. **Leeds P43, W13, D6, L24, Pts 45**
23. **Southend P43, W10, D12, L21, Pts 42**
24. **Luton P43, W9, D10, L24, Pts 37**

The Colchester game had seen Phil Brown recall Jon Parkin from his loan spell at Stoke. City had been dragged back into the relegation reckoning, and Parkin had hit a spell of good form at Stoke, scoring in three successive games. It was the kind of form that couldn't go ignored.

Jon Parkin: It was strange for me coming back. Stoke were trying to get in the play-offs and I was helping them do that, then not long after I'm there playing against them. Phil Brown hadn't contacted me at all in the five or six weeks since I'd last spoken to him, even though he'd said he'd get back to me. First day back, I went to see him and said: "Why have you never phoned me?" He couldn't answer. I said: "I'm not being funny, but you can fuck off. You're bang out of order and you know you are. You've not had the balls to phone me, you're an absolute shitbag. If you pick me, I'll play for the lads, but I'm not doing it for you." That's the thing in football, even if you hate the manager or you're not getting along with him, you're playing to do well for your team and yourself but inadvertently you're still doing well for the manager. But I told him if he picked me I'd try my hardest, I just wanted him to know it wasn't for him. Obviously he never spoke to me after that. I wasn't involved much for the rest of the season.

With three games left it was looking like a shootout between Yorkshire rivals Hull City and Leeds United to fill the last relegation spot. On April 21, Leeds travelled to Southampton and City travelled to Stoke.

The Stoke game will live long in the memory. The home side went 1-0 up after 45 minutes through Liam Lawrence, and that's how it stayed for most of the second half. Leeds were holding out at St Mary's. City were heading for the bottom three. Nick Barmby and Jon Parkin had come off the bench, but the home defence couldn't be breached. Then news came through from the south coast. Bradley Wright-Phillips had scored for Southampton. Leeds were losing and City were out of the bottom three. Injury time came, and if either team could snatch an equaliser it would strike a huge psychological blow. Step forward Nick Barmby...

Nick Barmby: It was a pretty hostile atmosphere at Stoke. They'd gone 1-0 up and were close to the play-offs. We had a goal disallowed after their goalkeeper kicked it against Nick Forster, and it was a perfectly legitimate goal. I was coming on thinking: 'We need a goal here.' The ball came across and I lashed at it; it took a deflection and went over Steve Simonsen's head. I was pretty euphoric, though I ran over to the Stoke fans, which was a silly thing to do. Obviously Leeds drew that day, meaning they had to better our results...

Jon Parkin: I can't remember what I did in that game.

James Richardson: I'm pretty sure I still have the bruises from the ensuing celebratory pile-on. It wasn't the great man's finest goal, but possibly his most important, in view of Leeds' late cede at Southampton, and it set up the Cardiff game.

Phil Brown: All we had to do was finish fourth bottom. Finishing fourth bottom was like winning the league. We just had to keep the supporters believing we could navigate our way to finishing 21st this year then we could start afresh the next year.

20. **Barnsley P44, W15, D5, L24, Pts 50**
21. **Hull City P44, W12, D10, L22, Pts 46**
22. **Leeds P44, W13, D6, L25, Pts 45**
23. **Southend P44, W10, D12, L22, Pts 42**
24. **Luton P44, W9, D10, L25, Pts 37**

Advantage City. Next up for the Tigers it was Cardiff at Ninian Park. Leeds were at home to Ipswich. Neither opponent had anything to play for. However, as Cardiff seemed to hold a special disdain for the West Yorkshire team – partly because former Leeds chairman Peter

Ridsdale was now chairman of Cardiff, and partly because of a bad-tempered FA Cup tie in the not-too-distant past – City were on the receiving end of what may well be the most welcoming atmosphere that any English team has ever been afforded in south Wales. City knew that a win in Wales coupled with a defeat or draw for Leeds would all but secure survival, given City's superior goal difference (minus 16, compared with Leeds' minus 24).

Phil Brown: It was a very strange day. We went with a 1-0 game plan, a clean sheet mentality that I pride myself in. But we also had a threat up top.

Andy Dawson: Like the Yeovil and Swindon games, we knew what a win would do. There was pressure, but those experiences helped us as we still had a lot of players who'd been involved in them. It was a nervy occasion though, and we were looking at how Leeds were doing, praying that other results would go our way.

Damien Delaney: It was nerve-racking. Ninian Park was a bloody difficult place to go and play football. Cardiff were very good back then. Dave Jones was a great manager, and players like Steve Thompson, Danny Gabbidon, Roger Johnson, Steve McPhail and Joe Ledley were excellent. To go there and get a result at any time is difficult.

Andy Dawson: It was a red-hot day, there wasn't much in the game, but Cardiff weren't playing with a great intensity.

Ian Ashbee: There was a nervous energy that was different to games like Yeovil where you're going to be promoted. It was a horrible feeling where you felt like you could be letting people down and that all the hard work we'd put in to achieve what we'd achieved could be undone.

Peter Swan: I was completely behind Hull at the time. I want to see all of my old clubs do well, but because I'd been working with Hull City for so long, I felt part of them, so I wanted success for them. And I wanted to be working on a Championship club the next season.

Great intensity or not, City still had to find a way to score. News filtered through that Leeds had gone one up against Ipswich at Elland Road through Richard Cresswell. However, Dean Windass had promised Phil Brown on signing that he'd score eight goals and keep City up. He'd scored seven. In the 52nd minute he stayed true to his word.

Dean Windass: Sam Ricketts got the ball to Steve McPhee. He had a shot and it hit one of their lads on the chest. I remember wrapping my foot around the defender and volleying it. It was just an instinct. I just reacted.

Boaz Myhill: That summed Deano up. Whenever the club needed a big, special goal, Deano was there to score it. It was great for the area having local lads scoring these goals.

Dave Burns: Deano scored as only Deano can, because the bloke's got a sense of history and a sense of theatre.

The rest of the match was surreal. It was tense. How couldn't it be given what was at stake? But there was also a feeling of a pre-season friendly to matters too. The Cardiff fans didn't seem to care who won. The prospect of a Leeds relegation seemed more appealing than a win or draw that would ultimately mean nothing to them. And so the game was played out with Boaz Myhill being called upon to make a few saves, but City's clean sheet remaining intact.

Meanwhile, at Elland Road, Ipswich forward Alan Lee was about to become a Hull City hero. In the 88th minute he glanced home a header to tie the scores. If both matches stayed as they were, City were effectively safe – with three points more and a nine-goal superior goal difference with just one game left to play. The final whistle went at Ninian Park. City's three *points were in the bag. However, at Elland Road the Leeds fans had taken to invading the pitch after Ipswich's equaliser – causing the players to be led from the pitch by the referee – meaning City faced an agonising wait to see if safety had been achieved.*

Adam Pearson: To have to wait for the Leeds game to finish, with their fans coming on to the pitch, your whole life was flashing before your eyes, because at this time I'd agreed a sale to Russell Bartlett and he only wanted the club if we were in the Championship. For us to have been relegated would have been a disaster, both from the deal going through – because the club needed an injection of cash – and from a status point of view.

Damien Delaney: The game finished, and we're sitting in the centre-circle getting all these messages about the Leeds game. Some were saying it was over, others were saying it wasn't. You were just asking yourself: 'What's actually going on?' We were looking up at the big screen hoping.

Phil Brown: That pitch invasion meant we had to wait and wait and wait. I've had to witness it since at Southend when we were waiting for Millwall to finish their match and it brought back all those memories of that day at Ninian Park. We just walked around the pitch looking at the big screen, and the fans waiting. Then we went crazy.

Andy Dawson: We'd done what we'd set out to do at Christmas. A great achievement.

A great achievement indeed. City were three points above Leeds but effectively safe on goal difference.

Sam Ricketts: Being a former Swansea player, it was the first time I'd played at Cardiff so I was expecting plenty of stick, and I did get plenty throughout the game. But that just made it sweeter at the end. We were stood on the pitch at the end waiting to see the result from Leeds, and the feeling of staying up at the end was one of such relief. We'd worked so hard and it was a real tooth-and-nail job. I was making my way in football and I really didn't want to have to take a step back into League 1. It was important for the club and me as an individual that we stayed up and then tried to progress from there. It was pure relief.

Adam Pearson: Dean kept us up with his goals. He had a slow start but then started to score. I think he got eight in 12 and he was outstanding. His finish at Cardiff was brilliant. We had some real characters in the team that really dug in but Phil Brown was the architect of keeping us up, make no doubt about it.

Damien Delaney: There was no celebrating. We just breathed a huge sigh of relief. But it was a good day, and the rest is history.

Phil Buckingham: It was a real sliding doors moment, that game. You see where Leeds went, League 1 for three or so years, and that's the way it could have gone for Hull City. You knew they'd done well to get out of the bottom two divisions but it was very much on a knife-edge with regards to where the club went next. Would Paul Duffen and Russell Bartlett have gone through with the takeover? All the momentum was on the line. It was such a big deal to stay up that season. It ensured that there wasn't a backward step.

Martin Batchelor: The whole stadium celebrated as it meant Leeds would be relegated. Cardiff supporters smiled and shook hands with us after the match congratulating us, mainly for the fact we were not Leeds, I suspect. How good was it for Deano to be back in surely his last season for us?

Dean Windass: I never felt my life would get any better than that…

As the celebrations continued, one man started introducing himself to various members of staff and the media. His name was Paul Duffen. City's survival meant that he would become the club's new chairman.

Dave Burns: I just remember watching Adam Pearson pace a lonely walk on the far side of Ninian Park waiting for the news to come in from Leeds. He looked pained and anxious. He lived everything. And of course, that was the day Paul Duffen was introduced to everyone. We met him that day in the press box.

Paul Duffen: In 2006 I'd been introduced through a mutual acquaintance to Russell Bartlett who was trying to get a group together with Tony Cottee to buy West Ham from Terry Brown for £23m, but West Ham got promoted and the price went up significantly. It was too much for us. We then got introduced to Cardiff City and did our due diligence on that but that didn't work out, and then we got a call saying Hull City were available. I went to see it and it just ticked every box as far as I was concerned. It was all the things that appealed to my Boy's Own adventure of wanting to run a football club. The club hadn't played at Wembley, it hadn't been in the top flight, it had a really robust supporter base, it had a sole voice within a 40-mile radius, it had a great stadium which was – unbelievably – free of charge. It was a no-brainer really. I did a lot of research and got caught up in the whole romance of the Hull history. I just thought: 'What a fabulous place to try and do something!'

I moved up to Leeds in January 2007 to conduct due diligence and went to every home and away game in the second half of that season. I lived that experience and I was at Cardiff when we were waiting for the Leeds results to come in – which obviously had a mesmeric effect on the fortunes of the two clubs. I don't know if relegation would have ended the deal. There was a contingency plan to complete the transaction whether the club was in the Championship or League 1. However, I think that from both a buyer and seller perspective, the metrics were so different that had the relegation happened the deal would not have happened.

Phil Brown: I was introduced to a guy in a light grey suit with a Hull City tie on – our club suits weren't that colour so it looked a bit odd – and I said to Adam Pearson: "Who is this fella?" and he told me it was Paul Duffen. Adam told me that this was the club's new chairman – he was part of a consortium taking over the club and the proviso was that we remained a Championship club. So I'd fulfilled that part of the bargain. Adam then told me that part of the deal was that the new owners wanted me to be the manager, because having done the survival the way we did, they'd been doing due diligence on me and the club for the past 20 or so games of the season, and I fitted the bill. At a lot of teams, when the club changes hands or a new owner comes in, the manager is the first on the way out. Having met Paul that day, and then again in Leeds a couple of days later to discuss my plans for bringing players in, I realised that I could work with him and the new incumbents. The rest is history.

Of course this meant that Adam Pearson – the architect of the modern Hull City – would no longer be the club's owner. It was a tough bit of news for the fans and players to digest, given how he'd rescued the club from near liquidation, had banished the bitter memories of the 1990s, and provided the perfect antidote to the likes of David Lloyd, Nick Buchanan and Stephen Hinchliffe. He'd made mistakes, but had always been honest with the fans and had delivered on what he'd promised. Contemplating a Hull City without Adam Pearson was not an easy task.

Adam Pearson: The next owners had the bravery to borrow the money to have a crack at the Premier League. I'd built the club up prudently, it was break-even, everything was invested back into the club and it was in the right condition. I was never going to be of a mindset to risk the whole club by gambling on a drive for the Premier League. It needed someone else who didn't have the club at their heart to be able to take that gamble. I would never have taken that gamble and we'd have been marooned in Championship mediocrity for the rest of our lives. What was added next meant the story became really exciting but it was too high a risk strategy for me.

Peter Taylor: Adam is without a doubt the best chairman I've ever worked for. He was so supportive. We had a few little bust-ups, but we soon shook hands afterwards. He wasn't a yes man to me and I wasn't a yes man to him, but it was a bloody good relationship. He was a top chairman because he lifted the manager when he needed lifting. Nine times out of 10 in football, the manager has to lift the players and staff, but who's going to lift the manager? There are a lot of clubs that don't lift the manager. Adam would do that. He got the timing right for saying to me: "Do you want another player?" And he knew when to say: "Don't worry, we'll get it right."

Andy Dawson: Adam is a massive part of the football club. He'd brought me in as an individual, which worked out fantastically for me, but he was a good person as well. He was always approachable, he was always there to have a talk to, he wanted the club to do well and when you spoke to him that shone through. You knew he was somebody that cared for the club. But he sold the club for the right reason, as he felt he couldn't take us any further. So credit to him for that even, as he did it for the good of the club.

Nick Barmby: Adam bought the club when it was still at Boothferry Park, and straight away put in the money. He's backed every manager he's ever had. He got the ball rolling with the KC and the club's had nothing but success since then. Adam is a big part of Hull City's history. For me the perfect scenario was Russell Bartlett coming in and Adam staying, but he knew that he needed to sell the club for it to be able to go from Championship level to Premier League level. Adam and Peter Taylor got the ball rolling. We should never forget these people. Adam's not from Hull, but he has such a strong affinity with Hull as a city – not just the football club, not just Hull FC; he likes the people, he spends a lot of time here and he wants the city to do well.

Ian Ashbee: Adam was a hands-on guy and he'd speak to people all the time to find out bits and bobs. He was brilliant, particularly for people like myself who could go to him. Everything comes and goes in football and you just get on with it, but Adam was a big loss, for sure.

Martin Batchelor: Adam Pearson was the man who seemed to make it all possible, the only chairman I can remember whose name has been sung by the fans as a hero.

Ryan France: I like Adam a lot. He did extremely well for Hull City as a whole, a good man and a good chairman who was approachable, but when someone comes in with fresh ideas who invests a bit of money it's great. And boy did Phil Brown use that money well!

Stuart Elliott: Adam Pearson was a stalwart for that club. I had such a great relationship with him and he always looked after me and my family. I have the most tremendous respect for him. He sacrificed an awful lot for Hull City, and he spared no expense to get Hull City back to the higher leagues. He always put the club first in everything he did.

Simon Maltby: I was sad to see Adam go. He'd been good to me, and I found him really personable and approachable. But he felt it was the right decision for him at the time.

Rob Smith: I was caught out by it. It was a shock when he told us. He came around individually to tell us he'd sold the club. It knocked the wind out of all of us. There'd been no real talk around the building of it. We were gutted. It was a bolt out of the blue for me, and I think it was for everyone. I'd met Paul quite a few times in the preceding season though I'd never quite twigged what was happening. But it was a new person and you start to worry about what changes will be made.

Adam agreed to stay with the club in an advisory role, but left a few months later, severing (for now) his ties with the club he'd so diligently rebuilt.

Adam Pearson: I was intending to stay but I didn't think me and Paul would be able to work together. He wanted it to be his show, and rightly so. Russell was able to provide the funding to take the club to the next level though, and that was great. It meant I could leave with a clear conscience. We'd got the club into the Championship in a new stadium with a squad of good players and signed Phil Brown permanently. I did that deal.

I was sad to leave the club, and disappointed. I missed it immediately. But I stayed away and never came back. I realised I needed to get back into football very quickly so I made a very quick investment in Derby County, which in hindsight was too quick as it's very hard to transfer your heart and allegiance from one club to another. I should have had a year or two out of the game.

As the chairman's office saw a departure, so too did the playing squad: Scott Wiseman, Darryl Duffy and Nicky Forster headed for pastures new, while Ray Parlour's enjoyable spell at the club came to an end. Meanwhile the Jon Parkin saga reached a conclusion as the big striker returned to Stoke, but this time in a permanent move.

Jon Parkin: Brian Horton came in that summer as assistant manager. I'd gone in to see Phil Hough to sort everything out about leaving and I saw Brian who was saying: "Parky, why don't you just stay?" but I said to him that I couldn't play for Phil Brown and explained what happened. To this day I've not spoken to him. If he'd have explained what he said to me, I'd have been fine. I just wanted him to be honest with me. I've always been an honest player, even if I've been crap I've tried my hardest for my team, and that's all I want from a manager.

Hull City offered an opportunity for me to play in the Championship as a striker and it provided a platform for the rest of my career. I'm very thankful to Peter Taylor and Hull for giving me that chance. Things fizzled out at the end but I've a lot to thank Hull for and I still hope they do really well.

The rest of the squad looked forward to a 2007/08 season under new owners. History was waiting to be made.

2007/08 season

The elation of avoiding relegation had been tempered by Adam Pearson no longer being Hull City's owner. Pearson had resurrected a club that had spent a decade on life support. Hull City had been on the brink of extinction when Pearson took over, playing in a crumbling Boothferry Park to a loyal fan base of 4,000 or so. The club was now back in the second tier, financially secure and playing to crowds of 20,000 in a sparkling new stadium.

Little was known about the new owners – majority owner Russell Bartlett, chairman Paul Duffen and (reportedly at the time) Martin Walker – other than they hailed from Essex, Bartlett and Walker had made their money in property and they had tried to purchase West Ham. This is perhaps why expectations weren't particularly high when the players reconvened for pre-season training. Hull City were 50-1 with most bookmakers to win the division, alongside fellow outsiders such as Plymouth, Blackpool and Colchester. One man, however, didn't quite see things that way. Luckily he was sitting in the chairman's office.

Paul Duffen: I had run a public company for six years that I'd founded in the 1990s, and I was getting frustrated by fund managers who'd never had a proper job trying to tell me how to run my business with a spreadsheet. It was a good time for me to move on and the thing I'd always wanted to do since I was a kid was to run a football club.

Andy Dawson: The first time I met Paul was on a flight to Italy in pre-season. We were on the plane and the chairman was sitting in front of me. Half way to Italy he turned around and started having a chat with us all. It was really good, he seemed like a down-to-earth fella. He was as good as gold with me.

Brendon Smurthwaite: It was a shock when Adam left. A lot of us had been there from the start with him and you just think that that's never going to end. Apparently Paul had been to a load of games the previous season as Adam's guest, but I'd never clocked him. I found out about it all from Adam, and I just found it all very strange. Then I met Paul, and I didn't know what to make of him because he was so different to Adam and was very formal. We didn't know where he'd come from or what his history was, and we'd all loved working for Adam. But Paul was good to work for. Some people hammer me for saying that, but it was good fun at that time. Within a couple of weeks, Paul knew everyone's job and everyone's name, from the cleaners to the finance directors. He also spoke four or five languages and was very media friendly. He was a good frontman for the club. And the Christmas parties that we had under him – when everyone was invited, from the casual matchday staff to the players – were brilliant. It just made the club a fun and happy place to work. Paul was also very ambitious, coming out with all the 'dare to dream' stuff. Staff-wise, though, he didn't change a thing.

Simon Maltby: I had no issues with Paul Duffen. He supported me throughout the time he was there. He was a very different character to Adam, but from a personal point of view he was always very good to me. When you're going up through the leagues so quickly, it's hard to keep your department up to pace with all of the progress. Sometimes when you have rapid success, the infrastructure at the club doesn't keep track with that, so we had a few issues there. But I can't say anything bad about Paul.

Rob Smith: Paul was a brilliant communicator. He didn't try to change too much, he knew who we were and respected what we did and let us get on with our jobs. He was brilliant around the club, he knew everybody – no matter what job you did he'd stop to talk to you. He'd always encourage us to mingle with the fans before games and even during. That really galvanised everyone.

Technically, Hull City were managerless as Phil Brown's initial short-term contract had run its course. Even though he'd led City to survival there were no guarantees that he'd get the job full time. However, he appeared to have a kindred spirit in the boardroom.

Paul Duffen: While I was watching the second half of the 2006/07 campaign, I was watching Phil's body language and behaviour. When we were beaten at Barnsley in a performance where we looked like a broken team, as the players walked off in the corner of the pitch I remember Phil standing there and applauding them in. He was someone who clearly identified with his squad and with his team and I thought: 'I like that; that's the material I'm made of.' I watched him closely over the rest of the season and I thought that he'd earned the right in a division where staying up is notoriously difficult. I did look around – we did interview some other managers – and I interviewed Phil last of all and I was absolutely convinced that he and I could generate a good working relationship. I needed to work in a club where the management would teach me about football and enable me to add value as I wanted to be hands-on and very involved as executive chairman, and I knew I wouldn't be able to do that unless I understood what was going on at the training ground.

So Phil Brown was firmly ensconced in the manager's office, and Steve Parkin was given the full-time job as the first team coach. That left an opening for an assistant manager. To the delight of all Hull City fans, the role was to be filled by a familiar face – one who had unfinished business in East Yorkshire.

Brian Horton: I didn't know Phil. We weren't friends, though I'd seen him at games when he was number two to Sam Allardyce at Bolton. We'd generally speak and we'd sat together at times. I was out of work and was at a function. Phil was there and said: "What are you doing at the moment?" I told him I was doing nothing apart from playing golf and enjoying life. I knew he was at Hull and he told me that if he kept Hull City up he'd have a chance of keeping the job, and asked me if I'd consider being his number two. I was quite shocked because I'd never really been a number two before – save for a couple of months under Mark Lawrenson at Oxford – but I told him to give me a ring if he got the job. He kept City up and he rang me to tell me that he was going to interview five or six people around my age group and then would make a decision. Luckily he chose me. I went in and it just clicked straight away. The staff right through the football club – Steve Parkin, Bob Shaw, Mark Prudhoe, Sean Rush, Simon Maltby – just worked together brilliantly. It doesn't always work but the staff he inherited were great. That was one of the reasons why we did what we did. It was just fantastic, every day. The spirit of the football club was just fantastic.

Phil Brown: I'd spoken to Brian at a function I was attending on behalf of Hull City and there was an ex-Hull City players table. Brian was on that table, and at the end of the night I interviewed him and realised what an affinity he had with Hull City, what a respect he had for me, and what respect Hull City fans had for him. I wasn't frightened to take that on and use that relationship he had with the club as part of my backroom team. Steve Parkin was on board now, and Colin Murphy was moving more into retirement stage and I needed strength in depth in the backroom. It was a no-brainer. Me, my then wife, Brian and his wife Val decided to meet later that week for lunch. We'd said if the two wives didn't get on it would be a non-starter, but Karen and Val got on like a house on fire.

Brian Horton: Me and Phil had a great relationship where we had our ups and downs, disagreements – I'd always said to Phil from the off that if he wanted a yes man I wasn't the man for him – we were always honest with each other.

Andy Dawson: Brian's a great character. I really got on well with him. He was always one of those characters who you could have a full-blown argument with after a game but on the Monday morning it would be all forgotten. I have full respect for that. To this day he's someone I turn to for advice. He's a real, real top man.

Sean Rush: Brian Horton was like a father figure. He was massive for me.

The backroom staff were sorted. That just left the players. First in was a man who, given his age and the glorious manner in which he'd finished the 2006/07 season, would have been forgiven for contemplating retirement.

Paul Duffen: My first signing was some bloke called Dean Windass. Which clearly paid dividends nine months later!

Dean Windass: I scored the eight goals after rejoining, then I had to go to East Midlands airport to have a meeting with Paul Duffen. Bryan Hughes was there at the time, as was Richard Garcia. I went in and they offered me a two-year deal. That took me to being 39.

Bryan Hughes was indeed there, and it was quite a coup when City managed to pull off the signing of such an experienced, respected player.

Bryan Hughes: Charlton had just been relegated from the Premier League and over that summer I'd had a few offers. Everton were sniffing round me at the time, which would have been nice, but that was dragging on and on and not really happening. My agent called me and said Hull City were interested. I'd done a bit of background work on the club, and had seen they'd only just survived the season before. I told my agent I'd speak to them, and that's how it all came about. I met Phil at Faro airport, as we were both in Portugal at the time, and we flew back to the UK together where we met up with Paul Duffen, Brian Horton, my agent and a few others. We thrashed out the deal, and I was told what the plans were for the club – to get into the Premier League within three years. That was really pleasing to hear, and that's why I signed the three-year contract. It gave me a goal to aim for. I wanted to be part of that.

I knew Nick Barmby through playing against him and Michael Turner from my days at Charlton. When I first met Phil Brown and the board, Dean Windass was at the same hotel trying to sort out a permanent deal. The squad was a really nice group. I got a really good feel for the club. Going to Italy was really helpful too. It helped me get to know everyone, and the high-altitude training was great.

Further experience was added through an old colleague of Phil Brown's in Henrik Pedersen.

Henrik Pedersen: Phil Brown was a big factor when I signed. I had played for him for four years at Bolton when he was assistant manager, so when I heard about the interest from Hull, and heard that he was the manager, I was willing to listen. However, the main reason I signed for Hull was the three-year plan for the club. The new owners said the first season should be a mid-table position, the second season the play-offs, and third promotion. It was a very interesting plan that I liked the sound of; being part of something new, trying to reach the new owners' goals.

A year ago City had raided Colchester for manager Phil Parkinson, but had been banned from signing players from the club for 12 months. Parkinson had departed, but the year was up, and Layer Road was to provide two players who were to be integral to the season ahead.

Richard Garcia: I was out of contract with Colchester and we'd had a great season in the Championship, finishing 10th. I was looking at moving to a club that had ambition to reach the Premier League. There were a few options but after speaking to Phil Brown and Paul Duffen that's what cemented my decision. They sold me the vision of making the Premier League in three years, and that was in line with my goals, so it fitted perfectly.

Wayne Brown: Colchester had had a successful season but they let a lot of their better players go – one being Richard Garcia, two weeks before I signed – so we were going to struggle and I needed to do what was right for my career, so when Hull came in for me I was excited by the prospect of going to a bigger club. Once I got the chance to see the stadium and ambition from the chairman and manager, I was sold. I fully believed we could finish in the top six.

Richard Garcia: As always it takes time to get to know a new bunch of teammates, but there were a few new players so that helped and the guys that were there from the year before were very welcoming, so it was an easy transition.

Wayne Brown: I knew Michael Turner from Brentford and knew he was a good size and no-nonsense, which is great for me. I like playing with players like that. Ash had been there for a while, I knew a bit about him, I knew Andy Dawson as a reliable left-back, and with Sam Ricketts I knew we had the foundations for success. I was a little bit concerned with Hull finishing fourth from bottom the previous year but I fully believed that we could get into the top six in my first season.

Overall, given that Michael Turner, Sam Ricketts and Dean Marney also had a full season under their belts, the squad looked in much better shape than it had done a year earlier.

Paul Duffen: The difficult challenge was almost every season we had to refurbish the squad. That summer, clearly we wanted to give Phil some resources but there wasn't lots of money flying around so we had to be quite careful. That's why there were a fair number of free transfers, loan signings and some journeymen who came in with some experience. But everyone was picked for a purpose. In Michael Turner we had someone who we felt was an outstanding player but who needed a wise head around him and that's where Wayne Brown could add even more value: by buying one player you end up with two better players. Everybody had to improve the squad. Henrik Pedersen was a massive influence around the squad and one of the loveliest men you'll ever meet.

Dean Marney: A few people thought that I might look to leave in that first summer, but that was never in my thoughts as I wanted to prove to everyone at Hull that I could be a success. I had a few options to leave but I had a point to prove.

Henrik Pedersen: When I came to Hull I was struggling with an Achilles injury, so I spent a long time being in the gym with the physios. This gave me a lot of time to see how the other players were, both as footballers and also as people. And they were good players, but even better people. The changing room was very nice to be a part of, they took me in very quickly, and it was easy to fit in. I was living alone – my wife had to move to Denmark to finished her studies – and many of the other players were nice enough to invite me to their homes for meals and so on.

Ian Ashbee: I'd never seen a decent car in the car park at the training ground and on the first day back for training there's a Ferrari there, so I thought: 'Oh… here we go! We're in the deep end here.' But when you see that calibre of player signing and the money we've got, you think about your own personal job. Are they going to think you're OK, bring someone else in, etc… so there were a load of emotions going around at that point but that's good; that's what you want. You don't just want to go through life thinking it's all going to be hunky dory because it's not. That's not what life throws at you.

Sam Ricketts: I didn't think too much of the club being taken over in the summer, but when we came back for pre-season the first thing I noticed was that the training ground had had a really big change. Phil Brown had had some stuff ripped down and other stuff put up. You walked through the doors and thought: 'Hold on a minute!' All the standards were being lifted around the club. It was building to something, and the momentum was to grow and grow as new signings were being made. We went away for pre-season to Bormeo and Phil Brown was so meticulous; he knew what he wanted, he knew how he wanted us to play, and we started on that from day one. Gradually everything just dropped into place.

Paul Duffen: We had a backbone. And with Ash at the helm in terms of captaincy we felt that we could create an eclectic mix of players and that Phil and Brian's priority – apart from ensuring that these players improved us and we covered the positions – was that they had the right mentality; they were the kind of people who could get on board with our ambition.

Sean Rush: They were a squad, a set of players, who were so manageable. They set their own standards, they were self-policed, there wasn't one player who stood out on that score. There were five or six senior pros who set that standard and the younger lads just came along with it. We didn't buy a team, we got a group of lads who just really bonded. I don't know if I'll ever have that experience again. You had lads like Nicky Barmby and Ash who were senior pros, Wayne Brown came in and helped develop Michael Turner. It was the perfect blend.

Optimism abounded – as it usually does – leading into the first game of the season at home to Plymouth, a side expected to struggle that season. Phil Brown shocked many with his selection of Danny Coles ahead of Michael Turner – who'd finished the previous season so strongly. City lost a dispiriting game 3-2, despite an early Dean Windass goal and Dean Marney levelling the scores at 2-2 just after half-time.

Michael Turner: When Phil Brown first came in and dropped me from the team, obviously that was a huge disappointment, but I managed to get back. At the start of that season I just felt really disappointed not to start and I felt that my time at Hull might be at an end as the manager usually picks what he thinks is his strongest side for the first game. It was a blow. I was sitting on the bench watching and thinking: 'I have to get back in the side and prove what I'm all about.'

Andy Dawson: We'd worked so hard from Christmas onwards to stay in the Championship, and Phil Brown being the way he was wouldn't accept performances like that. But things had changed. We'd gone through two years of trying to stay in the division and now Phil was telling us: "It's time to kick on again," which was great to hear. The bigger names you bring in, the more you have to lift your game, the higher the standard gets, so we expected to have a really good season that year. The Plymouth game – no disrespect to them – was the type of game at home that you should be winning if you want to be challenging at the top of the table. It was just a poor all-round performance. We'd started like that the season previous, and the players and fans were thinking: 'Not the same again.' Phil had some serious words after that.

Bryan Hughes: We were hit by a bit of a sucker punch against Plymouth. I thought we played alright on the day, and they weren't a bad team. They seemed to enjoy the carnival atmosphere that the fans had created at the KC that day too. We just made a few individual errors and that cost us. Phil Brown made no bones about how unhappy he was in the dressing room afterwards. He made it clear that certain individuals wouldn't be around much longer.

Memories of the disastrous start made to the season before were already creeping into the minds of many City fans, and when Coventry went 1-0 up at the Ricoh Arena in the next league game, the levels of concern rose a few notches higher. It was to great relief, then, when Nick Barmby – all five foot seven of him – towered above the home defence to head home what would be a vital equaliser.

Nick Barmby: It was a free-kick from the right, it was whipped in and I just got ahead of one of the defenders. With heading the ball, I was always taught by Dave Sexton at Lilleshall that it's not how small or tall you are, but the timing of your header. If you jump right you can get above people, and I was always a pretty decent header of a ball. So it was all in the timing. That settled us down and got us the point. The biggest thing for teams in any division is just to get off the mark and get a point on the board so you don't see that nought on a Saturday any more in the league table.

The 'one' became a 'four' after the next league game at home to Norwich, with goals from Dean Windass and Richard Garcia giving City a 2-1 win.

Phil Brown: After two or three games that season, I think we were 17th or 18th in the table, Paul Duffen came to me and said: "We're strong enough to finish mid-table or above." He kept revising it up as the season went on.

City then beat a top-flight club away from home for the first time since 1972 as a spectacular Stuart Elliott goal secured a 1-0 win in the League Cup against Wigan. At that point City were rumoured to be on the brink of a move for one of the Wigan forwards in action.

Caleb Folan: I was aware of interest from a few different teams, Hull being one of them. I didn't really think too much about it though, I just focused on playing.

The rumours proved to be true, and Caleb Folan became Hull City's first £1m player.

Caleb Folan: Initially I was at a junction. I'd just signed a long contract with Wigan in the Premier League and the thought of moving on so soon left me a bit confused. I met with Phil Brown and there was something about him that I liked. I'd always had old-school managers, and Phil was relaxed and open. That helped me make my decision. I didn't feel any pressure of being the first million-pound signing. Phil had mentioned it but I was more just excited to meet everyone and get back into a normal routine.

Paul Duffen: In Caleb we thought we'd found somebody who could dramatically improve us. He had the physique, the stature and the talent to become a significant goalscorer in the Championship. And he turned out to be a supersub!

Nick Barmby: Caleb was a young kid who I knew from Leeds as an apprentice. And when you roughed Caleb up and he got angry, he was unplayable at times.

Caleb's debut at Blackpool gave City fans a glimpse of what £1m buys you, as he led the forward line brilliantly and played a role in Ian Ashbee's equaliser. However, a sickening clash of heads cut his debut short, and City went on to concede a last-minute winner when Ben Burgess scored against his old team.

Caleb Folan: I remember dummying the ball for Ian Ashbee's goal. I don't remember much of the game really, just the fans feeling on top of you. But then I just remember being on the way to the hospital. Phil Brown and Brian Horton came to visit though!

The match was to all but signal the end for one true City legend, however.

Stuart Elliott: I missed one or two chances and never got back in the team after that. I felt that I didn't deserve to be left out but Phil was bringing in his own players and wanted to try out his own ideas, so I knew then that my time was coming to an end. There was no bitterness though. It was just the way things were.

The first £1m player was through the door, but there was to be no letting up. Next in was a bona fide world superstar.

Phil Brown: With Jay-Jay Okocha, at Bolton he'd taken us to the next level on an international scale. I knew he was capable of playing great football, putting a smile on people's faces, and taking pressure out of situations by being himself. I had a bit of resistance on signing him – Brian Horton didn't think he'd be able to reproduce what he'd done at Bolton, and Steve Parkin agreed – but Jay-Jay helped make Hull City global. The camera crews and international media presence when we signed Jay-Jay Okocha was probably the biggest Hull City had ever witnessed. I was getting phone calls from Nigeria, Australia, America, all asking how we'd managed to sign Jay-Jay. And it was down to the relationship we'd had at Bolton Wanderers. Jay-Jay just enjoyed raising the level of expectation at any football club he'd been at. I knew he could get players to play better; the training sessions went up a level, the quality of our preparation went up a level, even having him on the bench meant that players would look across and see a player of his calibre there, a worldwide, iconic legend.

Paul Duffen: At the time we breached a lot of thresholds such as a record signing, though that said more about how little we'd been paying previously! Jay-Jay was somebody that Phil had had at Bolton who he felt had a mesmeric effect on the team in training, regardless of how much he was going to be able to appear on the pitch. Having his experience and enthusiasm was a really positive thing. He was a free agent and we met him at a hotel in Park Lane in London. He was keen to work with Phil again, and he liked the underdog story of Hull City. Sadly he didn't get as many games as we'd have liked but there were a few games where he was magnificent – one sticks in the mind against Stoke when there were four players trying to dispossess him on the edge of the area where he was just playing keep-ball and taking the piss. Even though he didn't feature towards the end of the season his influence on the squad was just fantastic.

Andy Dawson: When you're signing players like that, you're not bringing them in to get you to mid-table in the Championship. You're signing them because they're coming to get promoted. Jay-Jay had been a world superstar and he wasn't coming to have a leisurely season. I think he brought a lot of the players on too, those of us who'd been there for a long time. We thought: 'We have to raise our game here.' And not only were people like Jay-Jay top players, they were top people as well. It was certainly a statement from the club and Phil Brown, saying: 'This is where we need to be this season.'

Bryan Hughes: I knew Jay-Jay as I'd played against him numerous times, but his signing gave everyone a lift with regards to the direction the club was trying to go in. Phil and Paul wanted to make big marquee signings – there was talk about Juninho – to get the fans on the edge of their seats. But that signing gave everyone real belief. Jay-Jay didn't quite take off on the pitch at Hull City because of his injuries, but he was fantastic to have around the dressing room. He was never unhappy. His attitude was great and that rubs off on other players.

Dean Marney: Jay-Jay was not only a world-class player, he was a great lad as well. He was so down to earth, and a big help for the younger lads coming through. It didn't bother me from a competition point of view as my bigger picture is the team and the club's success. I just looked upon the signing as a massive positive.

Sam Ricketts: Jay-Jay was a really, really nice character. He probably didn't play as much or have as big an impact on the pitch as he'd have hoped, but off the field he brought an awful lot to the dressing room and did a lot to raise expectations around the club. When you sign a player like that it gives everyone confidence. It was another little piece of the jigsaw. It built belief that the club was possibly going to do something.

Nick Barmby: I loved Jay-Jay, a great guy, humble, and skill out of this world. Also, his shooting was amazing. He could hit a ball with both feet and his technique was fantastic. He gave everyone a buzz. I think the Hull fans were happy to see skills like that. It reminded me of when Peter Barnes came to Boothferry Park in the late 1980s. But Jay-Jay worked so hard in training and helped the young lads.

Brendon Smurthwaite: Jay-Jay was massive for the club. He was at the end of his career but it was still huge for the club. When I first heard the rumours I just thought it wasn't going to happen. Then Browny rang me and asked me to meet him at the KC reception to help show someone round the stadium. There was Jay-Jay, his missus, his kids and his Bentley. I just thought 'God!' He was a great bloke though, really easy to work with. The first press call with him took all day and he did everything that was asked of him without complaining once.

Phil Buckingham: When they started signing the likes of Jay-Jay Okocha and Caleb Folan, you knew it wasn't going to be an ordinary Championship season.

Damien Delaney: I'd been there since the Boothferry Park days, so to see the change from that to these big-name players coming in on big money, you were looking round thinking: 'Wow, we really have changed.' There seemed like very few players who were left from the very start of the journey. I was looking round thinking: 'This is madness!' Obviously Phil Brown had a plan about what he wanted to do, and the new owners came in and backed him. The club definitely changed that summer onwards. It was very different. But it worked out really well.

Henrik Pedersen: I have been lucky to have played with Jay-Jay Okocha twice, at Hull and also at Bolton. What a player he was; the best technically and a very lovely person. He has been at many big clubs in his career, but you couldn't sense it in him. He's a very down-to-earth person.

Brendon Smurthwaite: He trained really hard and helped raise the standards. He always had a smile on his face. And he was a bit of a wind-up merchant too. If I ever asked him to come down to a school or something, he'd ring me just as he was due to arrive saying: "Not today, Brendon." I'd get all worried and then he'd walk through the door with his phone in his hand laughing his head off. A great, great bloke.

Jay-Jay came on as a sub to a standing ovation to make his debut in a match at the KC against Stoke. City drew the game 1-1 thanks to a late equaliser from David Livermore. In Jay-Jay's second game, however, a masterclass was delivered in an unexpected 1-0 victory over Wolverhampton at Molineux. The goal came from a Dean Windass penalty but it was Jay-Jay that had both sets of fans salivating.

Martin Batchelor: Jay-Jay Okocha is the only City player I can remember being applauded by the whole crowd when he was subbed away at Wolves.

Away from the £1m signings and skilful superstars, the clean sheet against Wolves came in no small part because of the blossoming relationship at the heart of the defence between Michael Turner and Wayne Brown.

Michael Turner: He was naturally left footed and I'm a right footer so that worked perfectly for the two of us. And we are similar players, which sometimes doesn't work as a pairing but we seemed to click straight away. His reading of the game was fantastic and we both just got to know each other's games very quickly and formed a great partnership.

Wayne Brown: We didn't play in the first game against Plymouth – I was carrying a hamstring injury and Michael was on the bench – but then we played in a cup game against Crewe which we won 3-0. It takes time to build up partnerships and understandings but there was just a little click there where we knew where each other would be. You can get a good read from somebody who isn't going to try any fancy stuff. If they take good start-up position, you can then take up good start-up positions and keep a reasonable line. I knew if I was tight to my centre-forward he'd be behind me and vice-versa, and with Sam Ricketts and Andy Dawson, it wasn't just the two centre halves the whole back four had a good understanding. I enjoyed playing alongside him. It was one of the best partnerships I had in my career.

Boaz Myhill: They complemented each other very well; the young, up-and-coming player that wants to learn and show what he can do, and the been there, seen that partner to help him learn. I'm sure Michael would still say that Wayne helped him a lot in his career.

Sam Ricketts: The back four stayed pretty much the same except Wayne Brown came in as a centre-half. Wayne was the experienced one among us. He'd keep badgering us and controlling the back four. He was to play a huge role that season in educating us as much as anything. He helped Michael Turner, he helped me. I'd try to bomb forward as much as possible and Wayne would be shouting at me to tuck in behind as much as possible. We had a constant battle on that during games, but in a nice way. Wayne was a very, very good player for us. He brought a lot of calmness to the back four. He was there solely to defend. He wasn't bothered about playing pretty football – he'd quite happily stick it into Row Z, but he made us solid defensively.

City were to lose their next game at what had been a happy hunting ground in recent years – Hillsborough – 1-0, but came back strongly in the next game against Ipswich at the KC, with Henrik Pedersen finally fit and firing, scoring two goals, and a first City goal for Ipswich old boy Wayne Brown, giving the Tigers a 3-1 victory.

Henrik Pedersen: It took some time to get fit and ready to play, so it was very good to finally get my first start, and start giving something back to the club and the fans. As I remember it, the first goal was from a short corner taken by Jay-Jay which I headed in after he'd put in a cross, and the second was a long ball forward from Deano and a quick shot at the near post. It was a nice way to start my career at Hull.

Wayne Brown: It's always nice playing against your old clubs. You always want to do well against them. They had a few players playing who were there when I was there so it was nice to play against them. I mainly remember a fantastic bit of skill from Jay-Jay Okocha that he did on Alex Bruce, which I still remind him about. A really good game in which we were pretty dominant. Henrik scored two, and he was a great addition for us and gave us a different dimension.

While the wins were coming, so were the defeats. The next match saw recently relegated Charlton come to the KC. The visitors won a bad-tempered match that saw Ian Ashbee sent off. And with Charlton's dark arts on full display, no one did more to rile those of a black and amber allegiance than former City loanee Danny Mills.

Ian Ashbee: They'd gone round the block a bit more than us. They were a bit smarter. But I just wanted Danny Mills to be honest. I didn't like him, found him too opinionated. He was the type of person who would change the dressing room, who would be a bit of a snake, so I didn't agree with that and I'm not going to sit there and pretend to be alright to someone's face when I don't think it was alright, or that he was alright as a kid. It was a bit silly on my part to get sent off on that day. But you learn week by week, day by day.

Bryan Hughes: It was a high-tempo game. Lots of passion, lots of tackles, but Charlton used their experience in certain situations, certainly with the referee. It was a half-decent game of football but it was hard to take losing it. We deserved a draw at least.

A creditable draw with Crystal Palace followed, with Dean Marney scoring an injury-time equaliser to garner a result that was to ultimately cost Peter Taylor his job at Selhurst Park. Then, over the subsequent international break, a loan signing was made that would change the course of the club's history.

Phil Brown: Our chief scout had been scouring under-21 leagues – which Championship clubs have to do. If you want to be in the Premier League you have to have a Premier League mentality and that's exactly what Fraizer Campbell brought. He was bright, sharp and brought a Manchester United edge to us. We felt he would score goals because of his pace and the fact that we had big players around that could help him.

Fraizer Campbell: Warren Joyce was a big factor in my decision. I'd been on loan at Antwerp with him so we got on really well. When Hull came up as an option – they weren't in a great league position, about 15th – me and my dad went to meet everyone. As soon as we got there everything felt right. I'd looked round other places that hadn't felt quite right, but at Hull, in spite of the league position, it just had a good vibe. The manager was key to that. It was an obvious choice for me in the end.

Warren Joyce: I knew from having him at Antwerp he'd do well. There were a lot of clubs in for him – even some in the Premier League – but I said to him: "Look, the people there are so passionate and you'll do well. It can elevate you into the manager's plans back at Manchester United." I knew he'd be a crowd favourite because of the way he played. I was delighted to push him towards Hull.

Paul Duffen: Fraizer was an inspirational loan signing and it came about through contacts with Warren Joyce. Bob Shaw went to see him and reckoned he was the real deal. Bringing him in was amazing. As a personality and a talent he was so enthused and energetic that we may have got a bit ahead of ourselves seeing this starlet in our midst after watching him in his home debut against Barnsley. It was just incredible! The effect he had coming into the squad was galvanising.

Phil Brown: His dad's from Huddersfield – an electrician by trade and a former singer at a famous club called Johnny's – but when the two of them were travelling across to Hull City, they stopped on the M62 and rang me as they were having second thoughts. They'd just heard on the radio that Hull was one of the 10 worst inner cities in the UK according to some survey that had come out. My sales pitch was a two-fold one then: I told Fraizer that his dad was an electrician from Huddersfield, and Huddersfield was also named in the survey, and if you want to go to London to play football, 10 of the worst 20 inner-city areas were in London, so the survey is very misleading. I told them to continue on their journey and let me show them places where they'd go 'wow'. I took them to Swanland and places round there, the beautiful surrounding areas and it ended up being a no-brainer. You hear some rubbish about Hull – I've been to the cities of some of the biggest football clubs in the world, where there are proper slums nearby, and you wouldn't think twice about signing for those clubs. And I knew Hull was a lovely place to live.

Dean Windass: You could tell, coming from Manchester United, that Fraizer wanted to prove to people that he was a good player. We got on famously well as mates, as we did with Caleb Folan too. I just said to Fraizer: "When I'm in this area, I want you to be in that area, as I can't run around as much as you. I'll flick the ball on, I'll hold the ball up for you. You come short or long. I'll take the bangs and the bumps and I'll get you goals." It was a marriage made in heaven.

Fraizer Campbell: As a youngster you're just trying to learn, and that's what I did with Dean and Caleb, who were very different players. Dean would say: "I'll go up for the headers and take all the bruises and knocks and you just get in behind the defence," and Caleb was big and strong but I'd drop in deeper behind him.

Bryan Hughes: He was like a breath of fresh air. We had Dean up there as a target man, but we were maybe lacking a bit of quality perhaps from a number nine who could get down the sides of people. He was outstanding. He brought a new work ethic from the front. Everyone behind him appreciated his workload and it brought our games on as we were pushing even further for each other. It was a key signing.

Wayne Brown: You can never tell with young lads from big clubs – you don't know what you're getting. They can either be exceptional, or they can turn up thinking: 'Well I'm at Manchester United and I can just do a job for a few months then go back to my big club.' But the one thing that stood out for me with Fraizer was his work ethic. You sometimes get strikers who just want to look good on the ball but Fraizer's work ethic was phenomenal.

Caleb Folan: The injuries I'd had were frustrating and I hadn't been consistently playing. With Fraizer Campbell coming, we hit it off straight away. He's from Huddersfield and I've got family there, and I was one of the first people to greet him. Our friendship grew from there. We got on really well and that developed on the pitch; we had an understanding of each other. He was my roommate, and his mum used to make amazing flapjacks for away games that we'd munch on before the match. But the whole squad had a real togetherness that I'd never experienced before. It was amazing.

Fraizer Campbell: I love a bit of flapjack so that must have been the secret behind what we were doing.

Fraizer's debut – away at Watford – didn't go to plan as City lost 1-0 to a Marlon King goal. But Watford could wait...

Fraizer Campbell: I made my debut in a game away at Watford and I just remember standing in the tunnel next to Danny Shittu, who was grunting, shouting war chants. I was thinking: 'What have I let myself in for?'

Fraizer needn't have worried. Barnsley's defence, however, had cause to. In his home debut, in a televised match on a Monday night, Campbell tore them to shreds, scoring twice in a 3-0 City victory.

Fraizer Campbell: In the home game against Barnsley, the fans were brilliant and gave me a great welcome. I just really enjoyed it. I nearly got a hat-trick but ran out steam. It was a great night and the start of a great run for me and the football club.

City were struggling to put a run of victories together, however, and a home draw against Sheffield United, followed by a hugely dispiriting 2-0 defeat at Loftus Road to QPR, left the Tigers in mid-table. Few would have fancied City getting much out of the following game either; away at bogey side Burnley. Heading into injury time, City had an impressive 0-0 draw in their grasp. But there was something about this team. Why take one point when there's a possibility of all three?

Michael Turner: It was a tough place to go, especially on a Tuesday night, and they had some good, experienced players. Dean Marney put over a corner and it just seemed to land on my head and go in. It was the greatest feeling. To go there and win 1-0, coming away from that we were feeling we could do something special.

The provider of the goal, Dean Marney, was finally showing City fans what he was capable of too.

Dean Marney: I found a bit of confidence and started doing the things that I was good at. The season before I was maybe trying a bit too hard, and that can have the completely opposite effect. But I was going out, feeling confident, playing week in, week out, feeling good physically. The season under Phil Parkinson had been my first full season in a proper league. Once I got up to speed with the physicality of the league and built a good relationship with Ash we had a good time.

And the wins kept coming. The Burnley victory was followed by a 3-0 tonking of Preston, with the goals coming from Windass, Campbell and Dawson. That had been Dean's fifth goal of the season already. Not bad for a 38-year-old. Goals six and seven for the veteran were to follow in the next game at Glanford Park, Scunthorpe, as City came away with a 2-1 win.

Dean Windass: I missed a sitter to get my hat-trick! I always loved playing against Scunny. When Nigel Adkins was there he'd call me the fox in the box. I loved the local derbies and City fans would always pack the away end. But again, it was just natural ability. A header at the near post, and then one with my left peg. But I was gutted to miss the sitter at the end and as soon as I missed Phil brought me off. The Scunthorpe fans hated me and called me a fat bastard. My kids asked why they called me fat. I told them if they stopped calling me stuff like that it would be because I wasn't doing my job properly. I was never fat though!

These three consecutive wins were followed by two disappointing draws at the KC – 0-0 with Bristol City and 2-2 with Cardiff. Away matches at Preston and Southampton were next, and the season was about to take a worrying turn. The 3-0 defeat at Deepdale was bad enough, but in isolation could be written off as a blip. However, it being followed by a 4-0 defeat at St Mary's had City fans wondering if they were facing another relegation battle.

Phil Brown: You have lows as a manager, and those two games were a real low for me at Hull City. I felt as if I had to do something about the mentality at the club, and from the top: the chairman, the owner, the secretary, everybody at the football club. It was a big moment for me, as these people needed to see the whites of my eyes and see how serious I was about winning, and how serious I was about achieving something at Hull City. I remember reducing some big players to tears at that time, because it needed it. There was a point where I wasn't going to go any further, and if they weren't on board then they were out. That was the time when it all turned around. People need to see as a manager that you're serious about your work and what you want to achieve at your football club, but sometimes you don't get the time to have that moment. I was given time at Hull City, and I appreciated that as I felt that I had the backing of the owners and the chairman. I needed everyone to realise how important my time at Hull City was to me. That was a massive week.

Bryan Hughes: It wasn't the best of afternoons at Southampton. Jay-Jay played, and we played a diamond formation to accommodate him. Up until a certain point I thought we were on top, but we got hit by a sucker punch and didn't recover. Stern John got a hat-trick. It was the first time we'd played the diamond and I thought it worked OK for a while, but we knew we had to do something after the game. It was turning point for us. And I think Phil realised at that point that, because of his injuries, he could only use Jay-Jay sparingly. We went back to basics with a 4-4-2 after that.

Ian Ashbee: Phil had only been in charge a year, and for just three or four months permanently. He'd only just taken the reins where he could be the master of his own destiny and we were still waiting for him to get it right. It was a testing period, but not one we were overly concerned with. There was good quality within the side. It was just a case of getting a bit of momentum and confidence back within the squad.

Caleb Folan: I wasn't feeling: 'Oh no what's going on?' I was just focused on getting myself a consistent run in the team. I always knew I would score at some point. I wasn't concerned about that. I knew the connection I had with the other players and I knew it was just a matter of time. I was never worried about any defeat at any time.

Wayne Brown: Any successful campaign is going to have setbacks and that was a big down day for us. But with any good team, it's about how you react to these defeats. That game gave us a spur to think we had to start to do something. I think we reacted really well to that game.

Sam Ricketts: We were still growing in belief and confidence at that time. We never really expected to get promoted that year and we never really spoke about it. We knew what we wanted to do, we weren't being bashful, we just wanted to keep plugging away and improve. I wasn't looking either up or down the table, I was just concentrating on my own performances. As the season went on, the more confident we got as a team and the belief started to grow. What was possible started to dawn on us and started to focus us.

Paul Duffen: We trod fairly gingerly for the first few months. It's a well-worn soundbite from Championship chairmen but our only ambition was to stay in the division. In the first few games we did OK. My earliest memories of that season are getting to know all the stakeholders, from the sponsors to the local charities. I also wanted to build a better relationship between the stadium and the training ground, and get the whole club working together as one unit. The first real memory I have of a landmark result was losing back-to-back games against Preston and Southampton, shipping seven goals in the space of a few days, which I think was about 20% of the goals we conceded all season.

Michael Turner: The Championship is a tough league and you'll have a run of bad games and it's all about picking yourself up and going again. We did that. The team slowly started to pick itself – we didn't seem to make too many changes in the second half of the season – and that helps.

Phil Brown: Sometimes, though, it's not the 3-0 or 4-0 defeats that triggers these things; sometimes it's something as silly as my wife and my daughter leaving one of those games and having to walk a mile-and-a-half to get to a car that wasn't in the club car park, that wasn't in a safe place, the tickets that they had weren't in the directors' box, when there were people in the directors box who, as far as I'm concerned, weren't as important as my wife and my daughter. There were people at the club who were getting their priorities wrong. I have to thank Paul Duffen here, because he knew what I was talking about. He knew that every club has big players, and every club has important players, but when a manager has the support that I have, then I can achieve what I wanted to try to achieve, which was to achieve a greater standing in the footballing world for Hull City. We started to get somewhere near that at that point, and Paul Duffen played a big role in that.

Losing two games on the trot to an aggregate 7-0 scoreline was an unacceptable return. But those results had brought with them a realisation about what was needed for the rest of the season. After the final whistle blew at St Mary's, City were to play 28 more games in their league campaign and lose only five times.

Paul Duffen: Up until then we were just below middle of the table. But to get thumped twice like that was when I first thought: 'This is going to be a difficult ride.' Phil and I would meet at least twice a week to debrief the previous game and for him to offer his thoughts on how to approach the next game, and he was really accommodating with that. That week I was getting a better insight into how his mind worked and those few days gave us a real shock to the system. I thought it could be a very long winter.

Brian Horton: Phil likes his staff input and we had a massive meeting about it, right down to the youth team coaches, and we agreed that we had to change the system and the way we played. We went 4-4-2, which is tough as it meant leaving out the likes of Jay-Jay Okocha and Henrik Pedersen. Then we were unbeatable. You look at the side – Myhill, Ricketts, Dawson, Brown, Turner – that's solid. Then Garcia, Ashbee, Marney, Hughes, Deano, Fraizer, that's a solid 11. Ashbee was great in midfield, he'd let Marney go and play. Garcia was a good solid pro, Brian Hughes was a good player technically playing on the left but right-footed. Then there was Fraizer with his pace and Deano with his cleverness, who added a lot to that team and helped Fraizer an awful lot. Then you had the likes of Caleb, Jay-Jay and Henrik Pedersen coming on. It was just an excellent group.

The next game was at home to a struggling Leicester side, an ideal game to kick-start a season. The result – a 2-0 win – was most welcome, and the game's first goal came from a very relieved source.

Caleb Folan: I remember Deano helping it on over the top, in training we'd done that all the time, and I knew it was going to come at some point and I knew it would be a goal like that. I was feeling great with a sense of relief. It gave me a boost in confidence.

Just before Christmas, City visited the Valley to play Charlton, the side that had pulled every cynical trick in the book to beat the Tigers 2-1 in a game at the KC a couple of months earlier. This was a different Hull City, however, and the 1-1 scoreline, courtesy of a Fraizer Campbell strike, was kind on the hosts. Satisfyingly, Danny Mills was sent off for the opposition but City couldn't find what would have been a richly deserved winner.

Bryan Hughes: It was a good game. We came away from the game thinking we should have won it, which was a great feeling in a way given that Charlton had only just come down from the Premier League. It gave us a belief. We knew we could mix it with teams of that calibre.

Ian Ashbee: We should have won that game. It was just a case of learning. You make mistakes, but if you keep making them that's when you fall by the wayside. That afternoon we were brilliant on a big pitch against a side that had just come down from the Premier League. To go there and put in that performance – a really good performance not a lucky one – it showed that we were getting to grips with it. The players that hadn't played at that level before were getting to grips with it, the new players were doing well. We were all pushing forward and going in the right direction.

To play so well at one of the division's big guns provided a huge boost to City. And things were to get better on Boxing Day at home to Wolves, in a game that saw Richard Garcia playing a starring role.

Richard Garcia: We had been gathering momentum and improving as a group from the start of the season. Our performances and our understanding of what the management wanted was getting better but I still don't think we had any thoughts of going up. We were just chipping away at it.

Mike Hall: Despite this being our third season in the Championship, the club, to me, still hadn't attained the stature of the likes of Wolves. Wolves were having a good season when they visited the KC, but we comprehensively outplayed them in the second half, winning 2-0. Unless I'm misremembering it, the first goal seemed to involve about 20 to 25 passes before it was finished off by Richard Garcia. It was the kind of team goal also-rans just don't tend to score. After that game I definitely felt as though something special might be happening.

Fraizer Campbell scored the second to seal a 2-0 win. Attention then turned to a Yorkshire derby against Sheffield Wednesday at the KC. Dean Windass hadn't scored since his brace at Scunthorpe a month earlier. His introduction was to prove decisive here though.

Dean Windass: Phil left me out. I was a bit gutted being left out of a derby. But then Frazier pulled his hamstring, which left me and Caleb up front. With the free-kicks me and Daws would take them in training, and this one was left to me and it won the game for us.

The free-kick had gone in the postage stamp of the postage stamp, and demonstrated just what a wide array of skills Windass had at his disposal.

A New Year's Day tie at Stoke was a big test of City's recent run of form. Stoke were fourth in the table, but despite going one-nil up through former City defender Leon Cort, the Potters were pegged back by a 61st-minute Caleb Folan equaliser.

Caleb Folan: In among all of this, I never had a sense of how important certain goals were. After that game I was gutted with my performance. I walked off the pitch thinking: 'I was rubbish today.' That was the beauty of that season – we were just concerned with being better and that was the key to our success.

Three wins and two draws in the past five games, and spirits in the camp were high. But had expectation levels been raised a few notches?

Fraizer Campbell: From the beginning I was just overtaken by being out on loan and playing every week, so it was already a great experience for me, but around Christmas time we changed a little bit and we started getting those wins. People started to see us as promotion candidates.

Nick Barmby: Everyone was experienced in the Championship knowing what needed to be done. We had energy in the team. With Phil Brown, he'd drill into you in training that everyone closes down, we close down as a team. Even if we weren't playing well we were a hard team to play against. The back four was settled, the lads up front would cause chaos. Everyone knew that against a Phil Brown team you've got to work hard, and everyone bought in to what Phil was trying to do.

Dave Burns: After the new year I was talking about booking hotels near Wembley and only half joking. I could see something happening.

City had broken into the top 10 for the first time in the season, but were to lose their next two matches – a third round FA Cup game at Plymouth and a televised home match against top-of-the-table West Brom, in which both teams looked hugely impressive. However, on-pitch matters suddenly seemed unimportant as a devastating piece of news came out of the club. Popular goalkeeper Matt Duke was diagnosed with testicular cancer.

Matt Duke: I found a lump and went to see the club doctor, who sent me off for a scan. They called me back in the next day for an ultrasound scan. I had that scan and they asked me to wait in the reception as there was some paperwork to sort. At the time I just thought it was a bit strange but didn't think much of it. Two minutes later the doctor popped his head around the door and asked me to come in and explained what they'd found. The shock just hits you. I tried to contact my wife, but there was no answer, so I rang Simon Maltby but I couldn't talk to him on the phone. I couldn't get my words out. I was just in shock. But the club was fantastic. Phil Brown just told me to take all the time that I needed to get myself right, which I did. Thankfully it wasn't too long before I was back.

Simon Maltby: I have a medical degree, and I'd worked for the NHS, and part of your role is being able to spot serious issues such as testicular cancer. Dukey was different class. I wasn't involved too much in his rehab, because it's not the kind of injury we would deal with, but I directed him to the right places and when he came back, he was strong. It was devastating for him though, as it would be for anybody. Everything had been going so well for him, then you get hit with that. I felt for him. But it was caught early and he went on to do some great things. When he came back to the club all you could do was be supportive and ease him back into training. We did everything we could to look after him.

Matt Duke: I was getting loads of messages from my team-mates, which I kept for a long time. When I came back to see people during the treatment everyone was great. The lads were amazing. I can't thank them enough for how they were with me.

Boaz Myhill: You are just there for people when they need you, when they want to talk. It was unreal really, but Phil Brown at the time was telling us before games: "This is for Dukey." When the lads were down or when things weren't going so well, Phil would say: "You don't know how lucky you are, lads. You've got a perfect example of how things can change at the drop of a hat." To see how he came back afterwards was the most impressive thing. He really did fight it. He's a brave man.

Ian Ashbee: It's one of your family members going through a tough time. There were a lot of tough things that happened over my years at City that brought us closer together as a team, but we knew this was a tough one. People like Boaz, Ryan France and Daws were terrific at the time, being Matt's close friends, and you can only offer as much support as possible. Matt had a lot of good people around him. But as a team were we always there for each other, no matter what, and we were there for Matt Duke throughout that time. It was a tough one for Matt, but he came through it. He's a great bloke and he was fantastic throughout that time.

Nick Barmby: For me, the model of a professional footballer is seen not when he's playing, but when he's not playing. What is he like around the players? Yes, you're not going to be happy, you want to play, but you train hard and you let the manager know that you're there, banging on the door. Dukey knew that Bo was number one and was a fantastic goalkeeper, and Matt Duke helped him no end. The relationship they had was competitive – as it should be – but Duke's support of Bo was fantastic, and vice versa. When the bad news came in it hit all of us because he's one of us, a great lad. You feel for him and his family. But he never moaned. He was never saying: "Why me?" I think very highly of Matt Duke and his family.

Paul Duffen: Any football club training ground is a very closely knit group of players, especially one that isn't populated by prima donnas and world stars. The work ethic, the unity and the fraternity of a training ground is quite something. Everybody just supported him as one. The only focus was on Matt getting the best possible care he could and of us supporting him as best as we possibly could, but that was only ever going to be with moral support and love and friendship. That time brought out the best of the football club. It became something that was a focal point for everybody and it was very important for us.

After the West Brom game, City were due to set off for some warm weather training. However, one player, one of the most popular at the club, wouldn't be going. Damien's Delaney's time at Hull City was sadly at an end.

Damien Delaney: It came out of nowhere for me. We were getting ready to go out to a warm weather training camp. I was in Princes Quay doing some shopping and my phone rang. It was Gianni Palladini from QPR. I thought it was a wind-up, and I was thinking: 'What's going on here?' He said they'd agreed a fee with Hull and could I go down there. We were going away the next day and it was the first I'd heard of any of this. About five minutes afterwards Phil Brown rang me to say they'd accepted a bid from QPR. Once the club's accepted a bid for you, you know you're done. It wasn't a case of me wanting to leave or throwing my toys out of the pram. I was getting ready to go away with the team. You've got to be realistic though. When a club is willing to sell you it means they don't want you any more. I was never going to hang around where I wasn't wanted.

Phil Brown: Some of these decisions have to be made for the betterment of the team, and to be brutally honest I didn't think that Damien would go on to have the career that he's had, and I take my hat off to him. I don't think I got much wrong, but Damien would be one I got wrong. But he wouldn't have got in the first team ahead of Wayne Brown – who was outstanding for us – or Andy Dawson – who was also outstanding. But it may have been the wrong move to get rid of him.

Andy Dawson: I forgive him for injuring me within a couple of weeks of me joining Hull City! Damien could play centre-half, left-back – he took my place at times – and he was always a true professional who'd give everything he's got, every day. And he was another winner. In those promotions that we had, there's no coincidence that we had a lot of winners in the group who demanded from each other. Damien went on to do fantastically well and it doesn't surprise me.

Jason Price: He just stood out. Left-footed, quick, 6 foot 3, and he could play. You knew he was a player for the future. He's done really well for himself.

Nick Barmby: He was a player you knew would go on and do well. There was something in Damo. He hadn't been coached much before he came to City, playing in Ireland, but he was athletic, willing to learn, a great lad, but a tough kid who wanted everything to be done professionally. You knew that he'd go on to do well, and I'm really pleased that that happened for him.

Damien Delaney: My time at Hull City means everything to me. It was the place that gave me a proper start in the game, a platform for my career. It was a club that believed in me, and the fans eventually believed in me. To be part of what was arguably the best period in Hull City's history is fantastic. The day you sign for a football club and the day you leave; if you can leave it in a better state than when you joined, then you've done your job. I felt that the club had changed in my time there, both on and off the pitch, and it was fantastic. You can look back in 10 or 20 years' time and say you were a part of it. It was such a special period. I enjoyed every minute of it. I always look for Hull's results on a Saturday to see how they've got on. It's a place that will always be special to my heart.

Peter Taylor: Damien was always such a lovely lad, and seeing him playing in the 2016 FA Cup Final for Crystal Palace was a very nice feeling.

Damien Delaney: When Hull were relegated at Selhurst Park in 2017 I went over to the Hull fans to commiserate and show them I cared. All of a sudden, in the middle of that despair, they started singing: "Damo's a Tiger!" I just thought: 'Jesus.'

Another legend of the back-to-back promotions was to see his time at the club come to an end, as Stuart Elliott – who had just months left on his contract – joined Doncaster for the rest of the season. It was a sad end for one of the club's greatest ever goalscorers.

Stuart Elliott: It was a new regime, new manager, new chairman, and Phil had asked me if I wanted to go to Southend as they'd offered £250,000 for me. I didn't want to move there and there was a bit of a tug-of-war as Phil wanted the money. There was a bit of tension at that particular time and I was made to train with the reserves, which I felt was a bit disrespectful considering what I'd given to the club over the years, but it was nothing major. Towards the final few days of the January transfer window Phil told me I was free to go speak to other clubs, and Sean O'Driscoll at Doncaster showed an interest in signing me on a free transfer. My family could stay in Hull, so it worked out well for me. But it was tremendously emotional for me to leave though, as Hull City were more than just a football club to me. The club meant everything to me. I could never have achieved what I achieved at Hull City without the players that I had around me. I know it sounds like an old cliché but it's more than that for me as my team-mates were absolutely brilliant. It was such a family atmosphere at the time. From the backroom staff to the media guys, it was one big family. No one thought they were better than anyone else.

I did want to stay in Hull because I had a very good church there which had a lot of people that I loved and cared for and I didn't want to upset the applecart as far as that was concerned. That's why the move to Doncaster was important to me. As much as I loved football, my Christian faith always came first.

Andy Dawson: A fantastic fella, but a matchwinner. When we got promoted from League 1 I remember sometimes there'd be nothing in certain games and Stuey would just score for us. I'll never forget the Brentford game, when Stuey was just inside their half and he turned and hit it after getting the ball from a throw in. I said to myself: 'Stuey, what are you doing?' which I used to say a lot, and it ended up in the back of the net. But that was just him as an individual. He was a matchwinner. Somebody scoring 30 goals from left wing? That just doesn't happen. It won't happen again, in any league. He's a massive, massive part of why the club is where it is now. Those players are hard to find.

Alfie Potts Harmer: Stuart Elliott epitomised the most enjoyable time supporting Hull City for me. He was, of course, incredibly prolific for a wide player, and simply unstoppable in that 2004-05 season, then there was his unerring ability to seemingly get up early and float in the air before powering the ball past the goalkeeper with his head. Elliott was a real joy to watch during what was a great time to be a City fan.

Ian Bunton: The one player that sticks with me is Stuart Elliott. I felt he was pivotal in those early promotions, ghosting in on the back post. Everything he seemed to hit just went in!

Rob Harmer: You always knew that while Stuart Elliott was on the pitch, something special could (and probably would) happen. I've yet to see another player, at any club, who could hang in the air like he could.

Mike Scott: Stuart Elliott was my standout player for the 2000s. He had a fierce desire to run, he was as direct as a punch in the face, he had an interesting back story and he contributed freely to our ascent up the leagues. Ash was the undoubted fulcrum of that team, with Barmby added later, but Stuey provided the flow of goals that delivered for Peter Taylor's Tigers.

Jason Price: He'd score from anywhere. He could shoot from 40 yards and score. Sunderland wanted him at one point but he didn't seem to want to move!

Steve Lee: Jan Molby could certainly spot a player and, for me, Stuart Elliott became the single most important cog in a team that just seemed to click. When you consider we paid £230,000 for him, he also had to be the biggest bargain since the £40,000 we stuffed down Mansfield's bra for Ken Wagstaff.

Rich Lusmore: My favourite City player of the era has to be Stuart Elliott, and not only because he was such an integral part of a very successful City side. He also garners my affection due to being a naturally left-sided player (like me) and the clincher that he's a Glenman (my favourite Northern Irish team)! The late winner against Doncaster in December 2004 in front of a near full house readily springs to mind. It was one of 29 goals for the winger in that promotion year – which, given he missed several weeks out due to injury, was some achievement.

Craig Sargent: A bit like Andy Payton back in the day, Stuart Elliot seemed to be able to score at will and made it look easy. Never had I seen a City player leap so high to head the ball and his shooting technique just seemed to be 'hit it really, really hard'. It worked though, and for a couple of seasons he was simply unplayable. I even remembered travelling up to Old Trafford to watch his Northern Ireland team play England, secretly hoping he would hit the net. He didn't but back in 2005 an international footballer with 'Hull City' next to his name was still relatively rare. I was proud he was ours, and proud to have witnessed the flying winger from Belfast.

With legends filling the departure lounge, City fans were cheered by the return from injury of one veteran from the Peter Taylor years.

Ryan France: When I returned the team was more competitive to get in, and I couldn't get in. They were doing really, really well. We'd got a bit more of that team spirit that we'd had a few years previously. We felt as though we were going to win each game we went into. I came back at Plymouth away and played quite well. It was nice to get back to playing football.

Good teams 'win ugly', as many a pundit will claim, and Hull City were to prove that this quality was part of the club's armoury. A miserable late January night match at the KC against Coventry saw City win 1-0 thanks to a last-minute goal from Caleb Folan.

Caleb Folan: It was one of those goals – it wasn't a lump forward it was a ball for me to run on to, which was one of my strengths. The players knew I'd get on to it. Wayne Brown played it forward, I remember the defenders misjudging it, it bounced up to me and I'd seen the keeper off his line and my only choice was to help it over. As soon as I hit it I knew it was going in.

A few days later, another single-goal victory came at Home Park, Plymouth, with Dean Windass poaching the winner to claim the three points. City's good form – 17 points out of the last 24 on offer – was starting to prick up a few ears.

1. **West Brom P30, W16, D6, L8, Pts 54**
2. **Watford P30, W15, D7, L8, Pts 52**
3. **Bristol City P30, W14, D9, L7, Pts 51**
4. **Stoke City P30, W13, D11, L6, Pts 50**
5. **Charlton P30, W13, D8, L9, Pts 47**
6. **Ipswich P30, W12, D9, L9, Pts 45**
7. **Crystal Palace P30, W11, D12, L7, Pts 45**
8. **Hull City P29, W12, D8, L9, Pts 44**

Paul Duffen: We had a good blend. We had the old heads such as Dean Windass and Nicky Barmby, we had the experience of Ryan France, Bo Myhill, Ash, Andy Dawson and the combination of those things really started to gel. The whole squad was acting as one unit. We knew we had the capability on our day to beat anybody. By the time we got to the turn of the year we'd had games such as the draw at Charlton where we'd started believing in ourselves. And that's the hardest thing. Also, Phil and Brian had worked out what the best team looked like and what the best formations were. There wasn't one trigger point but the momentum and self-belief was building and certainly from the turn of the year I just felt it had become a self-fulfilling prophecy. We'd ridden our luck a little bit but after January we were the form side and suddenly there was talk about automatic promotion.

Any promotion talk quietened a little in February when three draws in three games provided a disappointing return. City came back from 2-0 down at the KC to draw with Blackpool thanks to goals from Folan and Windass. A Fraizer Campbell goal gave City a share of the spoils at Norwich, and the same player was again on the mark in a home 1-1 draw against lowly Colchester.

Every successful season needs 'the game'. Hull City were about to have theirs at the Hawthorns.

Wayne Brown: When you go to the bigger clubs, the bigger stadia, there's always a good atmosphere. There was a lot of expectation on West Brom to do well that season – which they did – but you want to pit your wits against the best in the division.

The Tigers shocked their hosts by taking the lead through a goal by Fraizer Campbell that was so good it looked like the City team was being controlled by a particularly advanced 12-year-old playing FIFA on the PlayStation.

Fraizer Campbell: I remember getting fouled and having a dead leg. I was hobbling a bit and then Jay-Jay passed me the ball and I turned. I'd have liked to have run with it but my leg was hurting so I thought: 'Well I'll just have to hit it from here.' It couldn't have come off any better. Henrik Pedersen was shouting to me on my right, and he told me after the game he'd have been fuming if I hadn't scored because he was totally free.

West Brom equalised in the 42nd minute through Roman Bednar, and going into the final 10 minutes it looked as though City were going to hold on for an unexpected point away to what many people considered the division's best team. However, in the 82nd minute the ball fell to Caleb Folan – who'd developed a nice habit of scoring crucial late goals – on City's left-hand side…

Caleb Folan: We were breaking forward after we'd won the ball in defence. I'd gone out wide because I wanted to see what was in front of me. Henrik Pedersen got the ball to me. As soon as I got it no one seemed to come and close me down. In my head I was hearing 'go at em, go at em' and I thought I'd just see how far I could take it. I remember getting into a position where I thought I might as well cut in, and it just felt so easy, it was so strange. I was just walking past players. There was no urgency to close me down. I remember thinking: 'Why not try a shot?' It wasn't a rocket, I just wanted to hit the target. Then I thought: 'Flipping heck it's gone in, that was alright.' After that I was looking at the fans thinking: 'Wow, they're going mental!' That's when it hit me and I started to get a bit emotional, standing there thinking: 'Come on!' That was a great performance, and it felt good. It felt like a Premier League game in that stadium with that atmosphere.

A famous 2-1 victory was sealed and City fans started to believe that something special was brewing.

Ian Ashbee: Back home to where I'm from. A great stadium, we were given no chance, and we played really well on the day again. It's a great place to go and things were beginning to look good for us. We looked powerful, we looked strong, set-pieces were looking good and we were working hard for each other. Once you've got that sort of determination, with a little bit of quality sprinkled in among it all, we were looking like a good outfit.

Michael Turner: They were near the top of the league. Going there and winning was just amazing. Coming away from that it was a massive confidence booster. Having Caleb, Fraizer and Dean Windass, we had the firepower there. We had the potential to do something special. We were always going to score goals. All three of them were a threat but in different ways and that made us the team we were.

Sam Ricketts: That was a really big game. They were at the top and my first game for Hull had been an away game at the Hawthorns. It was a hard place to go, we knew it would be tough, and to go there and win with a great goal like that which Caleb scored gave us a big belief that we could beat anyone in that league. I wouldn't say it was a turning point, but it was another piece of the jigsaw where our belief grew. We just carried on going and going and improving.

Mike Hall: This was really the game where we knew we'd arrived as a serious player in the promotion scene. West Brom were that season's stand-out Championship team, with a squad that looked like a Premier League outfit in all but name. They'd beaten us the previous month 3-1 at the KC Stadium and I'm quite sure I had expectations of a similar defeat as we travelled to the Hawthorns. Leaving the ground having won 2-1 with an assured, polished performance, I'm sure I wasn't alone in thinking that this was more than an impressive run of form – it was a genuine promotion push.

Martin Batchelor: That was the game we thought for the first time that this year really might be our season. It was so good we missed the train home.

Fraizer Campbell: We were just getting on with it. Everyone was honest, no star players. We got our heads down and worked hard together. There was very little pressure on us as no one expected us to be there and thereabouts.

Richard Garcia: For me this is the game where the belief and attitude grew into a promotion-winning team. We had been doing really well up to this point but we began to have the mentality that we wouldn't lose. And momentum really grew.

Phil Brown: We had quite a following that day. When you look at what West Brom have done over the past 15 or 20 years you've got to take your hat off to them. They are very memorable days and you start to wonder what is possible. That was one of the believing moments. When you go to places like the Hawthorns and win you start to think: 'This is possible.'

Boaz Myhill: You walk in the Hawthorns, particularly when you've been in the lower leagues, and you can't help but feel inspired. It was a good result as West Brom had a lot of top players at the time who'd come down from the Premier League. It was yet another example of us coming up against something different and finding a way through it.

Phil Buckingham: That was such a landmark game. Even after City had signed Jay-Jay and Fraizer they were still getting walloped in the December. At that point you'd have thought there was no chance of the club going up. But at West Brom, they were clearly the best team in that division that season, so for City to go there and not just win, but deservedly win, was terrific. They just looked the part. You suddenly felt that they had a swagger to go to a team like that. You can't underestimate what that win will have done for Hull City's confidence. Everyone was sitting up and saying: "Blimey!"

Paul Duffen: The nice thing about that game was that West Brom were a club with a lot more experience in the higher leagues than Hull City and had become a yo-yo club between the Premier League and the Championship. We went there and it was quite intrepid for us; it was very formal in the boardroom with men and women sat on separate tables, and there was a real formality about it, which was quite imposing. I think the game itself came at a time when we were in our stride and we had the confidence. It was Fraizer's masterclasses as a game. The most significant thing I remember was just before half time I thought: 'We belong in this company. We're not overawed.' That was a lovely feeling. I felt we had nothing to fear.

Brendon Smurthwaite: I remember thinking: 'Wow, we might get in the play-offs here.' Paul Duffen had been instilling the whole 'dare to dream' thing into all the staff, putting the logo in big letters in the tunnel. We were cynical among the backroom staff, but Browny got the players to believe it, and after we'd won at West Brom everyone believed it. We started to get national journalists taking an interest then too.

Andy Dawson: When you win certain games, people start looking at you and saying: "Wow!" That's what happened when we beat West Brom at their place. They were near the top of the table, had Premier League players and it had me thinking: 'We could actually go up here.' We all believed it and the run we went on after that was unbelievable. I went to the League Cup final – Tottenham versus Chelsea – the day after that because Mike was involved. I sat in Wembley thinking: 'If we could actually get here…'

1. **Stoke P35, W17, D11, L7, Pts 62**
2. **Bristol City P34, W17, D10, L7, Pts 61**
3. **Watford P34, W17, D9, L8, Pts 60**
4. **West Brom P33, W16, D7, L10, Pts 55**
5. **Plymouth P34, W14, D10, L10, Pts 52**
6. **Charlton P34, W14, D10, L10, Pts 52**
7. **Ipswich P34, W14, D9, L11, Pts 51**
8. **Hull City P33, W13, D11, L9, Pts 50**

The squad was strengthened when a familiar face was brought back to add further depth up front and in the wide positions.

Craig Fagan: I'd had a decent spell at Derby under Billy Davies and then Paul Jewell came in and he just wasn't right for me. I still had a house in Hull, and the club still meant a lot to me, so when they came in it was a no-brainer. I just wanted to get playing again and get some form back.

The standard had risen again. The players that had been signed had put loads of goals in the team, and confidence was high. It was just like Derby when I'd gone there a year earlier.

March was to prove a busy month for City, with eight games to be played. The first was a trip to Ashton Gate to play a Bristol City side that stood second in the table. The home side ran out 2-1 winners on the day, but Bristol City would keep.

City needed to get back on track, and a midweek home game against Burnley provided just that opportunity. The Tigers won 2-0 with goals from Fraizer Campbell and Richard Garcia, a scoreline that flattered the visitors as City played some dazzling football that had even the most cynical of fans drooling. The match was marred, however, by some typically inept refereeing from Mike Riley, who sent off four players, including Jay-Jay Okocha and Caleb Folan for City.

Matt Rudd: Richard Garcia's shot against Burnley at the KC in 2008 seemed to be initiated from an adjacent postal district.

This was followed by a derby match against Scunthorpe, in which City played a brand of football more akin to the Dutch sides of the 1970s. Michael Turner sealed a 2-0 win after Henrik Pedersen had broken the deadlock.

Henrik Pedersen: Scoring in a local derby is always a great feeling, and of course the fans love you even more if you score against the local rivals. I remember that we missed a big chance after just a minute or two, and my goal came after a long throw, and some ping-pong in the box, and then a header from close range. A win in a local derby is the best feeling.

A trip to Wales saw City lose by a single goal to Cardiff. This was followed by a big game for City. Southampton – the side that had dished out a four-goal thrashing in December – were to visit the KC. Revenge was secured, and a famous 5-0 victory saw five different goalscorers hit the back of the net: Fraizer Campbell, Henrik Pedersen, Michael Turner, Dean Marney and Bryan Hughes.

Paul Duffen: If you wanted any clear indication of progress or how the team had evolved, those two games against Southampton provide it. A nine-goal swing was an indicator to us that we'd got it right.

Phil Brown: We had five different scorers that day, and that's a really good tell-tale sign, and we had a nine-goal turnaround within the space of a few months. All of those things were really vivid in my mind at the time, telling me we were going to run automatic promotion close. We were building momentum and belief. It was like we were walking on water. It was surreal. The people of the city were just breezing through things. It was above normal.

Bryan Hughes: You could just see the confidence now. I'd been injured against Blackpool and out for a little while. I'd been watching from the sidelines, with Henrik Pedersen playing very well on the left. We started to get a real team spirit, and we were growing in confidence. You could see it off the pitch too. There were many times when we'd all be going out together or going for meals together. That helped us that season massively.

Dean Windass: I'd been out for seven or eight weeks. I had a baker's cyst on my knee. I didn't think I'd get back playing. I thought that was it. Something exploded behind my knee and my calf was like a rugby ball. I stayed at home for two or three weeks because I was on crutches and couldn't move. But Simon Maltby was brilliant. He worked wonders and got me back. In that game, I just sensed something in the group, that we had something special. We went out together, we'd go out with the wives and the girlfriends, we had a great group. We trusted each other, and we still meet up to this day. We all seemed to be sensing the same things. I trusted Sam, Daws, Turns and Wayne at the back, Boaz in goal, Ash sitting in midfield, and they trusted me, Fraizer and Caleb to score goals. When you add to that Brian Hughes or Henrik Pedersen on the left, Richard Garcia on the right and Dean Marney pushing on in midfield, that was a good team. After that game we thought: 'Oh, hang on a minute…'

Mike White: The near symmetry of it told me that something special was happening. The 4-0 defeat in December had seemed like a real low point, so that was put to bed. But when you looked at how dominant we were, you thought: 'This looks like a team that will really contend things for the rest of the season.' We found out that that fifth goal cost a City fan a few thousand quid. He'd had a bet on City winning 4-0, but then Hughes burst down the left-hand side and slotted it away in stoppage time.

Dean Marney: I remember after that Southampton game, as they still had some good players, thinking we were going to take some stopping. It could easily have been 7-0 or 8-0 and Nigel Pearson, their manager, was apologising to their fans after the game. I felt that we were the team that everyone didn't want to play.

Indeed, the thrashing had been so comprehensive that the opposition manager Nigel Pearson – a future Hull City boss and the great-nephew of City legend Paddy Mills – issued an apology to the travelling fans. He needn't have. City would have hammered any side from the division that day.

Ee-aye, ee-aye, ee-aye o, into the top five we go.

1. **Stoke P39, W18, D13, L8, Pts 67**
2. **Bristol City P39, W18, D13, L8, Pts 67**
3. **Watford P38, W17, D13, L8, Pts 64**
4. **West Brom P37, W18, D8, L11, Pts 62**
5. **Hull City P38, W16, D11, L11, Pts 59**

Rob Smith: In February I'd started doing the BBC predictor, and was thinking: 'Wow, that result would put us in sixth, that result would put us in fifth.' Then when we played Colchester away, all of a sudden I started to really get excited.

Colchester away was a rearranged fixture from January, when the game had been cancelled at a very late stage with a lot of bad blood involved. Layer Road had also been the scene of one of City's most depressing defeats of the past few years when a 5-1 hammering had all but put an end to Phil Parkinson's tenure at the club. There was to be no repeat this evening. Not with this team.

Paul Duffen: I'd always had an indelible focus on how football fans are the emotional shareholders of a football club. To me, filling a football ground is the most important thing. The away support Hull City had enjoyed for decades had been resilient through hell or high water. I felt the way the first Colchester fixture had been cancelled at such short notice was completely unreasonable and apart from doing all we could do as a club for the rearranged fixture – such as providing travel – I felt it was appropriate to go in the away end. I also went to the pub before the game to show solidarity with the fans.

Fraizer Campbell was to destroy Colchester on the night, causing Phil Ifil to get himself sent off after 14 minutes, and then scoring in the 20th and 33rd minutes to put City 2-0 up. Colchester pulled one back in the 37th minute to cause a few palpitations among the City faithful, but the Tigers still had supersub Caleb Folan to come off the bench. However, the reason he was on the bench was unknown to all but a few.

Caleb Folan: We'd had a big win on the Saturday. I'd see Paul Duffen round Leeds quite a lot as that was where he was based. We had a Tuesday game so the gaffer said that we'd be in training on the Sunday and no one was to go out that night, they should just relax. Paul was in the changing room and he looked at me and smiled...

I decided to go into Leeds that night for a few drinks and I bumped into Paul in one of the bars! He looked at me and I thought: 'Oh shit.' He came over to me and said: "What are you doing? You've got training in the morning," so I told him I was just leaving. I was thinking: 'Oh no, I've had a nightmare here.' And then it got worse!

On the Sunday morning my phone started going off. I thought it was my alarm clock so I was trying to press the snooze button. The noise stopped but then it kept going off and I realised it was my phone ringing. It was Brian Horton. I was half asleep and he hammered me down the phone because I'd slept in. He hung up on me, and he wouldn't pick up when I rang back, so I rang Simon Maltby to ask what to do. He said to ring the gaffer. It took me an hour to pluck up the courage. When I finally explained myself Phil started chuckling. He said: "It happens, thanks for calling, see you tomorrow." The next day I got a bit of a telling off, and the day after we travelled down to Colchester. Obviously I was dropped from the starting 11, but I was on the bench.

Brian Horton: We were out training on the Sunday and all of a sudden someone said: "Where's Caleb?" Phil said to me: "Give him a call to see what he's doing and what he's thinking." So I rang him and woke him up. It must have been 11 o'clock. I said to him: "Caleb, we are training you know," and he just said: "Oh my god, I'm still asleep." He was fined, which he accepted, and we got on with it…

Caleb was to come on and score the goal that would seal the game.

Caleb Folan: When I came on and scored – Dean Marney put me through one on one – I put my hands to the side of my head and people have always asked me what I was doing. I was acting as though I was sleeping. After the game Brian Horton saw me, laughed and clipped me around the ear. But it was all forgotten about after that goal. It was like a family in that you'd get told off, but it was like your dad telling you off. You just had to show you were taking things on board.

Brian Horton: We gave them a right good hiding that night. It was a good spirit. The work rate and the spirit throughout the whole club was just incredible.

Mike Scott: A spring Tuesday evening in Essex, a Fraizer Campbell masterclass that left Channel 5 pundit Adam Virgo in an advanced state of vertigo, a raw screaming away end and the continued realisation that these Tigers really did mean it, they were headed for the top three. Palpable excitement at the end of the game as Paul Duffen mingled with the fans outside the away end. Innocent times, yes. When supporting City was a pleasure, not an endurance test.

Leicester at the Walkers Stadium were up next. No problem. A 2-0 win ensued, with goals from Dean Marney and Caleb Folan. City even had the luxury of missing a penalty.

Alfie Potts Harmer: The Leicester game seemed like such a routine 2-0 win, and very un-City'ish.

Ee-aye, ee-aye, ee-aye o, into the top three we go.

1. Stoke P40, W18, D14, L8, Pts 68
2. Bristol City P40, W18, D13, L9, Pts 67
3. Hull City P40, W18, D11, L11, Pts 65
4. Watford P39, W17, D14, L8, Pts 65
5. West Brom P38, W18, D9, L11, Pts 63

The routine wins were coming thick and fast. A Watford side that were level on points with City but had a game in hand were next. What looked likely to be a close game proved to be anything but. Michael Turner scored in the first minute, with Frazier Campbell adding a second in the 13th. Substitute Caleb Folan did the business again by sealing a 3-0 win in the 73rd minute, just before the visitors had Steve Kabba sent off. A victory by a three-goal margin against Watford at the KC. That's got a nice ring to it, don't you think?

However important the win was, more important was the presence on the bench of a certain goalkeeper.

Matt Duke: The club were doing well pushing for the play-offs and I just wanted to get back. It came a bit sooner than I'd expected as Mark Tyler was in on loan and he got injured, so Phil asked me if I was OK to come back. I'd been training for a few weeks and I just wanted to get back to normality.

A 1-1 draw against QPR at the KC only came thanks to an injury time Michael Turner goal – though TV footage was to suggest that the QPR 'goal' hadn't crossed the line. This point left the table looking particularly enticing.

1. Stoke P43, W19, D15, L9, Pts 72
2. West Brom P42, W20, D11, L11, Pts 71
3. Bristol City P43, W19, D14, L10, Pts 71
4. Hull City P42, W19, D12, L11, Pts 69
5. Watford P43, W18, D15, L10, Pts 69

Just over a season ago, Hull City's 3-0 defeat at Barnsley had represented a particularly grim low point in a season full of low points. City were utterly abject, and the shoulder shrug by Ian Ashbee after the final whistle had, however unfairly, brought much condemnation upon the inspirational skipper.

Such memories were now firmly banished. The Ian Ashbee that strode out onto the Oakwell pitch on Tuesday, April 15th was our gladiator, our lion, our colossus, our leader. His never-say-die attitude and his inability to accept second best had set the template for this Hull City side. He scored City's second goal with a brilliant glancing header off a corner in the 52nd minute after a Dean Marney penalty – awarded after Frazier Campbell had been fouled – had given City the lead. Then on came Dean Windass...

Dean Windass: I knew I wasn't going to be playing two games in a week, so Phil would say: "You're going to be sub on Tuesday night against Barnsley but you'll be playing Saturday against whoever." But the bond that we had with me, Fraizer and Caleb was unbelievable. Me and Caleb accepted that Fraizer was number one and me and him would be taking it in turns to be number two. As Phil would say: "Everybody was singing from the same hymn sheet."

When Ash scored the header the atmosphere was unbelievable. Phil said: "Go on and get me a goal to wrap this game up." And with my first touch, Fraizer back-heeled it and I scored. Maybe the keeper should have saved it but I didn't care. It was just incredible.

Alfie Potts Harmer: That header by Ash, the celebration and Deano coming on to score with his first touch all live long in the memory, and automatic promotion looked like a real possibility.

Craig Fagan: Games like that are what I enjoy. Knowing we'd be in second place if we won was just motivational to me. And what a result! It was a massive step towards us getting promoted. Barnsley's a tough place to go so that was a big result.

Bryan Hughes: That game stands out for me. That was the game that showed we were on the cusp of doing something special. We were already building momentum but on that night we played some great stuff. The fans behind the goal, Ian Ashbee scoring that header from the corner, it was just electric. You could see the team was growing together. Everyone knew everyone's roles and responsibilities. I was playing on the left, even though I wanted to be in the centre, building up a good partnership with Andy Dawson. Everything just seemed to be clicking. There were great partnerships all over the pitch: Sam Ricketts and Richard Garcia on the right, Daws and myself on the left, Ash and Dean Marney were starting to get a bit of a partnership in the midfield, Dean and Fraizer had hit it off up front, and then obviously the partnership at the back between Michael Turner and Wayne Brown was phenomenal. And everyone would dig in for each other. You'd have spells away from home where you'd be under the cosh for five or 10 minutes, and we were standing up to these teams.

Andy Dawson: Fraizer could win a game from nothing. That's a tough game. We'd been on a good run of form but you're thinking: 'Can we continue it?' We kept on answering the questions that everyone was asking though.

Paul Duffen: It signified the fact that we had the most momentum. Bristol City had been in the top two slots for much of the season and were then on the wane, and at that time we looked like we were powerful and potent. Going to Barnsley and winning 3-1 at that time in the season was one of the most satisfying games. It felt like a job well done.

Phil Brown: All the games just married up; it was a miasma of great wins. But then you get a bit expectant of it. The supporters must have been thinking: 'Where did this come from?' The people of Hull, the staff, the players, we were floating six foot above everybody.

Ee-aye, ee-aye, ee-aye o, into the automatic spots we go.

1. **West Brom P43, W21, D11, L11, Pts 74**
2. **Hull City P43, W20, D12, L11, Pts 72 (plus 20)**
3. **Stoke P43, W19, D15, L9, Pts 72 (plus 12)**
4. **Bristol City P43, W19, D14, L10, Pts 71**
5. **Watford P43, W18, D15, L10, Pts 69**

As City fans were staring disbelievingly at the table, some tragic news was to break. A 10-year-old City fan on his way to his first away game – Billy Fletcher – had been killed in a car crash en route to Barnsley.

Paul Duffen: We didn't know the details before kick-off. We knew there'd been bad traffic but we didn't know the details. It was incredibly humbling. As a group of footballers, the team are focused on their performance and on winning, and the management are focused on supporting them, which can make you blinkered. It's about results. We were feeling pretty good about ourselves, thinking we'd broken a threshold regarding our performances. To have something as levelling as the death of a young lad travelling to a game of football, it does give you a stark reminder of perspective. It was a horrendous shock. His family were great and wanted the team to keep on playing positively and the lads were great in supporting the family. It was a very sad moment.

Ian Ashbee: A lot of the lads had young children around that age. A young kid travelling to a football game and losing his life… it's just devastating beyond words. The club did right by the family. It was something that the lads were affected by.

City went into the final three games of the regular season knowing that they just had to better what Stoke, Bristol City and Watford did to clinch a first ever promotion to the top flight, and thus avoid doing it the hard way through the play-offs. An away match against Sheffield United is never an easy prospect, and so it was to prove on Saturday, April 19th. An injured calf meant that Wayne Brown was out. City had sold Damien Delaney in January and loanee Neil Clement had been recalled by West Brom. Desperate times call for desperate measures, and David Livermore – a midfielder who had been out on loan at Oldham and hadn't featured in a league game since New Year's Day – was selected alongside Michael Turner in City's defence. Even though the home side had Chris Morgan sent off on the stroke of half-time, City just couldn't get to grips with the Blades. Future Tiger Stephen Quinn scored in the 51st minute and James Beattie sealed a 2-0 win with a 72nd-minute penalty.

Brian Horton: We had a disjointed side with David Livermore at left centre-back. We had a few injuries, played poorly and didn't deserve anything out of the game. But you're not going to go through the second half of a season without losing games. Apart from that game and one or two others, we were the best side in the division in that second half of the season.

Michael Turner: I remember Gary Speed playing for Sheffield United and we were all saying before the game that his legs had gone and we should try to get about him, but on the day he was fantastic. That was a tough afternoon and we had great travelling support. Dave Livermore was a great player and a very good midfielder. He was capable of playing centre-back but things didn't go our way that day.

Bryan Hughes: Things didn't quite happen for us that day. I wasn't very well and had been up all night, but I decided to play against the advice of the medical team. But you sometimes need a bit of a jolt to kick-start it again. Sheffield United were very confident that game, knocking it around despite being down to 10 men, and we couldn't get near them. It was a setback and we had to respond.

Paul Duffen: It was a physical game, an intimidating Yorkshire derby. I think it was timely though. Having a setback like that is the launchpad that the manager needed to reset expectations and the realities among his team who may have been playing like they had cigars in the mouths the week before, and now they'd had their pants taken down. So things like that are quite good because you've got to maintain the intensity and motivation throughout the squad. At the time it was horrible but it proved to be very, very useful.

Stoke beat Bristol City 2-1 to move into second, while West Brom pulled further ahead at the top.

1. **West Brom P44, W21, D11, L11, Pts 77**
2. **Stoke P44, W20, D15, L9, Pts 75 (plus 13)**
3. **Hull City P44, W20, D12, L12, Pts 72 (plus 18)**
4. **Bristol City P44, W19, D14, L11, Pts 71**
5. **Watford P44, W18, D15, L11, Pts 69**

In sixth position were Crystal Palace. Managed by Neil Warnock, they had been, along with City, the division's form team in 2008. They came to the KC having won six and drawn four of their previous 10 games. After winning just two of their first 16 games of the season and hovering around the relegation places, they were now in the play-off positions, and were probably the team to avoid within that quartet.

Warnock teams rarely lack confidence, and so it was to prove when Palace came to the KC for the penultimate game of the regular season. However, they soon found themselves 1-0 down thanks to another Fraizer Campbell goal, netting with a deflected shot from just outside the area after brilliantly making room for himself. Dean Windass was having a stormer, but was soon to find himself on the end of a shocking Sean Derry tackle that was to end his game, and potentially his season.

Dean Windass: Phil changed the formation. We went with a diamond and I played behind the forwards. I was running the show. I was told by Michael Bridges that Neil Warnock had told Sean Derry to do me as I was causing too many problems. I saw Sean coming and I didn't feel the impact. But I've since seen it and if I hadn't jumped up he'd have broken my leg. Clint Hill, who was playing for them and who I knew, said: "Dean, you'd better go off, look at your leg." You could see the bone through a rip in the sock. My head went at that point. I was trying to get hold of Derry. It was then when Michael Bridges came into the physio room and told me what Warnock had said that my head really went. That's why I lost my rag at the end when I was on my crutches. I had 55 stitches in my leg. I wanted to hit him with a crutch. Brian Horton was having to stop me. Warnock denied it. We had history from when I was at Sheffield United. I get on with him now though, and that happens in football. Fall-outs like that are part of the game. Thankfully – again – Simon Maltby was unbelievable and got me playing in no time. Simon was a great lad.

Palace equalised through a soft Scott Sinclair goal, and going into the final minutes it seemed that Stoke – 1-0 up at Colchester – were going to seal the second promotion spot. Ian Ashbee, however, had other ideas and in the 85th minute towered above everyone to head home a deliriously celebrated winner. Stoke's champagne would have to stay on ice.

Ian Ashbee: It worked out that that goal didn't mean anything but it kept the season alive and kept the momentum going. It could have fizzled out after that game had we drawn. It was a big, big game against the form team of the division, and the pressure was on. I loved that goal though. It bred a bit of confidence and you need that going into the play-offs.

Paul Duffen: A rare but always cherished Captain Fantastic goal. We turned the Sheffield United game on its head because we were the battling side, we came out looking like we were going to do business, whereas at Sheffield United the week before we were a little bit too showy. We applied ourselves – it was workman-like, it was beautifully organised, it was such a solid performance. We were back focused on the job in hand.

Another positive in the game was the return from injury of Nick Barmby, who came off the bench in the 68th minute.

Nick Barmby: That season – injury wise – was frustrating and disappointing but I was buzzing for the lads. The momentum was growing a long time before this game – the catalyst was the West Brom away game, when the lads thought: 'We've got a chance here.' Momentum is everything in football. To beat Palace, with me sneaking in as sub, was great.

1. **West Brom P45, W22, D11, L11, Pts 78 (plus 31)**
2. **Stoke P45, W21, D15, L9, Pts 78 (plus 14)**
3. **Hull City P45, W21, D12, L12, Pts 75 (plus 19)**
4. **Bristol City P45, W19, D14, L12, Pts 71**
5. **Watford P45, W18, D15, L12, Pts 69**

West Brom were effectively promoted given their vastly superior goal difference. City could finish no lower than third, ensuring their highest league position since 1910. But it was all about the fight between City and Stoke. City had to win at Ipswich – who were eighth and still in with a shout of clinching a play-off spot – and hope that Stoke lost at home to Leicester, who were in 21st position and still in grave danger of going down.

Sadly, a sluggish City never looked like getting anything from the game at Portman Road and lost 1-0 to a 70th-minute Alan Lee goal. Stoke's 0-0 draw against Leicester was enough to clinch them second place, while West Brom sealed the title with a 2-0 win at QPR. City finishing third meant a two-legged play-off against sixth-placed Watford, while Bristol City or Crystal Palace would await the winners at Wembley. So how was the mood in the camp immediately after this disappointment?

Nick Barmby: The best thing that Phil Brown did came after the game when we stopped off at a service station on the A1. We had a beer – just the one! – and Phil said: "Lads, we'll go up through the play-offs. We haven't done it now, but we've got the momentum and we'll do it." I wouldn't say it galvanised the lads as we were close and we were looking forward to the play-offs, but it was just a little thing like where you thought: 'Yeah, we can do this.'

Phil Brown: They're the moments you're born for. It comes from within. Sometimes you look back and you don't know where it came from. I needed to galvanise the group and we stopped off for a bite to eat on the way home and I had to say what needed to be said and get things off my chest. We'd finished the season on a low, but the whole year had been a great high and we deserved to be where we were. If we didn't get in the automatic spots, then we didn't deserve to be there. We just needed to understand what was in front of us. We can only control what we can control and what was in front of us was a two-legged affair against Watford. For it to end up that way left us in the lap of the footballing gods, but we were so tight as a group and the Nick Barmbys and Dean Windasses of this world would have been hurting more than anyone, and for them to be up for the challenge was a testimony to them as people. Nicky and Dean wore that shirt with pride. If anyone ever questioned that we shouldn't have brought them back to their home-town club, then they're deluded.

Bryan Hughes: I was disappointed that we hadn't quite done it automatically, because we had the opportunity. And people were maybe questioning us after the Ipswich game, saying that the bubble had burst. But that led to people underestimating us again. It was a personal goal of Phil's at the start of the season to get us to the play-offs – it wasn't necessarily about us getting automatic promotion – so the fact that we'd got there, he was buzzing about it and that rubbed off on everyone else right through the play-offs. He kept this exuberance going around the training ground and everyone reacted to that. We were quietly confident going into that first Watford game.

Wayne Brown: It was one of those situations where realistically things had been stacked against us in the Ipswich match. There wasn't any resignation to us finishing in the play-offs. We were trying to put pressure on Stoke. You always get to know how other teams are getting on, which is a funny situation to play in. We knew how Stoke were getting on. We lost 1-0, which was disappointing, because I just want to keep clean sheets. But we brushed ourselves down and got on the coach and our preparation was now: 'Forget the game, that's gone, we can't worry about things we can't change, so let's look forward to the Watford game.'

Fraizer Campbell: Obviously we were a bit gutted and frustrated, though it wouldn't have mattered even if we'd won. That mood soon changed to excitement about the play-offs, as that's the best way, if you can hold your nerve, to get promoted. It drags it out that little bit longer and makes it that little bit more special. We knew it was going to be difficult though.

Boaz Myhill: The manager was very upbeat. A lot of us were inexperienced at the level we were playing at, so it was going into the unknown and it was exciting, which was a massive plus for us.

Sam Ricketts: When we were in the top 10 we started aiming at the play-offs. When we got in the play-off position we started aiming at the top two. Had the season had a few more games we'd have got there.

Paul Duffen: After that Palace game we were very much in the mix. The Hull Daily Mail interviewed me before the game and part of my response was based around not wanting to pile pressure on the team and the management, but it was also based around how I felt having come into this incredible family, so I said yes automatic promotion would be fantastic but I feel there is some ridiculous journey that we are travelling on, and the most applicable fulfilment of that journey would be going to Wembley and winning 2-1 with Dean Windass and Nick Barmby scoring the goals. That was the way the story was written in my mind. And winning the play-off final is so much better than winning the league or finishing second.

It undoubtedly is. But you have to get through a two-legged semi-final and then win at Wembley to do it. And should this group of incredible men be successful, they would make history. Hull City had never played at Wembley. Hull City hadn't played top-flight football in the club's 104-year history. Three games stood in our way. There were nerves. There was excitement. There was hope. It was brilliant.

The play-offs

The play-offs weren't exactly new to Hull City. The two prizes on offer should City triumph over Watford, however, were.

Hull City had never played at the old Wembley. This was a source of frustration. Both rugby teams had played there numerous times in the Challenge Cup final. Even local non-league sides North Ferriby United, Brigg Town and Bridlington Town had played upon the hallowed turf. The only time City had been represented at the home of football was when Leigh Jenkinson appeared in the Rumbelows Sprint Challenge in 1992, which didn't really count.

City were two games away from a first ever visit to new Wembley, which had only restarted hosting play-off finals the season previous. And, should they manage that, one game away from a first ever season in the top flight. The stakes couldn't have been higher.

Ian Ashbee: The mood was still good. We'd not been expected to do anything at the start of the season and then we had that lull in the middle. So to go and be in there, we were still confident. There was also an air of never having been in that situation before from many of the lads, and that meant we didn't have that fear, and that helped us. It was just another game. You can't fear something you've never been through. We had to win a couple of games but we'd been beating the big clubs so we didn't feel we had to worry about Watford. Phil's sessions were really good, upbeat, and you didn't feel that if you made a mistake you were going to get ruined for it. Phil was great on the fitness side of things too, which he'd got from Sam Allardyce. We were ready. More ready than we even thought we were, and that's down to Phil getting it right.

Craig Fagan: I didn't doubt anything to be honest. Having been there with Derby I sensed how the lads were. We turned up in big games. Going into the Watford games I had a sense we'd have enough. Browny was tactically right in everything we did, he never left a stone unturned. I just felt confident.

Paul Duffen: I was nervous in the Watford away game. They'd impressed me at their place earlier in the season. They had a lot of seasoned players. But we had the comfort of knowing we had momentum going into the play-offs and they were going the other way. All of us felt a degree of suspending disbelief on a daily basis, but genuinely a sense of destiny. We weren't frightened, we weren't euphoric, we just felt this was part of some unstoppable momentum towards a destiny. It makes me shiver now just talking about it.

Boaz Myhill: If I'd have known what effect those three games would have on my life, I'd have been a lot more nervous. A lot of us didn't know what was happening and just embraced it!

The team selection was slightly complicated by the injury to Dean Marney. But with Bryan Hughes comfortable in the centre of midfield, and Nicky Barmby back in the fray, that blow was softened.

Dean Marney: I've had some nasty injuries but that was the cruellest. That one hurt, being out for that three or four weeks. I was confident I would play in those play-off semi-finals but just got one of those stupid tackles in training from Nathan Doyle and tore a medial ligament. At the time of doing it I didn't even think I'd have a chance of getting back for the play-off final.

Bryan Hughes: The game itself saw me playing centre midfield, because Dean Marney was injured. I wanted to be playing in the middle for the biggest games so that was good for me. I'd played there before in play-off games and I felt that I knew what to expect with game management and certain situations that would arise during the games.

The night before the game, City stayed in the Grove hotel just north of London.

Andy Dawson: We'd stayed at the Grove a few times before, and we'd watched the play-off game between Palace and Bristol City there the previous day. I can't remember feeling nervous. I think it was just pure excitement because we were on such a good run of form and we had such good players. From February onwards I think we only lost about three games. We were full of confidence.

The game kicked off in glorious sunshine, with City defending the end in which their fans were housed.

Craig Sargent: This was when things were suddenly getting serious. We'd all enjoyed the ride to the play-offs over the previous few months but there was still one momentous job to be done and on that boiling hot morning the reality of the situation hit home. Everything seemed to add to the pressure and the sense of this being one hell of a day; the lunchtime kick-off, the sun beating down on a furnace-like Vicarage Road, the Wembley prize. This was a special, special day and we all knew it.

Nick Barmby: It was boiling, and I joked with Daws that I hoped we got the stand end in the shadows so we didn't have to run in the sun. Luckily we did.

While there are those who will claim that it was City's destiny to go up that year, in some ways that disregards the hard work and not inconsiderable skills levels on display within the City ranks. However, any team that goes up needs a bit of luck, and Hull City certainly got that in the fourth minute when what looked like a perfectly good goal by Danny Shittu was disallowed by referee Kevin Friend.

Michael Turner: It was my job to mark Danny Shittu but he's such a powerful bloke. The corner came over and he just powered over me. I had no chance of stopping him and I just fell to the floor and the ref gave a foul, luckily, but it definitely wasn't one.

Andy Dawson: I didn't see any foul. When it's your year, it's your year. For me it was a perfectly good goal. When we needed that bit of luck we got it, and after that we were comfortable.

Wayne Brown: I didn't see the push or any sort of foul, but I do remember their fans going absolutely mad!

Boaz Myhill: I remember turning around thinking: 'Oh no!' There was a little bit of contact on me but I'm pretty sure that that can't have been why it was disallowed. I've no idea why it was ruled out but I'm delighted it was. Everything could have been so different…

Dean Windass: We got lucky. It was a good goal. The ref must have thought there was a foul on the goalkeeper, but Boaz said there was nothing.

To add insult to injury, City were soon to go 1-0 up. In the eighth minute, Nick Barmby was to score a goal that sent the away fans into raptures.

Nick Barmby: Fraizer pulled it back, I mis-hit it, it went through someone's legs and just rolled into the bottom of the net. It was great for me but more importantly it calmed us down and put pressure on the home side.

Richard Garcia: It was a nervy start and I think they were on top early and had some good chances, but when they didn't go in our confidence grew and then once we scored it settled us right down and we played our normal game.

The dream start was only to get better 15 minutes later, when Dean Windass made it 2-0. Both Hull-born veterans had scored.

Dean Windass: Our game plan was to come away not conceding. We always fancied ourselves at home. But with Barmbs getting the first one, I knew then we were going to get to the final, because I trusted my team-mates. I trusted those two banks of four. Then for my goal, someone hit the bar and I just used my instincts, followed it up, as I always did, and it's one of the easiest goals I've scored.

Nick Barmby: Two-nil is a precarious scoreline in football. I don't know why. You'd rather be 2-0 up than 2-0 down.

Craig Sargent: Surely not even the most optimistic of City fans could have predicted being 2-0 up within half an hour. The dream was on and everyone in the packed away end was going to milk it for all it was worth. I struggle to think of a more ecstatic and loud City away end.

Fraizer Campbell: It just felt like we couldn't lose. We battered them. They thought it was a fortress down there but we started so well.

Dean Windass: We got to half-time and we said: "Let's treat it as 0-0 – just don't concede."

Half-time among the City fans in the away end had a surreal feel to it. A quarter of the way through the tie and we had a strangle hold. But 2-0... Radio presenter Danny Baker has a challenge for football fans; when their team goes 2-0 up with a decent chunk of the game still to play, he dares them to stand up and exclaim: "Nothing can go wrong now!" because everything can still go wrong. That said, it helps if you have a goalkeeper of the calibre of Boaz Myhill in your side. As Watford flew out of the traps in the second half, Boaz was to pull off one of the great saves to protect his clean sheet.

Boaz Myhill: Danny Shittu crossed it and I was thinking: 'What's going on here?' Then it was just one of those things where I saw it off Mat Sadler's foot and flung myself to the right. Sometimes you save them, sometimes you don't. It was such a good day.

Andy Dawson: What a save! I've seen the highlights recently. I was closing the lad down, he hit it with his left foot. All I could do was run up to Boaz after and say: "Wow, what a save!" Again, big players, when you need them, pull these sort of things out, and that was a top, top save. It would have been different if that had gone in.

Nick Barmby: In the second half Bo pulled off one of the best saves I've ever seen. I've been lucky enough to play with some very good goalkeepers, but that save was out of this world. But it's what he's capable of.

Sam Ricketts: All I remember about the first leg is Boaz Myhill. He was amazing in that first leg. He made three or four unbelievable saves. He was the main reason why we won that game. It was nice for him too. The team had been so good he hadn't had that much to do in the previous games, so it was nice for him to be able to show how good he was in that one game. He was the difference between the two sides.

The battle for supremacy in midfield had centred around captains Ian Ashbee and John Eustace. The two had been chipping away at each other all game, but it was Ash who was winning out. Then, in the 61st minute, a flare up saw Eustace push Ash and receive his *marching orders. It wasn't unfair to ponder whether the Ian Ashbee of a few years previous would have been following the Watford skipper down the tunnel. Instead he stood back and let the ref get on with it.*

Ian Ashbee: I stood on his foot – which the ref didn't see – and then just put my arms out. They push you and they're the ones who get done. I'd learnt that over time. I knew John Eustace was after me, trying to put a bit of a stamp on the game, so he fell into the trap really. On the way out I nearly had a fight with one of their fans who was having a pop at me as I was trying to get on the bus, so it was adventurous to say the least!

Two-nil up and playing against 10 men, City rarely looked like conceding. Indeed, had Fraizer Campbell or Nathan Doyle made the most of their one-one-ones with Watford keeper Richard Lee, the tie would have been all but over. Not that anyone was complaining about the two-goal advantage.

Matt Rudd: I loved Watford away because even though we'd finished third and were favourites to go up, it didn't feel like we were under great pressure to succeed. For such a huge occasion, unique to the club at the time, the team dispatched the hosts and braved the sweltering conditions to make it look like one of the easiest wins ever. When a full back in Nathan Doyle, barely seen on the pitch since joining the club, can come on as a sub and do some fancy-dan, foot-over-the-ball gubbins in midfield before curling a shot against the post, you know you've had a decent day.

Brian Horton: Going to Watford and playing the way we did was incredible. It just should have been more than 2-0.

Wayne Brown: Playing against a former club and doing well is very memorable. We did really well on the day. We were the better team. We were full of confidence. When Barmby scored it was fantastic. When we went 2-0 up – we knew it wasn't over but we were a long way in the right direction. We kept out feet on the floor in the changing room after the game, we knew that the second leg was coming up.

Bryan Hughes: I thought we were absolutely outstanding in that first leg. Every man to a T. We grasped the opportunity. We got a bit of luck but we took our chances when we needed to and defended resolutely.

Dean Windass: I knew when we were on the bus on the way home that we were going to get to the final.

Rob Smith: Travelling back from Watford, on a beautiful sunny day, you sensed there was a professionalism that would get us the results we needed.

Ian Bunton: Those two goals and the goalkeeping masterclass by Boaz Myhill were enough for me to book my train tickets and hotel for London, I was that sure we'd be playing at Wembley.

Dave Burns: The two Hull boys scoring the goals. They were a likeable bunch of blokes but they were hard men, and we'd heard that they'd got tucked into Watford in the tunnel and psyched them out a bit in there. They showed no fear.

Phil Buckingham: After that first leg I was just thinking City were going to Wembley. It was scripted brilliantly with the two Hull lads scoring. Though no one should forget how magnificent Boaz Myhill was in that game. If you'd have offered any City fan a draw in that game, they'd have snapped your hand off, so to come away with a 2-0 lead was just a dream.

Ian Farrow: We travelled back from Watford after the first leg of the play-offs full of confidence. The away leg couldn't have gone better. We wouldn't have said it too loudly but I do think we all quietly presumed that it was safe to book the Wembley hotels.

Paul Duffen: To come away from Watford with that result might have been where the nerves started. Because then there's expectation.

Expectation indeed. Bristol City had booked their place at Wembley by the time of the second leg, so City knew who they'd be facing. And, in truth, a final against Gary Johnson's Bristol City, who'd stuttered after an impressive start to the season, was marginally more preferable to a match up against Neil Warnock's Crystal Palace, who'd been in such blistering form throughout 2008.

But City still had to negotiate the second leg. And however confident the fans had been coming away from Vicarage Road on that sunny afternoon, every single Hull City fan would have had a 'but what if...' moment keeping them awake between the two games. That said, and without tempting fate, some preparation for a potential date at Wembley needed doing.

Brendon Smurthwaite: All I was stressing about was the fact that there were only 42 seats in the press box and that was nowhere near enough. We had to go through a load of workshops with the FA in London the week before too, in case we did get in the final.

At kick-off, it seemed as if the game was City's to lose. But would 'Typical City' rear its ugly head?

Michael Turner: Going into the game we were full of confidence, but 2-0 is a tricky scoreline for some reason.

Boaz Myhill: It was all very surreal but it dawned on me that it was a bit scary. There were very real consequences to what we were doing.

Ian Farrow: The talk in the pub before the game was basically that as long as we didn't concede early it was in the bag. So what happened? Watford came out full of running, full of passion, full of endeavour, full of threat. They knew the task was difficult but were going to give it a go.

Phil Brown: Aidy Boothroyd had a reputation of playing direct football, and he played direct football in the first leg. He must have realised that that wasn't the way to play against Hull City and he changed his philosophy; after going through 47 games of that season playing long-ball football, he decided to try to pass his way through our team. That put me on the back foot a bit. They played football for the first 10 minutes or so, and I thought: 'This is massively different.'

The 'but what ifs?' and 'Typical City' worries grabbed every City fan by the throat on 12 minutes. Darius Henderson, absent from the first leg, played a one-two in the box and curled a low shot past Boaz Myhill's left hand. The cheers from the Watford fans were all but drowned out by the audible thuds of several thousands hearts hitting the pits of stomachs in the home stands.

Andy Dawson: I've managed Darius Henderson since, and he told me that's one of the few goals he's scored with his right foot. All we'd said was: "Don't concede early, don't concede early," and then what happens in the first few minutes?

Brian Horton: Aidy Boothroyd always played 4-4-2 and our 4-4-2 was better than his 4-4-2 without a doubt. He shocked us completely by playing a diamond shape, and they outplayed us at the beginning and scored. The whole stadium went silent.

Nick Barmby: Do you stick, do you twist? Do you sit back? It wasn't in our nature to sit back. When they scored that early goal, the lull at the KC from such a great atmosphere was so noticeable.

Dean Windass: We got a bit of a fright. They were a big physical side, but Aidy Boothroyd started playing a diamond. They passed and passed and we couldn't believe it. Then when Darius scored I thought: "Oh god, here we go!"

Mike White: I was still fairly new to commentary back then, and I had a mixture of wanting to find the right words to convey what had happened, but also there was the City fan in me, which I'd managed to keep locked away when I was commentating until that point. I said something like: "Oh god!" which is one of the expressions that you're not supposed to use on local radio.

Wayne Brown: There was a confidence that we'd do it. But there were nerves in the respect that we needed the result. We were looking to win the game, not draw. We were looking to be positive. After they scored I was thinking: 'Let's not panic.' You could sense the crowd were nervous. But I thought we were still holding the aces. There was still a long time to go.

Ian Ashbee: I was thinking: 'Here we go!' We weren't going to roll over. There were too many people in that changing room, in that club, who would not let that happen. We were still winning the game. I was reminding people of that, telling them not to panic, tucking people in around us to make us harder to play against. If you start tear-arsing around just because you've let a goal in in a game like that, you're going to get picked off. I was trying to get people not to panic and wait for our chance, making it a bit more boring than people would have wanted it to be.

Bryan Hughes: I didn't think anything. I just thought we'd win the game, because that was the confidence I had in everyone around me. The nervous tension after they scored seemed to mostly be coming from the fans. You could sense it. But we didn't think like that. This was our home pitch and we'd just beaten them 2-0 away. We were still in the lead.

Caleb Folan: We didn't think we had it won after the first leg. When they went 1-0 up, I was a bit nervous but deep down I knew it would wake us up. That game is the best atmosphere I've played in in my career. The KC felt like it had never felt before. I knew we'd fight back. We always did. We'd always come back somehow.

Phil Buckingham: It was City's to lose and that's when the fear factor that creeps in. Every player and supporter would to some extent have been mentally planning a trip to Wembley, so to go 1-0 down and the pattern of play being the way it was, everyone in the ground had every right to be nervous.

Ian Farrow: The fear was that City would crumble. Could they make it to half-time and re-group and re-energise? Why did we have such little faith? I suppose it comes with the territory of being long-time Tigers fans.

Paul Duffen: I just went cold. That game is the most seared into my consciousness because of the way it started, conceding that early goal. It meant suddenly anything was possible. I had no other ambition for us other than getting to Wembley for the first time in our history. It was already the best season in the club's history and in the context of getting to Wembley, when that goal went in the whole stadium froze. But that just suppressed the spring even more for what was to come…

What was to come was an exceptional piece of professionalism from an exceptional professional. Two minutes before half-time, Richard Garcia ghosted in between a number of defenders to head the ball over the Watford keeper and towards goal. Did it have the power to go in? Numerous Watford players were giving chase, but so was Nick Barmby. If Barmby gets there first, City go into half-time with the two-goal lead in the tie back intact. If a Watford defender gets there first the psychological advantage remains with the Hornets. But this is Nick Barmby we're talking about. There was only ever going to be one outcome.

Nick Barmby: We were given a lifeline before half-time. Richard Garcia looped it over the keeper's head. It was probably going in but you're always taught make sure it goes in. It was probably the easiest goal I've scored in my life. I remember Garc having a go at me, saying I'd taken the goal off him!

Richard Garcia: I remember heading it over the oncoming keeper and then it seemed like someone had pressed the slow-motion button. I was watching and willing it to cross the line and eventually Nick Barmby made sure it did… It was a relief and from then on the game was never in doubt. That goal came at the right time and we went into the dressing room at half-time with wind in our sails

Phil Brown: They were the most nerve-wracking moments of the whole season for me. Then just before half-time Nick followed the ball in. It was a crap goal but it was the most important goal of the season for me as it meant I could relax a little bit.

Ian Farrow: Cometh the hour, cometh the man. Richard Garcia did his ghost thing and headed the ball towards goal. It didn't have a lot of power. Would it have gone in anyway? Barmby and a defender both went for the ball. Others in Barmby's position may have just watched, hoping the ball would cross the line anyway. The former England international didn't. His experience, his professionalism, his will to win told him to power in. He was stronger than the Watford man and bundled the ball over the line.

Andy Dawson: It showed the character that we had though. We dug in. We'd done that all season. When you need the big players, someone like Barmbs steps up. It just relaxed us before half time.

Sam Ricketts: The goal that Nick got was so vitally important just before half-time. It relaxed us and really hit Watford. It was such a great moment for him, given how passionate he was about Hull, to score such a crucial goal. I was really pleased for him as an individual.

Wayne Brown: After a nervy opening we started playing a lot better, then when we equalised the roof was lifted off the KC.

Ian Bunton: Not the most stunning of goals, but Nick's determination to get to the loose ball was so important. The whole mood of the tie seemed to change.

Paul Duffen: We seemed blessed again. There were a few games that season where there seemed to be a force field around our goal. Watford had many chances in that second leg.

All of those feelings of sickness, the shortness of breath, the sheer and utter dread, it all dissipated in an instant. Half-time could be spent fantasising about an afternoon in north-west London, and not staring at your shoes trying not to throw up.

City controlled the game in the second half, and in the 63rd minute supersub Caleb Folan entered the fray.

Caleb Folan: I didn't get any specific instructions. Phil would tell me to keep hold of the ball but generally he knew you didn't need instructions. That gave me a bit of confidence.

Folan had made a habit of scoring late goals in games to seal important victories. He'd done it against Coventry, West Brom, Colchester, Leicester and Watford. And in the 70th minute, he did it to Watford again.

Sam Ricketts: Both semi-finals were as hard a two games as I'd had all season. I thought that leading up to that I'd dominated every winger I'd played against, even the likes of Victor Moses. But Jobi McAnuff was the best winger I played against that season and they were the hardest games I'd had, and two of my worst games, so it was nice for me to be able to impose myself on him a little bit. Eventually I was able to get forward, and it was something that Phil Brown worked on a lot with me – crossing balls to the back post. Crossing was one of my biggest attributes, and if I could get it to the back post we'd generally have either Caleb Folan or Dean Windass there. I got the other side of Jobi McAnuff for one of the first times and I looked up and saw Caleb so I tried to float a ball where I thought he'd be. Fortunately that's exactly where he was.

Caleb Folan: Sam Ricketts was doing an overlap down the right – he could do that all day, he had an incredible engine. As soon as I saw him go down the right I just knew I had to get in the box. I was trying to time my run. He just clipped it in. It felt so easy. There was no one coming for it, the keeper wasn't committed to it, and I had no doubts. It seemed like such a simple header. Then it was a mental feeling after that. I knew it was important – as easy as it was as a goal, I knew it meant something. I just ran and slid on the floor and I didn't want to get up. I just wanted to lie there. I was hugging Fraizer saying: "We've got this, we've got this." Watford looked broken after that.

Sam Ricketts: Given my celebration when the ball went in, it probably looked like I'd scored the goal! It was something we'd worked on so much in training. I crossed it, looked up, and it was perfect just seeing Caleb rise and finish it off. It was a fantastic relief.

Andy Dawson: When Folan scored, deep down we knew we were there.

James Richardson: The sealing of the tie. Elation, pure elation. I've never experienced an atmosphere like it at the KC before or since.

Mike White: Sometimes, when you're in a sporting event or a concert, the vibrations literally shake your whole body. That's the experience I went through when Folan scored. The atmosphere was shaking my whole being, right to the core. At that point, we knew we had it.

The release – the primal, guttural release – when Folan scored soon segued into a party atmosphere as Watford were beaten and Wembley awaited. But this Hull City side weren't a team to rest on their laurels. There was a thrashing to be handed out, and Richard Garcia wanted the goal that Nick Barmby had so callously denied him! In the 88th minute, it came.

Richard Garcia: I remember picking it up just over the halfway line and finding myself with a lot of space and thinking: 'Wow, where is everyone?' So I started to run with it and it eventually ended up in the back of the net.

Nick Barmby: They were chasing and had to come out and we capitalised on that very well. I was really pleased for Richard Garcia because he worked his socks off that season and was a really big player for us.

Brendon Smurthwaite: Richard Garcia scored a brilliant goal and no one really noticed. I always felt sorry for him for that.

The icing on the cake came in the 90th minute when substitute Nathan Doyle rounded off what was at that point the greatest evening in the club's history.

Caleb Folan: Nathan became my best friend in football. He was one of the first people I connected with at Hull City, and he helped me settle in. I've never forgotten that. He was critical in getting me through certain times, like my injuries. Before the game, all the shirts were hung up in the changing room. The sponsors were written on the back of the shirt, but on his shirt all the letters hadn't been ironed on properly and some of them had fallen off. But the ones that were left spelt out the initials of his new-born child. I said: "That's a sign, you're going to score tonight", even though we didn't think he'd get on.

He came on, and I don't know how he got the goal – it was going out for a throw in but took a deflection and went in – and he set off with his baby celebration. I was trying to celebrate with him but he was just in his own world.

The final whistle was blown by Mark Clattenburg and all that was left to do was celebrate like Hull City had never celebrated before.

Fraizer Campbell: It was a great feeling to know that where we'd come from earlier in the season, we were on our way to Wembley with a great chance of getting in the Premier League.

Michael Turner: It was a nice summer's evening, the pitch was the best it had been and scoring those goals and running away with the game meant we could enjoy knowing we were going to Wembley and having a shot at the Premier League. Coming out after the game and clapping the fans from the directors' box was one of the highlights of my time at Hull City.

Paul Duffen: It was just unbridled joy. You could feel it.

Dean Windass: It was incredible. With Neil Warnock leaving me out of the Championship play-off final for Sheffield United against Wolves years ago, I never thought I'd get the chance to play at Wembley. It would be the first time I'd ever played there – at 39 years old! I didn't think I'd get that opportunity.

Alfie Potts Harmer: That game was probably the best atmosphere ever at the KC, with even the West Stand in full voice!

Rob Smith: Everyone was arm in arm. It was hairs on the back of the neck time. I still get emotional talking about it. A lot of us had been there many years and we were doing something we thought we'd never see, and on the brink of something we *really* thought we'd never see. But to get to Wembley in such emphatic style, it was amazing. We were all as one at that time too – players, coaches, backroom staff, admin staff, everyone. When the lads came up after the game everyone was hugging and celebrating. One game to go and we could be in the Premier League. It was surreal.

Ian Farrow: The whistle went and many people invaded the pitch. I stayed in the stand looking. City were off to Wembley. My knees had gone all trembly. It was historic. It was emotional. It was City doing their rollercoaster thing yet again but this time we were enjoying the ride.

Mike White: I was in the tunnel after as the game was closing. It was packed. I couldn't get out. Players' heads would whizz by every now and then. I got out on to the pitch eventually after the final whistle went, and just saw a load of grown men with tears in their eyes. There were also people with big beaming smiles, you had people hugging each other, players were being mobbed. That moment stood out for me. Even though I had a job to do, I was thinking: 'Wow, what a thing to be a part of!'

Phil Buckingham: The final result belies how tense the KC had got that night.

As for the opposition at Wembley, Bristol City's manager was ambivalent towards who was standing between his side and a place in the Premier League.

Gary Johnson: I was a player at Watford, and they were my team. At the time, Hull and Watford teams were pretty similar in style but as a former Watford player and coach under Graham Taylor I was rooting for them a little bit, but it didn't really matter that much to me. I figured that Bristol City were going to be the underdogs either way.

This really was a journey into the unknown. Very few City players had played at the old Wembley – just Nick Barmby and Andy Dawson – and only Craig Fagan had played at the new version. No one was going to take Dean Windass's Wembley chance away from him, however.

Dean Windass: I'd said to Phil the week before on the training ground – when he told me I'd be playing – that I'd score the winner. He said he'd give me an hour, and I said: "In that hour, I'll score the winning goal." I don't know why I said it, I was just being cheeky. But I thought we'd win the game and that me or Nick would score.

As for the rest of the game preparation, Phil Brown was keen to 'normalise' things as much as possible.

Phil Brown: The preparations went very well. There were eight or nine days in between, and it went as well as it could. We tried to keep it on an even keel as there were a lot of excited people about – none more so than myself. It was important that we tried to prepare for a game of that magnitude with some semblance of normality, which was difficult. The most difficult part of a manager's job in those situations is keeping everybody calm because it is just another game in a series of 49. If you can maintain that philosophy then you can maintain some calm and play some football against a very decent side, which Bristol City were.

Paul Duffen: We always approached big games on the basis that we'd try to keep things as normal as possible for the players. Equally I believe in planning for success, and that had already been the most successful season in the club's history. So we decided that we'd take the team to stay in the Grove. We used Arsenal's training ground, which was fantastic. We planned a celebration party for after the game, win or lose, because we felt that that season had been something quite extraordinary and the players and coaching staff deserved it.

Craig Fagan: The preparation was spot on. Having done it with Derby I knew it was brilliant. I know it might sound trivial to supporters, but stuff like the tickets being sorted out was brilliant so you knew that your family were going to be there and sorted for seats. The hotel was brilliant. There were no excuses for the players not to perform. The physio treatment, the food in the hotel, everything was spot on.

Bryan Hughes: The preparation going into the Wembley game was spot on by Phil and his backroom team. He'd been there with Bolton so he knew what needed to happen. I'd been in a few big games before too – play-off finals and a cup final – and from what I'd seen I thought everything was done perfectly. He kept the squad together, we set off a couple of days early, we had spa days and massages. It was really nice. There was a good camaraderie feel to the squad. Phil kept everyone involved too, not just the 16 who'd be putting a shirt on, and you could see that in the pictures afterwards. The likes of Jay-Jay and Ryan France were kept involved. We weren't just a team of 11 players going down there to play on the pitch, we were a squad. That had been going on all season and everyone bought into it.

Away from the playing side of things there was a huge logistical operation to sort out and very little time in which to do it. Tickets, travel, media and various other tasks were stamped 'urgent' in a way the club hadn't experienced before. Thankfully City's backroom staff were every bit as hard-working, every bit as skilled at their jobs, as the men out on the pitch.

Brendon Smurthwaite: We had a massive staff meeting on the Monday and there was so much to do. Tickets were the major thing. For two days we couldn't get out of the office doors as there were people queuing there. You daren't go in the ticket office to sort out your own tickets as the girls were under such stress that they'd just throw you out.

Rob Smith: I was so nervous. I still get nervous talking about it to this day. It was uncharted territory for us and a lot of us were working seriously long hours to get it all planned. We'd had to get 40,000 tickets on sale within 24 hours of us beating Watford, and people were pretty much at their limit by the time we travelled down to Wembley. The players had prepared differently, but for the rest of us you almost wanted to get it out of the way. We were so sick with nerves.

Mike Scott: To get a ticket for the pivotal event one needed to deploy effort. City didn't make it easy for the average punter, especially ones who were representing an entire fans' group and had an order for 80-odd tickets to process. So it came to pass that your correspondent and two good friends, along with a few hundred similarly hardy souls, undertook shift work to queue up all night and acquire those golden tickets. Over the 10-hour wait the mood was dominated by weariness but never anything other than well-mannered and friendly. I had never met the guys in front of us in the queue before that night – I'm still on nodding terms with them 10 years later as our paths occasionally cross outside the East Stand.

Pizza deliveries came and went, night turned to day, the ticket office opened, the queue shuffled forward at the speed of a great Alpine glacier. We were cold as ice, but we were willing to sacrifice our rest time. Eventually the tickets were requested and the credit cards were caned. It was all worth it though – sleep is for the ticketless wimps.

Brendon Smurthwaite: Browny got the whole process nailed. We did the press day on the Tuesday giving all the press – local and national – access to whoever they wanted. After that he said no one else does anything. All the non-playing and non-coaching staff were staying in the Landmark hotel in Marylebone with the players' wives. Weirdly, Leeds United were staying in there too ahead of their play-off final.

Nick Barmby: The national press were obviously wanting to speak about the local lads. I don't know whether that took the pressure off the other lads at all, but it was unfair really as I'd hardly played for us that season.

As for the fans, getting a ticket was one thing. Then there was working out how to get to a stadium that hadn't been on the club's radar before. In 1987 Mark Herman had written a TV play about a couple on their wedding day eventually taking the decision to try (and eventually fail) to get to see City in an FA Cup semi-final. In 2008, life came close to imitating art.

Mark Herman: I nearly didn't make it to Wembley, which was to do with the first pre-release screening of The Boy In The Striped Pyjamas. Disney were delighted to have managed to secure the plum Saturday afternoon slot at the Hay On Wye Festival on Saturday, May 25. I heard this news while automatic promotion was still a possibility, and anyway, even if we were in the play-offs, getting to the final was far from guaranteed, but the risk was too great, so – advised by my producers not to use football as an excuse to Disney – I came up with so many alternative excuses (and 'personal matters'). I think they thought I had some life-threatening illness. They were therefore surprised when I said if they could move it to the Sunday it would be fine. (Ah, so he's not dying…) They then changed it to the Sunday. On hearing what my dilemma had been, a Disney executive later told me I was insane not to have told them, because "football's much more important than this crap".

Amid all the chaos and excitement Phil Brown and Gary Johnson had a tactical battle to consider. Each knew the other had matchwinners at their disposal.

Gary Johnson: The story was that it was all set up for Dean Windass. You always look for a story in these games, and the best story often wins the game. Because of Dean's age and him being a Hull lad there was a lot of publicity surrounding him in the week leading up to the game, so we were a little bit worried that the story was all about him.

Phil Brown: Bradley Orr was a player I really liked. Lee Trundle could open a can of worms with his left foot and Dele Adebola was a beast, but Michael Turner was a beast too and would go up in everybody's estimation in the way he managed to handle him.

After travelling down to the Grove the City squad visited Wembley on the Friday afternoon before the game.

Paul Duffen: We went to Wembley the afternoon before to familiarise ourselves, walk around the pitch. The lads were walking round taking pictures of an empty Wembley, which was a bit weird. But when the players walked out there on the Saturday, they weren't overwhelmed by it, they seemed very relaxed, because they got an enormous amount of strength from each other. Everything else happened as normal, and there was a quiet confidence. We were a very well-oiled, harmonious machine. We got to Wembley feeling quite relaxed.

Wayne Brown: It was daunting. It looked bigger without people in it. The lads had their cameras out taking pictures. On the day it then wasn't so daunting.

Nick Barmby: Browny took us to see Wembley on the Friday. He told us to take our phones out and film whatever we wanted to film, because when we're here on Saturday there'll be no phones, there'll be no waving at families. You were there to win. He was spot on. It was good man management. The lads were pretty relaxed really.

Boaz Myhill: We stayed in the Grove, which is amazing, a great environment to be in. Phil Brown took us to Wembley the day before, as a lot of us had never been there, and that gave us a little bit of something to sleep on. Me and Dukey watched East is East that evening and then went to bed.

Matt Duke: Me and Bo always roomed and we had a relaxed evening. People don't realise that you do the normal stuff even though it's the biggest game you're involved in. If you start doing anything different you can't relax. We just treated it like a normal game.

Dean Windass: I was a very experienced footballer at that point. I was more concerned about how the younger ones like Fraizer were going to cope, but Fraizer was so laid back he could go to sleep on a washing line. Him and Caleb were very good friends and were playing table tennis the night before, while me and a few others were playing poker. I didn't even think about the local story behind it all or there being any extra pressure on me. I thought we'd win the game as we were in such a rich vein of form. While we were playing poker, Ash was on the phone with Gavin Mahon, a mate of his who'd been the Watford captain when they'd won the play-off final a few years before. I said to Ash: "You'll do what your best mate did." He just said: "I hope so."

Paul Duffen: We kept it low key. Before every away game that season, the night before the game I'd had dinner with Phil and the coaching staff. We'd have a bit of banter and keep it relaxed. And we did exactly the same thing.

The only cause of worry for City was Wayne Brown's calf injury. There was no other centre-back near the squad – as had been shown by the experiment with playing David Livermore there in the Sheffield United game just weeks earlier – and splitting up the Turner-Brown axis at the back would have been hugely detrimental to the team. So, would Wayne be OK?

Wayne Brown: With about three or four minutes left of the home game against Watford I pulled my calf muscle. We'd used all our subs and I was thinking: 'We've won the game here, do I come off?' I was struggling. After the game we assessed it. There was a pull, and I'm thinking well maybe I'm out of the final. I didn't train once until we got to the Arsenal's training ground the day before the game when I had a light training session. I managed to get through that and declared myself fit but it was a nervy situation for me. I'd had a decent campaign and we didn't have loads of centre-halves at the time and the club did everything in their power to get me fit.

Michael Turner: He had a niggle and the club physios wrapped him up in cotton wool. For me there was never a doubt that he'd start the game, but whether he'd finish it… I wasn't too sure. The way he played that day, despite all of this, sums him up as a person and a player.

The financial impact of the Championship play-off final – for the victors at least – is emblazoned across the media, but of less interest to the fans who just want to see their team win. However, to Paul Duffen, who'd been City's chairman for less than a year, the implications of a promotion were dizzying.

Paul Duffen: As far as the financial impact goes, we turned over something like £8m in the 2007/08 season. The next year you knew it would be £40m if we went up. The difference it was going to make to the club was incomprehensible. We had to have a contingency plan in place for if we went up, as resourcing the club for the media frenzy that is the Premier League has an enormous impact on you. So we went down there quite wide-eyed but not overawed.

As dawn broke on a gloriously sunny morning in late May, 2008, tens of thousands of City fans awoke knowing that within a few hours they'd have witnessed either the greatest football game of their lives, or the most crushing. For the players, manager, chairman and backroom staff, it was a morning like no other they'd ever experienced.

Paul Duffen: I felt that the weight of burden for generations of Hull City fans who had never been to Wembley had been lifted.

Sean Rush: I went down to Wembley with the kit man and the physio about four or five hours before the team to set everything up. I just remember seeing Hull City fans playing five-aside in the car park. I was a massive City fan, and I knew that had I not been involved, that would have been me. That was when it sunk in. We all then went back to the Grove to drive in with the team, and the amount of City fans you saw, it was just one of those moments in your life that you'll never replicate. Being a Hull lad and a City fan from year dot, it just made the hairs on the back of your arms stand up.

Paul Duffen: It was so monumental for us as a club, and the media love a good story, and they start coverage about two hours before the game and have a huge inventory to fill. We were the Boy's Own story and that meant I was really busy doing media the day before on Wembley Way, as it wasn't just about Look North, Radio Humberside and the Hull Daily Mail, it was national and international press. On the morning of the match it was a frenzy. It was showbusiness.

Caleb Folan: In the build-up it felt like a normal away game. There were no nerves in anyone. There was a ping pong table and the lads were relaxing playing on that. The banter between the lads was normal. Everything was routine. We all knew the significance of it so there was no need to change anything in our routine.

Fraizer Campbell: It was my first time playing at Wembley. It just felt like we were on a journey that we couldn't get beaten from. Even when we were on the coach from the hotel to the ground, it felt like everyone on the streets were Hull fans. It was a sea of black and amber. It felt like it was our party. The odds seemed in our favour. I had such confidence in that team I was thinking: 'There's no way we're going to come out of here losing.'

Andy Dawson: The build-up was brilliant. Pure excitement. As a player that had come from where I'd come from five years previous, to be saying I'd be playing in the Championship play-off final, one of the most valuable games there is, I just couldn't believe it. Was I nervous? A little bit. But I honestly believed it was our time.

Boaz Myhill: I was anxious. We were pulling out of the Grove going to Wembley. I'd always sit at the back with Deano and Ash, and Deano was looking at me going: "Bo, what's the matter wi' you?" and I was just thinking: 'Shut up, Deano, leave me alone.' I went white. I was very nervous. The journey seemed to take about three days and I was getting more and more nervous by the second. We weren't allowed to go out to warm up until quite late on. Phil Brown had spoken to Sir Alex Ferguson who'd said that when he plays in cup finals or big games he keeps the lads in the dressing room so that they're chomping at the bit to go out on the pitch. That made things a bit different.

Wayne Brown: That night I was thinking I just need a good night's kip. I slept like a log and there was a buzz around the place. The preparation was excellent. We arrived there and I was doing the warm-up just thinking about my calf, hoping it would hold out, so I didn't do too much. The atmosphere before the game was fantastic, waving to friends and family, then it was down to business.

Sam Ricketts: I was really focused going into such a big game and I knew a lot about Michael McIndoe, having played against him a few times. I was respectful of what he could do, but at the same time I was confident of being able to nullify him. I looked at wingers and at the time there was no one really quicker than me, so I was confident I'd be fine in a foot race with anyone. With McIndoe I'd overshow him the line and he'd try to take me on there. I'd make him try and run me, and I knew that I was quicker than him and probably a little bit stronger too. I was respectful that he was one of their danger players though.

Nick Barmby: I'd been lucky enough to go to Wembley for the rugby and had played there several times. I was sat next to Sean Rush on the bus – a Hull lad – and I said: "Look at this" going down Wembley Way. All you saw was black and amber. You never saw any red. And we shed a tear but thought: 'This is it!'

Rob Smith: Saying goodbye to people getting off the coach at Wembley, we were all wondering if we'd be getting back on the coach together at the end of the game, or whether we'd have sacked it off to go celebrate a win round London.

Brian Horton: I just could not see us losing. I knew we'd win. Phil asked me on Saturday morning: "What do you think?" I said: "We're going to win this game." Seeing all our fans in the sunshine – their fans being in the shade – it just looked perfect. The whole thing was just meant to be.

Peter Swan: I just felt it was going to happen because Burnsy kept telling me it was going to happen. He just kept going on about a Dean Windass winner. I went there believing it was going to happen, thinking we were the better team. I didn't see anything other than promotion that day. It was weird. I wasn't nervous. But that's because Burnsy kept drilling it into me that City were going up.

Ryan France: I was up and down really. I wanted to be in the team – which I knew wasn't going to happen – or I wanted to be on the bench and I didn't quite make it. It was a heartbreaking moment. I didn't huff and puff and was there for the lads encouraging them. I didn't want the players to see that I was upset. I wanted Hull City to be in the Premier League more than anyone. I don't really support anyone, but if anybody asked me I'd say I support Hull City for what the club did for me and what the fans did for me. So on a personal note it was not so good, but I still felt part of the team.

Paul Duffen: The fascinating thing when you get upstairs at Wembley, in the royal box each team has about 200 tickets. The rest is Football League sponsors, other clubs, etc… and the Premier League are there. The first thing that happened was me and Steve Lansdown, the Bristol City chairman, had Lord Mawhinney – the chairman of the Football League – introducing you to Lord Triesman – the chairman of the FA – on the basis that by the end of that Saturday afternoon one of us was going to be moving. You have to go through a process, as the Premier League is owned by its shareholders and whoever got relegated from the Premier League had just voided their share subscription. Equally we had a golden share in the Football League, so you know that at the end of that afternoon one of you is going to have to resign your golden share in the Football League and sign the share certificate to become a member of the Premier League.

Rob Smith: I was in one of the main suites for directors. Half the room was Bristol, half was Hull. You just knew that at the end of that game one half of that room was going to be distraught beyond words. All I could do was hope it wasn't us.

Sean Rush: It was so hot. We did a really short warm up because of the heat. When we came out of the tunnel, I was gutted when I saw those flares at the side. It felt like they'd burned my face off.

Ian Ashbee: Even if my career had finished that day, I'd have played at Wembley, and that's what every boy dreams about when you're growing up. Most people never get to play there, so I felt lucky and privileged. And to be leading a team out that I'd taken as my own club – I look for Hull's games more than I look for Birmingham's – to the promised land where we'd never been before, that was something; I was never going to let that pass me by.

Unbeknown to Phil Brown and the Hull City team, Bristol City had been dealt a blow before a ball had even been kicked.

Gary Johnson: Before the game, Jamie McCombe had a stomach ache overnight. We'd built up for the game over the week and then on the morning Jamie couldn't play, so all the work we'd done with him was undone. And without being able to train again, we'd lost all the stuff we'd done on set plays. He was the last person we wanted to pull out.

Hull City had organised for a bunch of former players to be transported to the game, with other legends making their own way there. It all added to the historical significance of the occasion, with past generations willing the current generation on to do something that had eluded them.

Rob Smith: The chairman made sure that everyone was going to enjoy that day. We took coachloads of former players and people who'd been connected with the club who'd fallen away. Regardless of the outcome Paul wanted to make sure we enjoyed the day. It was an amazing gesture and for me made the day more special, having the likes of Tony Norman and Billy Whitehurst around.

Justin Whittle: I was asked if I wanted to go to the game, but it was my little girl's birthday party. I gave her the choice of coming to Wembley or having a party. She chose a party, despite my best efforts. I had to watch it on TV.

Adam Lowthorpe: I was there in a black and amber afro wig with black and amber face paint. It came from nowhere, getting in the play-off final.

And there were some touching (if brief) reunions.

Tom Wilson: When my wife and I were approaching the stadium the team coach went past us. Deano and Nick Barmby saw us and were banging on the window jumping up and down to wave to us, which made me feel great. They'd been my young lads at 12 and 13 years old.

All that was left was for 40,000 Hull City fans to get to the famous ground to witness their club play on a stage they never thought they'd see, playing for a place in a division that had for so long seemed an impossible dream. The significance of the occasion was lost on no one, and the emotions for many were poignant.

Ian Farrow: I remember in the 1960s and 1970s, as we walked down Anlaby Road before and after games, the number of people and the impending excitement or afterglow euphoria. I suppose I'd never known such a mass of people going forward in a common cause. I just wish all of those people were around to march on to Wembley. In that sense I think I've been very lucky to see City in their greatest times as well as their worst.

Mike White: I got up really early in the morning and went for a walk down Wembley Way. Even that early in the morning, the City fans were out in number and I just thought: 'Wow, we have finally made it!'

Raich Carter Junior: We got to Wembley at 11am, and went to a sports bar which let in eight Hull City coaches. A load of the kids went to have a game on a sports pitch next to the bar, home shirts versus away shirts, and all the parents had a beer. It was lovely. But in the distance you could see the arch.

Bernard Noble: Before the game I was very confident. We'd had the wins against Watford and we just seemed to be in the right position, coming on strongly going into the play-offs. When I knew we had Bristol City in the final I just felt so confident.

Rich Lusmore: I'd travelled on a Simon Gray coach to the game having promised myself back in the day that should City ever get to Wembley I'd use the same means of transport that had seen me to some of football's traditional backwaters during bleaker times. Amazingly we still got there on time (only joking Simon!).

Raich Carter Junior: I just remember feeling strange going on the escalators in Wembley. I was just thinking: 'I can't believe I'm going on an escalator to watch Hull City!'

Robert Crampton: It is still one of the best days of my life. I was there with all my family, including my in-laws. I'd seen about 20 people that I knew walking there. It was a party atmosphere and I was thinking: 'This could happen.'

Ian Bunton: Wembley 2008 was an occasion never to be forgotten. I remember being slightly in awe, on the day, of the whole place, but delighted that three generations of my family sat next to each other to watch it. My dad sat in his seat, nearly too slow to get out of it when something exciting was about to happen. My son, too small in his seat, his legs dangling from it as they were too short to reach the floor. And me sat on the edge of mine nervous as hell.

In the referee's room, just as in both changing rooms, the emphasis was on treating what was to come as an ordinary game.

Alan Wiley: I didn't feel under pressure. The main thing you have to close out of your mind coming into the play-off final is the media hype in relation to the value of the game. It was the £60m game at that point: it's something like £200m now. That's something that's a sideline of the game. You do realise that for the winning team that it can be life-changing for the players and the foundation of something really big for everybody. The big thing before the game from a referee's point of view is concentrating on the fact that, as much as there's all the hype, once the game kicks off it's just another Championship game. I stressed to my two assistant referees that once that first whistle goes it's a just football match and we have to deliver.

Finally, after all the waiting, all the razzmatazz, all the build up, it was time to get on with the actual match. The players emerged from the tunnel on a boiling hot afternoon with flame-throwers flaring at either side of them.

Richard Garcia: It was a fantastic feeling to walk out the tunnel and see half the stadium in amber and black and the other half red.

Paul Duffen: Going into the royal box and seeing that end of the stadium completely black and amber just left me in shock. I was in shock for the first 10 minutes of the game. It was just incredible.

Boaz Myhill: When the game kicked off I was fine. I felt like I was playing in my living room at home with my dad. It just never occurred to me that we'd lose once the game started. I just presumed we were going to win. Because I'd had no experience of losing play-off games, I made up my own ideas about what was going to happen. More experienced players might have reacted differently.

Wayne Brown: That game's like no other. But when the game starts it's just like another game. It's business. You play your own game.

Bryan Hughes: I was one of the more experienced players on the pitch. I felt like I needed to be organising the team as younger players can get caught up in the moment and lose a bit of discipline. And that Wembley pitch can be quite sapping.

Nick Barmby: Championship play-off finals are very rarely classics: everyone's tense, it's 100mph, no one wants to make a mistake, and people want to sit deep. It was scrappy. I only had two or three touches of the ball in the opening stages. Neither team kept the ball well. Then on about the half-hour the game started to open up a little bit.

Mike White: I remember those first few minutes and Bristol had a few half-chances and all of a sudden it became more real. Reality kicked in and you thought maybe the fairy-story wasn't going to come with a happy ending.

Wayne Brown: We'd played against big Dele Adebola and Lee Trundle. We didn't have any certain players to mark, it was just who came on your side. Trundle liked to come off shorter and play in the pocket, which caused a few problems on the day, and big Dele likes to pin you. He doesn't like you to jump for the ball in the air so he gets between you and the ball and makes it difficult for you to attack the ball, so you have to be quite cute with him and not get too tight.

Ian Ashbee: The day was boiling hot. On the pitch-side it really was boiling. It was tough on the pitch. It wasn't a great game and we weren't at our best. But there was a resolve in us that would never be beaten. You had lads like Wayne Brown at the back, you had Richard Garcia in midfield who had a work ethic that was second to none along with Barmbs on the left, and Yozzer in midfield with me – that was a solid core. I just don't think on the day we played well. And I think Bristol played well-ish. But we had gone away from home with our fitness levels – which Phil Brown had got right – and we dug in.

Roy North: It was like watching ants, we were so high up! I remember queuing for the whole of half-time just to have a waz! It was fabulous. It couldn't have been more exciting. Deano looked all tarted up with his hair dyed.

Ian Farrow: I don't really remember it being much of a match. I recall a great tackle in our box by Michael Turner early on in the game but don't recall Bristol City worrying unduly. Obviously with what's at stake you are apprehensive each time they had the ball in our half but I think we basically controlled the game.

Michael Turner: The first half was cagey. Not too many chances. Very stop-start.

With the 38th minute approaching the ball fell to Nick Barmby just inside the Hull City half. He surged forward as City counter-attacked.

Nick Barmby: I got the ball on the half-way line and was running through. Fraizer had made a good diagonal run so I slipped him in.

Dean Windass: It was a boiling hot day. I'd headed it down to Nicky. Nicky slid it down the side to Fraizer, and it was the first counter attack we'd really had. I remember Fraizer getting to the byline and Lewis Carey slipping. Fraizer then had an opportunity to cross the ball.

Fraizer Campbell: Barmby slipped me in and I ran past one, and then faked a shot when another defender came up. He then slipped, and if I'd known he was going to slip I'd probably have carried on with my run and had a shot, but I ended up coming back and looking up. There was only Deano about so I lifted it to him…

Dean Windass: Nicky had gone in to the back stick. I saw him there and thought that if I ran into the box Fraizer wouldn't be able to pick me out so I thought I'd hang about on the edge of the box. It sounds big-headed but it was just a natural instinct that I had. If I'd gone in the box someone would just have marked me. But because we'd got them on the counter attack, their midfielders were still a bit behind us. I stood on the edge of the box and just waved to Fraizer, and obviously he clipped it back to me.

Wayne Brown: I was right behind it and as soon as it left Dean's foot I was thinking: 'The keeper isn't getting that.'

The keeper couldn't get that. Dean Windass, the 39-year-old lad from Gipsyville with his hair dyed peroxide blond, had scored an unimaginably fantastic volley from the edge of the box.

Dean Windass: I couldn't believe it when I hit it. I knew I'd made good contact, but when it hit the back of the net I couldn't believe it. I could not believe what I'd just done. I'd done that in training every day and the balls had been getting stuck in the trees.

Phil Brown: I thought the way Fraizer was that he'd pull the trigger at some point, but when he was sent back away from the goal and he clipped that ball to Dean it played out in my eyes as a slow-motion goal. Dean's technique was never in question in terms of heading, passing and control – that's the main reason why I wanted to bring him back – and when he shot he would invariably work the goalkeeper. Except in that moment he didn't work the goalkeeper, he worked the back of the net. And at that moment, time stood still for me.

Alfie Potts Harmer: Maybe it's just looking back now, but time seemed to slow down a little as the ball dropped down onto Deano's boot. I remember all my companions hugging during the celebrations. Obviously we were ecstatic when the goal went in, but it was nail-biting for the next hour or so. I had been fairly confident up until that point, but once we were winning it got pretty nervy.

Ian Farrow: The world stopped. For what seemed like 10 minutes but was probably a tenth of a second it was as if I had suddenly been plunged under water. Everything I looked at was blurred and all sounds were muffled. My mind was shocked. Neurons stopped firing. Various constituent parts of my brain were trying to talk to each other to find out what had happened but were failing. It was as if I was dreaming but fighting not to wake up. Someone pushed me, shoved me or hugged me. There were faces. There was movement. I came awake as if out of a coma. Yeerrhhsss!!!!! It was that moment. The moment. Nothing in football, or much in life, will ever be the same again. It dawned that City had scored at Wembley in our cup final.

Brian Horton: The goal was fantastic. It was what Deano was about, even as a kid. He could do those volleys all day long. It was a great pull back by Fraizer Campbell too.

Keith Edwards: Beautifully timed. Volleying is all about timing, and he timed it absolutely perfectly. That goal will never be forgotten.

Nick Barmby: To score a volley like that for your home town to go up at Wembley… it's what dreams are made of. I remember looking over my shoulder and I just knew it was in. It was very poignant that a kid from Hull should score that goal.

Bryan Hughes: Dean was the best man at my wedding and we'd roomed together. In the morning I'd woken up in the bed next to him and I told him that he'd score the winning goal. There was just this feeling that it would happen. I didn't expect him to score it in the manner in which he did though, as I've seen him try that many, many times in training and it didn't often end up in the back of the net.

Paul Duffen: There's a protocol that when you're sitting in the director's box you don't react to things. I was thinking about my prediction that we'd go up at Wembley and Dean Windass and Nick Barmby would score, saying to myself: "Jesus Christ, this is spooky!" It was just ridiculous, extraordinary. I did try to behave with dignity, but I was on my feet. It's a weird feeling though, as you do feel the tension between you and the opposition.

Ian Bunton: What a goal it was! I can still see it now with my eyes closed. On a couple of occasions since that day, if my son hears me moaning about City, he just texts me a video of that goal. It always puts a smile on my face.

Caleb Folan: I'm still speechless when I think about that goal. I can still remember it so clearly. It was just so effortless from Dean. It was just so normal to him. But he would do that in training all the time. Not many would take on that volley as it wasn't straightforward, but his technique was so perfect. It couldn't have been anyone else. I don't know if any of the other lads would have scored that goal, as good a bunch of players as we had.

Rob Harmer: If you're going to get promoted to the top flight, for the first time in your 104-year history, then that's the sort of goal that you want to see take you there. I can clearly remember thinking, as soon as I saw Campbell's ball falling to Deano, he's going to score this. I was on the front row of the middle tier at Wembley and nearly went over the edge when it went in, one of the best goals ever scored at the new Wembley, the most important goal ever scored for Hull City and rarely will you see a goal celebrated with so much joy and relief at the same time.

Ken Wagstaff: It was a good goal. It was one I'd have been proud of. He struck it well. I still tell him that when I die he'll be the greatest living Hull City player.

Mike White: I was sat in the commentary box when Deano scored. Me and James Hogarth had to celebrate under the desk with fist bumps and the like as the etiquette says you're not really meant to celebrate goals in there. To this day it still doesn't feel real that we witnessed that. I later found out that my wife and son hadn't witnessed it as he'd needed the loo at precisely that moment.

Craig Fagan: When you score a goal like that in a game I just think you're destined to win.

Dave Burns: The Hull Daily Mail did a Wembley supplement. In it I said 1-0 City and it was going to be a Windass Wembley winner, as he might be a daft lad from Gipsyville but he's got a sense of history, a sense of theatre and it's just made for him. When he scored I was just concentrating on getting: "Is this a Windass Wembley winner?" into my commentary. I was also thinking: 'Why didn't I put some money on this?' I just sensed that he would do it.

Phil Buckingham: I don't think I'll see a better or more significant goal if I cover Hull City until the day I die. It was the absolute game changer, and it wasn't a scuff over the line or coming off someone's backside, it was one of the most beautiful goals that you're likely to see at any level. The way Frazier held it up and put it on a sixpence for Deano… the way it hit the back of the net was fantastic.

Gary Clark: I sponsored Dean's socks when he was a 16-year-old. It cost me £10, and no one else sponsored any of the rest of his kit. But after *that* goal at Wembley everyone knew who he was.

Dave Richardson: Being fortunate enough to sit on the touchline is really odd at times because you have to control your emotions and it's awkward and embarrassing if you jump up off your stool in celebration! For Dean's goal I was sat on the opposite touchline to where he took the shot from. I was tracking Frazier Campbell and then heard the City fans erupt. Swinging the camera round to where Dean was I saw him start to run in celebration, but he was running away from me, so all the photos I have are of his back!

Ian Farrow: A sublime volley that was always heading for the net. It came from an imaginative chipped pass from arguably the man who made the biggest single difference to our season, on-loan signing Fraizer Campbell, and followed great work taking the ball forward from another local lad and fan favourite Nick Barmby. A perfect goal on the perfect occasion. It just couldn't have been better.

Steve Lee: Looking back it seems crazy that we witnessed such a cartoonishly fabulous goal scored by a local boy on, historically, our most important match – and on our first ever visit to Wembley. First reaction was obviously to go nuts, which of course we did. That lasted maybe 10 seconds after which we, as one, seemed to realise that all we could do now was screw it up. We'd obviously scored too early and 'typical City' are bound to piss us all off by conceding two late goals to send us off into the early summer evening deciding: "You know what, we've had a few great years but this is where we wake up."

Martin Batchelor: It was the most fantastic goal, Barmby, Campbell and then Deano. It meant so much. I thought of all the people who were not there that day including my late dad who had taken me to my first match so many years before.

James Richardson: I was physically shattered and mentally drained by the time Deano had scored. My brain's decision to allow only an hour's sleep prior to boarding the coach to London didn't feel like a good one at kick-off as caffeine, nerves and adrenaline fought for superiority of my brain. In spite of my fatigue, I spent the seconds prior to Deano's goal shouting at Campbell for not making use of Carey's slip to get a shot away. Thankfully, he didn't listen. There was a split-second silence prior to ball arcing past Basso. I can't remember an awful lot about the moments after: Just chaos. I'm sure we either went over or pulled someone over chairs (it was a friend if it was, honest) but it was such a release after all the anxiety, I just remember the joy and it seemingly lasting several minutes. The next thing I clearly remember is slumping in my chair, spent, and the whistle going for half-time.

Nick Turner: Ten seconds of incoherent bellowing with clenched fists, then a glance at the clock and thinking only seven minutes till half-time – just hold it till half-time.

Gary Johnson: When you see Dean Windass's goal you see the ball fly past Bradley Orr. I can't help but think that maybe – if he hadn't had a depressed cheekbone and knew where he was – he might have got his head to it. It was a fantastic goal though. But it wasn't going to be our day once that all happened.

Alan Wiley: I had a great view of it. Fraizer Campbell went on his run, went down the left-hand side of the penalty area. There was a small challenge on him which got nowhere near him, but I'd moved wide left to make sure I could see the challenge in case I had to make a penalty decision. Then Fraizer Campbell laid it back. I was on the edge of the box with Windass, but 15 yards to his left, so I just saw him hit it. I realised how well he'd hit it, and your next thought as a referee is: 'You've watched the shot. Is it going anywhere near a Bristol City player? Is there a potential handball?' Then when it hits the net you could only think: 'Wow, what a goal!' Knowing Dean's back story your thoughts were also that it couldn't have happened to a nicer player.

Tom Wilson: Seeing Deano score that goal, and to know that I'd helped him just a little bit along the way, I felt so proud for him. It brought tears to my eyes. It still does.

Craig Sargent: My main memory is one of collective joy. It was a day when everyone I had ever known connected to City was there. My mates from back up north, all the Southern Supporters; most people had brought wives, girlfriends and kids. We were all there and for that crazy few seconds after the ball hit the back of the net we ALL knew what it meant. No words needed to be spoken. That was special and we all knew it. It was only after we'd all composed ourselves that we realised there was still two-thirds of the game left to play. This was getting serious! It was only after the event that I realised how great a goal it was. At the time I literally could not take it in.

Ian Thomson: It was too early in the game for anyone in their right mind to be thinking in terms of it being a matchwinner, and I celebrated it purely for the fine goal that it was and the fact that it put us into the lead. We all bounced about and hugged each other, but to be honest if Deano had scored exactly the same goal at the KC in a league game against Oldham or somebody we'd have celebrated it in exactly the same way. The only other thing I thought was: 'Just had to be Deano, didn't it?'

Matt Rudd: I was right behind it. We saw the mild swerve in the volley from the other end and knew it was in. I just jumped up and down like an idiot, what more can you do? Personal reactions to those biggest moments of all tend to get lost when things calm down afterwards.

Ian Bunton: Once Deano scored I actually started to believe we would win, and felt reasonably confident of keeping a clean sheet.

Sean Rush: When Deano scored, he ran past me. You can see it on the TV, I'm just desperate to get water to them because it was so hot. I was screaming: "Where are you going, Wayne? Come over here!" It hadn't really sunk in with me that we'd scored to go 1-0 up in the final!

Mike Hall: I had the kind of view I was unaccustomed to for Deano's Wembley goal, located near the front and in the left-hand corner of the City end, but the moment it left his foot it was obvious it was heading in. I remember the celebrations feeling long and almost dream-like, and then I just wanted us to waste as much time as possible – a mindset I held for the rest of the match. I realise now that with a one-goal cushion and over half of the match left, this would hardly have been the best course of action, but that was the mode I went into from that moment. I think it felt like you could just almost touch the prize on offer and didn't want anything – not even the chance of us being undone on the counterattack – to get in the way.

Sam Ricketts: Dean ended up celebrating by running up my side of the pitch to the Hull fans, and I don't know if anyone has clocked this but the rule is that as soon as all of the team that have just scored are back in their own half the opposition can kick off. I just stood in their half making sure that someone was there so that Bristol City couldn't kick off. So that meant that I never went into the corner and celebrated with Deano. He ran past me and everyone was following him. I missed out on the celebration but that was just being focused on what I thought we needed to do to win the game.

Alan Wiley: I can assure you now, that even if Sam Ricketts had been celebrating down the other end, that game would not have restarted until Hull City were ready.

Ian Ashbee: When Dean scored I switched on and started panicking. I thought: 'I'm not letting this go,' so I was on people more.

Dean Windass: I just focused on the game after that. I didn't know it would be the winning goal, but it was one of them where we'd got our noses in front and I thought we'd go on to get two or three, because we were playing so well at the time.

The next moment of note in the game came when Bristol City's inspirational right-back Bradley Orr collapsed on the pitch. Both sets of players and fans looked on concerned as the physios dealt with a player who wouldn't go down without good reason. It turned out that Orr had depressed his cheekbone in a challenge with Nick Barmby a few minutes before Dean Windass's goal. The delay lasted several minutes before Orr could leave the pitch, without too much assistance. He was replaced by Lee Johnson, forcing Bristol into a reshuffle.

Gary Johnson: Because of the situation with Jamie McCombe pulling out, Bradley Orr had become a lot more important in our set plays, and within 20 or 30 minutes he got a depressed cheekbone. The doctor wanted to take him off initially, but Bradley being Bradley he ran around the pitch and got the referee to call him on. But our doctor was saying he shouldn't have been on the pitch.

Michael Turner: Bradley Orr going off injured was good for us as he was one of their better players. As well as being a good defender he'd bomb up the right wing for them.

Alan Wiley: The game was played in a very good spirit. But when a player goes down with a head injury like that as a referee you're going to start asking yourself the question: 'How's that happened? Have I missed anything?' I asked my two assistant referees if they'd seen anything. I asked the fourth official. No one had. And I was thinking: 'If I have missed something the Bristol City players would be around me.' But nobody came. We got the injury sorted and at half-time the floor manager for Sky, Mick Beard, came in and asked if we'd seen anything, as obviously Sky would want to make a story out of it. We asked if Sky had picked anything up and he said they had no idea either.

After the delays City got into half-time with their lead intact. The key issue during the interval was ensuring that Wayne Brown would be able to stay on the pitch.

Wayne Brown: After 30 or so minutes my calf went again and I was thinking: 'Oh no, here we go!' So I got in at half-time, and the lads were buzzing. I had an injection in my calf. I said I don't know how long I'll be able to get through this. Simon Maltby said: "This should help, you shouldn't feel it that much. You'll probably feel it at the end of the game when it starts wearing off." That was the case and the more the game went on, the more I felt it. On the day we dropped a bit deep which was down to me so we didn't get exposed in behind with their pace. It was an odd feeling, there was a lot of pressure on the game and I just wanted to grind a 1-0 win out.

Phil Brown: Wayne had felt his calf at half-time but I couldn't make any changes as I was catering for the lack of legs of Dean Windass and Nicky Barmby in the latter stages, so they were two of my subs taken up already. If I made a third as early as half-time I might have been struggling later on in the game. This meant we had a different game plan in the second half, and it was quite simply not to come out of defence and rely on the pace of Fraizer and Caleb from the bench, and defend deep. That was because Wayne was playing in the second half on 50% of what he could do.

Simon Maltby: Wayne was struggling a little bit, but we managed it and got him through the game. That's exactly what he'd asked us to do. We imaged his calf and there wasn't too much going on, so it didn't seem like too big a risk. Nobody made him play; we explained what the situation was with his calf and he said he wanted to play. In all my time at the club, not once did we play anyone where it could potentially have had a detrimental long-term impact on them. And I'd never play anyone without them knowing what the full situation of their injury was. If you're only playing players who are 100% in every game throughout a season, you'd be starting with five or six players some weeks. You have to make judgement calls and we made the right call with Browny because he got through the game and there were no long-term issues. I was more concerned about fatigue-related things.

Gary Johnson: You don't know for sure about these things. I didn't know whether it was a major injury or just a knock from which he was going to come out OK. You can't change your tactics around that. We knew Dele Adebola was causing problems anyway with his strength, with or without Wayne Brown's bad calf, and we did create some decent chances.

Sam Ricketts: Phil said at half-time that Browny was struggling but he wanted him on the pitch so we're going to defend deeper. That fed into the second half and I felt that we defended for the whole 45 minutes. I've never watched the game back, but that's what it felt like: a real backs-to-the-wall defensive effort where we were throwing ourselves at everything and trying to get our blocks in. I don't think we had any great chances in that half. For me as an individual – who'd spent all season getting forward and trying to get his crosses in – I used to look at the league stats and my ambition was to get the most crosses in out of all the players in the league. In that final I just couldn't get forward. Part of the reason was because Bristol City played so well, but we also played deep. It was a game of out-and-out defending.

The second half. Forty-five minutes away from unimaginable glory. But at the same time everything to lose. The game took shape with City defending a little deeper and neither side able to gather any sort of momentum.

Andy Dawson: The game was a blur to me. In a normal game of football you're just concentrating on the 90 minutes, but the build up was that big that you can't help but think about the outcomes. There were that many things going through my mind that when I think back it's just a blur.

Gary Johnson: I thought the game was fairly even but we couldn't put the ball in the net, and as we feared it was becoming the Dean Windass story.

Alan Wiley: You firstly say to your two assistants – mainly the one looking after the Hull City defence – that Hull are dropping deeper and most of the play is going to be in that half and there'll be a lot of decision for offside. Then you have to keep the other assistant alert just in case of a Hull City counter-attack. The longer the game went on at 1-0, you knew that Bristol were going to throw everything at Hull. They had nothing to lose. There were a few last-ditch challenges.

Sam Ricketts: We were very strong as a defensive unit. I was a fit player and after going up for a header on around the hour mark I'd got cramp. I thought: 'Hang on a minute, I have not had cramp in my career.'

Rob Smith: I couldn't enjoy the game. I was shaking throughout the 90 minutes. I was a bag of nerves counting the time down. Even when we scored, all I was thinking was could we hang on?

Dean Windass: In my opinion Bristol were the better side on the day. We didn't play well. We had a game plan – to get the ball up to me and Fraizer – but we didn't really pass the ball.

In the 67th minute, Craig Fagan came on for Nick Barmby to play on the left of midfield.

Craig Fagan: Phil would always just say: "Go on there, work hard and enjoy it." To be honest we seemed quite secure so I think I was brought on to give us a bit of energy. I just felt that their players didn't think that they were going to win it. They didn't seem to have confidence they could get back in the game, and that gave me confidence.

Then, in the 71st minute, goalscorer Dean Windass was replaced by Caleb Folan.

Caleb Folan: That was one of the few times I felt really nervous because I knew what was at stake and I knew it would only take one mistake. I was just trying to keep it simple, which was what I'd been told coming on. I just didn't want to let anyone down. And there were some nervy moments.

Defences remained on top with the prize getting ever closer as the game wore on.

Fraizer Campbell: It was hard work. I got cramp in the end. We had to work our socks off, but we knew that was how it had to be to get what we wanted.

Sam Ricketts: With about 78 minutes gone there was a little break in play and I looked at Michael Turner and said: "Turnsy, if we don't concede in the next 12 minutes we're in the Premier League." It was a surreal moment. We looked at each other, and I said: "Twelve minutes Turnsy, come on, we can do this."

Sky's cameras kept cutting to Dean Windass and Nick Barmby sitting side by side on the bench, two Hull lads whose careers had got off to vastly different starts but had converged at the right time in the most wonderful way imaginable. Two Hull lads who represented different sides to the city we loved so much.

Nick was the schoolboy prodigy, the former Tottenham, Liverpool and England player whose cultured style had won him admirers all over the country. Dean was the council estate kid who was released by the club as a teenager only to battle his way back to become a Premier League player. Nick represented the Hull we like to show to outsiders; the Sunday afternoon walk around the Marina, the cappuccino in the café at the Ferens Art Gallery, the trip to see the new John Godber play at Spring Street Theatre. Dean represented a different – but equally wonderful – side of the same city; the 10 pints in Cheese on a Saturday night, the patty and chips, the liaison with the 32-year-old grandmother round the back of Tower. We couldn't love either of them more, but now they were as powerless as the rest of us, reduced to the status of fans watching as their team-mates gave their all to secure the club that meant everything to us top-flight football for the first time ever.

Nick Barmby: I can't remember exactly what Deano was saying. He'll have just been talking and talking. You can't shut him up. He'll have been talking about his goal.

Hull City had had the attacking 'moment' they needed back in the 38th minute. Now they were in need of a defensive moment. Two to be precise. In the 85th minute the ball was looped into the City six-yard box. Boaz Myhill punched it out straight to Lee Trundle who chested the ball on to his trusty left foot and struck it goalwards. However, having Michael Turner in your defence had been tantamount to having two goalkeepers for much of that season. And, as he'd been doing for the past 18 months in a Hull City shirt, Turner made a vital intervention.

Michael Turner: I remember a cross coming in and it being knocked down and falling to Lee Trundle. I just tried to get in the way of it really. As a defender I've always loved blocking shots – blocking a shot coming towards your goal is as good a feeling as a striker scoring a goal for me at times – and I just tried to make myself as big as I could. Then it hit my thigh and went over the goal. Looking back at that I was spread out and my arm was quite high. On another day it could have hit my arm and I'd have given a penalty away, so it was a little bit of luck maybe.

Wayne Brown: We got a bit of luck and Michael Turner put in a fantastic block from about seven or eight yards out which was phenomenal. Bo pulled off a few good saves and kept us in the game.

Four minutes later it was Sam Ricketts' turn to break Bristolian hearts. Ivan Sproule hit a low ball across the City six-yard box. All it needed was a toe poke from a Bristol City player and it was 1-1. Just as Darren Byfield stretched to pull the score level, Ricketts appeared and cleared the ball from danger. We could breathe again. Just.

Sam Ricketts: Michael Turner had blocked a shot just before, then I got mine in. You don't ever want to make last-minute blocks but it's really satisfying for me as an individual, but also for the coaches, as that sort of thing is the result of hours and hours of work on the training ground, ensuring you're in the right position all the time and stuff like that. That goes unnoticed to some extent.

Michael Turner: Sam Ricketts made a great clearance from a good cross they put in. As a team we defended brilliantly.

Dean Windass: I always felt we wouldn't concede. Michael Turner and Sam Ricketts' blocks were *the* big points, not my goal. Those blocks – and keeping a clean sheet – that's what wins you football matches.

Andy Dawson: There were nervous times in the game, but when you need people to stand up and be counted we had those big characters. It was certainly an occasion that I'll never forget. I still get goosebumps now if I see any of the highlights.

Gary Johnson: I was trying not to think it, but by the end I was just thinking: 'This isn't going to be our day.' Right at the end, Darren Byfield was within an inch of putting the ball in the net, and that was when the realisation hit me that it was going to be Hull's day.

The efforts of Michael Turner and Wayne Brown had not been lost on a couple of former City players who knew a thing or two about defending.

Tom Wilson: Michael Turner and Wayne Brown were terrific together. They just never got split up. Wayne Brown reminded me a lot of Pete Skipper as a player.

Pete Skipper: Michael Turner is one of the best centre-halves to have ever played for Hull City. And Browny was one of those lads where you don't really appreciate what they do because he just gets on with his job. He wasn't the quickest but very rarely got done. It was a terrific partnership.

The clock ticked on, too slowly for Hull City fans, too quickly for Bristol City fans. It was agony. Beautiful agony, but agony nonetheless.

Matt Rudd: My main memory of that game was spending the second half gibbering like a child, convinced City would concede an equaliser, because that's what City usually do.

Andy Dawson: I remember thinking there wasn't long left and looking at the clock – something I'd never usually do.

Paul Duffen: It had been the longest hour of our lives. We were all stupefied. I loved the shots of Dean Windass on the side chewing his fingernails. It was a nightmare! Every time they came into our half I didn't want to watch.

Bryan Hughes: We did a lot of running in midfield because we were so deep. It was just one of those things – one of our team-mates had an injury and we had to get round it. Some of the last-ditch stuff we did to keep Bristol out, that was a squad coming together for the whole season and digging in for the last 45 minutes of it. That's just what we had. We were never going to concede that day. That was the belief we had going through the squad.

Richard Garcia: I remember the defending the team did in the last 10 to 15 minutes when Bristol really threw everything they had at us. Every one of us was willing to run that extra yard for each other.

Martin Batchelor: How long was that last 15 minutes? It seemed to last forever.

Michael Turner: I think defending deeper suited my game a little. We were confident of not conceding given how we'd defended all season. Coming towards the end of the game we were getting tired. Had it gone to extra time we'd have struggled as they were on the front foot and we were on our last legs. But I was quietly confident that we'd hang on.

Nick Turner: I must have looked at the clock at least once a minute throughout the second half. Sixty minutes gone – two-thirds of the game gone, 66 minutes gone, three-quarters gone, 70 gone – 20 minutes left, 75 minutes gone – into the last quarter-of-an-hour, and so on. City were keeping them at arm's length and Bristol did not have any cutting edge. Just avoid risks and unforced errors and it's ours.

On 89 minutes, Dean Marney – an integral cog to Hull City that season – got a deserved chance to contribute to the final act, coming on for Fraizer Campbell.

Dean Marney: I managed to train the day before and thankfully Phil Brown put me on the bench, which he didn't have to do. I was very grateful for that, as I'd felt I'd contributed throughout the season. But missing those key games at the end left a bit of a sour taste even though I was buzzing for the team.

Fraizer Campbell: It was tense. When you're on the pitch it's not too bad but when you're sat on the bench you're constantly looking at the clock and every time they attack you're thinking: 'Oh no, not this time.' It's just like being a fan from up close. It was agonising.

The board went up. Four minutes of added time. Technically it may have been four minutes, 240 seconds, but to several thousand Hull City fans it was a lifetime. So close. So agonising. Four minutes became three, which became two, which became one. Then, in the 93rd minute, Dele Adebola headed goalwards. Boaz punched it out under pressure but the ball fell to dangerman Lee Trundle on Bristol City's right. Seconds left. Just seconds. Fucking seconds. Trundle looped in a high cross. Boaz raised his hands and got under the ball. It landed safely in them. We knew then. We just knew. Wayne Brown knew too, and provided – with the unwitting help of Boaz – one of the most iconic images of the day.

Wayne Brown: It was a cross that came in. I shielded the attacker to help Bo. When he took it, I'm thinking: 'That's it, the game's over', because I'd already asked the ref how long was to go. So as soon as Bo caught it I was just relief, thinking: 'We've done it.' I don't know why, I just jumped on his back with excitement. A strange moment. I don't know what came over me!

Boaz Myhill: Getting kissed by a sweaty Wayne Brown, urgh! To be fair, he'd done amazingly to stay on the pitch. He'd been struggling quite badly and we ended up sitting back deeply to cope with that and in the end it all worked out. It was just meant to be.

Nick Barmby: That last 10 minutes seemed to take an eternity. Bo made saves, Michael Turner and Sam Ricketts made blocks. When Bo caught the ball and Wayne Brown jumped on him I was just thinking: 'Put that whistle in your mouth ref and blow it.'

Raich Carter Junior: I'll always remember those two tackles by Turner and Ricketts. They were amazing. Then when Bo caught the ball to get the kiss from Wayne Brown, that was sheer relief. It still sends shivers down my spine.

Bristol City had statistically had the best of the match. They'd had 21 shots (13 on target) compared with Hull City's 11 shots (four on target). Only one of those 32 shots had met with the back of the net, however. The man responsible for that shot was sat on the bench but was desperate to be back on the pitch.

Dean Windass: Mark Prudhoe had his stopwatch set, and when the fourth official put up how many minutes were left, Pruds was leaning over to me and Barmbs saying "two-and-a-half minutes", "two minutes", "90 seconds", "one minute"… I was going to Barmbs: "Just blow the whistle, ref." Then when Wayne jumped on Boaz's back, Nicky said to me: "When the referee blows the whistle, we're running over there." And that's what we did.

Alan Wiley blew the final whistle. Some Hull City fans celebrated. Some embraced those around them – friends, family, strangers, stewards. Some sat and stared wide-eyed, unable to take in what they had just witnessed. Others cried. They cried for the grandparents, parents, uncles, aunties, brothers, sisters, friends, even sons and daughters who were no longer around to witness this most incredible of occasions, but who had been the club's lifeblood throughout its history. They cried for their city – blasted to pieces by the Luftwaffe, brought to its knees by the Cod Wars, the 'Crap Town' derided and sneered at for decades by the ignorant and arrogant. They cried for their club – all too often the punchline to a joke that wasn't funny anymore, living on a hand-to-mouth existence for much of the past 30 years. Thousands of men and women from one of the toughest, most resilient, most fantastic cities in Europe sat and cried in public. And they were right to cry. Right then, at that point, there was no team anywhere in the world that was better to support, to love, to cry over, than Hull City AFC.

Dave Burns: I said at the end of the game, and I felt this way myself as I could feel my voice filling up and my throat going: "It's OK, you can cry now." From a personal and professional point of view I was pleased with that as it felt right. I knew there'd have been people listening and crying as it had been hugely emotional. It was an honour and a privilege to commentate on it.

Phil Brown: One-nil is never enough until the whistle goes and then it's the greatest scoreline in the world.

Ian Ashbee: When the final whistle went I felt like a job had been done, and I felt that in Hull's history I'd achieved something that was commendable. I'd never been the best footballer in the world but I've got something I can look back on and say I've achieved, especially having done it with one football club. I felt privileged and honoured to have achieved that. It's something I'm proud of.

Nick Barmby: When Alan Wiley blew the final whistle it was the quickest I'd ever run on that pitch, to the fans. We stayed out for a long, long time with the fans singing all the songs. Brilliant.

Dean Windass: That was the quickest I'd moved all afternoon.

Phil Brown: My emotions at first were tinged with a feeling for the opposition manager. One manager was going towards the top table of English football and the other was condemned to another year in the Championship. It would have been as big for Bristol City as it was for Hull. They are two fairly similar cities – a lot of working-class people, a lot of industry, a lot of reasons for being on the terraces on a Saturday as an outlet in their lives. We'd fulfilled the dreams of 40,000 people to my left, but shattered the dreams of 40,000 people to my right, and that put me for a split-second in a reflective mood, thinking of what a great game it is. I still get emotional about it now.

Having had that moment of respect for Gary Johnson and shaking his hand, I then had Brian Horton and Steve Parkin hanging off my neck, which took it up to the next level of excitement and realisation. It was party time. That was the moment we realised that all our hard work was being rewarded. A couple of years of hard work had gone into that day, a relegation avoidance campaign and then a promotion campaign. Both had ended in an achievement, but the euphoria and the feeling of success from promotion lasted longer.

Bryan Hughes: It was pure elation. You could just see the team spirit. It was there in that moment. The reaction from everyone, not just the lads that were on the pitch, but the bench, the guys who weren't involved, the elation through everyone was amazing. We weren't individuals, we were a team. On paper we weren't the best team in the league, but as the season went on no one enjoyed playing against us because they knew what they were going to get from us. And we had a bit of quality in there. We had experience and youth. We had runners and guile. We had a bit of everything. Hats off to Phil Brown, he put that together.

Dean Windass: I'm a very emotional person. I'll cry at soaps on the telly so you can imagine what I was like. When I got to near the City fans I was thinking: 'What have I just done?' I was just staring at the supporters. It brought back being a six-year-old kid watching Hull City at Boothferry Park with my dad. And then I'd just done that. It was unbelievable!

Caleb Folan: When the whistle went the ball dropped on my chest. I picked it up and just started crying and fell to the floor. Sometimes the enormity of something doesn't hit you immediately but that hit me straight away.

Wayne Brown: My immediate reaction was to go to their players. I was just thinking how devastated they were. Then I hobbled off and joined my team-mates. We celebrated with everybody from the kit man right the way through to all the players and the fans.

Matt Duke: It's always worse watching, as you can't control anything. On the pitch you're concentrating on the game, not thinking of certain scenarios. Those last few minutes were horrible, but the relief when the final whistle went was just incredible. We'd had a bad start to the season and no one was talking about promotion. It was just amazing.

Sam Ricketts: When the final whistle went it was just a realisation that our dream to play in the Premier League was there. A lot of us had probably thought we'd never get to play there. It was just such an amazing feeling of satisfaction, and the celebrations around the pitch could have gone on all night. It was such an amazing experience to be on such a high that lasted months and months and months.

Richard Garcia: I was near Sam Ricketts and we hugged while screaming things. I can't remember what we were screaming but it was just pure joy and relief. Walking around to the fans and celebrating as a group was fantastic but it was only when I got back into the dressing rooms and had some time to reflect that it actually started to sink in.

Michael Turner: It was just relief and pure joy. Such a great feeling. We've all watched games at Wembley – play-off finals, cup finals – where you see teams celebrating at the end and it was a dream to be doing that on the pitch in front of 40,000 Hull City fans. The team spirit showed throughout the season but particularly in that game.

Andy Dawson: The final whistle – I'd never had a feeling like that in a game of football. All the emotions had built up, all of those things going through your mind from the morning just came out. I ran over to where I thought my family were and I saw them, it was just an emotional day.

Dean Marney: A lot of people questioned me for turning down the new deal at Spurs to go to Hull, and then when I struggled in the first season a lot of people thought I'd made a mistake. This felt like vindication.

Fraizer Campbell: I don't really remember the celebrations straight after. I was shattered, physically and emotionally drained.

Paul Duffen: My wife was there with my daughter and my four sons, sat in the royal box on the front row, and it was the most extraordinary euphoria. When the team started coming up the steps I thought I was in a dream or a Hollywood movie. It's quite a ridiculous experience to have that much focus – where everybody's there and you know that you've been part of something that is forever going to be important to hundreds of thousands of people. It's a rare opportunity and a privilege to be part of something that writes history. That's when I was overwhelmed, humbled. The time the fans stayed in the stadium at Wembley and the celebrations and tears – I'm a crier! – was nothing short of extraordinary. Life changing.

Craig Fagan: My instant reaction was one of delight. It felt better than it had done with Derby, and that was nothing negative about Derby but I'd been through so much with Hull, I knew how hard everyone had worked. Not just the players, but all the staff around the ground, the people in the offices, the groundsman. It was a celebration of everybody coming together and it did really feel like that at the party after. We were all in it together, it was a family club. And there was real excitement over what was coming up.

Mike White: You were just thinking: 'They've done it.' I was in the tunnel at that point, with a white bib on that allowed me to go out on the pitch. Phil Brown was getting interviewed by Sky, but in my mind he was the first person that I wanted to speak to. Then I just had a moment of realisation: I was at Wembley standing in the centre circle and City were going to the Premier League. The fan part of me kicked in and I thought back to playing on the Recker at Hessle pretending to be scoring for City at Wembley, daydreaming. Then I realised that Phil had finished with Sky and was walking up towards me and I had to be a journalist again.

Peter Swan: Even though I expected it, it was still a shock. I had to sit back and take it all in. Hull City in the Premier League? It just didn't fit right. But I knew it was a new chapter and I knew it was going to be fantastic. It just shows what you can do with a lot of hard work and the right people in the right places behind the scenes, as had been there under Peter Taylor and Phil Brown. At no point under them did City stand still. They'd keep moving forward, making difficult decisions if they had to.

Ian Farrow: At the final whistle I looked around with my camera to take photos. I couldn't find any of my friends who weren't crying. It was unbelievable. It was an ocean of emotion. Many people around me were carrying photos of fathers and grandfathers who had passed away having never seen, after many years as a supporter, City at either Wembley or in the top flight. They wanted these people to share the experience. I suppose that is, at its best, the loyalty and love football can produce.

Sean Rush: The senior players really came through on that day. I watch that final a lot, and you could say that Bristol were the better side on the day, but we had the players that would put blood on the shirts. We had lads out there who were dying for the cause. Wayne Brown was struggling with an injury, Caleb took a knock, it was full of Roy of the Rovers moments.

Nick Barmby: In my interview after the game I said that I've known a lot of people across the generations that have seen dark days at Hull City that weren't there to watch their team play at Wembley. It was for them. It was for the fans now. It was amazing. One of the best days ever for me professionally.

Gary Clark: My immediate thoughts were for the people I have known along the way who are no longer with us who would never have seen Hull City play in the top division. Also it shut up, for once and for all, those who had doubted and knocked us along the way.

Rob Smith: When you realised we'd won, the emotions… it just hits you. I've never watched the game back as I want the memories to be as I remember them. I just kept saying to myself: "We are in the Premier League." I looked round at the guys from the Football League who I'd known for years, and I was in tears. They just nodded their heads in approval as if to say: "You guys deserve that, after everything you've been through."

Frank and Margaret Beill: At the final whistle there was what seemed like several seconds of complete silence before the roar. It was a feeling of mass disbelief. Margaret often talks of that time when the world stood still. Hull City, the perennial underachievers, had done what we had waited for all our lives as supporters. Our party of 17 family and friends had tears rolling down their cheeks but all the cheering, screaming, crying and hysterical laughter came after a split second of eerie silence when your brain could not comprehend how you were supposed to feel. It wasn't supposed to happen because good things never happened to Hull City. Our son asked: "What do we do now?"

Alan Wiley: On a game as big as that, you don't want it decided on a controversial refereeing decision. That's your first aim. Second, you want to reach a stage that when people talk about the game the following day and people ask who the referee was, they can't remember. That's what you aim for. We were aware that with Windass scoring the goal, the media already had their headlines. We just had to concentrate on our own job. So at the final whistle we were just thinking: 'Job well done, nobody's talking about us.'

Paul Duffen: Phil, Brian, Steve Parkin and I had been a very close unit. I don't think we spoke very much when we saw each other after, it was more expletives than English words. More of an emotional vomit than anything else.

Steve Lee: The whole second half was spent in a kind of masochistic stupor just wishing it would end. In short I didn't really enjoy it. Couldn't enjoy it. I just wanted it all to be over and when the final whistle went I felt so drained I could barely smile. It was a mixture of relief and disbelief. I think it was only in the pub later that it finally started to sink in and we could revel in what had just happened.

Mike Hall: The rest of the match remains a blur, but at full-time when the subs ran onto the pitch to celebrate and the big screens confirmed we were in the Premier League I can clearly remember thinking that this isn't what supporting Hull City is like. Hull City do not do things like this.

Raich Carter Junior: Straight away, I was thinking: 'Shit, I've got to go to Old Trafford now!' It was the perfect day.

Gary Johnson: I felt the atmosphere was good. I remember the Hull City fans at the end were unbelievably jubilant but respectful. Both sets of fans were respectful to the opposition. It was a friendly cup final. Phil Brown impressed me too. All of us managers, when we've beaten a team, you always say unlucky to the opposing manager and you sort of mean it but sort of don't. On the day Phil was genuinely excited but after he'd gone to see the Hull players and fans he did come up to our lads and came to see me and seemed genuinely understanding of our situation. He was very humble in his comments but also in his persona. I appreciated that.

Phil Buckingham: If I went out for a drink in Beverley you'd often see the players out socialising together. We all knew each other on first-name terms. When you saw them walking up the steps at Wembley you knew what it meant to them all. You were genuinely choked for them.

Mike White: You always look for those moments that are going to be played eternally. One of them was the trophy presentation. It was coming towards Ash, who was about to lift it, and I said: "From League 2 to League 1, from League 1 to the Championship, and now from the Championship to the Premier League…" and just at that point Ash lifted the trophy and the crowd erupted. I couldn't have timed it any better!

Ian Ashbee – a man who epitomised everything we loved about both Hull City and Kingston upon Hull given how many times he'd been written off, the physical battering he'd endured, his against-the-odds comeback from injury – raised the trophy and then it was time to party.

Caleb Folan: When we were celebrating on the pitch I looked down and there was just a ribbon, my medal was gone. I must have lost it on the pitch. I couldn't find it. Ten minutes later Craig Fagan tapped me on the shoulder and he had it in his hand.

Dean Windass: Nick Barmby is a more intelligent lad than I am, and when we'd been interviewed on the pitch you could see he knew what it meant to everybody, not just what it meant to me and him growing up as City fans. Hull gets a lot of bad publicity and Nick said to the reporter: "It's not just the fact that Hull City are in the Premier League, it's going to have a big impact on the city, and on its businesses." We'd put Hull on the map.

Matt Duke: I'd gone from getting the worst news ever to going to the Premier League within the space of about five months. It was a bit of a rollercoaster ride.

Bernard Noble: It was the best day ever. We were all so emotional. When the whistle went, within five minutes half the stadium was empty, just the Hull City fans left.

Boaz Myhill: It was great to see what a big impact it had on the city and how much happiness it brought to so many people.

Paul Duffen: I can't think of anything more crushing than losing a play-off final. For us it would have been horrible, but for Bristol City, having been top for much of the season, it was a crushing way to finish it. My respect, because of the dignity shown by Steve Lansdown, Gary Johnson and all of the Bristol City officials, was immense.

Brendon Smurthwaite: The celebrations were quite low key for us doing the media and the websites. The after-match stuff took forever as everyone was in demand. We did the on-pitch interviews, then there's the radio stuff in the tunnel. I went into the dressing room to see Sam Allardyce in there with a big bottle of Becks. I had to do a load of stuff for Tigers Player. Then we did the stuff for the written press with Browny and Dean Windass. At the end, I went up to the players lounge seeing Dean sat on the floor with a bottle of beer just totally gone. Not drunk, just knackered. He had nothing left to give that day.

Rob Smith: Afterwards we were dignified, but were trying to work out what had just happened. Then Russell Bartlett came towards me – he's a big guy – he lifted me so high in the air I banged my head on the ceiling.

Brendon Smurthwaite: I always remember in the written presser a journalist saying to Phil: "Do you think this proves you as a manager after the Derby failure?" It was such a weird thing to ask on an occasion like that. Browny just said: "I'll let you decide."

Dean Windass: After the game in the dressing room, I saw Phil and we both had a bottle of beer. He chinked my bottle with his, and I just said to him: "What the fuck has just happened?"

Paul Duffen: I sat with Phil in the changing room with a beer with the boys going bonkers everywhere around us, and we were just thinking: 'This is bonkers!'

Gary Johnson: It was a big old day for our lads. Not many of them had been that close before. Not many of them had played in the Premier League. Although I was disappointed on the day we coped with it well. It's the supporters that get the most disappointed. I was more disappointed when I checked on my contract and saw what I'd be on if we'd got in the Premier League. That's when I really started crying!

Ian Thomson: I saw promotion to the Premier League as just reward for a group of fans who had for many years been the most loyal and long-suffering in the English game. I thought I would never live to see City in the top flight. It was and is the ultimate bogey laid to rest.

Rich Lusmore: It was enough to make a grown man cry. This was Hull City. Hull City! We weren't supposed to be in the Premier League! It was a time when those who you knew had followed the club through the bleakest of times could really enjoy the moment. And, of course, thoughts also turned to those who hadn't lived long enough to see it.

Nick Turner: One massive 104-year-old monkey off our collective civic back, a 100% success record at Wembley, a spectacular £60m volley scored the by the Hometown Kid, a historic moment that changed the club's profile forever, perennial forgotten underachievers transformed into the newest members of the world's richest league, every doubter silenced, every naysayer gainsaid, every scornful neighbour or smirking colleague put in his place, all the depressing defeats and disappointing draws consigned to the shade in the blazing Wembley sunshine, Hull Shitty no more, Yorkshire's number one, first time lucky after more than a century. Multiply all this by 38,000, add alcohol and turn up the volume to 11.

Mike White: I got Ash just before they were about to go into the dressing room. He was so emotional he could barely speak. I got enough out of him but he was on the edge. It just showed what it meant to him.

Mike Hall: As a spectacle it wasn't great, but as an experience it seemed to bring to the surface every visceral feeling I'd developed supporting the club. It was gut-wrenchingly raw to watch, of course, and to know what was at stake – how one error could take everything away and totally change the future direction of the club.

These feelings didn't come from just my 25 or so years of supporting the club at that point, and wondering whether I'd ever witness a City team at Wembley (let alone with a game to win promotion to the Premier League), they also came from generations of my family who are no longer with us – they didn't get to see anything like an occasion like that, so the privilege of being there was not lost on me.

The fact I was there to see it with my dad too meant an awful lot. The Hull City story has played a big part in our relationship and that realisation was laid bare that afternoon and as a result produced almost every emotion I'm capable of experiencing.

To me, supporting a football club is strange insofar as it often finds you paying good money to spend most of your time longing for the end, and I think that's a condition often lost on people who don't like football, or only casually watch it or loosely support a team. That match came as close to any for me to answering the question of why supporting a club can mean as much as it does. It took days to recover and an entire summer to let it sink in.

Roy North: I'll never forget it. Even – begrudgingly – Waggy told me we had a good team!

Gary Clark: It was the pinnacle of my life supporting my home-town club, to actually play at Wembley, to score at Wembley and to win a final at Wembley to put us in the Premier League. I could have dropped off my mortal coil that afternoon and died a happy man. My bucket list was complete.

John Cooper: I travelled down on the staff coach. You hope it's going to turn out right. I had access to the staircase under the royal box. As the players came up the steps at the end, we were at the top. We had a great view of the players coming up. I managed to get down to the bottom and see Brian Horton – who'd I've known for years – and we had a hug. It was a moment I'll never forget.

Raich Carter Junior: I was in shock. I cried once or twice. My grandad, who'd followed City all his life, once said to me: "I hate to say it son, but I don't think you'll ever see City play at Wembley." It was emotional for the people who weren't there.

Mark Robinson: I was at Sussex cricket club and we happened to have a day off and we were playing in London the next day, so it all worked our perfectly. The day was surreal. It was like being in a dream. There was a picture of the crowd celebrating in 4-4-2 magazine that I was in. Someone at Sussex got the picture framed and it got put up in my office at Hove. I'd won various trophies and achieved lots of things in cricket, but that poster of me and my friend celebrating was the best thing up there.

Paul Denman: I was asleep at the time! I was managing my son's band, Orange, and they played the last show of a long American tour in Portland, Oregon, the night before the game. I drove 14 hours straight through the night to get back to LA so I could listen to the game on the radio, but unfortunately I was so knackered I fell asleep and missed it all. A mate called me, woke me up, and said: "We're in the Premier League and Deano scored the winner!" I cried for three days solid, and I'm crying now as I write. It was probably the single most emotional moment of my life, and that includes having two children and getting married.

Nick Barmby: It's up there domestically. I wanted to play for my country, which I was lucky enough to do. I wanted to play in a major tournament, which I did. I wanted to win a trophy – a European trophy – which I did. But to be at Wembley with your home-town club and to see the black and amber army, including my wife, my youngest son, George (my eldest was in Spain with school, watching it from a bar, and hopefully not drinking!), my late brother-in-law, my family and friends; it was very emotional. Just great, great memories.

Matt Rudd: Credibility, excitement, justification for continued support in the lousiest times, joyous disbelief and, despite the obvious need to embrace a new, unprecedented future, a nostalgic look back at people who had helped us get there despite not being associated with the club on the day our Premier League status was confirmed.

Rob Harmer: Quite simply, it meant we'd arrived.

Robert Crampton: I just went crazy. Everybody did. It was a feeling of the most ecstatic happiness combined with shock, pleasure, delight… It was a sensation of the most pure, unbridled happiness.

Nick Barmby: You should be forever thankful to that whole team for being the first team to get us to the top flight.

Mark Herman: That week I had dreams, every single night, vivid, ultra-realistic dreams, of Wembley and all permutations of results; last-minute defeat, losing on penalties, a Myhill howler, etc… Each morning I'd wake up relieved that it was all a dream, the defeat wasn't real. Then came the actual day, it was so dream-like. Wembley Way a sea of amber and black, the sunshine and clear blue sky, then the stuff of dreams on the pitch, Windass, sublime, unreal. Totally unreal. The celebrations, then into the car and driving west along the M4, in an ocean of red, surrounded by miserable Bristol City fans, the scarves drooping sadly out of windows, surreal again. I start to think, is this just another dream? No, it can't be, this is so much longer than all the others. Then I get to the hotel near Hay Festival, I check in, freshen up, pinch myself once again before heading down to the bar where I see, lined up, Salman Rushdie, the comedian Dave Gorman (wearing wellies) and former US president

Jimmy Carter. I think, it *is* another dream. It was only waking up the next morning and reading the papers that I was finally convinced.

Nick Turner: If Carlsberg did historic Wembley wins... it would be just like this one, except Deano's goal would be at our end rather than the far one!

Simon Maltby: When I joined the club, I was expecting us to get in the Championship at some point, but getting into the Premier League was amazing.

Roy Bly: It was quite something – emotional – to go somewhere like that and see all those people from the city. It was like Hull was empty. The atmosphere was amazing. It was a great game, and we played ever so well. The strength of it was that we didn't let a goal in. Such an amazing day to experience.

Dave Richardson: I guess all City fans will say the same. It was the high point in any fan's experience. Considering the shenanigans at the club at the turn of the century it's a remarkable achievement. It doesn't matter when you started supporting the club it must be the best feeling ever that your club has reached the highest level of English football in the best league in the world. Not really for me to say but it might be that little bit more poignant for those of us who stood on the terraces at Boothferry Park singing: "From Boothferry to Wembley".

Dave Burns: I would say that one of the most fundamental things to have happened to the city, which helped bring success to the football club and Hull FC, and maybe even helped with attracting Siemens and becoming the City of Culture, was the decision by the local council to build the KC Stadium. That was a symbol of confidence, of optimism. There was a sense that things could be done in the city. That development lit the bluetouch paper for the city's future. Where would Hull City and Hull FC be if the stadium hadn't been built? I know the council get stick, but they deserve great credit for it. Wembley wouldn't have happened without the stadium. And the City of Culture might not have happened too, as City going up put Hull on the map and gave the people the confidence to say: "Actually we can achieve something. It's OK to be proud to be from Hull." City getting to the Premier League opened up that door. It gave the city a taste for success. It opened up the city to the world.

Sean Rush: Of the celebrations the main thing I remember is, on one of the hottest days of the year and everyone dehydrated, the boys are coming off and the champagne is flying and Andy Dawson gets a drug test and starts going mental because he couldn't join in the celebrations. We ended up waiting on the coach for Andy so that he could have a pee.

While the current players celebrated on the pitch and in the changing room, dozens of former players were delighted to have seen their old club achieve what had looked a long way off for much of its history.

Alan Fettis: I was delighted for Dean, delighted for the club, it was fantastic. Dave Burns rang me just before the game asking what I felt about the game. I told him that there'd be one goal in it and Dean Windass would have a big say. It just seemed to be written in the stars for him. I was delighted for everybody associated with the club, especially from my period there.

Ben Burgess: I was on a stag-do in Dublin. I was just watching it as a fan. It was such a great moment when Dean Windass scored. Sometimes you can be bitter when you leave a club but I've only got good feelings towards Hull City and good memories. It was just unbelievable. Phil Brown did a tremendous job. It was just really nice to see.

Warren Joyce: I felt pride. I was delighted for Hull City and the people of Hull, but I was delighted for Fraizer too because you want lads who you've helped along the way to have moments like that in their career. That moment will last with him throughout his life. That's what you want from the young players you're developing. I was buzzing for the Hull City fans and for Fraizer.

Brian Little: I managed quite a few teams in football. There are a couple that I don't bother for to be honest, but Hull City and Darlington are teams I have a massive affection for to this day. When I went to Hull, I knew the club was capable of going through the leagues. I always knew they'd go back up there. To see them go where they were was incredible. It was nice to have played a small part in that story.

Adam Lowthorpe: That second half seemed to drag on and on. When the final whistle blew and everything unfolded in front of you it was just brilliant. It was something we never thought we'd see. There was a massive sense of being proud of the club, a sense of being proud of being from Hull.

Marc Joseph: I was on holiday in Thailand watching the final and I was as proud that day as when we beat Yeovil in 2004 to get the ball rolling. I still had a few mates in that team, and mates around Hull, and seeing them achieve this was as important for me as anything else we'd done.

Damien Delaney: I made my debut for Ireland that night. A lot of people were asking me if I'd regretted leaving Hull that day, but it is what it is. We were playing Serbia at Croke Park and I woke up from a sleep in the afternoon, turned on the TV and saw the Hull players celebrating going up. I was genuinely delighted but I had a game to get ready for. It was fantastic though. The club had done brilliantly, Phil had done brilliantly, and they were obviously proved right in everything that they did.

Chris Chilton: I watched the play-off final in my back room that used to be my kids' playroom. I just wanted them to win because of the prestige it would bring Hull City AFC. I knew it would make a vast difference to the city and the club. It was wonderful to see. I was elated for Dean Windass but there are 11 guys who go down that tunnel and it was a collective thing. They defended very well indeed.

Pete Skipper: I couldn't believe we were there. The squad wasn't the best in the division, but they had some very good players and a fantastic captain who did remarkably well for the football club. And he was a far better player than people give him credit for. Everyone knew what fantastic players Nick and Deano were, but they had defenders who'd put their body on the line when they had to.

Billy Whitehurst: I went to watch my old boot boy Deano score his goal at Wembley, and then I drove to Wimbledon to watch the semi-finals of the greyhound derby. It was one of the best days of my life.

Billy Askew: I just thought it was great. I wish it had been me volleying that in! But it was fantastic. I always loved Deano.

Stuart Elliott: I was in London as I'd be playing in the League 1 play-off final with Doncaster the next day. Having to watch Hull City get promoted while sitting in a hotel in London with another team was very difficult for me considering my attachment with the club over all those years. My one regret is that I didn't get to go into the Premier League with Hull City.

Ken Houghton: I was there. Everybody said we'd never get to the First Division and you got it in your mind that it might never happen. But the lads did us proud. I was biting my nails more than I've ever done at the end. It was a nice feeling.

Martin Fish: I watched the game on television. I was delighted and proud. I sat back and thought that everything that I'd been through in the 1990s, all of that grind, was worthwhile.

Garreth Roberts: It wasn't the best game – a bit dour. It didn't really deserve a goal of that quality to win it, but it was nice that Deano scored because he was a youngster when I was at the club. Many people say it was a mistake for Brian Horton to get rid of him back then but Dean would be the first to admit he wasn't ready. Letting him go gave him the kick up the arse he needed to start taking the game seriously. I had loads of family at the game and to see them get to the Premier League was great. I'm sad that my generation never got to that stage but I'd never begrudge the players that did.

John Kaye: I was very happy. They'd been trying for a long time! I still follow Hull City. It's still one of the first results I look for.

Dean Windass's goal is to this day considered one of the greatest scored at the 'new' Wembley. One of its few rivals was scored one year later by former City striker Gary Alexander for Millwall against Scunthorpe. So how does he view the two strikes?

Gary Alexander: We'd both probably dreamt of scoring goals at Wembley for our boyhood clubs, mine being Millwall and Dean's being Hull. It's special. Both being centre-forwards though, we'd have both taken a tap in from a yard out. We can take great pleasure from scoring great goals for our clubs. Mine was better though!

Some Hull City fans who'd had the foresight to book London accommodation (or, indeed, those hundreds of City fans who lived in the capital) ventured into whatever pubs they could find to celebrate the night away. Others made their way back to Hull, still trying to take in what had just happened.

Nick Turner: The £60-a-go Thomas Cook special train back was officially dry (as designated by the nanny state) but resourceful Hull folk were not to be denied on this night of glory, and appropriate refreshments were taken as befitted such an occasion. The strong May sun was still shining as the train headed north with its dazed passengers in a state of blissfully euphoric disbelief. Weary travellers just gazed out of the window, barely unable to comprehend the magnitude of what they had just witnessed. Others jigged a celebratory conga down the carriage aisle. City had won at Wembley and got promoted to the Premier League. Things would never be the same again.

After all the media work was done and the stadium was emptied, Hull City's players, managers, boardroom and many others made their way back to the Grove where a party was planned.

Paul Duffen: There was a calm about it. Not to sound arrogant but there was a certain kind of expectation about this unstoppable destiny that we were actors in. We then went back to the Grove and there was a party.

Dean Windass: We went to the Grove. Paul Duffen told us that we had a marquee at the back of where the hotel was. I said to him: "What if we'd got beat?" He just said: "It was never in any doubt."

Rob Smith: When we got back to the Grove, the England team were staying there and formed a guard of honour for the lads as they got off the coach. Normally you can't stay in the Grove if England are staying there, but I think Brian Horton had used his influence to get us in. Again, you were thinking: 'Shit, we've arrived!' Throughout the night, not many people were drunk on alcohol; you were drunk on emotion. You couldn't stop pinching yourself. You'd wake up the next morning with Hull City as a Premier League club. Some of the lads still had their shirts on and were wearing their medals; the families were there and it was just a lovely way to get everyone together. But it wasn't a wild, rock-n-roll party. We were all in a daze, wondering what had happened, trying to take it in. It was the biggest thing that had happened in the club's history.

Dean Windass: I went back to my room and I couldn't believe what was happening. Even my then wife was saying over and over again: "I can't believe what you've just done, I can't believe what you've just done."

Simon Maltby: I was exhausted. Absolutely knackered. We went to the party on the night but I didn't stay up very late, when normally I'd have been one of the last to bed. My celebrations came later on. It was a great, great day though. You can't beat that. I don't think you could ever match that: League 2 to the Premier League in five years was just incredible. Great staff, great players, the people who worked at the stadium were superb, the fans gave us a great atmosphere. Great, great times.

Dean Windass: I was dragged to bed by my wife, because I was that drunk. On the way out, I remember seeing Phil, Brian and Steve Parkin smoking cigars outside the tent. My missus just dragged me past them.

Brendon Smurthwaite: The players all went back to the Grove, and I understand it was Matt Duke who was seen at 6am with a bowl of Corn Flakes that had beer on instead of milk. Nick Barmby asked us all to come back to the party – he said he'd organise the transport – but those of us on the media side of things just went back to the Landmark and went to a little Italian restaurant and listed all the grounds we'd be visiting the next season. We were knackered and were all in bed by 11pm.

Dean Windass: At breakfast the next day a few of the lads were having champagne on their Corn Flakes.

Paul Duffen: The next morning I came downstairs and there was a hardcore – led by the captain – who hadn't been to bed and were putting beer on their Corn Flakes. It was an incredible celebration. The happiness spread everywhere.

Ian Ashbee: There was no lager on my Corn Flakes! There was a wild party – I was never going to let that pass by – so I had about two hours' sleep. I was running on adrenaline though. You're looking round at what people have achieved who'd been involved in the club for a number of years, including all the backroom staff. Fair play to Paul Duffen, he got everyone down to the Grove and laid a massive party on that everyone was invited to. Everyone enjoyed it for what it was. And it continued for four or five days when we got back to Hull. But that night there were people who sorted the tickets in the office, people who'd clean the kits, all those people who never get the credit they deserve, Paul repaid them. Having a party together with them was great. I knew individuals around who it meant more to and I sat and had a quiet beer with them. We'd all had our own little journey.

Phil Buckingham: Phil Brown saw me and said: "Ring me tomorrow morning." So the next morning, when he's travelling back from London, I rang him. I don't think he'd been to sleep but he still took my call and that's about as good as it gets in sport journalism. That sums up the bond he had with the local media and the local supporters.

Mike White: Driving back the next day down the M1, we were near Watford and had hit a load of roadworks. I noticed a 4x4 next to us, and I looked across and in the passenger seat was Paul Duffen with the play-off final trophy. He clocked us and started cheering and waving his City scarf and the play-off trophy. I just saw someone who was loving the moment and loving the occasion. That epitomised Paul for me.

Hull City hadn't just been promoted to the top flight of English football – the most visible domestic competition in the world – for the first time in their history, a whole city had been given a shot in the arm. On the Monday after the match it was time for Kingston upon Hull to come out on to the streets and celebrate with the players, who were being paraded around the city in an open-top bus before being honoured with a reception at the City Hall.

Brendon Smurthwaite: The open-top bus parade was another nightmare as we had so many council regulations to fulfil that I hadn't really bothered with as I was busy doing stuff to get to Wembley.

Dean Windass: All I was doing was crying. I couldn't stop. Every interview I did, be it with Burnsy or with Sky, I just cried. I couldn't carry on with the interviews. On the open-top bus there were loads of fans in Deano masks and everybody was shouting my name. Bryan Hughes said: "This is for you, all this." I said: "No it's for all of us." I was getting a bit embarrassed by that point as I was getting all the attention and accolades, but Ian Ashbee, Boaz Myhill, Andy Dawson and Ryan France had come through all the leagues. I wouldn't change anything but I did get embarrassed as it wasn't just about me. I know it's boring to say, but there's no 'I' in team.

Dave Richardson: The celebrations in Queen Victoria Square were amazing. The city really took the club to its heart that day. From my vantage point in a cherry picker I had a really good, if precarious, view of the crowd and City Hall balcony. I'd never seen crowds like it. The city council also played their part on the day. The town was full of images and banners of City players. Absolutely fabulous!

Dean Windass: Coming round the corner of the main square… I was at the front with Dean Marney and our Josh, who was about 12. When we came round I couldn't believe what I saw. It was a sea of people. I broke down again. The scenes were incredible all around Hull but when we came round that corner, I just thought: "What the fuck is this all about?"

Brian Horton: It's a big city and it has been a big part of my life and it holds special memories for me.

Paul Duffen: I'm just glad Deano lived through it to be honest, particularly when he stood on the balustrade at the front of City Hall. We all met at the KC in the morning and the buses turned up, the media were there. It was clearly meant to be a celebration and I don't think that dignity necessarily became a big part of that. Everyone was so overwhelmed by the joy of it. It was nuts. I'd never contemplated how many people could be on the streets of the city. Driving along Anlaby Road, then the closer you got to the Town Centre you couldn't believe it. Standing on that balcony, every road leading out was crammed with black and amber. Astonishing. But that was a real piss up.

John Cooper: I saw Dean Windass, absolutely kay-lied, climb up on the balustrade. One of the council staff asked me to have a word with him. Everyone saw that photograph of him standing on the balustrade, but what you can't see is me on the floor holding his ankles.

Fraizer Campbell: For a couple of weeks after it was like living on Cloud Nine. We felt like the kings of the world.

Henrik Pedersen: Unfortunately I didn't play in the final at Wembley, and that was a big disappointment personally, but it was a great day, and there were some great days celebrating after. The bus ride through the city is something I'll never forget.

Sean Rush: I remember thinking back to that day at Cardiff. Me and Adam Pearson were watching the end of the Leeds game together as it had over-run, and celebrated together when we stayed up. From that we got promoted. If you tried to write down what makes a successful, winning team, I don't think you'd be able to do justice to what we did in words. Some of it was luck, but the spirit that Browny got into that team was amazing. He deserved massive credit. The spirit that he'd bring to training every day was unbelievable.

Rob Smith: Paul Duffen and Phil Brown were the catalysts to that promotion as they got people believing, from the players to the marketing teams – everyone. They just brought such belief.

There were a few goodbyes to be said after the celebrations were over. Jay-Jay Okocha had started a mere 10 games for Hull City – coming on as a sub in eight more – but his impact on the club was colossal. Seeing Jay-Jay in a Hull City shirt was a privilege that few of those lucky enough to have witnessed will ever forget. But it was pastures new for the great man.

Boaz Myhill: Jay-Jay was the most talented player I played with. Watching him in training, one day we all realised that we weren't good enough to play him at his own game with all the flicks. We all realised we'd have to kick him. And the best thing about him was he just laughed. He was used to it, and it was amazing watching people try to kick lumps out of him and him just flicking the ball over their heads and laughing while he was doing it. He was unbelievably gifted.

Rob Harmer: Though he didn't have an enormous impact on the pitch, I'd say the impact of signing Jay-Jay Okocha is possibly underestimated by many. Not only was he an absolute joy to watch when he did actually make it onto the field, but you could almost sense the fear in the opposition when he was around and it sent out a massive statement of intent.

Henrik Pedersen's popularity in East Yorkshire was, and still is, unquestioned. Wholehearted on the pitch and both liked and admired off it, he'd done the club proud in his season at the KC, weighing in with some important goals. However, his family situation meant it was time to go.

Henrik Pedersen: You could say it was crazy leaving the club, as we had just won promotion and were going into the Premier League for the first time in the club's history. But my wife was pregnant and we felt it was the right time to move back to Denmark, as we wanted our son to be born and raised near his grandparents. I had been fortunate enough to have played football in England for seven years at the time, so we decided it was the right thing to do. Had my wife not been pregnant, I would have played the last year of my contract and possibly even more after that. I loved playing at the club, and was lucky to make some great friends.

James Richardson: I had a massive soft spot for Henrik Pedersen. Hugely under-appreciated in the promotion season, he was solid in whatever position he played and I loved his 'just belt it as hard as you can' shooting and the regularity with which opposing players bounced off him. Also a really nice man, not only at the time he was at City but afterwards, and he held court with my mates at the 2008 team reunion for Andy Dawson's testimonial, even suggesting we should head to Silkeborg and his pub for a then forthcoming stag weekend. It never came to pass sadly!

David Livermore had never let Hull City down in his two years at the club. Even his ill-fated attempt to fill in at centre-back saw him give everything. His contract was up, however, and his departure was confirmed.

Ian Thomson: Dave Livermore was a player of real quality but was overshadowed by Ash. Granted he couldn't match Ash in terms of leadership of men, but I always thought that he was a better player technically. I remember with great fondness his late volleyed equaliser at Premier League-bound Derby in 2007.

In a few short weeks, the rest of the squad would be reconvening to prepare for a Premier League campaign. It was a journey into the unknown. We couldn't wait to get there.

2008/09 season

For decades the top flight of English football has been billed – domestically, at least – as the best league in the world. The truth of that with regards to quality is questionable given the players that had graced the Bundesliga in the 1970s, Serie A in the 1980s and 1990s, and La Liga since the mid-1990s. However, in 2008 the Premier League had as strong a claim to that title as it had ever had. That year's Champions League final had been contested between Chelsea and eventual victors Manchester United. Chelsea had beaten Liverpool in the semi-finals, who themselves had beaten Arsenal in the quarter-finals. The only teams capable of knocking out the English clubs were the English clubs themselves. The season before had also seen three English clubs take three of the four semi-final berths. The same would occur in the coming season too. It was at this time that then UEFA president Michel Platini would famously complain that the strength of the top Premier League teams was unfair and needed curtailing. The top flight in English football had arguably never been stronger. Such dominance has not been demonstrated since.

Not only were the world's best teams in the Premier League but many of the world's best players were too. European champions Manchester United were spearheaded by Cristiano Ronaldo, already pencilling in his name as one of the finest footballers of all time. Joining him at Old Trafford under the great Sir Alex Ferguson were legendary figures such as Rio Ferdinand, Gary Neville, Wayne Rooney, Ryan Giggs and Paul Scholes. The squad also boasted the likes of Edwin van der Sar, Nemanja Vidic, Dimitar Berbatov and Carlos Tevez.

Defeated Champions League finalists Chelsea were still considered the richest club in the world under Roman Abramovich. Their starting XI could boast the likes of Petr Cech, John Terry, Ashley Cole, Frank Lampard, Nicolas Anelka, Didier Drogba, Michael Ballack and Joe Cole.

Arsenal were still considered a footballing superpower, even though they could no longer call upon the likes of Thierry Henry and Patrick Vieira. They still had Robin van Persie and Cesc Fabregas, who would have got into most clubs in Europe at that point (and were soon to move to Manchester United and Barcelona, respectively).

Liverpool were a force, with Steven Gerrard partnered in midfield by Xabi Alonso and Javier Mascherano. Behind them were Jamie Carragher and Pepe Reina. Ahead of them was one Fernando Torres.

Elsewhere Manchester City were newly minted, signing Brazilians Robinho and Jo for a respective £32.5m and £18m, as well as Nigel de Jong (£16m), Craig Bellamy (£14m) and Wayne Bridge (£10m). Everton were an upwardly mobile club under David Moyes, with Tim Cahill scoring freely from midfield, now joined by Marouane Fellaini. Aston Villa under Martin O'Neill were considered to have the best youngsters in the top flight, with Ashley Young, James Milner and Gareth Barry widely tipped to push the club into the top four. Newcastle's frontline contained former Ballon d'Or winner Michael Owen, fresh from a stint at Real Madrid. Tottenham's reserves were fielding a left-back by the name of Gareth Bale.

Of Hull City's 16-man squad that had been named at Wembley (minus returning loanee Fraizer Campbell), Wayne Brown and Dean Marney had had fleeting glimpses of Premier League football. Nick Barmby and Dean Windass had plenty of top-flight experience but it had been years since either had played at that level. Caleb Folan and Craig Fagan had played in the Premier League the season before but neither had been consistent starters for Wigan and Derby. Only Bryan Hughes had a reasonable level of recent Premier League experience. In contrast, Boaz Myhill, Matt Duke, Sam Ricketts, Andy Dawson, Ian Ashbee and Ryan France had played fourth-tier or non-league football within the past four years.

Such worries were for the pundits, however; for the fans and the players that summer was one of pure excitement.

Ian Ashbee: It was excitement, tension, people telling us we were going to be worse than Derby, the quality wasn't going to be there, I wasn't going to be good enough as an individual. All of those things were being thrown at us but we were heading into something we'd never been in so it was interesting to think about how we could deal with those pressures individually and collectively. You can't answer those questions until you start playing football. But we had a good pre-season – we only had three weeks off as Phil got us back in early and got us all fit – and we had it all nailed down.

Alfie Potts Harmer: I was still in school and like so many I had grown up in classrooms of Manchester United, Liverpool and – although a dying breed by this point – Leeds United 'fans'. So it felt good for City to be at the top table, and seeing some of these classmates discretely try to convert. The thought of City facing the top teams week in, week out seemed so exciting at that time.

Michael Turner: The previous season in the Championship had given me so much confidence going into the Premier League. But still it was a massive unknown for me and the club. We made some really good signings and had some matchwinners in the team but you never know when you're going into the unknown.

Nick Turner: One-hundred-and-four years of vain efforts and frustration expunged from the local psyche, the humiliatingly long and embarrassing shame of never having played top-flight football was finally at an end. The inexplicable failure in more than a century to do what so many other clubs seem to do regularly was a source of both anger and despair to many fans, some of whom could be forgiven for thinking the great day would never arrive.

Rightly or wrongly, towns and cities are often judged by the prowess of their sports teams. What type of city has a team that has never competed at the highest level in 104 years when far smaller places have managed to reach the top division? Who would want to be associated with a club or city that had the distinction of being the largest conurbation in Europe never to have played at the highest level in its national competition? That burden weighed more heavily on our shoulders than outsiders realised – probably because outsiders had rarely been given a reason to be interested in the fortunes of our club or city.

Some bold claims were made about the transformative effect of the Premier League promotion on the city. Full hotels for every home game, the marina seeing more visiting yachts, oligarchs helicoptering in, boom time for the restaurants – all of these were predicted. Sadly most of these would prove to be euphoria-driven hyperbole and the financial benefits did not ripple out or cascade down to the population as had been foreseen. But what the hell, we were up at long last and for many of us that was ultimately all that mattered.

Paul Denman: I used to ask my mum, Ethel: "Do you think we will ever get to Division 1?" She'd say: "Yes son but not in my lifetime." She was right. She passed away in 1997 seven years after my dad, Ken. I put them both in my back pocket and took them to every Premier League game we played. I only missed five or six of that first season, the ones around Christmas and New Year, which isn't bad going as it was a 10,000-mile round trip from where I lived in LA!

Nick Barmby: Wherever I've been I've tried to embrace it and give it the best I possibly can. I remember that summer, I just couldn't wait to get back. We went to Bormeo in Italy to train pre-season and had a couple of meetings where we just said: "Let's get at these teams and give it a go." Anyone who goes up through the play-offs isn't fancied the next season, and you can use that to spur you on.

Craig Sargent: Although I didn't realise it at the time, for me and I think a lot of others it was the end of the journey rather than the beginning of a new one. It was our prize for enduring the dark days of the 1990s. Things would never be the same again and, although some truly wonderful days lay ahead, the club changed for me; not for the better or the worse, it was just different. Maybe I grew up as the club grew up. I loved the national exposure that being in the Premier League brought to the area and that can never be underestimated. Suddenly, though, we all had to share our club with everyone else and I'm not sure I liked that!

Phil Buckingham: Hull City became front-page news, so my workload increased significantly. But the paper committed to sending me all over the place. I went to Bormeo. Paul Duffen rang me a week before I was due to set off and said: "How do you fancy driving there with me through the Alps in my Aston Martin?" I had to travel light as there was hardly any boot space. That was a unique experience.

Peter Swan: You didn't see too many in the starting XI as Premier League players. Few of the players would get in other Premier League teams. But that just shows how special they were as a team.

Sam Ricketts: I just felt huge excitement with a bit of trepidation added. We'd had such a good year before. In training in pre-season I was just doing my thing and I did something very simple, just a pass to Michael Turner or Wayne Brown, and Dean Windass said: "Oh, you can't do that in the Premier League." I just thought: 'Oh no, if I can't do that then am I good enough for this level?' And to be honest it took me 10 games or so into the Premier League to get rid of that and know that I was good enough, and that I could do this.

Sean Rush: You had to look at the dynamics of the game – we did studies on things like how long the ball was in play, and what the tempo was like, what running distances were expected. It gives you a real taster of the standards of players in that league. You make six mistakes in the Championship and you maybe concede one goal. You make one mistake in the Premier League and it's a goal. On distances covered it was bigger distances in the Championship, but in the Premier League it's all short, sharp runs.

Robert Crampton: Three massive things happened to Hull within the space of a few years, hosting the City of Culture, the Siemens deal and Hull City getting into the Premier League. You can't underestimate the importance of any of those things, but Hull City getting into the

Premier League was first and maybe it helped with the other two happening. You've heard of the cities in Germany that have teams in the Bundesliga but not the ones that don't. Being in the Premier League matters so much as it puts you on the map.

James Richardson: When you've been to so many games over the years, 38 of them shouldn't really mean so much, but at times playing those games in the Premier League seemed light years away. Even during my formative years we had a taste of the top flight when we visited Newcastle and Aston Villa in the cups in the late 1990s and, while it was fun being the David to their Goliath, now sharing a stage with them felt as surreal as it was exhilarating. Even after we became upwardly mobile following the move to the KC it still felt like it was one of those things that just wouldn't happen as it wasn't a very City thing, so I cherished the opportunity as there was no guarantee our heights would be higher and we'd be there for any more than those 38 games. What a rush!

Mike Hall: Hull City getting into the Premier League meant a huge amount to me. I've never given a thought to supporting another club, no matter which division or crisis the club has found itself in. Had it never happened it would not have diminished my support for the club, but to witness us get there in my lifetime felt like an honour. We may have another era like that or we may not, but even if that is the case the record books will always show that it happened first in 2008. I think being able to witness that achievement – and in the way it was done, and with the people I saw it happen with – played a significant part of what those years were about for me.

I think it meant something big for the city too. After so long as the butt of any joke going, the city finally emerged into people's consciousness in a positive way. Suddenly you could go abroad and the people you spoke to would have heard of Hull City. It happened to me in Madrid, speaking to a Real Madrid-supporting taxi driver. A Madrid-based Real Madrid supporter talking to me with some knowledge about Hull City. I think it's difficult to estimate how much that means to the city the club represents. It probably means more than just what it ended up doing to balance sheets in the short term; I think it raised the city's profile in the minds of people all over the world, and that can have knock-on effects in ways that might be felt for many years down the line.

Ian Farrow: It was the impossible dream come true. I always remember my grandfather and others saying that they'd never see Hull City in the top league. He never did, and even though Dave Dewberry called his supporters association the Division One Society as we went through lock outs, liquidations and relegations, I was certain I would never see the club climb from the lower leagues. I remember having a long conversation with a group of friends sometime during the David Lloyd era when even the most optimistic of us were saying that the very best Hull City could ever now amount to, given the money that seemed to be concentrating with the higher echelon clubs, would be a stable second-tier side.

It was my club playing the best teams in England, maybe the world, on equal terms, week after week. It meant national and international recognition for the city of Hull. We were no longer repeatedly told we were the biggest city in Europe never to have a top-flight football club. We were Hull and we were Premier League.

On the subject of Hull being the biggest city in Europe to never have hosted top-flight football, it was a fact trotted out so frequently, few sought to question it. However, depending on the definition of a city, or, indeed, where exactly the boundaries of Europe stop, it probably wasn't true. Ufa in Russia has a population of more than 1 million but has never played in the Russian top flight. Closer to the UK, Wiesbaden in Germany has a larger population than Hull and has never hosted Bundesliga football. None of this altered the fact that it was something of an embarrassment that Hull City had spent 104 years outside the top flight.

In the Premier League everything needs upsizing – the backroom staff, the media facilities, the wages paid, and the squad itself. So how was the chairman coping with this?

Paul Duffen: It was difficult because we were the last to be confirmed in the Premier League, so clearly we knew we had to overhaul the side. We were now having to feed in a pond where a lot of the fish had already been taken. Equally in June you have a lot of ambition and thoughts – we had a list of three players for every position, and the scouting team had been amazing with the lists ready for us. But we didn't have any money, because you don't get the first payment until the end of August. They've changed that now but back then it was really difficult because we were having to do deals when we were taking players on deferred payment, free transfers or loan deals.

John Cooper: The stadium had to meet certain criteria to be in the Premier League, including the brightness of the floodlights, media facilities, etc… and that had to be done in a short space of time. You don't have time to think. It was an interesting time, especially the planning and security.

In total, City signed 10 players. Former Barcelona and Brazil player Geovanni arrived on a free from Manchester City. Experienced midfielder George Boateng came in from Middlesbrough. Gabonese centre-forward Daniel Cousin signed from Rangers. Craig Fagan rejoined on a permanent deal. French full-back Bernard Mendy came in from Paris St Germain. Hungarian winger Peter Halmosi – so impressive against City for Plymouth – joined for £2m. Tony Warner and Mark Oxley added depth to the goalkeeping pool. Former England international Anthony Gardner joined from Tottenham for a club record £2.5m. Centre-forward Marlon King joined on loan.

Phil Brown: While we made some really good signings we still had a squad from which I'd said we'd give everybody an opportunity. I was delighted with who we brought in though as not only had we brought in experienced players like George Boateng, we brought in a bit of flair as well and strikers we thought could score goals at that level.

Paul Duffen: The thought of building a Premier League squad was quite daunting but the scouting network had been brilliant. We had an incredibly wide list of potential targets, and I think we managed to navigate that minefield quite well. We brought in 11 or 12 players but we must have been dealing with another 40 players. You have to kiss a lot of frogs to find your prince, particularly when you're in our situation – a minnow club. We seriously needed to resource the club with people with Premier League experience because there's no substitute for such experience. We were still doing transfer business on our pre-season tour.

Brendon Smurthwaite: As we were signing a load of players from overseas, they came with a bit of an entourage. You'd have Canal Plus wanting to speak to Daniel Cousin and Bernard Mendy, Brazilian channels wanting to speak to Geovanni and so on. We weren't used to that. Sky were there every week, usually Rob Palmer. The interest in us as a club was massive. And everyone seemed to want us to do well.

Simon Maltby: It was a big step-up for everyone. From the medical side of things we should have brought in more staff, but I had Liam McGarry doing his degree and I didn't want to bring in anyone above him. We talked about bringing in more people and developing the training ground – all of which was put into the next stage – but when the funding was pulled on that things started to go back to square one.

As far as the signings went one of the better bits of business was getting George Boateng's vast experience on board.

George Boateng: I had had six years at Middlesbrough but felt that my time was coming to an end and I was due a new challenge. I still had the spark and the qualities to play in the Premier League though. Then I had a phone call asking if I was interested in joining Hull City. I thought that talking to them couldn't do any harm, to see what they had to offer. I agreed to meet Phil Brown and Brian Horton in Amsterdam. The team had already gone to Italy but they flew to Amsterdam airport. It was a really positive chat. They explained to me what they wanted to do and that they needed some Premier League experience. They were looking for someone who knew what it took to win matches at that level, and I fitted the bill. The issue was that I had a year on my contract at Middlesbrough. I said that I wanted a two-year deal, with the second year added automatically if we stayed up, as I figured that there'd be a lot of responsibility on my shoulders. They agreed. The interview went so well that Phil asked me to fly to Italy that night to meet the players! There was no chance of that, sadly.

A wow factor was added in Brazilian Geovanni, who'd scored the only goal in a derby match for Manchester City the previous season.

Geovanni: My reaction upon joining Hull City was a one of joy because I wanted to play the Premier League again. And with Hull going up for the first time in their history, I knew that it would be particularly important to the club.

Phil Brown: I thought that Geovanni gave us a similar feel to when we'd signed Jay-Jay Okocha. It meant we were putting a similar marker down to the footballing world; we could attract a Brazilian superstar at little old Hull City.

Brian Horton: I'd seen him play at Manchester City and I was surprised that they'd let him go. I said to Phil: "He's on a free transfer, do you want me to make some enquiries?" And Phil told me to. Phil set it up with the agent and the deal got done. I got on great with him. He had great technical ability. He came with us pre-season and scored in a game and showed what a talent he was.

Paul Duffen: We did a cracking piece of business with Geovanni, and that was the thing that defined the beginning of our season. He had such an impact.

Nick Barmby: I love Geovanni: Great player, great man. And never get in the way of one of his shots, because it hurts!

Sean Rush: Geo was a nightmare! In the end we'd just give him the ball. He wasn't one to be running or doing long distances. Geo liked short, sharp runs.

Bryan Hughes: I thought Phil's recruitment was good with the likes of Geovanni and George Boateng. I felt we had a good chance of staying up.

One player who sadly wouldn't be joining City was Fraizer Campbell. He expressed a desire to break into the Manchester United team, and then moved to Spurs on a season-long loan as part of a transfer deal that saw Dimitar Berbatov move in the opposite direction.

Fraizer Campbell: It's difficult because the press made out that I was in Hull ready to sign papers but it was never as close as was being reported. Any opportunities to go back to Hull were last minute when I'd already got my heart set on something else. I get that people don't know the full story but I always look back at my time at Hull with nothing but fond memories. It was sad that I got a bit of stick when I'd go back there, but I always had good memories of that time.

Paul Duffen: Fraizer was someone we really wanted to sign – either on loan or as a permanent transfer – and I was talking to David Gill constantly throughout the period, but these clubs work in mysterious ways, and rather than coming and playing a starring role with us he went to warm the bench somewhere else for a season, which was part of a bigger transaction with Dimitar Berbatov. It's just one of those things, but it was very frustrating.

Caleb Folan: I was gutted. Fraizer was massive for us. I wanted us all to take the next step together too, so I was gutted when we couldn't get him back, but Tottenham are a big club and you have to take those chances.

Martin Batchelor: Whatever happened subsequently, Fraizer Campbell's magnificent contribution to the 2007/08 season should never be forgotten.

'Hull City will do a Derby' was a phrase commonly bandied about in the summer of 2008. Derby had accrued a feeble 11 points the season previous, and some pundits – including cretins such as David Mellor – couldn't be bothered to look at the spirit within the City squad when compared with the Rams. One man had a unique insight into both clubs' Premier League preparations, and he wasn't too concerned.

Craig Fagan: I wasn't worried about that. There was a different aura around Hull, more of a togetherness. When Derby were promoted they signed some players who weren't a good fit for the squad, more like marquee signings, and at the end of the play-off finals Billy Davies was having problems with his contract. That kind of thing shouldn't happen. That all bled in to the next season. We didn't have any of that at Hull. Everybody was pulling in the same direction. And we had a good group of lads, and the lads that came in knew they had to work hard to earn our respect. It was all about the team though.

The manager had no worries either.

Phil Brown: When we were promoted I thought that we were capable enough to play in the Premier League, having been there with Bolton. If you were organised, if you were hard working, you could have a DNA that would frustrate the opposition, but you also had to have goals in your team. That was the combination I was trying to get, the hard-working, organised team with players who could score goals. I was delighted with what I'd achieved.

And the new signings were already finding just what a strong spirit existed within the squad.

George Boateng: I was very professional in my training and wanted to win everything. I was always on time. My body language was good, and I'd support everyone. I knew that the whole squad was going to be important as I knew that we'd need every single one of them if we were going to stay up. I like to think I raised the bar a little within the squad. But everyone within the squad was so humble and so nice; not one of them was big-headed. I got on really well with the likes of Ian Ashbee, Andy Dawson, Dean Marney, Caleb Folan – they were so nice to me, very respectful. Within a matter of days I felt really at home.

The preparation was done. The first game couldn't come soon enough.

Paul Duffen: We started the next roller-coaster ride with an assembled cast that was for purpose. But the only objective – for the second season running – was to stay in the division.

The fixture list had been kind to City. Fulham at home was to be the first game of the season, which was ideal in many ways. Fulham weren't expected to be in a relegation battle – so there was no danger of City immediately losing ground on a potential rival on that score – but they were a beatable team in a way that, say, Arsenal weren't. Before the game kicked off, however, the occasion needed to be marked.

Paul Duffen: We were building up to the start of the season and we had the Premier League bell in the West Stand. We didn't even know if it worked. It was very difficult at the time – as we were thrust into the spotlight – but I believed it was a chance to benefit the city and the region, as people wanted to know about Hull. Telling the story was important and we had ridiculous media value thrust upon us, and we embraced that as much as we could.

I always had to walk a thin line between trying to make sure we discharged our duty to record the fact that this was in the name of the former generations of the Tiger Nation who hadn't lived to see that moment, and it sounded a bit cheesy and softly romantic. But I really felt it. I'd come into the city and been welcomed and embraced, as had my family. I was then living in Kirkella. It was something I was overwhelmed with. I really did catch the spirit of that. There were people who'd worked at the club, their parents and grandparents had been fans.

The history of the club was something I made a point of becoming very well aware of and I felt that ringing the Premier League bell – I was mindful of the fact that the club had 104 years of history and I was ringing the bell. I didn't mean to break it though! That was just witness to the fact that no one had rung it before and we didn't have a dry run. We were in the Premier League, and that day – before the Fulham game – Steve Wilson was commenting live for Match of the Day, and he presided over me and Phil ringing the bell. It was incredibly emotional and it did feel like that was the moment when everything that had happened up until then was punctuated. It was an amazing moment.

Rob Smith: We were prepared. We had a beautiful stadium, we had the facilities. We had to change a few things, but it wasn't a massive change off the field. The problem we had was trying to get everyone in the ground who wanted to be there. It was a long way away from trying to entice people into Boothferry Park. There was more money at stake, but we tried to keep things on a level.

Sam Ricketts: We didn't get too engrossed in the history. It was maybe something that affected the Hull lads a little bit more. I wasn't trying to think about it too much as a player. I thought about that sort of thing more when we were getting promoted as Hull had some notoriety as being the biggest city in Europe to never have been in a top flight, but in that first game you didn't really get too concerned about what it meant on a wider scale.

Phil Buckingham: Football Focus were live from Hull. It felt like a landmark day for the city, not just the football club.

Nick Barmby: As soon as I put the shirt on and saw the Premier League badge, I sat there and thought 'yeaah'. I'd always wanted to do it. Me and Adam Pearson had had a little dream a few years before and I'd managed to fulfil it.

Andy Dawson: A dream come true. When I first played in the Championship I was thinking: 'Can I do it?' I answered those questions. But this was another level again. But what an occasion. I just thought I should go and enjoy it. Five years previous we were playing Darlington at home in League 2; now we were playing Fulham in the Premier League. If someone had told me that was going to happen I'd have just laughed. It just doesn't happen.

George Boateng: I only realised how historical the game was afterwards. In my mind I just had to do a job and part of that job is when you walk out at 3 o'clock on a Saturday to not be captivated by the occasion or the fans or the media. You have to stay focused, so my mind was solely on getting the three points. We had a tactical plan and we stuck to it very well.

Ian Ashbee: We could probably have lost 5-0 that day and the fans would not have been bothered because they were just thinking: 'Wow, we're playing in the Premier League!' Leading the club out was very special. I remember it like it was yesterday. Living in the city and knowing what it meant to everyone, it was brilliant. Phil said everyone would get a chance and he was true to his word. A lot of managers would have just got rid of people. I thought maybe that Fulham game was my chance, but even if I only played the one game I could still say I'd played in the Premier League and I'd played in every division for Hull City.

Boaz Myhill: It was like playing against film stars. I'd been in a couple of international squads by then with Wales and met a few big players, but it was just insane. Never in my wildest dreams did I think that when I signed for Hull in League 2 five years later they'd be in the Premier League. I knew there'd be a good chance that they'd get out of League 2 and maybe League 1, but to then be in the Premier League, it's so much faster and everything just looks different, the players, the balls, the stadia, everything.

Andy Dawson: I kept saying to myself as the game was going on: "This is the Premier League. I can watch it on Match of the Day later. It'll be brilliant!" And I think that was a massive part of why we did so well, there wasn't pressure on us, it was all just enjoyment. We all just relaxed and did what we loved.

City got off to a terrible start. South Korean forward Seol Ki-Hyeon scored after eight minutes. The pundits who'd already written City off, who couldn't open their mouths without parroting 'Doing a Derby, doing a Derby', looked on smugly. As far as they were concerned, a 10-month-long avalanche had commenced.

Mike White: When they scored I was thinking: 'Here we go. This is how it's going to be.'

Phil Buckingham: I didn't expect them to win if I'm being honest. I thought they might get caught up in the occasion. And when Fulham scored first I feared the worst.

Ian Ashbee: Going 1-0 down I was thinking: 'This could be a tough afternoon.' But then the game changed…

In the 22nd minute, the ball fell to Geovanni about 40 yards from goal on the City right-hand side. He turned and advanced to the edge of the Fulham box. No one closed him down. The Brazilian hit a low, curling left foot shot to opposition goalkeeper Mark Schwarzer's right. The back of the net rippled. History had been made, and City were on level terms. The first ever goal scored by a Hull City player in the top flight of English football had come from a Brazil international. The surreality meter cranked up a few more notches.

Geovanni: When I ran onto the field in that game I knew what the expectations of the fans were, and also those of the players. But, as I always do, I prayed to God and I gave my best and that day. And I was honoured to score a goal that went down in the history of that wonderful club.

Andy Dawson: The big players we brought in won us games, and Geo helped win us that Fulham game.

Phil Buckingham: A Brazilian playing for Hull City and scoring a goal in the opening day of the Premier League season at the KC... Amazing!

Mike White: When Geovanni scored, and it was the first time we'd really seen him, it changed everything. I'd been a bit underwhelmed with it being Fulham – with all due respect to them – before the game, but after that it became one of the most memorable games in the club's history.

Phil Brown: It was a beautiful day, and the bell was rung in the reception. That was Paul Duffen's idea and he was a master of branding. Geo's goal settled everybody down. Then with 20 minutes to go, it's still 1-1 and the sun's still shining, we realised we had a chance of our first point in the Premier League when everybody was telling us we'd 'do a Derby'. Then Caleb Folan started another fairytale.

Caleb Folan had scored two of the most celebrated goals in Hull City's history – the winner in the 2-1 win at West Brom, and the goal that settled the second leg of the play-off semi-finals against Watford. In the 81st minute of Hull City's first ever top-flight game he scored a third. This one, however, had as much to do with Craig Fagan's unselfishness and boundless energy as it did anything else.

Craig Fagan: I was annoyed at not starting, as I'd had a good pre-season. I used that as motivation though. I managed to cut inside Paul Konchesky and then I could have shot and maybe scored myself and taken all the plaudits but Caleb was in an easier position for a tap-in. Sometimes fans don't realise that simple passes aren't as easy as they look as you don't always see the players that are free. As I was running with the ball it was all going through my head, how I hadn't started the game, this was my chance to prove people wrong. But then you see Caleb totally free with a chance to win the first ever game in the Premier League, so what do you do? There's no choice. The club comes first.

Caleb Folan: I'd laid it off on the halfway line, and I'd turned and run towards the box. I just tried to stay in the right area. Craig intercepted it and I was so wide open and I was screaming at him for the ball. I wasn't sure he was going to pass, but then he clipped it back to me with a perfect pass, perfectly weighted, and I knew where I was going to put it. I just tried not to blast it and keep it simple, put it where I wanted to put it. I sidefooted it into the near corner and just thought: 'Oh my God, this just gets better and better!'

City held on and a whole new wave of celebrations could commence.

Sam Ricketts: Caleb scored the winning goal wearing my boots. He hadn't brought any boots, largely I think because he wanted the ones I had at that time. So I said to him before the game that he could wear them, because I was wearing studs and he wanted to wear moulds.

Phil Brown: When your subs do that, it's incredibly satisfying for a manager. It's one of the things that supporters measure, whether you've got tactical nous, whether things like your substitutions work. A good day at the office.

George Boateng: I did a lot of mileage that day. But it was only after the game had finished that I realised that we'd made history and how important the day was.

Brian Horton: We'd been to Scotland pre-season to play Hearts and Roy Hodgson came to watch us play. He stayed until the last minute and we had a good chat. He'd done his homework but we got away with our first win, which is always very important.

Michael Turner: Derby had had a shocker just getting 11 points and that was in the back of our mind pre-season, but that win set us up for that early period of the season.

Richard Garcia: It was great. I think we played pretty well for our first outing as a group in the Premier League. It was a great honour to be part of the club's history and you could feel the support of the whole city.

Paul Duffen: Obviously, comparisons were being drawn with Derby. We got to see Geovanni firing, which was impressive. Fulham at the time felt like a big club. They were a long-term constituent of the Premier League and had a great history. It's the kind of fixture where you're thinking: 'OK, there aren't any expectations, but if you lose to Fulham you're automatically going to be categorised as being in a relegation fight at the end of the first game of the season.' That's where we benefited from finishing our previous season late – a short summer break, back into training, the buzz in the dressing room still there, the core of the squad still there – and there really was a carry over of that march towards the end of the previous season. You couldn't wish for a better start to the season. That set the level of expectation, and we were bouncing.

The win meant that City were already one-quarter of the way towards surpassing Derby's points total. Not that that was the club's sole aim. The 40-point relegation survival threshold was the target. But ramming the words of those arrogant and ignorant critics back down their throats was always going to be hugely satisfying.

The next game, away at Blackburn, saw City surprise a few more people. A Richard Garcia header claimed a 1-1 draw. Four points. One-third of the way to surpassing the Derby total.

Richard Garcia: Craig Fagan played a diagonal ball into the box and I was just thinking head it back hard across the keeper into the far post. I didn't catch it exactly right and it ended up floating back over him instead. It was a great feeling

Phil Brown: When we went to Blackburn, I felt we'd got a good point there. I looked at the games in our analysis department on the training ground. It was there we'd educate the players, let them know what our DNA was and what was expected of them. The energy levels of the team were going to be important as we knew we had to work hard. We weren't going to be as talented as the opposition so we had to work hard. I thought the training ground complex was brilliant for that – we had a lovely family atmosphere, and that provided us with points, just as the supporters provided us with points, but the education programme – the coaching and strategy – also put points on the board. The two people that looked after the training ground – Paula and her husband – lived at the training ground in Cottingham and they'd make it like a home. The players would come to training but it was like they were going to their home to train. It was such a wonderful environment to cultivate the family atmosphere that I wanted to have. Brian and Paula were priceless.

Then, with the summer transfer window about to close, came what we'd all been dreading. Steve Bruce's Wigan came to the KC and, inspired by an outstanding forward display from Amr Zaki and Emile Heskey, ran out 5-0 winners. The arrogant critics looked on, smugly. Our honeymoon was over, we'd been found out, this was the reality of the Premier League.

The match was particularly tough on one of the heroes from the 2007/08 season – Wayne Brown. He was run ragged by Zaki in difficult circumstances and was never to play for the club again.

Wayne Brown: I'd struggled in pre-season with my calf and then my hamstring. We played Swansea in the League Cup on the Tuesday and that went to extra-time, which wasn't great for me and my injuries. Then Anthony Gardner got injured in training on the Friday, so Phil Brown asked me if I was okay to play. I told him I was. I'd waited a long time to play in the Premier League again.

Amr Zaki was flying and it was a tough game to play in. I made a mistake when I'd tried to head the ball back to Boaz, got under it slightly and Emile Heskey went on to score, which led to my downfall. Did I feel a scapegoat? Yes, probably. The manager made his mind up, saying to me on the following international break that I wouldn't play again for him while he was at the football club – three days after the transfer window had shut – was a little bit harsh given that I'd played over 40 games in the Championship and I thought I'd been a pretty big part of us getting promotion.

Phil Brown: I witnessed what I thought was the poorest defensive display that I'd seen from one or two individuals. It was a rude awakening. If anybody thought that it was going to be a breeze because we got four points from the first two games, this was the eye-opener.

Ian Ashbee: Wayne Brown was playing against Amr Zaki, who was rapid, and Wayne was never known for his pace, as much as he had other qualities. It was a bit of an eye-opener, but the best thing to do with one of those games is to get rid of it straight away. Phil said: "It's happened, let's move on and try to pick up more points." If you start dwelling on things like that throughout a season, you can start to diminish very quickly and confidence goes. But we were back on the training ground very quickly working hard, putting good sessions in, getting the lads upbeat.

Sam Ricketts: We took it as a little bit of everything: a reality check, a feeling that we'd been beaten 5-0 by a club like Wigan, not Manchester United, which was worrying, and it probably changed a lot about the club. We went into an international break and I think we signed a few players then to really bolster the squad. Maybe that game pushed that along a bit. It was certainly a wake-up call but we were still fresh into it and we weren't too worried.

Paul Duffen: I don't think there were any issues. It was embarrassing but the expectation was very sober – it was about competing in the division and finding our feet. This game probably had the same effect as the Sheffield United defeat at the end of the previous season, because it was a line in the sand. The Fulham game had been so euphoric and we probably needed to reset a few realities and expectations. It was just a game of football. We'd lost but it was early enough in the season not to have any particular effect on the eventual outcome.

Phil Brown: We didn't think it was the end of the world. We'd planned for this. Before a ball had been kicked I took all the coaching staff on an away day in a hotel in York – something Sam Allardyce used to do – where you get them away from the training ground, away from the stadium, away from Hull, and we sat down and talked about certain things that could be coming our way, such as a heavy home defeat, or three or four defeats on the bounce. We talked through what we'd look like, what we'd do when these moments arrived. When you talk about these things you're opening up a pathway to preparing for these moments, which helps you accept them when they come along. So we got back to training on the Monday and simply prepared for the next game. I thought the away days that we did were key, and an integral part of our planning to survive in the Premier League.

It was sad to see a brief but illustrious Hull City career ended this way. Wayne Brown had been as important as anyone to the club's historic promotion, but such are the realities of life in the remorseless Premier League.

Wayne Brown: I didn't want to leave. I thought I'd done well for the club and I wanted to play in the Premier League. The club had turned down a couple of offers for me in the summer which I thought showed that they wanted to keep me. I thought I'd be given an opportunity, but when your manager says he doesn't want you, what can you do? I decided to go out on loan to Preston because I just wanted to play football. In January Leicester came in and I knew that their potential and ambition was there.

I was sad to leave Hull. Not only my team-mates and the people at the stadium, but the Hull people in general had made me feel very welcome and I've still got many good friends there now. The Hull people were exceptional to me and it's something I was very grateful for.

Mike Scott: A single season was all it took to place Wayne Brown in the 2000s hall of fame. Signed from Colchester, like so many before him, Brown was a no-nonsense centre half that struck up a fine partnership with the younger and more gifted Michael Turner during City's tumultuous 2007/08 season. Only missing five League games that season, his contribution climaxed in the closing seconds of the Wembley play-off final when he leapt excitedly on the shoulders of Bo Myhill after the keeper had snuffed out the 112th and last Bristolian cross of the match.

A single Premier League game was all it took for Brown's City career to end, as Wigan's future Tiger Amr Zaki took him to the industrial-scale cleaners. He moved to Leicester and did a similar lower league job by the Fosse that he had just completed by the Humber.

In the international break, Phil Brown made a few more moves in the transfer market. Guinean Kamil Zayatte came in from Swiss team Young Boys, originally on a loan deal, but one that would eventually see City parting with a record-equalling £2.5m to secure his services. Stefan Giannakopoulos also arrived in a short-term deal. Finally, a player who was to become a firm favourite with the fans arrived through the door when defender Paul McShane joined from Sunderland.

Paul McShane: I was at Sunderland and had been a regular in the first half of the season before, but then I lost my place in the team. I'd needed a pre-season to get back into the team but on my summer holidays in Mexico I fractured my kneecap, so that made me miss pre-season. At the end of pre-season Roy Keane said: "You've not trained so I can't have you in my plans. I want you to go out on loan." He'd wanted me to go to Charlton at first, but that didn't feel right, so I hung on and Hull City came in for me late in the window. I knew straight away it was the right move for me. But then I watched the Wigan game and was thinking: 'This is going to be a tough, long season.'

The next game was to mark the first time in the season that City would visit one of the great Premier League stadia – St James' Park, Newcastle. A revitalised City shocked the hosts – and much of the 50,000 crowd, by going 2-0 up before the hour mark, with both goals coming from Marlon King. A late Xisco strike made it a tense finish. However, when Andre Marriner blew the final whistle, City had a first away victory in the top flight and seven points to their name – four behind the Derby total and 26 behind the tally needed to avoid relegation from the previous season.

Paul McShane: I remember being quite nervous before the match. The last appearance I'd made for Sunderland had been at Newcastle. I'd played right-back and had a nightmare. I wasn't used to right-back. So for my first game to be against Newcastle was one thing, but I was preparing to play centre-back. Then Phil Brown said: "How do you fancy right-back?" I said: "Yes, why not," as I couldn't exactly say no. So I was anxious. Then we had to wear Newcastle's shorts because of a colour clash. I was just thinking: 'What is going on here?' It was a great win though. We ground a result out and that gave us a bit of momentum for the next five or six games.

Boaz Myhill: A lot of people will turn up at Newcastle and freeze. We turned up there and won. You get on a run and good things happen.

Craig Fagan: Marlon King brought us something different in that first part of the 2008-09 season. He had an aura about him, a real confidence and that brought a fear factor with it. When he came in he nicked a few goals, held the ball up, worked hard and he was vital to that start of the season when we were doing really well. He played a big part in that.

Michael Turner: Marking Michael Owen was daunting. I'd seen him play for Liverpool and Real Madrid and it was a game I was looking forward to, testing myself against players like him. I don't remember him doing much at all that game though! Their fans were protesting against the owners and it was a weird atmosphere and us scoring in the first half quietened them down and from that moment we were confident we were going to win that game.

Sadly, the win came at a cost. The in-form Craig Fagan was on the end of a disgraceful 'tackle' by Danny Guthrie that left the City forward with a broken leg.

Craig Fagan: I was coming into the best form of my life, I was loving playing in the Premier League, I thrived in every game showing what I can do. But that game was more notorious for me because of that tackle by Danny Guthrie. I think there were about four minutes to go and it wasn't like I was keeping the ball in the corner, I was just running after it. He'd already attempted to swipe my legs once, and then the second time he caught me. I didn't realise that I'd broken my leg. I just thought it was a dead leg. I thought it was my shin pad that had made the clicking noise. I tried to run for the last minutes but I just couldn't. Then when I got into the changing room they were saying that it wasn't right. I couldn't sleep that night because of the pain, and then went for an X-ray where I found out that I'd broken my leg. I was devastated. I was playing the best I'd ever played. If I'd kicked on that season who knows what would have happened.

The big games kept coming. The following Sunday saw Everton visit the KC, the first league meeting between the sides since 1952. City got off to a dream start thanks to Michael Turner.

Michael Turner: Marouane Fellaini was marking me and I managed to outjump him. I headed the ball but fell back so I didn't know it had gone in until I got up and people started running towards me.

A Phil Neville own goal put City 2-0 up, only for Everton then to rally and claim a point.

Michael Turner: We'd played really well that first half, 2-0 up at one point, and they brought Saha on at half time and he totally changed the game. Drawing 2-2 was a disappointment but looking back it was probably a good result in the end.

Paul Duffen: Those first few games were a great backdrop before we went to London…

London. Arsenal away on September 27th, then Spurs away on October 5th. The former were top of the table, having won four and lost one of their five games. Indeed, they'd only lost one game at their new home, the Emirates, since moving there just over two years ago. Setanta had chosen to televise the game, no doubt expecting the north London side to dish out a hammering that could be eulogised post-match, before spending a couple of minutes telling us how this was a 'reality check' for Hull City, before straining to patronisingly point out a couple of positives. To the outside world City were lambs to the slaughter, rank outsiders. There was an inner confidence within the City ranks, however, and it stemmed from the manager's office.

Phil Brown: Our mindset was one of to attack but with a formation where we were playing a diamond with Geovanni just behind the front two of Daniel Cousin and Marlon King. We planned too for set pieces, which was something high on our agenda when I was coaching under Sam – set pieces both for and against can define your season – so we were working towards a surprise campaign through the diamond. A diamond formation is known as a very attacking formation. It would expose our full-backs to a lot of two-on-one situations, which was tough considering that Andy Dawson had never played in the Premier League. It was a high-risk strategy but we felt we could catch Arsenal unaware.

Paul Duffen: Phil and I sat down at least twice a week to do a post-mortem and a preview on our games. The preview for that game was that in the Everton game we'd played in a certain way to counter their threat. Going into Arsenal Phil said to me: "What is your input to me about how you want this game to go, because if we get it wrong, we could get a spanking. We can either go to limit damage, or we can have a real go." I told him there's no prize in planning to come second so let's have a go. And we slightly apprehensively made our first ever visit to the Emirates.

George Boateng: I'd been out injured for some time but I was working towards being back for that game. I'd been to the Netherlands for treatment. But what a game to come back for! I remember early in the week Phil Brown changing how we did training from a 4-4-1-1 to a 4-3-1-2. Obviously I had to support the manager, but it was going through my mind that Phil was a very brave guy. We were off on the Wednesday, and then on Thursday it's the coaches' day, and again Phil did the 4-3-1-2. I just thought: 'Wow!' I remember talking to a mate about the training and I said to him: "You're not going to believe this but we're playing something like 4-3-3, with two centre-forwards." He thought I was joking. I told him that we'd either beat Arsenal 10-0 or lose 10-0.

Paul Duffen: We stayed in the Grove again, as we had done for Wembley, but for some reason Arsenal didn't want us to train on their pitch this time.

Andy Dawson: Arsenal at the time had only lost once in the league at the Emirates. They were nigh on unbeatable at home. Live on TV, a million miles from where we'd come from playing against top internationals… A great occasion.

Ian Ashbee: I was rooming with Dean Marney, because he'd make me great cups of tea on a night time, and I said to him the night before: "I'd take losing 4-0 tomorrow, that won't be so bad." But we went there, we knew what we had to do. Phil Brown had set us up as a 4-3-3, and I was thinking: 'What are you doing with a 4-3-3? We're away at Arsenal!'

Paul McShane: Arsenal were a very good team at the time and had a great home record. We were just going to try to get a draw as far as I was concerned. That would have been a great result for us. But we were well prepared going into the game. Phil Brown put a lot of trust in us, and was aiming to get the win. We were working on the tactic of Arsenal disrespecting us, attacking and throwing everyone forward, leaving two versus two at the back; William Gallas and Kolo Toure against Marlon King and Daniel Cousin. When we won the ball we knew we had to get it straight up to them. Daniel Cousin was a massive part of the success in that first season. He was as strong as an ox and would bully some of the world's best defenders. People would under-rate him. Then Marlon King was a great player, very intelligent, and he scored some great goals for us.

Phil Buckingham: It was impossible not to expect a hammering. In 2008, Arsenal had won the Premier League title relatively recently and had been challenging in the subsequent years. It was little old Hull City going there. No one gave them a prayer.

Ian Farrow: We set off with no expectations at all except to see our club playing one of the then 'big four'. Our group also had a quick two quid bet in London and got 14-1 for a City win. We visited a local Arsenal pub talking to their supporters who, in a condescending but friendly way, tried (without much conviction) to tell us that we were in with a chance, and that football was a funny old game. We in turn asked them if they could keep the score down to three or less. Arsenal sat at the top of the Premier League and their juniors had that week put six past a full-strength Sheffield United without reply in the League Cup.

Brendon Smurthwaite: The press facilities were amazing. We'd never seen anything like it – a pre-match meal, a free bar, a freezer just filled with Ben and Jerry's ice-cream that you could help yourself to, fish and chips at half-time, TVs everywhere. You wanted for nothing.

Michael Turner: We were so excited going into all the games. I'd never played at 5.30 on a Saturday before, and the Emirates was the best stadium I've played at, the pitch was immaculate. We were looking forward to it. There was no pressure on us.

Ian Farrow: The only person seemingly thinking we could definitely win the game was our manager. Surprisingly Phil Brown had chosen a very attacking side when the majority of us would have settled for damage limitation. A 4-3-1-2 formation with Geovanni just behind Cousin and King, with Marney, Boateng and Ashbee doing the work of six in midfield.

Paul Duffen: Arsenal are a very well-run football club, very dignified, very welcoming. They presented us with a silver cannon to record the first time we'd played at the Emirates: A lot of pomp and circumstance and formality. I had no idea what to expect in terms of the minutiae of how the game would run, but I was a little nervous that it could be embarrassing.

Brendon Smurthwaite: I'd seen the late Danny Fulbrook before the game, who'd reported on the Hull Daily Mail a few years before, and he said it was going to be a long day for our boys but we should enjoy the game.

Steve Lee: I think many Hull City fans regarded Arsenal with a certain degree of respect, if not admiration. We were led to believe they were a club that did things 'the right way' on and off the pitch. We'd had an unexpectedly good start to our debut Premier League season but were about to come up against our first real test against one of the big beasts and one that nobody I knew was confident about. I was thinking: 'I'd take a 4-0 whupping right now.'

A familiar face from the play-off final would be officiating matters.

Alan Wiley: If you offer Hull City a draw at kick-off time, they'd snap your hands off. You also think that if Hull City play Arsenal at their own game they might get a bit of a tanking. So what you're expecting as a referee is for Hull to play a spoiling game, try to slow it down and stifle in midfield with a load of niggly fouls to break up play.

The game kicked off, and though Arsenal were in the ascendancy, they couldn't quite break City down.

Andy Dawson: One thing that we were was organised and disciplined as a team. We were hard to play against – you have to be when you've just come up from the Championship. In that team there was me, Boaz Myhill, Ian Ashbee, who'd been playing lower league football not long back. We were miles off what Arsenal were. We all knew our jobs. It was backs against the wall at times, but we stuck in.

Ian Farrow: Talking to fans as we went into the Emirates the feeling was the same and everyone seemed to be taking the match as an occasion. We were all looking at watches and saying "five minutes gone and we're still level"... "eight minutes gone and it's still 0-0".

On 17 minutes it looked as if City's defence had been breached. Just 17 days prior to this game, Theo Walcott had scored a hat-trick in Croatia for England, confirming his status as one of the best young players in Europe. Today he broke the offside trap and advanced down the Arsenal right towards goal, moving towards a one on one with Boaz Myhill. He'd been gobbling up such chances for a long time now. Surely this was the opener. Then, seemingly out of nowhere, Andy Dawson executed a tackle that Paulo Maldini would have classed among his finest.

Andy Dawson: For me, playing so well against Theo Walcott had given me a lot of confidence as he was a big England international at the time. He'd gone through, and I was probably in a bad position, which was why the ball was played through. As he was running through I was thinking: 'No! No! Can I get back?' Then it was a case of can I time it and not bring him down, because it's a sending off as I'm last man. He took an extra touch, which gave me the opportunity. If he'd just hit it I wouldn't have got there. But that gave me my one opportunity to get round and luckily I timed it just right and got the ball. For me, after that day it gave me a bit of extra confidence. You question yourself as to whether you can play at this level, have you got the pace, and can you deal with it technically and tactically. I thought to myself: 'Yes, I can actually do this now.'

Nil-nil it stayed, on 20 minutes, 30 minutes, and then at half-time. As the players retreated to the changing rooms, a couple of thousand Hull City fans took commemorative photos of the scoreboard. It wouldn't, couldn't, get better than holding Arsenal to 0-0 at half-time at the Emirates.

Paul Duffen: Getting to half-time 0-0, and feeling that our full-backs were negating their threat, Andy Dawson had Theo Walcott in his pocket, it felt like it was going to be something that could be quite fantastic.

Ian Farrow: There was a jubilation at half-time when we had kept the then still mighty Arsenal at bay. Nil-nil at the break was an accomplishment. We quietly celebrated the fact while noisily supporting our team, even through the break.

George Boateng: When it was 0-0 at half-time, Phil was still really angry in the dressing room. We were thinking" 'What?' He was saying that we didn't realise how good we were and that we shouldn't be settling for a draw. He told us we could do better and win the game but we needed to put another 10% or 15% into things. We were all thinking: 'Is he serious?' We didn't say anything, but we were sitting down, all shattered, and here we were being told we had to do more. So we went out and conceded first. Normally you're disappointed when you go behind, but for some reason we didn't feel disappointed. No one's head dropped. We kept on playing our football and had a couple of small chances, I had a shot on target that was saved. We weren't down.

The game's opening goal came when Paul McShane, under a great deal of pressure from Cesc Fabregas, put the ball in his own net. Normal service was resumed. The football world could shrug its shoulders. Nothing to see here.

Paul McShane: I was covering across as the right-back. I still had the mentality of a centre-back. There was a bit of a melee in the mouth of the goal and I was trying to clear the ball. There was lots of dancing around, then Cesc Fabregas got a touch, it came off my heel and went in. It was only after the game that I realised it had touched my heel and was going down as an own goal. As a defender I'd do everything I could to clear the ball, and every now and then it would come off me and go in the back of the net. But I wasn't too fussed about that.

Steve Lee: When we went in at half-time 0-0, we were thinking we couldn't nick a draw here could we? That dream evaporated soon after when Paul McShane put the ball in his own net. Oh well, maybe we can at least keep it down to a respectable score…

Paul Duffen: When we went 1-0 down I was still really proud. I just felt: whatever happens now it's not going to be really humiliating, we've worried them. And then what happened after that was absolutely unbelievable. I was stunned by it.

'Stunned', in this instance, is an understatement. On 62 minutes, Geovanni took the ball 30 yards out on City's left, cut inside and unleashed an unstoppable shot into Manuel Almunia's far corner. The City fans went berserk. We'd scored at the Emirates. THIS was as good as it gets.

Andy Dawson: They went 1-0 up and we were thinking: 'We have to stay strong and stay in the game.' We'd seen what Geo was capable of, but that was absolute top drawer. I was overlapping, and as I overlapped he stepped in and just let fly. A world-class goal. I was thinking: 'We've just scored at Arsenal and it's 1-1. What's going on?'

Alan Wiley: I had a great view. He was on the left, coming back in, and the first thing that surprised me was that no one went to close him down. You got the impression that Arsenal thought: 'You can shoot from there as it will have to be one hell of a shot to beat us.' And it duly was.

Boaz Myhill: The Emirates is an unbelievable place to play. Arsenal were playing free-flowing football, but everybody remembers Geovanni's goal as one of the best goals you'll see. Not many people would have expected a Brazilian to be playing football for Hull! That in itself was a success, managing to get someone like that to sign for us.

Brian Horton: Geo had that in his locker. He was just a gifted technical player. He just had a quality that could do special things. The fans in that corner were having an unbelievable time.

George Boateng: What Geovanni did from that distance was incredible. For me it has to go down as one of the top 10 goals ever scored in the Premier League. The curve to get it in was just breathtaking. I just remember seeing Phil Brown running down the touchline celebrating like a madman.

Mike White: To witness that was just incredible. You almost knew when he cut in that he was going to have a go. I just said: "He's cracked one" and it went straight in the top corner. It was sublime. I think I said: "Quality, pure quality, from Geovanni."

Caleb Folan: In training he'd try these shots and they'd often end up on the roof, but in games he'd just do it. Some of those goals were unbelievable.

Matt Rudd: It was all about not having the right to do any of it; shoot from that distance, get it on target, score. We were Hull City, they were Arsenal. It was utterly bonkers.

Ian Farrow: City didn't panic but instead seemed spurred into playing some very nice football. So, when Geovanni scored 10 minutes after we went one down with a typically penetrating run and unstoppable, perfectly executed long range curler past the 'keeper, it was probably deserved. One-one at the Emirates. We would certainly accept that.

George Boateng: When we equalised that just lifted everyone so much. We felt like we became supermen instantly. Our mental strength got such a massive boost. I was thinking back to what the manager said about giving more and winning the game, and something just pushed us. It was amazing.

Four minutes after Geovanni's equaliser, in the 66th minute, City won a corner on the right-hand side. Andy Dawson ran over to take it.

Andy Dawson: I was thinking 'It's 1-1 and I'm taking a corner at the Emirates in the Premier League!' We were massively in the game and Phil Brown was big on his set-pieces as he knew at the level we were playing at it was a good opportunity to score a goal. We'd worked a lot on it.

Andy Dawson's inswinging corner was inch perfect. Daniel Cousin rose above William Gallas and glanced the ball into the net. Two-one. TWO-ONE!!! The City fans present thought their eyeballs were going to explode at what they'd just witnessed.

Alan Wiley: One of my assistant referees immediately said: "That's put the cat among the pigeons!"

Phil Brown: The Geovanni goal was a godsend but the set piece was one that we'd really worked on. We knew if we got the ball into the six-yard box with quality that we had more height and we were braver.

Robert Crampton: I went as a guest of an Arsenal supporting friend, sat in one of the posher bits of the Emirates. When the first goal went in I kept my counsel, as I was surrounded by home fans. Then I realised that they didn't really give a shit, so when Cousin scored I went absolutely mental.

Steve Lee: I'd been tolerating the shut-up-sit-down brigade around me but with momentum suddenly swinging City's way I made my way to the back of the stand and managed to squeeze onto the back row just in time to see Marlon King win a corner. I don't think I've ever so uncontrollably, rabidly squealed like a girl as when Daniel Cousin's header flew in.

Mike White: It's one of those goal commentaries that I would love to have back and do a retake. I don't think I quite captured truly what it meant. The adrenaline had really got to me. The City fan in me was coming out. I did eventually say, however: "Check out this scoreline: Arsenal 1, Hull City 2." So I got there in the end!

Ian Farrow: Cousin rising high above everyone and placing a header in the far corner. I remember the chants of "we are Premier League" and "we're by far the greatest team the world has ever seen" been sung with little sense of irony. Suddenly everyone believed. Even the players.

Phil Buckingham: I had the Hull City media team sat behind me. They were allowed to show their emotions but I wasn't. There are not many goals that have got me out of my seat as a reporter, because in a press box it's not the done thing, but Deano's goal at Wembley and Daniel Cousin's at the Emirates did just that. It was impossible not to get swept away in it all.

Craig Sargent: Football is at its best when the unexpected happens and all logic is thrown out of the window; the peak for me of the Phil Brown era. It was the time when everything was right. On this late Saturday afternoon it felt like anything was possible. Geovanni's goal needs no introduction but the outpouring of joy that met Daniel Cousin's goal was something to behold. The fact that we were all still in dreamland because of Geo's sensational goal minutes before led to a state of delirium I'm struggling to remember experiencing since.

But still Arsenal came. On 74 minutes Adebayor was millimetres away from connecting with a cross to bring the scores level. On 81 minutes Robin Van Persie hit a shot narrowly wide. But Arsenal were always going to have some chances. Their problem was, however, they couldn't take hold of the midfield. Ash, George Boateng and Dean Marney – with Bryan Hughes later joining them – ran their blood to water and the likes of Cesc Fabregas and Denilson didn't know what had hit them.

Ian Ashbee: I don't think I've run so much in any game as I did that game. With George Boateng, Dean Marney and myself, there are legs in there. There's tenacity. To go up against Fabregas, with Van Persie dropping deep as well, you have a lot of respect for them, but we were on the pitch now and that's where my respect for anyone goes out of the window. George was good because he had the experience, he'd done stuff like that. We worked extremely hard on closing down throughout the week, and setting ourselves up right, and we didn't give them a second. We did a job on them.

Bryan Hughes: It was tough, as they were putting pressure on us. But there was still an element of resilience about us from the previous year. We'd dig in for each other and we had to towards the end. What a moment that was for the club. At the start of that season no one expected anything of us, but we just got on with our job. We embraced every moment of it.

Ian Farrow: This could have been Dean Marney's finest hour (and a half) in a City shirt.

An incredible injury time save from Myhill to deny Fabregas was the last meaningful action of the match. Alan Wiley blew the final whistle and the football world was put into an advanced state of shock. Hull City AFC had beaten Arsenal on their own patch by two goals to one. All these years later, that still feels enormously satisfying to type.

George Boateng: The last 10 minutes were backs against the wall. It would have been such a shame if we'd drawn. But you can imagine coming in the dressing room after that. We were so tired but the victory was so sweet. Arsene Wenger couldn't comprehend that he'd lost the game. He was in shock.

Paul McShane: In the last few minutes, on the pitch it felt like we were going to win. We were so well organised and every player was helping every other player out. We were like dogs working for each other. We'd do anything to get the win. Our fitness stats were very high and we had an amazing hunger to get the result. The work rate of everyone was incredible. Such amazing cohesion within the team. It was a great, great, great result!

Geovanni: The game against Arsenal was incredible, not only for my goal, which was sensational, but above all after the game to see the faces of each player, the joy of our dreams coming true to beat one of the greatest powers of world football. It was priceless. We had faith and believed that the impossible was possible.

Brendon Smurthwaite: We were getting requests for interviews from all over the world. We were *the* story in world football. It had been crazy but Arsenal sent it even wilder. We shocked the world.

Boaz Myhill: It was a lot of hard work that won us that game. Phil Brown was still talking about Daws's tackle on Theo Walcott years later.

Paul Duffen: The way the media reacted was ridiculous. I had Sky at my house the next day, in my garden doing a piece.

Brendon Smurthwaite: In the press conference at the end, when Browny walked in, the London-based press seemed to be in shock. They didn't seem to know what to ask. And for once I don't even think Browny knew what to say.

Alan Wiley: The one thing that stood out to us in the second half was not only that Hull City had scored two goals, it was that they'd deserved them. They'd played some really good football. We were pleasantly surprised by that. It wasn't a smash and grab. Hull deserved that victory.

Phil Buckingham: I'd known a lot of the lads on the pitch for years, seen them come up through the lower leagues, so to see them get to that point, it was impossible not to feel part of it.

Ian Farrow: Towards the end, Van Persie spurned the sort of chance he would normally score, but that's football, and I don't think that Arsene Wenger could have many complaints at the final whistle. He inevitably did, of course he did, but that's another story and not for this memory, which is one of jubilation that finishes with everyone hugging anyone and everyone else they could find who had a City heart.

Robert Crampton: Afterwards the Arsenal fans were great. I went to a pub on the Holloway Road, and their fans in there were just saying: "Well done, mate." It felt bigger than Wembley in a way, because it was more unexpected.

Brian Horton: Not bad memories these, are they? Phil's brilliant tactically. We'd seen them play and devised a system we were going to go there with, and identified the areas we were going to let them have the ball, and the plan worked perfectly.

Michael Turner: We kept them quiet but when they scored I just thought: 'Oh no, we've played well here and now we look like losing it,' so to turn it round in the manner we did was such a great feeling. Beating Arsenal away… it was unheard of for a newly promoted side.

Frank and Margaret Beill: We were among the Arsenal supporters as one of our daughters had friends with season tickets who were unable to attend the match. We kept any sign of supporting City hidden but it became obvious who we were. At the end some of the Arsenal supporters said: "Well done."

Paul Duffen: The three greatest moments in my life other than marriage and the birth of my children are undoubtedly that Watford home game, Wembley and the game at Arsenal.

James Richardson: Arsenal felt otherworldly, I'm not sure I'll ever quite match that high outside of City winning a trophy. Dancing through the streets of Islington, past Highbury, as my fellow travelling companions smoked cigars will live with me for ever.

Mike White: The commentary box was in among all the Arsenal fans, and at the end of the game you could hear them all walking past chuntering various excuses. Then after the programme had finished we ended up walking out of the stadium with Martin Keown, and he was the same. Just making up excuses. I lost a bit of respect for him that day, as I thought City warranted more credit than that. I thought we deserved the win for the way we defended.

Craig Sargent: Following the final whistle I remember walking out of the ground, seeing a fellow member of Hull City Southern Supporters and trying to explain how I felt. I couldn't. We just kind of stared at each other with big grins on our faces, exhausted from the emotion of it all.

Rob Smith: I was ringing people up, crying, telling them about the game. We'd just beaten Arsenal. We'd done something you'd never have believed in a million years. I think I was more emotional after that than I was after Wembley. Stuff like that just shouldn't have happened to Hull City. Another part of the fairy-tale.

Robert Crampton: Before the season started you're looking at the fixtures thinking: 'Where are we going to get 10 wins from?' You wouldn't have put the Emirates down as one of them. It was Arsenal, a massive club. It was magnificent.

Phil Buckingham: I struggled to put it into words then, and I do to this day.

City were sixth in the table with 11 points. They'd 'done a Derby' alright, it's just they'd done it after six games, not 38.

1. **Chelsea P6 W4 D2 L0 Pts14**
2. **Liverpool P6 W4 D2 L0 Pts14**
3. **Aston Villa P6 W4 D1 L1 Pts13**
4. **Arsenal P6 W4 D0 L2 Pts12**
5. **West Ham P6 W4 D0 L2 Pts12**
6. **Hull City P6 W3 D2 L1 Pts11**

Tottenham had been struggling that season and were bottom of the table as they prepared to face the Tigers. But going to White Hart Lane was still a daunting task for a newly promoted side. Except Hull City didn't do 'daunted'. City left north London with another three points in the bag. Those 11 points Derby accrued? We'd smashed it in seven games. The moral of the story? David Mellor knows arse all about football (as had been evident to anyone who'd ever heard him present 606 on Radio 5).

Before the match, it looked as though a Dawson family reunion could be on the cards.

Andy Dawson: Me and Mike had talked about playing against each other for years. Obviously I was a million miles from where Mike was previously. Did we ever think we'd get the opportunity? Probably not, unless it was a cup game. Unfortunately Mike didn't get on.

The game's only goal came in the ninth minute, when Geovanni smashed home a spectacular free kick from 30 yards.

Geovanni: It has always been my speciality to take free-kicks, since I was young. I trained a lot and against Tottenham I didn't give the goalkeeper a chance!

Andy Dawson: That was one where I thought: 'I can't score from there!' Geo had scored against Fulham and Arsenal with top strikes and then he goes and does that against Tottenham. There was no argument from me when Geo wanted to take a free-kick after seeing those goals.

Dean Marney: I was at Spurs from the age of nine to 21. It was a massive part of my life but I never quite got the opportunities. I felt I had a point to prove to show them they made a mistake. It was great going back. A lot of players won't celebrate goals and the like against their old clubs. I understand that, but you've left for a reason. I was delighted to win!

Michael Turner: I was a Tottenham fan when I was younger so I was looking forward to this game. We had loads of confidence going into this game after beating Arsenal. Another unbelievable goal from Geo and as we had done the week before, we defended resolutely. To beat Arsenal and Spurs back to back away was amazing. We were pinching ourselves.

Craig Sargent: This goal often gets forgotten about due to what happened at Arsenal the week before but it really was a stunning free-kick and for a short period at least we were a bloody brilliant Premier League team with a Brazilian number 10 firing in free-kicks from 30 yards!

Paul Denman: That free-kick was right in the postage stamp – unsavable.

Nick Barmby: I was older and knew I wouldn't play week in, week out. I was happy to be sub and come on and make an impact – that was the way my career was heading then – but I still had the determination wanting to start. I just wanted to do what was best for the team. To beat Arsenal at the Emirates and Tottenham at White Hart Lane – that's no mean feat.

Phil Brown: Andy Dawson marked Theo Walcott and Aaron Lennon out of two successive games. For a lad who'd never played at the highest level, who was from a really solid family background, to be doing that was a great testament to him. He grew a couple of inches in that Arsenal game. Everyone would talk about 'little Andy Dawson' but at the end of that game he was about six-foot four. He looked like his Michael! He grew in stature with every game and it was no coincidence that Andy Dawson completed a very good year in the Premier League.

Dave Burns: The attitude of the players and manager, and the way they just went for it, was fantastic. It was just a dream.

Paul Duffen: We were never a one-man team but Geovanni was certainly starting to fulfil our expectation of him. By then we'd exceeded the Derby points tally too.

Phil Brown: There was one horrible comment from a former Derby County manager who said that Hull City wouldn't even get past Derby's total. Those sort of comments, that crass mentality, spurred me on, spurred the backroom staff on and spurred the players on to prove those people wrong. When we had more points than Derby after seven games was a real milestone. Then after nine games we were flirting with the big wigs at the top of the division. But answering those critics really spurred us on.

Paul Duffen: Coming back from a Premier League meeting on the train with John Williams, Blackburn's chairman, he said to me: "We feel like one of the best sides in England right now because you didn't beat us."

The wins kept coming. The 'London 0 Hull 4' prophecy of the Housemartins' 1986 album title came true when City beat West Ham courtesy of a Michael Turner header to complete an unlikely quartet of victories against sides from the capital. Next up were West Brom at the Hawthorns, the venue of the unexpected victory that had given City so much belief the season before. This time City were travelling there as the Premier League's in-form team.

Phil Brown: For the first 20 minutes or so, I just remember us being under the cosh to an unbelievable degree.

Sam Ricketts: I remember coming on. I'd been dropped after the Wigan game, and Paul McShane had come in. It had taken me a little bit of time to settle in to the Premier League – just as it had the Championship – getting that belief that I was good enough. But the year before, the game at the Hawthorns had been pivotal in us getting promoted in a hard game where we had to give everything until the whistle went. But in this game we blew them away. We were 3-0 up and we were head and shoulders better than them. We were quicker, more powerful, and we were thinking: 'Wow, this was one of our hardest games last year and we've come here and blown them away.' That was bigger for me than anything to do with our league position. We were going into Premier League games expecting to win, not hoping.

Alfie Potts Harmer: One match which has always stood out for me was the 3-0 win against West Brom in the Premier League in 2008. It was almost November, yet that win put us joint top of the Premier League. It was such a convincing win too. I think we scored the third goal just after the hour mark, and as soon as it went in the Hawthorns began to empty. It seemed like the last 20 minutes were played in front of only City fans, and I can recall the disbelief at what was happening that season as we left the ground.

City's goals came from Kamil Zayatte, Geovanni and Marlon King. At the end of play, the victory left the league table looking like this, with City joint top on points.

1. **Chelsea P8 W6 D2 L0 Pts20**
2. **Liverpool P8 W6 D2 L0 Pts20**
3. **Hull City P9 W6 D2 L1 Pts20**
4. **Arsenal P8 W5 D1 L2 Pts16**
5. **West Ham P8 W4 D3 L1 Pts15**

Paul Duffen: No one wanted to play us.

Ian Ashbee: I'd done the hard yards like so many of the fans and I was just laughing. I'd get up and have my breakfast in a morning and I'd look at the tables and laugh, thinking: 'What's going on?' You've got to ride that wave while you're there and carry on with what you're doing, but obviously that didn't materialise. But to say you were that high up the league in the first season that you were in there – and I was taking pictures of the table when we were joint top – it's special, in anyone's world.

Phil Brown: It was brilliant, really enjoyable. All the coaching badges you take, all the courses you go on, they don't prepare you for this. I was sitting in Medici's restaurant one night and I got a phone call from Australia asking me about the Tigers branding side of things as we had a supporters club over there. We had another one in America. We were all over the world. It was just a wonderful period of my life and a wonderful period in the history of Hull City. Nobody can prepare you for these things though. Maybe to a certain extent I was far too honest at this point in the media's eyes. They will tell you now that you have to be slightly dishonest, you can't give the full picture as they'll exploit that, and that's what happened.

Paul McShane: We had a great team spirit. I think it had originated from the season before. There was a great group of lads who were very senior, who'd brought the club so far. At half-time, everyone would chip in to solve the problems. The likes of Ian Ashbee, Nicky Barmby, Dean Windass, Andy Dawson, Boaz Myhill, George Boateng – they were senior lads and good characters. That created an excellent atmosphere around the training ground.

Mark Robinson: In the Sussex dressing room people like Michael Yardy would slaughter me over City saying we were a pub team, with a council-owned ground, calling us the Dog and Duck, but it was nice to actually be on their radar!

George Boateng: It was one of those situations – my mental strength has always carried me forward. Even though it was unreal to see it, it was not something that I felt was unachieveable. Looking at the table, our confidence was so high that we weren't even shocked to see ourselves there. We were playing good football and we were finding ways to win. What pleased me at the time was that everyone had had us down to get relegated and it really didn't look like that would happen.

Phil Buckingham: On the media days, usually on a Thursday or Friday, the interest in the club went crazy. It had been high from the beginning of that season, but then it would normally taper off pretty quickly when the novelty had worn off. But when City were going to the likes of Arsenal and Tottenham and winning, all of a sudden the interest peaked. It was standing room only in the media room – which doubled as a gym – at Millhouse Lane. Everyone wanted a piece of Hull City. The club was *the* story, and journalists were clambering over themselves to be a part of it.

Sean Rush: Those first 10 games were unbelievable. We were under the radar because nobody knew what we were about.

Geovanni's spectacular goals were grabbing the headlines, but it was the form of Michael Turner – by this point the highest scoring defender in the Premier League's official Fantasy Football competition – that had City fans wondering if they were watching what would be the club's first ever England international.

Michael Turner: There was talk of me playing for England, but it was only when I moved to Sunderland that I got in the provisional squad a couple of times. I wasn't aware of anything when I was at Hull. All the talk was a bit premature as I'd only just started playing in the Premier League. I was just loving life, being part of something special.

City were brought down to earth with a bump in a midweek home defeat to Chelsea, with the Blues winning 3-0. But next on The Hull City hit list was arguably the biggest of them all: Old Trafford. In the opposition dugout was Sir Alex Ferguson, who was keen to heap praise on his one-time cross-city adversary Brian Horton.

Brian Horton: I had my battles with Sir Alex, dating back to my first spell with Hull City. But when I came to Manchester City I got to know him very, very well. When you have a manager of his stature saying nice things about you, it's great isn't it?

Paul Duffen: I had lunch with Bobby Charlton and his wife! For anybody who loves football you feel like a kid living your dreams going to the boardrooms of Liverpool, Newcastle, Arsenal, Spurs, Everton, Manchester United…

The Manchester United line-up was star-studded, but on the right-hand side of their attack was the biggest star of all: Cristiano Ronaldo. Five years ago, in October 2003, Andy Dawson had been worrying about Macclesfield Town's Chris Priest and Matthew Tipton. So how did he feel about pitting himself against a player on his way to becoming one of the best of all time?

Andy Dawson: The better the player I was playing against, the more I embraced the challenge. I was thinking: 'Bring it on. Let's have it!' I loved every single minute of playing against world superstars. When they were one-v-one I was thinking: 'Great, let's have a go at it!' I wasn't an arrogant person, I just embraced the better players coming and having a go at me. Looking back on my career now, that's probably what drove me forward and it's why I was able to step up at each level, because I challenged myself.

Paul McShane: I really look forward to those challenges. They are the best players in the world, and you look forward to that test. But at the same time I didn't think about it really. You become a bit ignorant about it in a way, as if you get sucked in to the whole 'it's Cristiano Ronaldo, Wayne Rooney, Ryan Giggs and so on…' then you've already lost. You have to switch your mind off to that. Once you click off it's just 11 versus 11. Everything else goes out of the window. Whoever plays the best on the day will get the result.

Manchester United scored first through Ronaldo, but City showed that no stage could daunt them when a Daniel Cousin header brought the scores level. Michael Carrick put the home side back in front before a contentious goal – the referee missing a foul on Bryan Hughes in the build up – saw Cristiano Ronaldo score his second and Manchester United's third.

The game looked dead and buried when Nemanja Vidic made it 4-1, but Phil Brown made a substitution in the 59th minute, bringing on Bernard Mendy for Bryan Hughes. Suddenly the much-vaunted Manchester United defence of Gary Neville, Patrice Evra, Rio Ferdinand and Vidic couldn't cope, with Mendy's pace in particular causing problems. The Frenchman pulled one back in the 69th minute. Game on. Alex Ferguson's response was to attack.

City were facing an attack that effectively comprised Ryan Giggs, Ronaldo, Carlos Tevez, Dimitar Berbatov and Wayne Rooney. It did no good. They couldn't find a way past an inspired Boaz Myhill and City kept pressing. Mendy was brought down in the area on 82 minutes by Rio Ferdinand to give City a penalty, which Geovanni duly despatched. Four-three. City's couldn't win this, could they?

This was to be one fairy-tale too far. Manchester United held on, with their manager and fans pleading for the final whistle. City had lost their first away game of the season 4-3, but had shown that there was no opposition, no situation that daunted them.

Geovanni: It was a spectacular game against Manchester United. We imposed ourselves, applying pressure all the time, wanting the result all the time. I am proud to have been part of this wonderful group!

Paul Duffen: To see Alex Ferguson making defensive substitutions at the end of the game… he just wanted the game to stop. There was no question of 'Fergie time' that day. We played with such spirit and adventure.

Phil Brown: Sir Alex was the first person to point out to me that we were the first opposition side to score three goals at Old Trafford in about seven years. Bernard Mendy transformed the game on the right-hand side as a winger. His pace was a huge threat, he could run like the wind, and he got at their left-hand side and made a game of it.

Michael Turner: We were always behind in the game but we wouldn't let it lie. We kept going and kept going and rightly got a lot of plaudits from our performance.

Brian Horton: It was a great game of football. We had them on the rack. Sir Alex wasn't happy about the penalty decision, but it was a penalty. Bernard Mendy on the right wing caused them untold problems. The games against the big sides were coming thick and fast. It was great to be involved in.

Phil Brown: When you go into Alex Ferguson's office after the game, there's all the legendary stuff there, including all the great wines. It was a bittersweet moment though because I was at the top table in football management, but we'd lost a game and that was disappointing. It doesn't matter who you're playing. We received all the plaudits from the media, but we still lost the game.

The next game at the KC, against Bolton, saw City lose their first game against non-stellar opposition since the Wigan thrashing. Even still, it took an inspired display from Bolton keeper Jussi Jaaskelainen to keep the Tigers at bay, while Matt Taylor got the winner at the other end. A creditable 2-2 draw with Manchester City at the KC followed – with goals coming from Daniel Cousin and Geovanni – before a long trip to Fratton Park, Portsmouth.

On the south coast, Peter Crouch put the home side ahead after 20 minutes only for Michael Turner to equalise just before half-time. Glen Johnson then scored with an incredible volley from 35 yards to hand the advantage back to Portsmouth. In the 72nd minute, Phil Brown brought on 39-year-old Dean Windass. In the 89th minute a cross came the veteran's way. He headed it towards goal, the ball bounced off Portsmouth defender Noe Pamarot and nestled in the back of the net. City gained a vital point and Dean Windass became the second oldest goalscorer in Premier League history (after the Dubious Goals Committee ruled that he'd be credited with the goal) at the ripe old age of 39 years and 236 days.

Dean Windass: It was just instinct. Ash put the ball back in the box, it was being knocked about and I jumped early. I headed it on to a Portsmouth defender's head and we got back to 2-2. People said it was an own goal, but I always say: "Well I got the goal bonus and I got the goal in the end."

The next game at Stoke was notable for City's innovative attempts to quell their opponent's long throw threat from Rory Delap. This saw Dean Windass warming up in front of Delap as he waited to take a throw, Boaz Myhill putting the ball out for a corner instead of a throw-in, and, most ludicrously, Paul McShane being denied the use of the towels that Delap had been using to dry the ball pre-throw. City drew the match 1-1, with a Marlon King goal being equalised by a penalty after Ricardo Fuller had theatrically thrown himself to the ground. Three draws on the trot proved that City were still no mugs at this level.

Paul McShane: We were so well prepared in the lead up to games. Phil Brown has to take a lot of credit for that. We were finding ways to deal with all these teams, and Stoke had the long throw, which was their biggest threat. We had a discussion the day before about how to deal with it, asking things like: 'Do we want to give away a throw-in or a corner?'

Boaz got it on his left and knew he couldn't get the ball up to the half-way line, so he had a little look and – as we'd told him to do the day before – he kicked it out for a corner. All the Stoke fans gave a big cheer but we knew what we were doing. The instruction from the sideline was: when you get a throw-in, you demand that towel and waste a few seconds if we're level or ahead. Initially they weren't giving me the towels, but that's against the rules as both teams have to have access to the same things. So I grabbed a towel and thought I'd take the mick a little bit and started drying my hair and stuff like that. It was just one of those things to waste a bit more time and secure the 1-1 draw.

The Tigers were still in a dizzying sixth position in the league as they prepared for the visit of Middlesbrough. The game had added importance for former Boro man George Boateng, so when Tuncay put the Teessiders 1-0 up on 79 minutes, City's Dutch midfielder was having none of it.

George Boateng: It was such a big game because you still felt it could be important in the relegation fight at the end of the season. The chief executive at Middlesbrough at the time had let me go when I asked, probably thinking Hull would be relegated, so I didn't leave on great terms. That played on my mind, and I wanted to win. The sentimental side of things didn't bother me. When we went a goal down, I just thought: 'No way, this is not happening!' It was like a bad dream. I was trying to think of what I could do to change things, turn it around. When we got that equaliser our mental side came through. I wanted to prove to Middlesbrough that they made a mistake by allowing me to go and show them that we could stay up and they might go down!

City had equalised in the 82nd minute through a Ross Turnbull own goal, and then scored a winner in the 85th minute through a Marlon King penalty after David Wheater – who was sent off – had brought down Geovanni.

Meanwhile, it was mid-December and City were a comfortable sixth in the Premier League. The 26 points accrued was more than double the tally Derby had managed, but no one was talking about 'doing a Derby' anymore. The chat was about where Hull City – and Phil Brown – were going to go from here. European football? The next England manager? Nothing seemed impossible.

1. **Liverpool P16 W11 D4 L1 Pts37**
2. **Chelsea P16 W11 D3 L2 Pts36**
3. **Manchester United P15 W9 D4 L2 Pts31**
4. **Arsenal P16 W9 D2 L5 Pts29**
5. **Aston Villa P16 W8 D4 L4 Pts28**
6. **Hull City P16 W7 D5 L4 Pts26**
7. **Portsmouth P16 W6 D5 L5 Pts23**

The big games kept coming, and for football fans brought up in the 1970s and 1980s, Anfield held special appeal. City were unbeaten in four games, but the opposition – who were top of the table – had in their ranks the likes of Pepe Reina, Sami Hyypia, Jamie Carragher, Xabi Alonso, Javier Maschereno, Dirk Kuyt, Steven Gerrard and Robbie Keane. Fernando Torres was to miss the game through injury.

Ian Ashbee: Alonso and Gerrard. You pinch yourself being on the same pitch as them.

Liverpool didn't seem to get the memo that City didn't do daunted and were no respecters of tradition. Sparked by an inspired display by Bernard Mendy on the right wing – in which he destroyed the hopeless left-back Andrea Dossena – City took a 2-0 lead after 22 minutes. The first came from a Paul McShane header, the second from own-goal specialist Jamie Carragher.

Paul McShane: Dean Marney was on the bench and in the dressing room beforehand I remember saying to him that I might score, and if I did I'd run over to him and give him the peace sign. I've no idea why. We started really well and I went up for a corner – something I didn't do very often – and I thought I'd do my best to make the most of it. The ball was cleared out, I think Daws crossed it back in and I was at the back post with Dossena, who wasn't the best in the air. I knew it was my chance, and I concentrated on getting a good connection and thankfully it went in. Then I ran over to Dean and did the little celebration.

Sadly for City, in the 27th minute Paul McShane had to leave the pitch with an injury, causing Mendy to move to right-back as Dean Marney came on to play in midfield. Liverpool, who'd just pulled one goal back through Steven Gerrard, could rest more easily as City's chief attacking threat was now encumbered with defensive duties.

Paul McShane: Not long after my goal I got an elbow off their winger, Riera, and it caught me flush, right on the sweet spot of the temple. I felt a bit shook up, but I didn't think anything of it. But then players started to disappear in my vision, and then the ball did too, and I felt like I was in a dream. Everything was fuzzy. I was struggling and I thought I'd have to go off. It was such a shame as Bernard Mendy and I were flying down that right-hand side. We could have been further ahead. I was gutted to have to come off.

Gerrard was to score a second in the 32nd minute. However, for both of the Liverpool captain's goals, it appeared that he'd fouled Michael Turner.

Michael Turner: We were all really angry because it was a clear foul by Steven Gerrard on me for both the goals. But even with those refereeing decisions we still got a draw at Anfield, which was a massive point.

Sam Ricketts: I'm a Liverpool fan so it was a boyhood dream to play at Anfield. Bernard Mendy was like Usain Bolt on the right wing. He was unbelievable that day. That was another surreal moment, thinking: 'Hold on, we're 2-0 up at Anfield here!' I was a little bit disappointed to come away with a draw, but at the same time you thought it was quite an achievement to get a draw at one of the biggest clubs in world football. It was another measure of how far we'd come as a team.

Nick Barmby: Liverpool fans had always been really good with me. I've come off twice for Hull City there and always got a good ovation. But to get a result at Anfield is incredible, and we should have won. There were decisions by the ref that day where you had to think: 'No, that was a foul.' But we can still say we were 2-0 up at Anfield.

Ian Ashbee: Lining up next to Steven Gerrard in the tunnel leading our teams out at his ground – the legend that he is in football, not just at Liverpool – was amazing. And I was dealing with him okay, to be honest. But good players score goals. I always felt that I could keep the other opposition players in front of me, or have them in my periphery vision where I could feel where they were, and I'd have Michael Turner chatting in my earhole saying: "He's left side, he's right side" – I had a good understanding with Michael like that. But Steven Gerrard was different. He was like a ghost floating into places that would take me off my game. Frank Lampard I felt I dealt with really well as I'd just track his runs straight, but Steven Gerrard on that day was the most difficult of opponents. It was an eye-opener to how good somebody like him really is.

George Boateng: We were very focused on what we had to do. And that game showed that it's not just about having more quality than the opposition – it's about making yourselves effective in what you have to do. Liverpool struggled to deal with us. They thought that we maybe had one or two quality players, and if they kept them quiet they wouldn't have a difficult match. But the reality was that the players we had were all fit, all capable of finding football solutions against quality opposition. It was a great game to play in. Most of the team hadn't played at Anfield so it was memorable in lots of ways.

Paul Duffen: With the Manchester United and Liverpool results, I came away feeling we've done ourselves a real service as a football club, we've justified our place at the top table, but we got one point from two games. As is the case in every league, you've got to take points off the sides around you, and the games against the likes of Liverpool are the days you can just relax with no pressure and have a go. And that was real pride. The then owners of Liverpool weren't the most beloved by their fans. I was sitting in the front of the directors' box next to Tom Hicks and for the whole game the fans in front of us were just turning around shouting insults at him. They weren't even watching the game. That was a bit weird.

Phil Brown: We went 2-0 up and then there were a couple of fouls, meaning both of their goals were questionable. The fine margins were starting to work against us and I didn't know whether it was my public persona, being so honest, which was causing myself and the club more harm than good. It's a minefield and you have to understand that the media need to sell papers, and the story of our success was selling papers. But what was going to sell more papers was our demise. At Anfield I thought that the powers that be were turning against us.

Dave Burns: One of my favourite moments was Paul McShane scoring at Liverpool. One of my great pleasures is working with Swanny, and that day he'd decided to put a bit of money on McShane to score first at 66/1. When he went to collect his money, the woman in the betting office said she'd stayed late to see which kind of idiot would put such a bet on.

Paul Duffen: I had the privilege to be the chairman of Hull City for more than 100 games, and I was the luckiest man in the world because a very high percentage of those games were remarkable.

Sean Rush: Mark Prudhoe turned round to me after that game and said: "It's like Phoenix Nights, isn't it? You don't know what's going to happen next."

Within three months of City drawing at Anfield, Liverpool were to host Real Madrid in the Champions League and win 4-0.

Going into the festive period, City could start to reflect on an amazing year, and a dizzying start to life in the top flight.

Boaz Myhill: The manager had broken down what he wanted from us in each 10-game section, and to say we exceeded expectations in that first half of the season is an understatement.

Caleb Folan: It was such a family unit and it was progressing like that. Everyone made everyone feel at home. We had such togetherness. We knew it was going to get tough though so we knew these points were important.

A potential fly in the ointment came when Roy Keane was sacked as Sunderland manager. Phil Brown was both hot managerial property and a Sunderland fan, meaning speculation of a move was rife. Was an offer ever made? And would Phil have been tempted?

Phil Brown: Given the success we were having, that speculation was always going to follow. And it's the type of thing you're not really educated to be able to deal with. But at that time people were getting two and two and making five. The reason for that was my childhood being spent on the terraces of Roker Park. I was delighted with the job I was doing, and the time I was having at Hull City, and I didn't think anything was going to spoil that. Would I have been interested in the Sunderland job? Of course I would, as that was my club. But at the same time I was believing that Hull City were becoming a force to be reckoned with, and I'd started a job that I wanted to finish.

Paul Duffen: It was never anything that was an issue as far as we were concerned. Sunderland never asked to speak to him. It was all just speculation.

In one of those quirks that the football fixture list throws up, Sunderland were the next visitors to the KC. Steed Malbranque put the Black Cats ahead on 10 minutes, but City were soon back on level terms through Nick Barmby, who'd not only scored his first top-flight goal for Hull City, he'd also equalled the record as the player who had scored for the highest number of Premier League teams – six – though Craig Bellamy has since broken this record.

Nick Barmby: It's nice [becoming the second player to score for six different Premier League clubs], but it was more just that I'd wanted to score for Hull City in the Premier League and I managed to do that. The ball dropped to me and I put it through the goalie's legs, but it's immaterial when you get beat.

And beaten City were. Sam Ricketts was sent off on 81 minutes just after Sunderland had taken the lead through a Kamil Zayatte own goal. Sunderland cashed in, scoring twice more to end the match with a flattering 4-1 victory. But this could be classified as a blip. City were still exceeding expectations, and had still only lost one match away from home all season. However, maintaining that record on Boxing Day at big spending Manchester City was a tough ask. Phil Brown also had to ponder how to approach a game the day after Christmas.

Paul Duffen: Football clubs generally have a two- or three-hour travel threshold as to whether they travel on the morning of a game or stay in a hotel the night before. Going to Manchester from Hull on Boxing Day was doable on the day, and it was the end of a year in which we'd achieved amazingly but had perhaps lost our way a little bit. Phil is a very creative manager and was seeking to find any solution he could that would reset our fortunes that season. Other than the Middlesbrough game at the beginning of December, we'd been short of points. You have two choices as a manager – team hotel on Christmas night and you're all going to be locked down away from your families, or you can make a bargain that says I will trust you, you can spend Christmas with your families, meet at the team hotel at 11 o'clock in Manchester and go through the usual ritual.

George Boateng: The game was on Boxing Day, and the manager would normally make you train on Christmas Day and you go away with the team and stay away with the team. But Phil Brown, because it was Christmas, wanted to show a caring side and let us spend time with our families. So we did a light session on Christmas Day and then were allowed to go back to our families. We would then meet early on Boxing Day morning. We all thought that was very generous of him, very nice. Everybody had been working their socks off and we had a good understanding.

What killed us was that Man City had done their homework very well, and we didn't see it coming how they were set up. They had good players like Steven Ireland, and had a really good team. Before we could even blink we were 2-0 down. They just kept coming at us like a train. They had different sorts of tactics and ways of opening us up, and we didn't know how to stop with it.

We went 3-0 down, and I was at fault for the third goal. I gave the ball away in midfield, they countered and scored. That really pissed Phil Brown off. He decided to take me off after 35 minutes, which was for me one of the most disrespectful things he could have done at the time. I'd been brought in as a leader, and that sort of thing had never happened to me. Nobody had substituted me after 35 minutes before. To say that I was playing bad was wrong. But I knew why Phil was angry because I made the error for the third goal. But those things happen. That's just football. I felt really disrespected.

The move did little good. Robinho – who'd scored in the 28th minute to add to two Caicedo goals – scored again a minute after Boateng was taken off. A livid Phil Brown was to then make a decision that was to see the club beamed to TV screens all over the world, but in a much less positive manner than had been the case for, say, the win at the Emirates. When the referee blew the half-time whistle, Phil Brown signalled for the players to march towards a section of the pitch in front of the Hull City fans, and not to the sanctity of the changing room. It was here that his now infamous team-talk would take place.

Phil Brown: I exposed the changing room for what it was. I won't mention their names, but there were two players that let us down that day by going out on Christmas Day and over-celebrating. Therefore the reason why I did what I did was to expose that. Maybe in hindsight I should have just exposed those two players instead of the whole changing room, but I had so much support from the likes of Nick Barmby, Ian Ashbee and Paul McShane, the stalwarts, the backbone of the team. If I hadn't had their support they wouldn't have followed me, but they followed me in front of thousands of Hull City fans who'd sacrificed their Boxing Day to come and see us, and quite frankly we didn't play. We were 4-0 down at half-time, and I felt those two players had compromised our whole season by doing what they did. As far as I'm concerned, it was the right thing to do.

Paul Duffen: As it unfolded, Phil felt the weight of the decision to let the players meet on Boxing Day, and as far as he was concerned they didn't turn up and he was furious. He felt they'd broken a commitment to the fans, to him, and he decided minutes before half time to keep them out there. His feeling was only that: 'I'm not going to let them run and hide.'

Brian Horton: Just as I was coming down from the stands for half-time, Phil told me he was going to do it. But at the end of the day, he was the manager. If that's what he wanted to do, I said he should do it. If you want to do something, do it. If you have to live with it, so be it. A lot of people liked it. I think our fans liked it.

Mike White: Back then we used to have a half-time bulletin back in the studio. Burnsy would have been doing the half-time wrap up, chatting to Swanny, then been about to go to Scunny or Grimsby. We then realised that Browny was keeping them out on the pitch. People said it had never been seen before, but Radio Humberside had experienced it a couple of years prior to that with Russell Slade when Grimsby were getting walloped by Lincoln. But it was still utterly bizarre.

So how did the players feel? They'd given Phil Brown and the fans the best year in the club's history, and continually defied the odds. Yes, they were 4-0 down, but they were 4-0 down to a team that in Robinho, a £32.5m signing, had a player who'd cost more than every incoming transfer in Hull City's history combined.

George Boateng: I felt, it's his decision, it's fine. I went to sit down and then the half-time team-talk came, which took it to another level. I remember sitting there thinking: 'This is a dream.' We could barely hear him because, even though he was screaming, there were 50,000 people in there. We could tell he was angry but we couldn't tell what he was saying. Initially when we were walking there we thought we were going to clap and apologise to the fans. But then he sat us down…

Boaz Myhill: I didn't know what was happening. I was walking off the pitch, looking at the floor having conceded four goals, and then I saw people walking past me going to the edge of the penalty box and I thought: 'What's going on here?' Then all of a sudden the team talk was happening. It was a low point for us as a club and for the players. Manchester City were a good side and we were at the opposite end of the football spectrum for resources. Managers are under a lot of pressure. Phil felt let down after giving us Christmas Day off and he wanted to fight back a bit. It's not something we enjoyed as players, but I'm sure he didn't do it for us to enjoy it. Life's not always ethically perfect and sometimes people make mistakes. We make mistakes as players and you have to deal with the consequences.

Ian Ashbee: I think it was a massive turning point within the season. Phil Brown has said he'd still do it today but I disagree with him and I'd have no problem saying that to Phil. I think it turned the season, even though Phil won't want to believe that. I was in the changing room with those lads, and it did affect people. It affected me and the way I looked at certain things. To think that you could be joint top in the Premier League at one stage and still be in the top half, playing against the likes of Robinho, and just have one bad half – don't forget we'd put the club on Match of the Day and in the press from a group of lads who weren't expected to do anything – to be sat down like that at half-time was a little bit disrespectful. Everyone had put a proper shift in that season up to that point, and I feel that when he sat us down on that pitch, it wasn't the right thing to do. I don't think he would do it again. It changed everything that day. The changing ground had been buoyant, people wanted to train, they'd stick around after training having a game of darts, but after that there was a difference, and the cliques started to form and I felt it was all down to the team talk. I felt Phil should have dealt with it the way he dealt with it after the 5-0 defeat against Wigan, and just moved on. The way the season went after that… only he knows why he did it.

Bryan Hughes: That was the season's turning point. It affected the mood within the squad. That was what brought our downfall. There were a lot of experienced heads in that team and they were being treated like school children. Some of the players really weren't happy about it. Phil maybe did it for the right reasons, and he got a response in the second half, but after the game there were words said in the dressing room. I think Phil lost a lot of the players that day. But managers do things on the spur of the moment and you just wish he'd been able to take away the moment and look at the bigger picture. We were sixth going into that game. We'd been favourites to get relegated. We were punching way above our weight and some of the players thought that there was no appreciation of what we'd achieved. There was definitely a mood change within the camp.

Craig Fagan: In the squad we had, the British lads took it better than the foreign lads, and I think we lost a couple of the foreign lads due to that. Their attitudes changed to some extent.

We were 4-0 down so Phil was either going to go mad on the pitch or the changing room. Does Phil regret it now? I don't know. Would he do it again? I'm not too sure.

Dean Marney: If Phil Brown is truly honest, I think he'd look back on that and see it as a mistake. We had an unbelievable spirit – staff and players – and we had a lot of influential older players. When something like that happens – and we were getting beat comfortably, but that happens in the Premier League – it's an embarrassment. Looking back should we have just said 'no' and gone in the changing room? Possibly. It might not have been the moment it all changed for us but it played a massive part.

Nick Barmby: Some things just didn't go for us that season, but you can't just blame one incident – the Man City game at half-time – because we could have been in the dressing room getting a roasting and then get beaten five or six times on the trot, so I don't think you can blame that really.

Paul McShane: At the time I just went along with it because I was 22 or 23 and I didn't know anything else. It was a poor performance and I didn't think too much about the team talk at the time. But looking back, I think I might have made a bit more of a fuss about it if I'd been a bit more experienced. I might have said to Phil: "This isn't on." Looking back. I don't think Phil made the right decision. I would imagine Phil feels the same way. But it was a memorable day alright!

Michael Turner: I'm not sure if it had a long-term impact on the team. It was a bad performance in the first half and we were disappointed but the way we were kept on the pitch was embarrassing. We were thinking: 'What are we doing here? We should be in the changing room getting a running down not sitting here in front of our fans getting spoken to like that.' It was embarrassing really, and the way we'd performed in the early part of the season, to be treated that way was disappointing and I don't think we deserved it. But I wouldn't say it was the catalyst for our downfall – after that game we put in some good performances.

Sam Ricketts: From my point of view I don't think the team talk changed things as much as those on the outside thought it had done. We had an unbelievable team spirit. They were a really, really good group of players. We were honest, and the type of players who wouldn't turn on the manager. I felt we stuck together. I can't remember anything happening too much after it to be honest.

Simon Maltby: I wasn't aware of it making a huge impact beyond a couple of rumblings from players who weren't in the team anyway. I didn't see a massive impact. I don't think back now and see it as a turning point. My main memory of it is how cold it was out there. I wanted to get inside where it was warm.

George Boateng: It was a breaking moment in the team, because that kind of thing spoils everything you've built up in terms of confidence in the manager and the staff, players having confidence with each other. That all disappeared that afternoon. I believe that was the beginning of the end.

For one player, the location of the team-talk had him worrying that he'd somehow managed to lose his team.

Craig Fagan: I was on the bench. It was a strange game. I'd been out for three months so I was delighted to be in the squad. After about 30 minutes, Browny turned around and said to me "You're going on at half-time." I was delighted, even though we were losing. I just wanted to get back out there. At half-time the whistle went so I quickly ran off to the changing room to nip to the toilet and get changed because I wanted to do a warm up. I came out of the toilet and there was nobody there! I was thinking there must be some fighting in the tunnel, so I ran out there but there was nobody there too. So I walked out onto the pitch and I could just about make out Browny going mad. I had to walk over because I needed to know what was being said. He was laying into the lads, rightly or wrongly. Was it embarrassing? Yes, because you knew it was going to make the news.

For those watching in the media, it was difficult to know what to make of it all.

Dave Burns: We just thought it was bonkers at the time. Hugely entertaining, but bonkers. No one came out and said it at the time, but eventually a few players would say: "That cost us; that destroyed us. We'd done so much for him." I also felt that Phil was to blame a little bit that day. He'd picked the wrong team. The full-backs weren't quite right. The players felt they'd given so much for him throughout the season, for him to humiliate them in that way was unforgivable in some eyes. I'm sure he regrets it. His man-management was good, and I really liked Phil, but that was a mistake.

Phil Buckingham: My immediate take on it was that I didn't quite grasp the enormity of it. In my match report for the Hull Daily Mail, the team talk only gets a mention in the sixth paragraph. In retrospect I should have led with that! I remember thinking it was unusual but I didn't think it would have the lasting consequences that I think it probably did have. Each player will tell you a different story about how they reacted to it, but I think it damaged what Phil Brown had built. He'd built such a close-knit unit that were willing to fight tooth and nail for each other, and then on the back of a couple of defeats he's hanging them out to dry. The more you think about it looking back, the more absurd it seems. They'd played dreadfully in that first half, but that group of players had done wonders to be in the position they were in. It felt all so needless to do that to them. I think it did have lasting damage. How could it not?

Mike White: I think it affected the mood of the club. At the time people tried to straight bat it and play it down – and they managed to get people to stay on message – but later on I think it started to chew into people. I interviewed George Boateng when he became one of the first people to speak out about it later on in the season. At the time, I thought 'fair play' to Phil. They had been embarrassed and the fans had travelled across at Christmas. But with the power of hindsight I can see he shouldn't have done it. It seems as though he was maybe trying to protect his self-image, though I didn't feel that at the time.

Phil Buckingham: That became the story about Hull City, a sort of sideshow: 'Here they are, the group of players who were chastised by their manager on the pitch.' I suspect that deep down Phil Brown will know that it created something else and it tainted what had gone on before. It wasn't a case of the players chucking in the towel – they were very unlucky a couple of days later when they lost to Aston Villa – it did seem that that was the point the bubble burst.

With the players having mixed feelings about the event, those closest to the manager offered nothing but support.

Paul Duffen: A lot of people have said to me since that they felt it was all about him and that he did it to make a big gesture, and that he'd lost the dressing room. I'm sure these things are not true. I felt he did it because, yes, it was dramatic, but in terms of having an effect on the side, we drew the second half, so it had an impact. It wasn't the start of our declining results; we'd only got a handful of points since the end of October. He did it for reasons he felt were the right reasons, and it set up a wonderful opportunity for Jimmy Bullard a season later…

Brian Horton: I've had many worse things done to me as a player, particularly by people like Alan Mullery. Phil did it for a reason and the reason, I thought, worked. We used to go to horse race meetings and you'd get 20 or so guys doing it in front of him for a laugh, so he got a bit of good publicity from it too! The players need to know that whatever you say and whatever you do, it's for the right reasons.

Paul Duffen: I have a firm belief that if you support people, you support them 100%. If you value people, you value them for their entirety. You can't choose to value bits of people. It doesn't mean that you might not think on occasion that their judgement could have been better, but I would never ever deal in the business of retrospective analysis of decisions I know were made for the best of reasons with the right intention. From a professional perspective I fully supported Phil throughout all that because I understood that he did it for reasons that he felt would get the best out of the team on that day.

And the fall out seemed to continue after the final whistle.

Brendon Smurthwaite: There was a hoo-ha in the dressing room after the game. I was stood at the dressing room door and you could hear shouting and the tactics board going over. The floor manager for Sky asked me if I could get Phil out for an interview as they needed to get everything in the can. I just said: "I'm not going in there, mate. If you want to, be my guest." It gets debated so much as to whether it was a turning point, but I don't really know.

The move was to have a positive financial impact, however.

Sean Rush: Each shot on TV of the Lucozade logo on bottles earned the club £1500. Me giving the lads fluids during the team-talk earned the club £15,000 through Lucozade endorsements.

So how does Phil Brown feel about it looking back?

Phil Brown: I've never regretted it. I've never looked back and thought it was the wrong thing to do at that moment, because whatever anybody says about it, my job was to survive in the Premier League and we fulfilled that, so I don't think you can say it was a failing or the wrong thing to do. It might have been the one thing that kept us in the Premier League, I don't know. If we'd been relegated it would have been the wrong thing to do. If we'd gone down I'd have regretted it.

Lost amid the hubbub of the team-talk was the fact that the game was to bring down the curtain on Dean Windass's incredible Hull City career.

Dean Windass: I knew I wasn't going to play regularly. Hindsight's a wonderful thing, but maybe I should have retired after scoring against Bristol City. But I had a year left on my contract, and when I came back that summer I was so fit. Phil couldn't believe the shape I was in in Italy in pre-season. My last game for City was when I started in that infamous game at Manchester City. Phil said he was starting with me and Marlon. I had a chance in the first half – I should have volleyed it, but I didn't and it didn't come off. Brian had a go at me at half-time for that. Then I was brought off. I never played again after that.

I had an unbelievable 20-year career where I played in almost every game I was available for. But I was nearly 40 years old. Me and Phil had a few run-ins around then but that's just part of being a man.

Andy Dawson: Dean is a great character and scored the most famous goal that Hull City are ever going to score. Deano's an absolute Hull City legend and always will be. Not only that, he's a good character and a good, good person.

Bryan Hughes: Dean deserves special praise. He's someone who'll talk about his goal all day, but deep down he knows he wouldn't have been able to do that without the rest of the team.

Frank and Margaret Beill: Deano is the proverbial prodigal son who returned home to deliver what everyone had dreamed of for so long. Maybe clown prince is a more appropriate title. On behalf of the Tigers Co-op we applied to the Hull City Council to have Deano made a Freeman of the City. We hoped to see him herding a flock of sheep over Monument Bridge. However, the application was turned down on the grounds that whatever he had done it was only 'part of his job'.

Ian Thomson: Dean Windass was the stand-out player during a period when the club was desperately impoverished, whose departure heralded the looming and near-terminal decline, returning to the club pushing 40 years of age, making a huge contribution to the 2007/08 League campaign and then scoring, in breathtaking style, what will surely always be the most significant goal in City's history. You absolutely could not have made that up.

Paul Denman: Deano played in midfield when he first came back and you could see he really wanted to be a footballer. He just got stuck in and ran and ran and ran. He moved on to 'Aberdeano' as we needed the money and when he came back he was a different Deano, a proper striker. He sent us to the promised land with a strike that Ronaldo would have been proud of. I always thought that Phil Brown should have let Deano kick off in the first game against Fulham, that way he could have claimed to be the first City player to kick a ball in the top flight. He deserved it.

Mark Greaves: Deano is more of a local lad than anyone. He'd drink with the fans in Gypsyville Tavern, buying everybody a pint, being everyone's friend. A true cult hero. There was nobody better to score the goal that got the club in the Premier League. He does tell us all about it every time we see him though, and rightly so. Deano lived a couple of streets away from me when I was growing up and we went to the same school, so I wasn't even the best footballer on my estate or my school! He took all my glory away from me when I was a kid. But I'm a huge admirer of him and very proud of him.

Dean Windass: I'm an ambassador of Hull City now, and if my dad was still alive he'd be very proud of me. I remember going to Boothferry Park as a kid and I always dreamt of scoring a goal for City there. When Brian told me I wasn't good enough at 18, I didn't think that was going to happen. Then 20 years later I go smash one in the top corner at Wembley. It was Roy of the Rovers stuff. I wouldn't change anything. I had a great time as a schoolboy training in City's gym from being 10 years old. I had an unbelievable two years as a YTS. Being rejected broke my heart. But my dad said to me when Brian released me: "It's one man's opinion, so prove him wrong." And that's all I tried to do all my life – prove people wrong. I never thought it would end like it did, scoring such an important goal for the football club that I've always loved and I will love until the day I die. I'll always be thankful to Terry Dolan and Phil Brown for giving me the opportunities to do the things I did with Hull City.

Dean joined Oldham on loan for the rest of the season before leaving permanently to take up a player-coach role at Darlington. After playing in the non-league network again for a handful of teams, and going public with his battle against depression, Dean was made an ambassador of Hull City.

A few days after the Manchester City game, Aston Villa came to the KC. A much-improved City performance saw Nick Barmby have an early goal harshly ruled out as Villa – fourth in the table at that point to Hull City's eighth – struggled to break down the home defence. A Kamil Zayatte own goal in the 88th minute looked set to cost City dear, until a penalty was awarded in injury time. Incredibly, after much discussion with various officials (including a fourth official who had access to TV replays), referee Steve Bennett opted to change his mind about the handball decision, correctly as it turned out, and withdraw the award of a penalty.

Phil Brown: If you look at the decision made in that game, you'd have thought that the powers that be, the referees, the Premier League, the media had turned against us. I thought that was a really poor refereeing display. He gave a penalty and then pulled it.

A blow came when Paul McShane, one of the club's defensive lynchpins, was recalled prematurely from his loan from Sunderland.

Paul McShane: Initially it was a six-month loan with a view to extending it to the end of the season, but when we were on our way to Newcastle to play a cup game, Phil called me and told me that Sunderland were calling me back. Roy Keane had just got the sack so they wanted me back. I was disappointed at the time as I was in my stride and I just wanted to keep playing football. Sunderland were playing games, and essentially wanted to weaken and disrupt what they saw as a relegation rival. I felt it was a bit of a dirty tactic. I didn't start one game for the rest of the season. I had very strong words with Ricky Sbragia after that.

The FA Cup offered a welcome distraction from the league, with Newcastle coming to the KC. This meant a first reunion between Craig Fagan and Danny Guthrie, the player who had broken his leg a few months earlier.

Craig Fagan: I hadn't heard from Danny Guthrie after the injury. Just before we were due to play this game he sent me a text message and I replied saying that it was a bit late now but that I didn't want to drag it on. There was talk of me trying to sue him and the club saying they were going to back me but I just didn't want to be one of the first players to sue another, even though the tackle was ridiculous. If you did that to someone in the street you'd get arrested. But I just wanted to get back and playing. It took some self-control to not do anything in that game though. Did I want to do something back? Yes, but I just tried to not let myself or the club down.

City exacted the best form of revenge in beating Newcastle 1-0 in a replay after the first match was drawn 0-0. In the league, however, the defeats kept coming. Everton beat City 2-0 at Goodison Park before Arsenal – the team so memorably conquered a few months earlier – came to the KC. This game saw the famous three – Boaz Myhill, Andy Dawson and Ian Ashbee, who'd represented the club in all four divisions – become the famous four, as Ryan France finally made his Premier League bow.

Ryan France: I'd finally done it. I wasn't in awe. I asked Robin van Persie for his shirt before the game because a pal asked me to. Then I just concentrated on the game and I enjoyed it. In anything you do, have a go. I'm not as good as the Arsenal players but I just gave it my all. That said, at times it was like watching Brazil. Then I went home and watched myself on Match of the Day.

A much-improved City display saw Arsenal win, but only due to two late goals as the match finished 3-1. But it was another defeat. Something needed to be done. Something spectacular was done.

Paul Duffen: In January we were looking for a solution. The most important thing, Phil felt, was that we weren't scoring enough goals from midfield, we didn't pose enough of a threat from midfield, and that's where we were being over-run in the games that we were coming a close second in. At the time the three best midfielders in England were Steven Gerrard, Frank Lampard and Jimmy Bullard. In the September Jimmy Bullard had been called up to the England squad and there was an opportunity. Fulham were going through something of a renaissance at the time, and under Roy Hodgson were looking at how they could change the club going forward. Jimmy hadn't been offered a new contract and he was identified by Hull City and the scouts as the player that could made a significant transformation to our squad.

I did what I was tasked with doing, in that I made the negotiations with the other club, spoke with him and his agent to see if we could get a deal to get him to come to the club. Fabulously we were successful. The day we signed Jimmy Bullard every single news and media outlet in Hull and England declared it as an amazing coup for Hull City. Of course he had a medical. The crazy thing is that Phil and I felt more exposed than ever because he was our record signing. And yet we felt, and it was said and echoed by most at the time, that it was a coup to get him and at a bargain price. To tempt him to come to Hull City was the hardest job, to sell him the dream of what we wanted to do.

Phil Brown: We were paying £5m for a player, and a lot of people have been saying he was already crocked. He wasn't already crocked. He'd had a cruciate ligament go, and people say you can't recover from them, but of course you can. The medical profession and the science we had shows that this player was fully tested and he passed it with flying colours.

Paul Duffen: There had been players previously who we wanted to sign and the medical department told us we couldn't, so we didn't, such as Richard Cresswell. If you have a sports science department you have to listen to what they say. Bullard had played something like 40 games for Fulham since his injury. We were happy it was a coup.

Jimmy was renowned as one of football's big characters, a favourite on Soccer AM. So how did his new team-mates react to the news?

Andy Dawson: We all knew Jimmy as a joker. But when he came in he showed that he was a very, very good player, which he showed at times at Hull City. But with his injuries it just didn't happen for him. But not only for him, but for us as a club, as Jimmy would have made us – had he been consistently fit – much better. It's just a shame for everybody that we didn't see the best of Jimmy for long enough spells.

George Boateng: I was sceptical about Jimmy Bullard coming in as we had a similar kind of player in Geovanni. It wouldn't change much for me personally. Jimmy is a great player offensively but when it came to on-pitch discipline not so much. He's great when you have the ball, but when we didn't it was like playing with a man less. We were collectively so strong, working our socks off for each other. But I thought that signing would bring problems.

City did three other bits of incoming business in January, with the experienced Kevin Kilbane joining for £500,000 from Wigan, Angolan forward Manucho coming in on loan from Manchester United, and Kamil Zayatte's loan move being made permanent for a fee of £2.5m. Meanwhile Marlon King returned to Wigan. His time with City had soured after a bright start, following an unsavoury incident in a Scarborough casino that ended in a confrontation with Dean Windass, and his arrest for assault on a woman in a London nightclub, which ended with him being sentenced to 18 months in jail. Regardless of how effective he'd been on the pitch, no club would want to be associated with such behaviour.

Paul Duffen: We were having to try players who weren't exactly proven. We brought Manucho in to give us something different. But we didn't have the resources. It's hard signing someone in January, and you often find you're bringing in players that upset the balance and the chemistry in the dressing room. It's a false marketplace.

A visit to Upton Park was next, and it was an eventful evening. Rumours were swirling that Michael Owen was coming to Hull City in exchange for Boaz Myhill. Myhill himself was dropped for Matt Duke, who would make his Premier League debut just over a year after his operation to remove a cancerous tumour. Record signing Jimmy Bullard would be sat on the bench, waiting to make his debut for Hull City.

Matt Duke: I was pinching myself. But whenever a challenge gets put in front of you in football, you just try to do your best. I had a fantastic coach in Mark Prudhoe and we worked hard. Me and Boaz had a great relationship and we always supported each other. Browny pulled Boaz first to have a word with him, and it was Boaz who said to me: "You're playing tomorrow, well done." Then Browny confirmed it and I was delighted. But the reaction of Boaz and his delight for me shows what a great character Boaz is, because he could have been upset but he wasn't. The team was going through a bad spell and when that happens sometimes you change your goalkeeper. I don't think it was anything to do with the way Boaz was playing, because he was doing alright, it was just a way to change something.

Boaz Myhill: Some of the stuff that Matt has been through, not many people will have to go through, hopefully. Also, he'd had to turn up every week and not play, and that's not easy. So while I was disappointed to be dropped there was part of me that was looking at him thinking: 'Yeah, well done. Brilliant. Fair play.'

Matt Duke: You don't get much bigger than having your first Premier League game on TV, which was great as so many people got to see it.

Duke put in an incredible performance, saving a penalty and keeping the score respectable, although West Ham were 2-0 up soon after half-time.

Matt Duke: It was one of those nights when you save pretty much anything. Apart from the result it probably couldn't have gone any better for me. You can't think about what's happening, you just get on with your job. I was playing at the highest standard I'd ever played at, and your tensions and emotions are high, so you have to be on it. I'd done a bit of homework on the penalties. And then I saw a penalty Carlton Cole had taken on the big screen before the game and I got an idea of where he would put it. Thankfully I went the right way. All the players ran up to me celebrating but I was just screaming at them to concentrate on defending the next attack. As much as you want to run off and celebrate you can't. It was an unforgettable night for me. It will stay with me forever.

In the 53rd minute, Jimmy Bullard came on for Hull City to replace Geovanni. Within half an hour he was stretchered off after a tackle by Scott Parker. Bullard had done his cruciate ligaments in the same knee that he'd dislocated playing for Fulham (also after a tackle by Scott Parker).

Paul Duffen: The guy who'd crocked Bullard previously does it again… It was sickening. We'd had a glimpse of what he could do. He'd been magnificent around the club. He'd actually had a bit of flu that night. It was horrendous. I felt sorry for Jimmy and I knew it would deprive us of a talent.

Phil Brown: It was just very, very unfortunate the way it all happened. It was one of those defining moments, 20 or 25 minutes into his debut at West Ham he does his knee again against the same player – Scott Parker.

Mike White: The day Jimmy Bullard signed, Phil had invited the local media to Cottingham for a curry along with Brian Horton and a few of the backroom staff. We did that, then the next week was West Ham away. After the game I went down pitchside to do the interview. I didn't know that we were getting messages suggesting that Newcastle were selling Shay Given and looking to sign Boaz Myhill. I asked Phil why Matt Duke had been selected ahead of Bo, and he was a bit cagey about it, saying "football reasons" or something like that. My instincts kicked in, so I just followed it up with: "Have you had a bid for him?" He looked at me, scoffed and walked off, saying: "Interview over." I think that summed Phil up at that time. But I still really like him as a bloke and I still love bumping into him. There's no issue, but at that particular time I felt that certain things were starting to creep in. You did see a change in him. He perhaps got a little caught up in the ride of it all, but then everyone did in one way or another.

The rot was stopped in a 2-2 home draw with bottom-of-the-table West Brom. It was the type of game that City should have been looking to win, but goals from Bernard Mendy and Craig Fagan secured the point and brought to an end a six-game losing streak in the league. This was just as well as City's next game was Chelsea away, a game in which the home side were expected to win comfortably. However, City put in a terrific shift to secure a 0-0 draw.

Michael Turner: We were going away after the game to Dubai for some warm weather training, so it was a massive game. We'd had a bad run of results and were getting a bit edgy. But we defended really well. We were on the back foot for most of the game, but it was a terrific result. I just kept thinking about playing against Didier Drogba – he's a colossus of a man and was just overpowering defenders.

Sam Ricketts: It was another one of those games. You get into the Premier League to play against these players. I remember they'd just signed a new winger, Queresma, and I think he was on debut. I tried my hardest against him and it came off. The team seemed a bit more like the team that had got us promoted now too, as Richard Garcia was back in the team round this point and people like Ryan France were coming back into it.

Ian Ashbee: Up against Lampard and Ballack… I remember the game well. It felt we were back a little bit after the half-time team talk. It took that long to move on – this was the February – from that game. People would say that we should have just moved on, but it affected people. Going to Chelsea and getting a 0-0 – and we could easily have won 1-0 – against a team you wouldn't expect us to get anything from was another big plus for us to kick on a bit. Then we had a good time in Dubai.

Matt Duke: John Terry missed a great chance early on. I'd made a reaction save and it fell into his path, and he hit it over. We were sat in Heathrow Airport that night on the way to Dubai, and I was thinking: 'Is this really happening?' While Phil Brown was in charge we were a well-travelled team because he liked to get away to the sunshine!

Ryan France: That is my most frustrating memory of football. We'd played well, it was 0-0, and I'm stood warming up with Didier Drogba which was a bit surreal. Phil sent me on – he said: "You're defensive centre midfield, don't move!" – but the ball broke down the left with Craig Fagan and I just started moving forward. I went past Frank Lampard, he didn't pick me up, so I started running a bit quicker, went past the centre-halves picking up speed and no one was picking me up. Fages was running toward the left corner and I'm shouting: "Square it, I want a one on one with Petr Cech." I just wanted that opportunity. All I wanted Fages to do was lift his head up, see me and square it and let me do the rest. But Fages had got it into his head to go into the corner, which I can't blame him for as we needed the point. Then I looked back at the bench and the gaffer was screaming at me to get back.

Craig Fagan: During the game I'd played up front on my own, which I liked, though normally I'd have someone like Barmbs behind me. It meant I could run either side and hold the ball up. It was a great performance team-wise. But for me, playing against the likes of John Terry, Ashley Cole and Frank Lampard was amazing. I was always going to give my all. We played really well as a team and I never stopped running. I'd given John Terry and Alex a bit of a torrid time. At the end of the game John Terry came over and said: "Well done, mate, you played well today; do you want to swap shirts?" I was gobsmacked. I took his shirt and he was still stood there. He then said: "No, I want your shirt as well!" so he took mine. I didn't think he'd care or be bothered about who I was or want my shirt. It was a massive compliment. I went into the Chelsea changing room after to get it signed, and John, Ashley Cole and Frank Lampard said how well I'd played. It was a massive boost for me.

Paul Duffen: I used to worry about how many points the players had in their legs, and please don't use too much of that energy up getting a draw at Chelsea. I'd trade losing 2-1 at Chelsea to going out and beating Newcastle 3-0. I wanted to beat the sides around us.

After the draw, Chelsea sacked their manager 'Big Phil' Scolari.

Mark Robinson: We saw off a few managers that season. If you failed to beat Hull City you generally seemed to get sacked the next day.

10. **Fulham P23 W7 D9 L7 Pts30**
11. **Sunderland P25 W8 D6 L11 Pts30**
12. **Hull City P25 W7 D8 L10 Pts29**
13. **Newcastle P25 W6 D9 L10 Pts27**
14. **Bolton P25 W8 D3 L14 Pts27**

The trip to Dubai made little impact on the pitch. City drew 1-1 at Sheffield United in the FA Cup, then lost 2-1 at the KC to Spurs, with Jonathan Woodgate getting a late winner after Michael Turner had equalised Aaron Lennon's opener. City then beat Sheffield United 2-1 in the FA Cup replay to set up a quarter-final tie at The Emirates against Arsenal. After this came a home match against Blackburn. The match was memorable for three reasons: a strange team selection from Phil Brown that saw Richard Garcia starting up front on his own; Phil Brown looking visibly shaken and hurt when his decision to take Geovanni off in the 53rd minute was booed by the City faithful (Brown was also to joke in a post-match interview that he hoped Geovanni failed a drug test – something that was intended in good humour but which was pounced upon in some areas of the press); and Ian Ashbee becoming the only one of the 'famous four' to score in all four divisions, as City lost 2-1.

Ian Ashbee: Those sort of records don't bother me. I was just more bothered about trying to win the game. I can't remember who crossed it and I smacked it in the net, grabbed the ball and tried to get it back to the centre circle. I thought we should have beaten them on that day. Those kind of games tally up at the end of the season and we had chances on that day.

An away match at Fulham followed. On a Wednesday night in early spring, City put in a titanic defensive effort to keep the hosts at bay. In the 89th minute, with City looking to shore up a priceless away point, Phil Brown brought on Richard Garcia. Deep into injury time, the Australian winger was first to a ball and advanced towards the Fulham box. Challenges were flying in and the ball wouldn't come down for him, so he ended up running towards the left-hand corner, pursued by defenders in white. Somehow Garcia managed to whip in a magnificent cross that found Manucho unmarked just inside the six-yard box. The ball hit the back of the net. City had the hardest fought three points they were ever likely to take and the celebrations were exuberant.

Richard Garcia: At the time I was disappointed at being on the bench. I had spoken to my brother the day before and he was giving me words of encouragement and told me not to be disappointed and to be the difference when I got my chance to come on. As I was coming on Phil Brown said: "Give us a spark, Garc," and that's what I tried to do. I ran with it and wouldn't give it up and eventually it ended with the ball across for the goal.

Ian Ashbee: It was such a relief. We hadn't had a win for a long time. Manucho had been threatening to score a goal, a big lad, good with his feet though a frustrating lad to play with, and it was another three points closer to where we needed to be. But I felt like a fan when we scored goals like that.

Matt Duke: The first half wasn't very memorable. It was a bit of a dull game. But the second half they got on top and I made a couple of good saves. The one off Clint Dempsey was a particularly good one. But when you're thinking: 'We'll take a 0-0', and then you score, it's such a relief. It was a massive win as we'd struggled away from home. I remember being on the coach afterwards and Paul Duffen coming up to me and giving me a kiss.

Michael Turner: It was massive for us; we were fighting for our lives. After the start we'd had we never thought we'd end up in that situation. It was a tight game and nicking it 1-0 was key to us surviving. It made us believe we were capable of staying up.

Sam Ricketts: That was an unbelievable night. We probably didn't deserve to win that game. It was at that point where we thought that one more win would do.

Nick Barmby: It was do or die for us. We had a great away following – as we always do in London – and that night was just unbelievable. Everyone played a part – even if it was just a small one – in that season to help us to stay up, and that was what Manucho did that night. A very important goal.

Mike Hall: Rarely have I seen us as comprehensively outplayed as we were that night, only for Manucho's injury time winner to give us a truly unexpected win. I think we all felt then that that win might just keep us up...

City reached 32 points with 10 games of the season left. Seventeenth-placed Fulham had stayed up with 36 the previous season.

The next point came the following Saturday at the KC, when City had the better of a 1-1 draw with Newcastle, but couldn't build upon Geovanni's early goal. Avoiding relegation was all that mattered to City, now in 13th position. Third-from-bottom Stoke had 29 points. It was going to be tight.

Four points from two games led to a belief that City had turned a corner. To add to that City were in the last five of the FA Cup, facing Arsenal in a delayed quarter-final tie. Nick Barmby gave the Tigers an early lead, which remained intact until the 74th minute when Robin van Persie equalised. Then, infuriatingly, William Gallas scored a winner that was clearly offside. At the final whistle tempers flared, with Arsenal captain Cesc Fabregas – who hadn't been playing – coming onto the pitch to remonstrate with the Hull City players. Not long after a visibly angry Phil Brown appeared in a press conference and accused Cesc Fabregas of spitting towards Brian Horton.

Paul Duffen: That was unfortunate as it brought negative publicity. The thing that annoyed me was that Brian is one of the people I respect most in the world. I believe anything that Brian says, but I particularly believe Brian when I'm there with him at the time and I see it. Brian's managed more than 1,000 games of football – he's an icon. He doesn't need to get involved in some scrappy argument. But incidents like that didn't do us any favours.

Phil Buckingham: Everyone I've spoken to at Hull City is adamant about what happened, but it was the way Phil dealt with it so publicly, taking on a club like Arsenal; I don't think that was a wise thing to do. The morning after Phil went on Victoria Derbyshire on Radio 5 Live and she even had to ask him if he was feeling alright, as he sounded so upset. The pressure seemed to be starting to show.

Sean Rush: There was a picture of me on the back pages of the newspapers having an argument with Cesc Fabregas. They were mad times!

The aftermath of the incident did not reflect favourably on either Hull City or Phil Brown. With no way of proving what had happened, the London-based national press – consisting of a large number of Arsenal fans – ruthlessly went for the City manager. Months earlier he'd been the next England manager, the new Brian Clough, the man everyone wanted a part of. However, he'd gone from messiah to leper. Finding a positive story about Brown – who'd already hugely exceeded what most people were predicting for Hull City – was nigh on impossible. So how was it affecting him?

Phil Brown: I was feeling that the media were coming for me. It saddens me that I've got a lot of good friends in the world of the media who were all there at the start, but then the bosses, the powers that be, caused the friends to disappear and the enemies to come out. They would ask the same questions in a different way and then write about it in a detrimental way as opposed to a positive way. So regardless of whether you're defending your team's tactics or defending a scoreline or attacking a referee's decision, it would be construed as: 'Here he goes again, he's moaning, blah, blah, blah.'

It became a bandwagon that started to roll. To stop it is difficult; the only way you can stop it is through performances. For me to pull away from the media and press conferences would have been construed as 'ah, he's gone into hiding, he's sulking' so I had to keep performing myself. The one thing I had was the full support of the changing room – if I hadn't had that I'd have been a worried man – I had the full support of Paul Duffen, and that of the owners. I'd say I had the support of about 99% of the supporters too, and that was key to me, being able to still be myself.

Paul Duffen: It was interesting. It got to a stage in October 2008 where most of the questions I was asked were about Phil and how I was going to keep him at Hull City. Within three months, I was being asked was his job safe? Was I going to sack him? Phil is a larger-than-life character, he wears his personality on his sleeve, and because of that he's a Marmite personality. The media loves to love him and loves to hate him. There's no question that at the beginning of 2009 they were on his case. We started to talk about having roundtable meetings with the press to ask what their perceptions of Hull City were and why this relationship seemed to be going sour. I just think it's the British condition, our media building up the underdog to being a hero, but they also want to be first in the queue if that's going to go the wrong way. You don't see many articles defending the slide, as it's not going to fill column inches. It was a reflection of that combined with the fact that we'd had an incredible 2008 and when 2009 came in it did all seem much tougher. We were aware of the fact that there was a certain pursuit against Phil.

Brendon Smurthwaite: The press were out for Phil. The Arsenal game was dressed up as a total fabrication on Phil's behalf and there was an air of: 'How dare you come down here and question someone like Arsene Wenger.' If Browny had his time again he might not have gone in so quickly and said what he said, but he was emotional and was torn to bits in that presser. It was almost as if the press wouldn't have what he was saying. I'd been in the tunnel, and didn't see what happened, but I saw Fabregas bulleting into their dressing room with two or three City players bulleting past trying to get after him. Their security guards were trying to work it out. When we won there in the league everyone thought that Phil was great, but by now they'd turned on him. And we were never going to win that argument. It was a shame.

Phil Buckingham: I sensed a change in Phil. I'd sensed a gradual change in Phil from his very first day as Hull City's boss, when he was a tracksuit manager. I think he wore shorts in his first game in the dugout. Then he slowly became this very slick guy, and I think image became a big thing for him, whether it was on purpose or not; he seemed to want to look the part. At times it did seem like the success he'd had might have been too much too soon. Because he was – for a while – the media darling, he thought he could say anything and sometimes he would tie himself up in knots. That Arsenal game was a prime example of that.

Nick Barmby: That's football in a nutshell. If you're doing well, everyone catapults you two or three notches up. If you're doing badly the same people will shoot you down. The Premier

League is a hotbed and everything is judged – what you say, what you do – but there was no massive change in Phil. Towards the end of the season he was pretty calm and just focused on what needed to be done.

Andy Dawson: It was a difficult time. Phil wasn't any different to how he'd been in the Championship, because he demanded that we win every game. But confidence was low. When you're winning games, you don't think you'll lose them, but when you start losing games, especially games in that Premier League, where you'd maybe lose two or three and then find yourself playing Chelsea away, it's all the more difficult. And we were getting dragged into it more and more. But that's when it's time for the big characters to stand up. The start we'd had to the season gave us a bit of a cushion but we knew we were getting closer and closer to the relegation zone and we knew we had to start winning games, or at least picking points up. But the attitude – particularly of the lads who'd been there for a while and knew where we'd come from – was that it wasn't time to let it slip. We knew we had to stick together and get over the line somehow.

Mike White: I sensed a change in him, and it was a shame. For the most part I got on well with Phil. But every now and then you'd see a different side to him, and you felt it was because the pressure was mounting. I don't like being too familiar with players, but I remember shouting across the training ground "Browny" at Wayne Brown. Phil was walking past and he said: "Oh, it's Browny now is it, and not 'Phil 'or 'the manager'." I smiled but thought: 'Where has that come from?' Then not long after I was sat at Beverley train station and my phone went, and it was Phil. He was asking me for some travel news as he was stuck in traffic. So one minute you'd be getting calls like that, and the next he could be a bit snippy with you.

One way in which Phil Brown could silence his critics was with wins. Wins that would secure a survival that no one had been predicting in August. The next four games – against Wigan, Portsmouth, Middlesbrough and Sunderland – all looked like the type of fixtures that City should be capable of getting something from. Alas, only one point – from a dour 0-0 draw at home to Portsmouth – was forthcoming. City entered the bottom five.

16. Hull City P33 W8 D10 L15 Pts34
17. Blackburn P33 W8 D10 L15 Pts34
18. Middlesbrough P33 W7 D10 L16 Pts31
19. Newcastle P33 W6 D12 L15 Pts30
20. West Brom P33 W6 D7 L20 Pts25

A trip to the KC from second-in-the-table Liverpool wasn't ideal but that was the task ahead for City. However the Anfield club's class told in a 3-1 away win. To add insult to injury Caleb Folan was sent off.

Caleb Folan: I'm a boyhood Liverpool fan and the night before the game I was really amped. I was so looking forward to it. I was so up for the game. The incident with Martin Škrtel was mad, a freak incident where I was frustrated and just kicked out. I wasn't thinking of any consequences. He was just trying to shield me off the ball and I just kicked him. When I saw the red card I was gutted. It was just a build up of stuff.

From Liverpool to fifth-placed Aston Villa at Villa Park, the matches didn't get any easier. This fixture held particular significance for Boaz Myhill – who'd been recalled as the first-choice goalkeeper – as it was his first return to the club where he'd served his footballing apprenticeship.

Boaz Myhill: It was just great – my job in the youth team at Aston Villa was to blow up balls and then sit and watch the games with the kit man. In my time there, from being 12 until when I left, I would dream of playing on there. To actually get out there and play on there was unbelievable.

If Boaz felt affection towards Villa, the opposite was true for boyhood Birmingham City fan Ian Ashbee. The match was something of a disaster for City – culminating in a 1-0 defeat –but it was calamitous for the skipper, who suffered another knee injury that was to rule him out of not only the rest of this season, but the whole of the next season too.

Ian Ashbee: I knew something was wrong. I'd ruptured the big ligament in my knee. I felt something go in a tough tackle with James Milner. I'd tried to do him, to be fair, and I think I did, but his trailing leg caught my trailing leg and got it in a bad position. Then I saw the scar on the front of my knee – it had gone white and then blood started coming out of it, so I thought it was just a bit of a kick that I'd got. I went back on to play, and when I started to run my leg felt like jelly so I said to Simon Maltby that he'd have to take me off.

They checked my knee, and when they went in there they saw that the osteochondral defect had come back tenfold. At a consultation in Sheffield I was told I wouldn't play again, but Phil Brown and Paul Duffen said: "There's one more chance, do you want to go to America to see knee specialist Richard Steadman?" The club got the insurance sorted and I went there. That's when they drilled all the holes in my knee. Dr Steadman was great but he said he'd never seen a lesion as big as that on anyone's knee so he was either going to chop it off and turn it round, or scrape it all off and drill, and they did the latter. I'll always be grateful to the football club for what they did.

Phil Brown: We'd played a 4-3-3 the majority of the time, with Ash sitting deep with Dean Marney and George Boateng either side of him. Ash just couldn't get about the field at that point – and I know he won't thank me for saying that – but the fact that he was in the centre of the field and he stayed there was pivotal to the two centre-halves having good performances, to our clean sheets, to our two full-backs being able to go forwards. Sometimes you have to have people who don't run everywhere. They allow those that do run to run further, and Ash was one of those players. When he got injured in the Villa game it was no surprise as Birmingham were his team and he hated Villa. He'd have been giving maximum effort, maybe a bit too much!

It was a bad impact though. He was a great captain, hence why I took him to Preston with me even though I knew his knee was maybe on its way out. He played as many games as he possibly could there. He'd run through a brick wall for me, and I believe that he'd even do that now. Verbally he'd dig people out. If you got praise from Ash you knew you'd done something good. He'd get the best out of you by having a go at you, so if he said "well done" then you knew you'd done well.

Simon Maltby: It was a bit of a recurrence of the old injury but a bit of a new thing as well. His attitude was excellent again, and he came back again. He was a bit older this time and that often means it's harder, and with it being the second time around that can take it out of you mentally. From my point of view, he was as good as gold again. I always got on really well with Ash.

So, facing a relegation fight without their inspirational skipper, City took on Stoke at home. After spending much of the season in the relegation zone, Stoke had reached mid-table thanks to a fine run of form. However, even with nothing to play for, the away side eased to a 2-0 lead that was cut back in the last minute when Andy Dawson scored his first Premier League goal. A 2-1 defeat put City in the bottom three with two games left...

16. **Sunderland P36 W9 D9 L18 Pts36**
17. **Newcastle P36 W7 D13 L16 Pts34**
18. **Hull City P36 W8 D10 L18 Pts34**
19. **Middlesbrough P36 W7 D10 L19 Pts31**
20. **West Brom P36 W8 D7 L21 Pts31**

Bolton was where Phil Brown had made his name as a coach under Sam Allardyce. Now, more than ever, he needed a result at the Reebok as City travelled to Lancashire knowing that their final game was against the all-conquering Manchester United.

Phil Brown: We thought we needed four points. We felt we had to win one of the games at least. If we didn't beat Bolton we were thinking that we'd have to beat Manchester United. We took the lads up to the Lake District, Lake Windermere, which is a beautiful part of the world, but also a place where your mobile phones can't pick up a signal. That was a key factor. Coming into those games, with the rigours of the season and the pressure that the players had come under from everybody – myself included – I felt we needed to relax and communicate better. We shared rooms of four there, instead of our usual single rooms or twins, so we were living on top of each other. The likes of Geo couldn't speak to anyone without his mobile phone, so he had to communicate more with his team-mates.

Michael Turner: Playing Manchester United at home on the last game of the season was always on the back of our mind so we knew we had to get the points in the bag beforehand. Before the game the manager took us to the Lake District to do a bit of team bonding and that really helped. We travelled from there down to the game and it was such a big game for us.

City kicked off against Bolton as Newcastle – the club City were effectively in a two-way battle to avoid relegation with – got their game at home to Fulham under way. Disaster struck for City in the 26th minute when Grétar Steinsson put the home side 1-0 up. However, after 41 minutes at St James Park, Diomansy Kamara scored for Fulham. No advantage had been gained. Then, in the 47th minute at the Reebok, Craig Fagan's tireless running was rewarded.

Craig Fagan: I was playing up front on my own and I felt I was playing well. Richard Garcia played the ball forward and it went over the top of Danny Shittu's head into the channel. I just fancied myself. I knew that Danny wasn't comfortable with how the ball was bouncing and I just fancied myself to close the ball down. I knew if I got there I'd create a problem. I managed to nick in, nudge him off the ball and put a left foot shot into the goal. You can see the relief in the celebration after. But people kind of forget that goal. Maybe I should have spoken about it more, as I never really mentioned it at the time.

Phil Brown: We went 1-0 down and that was a tight situation. We needed big players to step up and Craig Fagan got the equaliser. It was one of the most important goals of the season.

Andy Dawson: Let's not forget what Fages was as a player. When things aren't going well, he's the type of player you want in your team. He'd just run tirelessly and that's what got him this goal, closing Danny Shittu down. We knew we needed something as that game was a big opportunity for us, with Manchester United coming up. When you go one down that's when you need your characters. Fages's finish gave us that opportunity, that glimmer of hope.

Boaz Myhill: At Bolton Ian Ashbee and Jimmy Bullard hadn't played but travelled with us and they were saying that was the goal that was going to keep us up.

Paul Duffen: Because of Phil's history, it made any time we went to the Reebok more significant. It's not a glamour game, it's not a highlight when you look at our achievements that season to stay in the Premier League, but it was hugely significant in what it meant in terms of our survival. Because of injury and form Craig was in and out of the team, but he grabbed his opportunity with both hands.

Michael Turner: A draw was a great result because it left it in our hands for the final game.

Nick Barmby: I had a chance on the back stick in the second half – should have scored. At the end Browny came on the pitch and put his arm around me and said: "What do you think?" I told him we were staying up. It was a good result because they were down near the bottom as well, but any point towards the end of the season is worth its weight in gold. The commitment of the lads showed that day. They showed how much they wanted to stay in the Premier League.

The point earned looked all the more crucial when the score came in from the north-east: 1-0 to Fulham. Newcastle had a Kevin Nolan goal harshly disallowed by Howard Webb, and key defender Sebastian Bassong was sent off, meaning he'd miss the final game of the season. A glance at the table was enough to shred any City fan's nerves, but it looked much better than it had two hours earlier.

16. **Sunderland** P37 W9 D9 L19 Pts36 (-19)
17. **Hull City** P37 W8 D11 L18 Pts35 (-24)
18. **Newcastle** P37 W7 D13 L17 Pts34 (-18)
19. **Middlesbrough** P37 W7 D11 L19 Pts32 (-28)
20. **West Brom** P37 W8 D7 L22 Pts31 (-31)

City would go into the final game of the season knowing they simply had to match or better whatever Newcastle United did at Villa Park.

Phil Brown: Going into the last game of the season, we knew we had to do as well or better than Newcastle. But we had Manchester United in town! They were preparing for the Champions League final, so we knew Sir Alex was going to make changes, but even their third team would have been good enough to stay in the Premier League. Newcastle were away to Villa with the resurgence under Alan Shearer not really happening.

Nick Barmby: It was weird. In the build up it was all about: 'Is Ronaldo playing? Is Rooney playing? Is Scholes playing?' They had the Champions League final on the Wednesday so in the back of your mind you were thinking Sir Alex Ferguson wouldn't be playing the big players as they'd wrapped the league up and Sir Alex always liked to play the kids when he could. So we were sure he'd play some kids.

Andy Dawson: It was a strange game. It's Manchester United at home, they're in the Champions League final on the Wednesday and we'd been on a bad run.

Boaz Myhill: I remember Alex Ferguson playing a game with Phil Brown, walking into the dressing room telling him Ronaldo and co were playing. They still had a really good team but it was mainly the reserves. We knew we were going to be up against it.

The game kicked off in a muted atmosphere. Even though Manchester United were effectively playing their reserves, with future City players Corry Evans and Ben Amos on the bench, they still had enough about them to keep the home side at arm's length. Then, in the 24th minute, Darron Gibson put the visitors 1-0 up with a terrific long-range strike. City were in the bottom three.

Phil Brown: On the day, hell fire, it was difficult to control matters given what was going off at Villa Park. Gibson stuck one in from 25 yards, and that's when I started listening to Ash and Jimmy Bullard, who were sitting three rows behind the dug-out keeping up with events at Villa Park.

Boaz Myhill: It was vile to play in, horrendous, knowing you're losing, listening to stuff going on in the crowd and wondering what's happening.

Michael Turner: It was a strange game. We didn't play very well and it had an end-of-season feel about it.

Sam Ricketts: We went into the game thinking that we had a chance because we weren't playing against their first team. Then Darron Gibson scored. You then kind of want to know what's going on with the other game while wanting to concentrate on your own. But we never got back into it.

However, good news was soon to filter through from the Midlands. On 38 minutes a Gareth Barry shot cannoned off Damien Duff and squeezed past Steven Harper to end up in the back of the net.

Nick Barmby: We just never really got at them. They were comfortable, and the atmosphere was tense. Then we heard a little bit of cheering because Villa had scored. But we were wondering: 'Well have they, or is it someone joking?' while trying to concentrate on what's happening on the pitch.

Paul Duffen: I hate seeing people in the directors' box checking their phones; I find it disrespectful. To me, you're there and you want to give as much positive mental energy to the team as possible. That's what I was focused on doing. I was aware of the Newcastle score at half-time, as everyone in the ground was aware of it!

Andy Dawson: Obviously we heard the cheer that Newcastle were losing, and I remember thinking: 'I hope I don't hear a big sigh now.' We knew the importance of it. I don't think we ever looked like scoring so we were basically waiting for the other result.

All that mattered now was that Newcastle didn't score. If that remained the case, City would stay up. And it was just as well, because at no point did the Tigers look like breaching the Manchester United defence.

Craig Fagan: That game was horrific. Horrible. We never played well. They didn't have a full-strength team but they just looked so much stronger and had so much more energy than us. I don't know if it was because we'd given our all the week before against Bolton, I think that affected us.

Dean Marney: It was horrible. All week we'd been saying about how we needed to just concentrate on ourselves and not worry about Newcastle but that was impossible. You were listening for every little noise in the crowd. We were poor on the day, even against an understrength Manchester United.

After what seemed like an eternity, Alan Wiley blew the final whistle at the KC Stadium. Moments afterwards Chris Foy did the same at Villa Park. City had finished the season on 35 points, Newcastle on 34. Hull City, the side no one had given a chance to from the second Alan Wiley had blown the final whistle in a very different match the previous May, had finished 17th and ensured that they'd be playing Premier League football the next season. Yes, it had been achieved after the club had won just two of their last 29 league games, but it had still been achieved. And that was something to celebrate.

Phil Brown: Our final whistle went and we'd been beaten, and we were just waiting for the final whistle at Villa Park. It was about 30 seconds and then the news came across the stadium Tannoy that we were safe.

Michael Turner: When the final whistle went it was just huge relief. Although the second half of the season hadn't gone well for us we felt we deserved to stay up after the unbelievable results we'd had earlier on in the season.

Sam Ricketts: Gradually the news filtered through at the end about Newcastle getting beat and it was yet another unbelievable thing. It was such great satisfaction. You just want those moments to last forever.

Richard Garcia: At the end of the game it was bittersweet, relief and happiness of staying up but disappointed that we slipped so far from how we started the season.

Nick Barmby: It was just sheer relief from everyone at the end. But whether we stayed up by goal difference or a point, it was an unbelievable achievement. It's what we set out to do and we did it. Hats off to everyone who was involved for everything they did – apart from Phil's singing at the end.

Craig Fagan: We stayed in the Premier League. If you'd offered that at the start of the season we'd have taken it.

Boaz Myhill: All of a sudden it was over and what was a struggle turned into a success.

Dean Marney: Thankfully that start kept us up. But when you make that sort of start, to only get the number of points we got is alarming.

Dave Burns: There was a sense of relief and a sense of reward. It was a wonderful achievement. For City to stay in the Premier League was stunning.

After the initial news had sunk in, the mood at the KC turned from relief to celebration. It was party time, and Phil Brown was providing the music, courtesy of his rendition of Sloop John B on the stadium's public address system...

Phil Brown: All of the emotions of what we'd done, and the 10 months of build up and preparations, the half-time team talk, all of that, and then getting to the end of the season where it was in our own hands; all of those things spilled out in the terms of the song and my emotions.

Paul Duffen: I was standing next to Phil. We all express ourselves in different ways. He's a human being. If I felt the pressures of those two years, having been on that enormous roller-coaster, I'm sure he felt the same way. If you look at what he did, he thought he was doing something to assimilate with the fans. He was cheerleading one of our anthems and I don't care what his voice sounded like, it was about him expressing his delight that we were still on that journey.

Dave Burns: The singing was just funny. That was just Browny. Some people could get po-faced about it, but that was just him, doing something different. His goatee offended me more than the singing. I was so pleased for him though, and pleased for the city, as it had been such a fantastic experience, life-changing for lots of people. It had given the city such a warm glow. To stay up was a humungous achievement.

Andy Dawson: We didn't hear Phil's singing. As soon as the whistle went it wasn't long before we knew Newcastle had lost. Then you get all the emotions, the ups and downs from the start of the season and then the bad run we went on. But for a club to get promoted and stay up, in those days, was hard. It was a lot more difficult for new teams to stay up then. It was an amazing feeling.

Ian Ashbee: It's horrible as a fan waiting, but obviously it was elation when Newcastle lost. We could go again next year, but obviously I wasn't going to be part of it.

Geovanni: One of my best memories of this game was when I picked up my son Daniel and walked with my daughter Giovanna holding my other hand. When I looked at the crowd, they stood up and shouted: "Geo, Geo, Geo, Geo." This was the best moment of my 17-year career. Emotional!

Caleb Folan: It was crazy. They'd not fielded a strong team. I was feeling good about the whole thing. But when that final whistle went and we knew, that feeling of staying up was unbelievable. We just deserved it. The season had its ups and downs but we deserved to stay up because of the way we'd started it. There was a sense of achievement. Throughout my whole time at Hull everything felt like an achievement, I felt like I'd achieved something in my career. I felt we'd earned it. We're a part of history! I wouldn't have it any other way – the players, the coaches, the manager, I just couldn't have it any other way.zIt was unbelievable.

George Boateng: It was weird, because it was a big game that we wanted to win. When we heard that Aston Villa had scored I felt that the pressure went off us a little and we were relaxed. On that day, the only thing that mattered was the fans. They were magnificent. Even though we lost the game, I remembered parading around the pitch afterwards and all the fans staying to cheer us. I was so pleased for them. I knew that we'd given them something they would cherish for a long, long time. I was really proud and happy for everyone involved in the club, like the people in the offices, the amazing secretary, the tea girls who'd work crazy hours for very little money, people like Simon the physio, so many great people who I was so pleased for. If we'd been relegated that could have affected their wages. I was so pleased that they had that security for longer.

Phil Buckingham: Straight afterwards I felt a bit flat. It was Manchester United's reserves and City still lost to them. It didn't feel like a good way to survive. It was a strange mixture of emotions. But then you felt that ultimately it was mission accomplished, as the only goal at the start of that season was to stay up. Although they scraped it, that's exactly what they did.

Paul Duffen: That game didn't have the same feeling as destiny as our 2008 season had, but I can honestly say that the emotion that was strongest in me at the beginning of that game was I was absolutely exhausted. It was the culmination of two seasons where our feet hadn't touched the ground, and I was quite sanguine. We were either going to win or lose, and if we went down we'd have to face life back in the Championship, but we'd still have made Hull City a Premier League club for the first time. If my record was going to be a year in the Championship, a year in the Premier League and then a year back in the Championship, then I was reconciling that that might not be the worst outcome. We had no money, and if we went down it would give us the ability to press again with whatever finances may be available. Staying up clearly was the most important thing, but if we had gone down that afternoon then it was something we were planning for. Every season we were planning for two scenarios. But I did feel that everybody was tired.

After the dust had settled, it was time to say a few goodbyes. A particularly tearful one was that of Ryan France, a player who had taken the field in all four divisions for Hull City within the space of little more than five years after signing from non-league Alfreton Town. Everyone loved Ryan, and it was a sad day when he left the KC as a player for the final time.

Ryan France: I have nothing but very fond memories. I have so much time for Phil Brown and how he handled my leaving. He knew Hull City meant the world to me. I'd been there six years. He rung me up and told me to come in. He just said: "It's better for you to go out and get football," and he was right. It was an extremely sad moment. I don't mind admitting that I had tears rolling down my cheeks as I drove out of the car park.

Peter Taylor: Colin kept going on about him. He trained with us before we signed him and I kept looking at him and thinking: 'He's one of us, he's already good enough.' He was good in the air, he could cross, he could score a goal. We thought: 'Blimey, what a steal!' People like Ryan France are such a good story. He worked hard to be a success. For me personally, thinking of someone like Ryan France and the way he developed is a really nice memory.

Robert Crampton: Ryan was always busy, and you could see that he cared. As a man on the terraces, you can identify with that. You got the impression he would be on the terraces if he wasn't on the pitch.

Mike Hall: There were times during our ascent where I would genuinely struggle to pick out a player in our squad who I didn't either rate or like. Ryan France seemed to embody that type of character. A good player picked up at a bargain price, seemingly without ego and who served us well over some of the most impressive seasons in the club's history. I loved the fact France became the fourth player to represent us in all four divisions and thought it no less than he deserved.

Dave Richardson: Coming to the professional game relatively late, Ryan France showed himself to be a versatile player who could play in defence and midfield. It was a shame he damaged his cruciate or I think he would have played in more Premier League games. He's still one of that elite group who has represented the same club in all four divisions. He's also one of the nicest people you could wish to meet.

Bryan Hughes had only been at the club for two years, but what a two years! It was time for the popular midfielder to leave, however.

Bryan Hughes: My time at Hull was fantastic. Not knowing what to expect when I first signed, to get promotion in that first season was incredible. It was really enjoyable and I made some really good friends along the way. The fans have been great with me too.

Mike White: Bryan Hughes was a very down-to-earth character but carried a presence about him because of the career that he'd had. You could see how respected he was among the other players, and he was always a really approachable person.

The legend of Colin Murphy still lives on among those lucky enough to have played under him. However, at the end of the 2008/09 season ill health meant that the man affectionately known to everyone as 'Murph' was to end his association with Hull City, and football in general. It was a loss.

Damien Delaney: Colin Murphy was the old head at the club. He really understood lower league football and what it was about. He was really good for Peter, as he could bounce off him. But Colin Murphy meant a lot to me as well. I played for him at Cork City, and he was the one who brought me to Leicester and then to Hull, so he's someone who I owe a lot to. When I made my debut for Ireland, Colin had had a stroke not long before. I kept my shirt, signed it and gave it to him. I thought he deserved it more, after all he'd done for me. Not a lot of people will know a lot about him but he was so important to us, and he's a really good guy. He was a real football man, old-school and wouldn't last in today's game. If you told a modern player about the stuff he used to do, their jaw would be on the floor. He'll always mean a hell of a lot to me, and he played a bigger part in Hull City's history than a lot of people will appreciate.

Simon Maltby: I loved Murph. He was so good to me and a real character.

Also to officially depart were Jon Welsh and Michael Bridges, who'd been away on loan deals. The rest would get another shot at Premier League football. And there was no talk of 'doing a Derby' this time.

August 2009 to December 2009

The sequel is rarely as good as the first instalment. The Hull City side preparing for the 2009/10 season had a lot to live up to. As the summer wore on, fans that had been as embroiled in the relegation fight as the players could afford to look back on the season just passed as a whole. Yes, we'd won one league game in the whole of 2009, but... Arsenal away, Spurs away, Manucho at Fulham, the games at Anfield, Old Trafford, Stamford Bridge... City were still in the Premier League and they were there on merit. And looking at the season ahead, three clubs – Wolverhampton, Birmingham and Burnley – had been promoted with a 17th-place finish now their only goal. City had a season's experience on these sides. The Duffen/Brown rollercoaster ride had hit a dip, but there was nothing to say it was going to be terminal.

Nothing that the fans were aware of at least.

Off the pitch the club had been put up for sale with the owners keen to make the most, financially speaking, of the club's top-flight status.

Paul Duffen: As soon as we stayed up the club was for sale. That's one of the reasons why the Michael Turner thing happened at the very death. The club was put up for sale with Corporate Finance House in the May. Through the summer we had a couple of bids. Vantis were trying to sell it for us. Then another finance house that Russell knew tried to sell it for us too. Seymour Pierce had a look at it. Russell was told he could get £60m for the club, and I was on a deal, so that was fine. I'd have a piece of that. But we had decided to sell the football club.

Phil Brown: I knew there were one or two financial problems. But did it affect my plans? I don't think so. We knew how difficult the second year in the Premier League would be though. People would respect you from day one, whereas in the first season I think opponents had been believing the press that we'd be even worse than Derby the year before. It was a

411

massive difference, and people were better at weighing you up tactically in a way they hadn't done the previous season. The off-field activities weren't helping though.

On the pitch the second half of the 2008/09 season had made it clear that strengthening was needed. It was unlikely the club would see anything of captain Ian Ashbee, while Jimmy Bullard was still on the treatment table. However, it was goals that were a chief concern. Marlon King had never really been replaced since his return to Wigan, while Manucho had flattered to deceive and no further interest was shown in the Angolan. Daniel Cousin hadn't pushed on from his bright start, while Caleb Folan seemed out of favour with Phil Brown. This left Craig Fagan as the most prominent centre-forward on the club's books, meaning the rumour mill was going into overdrive.

Paul Duffen: Marc-Antoine Fortuné and Bobby Zamora I thought were seven-out-of-ten potentials. We met with both of them, pursued them, had a conversation. Michael Owen – I don't know where that came from. With Darren Bent, I don't know about that either.

Alvaro Negrado was the most serious one. It was potentially a fantastic deal. I went to Real Madrid a couple of times. He'd been on loan at Almeira and Real Madrid had decided that he wasn't quite ready for their first team. We thought that we'd take him, pay his wages with a clause at the end of the first season that we'd either buy him for a pre-agreed price, send him back (as in release him from his loan), or – if he played anywhere else in England – we'd be on a percentage of the transfer fee. So it was a creative deal and we got very close to making it happen, and Real Madrid were really keen that he didn't play in La Liga as they didn't want him playing against them. But when push came to shove they couldn't make him leave Spain. He went to Seville and then turned up Manchester City not long after. He would have been a great signing. We got ever so close to making that happen.

With Fraizer Campbell we got pipped by Sunderland. We put a good bid in but we couldn't put in the same money up front. I think he went to Sunderland on the same money, but I was having to bid on the basis of half now and half later and Sunderland were able to pay the £7m on the nail.

One departure that summer did shock City fans. Popular right-back Sam Ricketts – who'd excelled in the top flight once he'd found his feet – was allowed to join Bolton for the derisory sum of £2m.

Sam Ricketts: It was a bit of a long time coming. When we got into the Premier League I was still on my Championship contract. Dean Marney had got a new one early on, as had a few others. The chairman had said to me in January that they wanted to give me a new contract – I had about 18 months left on it then – and I said: "Yes, brilliant, I want to sign as soon as possible." I was really keen to stay. Then they kept delaying, saying they wanted to make sure we were still in the Premier League first, explaining that they'd given out a lot of new contracts to players earlier on in the season who'd then seen their form dip. I said "fair enough" and they told me that with one more win they'd offer the contract. We won at Fulham and my agent spoke to the chairman and said: "There's the win. Can we sort it out?" The chairman said they'd fax the offer over in the next day or so. One day went by, two days, then weeks and nothing came through.

With that I thought I wouldn't chase it if they didn't want me. It went on and on, and Paul Duffen told my agent that I had to go and speak to the manager about it to iron out a few things. So that's what happened. I spoke to Phil Brown. He said he didn't want to offer any new contracts. At the end of the season we all had player appraisals, meetings with the coaching staff. Phil told me then that I had 12 games to prove myself – the first 12 games of the season. I thought: 'Well I've just played under you for nearly three seasons, you know what I'm about,' so I figured he didn't want me to stay. I didn't know about anything financial at the club, but I knew that they weren't going to offer me anything and I'd had a bit of interest from a few other Premier League clubs, so thought: 'If you don't want me to stay then I'll go.' But I didn't want to go. If they'd have offered me a contract at any point I'd have signed it, but it never came and my hand was forced so I had to go.

Phil Brown: Sam Ricketts leaving was a footballing decision. I believed that we'd got as much as we could out of Sam and that there was maybe better out there.

Paul Duffen: Phil and Sam Ricketts had a very interesting relationship, a bit edgy, probably because they were both full backs. For whatever reason it was time for Sam to move on.

Sam Ricketts: I joined the club full of hope that I'd be able to continue my career. Naïvely maybe, I was wondering, on coming into the Championship, if I'd ever be able to get into the Premier League, and my time at Hull surpassed that. We got into the Premier League, we stayed there and I moved to another Premier League club, so from a footballing point of view it couldn't have gone any better. My final two years were hugely successful, we couldn't have done any more. In that year we were promoted to the Premier League, I played some of the best football I'd ever played in my career. Phil Brown – who I have huge respect for – hadn't given me any real praise in that 2007/08 season, but after we'd lost to Ipswich in the last game he walked past me and said I was magnificent all season and in the appraisals he told me he thought I was player of the season. To get that from a manager is one of the best things you can hear. He gave me a platform to play some of my best football and I thoroughly enjoyed it.

Richard Garcia: Sam and I were similar in age and had similar ambitions. We got along pretty much straight away and would always joke around with a quote from Remember the Titans – a film that came out around that time – which was 'right side, strong side'. In the film it was left side, but we used it to celebrate good performance and motivate ourselves at times. All in all I think we just worked hard for each other and complemented each other well. I remember we would talk about each other's movements and iron out what worked best. Phil Brown would always talk about partnerships all over the park and Sam and I took that on board and would work tirelessly to help each other in both attack and defence.

Matt Rudd: Sam Ricketts is, to many, the finest right-back City ever had. Already an international when he signed, he played three solid seasons on the right of a very strong defence that would write itself into legend, and while his forays down the flank, his combinations with Richard Garcia in the promotion season of 2008 and his superb crossing will be always recalled fondly, there was little doubt he was also a committed, tough-as-old-boots defender who could read the game, intercept passes and tackle like a tank. A textbook defender and a fine player.

A number of signings were made. The forward spots were filled by USA international Jozy Altidore, who joined on loan from Villarreal in Spain, and Algerian Kamel Ghilas, plucked from Celta de Vigo for about £2m. In midfield Stoke's Seyi Olofinjana was brought in for £3m, while in defence the signing of Steven Mouyokolo from Boulogne was made official. Best of all, however, was the capture of some serious Premier League quality, as left-midfielder Stephen Hunt joined from Reading for £3.5m.

Steven Hunt: Reading had held on to me for a season in the Championship, probably against my wishes, knowing that I'd still get my head down for them. Hull City were the first to come in for me in the summer after that, with about two weeks to go in the transfer window. Brendan Rodgers was the Reading manager at that point. I'd had a hernia but was back fit. I'd played for Ireland and was over there trying to sort out all the details. The fax machine in the hotel wasn't working so the local police let me use theirs in the local cells to fax off my contract.

Was Hull City unknown to me? Maybe. Did I know what I was getting myself into? No. But it was Premier League and it was an opportunity.

Mike Hall: After such a narrow escape from relegation in our first Premier League season it was obvious we needed to strengthen in the summer, but it wasn't until Steven Hunt was signed just before the season started that I started to believe we were ambitious enough to take another step forward.

So, the squad was bolstered and the club was no longer venturing into the unknown. But how was the mood in the camp?

Andy Dawson: Staying up is difficult, but the second year is still not easy. You think: 'Where do you go from now?' Do you try to kick on? Do you try to consolidate? In terms of the players we brought in, I felt we were trying to kick on.

Boaz Myhill: The club and the infrastructure had to catch up with the on-pitch success we'd had. In my first year in the Premier League I was still washing my kit at home, which I'm sure not many other goalkeepers were having to do. Stuff like that doesn't make a huge difference, but it does make some difference. Improvements were made for this season and every little helps on that score.

George Boateng: I felt there were more problems this time round. We should have strengthened the team, but we weren't working towards that. We weren't doing it how it was supposed to be done. We weren't standing still, but I knew that other teams had seen what we were about now. Also the atmosphere was different. Upstairs things were changing.

Another heart-warming piece of business was done when an injured Ian Ashbee was offered a new contract.

Ian Ashbee: Paul Duffen knew that I was going to be out for the year but he thought it would only be fair to offer me the new contract. I'll always be thankful that they did that and got my knee right for me.

The club started pre-season preparation with another trip to Bormeo in Italy. It was here that one local journalist was to get a taste of Jimmy Bullard's somewhat unique approach to life.

Dave Burns: Jimmy Bullard came out for a night out. The players had invited me and Phil Buckingham, and everybody was dressed smart-casual. Then Jimmy turned up in Björn Borg tennis gear. A full Fila kit, with tight white shorts and white sannies. I said: "What are you doing?" He just replied: "Burnsy, they'll all be wearing it. I'm a trendsetter." You could tell he was bonkers. Later in the night I walked down the main street and there was a big circle of local women chanting, dancing and laughing. I went to have a look at what they were laughing at, and in the middle was Jimmy dancing for all these Italian women. You just thought: 'He's nuts.' It's a shame it didn't work out for him because he was a lovely lad.

After Bormeo came a real 'is this really happening to Hull City?' moment, as the club, by dint of finishing 17th the season before, were invited to take part in the Barclays Asia Tournament held in Beijing, the capital of China, along with Tottenham, West Ham and local side Beijing Guoan. City lost the final 3-0 to Spurs after beating Beijing on penalties in the semi-final.

Sean Rush: I'd done a bit of research on humidity and said to Phil that we'd have to keep the training times really short. So we went out the stadium in Beijing to train, and we had to half the pitch, with West Ham on the other half. Gianfranco Zola was their manager then. I told Browny to keep it to 20 minutes. Half-an-hour later and Phil's morphed into Sven Goran Eriksson, dictating every last thing, and all because Zola was on the other side. It was like a competition to see who was the better coach. The lads were dying, dead on their feet, sweating stones off.

With the pre-season stuff done, Hull City were given the honour of kicking off the new season at Stamford Bridge. Few expected anything other than a Chelsea win. However, when Stephen Hunt scored the first goal of the season after 28 minutes, it seemed that the spirit of 2008 was back.

Stephen Hunt: To start the game was a surprise as I'd only played 45 minutes pre-season. But I'd probably looked sharp in pre-season training for the couple of days leading up to the game. And I scored the first goal of the Premier League that season, which will forever be a highlight of my career. I scored the goal from about eight yards out, and started to run towards the Chelsea fans as my momentum was going that way. I thought twice about that and turned towards the Hull City fans and enjoyed what was a special moment. I had no connection with the fans at that point, as I was new, but I was a Premier League player again and was very proud.

Sadly, Chelsea were to equalise through Didier Drogba in the 37th minute, and then City were denied an unexpected point when Drogba claimed a fluked winner in injury time.

Boaz Myhill: The Sky blokes were about to announce George Boateng as the man of the match but then had to change once Drogba got the winner. It's such an unforgiving league.

Stephen Hunt: Drogba scored a flukey goal for the winner in the last minute. I'd played about 75 minutes and we deserved to win or draw the game.

City then welcomed Spurs to the KC and were given a thrashing that was worrying on many levels. Jermain Defoe scored a hat-trick in the 5-1 win, with Stephen Hunt grabbing his second goal in two games for the Tigers.

Stephen Hunt: I scored with a fluke against Spurs on my home debut. It was a well-taken free-kick that I put into a good area that happened to go in the goal. Scoring on my away and home debuts got me off to a great start. In pre-season we'd gelled together and I was getting to know the team.

A much-needed win against Bolton gave City some breathing space, with Kamel Ghilas scoring the only goal of the game. However, rumours were emerging that City were on the verge of selling defensive lynchpin Michael Turner, with figures of between £9m and £12m being touted in the press and the likes of Tottenham and Liverpool being linked with the player. As City travelled to play Wolves at Molineux, many were wondering if it would be the last that they would see of our player of the season for the past two years.

Michael Turner: I knew that that was the last game before the transfer window was going to shut. There'd been a lot of rumours about me leaving and I remember that game clearly. We were on the back foot a little bit and I made a clearance off the line and a couple of good blocks. It was a game made for defenders really. I did feel it could be my last game though.

City drew 1-1, with an early Geovanni goal giving the Tigers the lead, but the star of the show was Turner, who put in a brave and committed defensive masterclass. All of this made it all the more difficult a couple of days later when he departed to Sunderland for what was rumoured at the time to be a fee of £6m, but was later revealed to be nearer £4m.

Michael Turner: It was an emotional time, but that's the way things go. There'd been loads of rumours and it is flattering as a player when that happens. The first I knew was when Sunderland put an offer in and the club said they were prepared to accept it. So I felt in my head that the club were prepared for me to go. I spoke to Steve Bruce at Sunderland and felt it was an opportunity I didn't want to let go by. My memories of Hull were all so good and I'd had such a good three years there but these things happen in football, people move on and it was the right time for me.

Phil Brown: Where Michael Turner was concerned, I was given a wrong steer. I was told by the football club, by the powers that be, that the deal would be worth £10m to Hull City, and had that been the case it would have been a no-brainer. Having let Michael then go, I went to a sponsors meeting with BMW not long after, where it was categorically stated to be that the fee was only £4m. If I'd known that was going to be the fee, I wouldn't have sold Michael.

Paul Duffen: With Michael Turner, it was about the imperative I was given about how we were going to pay the wages in August.

Phil Buckingham: The financial worries were apparent in the summer business. It was becoming obvious that Michael Turner would leave the club. I remember Paul Duffen saying that they'd want eight figures for him. When you see what Turner went for… warning bells were sounding loud and clear. When he was replaced by Ibrahima Sonko, that told you a lot about Hull City's financial situation.

Dave Burns: I knew we were being fed bullshit at the Sunderland away game. Michael Turner had gone, but Paul Duffen was always available for an interview and he came up before the game. I knew from his body language that he wasn't telling us the truth. I was thinking he was feeding me bullshit. I didn't quite know that Turner had been sold to pay the wages, but that was to emerge.

Whatever the fee, one of the finest players in the club's history had gone. It was a hard one for his team-mates and the fans to take.

Andy Dawson: Michael had shown in the Wolves game what he was made of. Captain and man of the match. Not a loud character but a leader on the pitch who set an example with his performances. We lost a player that had won player of the year the previous year.

Craig Fagan: Losing Turns was massive. He was unbelievable at the back for us. He'd put his head in places where most people would never dare. We missed him. Some people maybe took him for granted but I thought he would be tough to replace. We needed players who were there for the fight.

Sam Ricketts: As a person, I got on really well with Michael. And as a defender he was so, so good. He very rarely made a wrong step or missed a header. He was phenomenal in the air.

Nick Barmby: The lads were sad to see him leave because he was outstanding for us, both defending and he'd nick you a goal. He was assured coming out of the back and was a good defender and a great lad. The lads were gutted. There'd been talk of Liverpool, and at that time – with the way he was playing – he'd have done a really good job for them.

Dean Marney: Michael Turner came from the lower leagues and really stepped up. He took to the Championship like a duck to water and would hardly ever have a bad game. Then when we went into the Premier League he went up another level. He had loads of opportunities to leave. Losing him was a massive blow but he'd done so well it was impossible to keep him. And he played most of his career in the Premier League.

Paul McShane: Michael Turner was a magnificent defender who made a huge difference to that team. He was deceiving, as he didn't look like he was quick or a good a reader of the game, but he was fast and he read the game very well. He was a very intelligent player. He was brilliant in the air and could score some vital goals. He's a big stand out for me.

Ian Ashbee: Michael Turner was one of the best players I played with. He always played extremely well.

Matt Duke: When you lose your better players it's going to leave a hole. Michael had been fantastic, so it was going to be a big loss.

Phil Buckingham: Michael Turner remains one of my favourite Hull City players. Given the first impressions I had of him – a spindly, Bambi-on-ice character – to what he became when he left the club, I just thought it was an incredible transformation. He was heroic at Wembley in the play-off final, and in that first season he played every minute in the Premier League. That is some going. Even in a struggling team he always stood out. In his last game away at Wolves, he'd have known he was on the verge of leaving the club and yet he was magnificent, throwing himself at everything and anything. He won City a point almost single-handedly. When the pantheon of great City defenders is written, he'll never be far from the top. He was brilliant.

Ian Farrow: I voted for Michael Turner as City player of the year each year he was with us. I even voted for him in an all-time City XI on a local radio show. At that point Turner had only been with us for about a year and everyone else was voting for Pete Skipper and Richard Jobson, which I could understand yet I felt Turner had shown that he had a little bit more to offer than even those aforementioned City greats. He wasn't given the best start to his City career by being partnered with Danny Coles, yet Turner went on to play a major role in keeping us in the Championship that first season. He carried on the following season, being one of the main reasons we reached the play-off final. He was a colossus for us and didn't look out of place when we played the likes of Arsenal, Chelsea and Manchester United. He should have played for England, especially as Matthew Upson got a call-up during that period. Turner was a major reason we got to the top division and a very big reason we stayed there for that first season. We'd probably have had at least another season in there if we'd been able to keep him.

Steven Hunt: It was sad to lose Michael Turner but there were other promising players waiting to get in the team. Anthony Gardner was trying to stay injury free, and he had loads of Premier League experience, so it wasn't as if we had nobody to replace Michael. But there was a bit of uncertainty.

The club signed Ibrahima Sonko from Stoke to fill the gap left by Michael Turner, and Dutchman Jan Vennegoor of Hesselink bolstered the attacking options. Meanwhile, making the opposite journey to Turner was a familiar, popular face from the happy days of 2008.

Paul McShane: There was no hesitation for me, as I'd really enjoyed my time at Hull. Sunderland just wasn't for me. I needed to leave. I'd been injured again in pre-season and it just seemed that it wasn't to be there. Then Hull bought me.

As so often happens in football, fate dealt both City and Turner a cruel hand with the next league game, after an international break, pitting the Tigers against his new club. Without their defensive leader City looked woeful, and Sunderland ran out comfortable 4-1 winners.

Michael Turner: I had never felt so nervous going into a game. Seeing my first fixture as being against Hull City, it couldn't have gone any worse. It was the last game I wanted to play in. It went well for me personally that day, but I had mixed emotions coming out of it. I was just relieved when it was all over.

After the Sunderland defeat, City lost 1-0 at home to a newly promoted Birmingham side widely expected to struggle that season. In the next game, young centre-back Liam Cooper was given a debut at Anfield of all places. Fernando Torres scored a hat-trick in a 6-1 thrashing. A welcome win against Wigan at the KC followed – with Vennegoor of Hesselink and Geovanni scoring – but this was followed by a 2-0 defeat at Fulham and a dispiriting 0-0 draw at home to crisis club Portsmouth. The squad didn't seem to have the same feel to it that it had had in the wildly successful previous two-and-a-half years.

Ian Ashbee: The changing room didn't have the same feel to it. Wage brackets had been smashed, and that brings in a different breed of player. You had lads coming in on a load of money to not play football. I just don't get that. At a club like that, it felt slightly strange. And I was sat on the sidelines unable to do anything about it.

Mike White: Phil Brown worried me at that point. Liam Cooper was given his chance and then used as a scapegoat after. You had a sense of it all unravelling.

Steven Hunt: We had a good bunch of lads in certain parts of the changing room, and a not-so-good bunch in other parts. But that's what football is.

Matt Duke: The mood was a bit different. It's always got to change as the team needed to be strengthened and you're bringing new faces in. But you end up losing the spirit a bit. It was still good though. It was still a good atmosphere. We just didn't play well enough as a team. The table doesn't lie. It just didn't happen for us that season.

Paul McShane: The team felt different. Losing all the time dents people's confidence and it can become a bit of a habit, where you're just waiting to be beaten. The other teams were ready for us in that next season, too. A lot of teams really wanted to beat us because of what we'd done the season before.

Sean Rush: The finances that we earned in the Premier League were never really ploughed back into the club and the Academy and I felt that was a shame. From my side of things, when you look at other clubs they had such good facilities but we never quite got there.

With the club's financial worries intensifying, a big change was made at boardroom level, which saw chairman Paul Duffen leaving the club.

Paul Duffen: There were two things that Russell and I fell out badly about. One was Michael Turner, and the other thing was Ash, because when Ash got injured I was adamant that he'd get another year on his contract, even if he didn't play. I felt it was the right thing to do.

Though the club's finances were in a parlous position, under Duffen's tenureship Hull City had played at Wembley for the first time, been promoted to the top flight for the first time, and then pulled off a survival campaign in that first Premier League season when most had written the club off.

Paul Duffen: It was an unbelievable adventure. I've been very lucky in my life. I've been part of some extraordinary things, professionally and personally, and the journey at Hull City was something that absorbed all of my time, energy and emotions. I made life-long friends, and I still spend a lot of time in Hull. It had a defining impact on me. I didn't know anything about Hull before I went up there, I couldn't have put a pin on it on the map, but by discovering it and learning to love it and understanding the nature of the people in both Hull and East Yorkshire, that whole experience was one of growth for me, learning, unrivalled experiences. Sport in the city is obviously massive and it was something I loved. It was something I got huge amount of reward from and something I was fortunate enough to be very successful in, so for all those reasons for me it was just a glorious adventure filled only with memories of affection, shared success and enormous team spirit.

Phil Brown: Paul Duffen was a godsend to me. He's very intelligent and he understood me as a character. One of the best moments for Paul, according to him – and he was my boss so for him to say this shows his level of integrity – was one time when I took my backroom staff to Medici's for a bite to eat and I invited Paul. Paul listened to me talking, then I turned to him and said: "The reason why I invited you is because I firmly believe that you're one of my backroom staff, and that's not being disrespectful it just shows your stature." Paul knew he was my boss but he also felt like an integral member of the staff who felt he could give an opinion that wasn't falling on deaf ears. It was one of the best relationships I've had with a chairman in the 40 years I've been in football.

Dave Burns: Paul was a charming man and a very good communicator, but he turned out to be all fur coat and no knickers. He galvanised the fans, but ultimately for all his good things the club got into such a mess financially when he was chairman. Whose fault that was – his or Russell Bartlett's – I don't know, but it was a mess.

Phil Buckingham and I were invited out by Brownie to a couple of pre-season tours in Bormeo in the Italian Alps. We had full access to him and the players. We were invited on a night out with Browny, Paul and the backroom staff. I remember being in a bar in Bormeo with all the staff, and I said in front of everyone to Duffen: "You speak five languages, you have just driven across the Alps in your Aston Martin, you're the chairman of a Premier League football club, you're dapper. You must be flawed. What's the secret? No one has that good a life." I don't know how well that went down but I thought he was too good to be true. And ultimately that turned out to be the case, as he and Bartlett took the club to the brink of oblivion. I don't think we should ever forget that. I liked him and I still like him, but he was running things on a day-to-day basis so I hold him responsible.

Phil Buckingham: Paul Duffen was always gold for the media. He was eloquent and approachable and, as much as supporters will judge him by the club's financial position when he left, you have to remember the part he played in its rise. He played a huge part in whipping up the enthusiasm behind the club in his first year there. It might look daft now, but the Hull Daily Mail was doing a 'get behind the Tigers' campaign and we approached Paul Duffen to get dressed up in a kit. He was happy to do it, on the KC pitch kissing the badge and all sorts. That might seem hammy, but it was all part of whipping up something. He played a really big part in getting people behind the club at that point. It wasn't an empire built on strong foundations, but it's too easy to dismiss his role in the club's history simply as the man that came close to bringing it down, as he did such a good job of building it up as well.

Mike White: I won't say anything bad about Paul Duffen. I understand that City fans have a right to feel concerned about how the club was run in the end, but as a person for me to deal with, as a person in the media, I don't have any issues with Paul at all. He was brilliant for me. You could always pick up the phone, ask him a question and you'd get an honest answer. And he respected you as a journalist. If you had information that you were going to run as a story, he would respect that and wouldn't try to steer you off the scent. I was one of the first people he called when the club were trying to sign Juninho. You don't always get club chairmen trying to steer you in the right direction. I think he did a lot of good things for the club, which shouldn't be forgotten, and his close relationship with Phil Brown was just what the club needed.

Phil Buckingham: When Paul Duffen left I remember Phil Brown's press conference. He'd been stripped of his closest ally and it looked as if he would follow soon after. He looked very vulnerable all of a sudden. He looked like a man cut adrift.

With Paul Duffen on his way, Russell Bartlett brought back a man still hugely popular in Hull. Adam Pearson had rescued the club from financial oblivion before, but this time it was different.

Adam Pearson: I shouldn't have come back. The club had changed immeasurably. It was immersed in debt. They'd put so much debt into the club. It was unrecognisable from the one that I left. What they did wrong was gamble on subsequent deals in the Premier League that then risked the club, predominantly the Bullard deal.

These off-pitch events were followed by a 2-0 defeat away at bogey team Burnley, which meant that City had played all three newly promoted teams and picked up a solitary point. The press – both local and national – were reporting that Phil Brown was on the brink of the sack. Failure to beat Stoke at the KC would all but confirm this. One down with half-an-hour to play, the picture looked bleak, but Seyi Olofinjana equalised against his former team, then Jan Vennegoor of Hesselink netted a winner in injury time. Phil Brown kept his job and this game gave City a renewed vigour. A 3-3 draw at home to West Ham in the next game saw a returning Jimmy Bullard score to add to a Carlton Cole own goal (deflected in after a Bullard shot) and a Kamil Zayatte near-post strike. Then came a memorable game at home to an Everton side that had beaten City 4-0 at the KC in the Carling Cup a few weeks earlier.

Steven Hunt put City one up after nine minutes, and in the 20th minute a free-kick was awarded 25 yards from goal. Up stepped Andy Dawson…

Andy Dawson: I remember speaking to Stephen Hunt when we were warming up and saying what a great night for football it was. I just had a feeling it was going to be my night. We started really well, and for me personally it was a privilege to score in the Premier League. I'd scored the previous year but to go on and win the game and score a goal against a top team like Everton was just great. And that win took us out of the bottom three.

Nick Barmby: A great result. And a great free-kick from Daws. It's just his celebrations that he needed to work on… he'd always get a bit mad with himself when he celebrates.

Dean Marney scored after 28 minutes, only for Everton to then stage a second-half comeback. A Kamil Zayatte own goal (his third in 43 league games for City at that point) and a Louis Saha penalty made the closing stages nervy, but City hung on to record a morale-boosting win.

Steven Hunt: Ireland had been knocked out of the World Cup play-offs by France just before that game through the goal that came after Thierry Henry had handled the ball. For some reason, Everton's kit man decided to start saying things to me about that goal. All I remember is thinking: 'Right I'll prove this fella wrong. Who does he think he is?' After we won the game I ran down the tunnel after him saying: "Who the fuck do you think you are saying that sort of stuff to me." I don't know what I was thinking to be honest, but it shows I had the fire in my belly. I remember looking around and seeing David Moyes looking at me going: "What the hell's going on here? You've just won the game and now you're shouting at my kit man!" Maybe I should have calmed down but those comments had motivated me all the more. And my goal was one of the sweetest strikes I've ever hit. Everything was going right for us. That's Phil Brown in a nutshell. He had the capability to really get a team firing and then he'd go the other way sometimes and we'd go a few games without winning. In terms of tactics and preparation in the days before games, Phil is probably the best manager I've ever had in how he gets his point across and how he wants his team to play. I really liked his team talks. But there are other parts too. No manager is perfect though. They all have their flaws. And I got on well with Phil. I'd never do anything to disrespect him.

The match had also seen a key player from the season before recalled to the starting line-up.

George Boateng: There had been lots of incidents that season. I hadn't played much for six to eight weeks at one point around October. I'd fallen out with Phil Brown. We had our differences – not personal, it was about things on the pitch. We had different ideas on how to stay up. I felt my experience meant I knew what it took to win games. But Phil had kept us up the season before, and he felt he knew better. So we fell out. Phil tried to send me on loan to Ipswich, but I said I wasn't going anywhere: I liked the club, I liked the players, and sometimes not playing is just part of football. There are ups and downs. But sometimes I wouldn't even make the 18. I stayed calm and waited it out, and Phil changed his mind. Against Everton at home Phil asked me how I'd feel about starting again. I told him if he needed me I was always there. I'd been his best trainer over that time out of the team. I stayed professional. I still cared about the club and wanted us to win. I played well on my first game back and me and Phil were patching up our issues.

City then travelled to the Etihad to take on a Manchester City side that had spent even more money since the fateful game on Boxing Day 2008. But City's spirit was strong.

Steven Hunt: Team spirit was good at that point. We had characters, but not all of them were steely ones. We had me, Paul McShane, Nick Barmby, Andy Dawson, Kevin Kilbane and a few others who were strong characters in good times and bad times. We'd know how to behave. But when things go bad you get to see the real side of the others' performances. I had a great year at Hull – probably the most enjoyable of my career in terms of how I played and the banter that I had with Paul McShane and Kevin Kilbane, who'd I'd share lifts in with, and Nicky Barmby who I really admired as a player. When you get to know him you'd get to know why he'd had such a successful career. We had funny individuals in the team who kept the dressing room light-hearted in defeat, which was needed, but sometimes you need a bit of graft too. You need to hurt when you lose.

City started well but on the stroke of half-time Shaun Wright-Phillips gave the home side an undeserved lead with a deflected long-range shot. However, the mood in the squad shone through in the second half, with Dean Marney, Richard Garcia and Stephen Hunt, and later George Boateng and Nick Barmby, running their blood to water in midfield, allowing Jimmy Bullard the freedom to pose numerous problems for Manchester City. The Tigers got their reward in the 82nd minute when Kolo Toure was adjudged to have fouled Jan Vennegoor of Hesselink in the box. Bullard duly stepped up and converted the penalty. Immediately after, one of the all-time great goal celebrations was pulled off with perfect comic timing.

Paul McShane: The night before, I was getting ready for bed, brushing my teeth, and it just came into my head. I don't know where it came from. I thought it would be unbelievable to do the team talk if we scored, but I knew it had to be an equaliser or a goal that put us in the lead. If we were losing 4-0 and did that celebration, people would just have mocked us. But as it happened, it couldn't have been more perfect. Jimmy scoring was great, as he executed it really well. Though when he scored we had to shout at him to remind him to do it. Me and Hunty were screaming at him. But for it to take place in exactly the same place as the original team talk, that was perfect. It was a great game, a great performance and a great result.

Nick Barmby: Jimmy was unlucky when he first came in but came back from injury and scored a couple of goals and brought a fresh impetus to the lads. Paul McShane had said that if anyone scored we should re-enact the team talk, so it was good fun. And Phil took it well, the fans were laughing.

Steven Hunt: On the way to the game, Paul McShane mentioned the celebration idea. We said whoever scored would be 'Phil'. Typically it was Jimmy, who's a very funny guy. We wouldn't have done it if we were losing, but it made it 1-1 so it had to be done. It was good value, good entertainment.

Andy Dawson: It was the same end, the same position and it just had to be Jimmy. You still see it now when you're flicking through Sky on programmes about the funniest moments in football. It was a really good point, more importantly.

A vital point was secured by City but the game's drama wasn't done there. Craig Bellamy could start a mass brawl in a monastery, and Paul McShane was not a man to mess with.

Paul McShane: Craig Bellamy came on in the second half, and he likes to be a bit lippy and get in your head. The year before at West Ham he was giving me dog's abuse, so when he came on I was just promising myself that I wouldn't get in an argument with him. I just said: "I'll see you after the game in the tunnel," because at the time I did want to punch his head off. So all I said to him during the game was: "Shut your mouth and I'll see you after the game in the tunnel. We'll speak then." That meant I didn't get into his game. His strength was winding people up. When the game finished I ran into the tunnel to find him, and I got held back by the security guards. He was on the other side of the guards calling me all these names. I then went into our changing room, and Nicky Barmby came in and said: "Craig Bellamy's waiting for you outside." I sprinted out to try to get him again, but again the security guards were there and Craig was stood behind them all giving me yet more abuse. I honestly wanted to fight him. After that, he sent me his jersey into our changing room to wind me up further. He'd signed it: "To the hardest man in football, from Craig Bellamy." I saw him a couple of months later after I'd been playing for Ireland against Brazil at Wembley. I was out with Kevin Kilbane and Shay Given in London and we bumped into Craig. We had a chat and to be fair we got on really well and I still get on with him to this day. He was a great player, but he certainly knew how to wind players up. In that game against Manchester City, I wanted to have a proper, full-on fight with him but I couldn't get near him.

After some hugely worrying performances in the aftermath of Michael Turner's sale, City seemed to be settling into becoming a useful mid-table Premier League side. Fifteenth position represented real progress considering that the club had been in the relegation places little over a month earlier.

14. **Wigan P14, W5, D2, L7, Pts17**
15. **Hull City P15, W4, D4, L7, Pts16**
16. **Everton P14, W4, D3, L7, Pts15**
17. **West Ham P14, W3, D5, L6, Pts14**
18. **Bolton P13, W3, D3, L7, Pts12**
19. **Wolves P14, W2, D4, L8, Pts10**
20. **Portsmouth P14, W2, D1, L11, Pts 7**

So City were on the up. The past four games had seen a return of two wins and two draws. Stephen Hunt was in terrific form, and City fans were finally getting a glimpse of what Jimmy Bullard could do. However, in the next game, at Villa Park, Bullard was stretchered off as City lost 3-0 to Aston Villa. They would go on to lose or draw their next eight games.

As the year, and indeed the decade, drew to a close, there was a glimmer of hope. A festive match at the KC against the all-conquering Manchester United saw City start the game with as good a 45 minutes as they had enjoyed against top class opposition in a year or so, with Richard Garcia being denied a cast-iron penalty after drawing a foul from Nemanja Vidic. It was something of a travesty when Wayne Rooney put the away side one up on the stroke of half-time. Craig Fagan equalised on 59 minutes with a penalty, but Manchester United's class was to tell in the end, with an Andy Dawson own goal and a Dimitar Berbatov tap in seeing the visitors flattered by a 3-1 win. For all City's bravery they fell to 19th in the table after the defeat.

Craig Fagan: We had some good performances that season. Personally, going up against these players was a dream for me. You wanted to test yourself against them. In that first half we gave them a good run for their money. We made them buck their ideas up in the second half though and they turned up the heat. It showed what we were actually capable of, but it was a disappointment that we couldn't do it more. But scoring a penalty against Manchester United is what dreams are made of.

That left one more game in the greatest decade in Hull City's history. Bolton away on the evening of December 29th. City went two down on the hour mark, but rescued a point through the ceaseless work ethic of Craig Fagan and double goalscorer Stephen Hunt.

Stephen Hunt: Phil used to play me attacking on the right or the left, or in behind the front man, and I used to enjoy that. He used to believe in my goalscoring abilities. Craig was great that day, lots of pace and energy, and we were virtually playing up front together in that second half. We were chasing shadows before we went 2-0 down. We were getting battered.

City fans travelled back down the M62 in good spirits, and rightly so. Their team had shown real heart in rescuing a point. But these fans could also reflect upon a quite incredible decade for the football club.

When the game against Leyton Orient on January 3rd, 2000, kicked off, there was nothing to suggest that the club would rise through the leagues, be managed by a former England boss, welcome back two local football legends to incredible effect, bring in a former African footballer of the year, play at Wembley for the first time, win a place in the top flight of English football for the first time, win at Arsenal, Tottenham, Newcastle, draw at Liverpool and Chelsea, lose by the odd goal in seven at Old Trafford, stand joint top of the Premier League, avoid relegation after being written off by so many, make legends of the likes of Ian Ashbee, Andy Dawson, Boaz Myhill and co. The journey Hull City had been on would have been written off as unrealistic had it come from the pen of Mark Herman. Yet we'd lived it, breathed it, loved it, cried, laughed, cheered and celebrated in ways we didn't know were possible.

We now had stories to tell – stories we will never tire of telling – of Big Kev, Brabs, Jon Whitney's stare, Elliott's header against Swansea, Delaney's screamer against Rochdale, Ash at Yeovil, Barmby's volley at Hillsborough, the Beast, survival at Cardiff, Folan at West Brom, Folan against Watford, Dean Windass, it just had to be… Wayne Brown jumping on Boaz, tears at Wembley, beers after Wembley, the Premier League bell, Geovanni, Folan, our first three points, Andy Dawson's tackle on Walcott, Geo's screamer and Cousin's header at Arsenal, Manchester United fans screaming for the full-time whistle at Old Trafford, 2-0 up at Anfield, the half-time team talk, Manucho at Fulham, Phil Brown's song of survival, the half-time team talk re-enactment…

What a journey. What a privilege to have witnessed it.

2010 onwards

The rest of the 2009/10 season was speckled with moments of hope, but in truth City looked like a broken club. The first league game of 2010, after a 4-1 defeat at Wigan in the FA Cup, saw the Tigers travel to Tottenham and draw 0-0 thanks to a logic-defying goalkeeping display from Boaz Myhill.

Boaz Myhill: Is that the best I've ever played? It was certainly an amazing game. I walked to do the press after that game and found a tenner on the floor. It was just one of those days. It was unbelievable. I was diving the wrong way and still saving shots. It was enjoyable!

A 4-0 defeat at Old Trafford followed, then, as January was closing out, Stephen Hunt picked up an injury that was to mean his Hull City career was to last for only a handful more games.

Steven Hunt: There was some interest in me from Wolves. I went to see Adam Pearson with my agent because I knew how much Jimmy Bullard was on. I said to Adam: "You've got to give me as much as him, because I'm better than him and I deserve the same contract as I know what I'm doing for the team away from the matches too." He said if we stayed up I could have that contract. We then played against Wolves and I broke my foot. I thought it was bone bruising. I could barely walk but I was keen to play, so every Friday for weeks I was trying to train but just couldn't do it. I kept having injections in my foot. We played Chelsea not long after Wolves, and I played with an injection in my foot and it was just numbed.

It was worse than a broken foot. My foot had just collapsed. I was told it was a career-threatening injury. For about four games I tried to train the day before a game, and have an injection in the foot as I was flying and I really wanted to continue playing. It got to the stage where I couldn't do it anymore, and I needed to find out what was wrong. The specialist gave me bad news and I was devastated to be out for the rest of the season. I had six or seven goals before January. It was the best six months, playing wise, I'd ever had.

As Hunt played through the pain City went on a decent run, drawing with Wolves 2-2 at the KC, then drawing 1-1 at home to Chelsea in a game that saw the rapidly improving Stephen Mouyokolo give the Tigers the lead. Then came an excellent 2-1 win against Manchester City, with Jozy Altidore and George Boateng scoring their only Hull City goals. The win took City to 14th, but three insipid defeats were to follow: 1-0 at Blackburn, 3-0 at West Ham, and 5-1 at Everton.

16. **Sunderland P27, W6, D9, L12, Pts27**
17. **Wolves P28, W6, D6, L16, Pts24**
18. **Hull City P28, W5, D9, L14, Pts24**
19. **Burnley P28, W6, D5, L17, Pts23**
20. **Portsmouth P27, W5, D4, L18, Pts19**

Going into a televised game at home to Arsenal rumours were circulating that should City lose Phil Brown would be sacked. Arsenal scored early through Andrei Arshavin, only for Jimmy Bullard to equalise in the 28th minute with a penalty. Then, one minute into the second half, George Boateng went into a challenge with Bacary Sagna.

George Boateng: I picked up a booking early in the first half. Nicolas Bendtner had kicked me off the ball, which the referee didn't see, and I was booked for retaliating. Then in the second half there was a 50-50 ball between me and Bacary Sagna. I was favourite but somehow he accelerated – I don't know where he got the speed from – and got there before me. He touched the ball and I stood on his leg. The ref thought it was worth a second booking – which I thought was harsh, as there was no intent there – and that led to me being sent off. I was really angry and disappointed as we lost the game. But in that game, everything seemed to be back. What we had in the first season seemed to be back even after I was sent off. The lads were working their socks off.

City held on heroically, but in injury time a shot by Denilson was palmed back out into danger by Boaz Myhill. Nicklas Bendtner was first to the ball and gave Arsenal a lead that was to seal the three points.

All eyes were now on Adam Pearson. On the following Monday he put Phil Brown on gardening leave.

Adam Pearson: Phil was doing a good job and the owner asked me to get rid of him. I should have said no but I didn't. If Phil was going to go, it should have been the day that I came back. Once I'd made the decision to let him have a run at it, because he'd put some good performances together, he should have been kept until the end of the season. By the time we sacked Phil – after the Arsenal game – the club was totally and utterly broken. It was destroyed. Everything that had been built up – all its values, its financial prudence – had been destroyed. It was a squad littered with mercenaries who Phil would sometimes manage to get performances out of. It was toxic. People like George Boateng came out and said it but a lot were thinking it, the whole club was toxic. But Phil should have been given the opportunity to see that season out, and there is a chance, looking back in hindsight, that things would have gone differently because he would probably have got better out of the players than Iain Dowie did, but the club would probably have gone down the year after as it was rotten to the core and it was out of control financially.

Phil Brown: With about nine games to go I was asked by Adam Pearson to bring a bullet-point presentation to Russell Bartlett with regards to the survival campaign. This was after the 2-1 defeat to Arsenal. I thought that performance showed a lot of guts, that there was a lot of fight in the camp. To lose my job after that game – and I'd had a meeting with Adam Pearson in my office after the game saying exactly those words, with that kind of spirit, with that kind of fight we'll stay up – was the most disappointing thing that's happened in my life. To be told one thing late on the Saturday and then told that on the Monday, it meant the most successful period of time for me had become the most disappointing. It must have been a combined effort from them though.

Brian Horton: George Boateng got sent off, it was 1-1 and we conceded a goal in the last minute that Boaz would have saved 999 times out of 1000. Would that point have kept us in a job? On the Monday Phil got a call from Adam Pearson to say he was relieving him of his duties, which I found very hard to believe. I couldn't understand why he'd done it after all he'd done. I firmly believe that we'd have stayed up again. We had a big game coming up at Portsmouth. It was a winnable game for us. I think we'd have stayed up. Nothing will ever change my mind on that one. The spirit was still OK, the players were largely behind us, we'd just taken Arsenal to 94 minutes with 10 men. If the spirit hadn't been there we wouldn't have done that. I'll never understand it, but then I've been in football all these years and I still don't understand a lot of it.

Phil Brown: The bullet-point presentation was based on the fact that we had to go to Portsmouth, we had Birmingham coming to our place, we had Sunderland coming to our place, and these were winnable games. If we won three or four we'd have got 36/37 points, which would have been enough. Sitting on a beach in Egypt – which I did to get away from things after the decision – I was then asked by the chairman of Burnley to go and manage them. It was bizarre. But I was on gardening leave and I couldn't go there unless they paid the compensation. That was a surreal moment, being in the hot seat at Hull City and then nearly being in the hot seat at Burnley a week later. It turned out they didn't need me as they put Brian Laws in charge and won 4-1 at the KC!

Brian Horton: Phil went on the Monday and I was asked to take training for a couple of days, which I did, and I was asked to look after things on the Saturday if they hadn't got anyone in. But it didn't work out. Steve Parkin – who was fantastic – stayed and Phil and I went.

Phil Brown: Brian Horton is a Hull City great, and to have the support he gave me was incredible. Steve Parkin was one of the most trustworthy assistants you could ever have. Simon Maltby was a top physio – and quirky though he was, he knew where I wanted to go.

Ian Ashbee: I don't think Adam Pearson was ever overly keen on Phil, and he wanted to change something. The easy thing is to change is the manager. I don't think the timing was great, having just lost unluckily to Arsenal. I still felt we had enough and that Phil could claw it all back. The changing room was alright and together, and I still felt that Phil was the right man for the job.

Phil Buckingham: I got the impression that Adam Pearson was twitchy, but I thought that the manner in which they lost to Arsenal would protect Phil Brown. They were desperately unlucky. But Adam seemed to think it was then or never. You feel for any manager that loses his job, as you tend to work with them day to day, but this one was even more disappointing than usual as you knew what Phil had done for the club. He was such a key figure in it all. It was galling to see him lose the job in the way he did. He's always maintained that he would have kept the club up. I'd disagree with him as the statistical pattern would suggest that they weren't going to pick up the points needed, but City rolled the dice and that didn't work.

Paul McShane: I was a write-off at that time. I'd lost my dad unexpectedly on March 12th, just before the Arsenal game. We were due to meet up on the Friday and then stay in the hotel in Hull, but I was woken up by my brother-in-law banging on my door on the Friday morning and by the look on his face I knew something really bad had happened. He told me that my dad had died very suddenly, and I was just a zombie for the rest of the season. He was buried on the Sunday and I was back in training on the Tuesday but I couldn't stop crying. I was disappointed for Phil and that he'd left, but I can't remember exactly how I felt because I had so much going on in my family life. We deserved to be relegated though.

Iain Dowie was to take over the running of the team. But Phil Brown, the man who had taken Hull City to Wembley and into the top flight for the first time in the club's history, had managed his last Hull City game. City had won a mere six of his last 51 league games, but there was no clamour from the fans for Phil to be sacked. And irrespective of that tough final 12 months, Phil and his team made history, something the fans of the club will never forget.

Phil Brown: Hull City meant everything to me. My whole career came to a pinnacle. It was everything I'd worked towards. I had a playing career that wasn't the most illustrious in the lower divisions, but I'd put my life and body on the line, playing for whoever I was with, managing to get 700 games under my belt. Then I went into coaching, very fortunately, at the end of my career, which followed on under Sam Allardyce. I then failed – as people told me – on my first attempt at management at Derby County, where I lasted eight months. Then I got a chance at a club – even on my first day under Phil Parkinson – that I felt an affinity with. I felt for the people because they'd been through two or three generations of deprivation with the fishing industry going under among other things. I was a working class lad and worked hard for the money I earned, and that spirit was in place at Hull City. The people on the terraces wanted to see a hard-working, organised, creative team that worked hard for their shirt and respected it.

I took some of the players to see Boothferry Park long after we'd moved out. It was a crying shame to see one of the great playing surfaces in English football in that state. I wanted the players to see it – though some of the foreign lads were looking at me as if to say: 'What the hell are we doing down here?' – but I wanted to tell them the story of where we'd come from and why we had to wear the shirt with pride.

Caleb Folan: I was gutted when Phil left – I was in tears that day. It was upsetting that everything had got to that point. That's when things started to change.

Brendon Smurthwaite: It was quite a sad place when Phil came to Hull City, and he really brightened it up. I remember meeting him and thinking: 'Wow, he can talk.' He took a lot of the training and when Phil Parkinson went it seemed natural for him to come in. People still ask me about him and can be a little bit critical of him, but as a fan would you swap those years for anything? On the outside people created a perception of him because of how he'd dress and his tan and everything, and he could be bad-tempered – which all managers can – but he was what the club needed at the time, from a footballing and PR point of view. Browny would speak to anyone and the media loved him. For much of the time under him we were a lot of people's favourite second team.

Alfie Potts Harmer: I still think Browny probably deserves more credit than he gets. Although we invested that summer, promotion in his first full season was a truly phenomenal achievement. He got a lot of criticism in the next two seasons, some of which was obviously fair, but it's worth bearing in mind that he kept us up against the odds and I honestly think there's a chance he could have done it again.

Dave Burns: I liked Phil. He was a bloke's bloke. You felt you could have a pint and a laugh with him. We had a falling out or two, with him banishing me for a while at the KC, but he was terrific. I still feel a genuine warmth towards him. And he did a terrific job.

Peter Swan: I liked Phil Brown. He was different, and he wasn't scared of being different. If he was chocolate he would have eaten himself, but who cares? I still like the bloke for what he's done. He did brilliantly. He could handle characters too. Him and Paul Duffen worked really well together. You have to take your hat off to him.

Bryan Hughes: Phil was a big influence with that feelgood factor on the training ground. He was very bubbly, a very likeable character to have around. That rubbed off on a lot of players. He would get the best out of players. He was great at that.

Phil Brown: They were the greatest memories that I've had, but ones that I'll hopefully be able to recreate one day. A fantastic time in my life.

With Phil Brown went Brian Horton, one of the greatest names in the club's history.

John Cooper: Brian Horton was a fighter, a good footballer, a good thinker. He is just one of those people whose infectious in every way. When he was first at City he had Dennis Booth with him, and the two were unbelievably good together, as Dennis would be more like a comedian. Brian's a gem, lovely, honest and would do anything for you. When he was City manager in the 1980s, I was helping out with the Boys Brigade. I asked him to come down and say a few words. Not only did he come down, he brought a load of stuff with him and stayed as long as we needed him. I can't speak highly enough of him.

Iain Dowie couldn't inspire anything from the team. City won one, drew three and lost five of the final nine games of the season to go down with a whimper. The dream was over.

Richard Garcia: The second season was a hard season as we didn't really hit form too often. It was great to be able to come back into the side and we had a decent run of form but it was a very different environment from the two years before.

Steven Hunt: I went to Jimmy Bullard during the season and said: "Jimmy, we need you to get fit, can you stop messing about in the gym and train harder?" He laughed it off but I was being deadly serious. When you have one or two people who aren't pulling their weight in a team environment it can be disheartening, particularly when the rest of them are trying and failing. Bullard didn't help. But I would imagine that he was very disheartened with football too, given the injuries that he'd had.

City's fate was effectively confirmed after a 1-0 home defeat to Sunderland in a game that saw Jimmy Bullard miss a penalty. It had been a difficult season that had seen City lose the captain, manager and chairman that had led the club so gloriously into the Premier League two seasons ago. Iain Dowie was to be told his services were no longer required and the team was to be decimated, with the chief concern centring around managing the eye-watering debts that had been accrued.

The fire sale started almost immediately. Steven Hunt left as Wolverhampton stayed good on their interest in him from a few months earlier and City recouped their money on the player of the season.

Steven Hunt: If I'd stayed fit... one, we would have stayed up – that reflects the mood I was in when I was playing and what I felt I could have done – and two, I'd have had more choices than Wolves at the end of the season if I'd chosen to leave, no disrespect to them.

When Hull went down, I knew I couldn't do the same as I'd done at Reading and stay in the Championship. However, do I wish I'd had many years at Hull City? Yes, because of the great memories I have. When I look at Paul McShane, who stayed there for years and had more success, I was probably a tad jealous of him. The day we played Sunderland at the end of that season, the Hull City fans were singing their hearts out – "This is the best trip we've ever been on" – and it brought a tear to my eye. But I thought, fair play lads, you're going out on a high. I didn't live in the area – I lived in Leeds, though I don't know why – but for that day I'll always be grateful to the fans for how they were.

Mike Hall: When injury ruled Steven Hunt out for the season it immediately felt like a blow too far for a club that had barely looked like surviving throughout the campaign, and so it proved. I feel that Hunt's never-say-die attitude was at odds with the general malaise that hung over the club that season – his approach to the game would have been far better suited to the confident, honest and hardworking side that had been promoted two years earlier and initially taken the top-flight by storm. That's probably about as high a compliment as I can give. He was deservedly recognised by fans with the Supporters' Player of the Season award for his one season at the club.

Paul McShane: Steven Hunt was very good to play alongside. He's such an honest player who'd run himself into the ground. He was terrific in that second Premier League season and he was great to have in the changing room because he was never afraid to say what needed to be said. He had such a hunger to succeed. That stayed with him throughout his career. I was really glad to have a season playing alongside him at club level.

Boaz Myhill had etched his name alongside the legendary City keepers of the past century. He was also hugely popular with his team-mates and the fans. Known as one of the good guys, Boaz had played more than 250 games for City but was on his way to West Brom for £1.5m.

Boaz Myhill: All of the most important things that happened to me happened while I was at Hull. My children were born there, and the city and club are everything to me. It can't be described. I was very lucky to go there when I did, that's not lost on me. I had some good games and some bad games, but I was always well looked after by the fans. It was a great club to play for and it's been the highlight of my playing career. It was a shame when I left, but the way things were going with the club financially I don't think they had any choice. Administrators were coming in and a lot of money was taken from the players. When I left I had to write off money owed to me as they couldn't afford to pay it back. But people will still be talking about that time for years. It was such a positive six or seven years for the club. It's great to look back at that and think that you played your part in it.

Craig Fagan: Some of the games that Boaz Myhill kept us in were amazing. That game away at Tottenham was the best goalkeeping performance I've ever seen, live or on TV.

Ian Ashbee: Boaz Myhill was exceptional. The kind of player that drove the club forward.

Dean Keates: Boaz Myhill was an exceptional goalkeeper who has deservedly gone on to play right at the top level.

Jason Price: What a player he was on the floor! He could find a pass from 50 yards away. He'd smash it, it wouldn't go more than six foot off the floor and it would go straight to your feet. It was crazy. He was better than most of us as a dead ball specialist. He was unbelievable.

Matt Rudd: I always believe that if you have a spine to your team then you have a chance, and a good spine is made great by a consistent, reliable goalkeeper. Boaz Myhill was the best in three straight divisions as City rose through the football pyramid under Peter Taylor and Phil Brown. Capable of great saves, always focused on his job, strong in the air despite a comparative lack of inches and just very consistent indeed. And despite not being a local boy, he adored being at City and reportedly cried at being told he had to be sold.

Nick Barmby: Bo was the best goalie in League 1, the best goalie in the Championship and on his day one of the best in the Premier League. And then for him to go and play international football was fantastic. But that comes from the hard work he put in at Hull Ionians and at Cottingham. We're for ever indebted to him – not least for that save he did against Watford. One of the best goalies I've played with.

Dean Marney had shown that he could cut it in the Premier League, particularly in the 2008/09 season. This caused Burnley to put in a bid of about £500,000 for him, which was accepted by a cash-strapped City.

Dean Marney: Hull City took me from a boy to a man. I went from still living with my parents to moving 200 or so miles away, and it was only when my girlfriend – now my wife – moved up with me that I settled. That first season was a bit of a write-off and then I had a big point to prove after the criticism I – rightly – got. Thankfully it went well after that and I thoroughly enjoyed it. I enjoyed 99% of my time at Hull, it was just difficult how it ended. But I look back at that time with nothing but good memories.

Ian Ashbee: Dean Marney got a bit of stick at times but was a very good player. We worked very well together.

Michael Turner: Dean Marney was underappreciated. A lot of his crosses and corners led to my goals. He had a great delivery and his energy levels were incredible, he was always available to pass to.

City couldn't afford to keep the likes of George Boateng either, meaning the popular Dutchman was to seek pastures new.

George Boateng: When we got relegated I had a chat with Adam Pearson and said to him that I'd loved playing for Hull City, my family liked it up there and I didn't want to leave, so let's work something out. But my contract had expired and Adam said that it was too difficult and they couldn't afford me. I said I'd sign anything they offered me but I think Adam was embarrassed to offer me all the club could afford then. I would have taken a big pay cut though, as I wanted to stay another three, four years and maybe do what Nick Barmby did. But looking back I feel really lucky to have played for the club and I had a fantastic time. The players and the fans were great. People think I don't like Phil Brown but we get on really well. Our differences were only on the field. We got on well on a personal level. I know I gave a critical interview on Match of the Day, but when you look back I talked about only things on the pitch – how things could have been different. I loved my time there, and in a way we wrote history.

Ian Ashbee: George Boateng was a breath of fresh air. I think he was probably brought in to fill my boots, but I wasn't done just yet, so we ended up playing together.

And Geovanni – the attacking inspiration behind City's spectacular start to the 2008/09 season – was another to say goodbye that summer.

Geovanni: I usually say that players have great differences! But at Hull, despite being a group from different countries with different cultures and different languages, we had desire to win, fellowship, friendship and respect, a family that I will never forget. I was friends with everyone.

Bryan Hughes: He was fantastic, great to have in the dressing room. He was a Brazilian international who'd done it at the top level, walking into a dressing room that looked like it was full of Sunday League players, and he just embraced us straight away. George Boateng and Jay-Jay were the same.

City rebuilt in 2010/11, with Nigel Pearson taking over as manager and, in the December, the Allam family buying the club from Russell Bartlett. However, in January 2011 City fans had to contend with the uncontendable: Ian Ashbee – who'd successfully returned from injury, again – was allowed to leave the club, joining Preston North End where he'd be reunited with Phil Brown.

Ian Ashbee: My time at the club means everything to me. It's something that I can't put into words. To come to a club that had nearly gone out of business not long ago and to go through the promotions, gaining Premier League status, doing all I did in that time, I can't put it into words. I'm extremely proud of it, and no one can take it away from me, no matter what any fan has ever said about me, whatever any player has ever thought. It's a proud moment every time I think about my career or I meet an old team-mate. It was a special time for a young boy from Birmingham who probably wasn't the best footballer in the world but who's gone on to achieve something that many players better than me haven't. Hull City is very close to my heart even still. I didn't want to leave. I never wanted to leave. It gutted me to leave.

Peter Taylor: Ash was brilliant. He was a brilliant captain for me. Outstanding. He was an angry man at times; he had his targets and standards and if he felt players weren't hitting them he'd have a go at them, and that is so handy for a manager because if you're the only one giving the bollockings it's not healthy as you're only going to make yourself more and more unpopular with players. Ash was a leader, a winner, and he knew his limitations and strengths. He was an aggressive captain and like a member of coaching staff at times.

Bryan Hughes: Ash deserves so much credit for what he achieved at the club. Playing alongside him was very enjoyable and I just hope he learned a little bit off me. The fans loved him and rightly so – he's a hero.

Stuart Elliott: Ian Ashbee and I had a few ding-dongs but it was always in good jest as he was trying to get the best out of us as players. He was a leader in the dressing room. He came to the club at the same time as me and I saw how influential he was, taking the club from League 2 to the Premier League. He'll go down as one of the all-time greats at Hull City.

Michael Turner: Ian Ashbee was colossal. Having him in midfield in front of me all the time was great. When anyone was trying to get the ball to the centre-forward I was marking he'd cut it out nine times out of 10. He was always in the right position. As a captain and a leader he summed up everything that was good about us.

Paul Duffen: Because of the way he maximised his abilities, his leadership, his courage, his humanity, his sacrifice, what he went through surgically so he could continue playing for Hull City and his influence on every Hull City team that went on the pitch, Ian Ashbee had an enormous influence. I have great respect for him in terms of how he contributed over all the years he was at the club, throughout four divisions. Just outstanding!

Colin Murphy: Ian Ashbee was up there with Barmby for me in my time at Hull City. One of the better players I've been involved with.

Gary Clark: My star man is and will always be Ian Ashbee. That man's story with this club is straight out of a Boy's Own annual. Free transfer from Cambridge, then to captain the club through all four divisions is the stuff of legends. A feat that will never, ever be repeated and deserving of so much more recognition than the great man received. Ian Ashbee, I salute you!

Dave Richardson: Ian Ashbee led by example in every game he played, upping his game in every division to prove his critics wrong, coming back from career threatening injuries. He's the man!

Ian Farrow: Ian Ashbee was there from the beginning and played in all the many different mixtures of players that formed the teams that took us through the leagues. Importantly, he was the leader in name and in influence, even, I suspect, during the seasons he was out injured. Arguably not the most naturally gifted of players, but that makes his achievement even more remarkable. What a captain! What an inspiration! More than any other player, he made a difference. We were always a better team when Ash played. That is the respect he had on the field. I don't think City would be the team of promotions, of Premier Leagues, of Wembley appearances, if it wasn't for the inspirational Ian Ashbee.

Paul Denman: Ian Ashbee led from the front, ground opponents down, scored at Yeovil, captain in all four leagues. I hated it when he ran off the pitch when he played against us for Preston. You should have stayed on the pitch, Ian, and done a one-man lap of honour to let us show how much you were loved and missed! A legend.

Peter Swan: Ian Ashbee was a player I'd love to have played alongside. You'd have him in any team. Every club would love an Ian Ashbee. He might not have been the best footballer, but he'd always get the best out of the players around him. People like him are a dying breed. You can't teach that kind of leadership. Hull City were lucky to have him.

Dean Keates: Ash is a bit of an unsung hero despite his legendary status in Hull, which he most definitely deserves. People don't always appreciate the non-flair players who put that hard work in – the goalkeepers or goalscorers tend to get the pats on the back. But Ash will always stand out to me having achieved what he did at Hull City.

Fraizer Campbell: I always looked up to Ash. He was the captain and he'd come back from a terrible knee injury. The way that he overcame that and then played a massive part in Hull getting promoted and then doing so well in the Premier League, you've got to take your hat off to him. He's a real leader and I really enjoyed playing my football with him.

Greg Strong: Ian Ashbee has deserved all his plaudits. He was my vice-captain and then took over the team, to massive success.

Marc Joseph: The work that Ash put in at the club was outstanding and the role model he was as a player from day one – you couldn't ask for better. The fans got that from him both on the pitch or just from chatting to him. He was a leader of men and he was always going to get the best out of the whole squad. You wanted him on your side and definitely not against you.

James Richardson: Ian Ashbee typified the most important aspect of sport – mental strength. Captaining a team through all four divisions is impressive, more so as it wasn't always great for him at City, but he came back from setbacks and criticism time and time again to be the heartbeat of the team, underpinning City's best moments during his career at the club with a no-frills, natural leadership and carrying the team forward. If the team were struggling, Ash winning a 40/60 tackle got them, and the crowd, going.

Mike Hall: In that decade, Hull City had a rare team spirit that only very few squads are able to harness. The spirit that carried the club from the bottom division to the Premier League was surely embodied by Ian Ashbee. He seemed to epitomise however Hull City were perceived as we rose up the divisions; a captain who was the envy of other lower league clubs during the back-to-back promotions, then later, the less celebrated but indomitable force that propelled us from the Championship and, briefly, to thriving in the Premier League.

As Nigel Pearson built a new squad, more heroes of the previous few years were moved on. One was Caleb Folan, who went to play his football in Colorado in the US leagues.

Matt Rudd: Caleb Folan carried the tag of City's first £1m signing as if it was his destiny, at times a bit too cool for school when City needed bodies to be put on the line, yet when he delivered he did so consistently and with great timing. In 2008 he became a goalscorer of regularity as City were promoted to the top tier, often sealing games as a second-half substitute prior to scoring the winner in our first ever Premier League game with ice-cool composure. Never good enough to stay in the big league, his departure came as no surprise but his impact on the team and the culture of the club will be felt for a very long time.

Matt Duke had been on an emotional journey at City and, having sat on the bench for a number of seasons, eventually became a Premier League player, where he let no one down. In the summer of 2011 he was to join Bradford, where he would go on to finally play at Wembley in the League Cup final.

Matt Duke: The journey I'd been on was incredible. I'd never expected it to happen. I'm still friends with a lot of my former team-mates. Our kids are still friends as they grew up together. When I've been back to Hull I've had a fantastic reception from the fans and it's nice to know that they remember you. I love going back as I have a lot of love for the club.

Craig Fagan was another hero of the club's rise from the lower leagues who was allowed to leave the club.

Craig Fagan: That time means a lot. To be such a big part of history, to get to the top flight for the first time, was a privilege, as it was to go up through the leagues. And to do it with the people that had been there from day one when I signed, that was a big thing for me. It was such a family club.

Matt Rudd: Craig Fagan was occasionally frustrating but equally capable of winning games and ruining defensive reputations entirely by himself. Blessed with great pace, he had enough ball control and wherewithal in attack to make the right choice, especially when he first joined in League One and pretty much single-handedly ripped stout Tranmere and Bradford sides apart. Over his two spells he had enough confidence in his ability to do the right thing when required, such as scoring a deceptively difficult equaliser against Bolton in 2009 that effectively kept us in the Premier League, and even though his attitude sometimes needed work, it was evident that he liked playing for us and felt at home in a City team.

The likes of Kamil Zayatte, Anthony Gardner and Peter Halmosi were also released, and Jimmy Bullard finally departed the club in August 2011. City carried on improving in the 2011/12 season, and when Nigel Pearson left to rejoin Leicester in late 2011, Nick Barmby was given the managerial job. At the end of that season Richard Garcia returned to Australia.

Richard Garcia: That period of my life at Hull City will always mean a lot. We achieved so much and had so many highs, but we also had a lot of lows and experienced so many different situations that helped me grow as a player and as a person. I was able to meet and work with some fantastic people and live in a place where the people were passionate about their city.

Alfie Potts Harmer: Richard Garcia probably doesn't get as much credit as he ought to. He was superb in that promotion season on the right flank, creating and scoring a handful of goals, including a few fantastic strikes. He probably took some undue criticism due to Browny playing him out of position (sometimes as a lone striker) but even then he always gave his all and was a very good servant to the club.

Brendon Smurthwaite: I thought that Richard was a very under-rated player. He scored some important goals, played anywhere and was a genuine bloke. Nothing was ever too much trouble for him. And he still has an affinity with the area.

Matt Rudd: Richard Garcia was a crazily underrated footballer. He had an exquisite touch, a short and sharp turn of pace, good crossing ability, packed a decent shot and was always absolutely selfless in pursuing the team's cause ahead of any other.

Sam Ricketts: He was someone who I had a really good relationship with on and off the pitch. It was great having him in front of me. I don't know if the fans picked up on our relationship too much, but in the promotion year we worked so well down the right side. He'd make so much space for me. It was probably the best partnership I ever played in, and he scored a lot of vital goals for us. I don't think he gets the credit he deserves. Before games we'd say to each other "right side, strong side", which comes from the film Remember the Titans. And even now when we text each other we still sign off with 'RSSS'. We worked so hard together and he was a real team-first player. He was a big player for us.

Sadly Nick Barmby was removed as the club's manager that summer in harsh circumstances. Nothing, however, could alter the fact that this proudest of Hullensians had been an integral cog in creating history with the football club he loved so much.

Nick Barmby: It was always an ambition of mine to play for Hull City, even if it was just for one game. But to be involved in what we all did was amazing. Memories that will never leave me for the rest of my life. To be the first to do those things, with all these different people who've played a part – coaches, managers, players, chairmen, backroom staff – they can say we tried to help Hull City and we did. Coming from Hull, I'm very proud to have been one of those people.

Caleb Folan: Nick Barmby was important to me. He was at Leeds when I was a youngster there. I always respected him massively. I was starstruck by him because I was a Liverpool fan. But he was such a normal person. He was so chilled out. He gave me a lot of advice and helped me a lot.

Craig Fagan: From coming into the club to the time I left, Nick Barmby was unbelievable with me. He understood how I wanted to play, he helped me non-stop off the pitch, he helped me with all things to do with football. I would sit on his table on the team coach so, lifestyle-wise, I'd listen to what he did and how he lived his life. That helped me massively. And I had some great banter with him and Andy Dawson.

Peter Taylor: A lot of people say to me: "Who's the best player you ever dealt with?" expecting me to say someone like Rio Ferdinand or Frank Lampard. But I tell them for reasons of professionalism the answer is Nick Barmby. I used to look at players when they were warming down and getting a bit sloppy, talking about what they were going to do in the afternoon, and I'd say to them: "Just look at what's Nick's doing." It really helps as a manager having someone like that to point to. It was an easy signing based on what I knew about him regarding his ability and as a person. Of course you want to be sure that he was going to be fit, but he was a first-class signing and a first-class lad. But with that, with him being used to playing in the Premier League, it could make it hard to substitute him every now and then as he didn't like it. But that just showed his desire.

Michael Turner: For me to play with Nick Barmby – who I used to watch for Spurs when he was a youngster there – was a thrill. A great player to train with and a great pro. He was crucial for us.

Steve Bruce took over at City and achieved another promotion to the Premier League in his first season – this time automatically after a dramatic final day. That summer, however, legend Andy Dawson said a final goodbye to Hull City.

Andy Dawson: It was an amazing time. Personally I had four promotions at the club, two of them to the Premier League. If someone had told me that when I'd signed I'd have laughed. I saw things in football that I never could have dreamt would happen to me, or even happen to the club. I am really proud for me and my family – my kids are massive Hull City fans – to be part of that journey. My kids grew up at that football club. It was just a great journey for me; one, as a professional footballer, in that it gave me more than I could have ever dreamed of; and two, to have been the places I've been. When I go back it seems like yesterday. It's a great club, I've got loads of friends there and I enjoy going back. Hopefully I'll get the opportunity at some point in my career to go back and work there.

Craig Fagan: Andy Dawson was someone who I looked up to. I felt that he'd always give his all. If Daws was playing you knew you'd get at least a seven out of 10 every week.

Ian Ashbee: Andy Dawson was brilliant. Same as me, probably never thought he was going to step up, but he was always good, always wore his heart on his sleeve and never let anybody down. To the older lads like him, with whom I went through what I did, I will always be exceptionally grateful.

Nick Barmby: It says it all that Andy Dawson was player of the year in League 1, player of the year in the Championship and player of the year I think twice in the Premier League. He just got better and better. When I managed Hull City he never put me under pressure if I didn't play him and that's the mark of a true professional. A very good player who had a great career, and he's a great guy.

Paul Denman: The tackle Andy Dawson made on Theo Walcott at Arsenal away when we won 2-1 was total class; he was amazing that day. He had a great free kick on him too. Never let the side down.

Stuart Elliott: Andy Dawson was a gentleman and an absolute stalwart. He was Mr Consistency.

Mike White: Andy Dawson wasn't one of the biggest, brashest players in that dressing room, but he was so respected. He cared about the game and he cared about the club – he really took City to his heart.

Off the pitch, the likes of Brendon Smurthwaite – who'd been a huge asset to the club – were also departing.

Dave Richardson: Being a press officer must be a thankless task. Everyone wants a bit of the manager/players/owner and it's down to you to keep them at bay while keeping everyone happy. Brendon Smurthwaite was superb at the job. He's also a very funny guy and really good company travelling to away games.

Meanwhile, physio Simon Maltby was to move on.

Simon Maltby: I enjoyed League 2 as much as I enjoyed the Premier League. I loved my first seven years at the club. I still think about it every day. I had a real affinity to the club and the people there. I've done a lot since I left the club, but all my Hull City memorabilia takes pride of place in my house.

The man responsible for the fact that Boothferry Park's pitch looked like a snooker table, and who was behind the smooth transition from Boothferry Park to the KC Stadium, had also moved on in this time.

Ian Farrow: John Cooper doesn't get enough credit when people talk about our history, and the club going from the lowest of the low to the peak of our success. Whether as groundsman or stadium manager, John ensured that City had the best pitch in the Football League and one of the best run stadiums. As far as I can gather he played a major part in the functional side of the KC's development and, people forget or don't know, he played two very decisive roles in City still existing and still being at Boothferry Park rather than the Boulevard under David Lloyd, which would have made it a lot more difficult for Adam Pearson to come in and get the KC built. The Hull City of today would probably never have happened – or the happening would have been much delayed – if it wasn't for John Cooper.

Bit by bit, the heroes of the 2000 to 2010 era were departing. The last to go (though Fraizer Campbell would rejoin) was a man who'd become a huge cult hero at the club. They sold McShane, super Paul McShane. The fans didn't understand.

Paul McShane: The fans knew the shite I'd been through. I'd never really felt that comfortable at Hull, even though I'd had a great time in my six-and-a-half years there. I always felt on edge as I felt I was always having to prove myself to the management. I knew that Nigel Pearson didn't want anything to do with the players who'd got the club relegated. I was saying: "I want to play, I want to get the club back up to the Premier League," but he didn't give me the time of day. So I had a big bust up with him. That meant I had to leave straight away on loan to Barnsley. The season after, I did well in pre-season and it looked like I'd be back in the team but I popped my calf and was out for a couple of months. And then even me and Steve Bruce had words at the start of his time as well, as I just wanted to be given a chance. I had nothing to lose at this stage. I was on the warpath. But Steve eventually gave me my chance, I took it, and we ended up getting promoted. The fans seem to recognise what I'd been through. My time at Hull means an awful lot to me. It's hard to explain. I love the club. I had a great relationship with the fans – I loved how they'd treat me and make me feel. I felt as if all the hard work, the perseverance, had been worthwhile. I never wanted to give up on the club as I felt as if I owed them for when we got relegated. I remember that last game I played in, against Manchester United at home, with all the fans chanting my name. That will stick with me for ever and I can't thank them all enough.

Steven Hunt: He deserves so much credit. I jumped ship, but Paul dug out the bad times at Hull and got them back up to the Premier League. It was tough for him at times, but he really earned the right to get back up with Hull City.

Ian Farrow: Everyone loved Paul McShane. He was a no-nonsense, no pretence, hard-working, hard-tackling, brave defender who initially divided fans because he was not the most creative of players. He won everyone over, however, through his force of nature, his bravery and his sheer determination to get stuck in against some of the world's best. More often than not he won the battle. By the time the club were ready to sell him, no one, including the player, wanted him to go.

Hull City went on to further success, enjoying three more seasons in the top flight and even reaching an FA Cup final, which they lost 3-2 to Arsenal after quickly going 2-0 up. A brief stab at European football also ensued. Sadly, a cloud hovered over the era due to the new owners presiding over a number of controversial plans, such as attempting to rename the club 'Hull Tigers' and an unpopular restructuring of the offering of concessions. Attendances were eventually to suffer, with fans at odds with the club (and each other) and the feelgood factor that had been almost tangible since the move to the KC diminishing considerably. But the Hull City of 2019 is a very different beast to that we were supporting at the turn of the century – bigger, better and with a more illustrious history to look back upon. And for that, we owe our eternal thanks to the men listed in this book.

Thank you

The list of people to thank with regards to the publication of this book is a long one. First and foremost, however, I simply must mention Brendon Smurthwaite. Every book needs a hero, and this tome has no shortage of them. However, the whole project simply would not have been a possibility without Brendon's hard work chasing up interviewees, offering encouragement and generally being the all-round good guy that everyone connected with sport in Hull knows him to be. Thanks Brendon. You're a star. Anything this book achieves will be every bit as much down to you as it is to me.

Also a godsend when it comes to contacts and general assistance was Phil Buckingham at the Hull Daily Mail. Phil has been a constant source of encouragement throughout the whole process and I can't thank him enough. Thanks also must go to Radio Humberside's David Burns and Mike White for their early encouragement of the book and subsequent help.

Matt Rudd's long list of contacts for 1980s pop stars was of little use to me, but he was a great help in tracking down a number of the more obscure former Hull City players. Matt's a real force for good in life as well as in all things Hull City, and he's another I'm grateful to.

Having access to Dave Richardson's vast array of Hull City photos has been brilliant (all of the match photos in this book come from Dave, as well as the 2008 celebrations). It's been a pleasure getting to know Dave, and as a photographer he has few equals. His son James has also been an integral part of the book's creation, given his work on its promotional videos. No family has any right to be that talented!

Jamie Brown and I met at Sir Henry Cooper School in 1987 and have been close friends ever since. Being able to involve him in the project to design the front and back covers, along with much of the marketing, was an utter pleasure. His wonderful late mum, Judith Brown (pictured), is one of the many reasons why any money the book makes will go to Dove House Hospice.

Proof-reading such a weighty book as this is a thankless task, particularly as I'm such a grumpy sod when it comes to people altering my work. Mike Hall was at my shoulder for many of the games described within this work, and as well as being grateful for his lasting friendship, I'm also thankful for his expert sub-editing skills. Also, getting the book into some sort of physical form was proving a bit of a nightmare, until Matt Egan rode in on a white horse (figuratively) and saved the day (literally). Matt is a good friend (figuratively) and someone I'm very grateful to (literally).

I don't know if I'd have ever started writing about Hull City if it wasn't for the combined forces of the Tiger-chat email listing group (particularly the match reporters) and fanzine Amber Nectar (and the contributors to its forum). It would be remiss of me not to mention

those behind the City Independent and Not606 forums too. These people are the lifeblood of our club and keep the passion burning through thick and thin. Thank you to you all.
Certain websites have been invaluable to me in researching this book. Mike Scott's On Cloud 7, Matt Wales's Tigerbase, Soccerbase and Footstats are all excellent at what they do, but enter at your peril. You can lose hours. In addition to this, a number of books have been incredibly helpful for research purposes. Mike Peterson's A Century of City and Tiger Tales, Chris Elton's Hull City: A Complete Record and Douglas Lamming's A Who's Who of Hull City are must-haves for City fans. On top of that, the following books have been great as research tools, but more importantly they are terrific reads for any City fan:

Now Tigers: The Early History of Hull City by Nick Turner
Hull City in the 1920s by Nick Turner
The Boothferry Park Years by Nick Turner
Live Through The Dream by Ian Waterson
From Boothferry To Wembley by Gary Clark
This Is The Best Trip We've Ever Been On by Gary Clark
46 And Counting… by Ian Bunton
Look Back in Amber by David Goodman
Hull City a History by David Goodman

Many of the contributors interviewed in the book have also gone out of their way to provide me with contacts that I've been missing. I can't think those people enough. On top of this, I've also been helped in various ways by: Nic Johnson, Les Motherby, Martin Batchelor, Gary Chilton, James McVie, Rob Harmer, Geoff Bielby, David Batte, James Smailes, Louise Hodgson, Ian Thomson, Rob Thomson, Steve Savage, Andy Dalton, Chris Mumby (Scunthorpe United), David Gregory (Colchester United), Mike Dees, Gareth Baker, Phil Graham, Francesca Wagstaff, Chris Whiting, Stefan Curtis, Ash Lord, Matthew Holmes, Con Egan, Quentin Edwards, Stacey Francis, Harriet Edkins (Crystal Palace), Darren Bentley (Burnley), Stuart Hudson (Blackpool), Tom Jarvis (Southend), Craig Bell, Helen Bell, Dave Lofthouse, Nick Turner, Graeme Hull, Stephen Adamson (who kindly let me use quotes from his biography of Colin Appleton – all other quotes are from direct interviews), John Anderson, Janice Ward, Paul Cooper, Ian Farrow, Gary Clark, Peter Hopper, Rick Skelton, Mark Thompson, Paul Gibson, Ian Bunton, Jimmy Chu and Mark Preston. My most sincere apologies if I've forgotten anyone.

My first ever Hull City game was in November 1982. My teacher at the time, Margaret Robinson at Fifth Avenue Primary, was sick of me writing about Hull FC in my weekend diary so got her husband, Malcolm, and son, Mark, to take me to Boothferry Park. I was instantly smitten. To have Mark contribute to this book has been particularly poignant for me. His mum's actions just go to show what an incredible impact good, kind teachers – of which I had many at Fifth Ave, Endike and Henry Cooper – can have on a young person's life. Sadly Margaret and Malcolm are no longer with us, but I will be eternally grateful to the Robinson family for igniting the spark.

Pretty much everyone in Hull will at some point in their lives be touched by Dove House Hospice. To be able to raise money for the charity through this book has been a wonderful thing. Thanks in particular to Dove House's Dan Clipson for his assistance throughout the writing and production. Thanks also to the Hull City Supporters Trust for their help with the marketing and launch party for the book.

Whoever said "never meet your heroes" obviously hadn't met the Hull City players, managers, staff and owners featured within this book. Every single interview was enjoyable. Pretty much every single interviewee wanted to know how they could help further with the book. Brendon Smurthwaite said to me at the beginning of the project that there's not a bad egg among them all. That was an understatement. Thank you to you all.

I've been lucky enough to have a large, supportive family that has given me a security and confidence in life to take on tasks such as writing this book. I also have an incredible mum and dad. My relationship with the latter even survived his somewhat zealous proof-reading of every single bastard chapter. In truth, I owe everything to my mum and dad. They'll just have to make do with a thank you for now, however. And a couple of grandsons, to be fair.

There was a hole in my Wembley 2008 experience, and that was because my brother, Oli, was at a wedding in Italy. Hull City have been a huge part of our lives, and the decade in focus within this book saw us driving all over the country attending games and having great adventures in my clapped-out Seat Ibiza. Thanks for all of your help with the book, Oli, and for everything else besides.

When you've got a non-sleeping toddler and another child on the way (who, it turned out, was also not that keen on sleeping), telling your wife that you intend to write a time-consuming book could have been a tricky task. There was to be a protracted house move amid it all too. Fortunately I have the best wife in the world. Thank you, Alice. I'll paint the bathroom ceiling now.

Finally, thank you for buying this book.

Printed in Great Britain
by Amazon